INTERNATIONAL DEVELOPMENT IN FOCUS

A Balancing Act for Brazil's Amazonian States

An Economic Memorandum

MAREK HANUSCH, EDITOR

WORLD BANK GROUP

The analysis for this book was completed on September 30, 2022.

Contents

Boxes

Figures

Maps

Tables

Acknowledgments

This memorandum was prepared by a World Bank team led by Marek Hanusch (Senior Economist, Macroeconomics, Trade and Investment Global Practice [MTI]) under the guidance of Felipe Jaramillo (Vice President, Latin America and the Caribbean Region [LAC]); Seynabou Sakho (Director, Strategy and Operations, LAC); Paloma Anós Casero (Country Director for Brazil); Robert Taliercio (Regional Director, Equitable Growth, Finance and Institutions Practice Group [EFI]); Doerte Doemeland and Jorge Thompson Araujo (Practice Managers, MTI); and Shireen Mahdi and Rafael Muñoz Moreno (Lead Country Economists, EFI).

Peer reviewers of the concept note were Giovanni Ruta (Lead Environmental Economist, Environment, Natural Resources and Blue Economy Global Practice) and Tatiana Didier (Senior Economist, Finance, Competitiveness and Innovation Global Practice). Peer reviewers at a quality enhancement review were Richard Damania (Chief Economist, Sustainable Development Practice Group [SD]) and Kevin Carey (Adviser, EFI), with additional review by Elena Ianchovichina (Deputy Chief Economist, LAC). Peer reviewers at the decision review were Otaviano Canuto (Nonresident Senior Fellow at The Brookings Institution); Martin Raiser (Vice President, South Asia Region); and Stéphane Hallegatte (Senior Climate Change Adviser, SD).

The core chapter authors, including World Bank Group staff and consultants, are as follows:

- *Chapter 1:* Marek Hanusch, Jon Strand, and Claudia Tufani
- *Chapter 2:* Gabriel Lara Ibarra, Ildo Lautharte, Jorge Muñoz, Camille Bourguignon, Rovane Battaglin Schwengber, Michael Weber, Marek Hanusch, Stella Mendes Carneiro, Claudia Tufani, and Joaquim Bento de Souza Ferreira Filho
- *Chapter 3:* Marek Hanusch, Gabriel Zaourak, Joaquim Bento de Souza Ferreira Filho, and Diogo Bardal
- *Chapter 4:* Jorge Muñoz, Camille Bourguignon, Luis Diego Herrera Garcia, Marek Hanusch, Eric Arias, Fabiano Silvio Colbano, Alexandre Kossoy, Bryan Gurhy, Dieter Wang, Jon Strand, Rafael Amaral Ornelas, Claudia Tufani, and Guido Penido

- *Chapter 5:* Hans Jansen, Marek Hanusch, Giovani William Gianetti (University of São Paulo [USP]), Frank Merry (Climate Focus), Adauto Brasilino Rocha Junior (University of Nebraska–Lincoln), Claudia Tufani, and Daniele La Porta
- *Chapter 6:* Paula Restrepo Cadavid and Olivia D'Aoust, with contributions from Hogeun Park, and Giuseppe Rossitti, Jake William Schneider (Harvard University), and Laurent Troost (Laurent Troost Architectures)
- *Chapter 7:* Marek Hanusch, Ana María González Velosa, Tanya Lisa Yudelman, Sandra Berman, Jon Strand, and Claudia Tufani.

Individual chapters, or parts thereof, were externally reviewed by Marta Arretche (USP), Arminio Fraga (Gávea Investimentos), Clarissa Gandour (Climate Policy Initiative), John Hemming (formerly Royal Geographical Society), Alfredo Kingo Oyama Homma (Brazilian Agricultural Research Corporation [Embrapa]), Charly Porcher (Georgetown University), Luis Quintero (Johns Hopkins University), José Luiz Rossi Junior (Inter-American Development Bank), Marcelo Stabile (Amazon Environmental Research Institute [IPAM]), Jonas Steinfeld (Wageningen University), and Fernando Veloso (Getulio Vargas Foundation [FGV]).

The memorandum is accompanied by a companion report, "Urban Competitiveness in Brazil's State of Amazonas: A Green Growth Agenda," and closely draws on 13 background papers:

Fabio Artuso and Giulio Zanetti. "A Branding Strategy for the Amazon."

Mark Bernhofen, Flannery Dolan, and Christian Borja-Vega. "Water in the Legal Amazon."

Adauto Brasilino Rocha Junior. "Farm Scale and Productivity in the Legal Amazon."

Pietro Calice and Federico Alfonso Diaz Kalan. "Sustainable, Inclusive Growth: Rural Finance in the North Region."

Xavier Cirera and Antonio Martins-Neto. "The Role of Skills Relatedness and Spin-offs in Diversification to Green Sectors."

Joaquim Bento de Souza Ferreira Filho and Marek Hanusch. "A Macroeconomic Perspective of Structural Deforestation in Brazil's Legal Amazon."

Gabriel Kohlmann and Elis Licks. "Mapping Value Chains for the Amazon Bioeconomy."

Ildo Lautharte, Ursula Mello, and Lucas Emanuel. "Education as a Leverage for Future Skills in the Legal Amazon."

Charly Porcher and Marek Hanusch. "A Model of Amazon Deforestation, Trade, and Labor Market Dynamics."

Graciela Sanchez Martinez, Juliana Paiva, Gabriela Lima de Paula, Paulo Moutinho, Rodrigo Castriota, and Alberto Coelho Gomes Costa. "Indigenous Peoples and Sustainable Development in the Legal Amazon."

Jon Strand. "Valuation of the Brazilian Amazon Rainforest."

Maria Vagliasindi. "Key Challenges and Opportunities in the Power Sector of the State of Amazonas."

Dieter Wang, Bryan Gurhy, and Marek Hanusch. "Could Sustainability-Linked Bonds Incentivize Lower Deforestation in Brazil's Legal Amazon?"

Ana María González Velosa, Tanya Lisa Yudelman, and Sandra Berman from the World Bank's Amazon Sustainable Landscapes team provided detailed comments on most parts of this memorandum. A close collaboration with the International Finance Corporation (IFC) underlies this memorandum, including feedback from Diogo Bardal, Bruce Ian Keith, Cristina Catunda, Carolina Moreira Mariotto, and Mattia Bordon. The team also benefited from discussions with the broader IFC country team for Brazil.

The team is also grateful for insightful suggestions and comments provided by other World Bank colleagues, including Anna Wellenstein, Genevieve Connors, Diego Arias Carballo, Valerie Hickey, Renato Nardello, Ekaterina Vostroknutova, Mark Thomas, Somik Lall, Christopher Ian Brett, Garo Batmanian, Luis Alberto Andrés, Pablo Acosta, Alberto Coelho Gomes Costa, Eirivelthon Santos Lima, Kjetil Hansen, Mathilde Lebrand, Megersa Abera Abate, Daniel Alberto Benitez, Alexander Lotsch, Edson Araujo, Christian Borja-Vega, Maria de Fatima Amazonas, Jevgenijs Steinbuks, James Cust, Ana Waksberg Guerrini, Javier Morales Sarriera, Jean-François Arvis, and Ernani Argolo Checcucci Filho.

Maria Elisa Dias Diniz Costa provided outstanding guidance on external relations, while Flavia Nahmias da Silva Gomes, Adriane Landwehr, and Priscilla Nunes Cardoso de Sa provided stellar project support.

Very special thanks are due to Tatiana Schor, who provided early inspiration for this memorandum and accompanied it actively throughout its preparation, as well as to her colleagues in the government of the state of Amazonas, including Jório de Albuquerque Veiga Filho, Jeibi Medeiros da Costa, Karla Fabiane Soares Tavares, Natalia Sagaydo, Jonas da Rosa Gonçalves, Karoline Andrade Barros, Lilia Marina Ferreira de Assunção, Nina Best, and Lupuna Souza.

The team is also grateful for close research collaboration with João Maria de Oliveira (Institute of Applied Economic Research [IPEA]) and generous sharing of data by Marc Muendler (University of California San Diego) and Christian de Cico and Matheus Nagliati (Arquivei).

The team benefited from helpful conversations with Adriana Moreira (Global Environment Facility); Gustavo Fontenele, José Ricardo Ramos Sales, Klenize Favero, Leonardo Póvoa, and Vitarque Coêlho (all federal Ministry of Economy); Eduardo Sampaio Marques (federal Ministry of Agriculture); Dione Macedo (federal Ministry of Mines and Energy); Leonardo Pamplona (Brazilian Development Bank [BNDES]); Leandro Rodrigues e Silva, Tiago Henrique França Baroni, and Eduardo Dornelas Munhoz (all Company of Planning and Logistics [EPL]); General Algacir Polsin, Ana Maria Oliveira De Souza, Germano Augusto Coelho De Morais, and Arthur De Freitas Lisboa (Manaus Economic Zone Superintendence [SUFRAMA]); Carlos Nobre and Victoria Ballester (both of USP); Juliano Assunção, Arthur Bragança, Amanda Schutze, and Clarissa Gandour (all Climate Policy Initiative); André Guimarães, Marcelo Stabile, and Paulo Moutinho (all IPAM); Paulo Barreto and Brenda Brito (both Amazon Institute of People and the Environment [Imazon]); Gabriel Kohlmann and Elis Licks (both Instituto Escolhas); Virgilio Viana and Victor Salviati (both Foundation for Amazon Sustainability [FAS]); Bernard Appy (Tax Citizenship Center [C.CiF]); Vanessa Rahal Canado (Insper Institute of Education and Research); Carlos Klink (University of Brasília); Britaldo Soares-Filho (Federal University of Minas Gerais [UFMG]); Roberto Schaffer (Federal University of Rio de Janeiro); Felipe Nunes Coelho Magalhães (Center for Regional Development and Planning [Cedeplar] of UFMG); Luiz Braido (FGV); Wilmara Cruz Messa (National Education Media Center of Amazonas [Cemeam]);

Fernando Ramos and Aline Soterroni (both National Institute for Space Research [INPE]); Salo Coslovsky (New York University); Bruno Simões (Amazon Vital); Pedro Mariosa, Naziano Filizola, Marcelo Seráfico, and Waltair Machado (all Federal University of Amazonas); Claudia Azevedo-Ramos (Federal University of Pará); Amintas Brandão Junior (University of Wisconsin-Madison); Glenn Shepard (Museu Paraense Emílio Goeldi); David (Toby) McGrath (Earth Innovation Institute); Maritta Koch-Weser (Earth3000 and USP); Jens Brüggemann (German Agency for International Cooperation [GIZ]); Martin Schröder and Florian Arneth (both KfW); Claudia Melim-McLeod and Ellen Hestnes Ribeiro (both Rainforest Foundation Norway); Vanessa Pérez-Cirera, Carolina Genin, Caroline Rocha, Paulo Camuri, Rafael Feltran-Barbieri, Leonardo Garrido, and Henrique Corsi (all World Resources Institute); Eurydes Siqueira De Barcellos Junior, Rodolfo Pereira Clemente, Jéssica Camilo, Anderson Chaves, and Rafael da Silva Lourenço (all Yamaha); Roberto Moreno (Honda); and participants of individual presentations to the Concertação pela Amazônia, IPEA, and the Amazônia 2030 initiative.

A team at Communications Development Inc. (led by Bruce Ross-Larson and including Joe Caponio, Mike Crumplar, and Meta de Coquereaumont) edited an earlier version of this document. The World Bank publishing team comprised Cindy Fisher (acquisitions editor), Mark McClure (production editor), Mary Anderson and Elizabeth Forsyth (copy editors), and Ann O'Malley (proofreader).

Executive Summary

IMPROVING LIVING STANDARDS AND CONSERVING EXCEPTIONAL NATURAL WEALTH IN BRAZIL'S LEGAL AMAZON

Brazil's Legal Amazon, here called Amazônia, comprises nine states, most of which rank among the poorest in Brazil. It is a vast territory of 502 million hectares, larger in area than the European Union (EU), and home to 28 million Brazilians.[1] Although Amazônia is mostly known for its vast natural forests, over three-quarters of Amazonians live in towns and cities. Thirty-six percent of Amazônia's population lives in poverty.[2]

Amazônia is home to about 60 percent of the Amazon rainforest and also to parts of other important biomes like the Cerrado savanna and Pantanal wetlands. These natural landscapes comprise large contiguous, mainly forested, areas, many of which have remained relatively untouched by the past 12,000 years of human expansion into natural lands.

Amazônia is one of the world's last frontier regions. But economic expansion has moved into those ancient forests, destroying them at a rapid rate—especially in Amazônia's southeast, within what is known as the "Arc of Deforestation"—and threatening the ways of life of many traditional communities. There is an urgent need for an alternative development path for Amazônia that promotes inclusion and sustainable natural-resource use.

This memorandum presents a multipronged approach, a balancing act that seeks to simultaneously provide a pathway to higher incomes for Amazonians while also protecting natural forests and traditional ways of life by focusing on four strategic actions:

- *Increasing the welfare of Amazonian citizens* by fostering productivity through structural transformation in both rural and urban areas
- *Protecting the forest* by strengthening land and forest governance, including the enforcement of existing laws (command and control)
- *Fostering sustainable rural livelihoods* by unlocking the natural capital associated with the standing forest and protecting the poor and traditional ways of life
- *Marshaling conservation finance* linked to measurable reduction in deforestation and drawing on public and private resources or market-based solutions.

The cost of inaction is high

Recognizing the exceptional value of Amazônia's natural forests is critical to halt their destruction. Brazil is responsible for about one-third of the world's tropical deforestation, largely linked to cattle ranching (Pendrill et al. 2019). Amazônia is Brazil's hot spot for deforestation, most of which is illegal.

Moreover, the Amazon rainforest is at risk of reaching a tipping point where climate change and deforestation would combine to cause the permanent die-back of large tracts of rainforest. Although tipping points remain surrounded by uncertainty, including the thresholds at which they would be triggered, the cat-astrophic implications make this a risk not worth taking. Three-quarters of the rainforest has already lost resilience since 2000 (Boulten, Lenton, and Boers 2022). Deforestation puts at risk the value of Brazil's standing Amazon rainfor-est, estimated to exceed US$317 billion per year—up to seven times more than the estimated private exploitation value linked to extensive agriculture, timber, or mining (Strand 2022).

The Brazilian rainforest's public-good value includes its ecosystem services, which for the South America region alone are an estimated US$20 billion annu-ally, including precipitation needed for the region's agriculture and protection against soil erosion and fire (Strand 2022). Global public values associated with the standing forest are even higher, especially owing to the Amazon's role as a carbon sink: the annual value of carbon storage is estimated at US$210 billion, with option and existence value linked to biodiversity and forest cover adding another US$75 billion.[3] Private use values associated with the standing Amazon, such as production of nontimber products or sustainable tourism, are estimated at US$12 billion annually. Accordingly, the cost of inaction is high, both in the Amazon rainforest and in Amazônia's other biomes.

Stopping illegal deforestation is not only an economic and environmental prerogative but also consistent with Brazil's commitments under the Paris Climate Accords: land, land use change, and forestry is Brazil's leading source of gross greenhouse gas emissions, and accordingly, stopping illegal deforestation is an explicit priority in Brazil's original Nationally Determined Contribution. At the 2021 United Nations Climate Change Conference—also referred to as the 26th annual Conference of the Parties (COP26)—Brazil advanced its zero illegal deforestation target to 2028. Fulfilling this commitment is important for the Brazilian government to demonstrate its policy credibility to its citizens and the world while meeting its obligations toward arresting global warming as a mem-ber of the international community. Given its green energy matrix, decisively curbing deforestation would make Brazil a green country and unlock benefits in international trade as the world decarbonizes (World Bank 2023a).

Beyond the climatic and economic considerations associated with deforesta-tion, the cost of inaction also includes slow social progress. In most Amazonian states, especially the more remote ones, poverty has stagnated or increased in recent years. Living conditions of the poor remain precarious in both rural and urban areas, particularly disadvantaging Indigenous people, Afro-Brazilians, *caboclos* (people of mixed heritage), and female-headed households.

Amazônia has a strong foundation to control deforestation

In the 2000s, Brazil implemented a series of measures to shore up the protec-tion of Amazonian forests, especially the Amazon rainforest. The Amazon

Region Protected Areas Program, launched in 2002, created 60 million hectares of protected area (currently totaling about 209 million hectares of protected areas or Indigenous territories, equivalent to 42 percent of Amazônia's territory). In 2004, the government adopted the Action Plan for the Prevention and Control of Deforestation in the Legal Amazon, which initially focused on land tenure and territorial planning, sustainable production, and environmental monitoring and control. In addition, law enforcement was stepped up through remote sensing monitoring, including the Real-Time Deforestation Detection System (DETER). Since 2008, there has been an increase in targeted enforcement actions in priority (blacklisted) municipalities. In 2012, Brazil updated its 1965 Forest Code and introduced the Rural Environmental Cadastre (CAR), an innovative database and environmental management tool. These public actions were complemented by private sector commitments, such as the 2006 Amazon Soy Moratorium and the 2009 Zero Deforestation Cattle Agreement.

Some of these measures were more effective than others, but jointly they have contributed to a significant decrease in the rate of deforestation. From a high of 27,772 square kilometers in 2004, deforestation in Amazônia fell to 4,471 square kilometers in 2012, a reduction of 84 percent.[4] However, Brazil has not been able to sustain this encouraging trend: Amazonian deforestation has accelerated markedly again since 2015, reaching 13,235 square kilometers (the equivalent of 1.8 million soccer fields) in 2021 (figure ES.1).

Enforcing Brazilian laws to protect natural forests has thus become more urgent, and additional measures should be considered that can promote both forest protection and inclusive growth, as discussed in this memorandum. In the short term, political will is critical for Brazil's forest protection institutions to work effectively.

FIGURE ES.1

Deforestation is on the rise in Amazônia

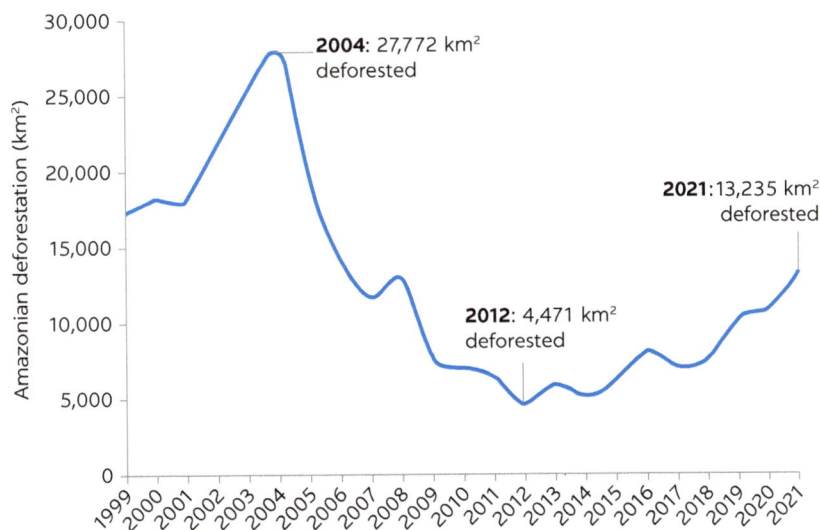

Sources: World Bank, using data from the Project for Satellite Monitoring of Deforestation in the Legal Amazon (PRODES) of the National Institute for Space Research (INPE).
Note: The figure shows annual deforestation in Amazônia. km² = square kilometers.

There is a strong need to reinvigorate social progress

There are important links between environmental sustainability and social progress, and any approach to development for Amazônia must recognize the legitimate desires of its nine states to improve their citizens' standards of living.

Amazonian economies are not particularly good in delivering jobs: unemployment among Amazônia's urban poor stood at 29 percent in 2019 and has worsened during the COVID-19 crisis.[5] Cities struggle to generate good jobs, and informality is high. Rural unemployment is much lower, but this masks relatively higher levels of low-productivity informal work. Given that Amazônia is already quite urbanized, most poor Amazonians, 6.5 million, live in urban areas, with 3.8 million in rural areas (figure ES.2).[6] In rural areas, poverty, however, is more precarious.

Significant gaps in public services also persist across Amazônia, especially in rural areas. Considerable progress was made in rolling out electricity, but many other services are lagging: in 2019, 34 percent of the rural poor had no access to improved sanitation, 46 percent relied on open defecation, and 86 percent had no access to solid waste collection.[7] Public services are better in urban areas, including for the poor, but housing deficits are significant and much higher than in Brazil overall. Many urban inhabitants live in favela-like settlements, ranging from about 2 percent of the urban population in Mato Grosso to 35 percent in Amazonas.[8]

COVID-19 exposed some of the weaknesses of health systems in Amazônia, many of which were overwhelmed by the pandemic. Preliminary data show that mortality in hospitals in the North region (which includes seven of the nine Amazonian states) was higher than in any other region of Brazil. In fact, mortality among patients admitted to intensive care units was 79 percent in the North (highest in the country), compared to Brazil's average of 55 percent. Even before the pandemic, the North region already had higher in-hospital mortality compared to other regions (Ranzani et al. 2021).

FIGURE ES.2

Most poor Amazonians live in towns and cities

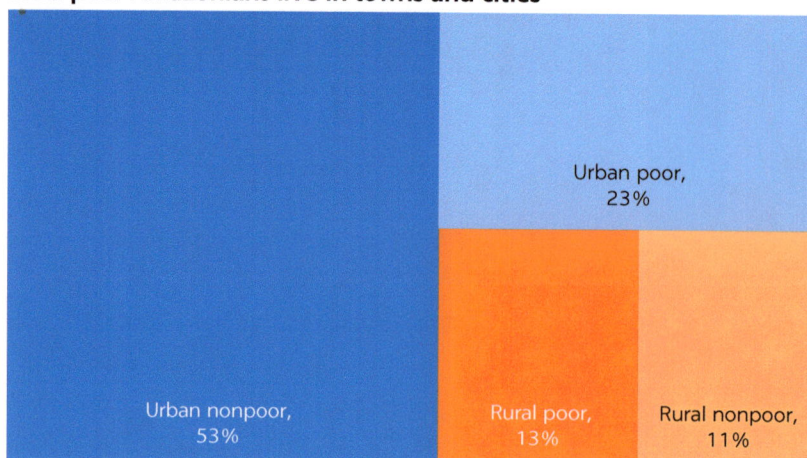

Urban poor, 23%

Urban nonpoor, 53%

Rural poor, 13%

Rural nonpoor, 11%

Sources: World Bank, using Socio-Economic Database for Latin America and the Caribbean (SEDLAC) and Brazil Continuous National Household Sample Survey (PNADC) 2019 data via the World Bank's datalibweb Stata package.
Note: The figure shows 2019 shares of Amazônia's population. "Poor" is defined as those living at or below the poverty line of US$5.50 per person per day.

Finally, crime is a major issue in Amazônia, connected to organized crime, drug trafficking, corruption, and smaller-scale armed robberies and personal conflicts, symptomatic of the region's weak rule of law.

Development solutions should include an emphasis on generating jobs—including productivity growth—and strengthening institutions for social progress across Amazônia.

Development solutions must account for Amazônia's diversity

Amazônia is rich not only ecologically but also culturally. It is Brazil's region with the largest number of Indigenous people—about 380,000, accounting for 1.5 percent of Amazônia's population, with nearly half of them living in the state of Amazonas (IBGE 2012). Many Indigenous Amazonians move across rural and urban spaces, and about 20 percent permanently live in state capitals.

Numerous small Indigenous communities continue to exist in complete isolation in remote parts of the forest. Other traditional groups in Amazônia include *ribeirinhos* (river communities) and *quilombolas* (descendants of fugitive African slaves). These groups tend to maintain strong cultural ties to Amazônia's natural lands. At the same time, they tend to have lower incomes and poorer access to services. Inclusive development in Amazônia needs to carefully account for the region's traditional peoples, whether they choose to embrace urban life, continue their traditional rural lives, or both.

Amazônia's mostly forested north is quite different from the southeastern parts through which the Arc of Deforestation has already passed. These parts account for most of Amazônia's population and have more consolidated markets and institutions. This is a region marked by in-migration from other parts of Brazil over decades as well as by commercial farming. Although this region tends to be more affluent, poverty remains an important challenge.

AMAZÔNIA IN BRAZIL AND THE WORLD

Amazônia's development context has global and national origins. As the world has become richer and the global population has grown, its demand for commodities has increased. Rising demand for agricultural and mining products has fueled Brazil's resource-intensive growth. It also led to deforestation, now especially in Amazônia, as agricultural production helps meet national and global food demand.

At the same time, the world is awakening to the impact of its demand on deforestation and its devastating natural, social, and economic consequences. Global efforts are increasing to promote deforestation-free value chains through consumer awareness and trade measures. Companies increasingly demand deforestation-free products from their suppliers. These trends are at times seen as a threat to economic growth in Brazil and Amazônia. But they also indicate an opportunity to upgrade the country's growth model to one that will simultaneously deliver natural resource protection and sustainable and inclusive development. A change in the growth model matters for Brazil and Amazônia.

Brazil has reached upper-middle-income status on the back of factor accumulation, including demographics and expanding education (labor accumulation), savings and investment (capital accumulation), and expanding the agricultural frontier (land accumulation). In this sense, defor-estation is a key part of the current growth model. Yet factor accumulation has its limits—and, in the case of Brazil, potentially devasting effects for Amazônia's forests. Brazil's future prosperity will hinge on its ability to raise productivity in sectors beyond commodities (the so-called "urban sectors" like manufac-turing and services), which are currently Brazil's least competitive sectors (figure ES.3). Meanwhile, Brazil's export basket remains dominated by com-modities (figure ES.4).

Because the Amazonian economies are nested within the Brazilian economy, accounting for less than 10 percent of Brazilian gross domestic product (GDP), solutions to Amazonian challenges are not limited to Amazônia alone. This memorandum shows that accelerating productivity growth across Brazil, including in urban sectors, would support sustainable and inclusive growth in Amazônia for three reasons:

- Productivity growth in other parts of the country would raise demand for goods produced in Amazônia, especially benefiting states like Amazonas that are integrated with domestic product markets.
- It would attract workers away from Amazônia, reducing the local labor sup-ply and thus raising local wages.
- It would reduce deforestation by attenuating the external competitiveness of Amazonian commodities, reducing pressures on rural lands and thus on Amazônia's natural forests.

A more balanced growth model with productivity gains across all sectors, including the urban ones, is critical for Brazil more generally and for Amazônia specifically.

FIGURE ES.3

Brazil's labor productivity imbalance between commodities and more-urban sectors, 1996–2021

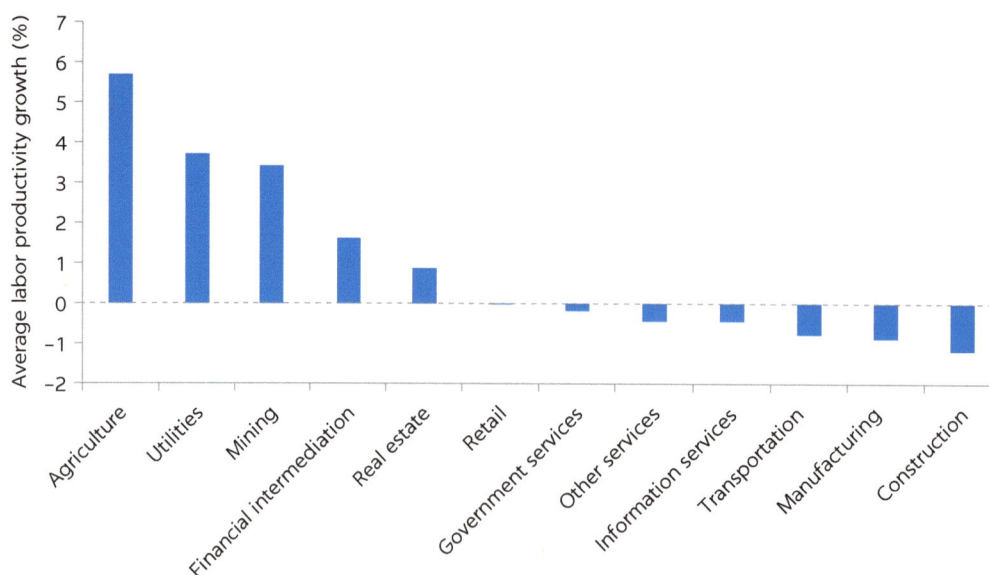

Source: Regis Bonelli Productivity Observatory database of the Getulio Vargas Foundation's Brazilian Institute of Economics (FGV IBRE).
Note: The figure shows average annual labor productivity growth from 1996 to 2021.

FIGURE ES.4
Brazil's commodity-heavy export basket

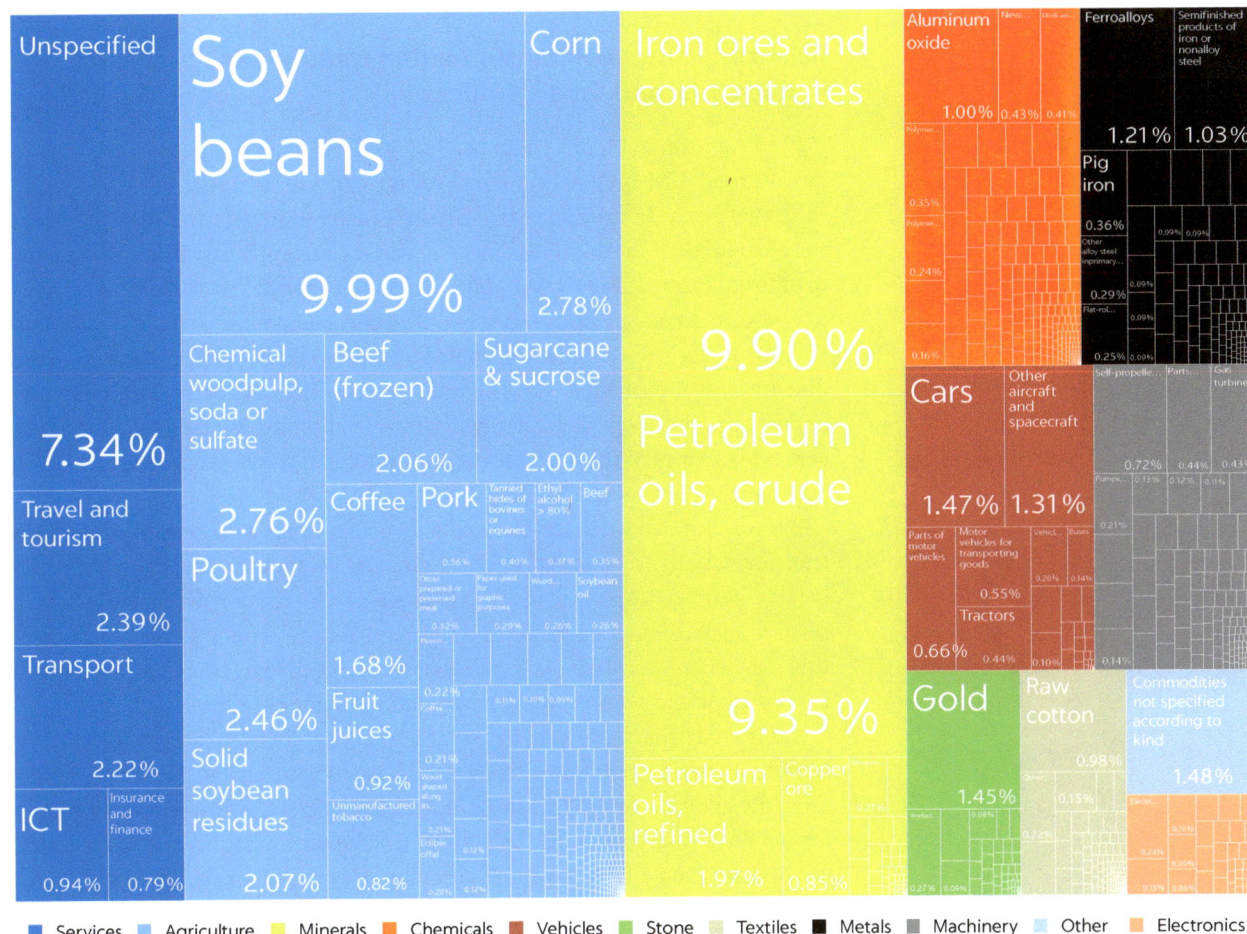

Source: Harvard University's Atlas of Economic Complexity research and data visualization tool (https://atlas.cid.harvard.edu/).
Note: The figure shows shares of Brazil's total merchandise exports in 2019. ICT = information and communication technology.

Regarding the dual objectives of meeting global food demand while curbing deforestation, agricultural intensification assumes an important role, as it implies that more demand can be met with a given amount of land. Accordingly, this memorandum shows that fostering agricultural productivity gains across Brazil raises food output while lowering deforestation. The main reason is that most of this increase in production stems from Brazil's more consolidated agricultural regions, where deforestation is less of a concern because few natural forests remain and land markets are relatively mature.

However, this report also suggests that agricultural productivity gains within Amazônia harbor risks: the availability of vast areas of natural land and their weak protection foster the "Jevons effect" whereby more-competitive farmers demand more land to gain market share ("intensification inducing extensification"). Containing the Jevons effect, especially in Amazônia's less consolidated economies, is critical. It requires effective land and forest governance and a more balanced structural transformation process. At the same time, fostering agricultural productivity across Brazil (where the Jevons effect is more likely to be contained) can help meet global food demand while reducing economic pressures on Amazônia's forests.

INCREASING THE WELFARE OF AMAZONIAN CITIZENS IN URBAN AND RURAL AREAS

Balancing structural transformation through improvements in both rural and urban productivity

Within Amazônia, Mato Grosso has followed the Brazilian resource-intensive growth model, turning the state into a large exporter of agricultural commodities, notably soy. It has made Mato Grosso Brazil's fourth richest state and by far the most affluent in Amazônia. In some ways it currently serves as a role model to other Amazonian states. Yet Mato Grosso's economic rise came at the largely unaccounted cost of vast forest loss: if other Amazonian states follow Mato Grosso's historical path, the Amazonian forests would be largely wiped out, with disastrous environmental and economic consequences. A different development approach is therefore needed, one that brings broad-based economic growth across all sectors of the economy in both rural and urban areas while reducing economic incentives for deforestation.

Increasing productivity in rural and urban areas will require structural transformation. To raise living standards and provide workers opportunities beyond agriculture, it is critical to achieve productivity gains in more urban sectors, such as manufacturing and services. Yet the economic performance of urban areas in Amazônia—as in other parts of Brazil—has been lagging, leading to poor labor market outcomes and precarious living conditions.

Increased urban productivity can also help contain the Jevons effect for two reasons: First, it strengthens other sectors relative to agriculture, thus attenuating the external competitiveness of Amazônia's agriculture sector. Second, it lowers the cost of machinery and inputs (like seeds or fertilizer) relative to the cost of land (and labor). This memorandum shows that urban and agricultural productivity gains are complements—promoting agricultural intensification and thus lowering deforestation. Notably, this complementarity does not depend on the sectors being integrated through value chains. In fact, the memorandum suggests that, where forests are at risk, deep rural value chains in manufacturing can be harmful to forests because productivity gains in the sector would raise the demand for agricultural inputs.

Removing market distortions

Several distortions facilitate the current growth model, many of which are linked to Brazil's colonization process (such as large areas of unregularized land) or to its historical industrial and trade policies. Removing distortions would support the shift to a less resource-intensive, more productivity-driven growth model.

In land markets, the following distortions are among the most significant:

- **Undesignated land.** A huge portion of Amazonian land comparable to the joint size of Norway, Sweden, and Finland remains without proper designation. These areas await designation as conservation units, Indigenous lands, agrarian reform settlements, land eligible for tenure regularization, or some other category of tenure. Undesignated areas have the highest rates of deforestation linked to land grabbing.
- **Tenure insecurity.** Many rural settlers remain without land titling, often for decades, limiting production potential.

- ***Inadequate land taxation.*** The rural land tax (Imposto sobre a Propriedade Territorial Rural, or ITR), originally intended to foster agricultural intensification in its current form promotes extensive agriculture and deforestation.
- ***Weak law enforcement.*** There is ineffective enforcement of the law meant to preserve the integrity of protected areas or Indigenous territories and to safeguard that at least 80 percent of private properties in the Amazon (and somewhat lower values in other biomes) remain forested. In practice, poor law enforcement lowers the cost of illegal logging and land use.

Collectively, these distortions in land markets constrain productivity and lock production factors into extractive practices that could otherwise be invested to promote balanced structural transformation. There are thus important links between policies focused on effective land and forest governance and economic development.

In labor markets, low human capital and skills mismatches undermine productivity and structural transformation—and this can also further contribute to deforestation if less productive farmers cannot transition to more sustainable rural or urban jobs. This highlights the criticality of policies focused on education, training, reskilling, and sustainable livelihoods.

Distortions also exist in input and product markets. Federal rural credit policies currently provide an implicit advantage to agriculture—a land-intensive sector—over other sectors. Rather, policy should focus on supporting climate-smart practices in agriculture, including integrated landscape approaches,[9] that require a shift from incentivizing private goods through relatively untargeted credit to incentivizing public goods, such as through Brazil's ABC Plan.[10]

At the same time, fiscal incentives to manufacturing in Amazonia have not helped incentivize productivity growth and should be reassessed. Generous fiscal incentives from the federal budget (amounting to about 0.4 percent of national GDP) have attracted firms to Amazonas State, arguably Amazônia's most urban economy. Goods from TVs to motorcycles, cell phones, and air conditioning units are produced in the Zona Franca de Manaus (Manaus Free Economic Zone), sustaining many jobs in Manaus, a city of 2 million people in the middle of the rainforest. Despite the substantial fiscal cost, Amazonas has been losing competitiveness, however, and finds it increasingly difficult to attract new businesses. The number of manufacturing jobs has also been declining, with a concomitant increase in capital intensity.

Clearly, more fiscal incentives for firms are not the solution, because they introduce distortions that incentivize companies to locate to places where they would not otherwise locate and result in reduced productivity—the exact opposite of what a productivity-focused growth model would try to achieve. Instead, Manaus should focus more on leveraging its significant urban capabilities by generating a conducive business climate (World Bank 2023b).

In addition, trade barriers significantly distort product markets. Brazil is among the world's more closed economies, and its participation in global value chains tends to concentrate on the export of primary commodities. Manufacturing and services are highly protected, introducing large distortions. Opening up those sectors would attract foreign direct investment, while greater competition tends to raise average productivity in Brazil more broadly and in Amazônia specifically.

Yet care is needed in the design of trade agreements. For one, they can directly hurt Amazonian states that depend on duty exemptions, notably Amazonas, further highlighting the need for a lower dependence on fiscal incentives. Second, they can harbor risks for Amazônia's forests. Under the trade agreement between the EU and the Southern Common Market (MERCOSUL, of which Brazil is a member), whose ratification remains pending, the EU will open its markets to more Brazilian agricultural exports while Brazil will gradually open its manufacturing sector. Various environmental safeguards are intended to reduce the impacts of this improved market access on deforestation. Such safeguards have a mixed record unless adequately implemented and enforced.[11] Trade agreements that include agricultural liberalization will remain a risk to the conservation of the Amazonian forests until economic and institutional maturity have sufficiently advanced.

Ensuring appropriate logistics

Lower transport costs would foster productivity, but transport systems need to be carefully tailored. Rural roads are often the most immediate cause of deforestation. They unlock the potential of land that is currently underpriced because of distortions in the land market. Proper pricing of Amazonian land, taking into account the value of standing forests, would reduce the attractiveness of rural land for agricultural production and unlock labor and capital resources for urban production. A greater focus on urban productivity and connectivity would also lower the need for rural roads. Most Amazonian cities are already connected to markets via road, rail, air, or water transport. In fact, within the Amazon biome, nearly all cities are connected by river, since they originated in the colonial period when settlers navigated the region by river.

Acknowledging the need to minimize adverse impacts on the biodiversity of Amazônia's extensive river systems as much as possible, river transport could be an effective and relatively cost-effective mode of shipping goods and could help reduce Amazônia's cost of remoteness. But there are significant challenges in the cabotage system, including low competition—a structural issue (that tax incentives partly aim to compensate for). Improving the competitiveness of river transport to connect Amazônia's cities could be a better alternative to rural roads.

This memorandum shows for the state of Amazonas that lowering transport costs by 12.5 percent (say, by reforming the cabotage system) would raise the state's GDP by about 38 percent (figure ES.5)—more than the annual amount of current fiscal incentives to the Zona Franca de Manaus.

Developing a network of cities

Given how fragmented the urban landscape is in the Amazonian vastness, only a few cities can likely become competitive. But since the Amazonian population is relatively small, a few successful urban centers could suffice for significant development progress. In the least developed states in Amazônia's north, the state capitals have the greatest potential to become economic nodes. Currently, they tend to be dominated by the public sector, but their urban density, infrastructure, and capabilities could also allow them to develop a more dynamic private sector. A few additional contenders as economic nodes, beyond the state capitals, can be found in the more developed and more populated states of Mato Grosso, Maranhão, Pará, and Rondônia. To the extent that

FIGURE ES.5

Tackling transport costs would benefit many sectors of the economy: Example from Amazonas State

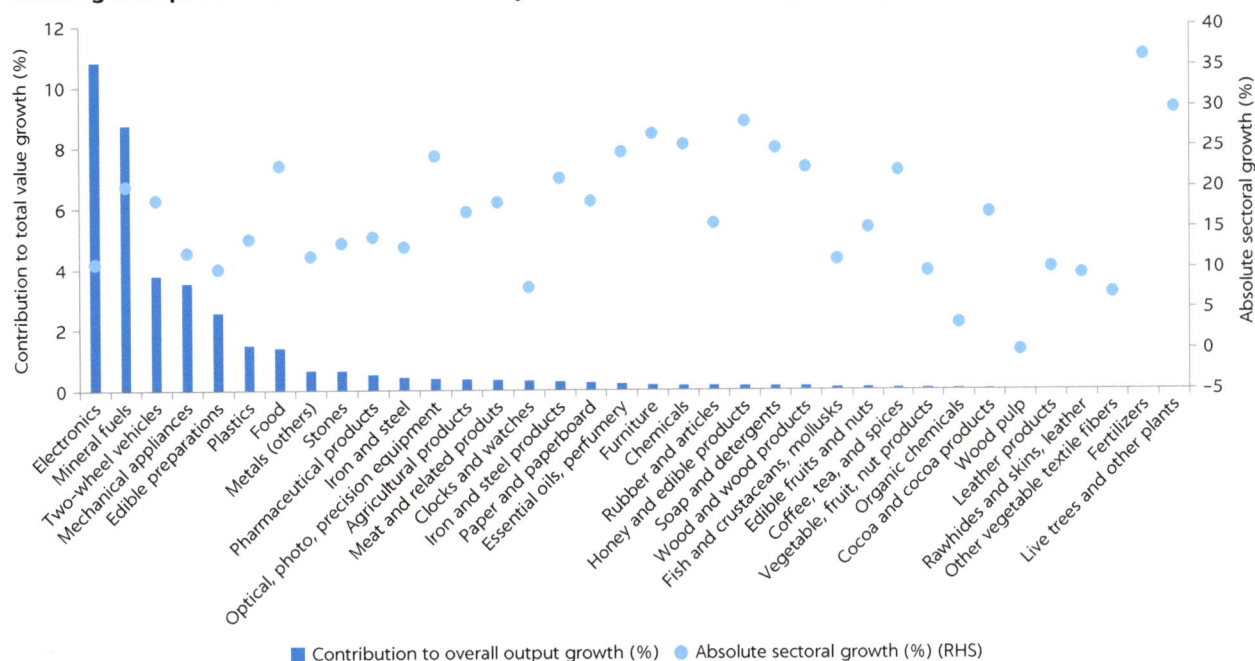

■ Contribution to overall output growth (%) ● Absolute sectoral growth (%) (RHS)

Source: See the companion report to this memorandum, World Bank 2023b.
Note: The figure shows the estimated impacts, by sector, of a 12.5 percent reduction in transport costs from and to Amazonas State. Contributions to growth account for interlinkages across sectors but sectoral effects do not. Larger sectors tend to make higher contributions to overall growth.

these cities already lie in more consolidated agricultural regions of Amazônia, strengthening rural-urban links there can further propel development with lower risks to forests.

While economic nodes have the potential to generate the dynamics supporting regional convergence, several smaller towns could become service nodes. They have less potential for competitive economic dynamism but can act as a bridge between urban and rural spaces. They are large enough to leverage the scale required to deliver certain public services, such as hospitals, and they are associated with better education outcomes than villages. Service nodes can secure a minimum service provision for more remote parts of Amazônia while generating human capital foundations for their inhabitants, serving as stepping-stones for economic nodes of Amazônia or even other parts of the country.

Strengthening institutions in Amazônia

Health and education. Skills pave the way for better jobs, whether in Amazônia, other parts of Brazil, or outside Brazil. Agriculture can absorb a significant amount of unskilled labor, but manufacturing and many types of services are more skill intensive. Strengthening Amazônia's human capital foundation is critical for the implementation of a sustainable and inclusive growth model. Amazonian states have lower levels of human capital than other parts of Brazil. Gaps in health are smaller than gaps in education, but poorer Amazonian states tend to have relatively wider health gaps. This reflects weaker health institutions in poorer areas and lower levels of urbanization, as many health services (such as hospitals) require a minimum scale to operate.

Education holds the key to raising human capital, and there has been some progress in improving education in Amazônia, including for Indigenous people, yet significant gaps remain. On average, 65 percent of 10-year-old children in Amazônia cannot read and understand a short, age-appropriate paragraph, well above the Brazilian average of 48 percent in 2019 (World Bank 2022). The COVID-19 pandemic has further weakened the region's human capital. Regaining ground and building on past achievements requires investing in teachers and strengthening systems for training and reskilling. These interventions at the basic level will also be critical to help raise Amazônia's enrollment in tertiary education—the foundation of modern urban economies.

Municipal services. Living conditions and sanitation services are considerably worse in Amazônia than in the rest of Brazil, especially among the poorer and rural populations. Although poor urban dwellers in Amazônia face worse conditions than in other parts of Brazil, there are clear advantages to living in cities, including near-universal access to electricity and better sanitation. Consistent with the notion of a frontier economy where both infrastructure and public service governance still need to mature, conditions are much worse in rural areas, especially for poor households. As noted earlier, about 86 percent of the rural poor have no access to trash collection, 65 percent have no household water connection, and 48 percent lack a private bathroom.[12] Poor service delivery is linked not only to limited budgets but also to weak governance, including for garbage, sewage, water management, and other urban services, albeit with significant variance in performance across Amazônia. Providing adequate municipal services is critical to raise living standards in urban and rural areas.

In rural areas, minimum service provision can be expensive or even infeasible given the distances and natural conditions of Amazônia, including seasonal flooding. Technology provides some opportunities, including green solutions (such as solar panels, mobile clinics, and satellite internet), despite limitations. Access to basic infrastructure services, such as electricity and water and sanitation, will be needed for all rural communities. Rural investments need to be future-oriented and consistent with economic transformation, which includes facilitating out-migration of rural populations. Ensuring a minimum living standard is important not only from a rural poverty perspective but also to reduce push factors for unproductive urban migration.

Law enforcement. Enforcing the law has been a challenge in Amazônia. This makes it difficult to reduce illegal activities prevalent in Amazônia, ranging from drug trafficking to wildcat mining to illegal deforestation. The magnitude of the challenge shows that although Amazonian states spend a considerable share of their budgets on the judiciary, budgetary outlays do not translate into effective upholding of the law.

In some cases, the attitude of governments toward illegal behavior is rather lax. For example, in the case of land grabbing, deadlines for the regularization of illegally occupied land continuously shift into the future. And certain environmental crimes—such as violation of the Forest Code—are not consistently prosecuted.

Weak law enforcement is often aided by an enabling political environment. Indeed, under a growth model anchored in resource extraction, it will be difficult to protect natural resources. A shift away from this model, as this memorandum advocates, could strengthen the political will to protect Amazônia's forests, because a productivity-led growth model is consistent with conservation.

IMPROVING FOREST PROTECTION

Effective natural capital governance rests on strong, enforced institutions. Protecting Amazônia's forests requires institutional reform to reverse the promotion of extensive agriculture (for example, through rural credit and the rural land tax), regularize lands, and enforce existing laws (command and control). Fostering sustainable value chains will be critical, and private investment must be responsible, supported by good corporate governance. Conservation finance should be leveraged to fund efforts to protect forests while laying the foundations for more sustainable and inclusive development in Amazônia.

Reform rural credit

Rural credit should favor productivity and sustainability. Rural credit policies currently provide an implicit advantage to agriculture—a land-intensive sector—over other sectors. The credit policies inefficiently promote agriculture because of both credit program fragmentation and the distortions arising from credit earmarking, which in fact reduces productivity. Central bank regulations to reduce the direct impact of rural credit on deforestation are an important advance. To further reconcile agricultural growth with environmental and fiscal sustainability, government support to agricultural finance should

- *Focus fiscal support on smaller, productive farmers,* with a greater emphasis on resilience rather than just production and using instruments other than interest rate subsidies, such as partial credit guarantees and support for agriculture insurance;
- *Revise subsidies and incentives to lending programs for large farms,* targeting them exclusively to programs that clearly contribute to public goods (including low-carbon agriculture and agroforestry methods);
- *Revise programs for midsize farmers* based on analyses of current market conditions, gradually phasing out credit quotas and interest rate caps; and
- *Remove quotas and interest rate caps for loans to large farmers* to avoid distorting competition.

Reform land taxes

The rural land tax (ITR) generates perverse incentives for deforestation and could be reformed in four ways:

- *Adjust the stocking rates* (heads of livestock per hectare) employed in calculating the tax to better reflect realistic levels of productivity, associating lower tax rates with much higher levels of ranching productivity. This would affect the tax burden regarding the productive taxable area (which notably excludes forests).
- *Update the definition of total property size* for ITR calculations. Both the productive taxable area and the total property area should be net of forests to reduce deforestation incentives.
- *Better integrate the ITR and the CAR* to ensure that environmental protection areas are respected.

- ***Replace self-declaration by owners with an independent assessment*** to avoid the underestimation of tax responsibilities and make the ITR more effective.

Raising the ITR rate could also reduce deforestation pressures, while returning the proceeds to farmers could mitigate associated welfare losses (Souza-Rodrigues 2019).

Accelerate land regularization

Tenure security affects both welfare and forest protection. In particular, land regularization should be prioritized as a public investment in an essential public good. For example, clarity in land tenure is important to allow an effective and fair conditioning of credit on compliance with forest protection laws. It is also important for accountability because land tenure uncertainty creates gray areas for law enforcement agencies concerning breaches of environmental protection laws.

Completing the designation of undesignated public rural lands is critical. Undesignated areas (figure ES.6) continue to be deforestation hot spots. They may even reflect an implicit policy preference in the states of Amazônia to develop agriculture: currently, land is transferred from public to private ownership at prices much below market levels (figure ES.7), while an unbalanced policy focus on agricultural expansion creates strong expectations that rural land prices will rise. This makes speculation on rising land prices rational, thus incentivizing land grabbing.

A more balanced growth model and a policy focus on agricultural intensification are internally consistent and could create a more enabling environment for land regularization that more strongly favors the conservation of natural lands over land grabbing and extensive agriculture. Conservation finance could provide further incentives.

To be effective, land regularization will first clarify the intention for undesignated areas, including the designation, mapping, demarcation, and registration of

FIGURE ES.6

Amazonas and Pará account for almost two-thirds of the undesignated land in Amazônia, 2019

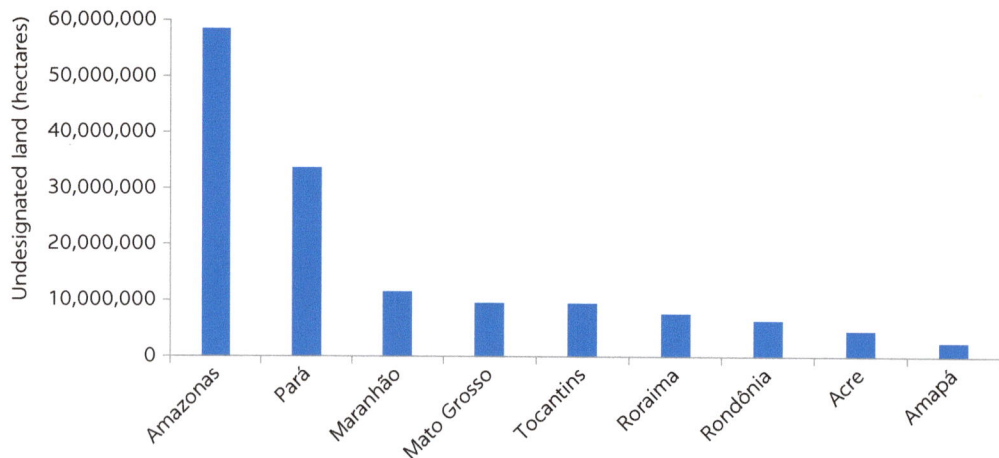

Source: World Bank, based on Brito et al. 2021.
Note: The figure shows hectares of undesignated areas in the Amazonian states. "Undesignated land" refers to public land awaiting designation as conservation units, Indigenous lands, agrarian reform settlements, land eligible for tenure regularization, or some other category of tenure.

FIGURE ES.7

There are significant implicit discounts in land regularization in Amazônia, 2019

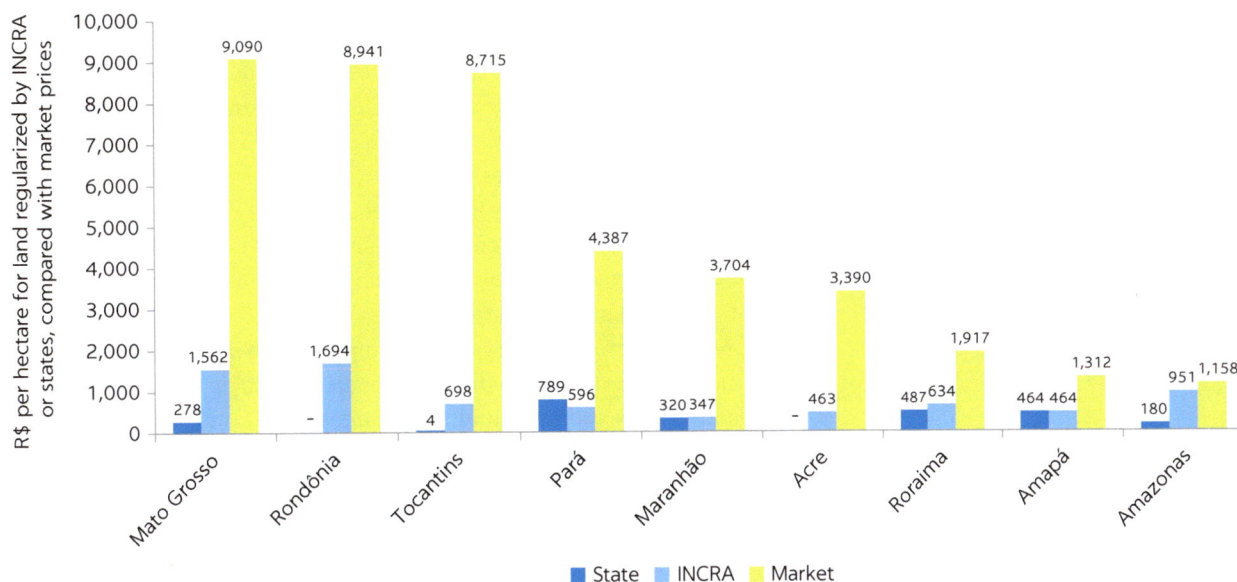

Source: Modified from Brito et al. 2021.
Note: The figure compares values (in reais per hectare) of land regularized by the National Institute for Colonization and Agrarian Reform (INCRA) or by states with market prices. The comparison between average market values per hectare and bare land values is used as a basis for land sales by Amazonian state and state governments. - = data not available.

all federal and state proposed protected areas, Indigenous people's lands, agrarian reform settlements, and other public land categories. Completing this process would clarify property rights and raise the expected legal cost of land grabbing.

Second, both federal and state land adjudication entities should reduce the gap between the low (private) cost of access and the high (social) value of undesignated public lands.[13] This can be achieved by adjusting statutory adjudication values closer to market values, assessing higher penalties for illegal deforestation on all public lands, halting changes to the cutoff year for valid unregularized tenure claims, and opening access to information on land tenure and market transactions to all public and private agents. In strengthening land administration and environmental institutions, federal and state governments should integrate land tenure and environmental regularization, giving special attention to equity. Because deforestation rates are much higher in areas without land tenure regularization, regularization should start with small-scale farmers in National Institute for Colonization and Agrarian Reform (INCRA) agrarian reform settlements, with complementary efforts to ensure environmental compliance.

Third, under the leadership of the federal government, Brazil should mandate the interoperability and integration of its multiple land cadastres, registries, and other land information systems.

Fourth, the government should invest in more accessible and simpler dispute resolution mechanisms and stricter enforcement of land tenure and use regulations. Simple alternative mechanisms for addressing disputes such as arbitration, mediation, and other administrative procedures can keep disputes out of the expensive, slow-moving, and often inaccessible court system. Enforcement should focus on credible penalties for illegal occupation and deforestation of land, document falsification, tax evasion, and registration of nonregularized land parcels in the CAR as a means of claiming ownership.

Strengthen compliance with forest laws

To enhance compliance, Brazil's Forest Code provides for a trading system for Environmental Reserve Quotas (Cotas de Reserva Ambiental, CRAs): landowners whose forest stock fell below the legal reserve minimum before 2008 would be able to cover their deficits by paying other landowners for maintaining an equivalent of forested area above the legal minimum. Operationalizing this system would reduce compliance costs across Brazil and is expected to reduce pressure on natural forests especially in Amazônia.

Command and control is another important tool to assure compliance. Environmental protection in Amazônia—if supported by strong political will to enforce it—can be enhanced by strengthening enforcement agencies and targeting resources to deforestation hot spots. In some cases, weak enforcement is due to institutional constraints, including inadequate resourcing and training of law enforcement agents and overlapping mandates. These shortcomings can be addressed through better resourcing, capacity training, and interagency collaboration. Recently, resources allocated to Brazilian forest law enforcement have been drastically cut (World Bank 2023a). It is imperative that this development be reversed. Ideally, these efforts should extend beyond Brazil's borders to achieve a regional approach to Amazonian protection.

Prioritizing municipalities with the highest deforestation rates can reduce deforestation more efficiently. At the same time, guarding against the danger that deforestation will be displaced to other areas is critical. Conservation finance could help shoulder associated costs and increase political will for better enforcement.

There are strong links between effective forest protection and protecting the integrity of Indigenous lands and livelihoods, which are all currently threatened by current patterns of resource exploitation in Amazônia.

Make value chains more sustainable

The private sector also has an important role to play in the conservation of Amazonian forests, including through effective environmental, social, and governance (ESG) standards. There is potential to strengthen and expand initiatives like the 2006 Amazon Soy Memorandum or the 2009 Zero Deforestation Cattle Agreement. In addition, companies should ensure that they source from sustainable suppliers. To aid this, monitoring and tracing systems should be strengthened, especially in the beef sector.

FOSTERING SUSTAINABLE RURAL LIVELIHOODS IN AMAZÔNIA

In Amazônia's rural areas, policy needs to be particularly sensitive to the local context. In the more consolidated agricultural areas where deforestation already occurred long ago, policy should focus on raising productivity by promoting innovation and value-added activities in established and emerging sectors; supporting a just strategy for climate change adaptation and mitigation (adoption of climate smart-agriculture, soil management, and recovery of degraded lands); and enabling the creation of value from ecosystem services (for example, biodiversity and carbon). The bioeconomy can play an important role in fostering sustainable rural livelihoods in the poorer and more remote areas of Amazônia.

Support the bioeconomy

The bioeconomy, unlocking the natural capital associated with the standing forest, is a small sector of the Amazonian economy. Besides sustainable extraction from the standing forest, the bioeconomy includes rural production like growing açai or cocoa and other nontimber forest products, nonforest production such as fisheries and aquaculture, and services like ecological tourism. Agroforestry production on private lands classified as legal reserves could also be considered as part of the bioeconomy, even though the exact scale of this practice remains unknown. It is a small sector but an important income source for many poor rural producers, including traditional communities. Bioeconomy production also holds considerable cultural value. Supporting these traditional livelihoods thus forms a key pillar of rural poverty reduction strategies.

The bioeconomy can also play a central part in Amazônia's structural transformation. As Amazonian farming professionalizes, smaller, less productive producers will come under increasing competitive pressure. To withstand this pressure, these producers may switch to more extensive production, notably cattle ranching, with strong incentives to turn forest into pasture, potentially illegally. It is thus a social and environmental priority to provide alternative intermediate pathways to such farmers, while future generations are more likely to look for jobs in cities. The bioeconomy offers such an alternative path.

Markets for sustainably produced forest products, as opposed to the same products produced as monocultures (for example, cocoa), remain small but they are growing. Especially if products are differentiated with a credible sustainability label, they can meet growing consumer demand for sustainable products and provide opportunities for bioeconomy producers. At the same time, however, such markets are bound to remain niche given the steep marginal cost curves of commodities sustainably extracted from the forest.

Strengthen social protection

Brazil's advanced social protection system (including social pensions and conditional cash transfer programs) will continue to be important in managing shocks in both urban and rural areas (whether from structural change, climate change, or other sources) and in alleviating poverty. Additional programs—perhaps modeled on the discontinued Program of Support to Environmental Conservation (Bolsa Verde) or the operating Forest Conservation Grant Fund (Bolsa Floresta) system in Amazonas State—may be warranted to preserve traditional ways of life in Amazônia. They can maintain standards of living in traditional communities as Amazônia undergoes structural change.

Strengthening social protection programs alone cannot curb Amazônia's large-scale deforestation but should be part of a broader development approach. Bolsa Verde generally operated in areas with lower risk of deforestation, and reductions in deforestation due to the program are estimated to be small (Wong et al. 2018). Bolsa Floresta's impacts on deforestation were also evaluated as limited (Cisneros et al. 2019). Targeting such programs more to deforestation hot spots may help reduce illegal deforestation by limiting the destitution that could fuel illegal behavior. A key challenge is that conditioning them on deforestation reduction would put beneficiaries, who tend to be among the most vulnerable communities, in direct conflict with illegal loggers, especially in a region where law enforcement is weak.

MARSHALING CONSERVATION FINANCE FOR AMAZÔNIA

Fostering sustainable and inclusive development in Amazônia requires innovative financing. Conservation finance is one source that leverages public and private resources or market mechanisms for climate finance, both domestic and international. Public resources can be motivated by the global public-goods value of standing Amazonian forests. Although such financing would focus on efforts to curb deforestation, it could also more broadly support a more sustainable and inclusive development model.

Most deforestation in Amazônia today is illegal, so financing could support governments in command and control efforts or land regularization. Focusing on governments and their jurisdictions is particularly important since deforestation can "leak" across territories, meaning that interventions successfully reducing deforestation in one area may inadvertently increase it in another. Amazonian governments' achievements in reducing deforestation could be rewarded with conservation finance, generating both resources and political will to protect forests, and conservation finance could support both direct protection efforts and policies aimed at sustainable and inclusive development.

To condition conservation finance on measurable reductions in deforestation at the jurisdictional level, a counterfactual is required: how much deforestation would have occurred if not for government efforts? Brazil's real effective exchange rate (a measure of the competitiveness of Brazil's commodities) and commodity prices (a measure of their demand) approximate Amazonian deforestation well (figure ES.8) and could thus be used to construct such a counterfactual.

FIGURE ES.8

Estimating "forest at risk" in Amazônia using macroeconomic indicators and accounting for policy action to curb deforestation

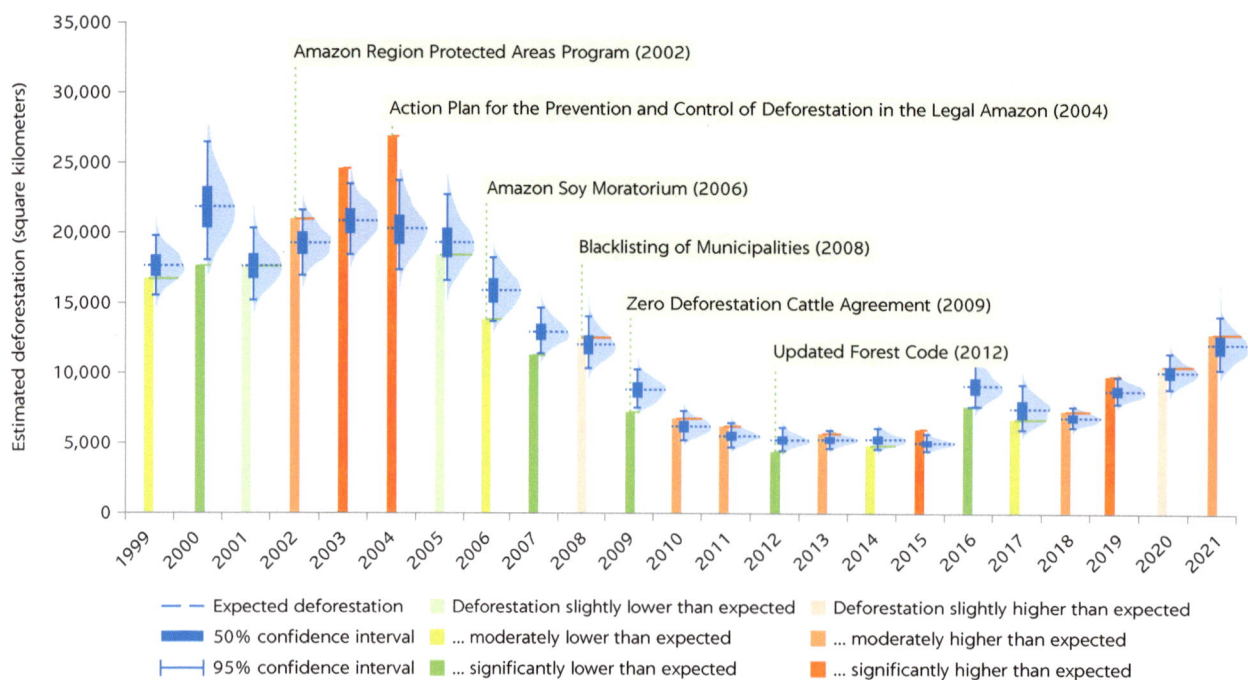

Source: Wang, Gurhy, and Hanusch 2022.
Note: The green and red bars show the level of observed deforestation, and the blue dashed horizontal lines show the estimated level of deforestation with bootstrapped confidence intervals. The model uses lagged commodity prices and the lagged real effective exchange rate, which were identified as the most important predictors using regularization methods. The flags show how various policy interventions coincided with statistically significantly lower levels of deforestation, which can be attributed to policy effectiveness.

When economic forces increase pressure on forests, governments require more resources to maintain the same level of deforestation, and linking the baseline to economic indicators would enable this. Because sufficient productivity growth will lead to a long-term appreciation of the real exchange rate, and because conservation finance helps consolidate forest governance, improving productivity and governance could ensure that deforestation pressures in Amazônia eventually moderate, potentially reducing the overall need for conservation finance.

Linking conservation finance to verifiable outcomes may make it more effective in raising adequate resources to prevent deforestation and promote development in Amazônia. Brazil already has experience tying financing to environmental performance: the Ecological Tax on the Circulation of Goods and Services (ICMS Ecológico) earmarks state tax revenues for well-performing municipalities. Because of the global public-goods nature of Amazônia's forests, there is also a strong case for international financing, for example through initiatives like the Amazon Fund. Generally, there is significant willingness in many countries to contribute to conserving especially the Amazon rainforest, particularly when linked to verifiable outcomes.

A broad range of market-based financing could be leveraged to raise conservation finance for Amazônia if clearly conditioned on slowing deforestation. Specific instruments include green bonds and loans, sustainability-linked bonds, and forest offsets as part of Brazilian or even global carbon markets. In fact, forest offsets are one of the main sources of carbon credits in global voluntary markets, and Brazil already has experience with selling them. Such financial instruments can be further supported by international development finance, through institutions like the World Bank. Beyond voluntary markets, forest credits could be linked to a Brazilian compliance market if the country were to introduce a carbon pricing mechanism like an emissions trading system (for which there is currently significant momentum in Brazil) or a carbon tax.

TOWARD SUSTAINABLE AND INCLUSIVE DEVELOPMENT ON THE AMAZONIAN FRONTIER

Development in Amazônia is a complex challenge, requiring concerted action at the global, national, and local levels (table ES.1). Amazônia belongs to Brazil, but because its forests have global implications, efforts to help preserve them should be shared globally as well. Curbing emissions from land use change would allow Brazil to meet its climate commitments and, since Brazil is otherwise a rather green country with a low-carbon energy matrix, it could unlock major opportunities from global decarbonization trends, from trade in green products to international carbon markets (World Bank 2023a). The timing of different interventions matters and can raise the overall effectiveness of complementary policy packages, guarding against unintended consequences.

Shared efforts

At the global level, but also in Brazil and Amazônia, more sustainably minded consumers, firms, and governments remain central to efforts to rid supply chains and global trade of production that contributes to deforestation. Less-resource-intensive diets will reduce pressure on natural forests, while closing crop yield gaps in the world and across Brazil will limit the demand for frontier expansion

TABLE ES.1 Shared efforts to support sustainable and inclusive development in Amazônia at the global, national, and local levels

OBJECTIVE	GLOBAL LEVEL	NATIONAL LEVEL	AMAZÔNIA
Global sustainable demand and supply			
Consuming more sustainably	✓	✓	✓
Closing crop yield gaps	✓	✓	Yes, guarding against the Jevons effect[a]
Promoting sustainable trade integration	✓	✓	
Balanced structural transformation across Brazil			
Removing distortions in product and factor markets		✓	✓
Fostering sustainable infrastructure and logistics and strengthening urban networks and municipal services in rural and urban areas		✓	✓
Reforming implicit incentives to extensive agriculture (including rural credit and land taxes) and foster climate-smart agriculture		✓	✓
Strengthening human capital		✓	✓
Improved forest protection in Amazônia			
Accelerating land regularization		Yes, for federal lands in Amazônia	✓
Strengthening law enforcement, including forest governance		Yes, for relevant federal agencies and regional collaboration	✓
Avoiding deforestation, promoting reforestation, and restoring degraded lands		Yes, for example, through the CRAs	Yes, guarding against deforestation leakage
Sustainable rural livelihoods in Amazônia			
Strengthening the bioeconomy			✓
Tailoring social protection			✓
Conservation finance			
Providing financing	✓	✓	✓
Receiving financing		Yes, for federal efforts in Amazônia	✓

Source: World Bank.

a. The "Jevons effect" refers to "intensification inducing extensification," whereby agricultural productivity gains locally increase deforestation.
CRAs = Environmental Reserve Quotas (Cotas de Reserva Ambiental).

(Searchinger et al. 2019). Conservation finance should benefit Amazônia but can, in theory, be raised anywhere in the world.

The productivity agenda is a shared one between Amazônia and the rest of Brazil. Factor accumulation and resource exploitation are no longer sufficient to propel development anywhere in Brazil; a much stronger emphasis on productivity, notably in sectors beyond commodities, will be critical for this, promoting more balanced structural transformation across the country. This agenda includes removing market distortions, fostering sustainable infrastructure and logistics, strengthening human capital investments, and repurposing implicit incentives to extensive agriculture and putting them at the service of climate-smart production and productivity. Within Amazônia, federal and subnational efforts should focus on promoting socioeconomic progress while protecting the region's exceptional natural and cultural wealth.

Policy timing and complementarities

Close attention should be paid to the particular characteristics of Amazônia as a frontier region, where both economies and institutions still tend to be relatively new (with the exception of traditional institutions) and require both time and dedicated efforts to mature. Maturity is already higher in some parts of Amazônia, notably in the southeastern part of the region.

Policies focused on institutional and economic maturity are complementary. For example, public investments in education raise economic growth, which generates job opportunities that make it more worthwhile for families to invest in education. Other examples apply to economic development and forest protection. For one, effective forest protection will release resources from extensive agriculture into more productive activities, including in urban areas. Recognizing that Amazônia's population is largely urban could help generate political will to promote productivity to generate more urban jobs. Jointly, effective forest protection and balanced structural transformation across agriculture and urban sectors will contain risks around the Jevons effect, intensifying agriculture and promoting both economic development and standing forests.

Gaining maturity is time-consuming, but protecting Amazônia's forests is urgent. This makes it particularly important to focus efforts and resources, including conservation finance, on land and forest governance. The foundations must be laid in states with low maturity while quickly closing gaps in states with overall higher maturity but nonetheless high levels of deforestation, such as those in the Arc of Deforestation. More gradually, all institutions must be strengthened—from education systems to municipal services to policing and judicial services—raising the overall level of institutional maturity across Amazônia.

Achieving balanced structural transformation is critical to strengthening economic maturity, and this transformation requires investments in productivity, including in urban productivity. For as long as rural poverty is high and urban areas struggle to absorb rural labor, investing in rural livelihoods and providing rural basic services will remain particularly important. Policy should support rural transformation by promoting sustainable, climate-smart rural production practices, including in the bioeconomy, while preparing rural populations for opportunities from the structural transformation and urbanization process. To ensure that traditional communities are not adversely affected by economic disruption (or other shocks, such as from climate change), social protection systems should protect their incomes and sustainable ways of life.

Certain policies promoting economic growth will become less risky to Amazônia's ecosystems when overall maturity is higher. These include trade agreements, especially if they disproportionately stimulate Brazilian agriculture. They also include transport infrastructure investments that raise the external competitiveness of Amazonian farmers—which, under higher overall maturity, is less likely to cause deforestation.

At the same time, certain policies directly rewarding higher forest cover are more efficient when maturity is higher: deforestation leakage is a lesser risk when effective governance suppresses land grabbing and illegal deforestation and when more balanced structural transformation reduces overall deforestation pressures. In these cases, policies incentivizing private agents to spare forested land, to reforest land, or to restore degraded farmland are less likely to be offset by higher deforestation in other areas, making the policies more efficient.

This memorandum suggests that an Amazônia that is rich economically, environmentally, and culturally is possible—but time is running out, and urgent action is needed to make it a reality. It requires a rebalancing of Amazônia's development approach.

NOTES

1. Data are from Brazilian Institute of Geography and Statistics (IBGE) population estimates.
2. Poverty data are from the World Bank, based on IBGE's Continuous National Household Sample Survey (PNADC) 2019 data and a poverty line of US$5.50 in purchasing power parity terms.
3. "Option value" refers to the prospective value of pharmaceutical innovation from the harvest of the biosphere's genetic resources, and "existence value" to the values attached to having the resources available to current and future generations.
4. Annual deforestation data are from the Project for Satellite Monitoring of Deforestation in the Legal Amazon (PRODES) of the National Institute for Space Research (INPE).
5. Unemployment data are from the World Bank, using PNADC 2019 data.
6. Poverty and population data are from the Socio-Economic Database for Latin America and the Caribbean (SEDLAC).
7. Data on public service provision and housing conditions, by demographic category, are from the IBGE's 2019 PNADC. Also see chapter 2, table 2.3.
8. Urban housing data are from the World Bank, using IBGE (2020).
9. An integrated landscape approach is one in which the organizing principle for management of production systems and natural resources is based on rational spatial planning and takes into account socioeconomic, ecological, and institutional considerations. It includes the integration of different agricultural activities, such as crop-livestock or crop-livestock-forestry systems, to maximize ecosystem services.
10. The Low Carbon Agriculture (Agricultura de Baixa Emissão de Carbono, or ABC) Plan promotes low-carbon agriculture.
11. One critical ingredient includes proper certification of beef.
12. Data on access to municipal services are from IBGE's 2019 PNADC. Also see chapter 2, table 2.3.
13. For equity reasons, land parcels below a certain threshold could be exempted.

REFERENCES

Boulton, C. A., T. M. Lenton, and N. Boers. 2022. "Pronounced Loss of Amazon Rainforest Resilience since the Early 2000s." *Nature Climate Change* 12 (3): 271–78.

Brito, B., J. Almeida, P. Gomes, and R. Salomão. 2021. *Dez fatos essenciais sobre regularização fundiária na Amazônia Legal* [Ten Essential Facts about Land Regularization in the Legal Amazon]. Belém, Brazil: Imazon.

Cisneros E., J. Börner, S. Pagiola, and S. Wunder. 2019. "Impacts of Conservation Incentives in Protected Areas: The Case of Bolsa Floresta, Brazil." Payments for Environmental Services (PES) Learning Paper 2019-1, World Bank, Washington, DC.

IBGE (Brazilian Institute of Geography and Statistics). 2012. "Os indígenas no Censo Demográfico 2010: primeiras considerações com base no quesito cor ou raça" [Indigenous People in the 2010 Demographic Census: First Considerations Based on Color or Race]. Report, IBGE, Rio de Janeiro.

IBGE (Brazilian Institute of Geography and Statistics). 2020. "Aglomerados subnormais 2019: Classificação preliminar e informações de saúde para o enfrentamento à COVID-19" [Subormal Agglomerates 2019: Preliminary Classification and Health Information for the Fight against COVID-19]. Report, IBGE, Rio de Janeiro.

Pendrill, F., U. M. Persson, J. Godar, and T. Kastner. 2019. "Deforestation Displaced: Trade in Forest-Risk Commodities and the Prospects for a Global Forest Transition." *Environmental Research Letters* 14 (5): 055003.

Ranzani, O. T., L. S. L. Bastos, J. G. M. Gelli, J. F. Marchesi, F. Baião, S. Hamacher, and F. A. Bozza. 2021. "Characterisation of the First 250 000 Hospital Admissions for COVID-19 in Brazil: A Retrospective Analysis of Nationwide Data." *Lancet Respiratory Medicine* 9 (4): 407–18.

Searchinger, T., R. Waite, C. Hanson, J. Ranganathan, and E. Matthews. 2019. *Creating a Sustainable Food Future: A Menu of Solutions to Feed Nearly 10 Billion People by 2050.* Washington, DC: World Resources Institute.

Souza-Rodrigues, E. 2019. "Deforestation in the Amazon: A Unified Framework for Estimation and Policy Analysis." *Review of Economic Studies* 86 (6): 2713–44.

Strand, J. 2022. "Valuation of the Brazilian Amazon Rainforest." Background note for this report, World Bank, Washington, DC.

Wang, D., B. Gurhy, and M. Hanusch. 2022. "Could Sustainability-Linked Bonds Incentivize Lower Deforestation in Brazil's Legal Amazon?" Background note for this report, World Bank, Washington, DC.

Wong, P. Y., T. Harding, K. Kuralbayeva, L. O. Anderson, and A. M. Pessoa. 2018. "Pay for Performance and Deforestation: Evidence from Brazil." Paper funded under Project No. 230860, Research Council of Norway, Oslo.

World Bank. 2022. "Brazil Human Capital Review: Investing in People." Report 173246, World Bank, Washington, DC.

World Bank. 2023a. *Brazil Country Climate and Development Report.* Washington, DC: World Bank.

World Bank. 2023b. "Urban Competitiveness in Brazil's State of Amazonas: A Green Growth Agenda." Companion paper for this report, World Bank, Washington, DC.

Abbreviations

ABC Plan	Low-Carbon Agriculture Plan (Brazil)
ACTO	Amazon Cooperation Treaty Organization
CAR	Rural Environmental Cadastre
Conab	National Supply Company
COP26	2021 United Nations Climate Change Conference (26th annual Conference of the Parties)
CRA	Environmental Reserve Quota (Brazil)
DETER	Real-Time Deforestation Detection System
Embrapa	Brazilian Agricultural Research Corporation
ESG	environmental, social, and governance
ESMS	environmental and social management system
ETS	emissions trading system
EU	European Union
FPE	State Participation Fund (Brazil)
FUNAI	National Indian Foundation (Brazil)
GDP	gross domestic product
GHG	greenhouse gas
HCI	Human Capital Index (World Bank)
IBGE	Brazilian Institute of Geography and Statistics
INCRA	National Institute for Colonization and Agrarian Reform (Brazil)
ITR	Imposto sobre a Propriedade Territorial Rural (rural land tax, Brazil)
NDC	Nationally Determined Contribution
OECD	Organisation for Economic Co-operation and Development
PAA	Food Acquisition Program (Brazil)
PES	payment(s) for ecosystem services
PNADC	Continuous National Household Sample Survey
PNAE	National School Feeding Program (Brazil)
PNDR	National Policy for Regional Development (Brazil)
PPA	Multiannual Plan
PRODES	Project for Satellite Monitoring of Deforestation in the Legal Amazon
REER	real effective exchange rate

RHS	right-hand side
SAEB	Evaluation System of Basic Education (Brazil)
SEDLAC	Socio-Economic Database for Latin America and the Caribbean
TFP	total factor productivity
UN	United Nations
WWF	World Wide Fund for Nature

1 Developing Amazônia, One of the World's Last Frontier Regions

MAREK HANUSCH, JON STRAND, AND CLAUDIA TUFANI

KEY MESSAGES

- Brazil's Amazônia is one of the world's last frontier regions, where economic expansion clashes with ancient ecosystems and traditional communities.
- High levels of social deprivations in the region coexist with the destruction of forested lands of exceptional biodiversity and major significance for the global climate.
- Given the Amazon rainforest's high public-good value relative to generally smaller values from economic use of converted natural land, deforestation is a massive destruction of wealth and implicit incentive for an inefficient, resource-intensive growth model.
- Not only does the rainforest deserve protection but Amazônia's other biomes also provide important ecosystem services.
- A delicate balancing act for policy protects Amazônia's natural forests while fostering sustainable and inclusive growth.
- Systems are already in place to protect Amazônia's forests. They urgently need to be enforced to stem the recent acceleration in deforestation.
- In the longer term, shifting from a resource-intensive growth model toward one based on productivity would help reconcile development and forest conservation.
- Conservation finance can straddle the shorter and longer term, incentivizing forest protection while funding the transition to a more suitable development approach for Amazônia.
- A more sustainable and inclusive development approach requires the following:
  - Improving the welfare of Amazonian citizens by fostering productivity through structural transformation in both rural and urban areas.

- Protecting the forest by strengthening land and forest governance, including the enforcement of existing laws (command and control).
- Fostering sustainable rural livelihoods, by unlocking the natural capital associated with the standing forest and protecting the poor and traditional ways of life.
- Marshaling conservation finance linked to measurable reduction in deforestation and drawing on public and private resources or market-based solutions.

AN ECONOMIC MEMORANDUM FOR BRAZIL'S AMAZONIAN STATES

This memorandum focuses on the nine states of Brazil's "Legal Amazon," referred to here as Amazônia—encompassing Acre, Amapá, Amazonas, Pará, Rondônia, Roraima, Tocantins, Mato Grosso, and parts of Maranhão. Amazônia is home to about 28 million Brazilians in a vast area of about 5 million square kilometers, so its population density is low. And while it covers nearly 60 percent of Brazil's territory, it accounts for only about 13 percent of the population.[1] It includes all of Brazil's portion of the Amazon biome and parts of other important ecosystems, such as the Cerrado savanna and the Pantanal wetlands.

Between natural riches and socioeconomic needs

The Amazon rainforest harbors exceptional natural wealth. Brazil alone accounts for about 65 percent of the Amazon basin, with the world's second longest river and the largest remaining primary rainforest.[2] The Amazon biome accounts for about 25 percent of the world's terrestrial biodiversity and 17–20 percent of its fresh water (Charity et al. 2016; Siikamäki et al. 2019). It also moderates global greenhouse gas (GHG) effects and thus has a major impact on the global climate. But more than the Amazon rainforest deserves protection, for all Amazonian biomes have high biodiversity and provide important ecosystem services.

Amazônia is not only home to important ecosystems; it is also home to many poor Brazilians, requiring solutions that sustainably improve living standards. Amazonian states, especially in the North region, count among the poorest in Brazil. In 2018, the average value added per capita in Amazônia was about 20 percent lower than the national average (figure 1.1).[3] The poverty rate is high, with 36 percent of Amazônia's population living on less than US$5.50 a day, and development outcomes (especially human capital) are low.[4] Only the states in Brazil's Northeast region are poorer. In purely economic and social terms, Amazônia's challenges are like those of other lagging regions across the world and even in Brazil nationally. But the social and environmental disruption associated with Amazônia's economic development draws considerable public attention, both within Brazil and across the globe. This memorandum explores policy packages that can simultaneously reduce poverty and curb deforestation.

FIGURE 1.1

Amazônia is a lagging region

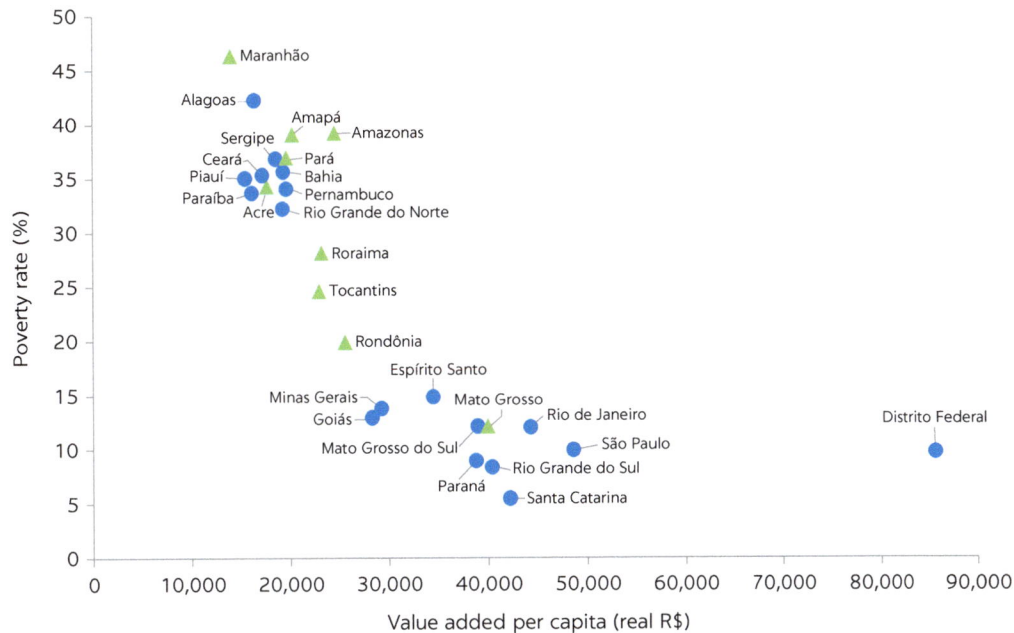

Source: World Bank, based on Brazilian Institute of Geography and Statistics (IBGE) data.
Note: The figure shows 2018 data for all Brazilian states; green triangles identify the states of Amazônia.
The "poverty rate" is US$5.50 per person per day.

A delicate balance

Fostering economic and social development in Amazônia, while maintaining the natural forests, is a delicate balancing act. Successive governments have attempted to improve local economic conditions in Amazônia. This has often put people and nature at odds, resulting in large-scale deforestation in some parts of Amazônia and, in some cases, conflict with traditional ways of life. In 2021 alone, the equivalent of about 1.8 million soccer fields was deforested.[5] This memorandum explores a new development approach where policy is carefully rebalanced to promote economic development for the diverse Amazonian population in greater harmony with this valuable yet fragile ancient ecosystem.

Economic development occurs through structural transformation, referring to rising productivity and the increasing concentration of economic activity in urban areas. It implies a transition from an agriculture-led economy to an economy increasingly led by industry (including manufacturing) and services. Amazônia is already highly urbanized; about three-quarters of Amazonians live in cities, and urbanization will further advance with structural transformation (figure 1.2). Policy needs to ensure that jobs and livelihoods are created where people live—and where people will increasingly move *to*. This requires growth to be based more sharply on productivity, including urban productivity. This does not require new cities; it requires making existing towns and cities work. Amazônia's current growth model is tilted toward agriculture. Rebalancing it to allow urban areas to take their due place in Amazônia's development story will promote economic development while attenuating economic pressures on natural forests.

FIGURE 1.2

Amazônia has been experiencing, and will continue to experience, structural transformation and urbanization

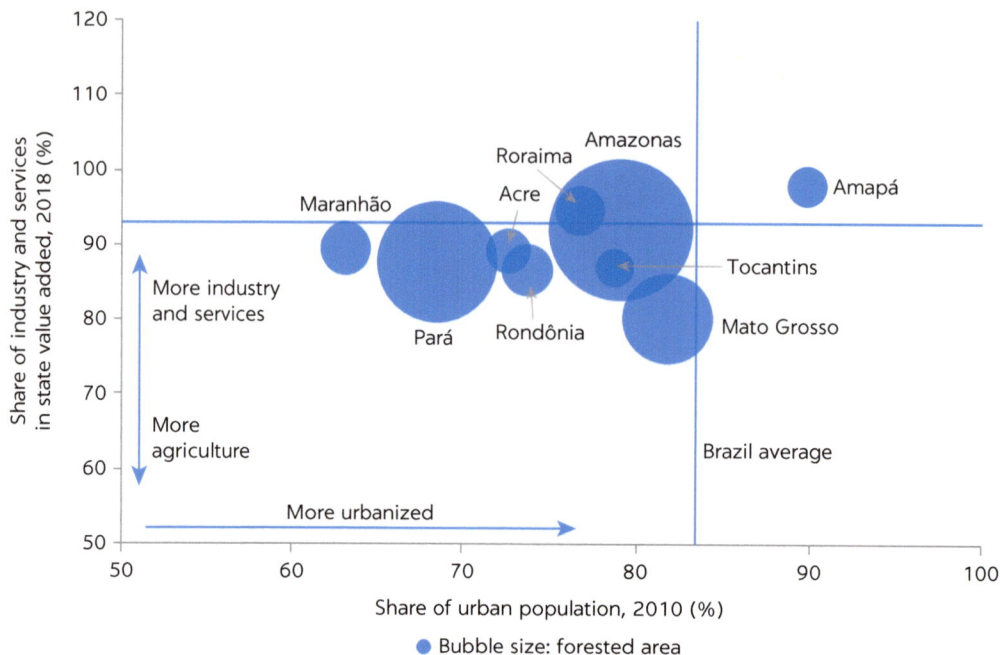

Bubble size: forested area

Sources: World Bank, based on Brazilian Institute of Geography and Statistics (IBGE) data and the World Bank's Hidden Dimensions of Poverty data set.
Note: Bubble size reflects the relative size of forested areas in 2015 within the nine Brazilian states constituting Amazônia. Structural transformation will imply a further shift of states toward the figure's upper-right quadrant (toward the Brazilian averages, which Amapá has already exceeded).

Structural transformation is a long-term process, however, and protecting Amazônia's forests is an urgent priority. In the 2000s, Brazil made impressive progress in protecting Amazônia's forests, especially the Amazon, including the expansion of protected areas and Indigenous territories, the Action Plan for the Prevention and Control of Deforestation in the Legal Amazon (PPCDAm), and blacklisting of municipalities, and various private sector initiatives in the soy and beef sectors. In addition, Brazil has a strong Forest Code. Yet the systems designed to protect Amazônia's forests, and their enforcement through command and control interventions, have recently been weakened. This has contributed to accelerating deforestation. Political will to build on past successes is critical to make Brazil a pioneer in forest protection once more, ensuring that economic growth does not deplete natural capital. This memorandum shows that forest protection and a productivity-led growth model are complementary.

Poverty is particularly severe in rural areas. As much as structural transformation will bring overall benefits, it does entail disruption, including for rural populations. The new development approach needs to also generate sustainable rural livelihoods in Amazônia. Amazônia is home to many traditional communities, including the largest number of Indigenous people in Brazil. Sustainable forest production ("extractivism") is intimately coupled with traditional ways of life. In addition, poor rural settlers in agricultural reform settlements (*assentamentos*) require prospects for higher living standards. Fostering rural sustainable livelihoods is critical to reduce poverty and to preserve rural and traditional cultures while also providing an important source of resilience to producers whose lives will be disrupted by structural transformation. The bioeconomy—unlocking the natural capital of the standing forest—thus is an integral part of a carefully balanced policy mix for Amazônia.

A new development approach for Amazônia should be bolstered by conservation finance, which leverages the substantial public-good value of Amazonian forests to raise resources to protect them and to invest in more sustainable and inclusive growth, promoting standing forests and higher living standards. It can tilt the balance toward the protection of public goods and help generate political will where trade-offs between economic development and forest protection are perceived. This memorandum shows that such finance can derive from public and private resources or from market-based mechanisms.

Amazônia's development challenges are nested in Brazil's growth model, calling for policy attention beyond Amazônia. Brazil's growth model overshadows the small economies of the Amazonian states, which jointly account for less than 10 percent of national gross domestic product (GDP). This memorandum shows that Brazil's growth has been stuck as the country's struggles to raise the productivity of its nonprimary, urban sectors. This struggle causes socioeconomic problems (for example, large favelas) while bringing vast deforestation to the frontier regions of Amazônia. To promote economic development while conserving forests, Brazil must address these productivity challenges because the current model is unable to sustain meaningful economic growth while depleting the country's natural wealth. A policy rethink has become even more urgent now as the global trading system focuses increasingly on sustainability concerns.

Opportunities from a new development approach

A more affluent, more sustainable, and more inclusive Amazônia is possible. If Brazil becomes a more productivity-driven economy, more balanced across economic sectors, demand will rise for Amazonian goods while providing new job opportunities in other parts of the country—and it will draw resources to more productive activities, making the economic expansion in Amazônia's Arc of Deforestation (further discussed below) less attractive. A growth model focused on productivity and more balanced structural transformation in Amazônia would be consistent with this national context and strengthen economic cohesion across Brazil while further improving income opportunities for Amazonians. Especially when coupled with human capital interventions and other measures to allow Amazonians to seek new opportunities, this approach will limit the risk of unemployment and of rising inequality.

Brazil would be a much greener country if not for deforestation. Brazil's energy matrix is 48 percent green (world: 15 percent), and its power matrix is over 80 percent green (world: 27 percent) (World Bank 2023a). Deforestation and agriculture are Brazil's most important sources of GHG emissions. Therefore, curbing deforestation plays a critical role in enabling Brazil to reach net zero (or even negative) emissions by 2050. It is also a requirement for Brazil to meet its Nationally Determined Contribution (NDC) under the Paris Climate Accords ("Paris Agreement") and its commitment made during the 2021 United Nations (UN) Climate Change Conference (known as the 26th annual Conference of the Parties, or COP26) to zero illegal deforestation by 2028. In a decarbonizing world, all of Brazil stands to gain from its green potential, notably in international trade.

For Amazônia, a new development approach would mean higher living standards, economic convergence with more advanced regions in Brazil and the world, and the preservation of its exceptional natural and cultural wealth.

Organization of this chapter

This chapter first presents the historical development of Amazônia as a frontier region, emphasizing the social groups that continue to shape its social and economic dynamics and the interplay with the environment, notably the rainforest. Next, the chapter argues that the land use conversion associated with the region's development is a form of redistribution of public wealth to private wealth—with massive destruction of wealth overall. This highlights the urgency to protect Amazônia's natural forests. Yet economic development can be a threat to natural forests if Amazônia does not pursue a development approach tailored to its environmental context. Such an approach would need to combine strong forest protection with a sharper focus on productivity, including in urban areas, while generating sustainable rural livelihoods, funded by conservation finance. The chapter concludes by embedding the memorandum in the public policy agenda and providing a road map for the remaining chapters.

THE AMAZONIAN FRONTIER: SOCIAL, ECONOMIC, AND ENVIRONMENTAL ORIGINS

Amazônia is one of the world's last frontier regions, where modern economies clash with traditional lifestyles and ancient ecosystems.[6] Indigenous peoples moved into the Amazon about 11,000–13,000 years ago, living mostly along the basin's numerous rivers. They not only are credited with living in harmony with the millennia-old rainforest but also may have shaped up to 12 percent of the Amazon's landscapes. This way of life came under threat from Portuguese colonization in the 1500s, which focused initially on the eastern coast of Brazil. The town of Belém, Portugal's administrative capital in the Amazonian territory of Greater Pará, was founded in 1616. From there, expeditions pressed deep into the Amazon rainforest, erecting forts and settlements.

Colonialism nearly annihilated the Indigenous people in Amazônia. Colonists relied almost entirely on largely enslaved Indigenous workers. Slavery and forced labor, armed conflict, suicides among despairing Indigenous people, and—by far the main cause—new diseases introduced by European settlers (including smallpox, measles, malaria, tuberculosis, and influenza) reduced Amazônia's Indigenous population from several million to about 300,000 today. Portuguese colonial legislation repeatedly outlawed Indigenous enslavement, but it was not effectively abolished until 1748. (African slavery was abolished in Brazil in 1888.) Today's Indigenous people descend largely from tribes that managed some level of accommodation with the Portuguese (like the Mundurukú), that migrated along the river (like the Tikuna), or that remained undiscovered and isolated—as some still are.

Today's *quilombola* (descending from fugitive African slaves) and *ribeirinho* (riverbank) communities are also associated with colonial history and its associated poverty. Brazil imported more African slaves than any other country, but Amazônia was too poor to import slaves and relied instead on

Indigenous labor. Thus, there are far fewer *quilombola* communities in Amazônia than in the rest of Brazil. The mixing of races in Portuguese Brazil—and, following Brazil's independence in 1822, in the Brazilian empire—meant that there were large groups of *caboclos*, people of mixed Indigenous heritage. As for other people of color, most *caboclos* were poor. Their resulting discontent erupted into one of the few attempted revolutions in Brazil, the Cabanagem Revolt in Greater Pará in 1835–40. After their defeat, some *caboclos* stayed in the cities, but many migrated deep into the Amazon. Living along the banks of the Amazon River, they acquired skills from Indigenous groups and learned sustainable hunting, farming, and fishing techniques. These *caboclos* were the ancestors of today's *ribeirinho* communities. They also played an important role in providing unskilled labor, as during Amazônia's rubber boom.

Despite considerable toil, violence, and loss of human life, the Amazon rainforest yielded little economic benefit for centuries, largely because of its unsuitability for agriculture. Unlike the temperate forests familiar to Europeans, which store nutrients and calcium in the soil, rainforests extract them from the soil and store them in their biomass.[7] This means that rainforest land was poorly suited for most agriculture, with lower-quality soils that degrade quickly. While relying more on fish- and turtle-based diets, Indigenous peoples circumvented this fertility problem by using rotating slash-and-burn techniques to create *roças*, or forest gardens, that were small enough to eventually regenerate.

European experiments with cattle and imported crops, by contrast, failed miserably. Instead, settlers focused on producing manioc (an indigenous crop) while sending expeditions into the forest to harvest forest products.[8] These extractivist products included sarsaparilla, ipecac, false cloves (used to conceal the taste of rotting meat), guaraná, and some herbal remedies. Cocoa, native to the Amazon and other parts of Latin America, was for a while a popular export crop to feed Europe's "chocolate mania," although production relatively quickly moved elsewhere, especially to Bahia State and West Africa.[9] Coffee, which is not native to the Amazon, was introduced to Belém in the 1800s, but production also quickly moved to other parts of Brazil.

The Colonial Frontier—and the New

A new dynamism began to emerge in Amazônia in the late 1800s, with two distinct frontiers eventually emerging: one along the major rivers (the Colonial Frontier) and one moving up from the southeast about 100 years later (the New Frontier) (box 1.1). The Colonial Frontier was linked to colonial expeditions and settlements, accelerating with the rubber boom in the Amazon from 1879 to 1912. The New Frontier was linked to the agricultural development of the Cerrado savanna biome to the southeast of Amazônia, supported by innovations in soil adaptation developed by the Brazilian Agricultural Research Corporation (Embrapa); the relocation of Brazil's capital from Rio de Janeiro inland to Brasília; and the construction of highways to support agricultural expansion into Amazônia.

The economy that rubber built
The rubber boom brought prosperity to Amazônia for the first time, demanding harsh toil by Amazônia's poor and vulnerable populations. Rubber grew wild in the Amazon rainforest, especially near Manaus in the state of Amazonas, as well as in Acre (which Brazil purchased from Bolivia during the rubber boom).

Amazônia's biomes and frontiers

Amazônia (officially called the Legal Amazon) comprises nine of Brazil's 27 states, in the Brazilian part of the Amazon biome, as well as parts of the Cerrado savanna and Pantanal wetlands. Amazônia includes the entire North region and parts of the Center-West (Mato Grosso) and the Northeast (selected municipalities of Maranhão) of Brazil (map B1.1.1).

The term *frontier region* is often associated with the westward-shifting North American frontier. Frontier regions are remote areas with low population density, an ongoing settlement process, and a relatively weak presence of the state. The expanding frontiers bring new institutions and production modes. This often comes with major changes in land ownership, notably toward greater private ownership (and associated land speculation), while the exploitation of abundant natural resources contrasts with the scarcity otherwise of many other forms of

capital (Johansen 1999). Such major socioecological transformations are marked by (at times violent) conflict, often to the detriment of Indigenous and other traditional communities (Schetter and Müller-Koné 2021).

Under Portuguese colonization, Amazônia's Colonial Frontier (including Acre, Amapá, Amazonas, Pará, and Roraima) extended along the major rivers. From the 1970s and 1980s, roads unlocked agricultural land in the southeast of Amazônia, giving rise to what is here called the New Frontier (including Mato Grosso, Rondônia, Tocantines, and the relevant municipalies of Maranhão)[a] (map B1.1.2). Deforestation is concentrated in the southeast of Amazônia, as economic expansion into the interior destroys natural forests in its wake. This is Brazil's agricultural frontier, synonymous with the Arc of Deforestation (map B1.1.3).

MAP B1.1.1

Brazilian states and biomes, and the boundaries of Amazônia

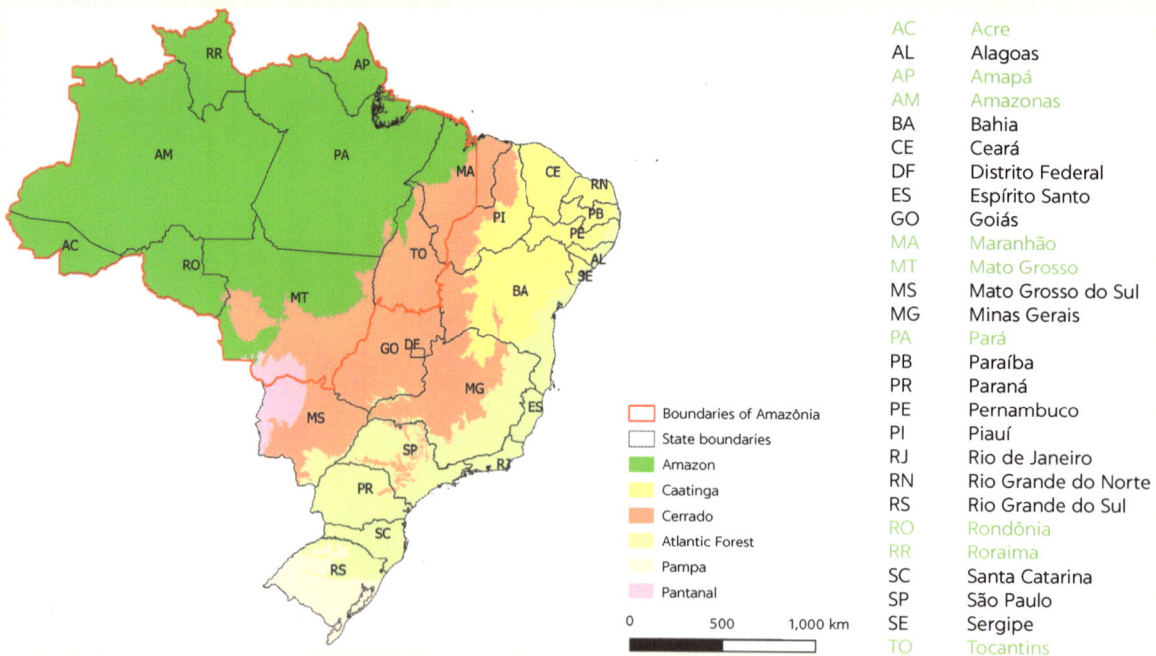

AC	Acre
AL	Alagoas
AP	Amapá
AM	Amazonas
BA	Bahia
CE	Ceará
DF	Distrito Federal
ES	Espírito Santo
GO	Goiás
MA	Maranhão
MT	Mato Grosso
MS	Mato Grosso do Sul
MG	Minas Gerais
PA	Pará
PB	Paraíba
PR	Paraná
PE	Pernambuco
PI	Piauí
RJ	Rio de Janeiro
RN	Rio Grande do Norte
RS	Rio Grande do Sul
RO	Rondônia
RR	Roraima
SC	Santa Catarina
SP	São Paulo
SE	Sergipe
TO	Tocantins

Legend:
- Boundaries of Amazônia
- State boundaries
- Amazon
- Caatinga
- Cerrado
- Atlantic Forest
- Pampa
- Pantanal

0   500   1,000 km

Sources: Brazilian Institute of Geography and Statistics (IBGE) and World Bank.
Note: The states constituting Amazônia are highlighted by red boundaries in the map and by green letters in the key.

continued

Box 1.1, *continued*

MAP B1.1.2

Amazônia's states of the Colonial and New Frontiers

■ Colonial Frontier
□ New Frontier

Source: World Bank.

MAP B1.1.3

The Arc of Deforestation in Amazônia

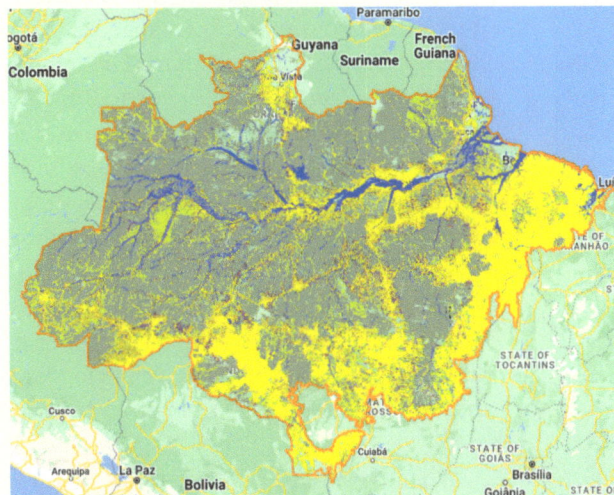

Source: Terra Brasilis platform of the Brazilian Project for Satellite Monitoring of Deforestation in the Legal Amazon (PRODES) of the National Institute for Space Research (INPE), http://terrabrasilis.dpi .inpe.br/app/map/deforestation?hl=en. Creative Commons attribution 4.0 SA license (CC BY-SA 4.0). *Note:* Yellow marks deforested areas; dark green is standing forest. The extensive deforestation along the southeastern border of Amazônia is the "Arc of Deforestation."

a. Although Maranhão also has an old colonial history, most of the relevant municipalities included in the definition of "Amazônia" are more like the states of the New Frontier.

With the discovery of the industrial capabilities of rubber (especially for tires) and the acceleration of the Industrial Revolution globally, rubber became a sought-after commodity and briefly became Brazil's biggest export. As rubber prices soared, Manaus became an affluent city, sporting the latest technologies (including a tram and electric street lighting) and lavish buildings (a magnificent opera house). Rubber was shipped along the Amazon River, with Belém, at the mouth of the river, accumulating wealth through related financial and logistics services.

However, as with cocoa before, rubber was soon being cultivated in other parts of the world, and large rubber plantations in British Malaya (today's Malaysia) and Dutch Sumatra (today's Indonesia) began to outcompete Amazonian extractive rubber. To break the British-Dutch monopoly, the Ford Motor Company briefly experimented with Amazonian rubber once again, but the attempt failed, largely because of damage from pests (the South American leaf blight), which wiped out entire monoculture plantations and left behind the now mostly deserted Fordlândia in the state of Pará. A second rubber boom, from 1942 to 1945, was short-lived, occurring in response to Allied supply disruptions during World War II as the Pacific region fell under Japanese control.

Promoting economic development

The Superintendency for the Development of the Amazon (SUDAM) was founded in 1966 to reinvigorate economic development in Amazônia. SUDAM's territorial mandate was defined to include the newly conceived area of the Legal Amazon (in this memorandum, synonymous with "Amazônia"), comprising nine states that were eligible for SUDAM support. SUDAM invested in infrastructure projects and, in 1967, developed the Zona Franca de Manaus (Manaus Free Economic Zone), Amazonas, with the objective of stimulating economic growth in this remote region of Amazônia. Manaus's main logistics connectivity is by river. In addition to Manaus, nine other (smaller) municipalities in the states of Acre, Amapá, Amazonas, Rondônia, and Roraima also received free trade designations. The zones were overseen by a new Manaus Free Trade Zone Superintendence (SUFRAMA). Their competitiveness derived from tax and import exemptions—a considerable cost advantage in the context of Brazil's policy of import substitution industrialization.

The government also built highways to open the interior of the Amazon rainforest and supported the settlement of poor farmers. The BR-230 highway, or Transamazónica ("Trans-Amazon") Highway, running roughly parallel to the Amazon and Madeira Rivers, provides west–east connectivity and directly or indirectly connects Belém in Pará to Porto Velho in Rondônia (and to Acre via the more recent BR-317 as well as to Manaus and Boa Vista in Roraima via the BR-319 and BR-174). The highway is currently in poor condition and rarely used.

When drought and famine struck northeastern Brazil in 1971, the military government embarked on a new policy summarized by the slogan, "A land without people for a people without land." The objective was to bring 1 million colonists to government-cleared 100-hectare plots (*assentamentos*). Far fewer people came, and in many cases their lands remain unregistered to this day. Poverty persists among these farmers, reflecting tenure insecurity, remoteness, and the low quality of the land, which distinguishes this frontier from the New Frontier in the south and southeast of Amazônia.

The Arc of Deforestation

Agricultural expansion from the south and southeast into Amazônia became the New Frontier, resulting in the Arc of Deforestation, destroying forests in the Amazon rainforest, Cerrado savanna, and Pantanal wetlands. Across the country, successive governments have been incentivizing agricultural development through expanded rural credit and a system of land taxes.

In the 1950s and 1960s, the government unlocked new agricultural land by building the BR-010 highway connecting Brasília and Belém, thus opening up large regions between the Tocantins and Araguaia Rivers for farming. Another major road was the BR-364,[10] which connected Cuiabá (originally an old mining town in Mato Grosso) with Porto Velho in Rondônia. Between 1976 and the 1990s, the government built the BR-163 (the "soy highway"), connecting Cuiabá with Santarém (and its river port) in Pará and linking to the Trans-Amazon Highway.

These roads (especially where paved)[11] provided new opportunities, especially for farmers in the more developed parts of Brazil who had large families and only had enough land to pass on to elder children. Younger children often would end up with nothing and migrate to Amazônia. These lands were largely Cerrado savanna that have been turned into arable land.

Massive deforestation (the original Arc of Deforestation) resulted and advanced into Amazônia, even reaching states of the Colonial Frontier (box 1.1). Today, most deforestation in Amazônia is taking place around 11 municipalities in Pará, Mato Grosso, Rondônia, and Amazonas, though deforestation is also relatively high in the Cerrado savanna in Tocantins and Maranhão. The panels of map 1.1 show how Brazil's transport network skirts Amazônia, supporting the economic expansion.

MAP 1.1

Brazil's transportation networks reveal Amazônia's remoteness from markets

a. Railroads and state capitals

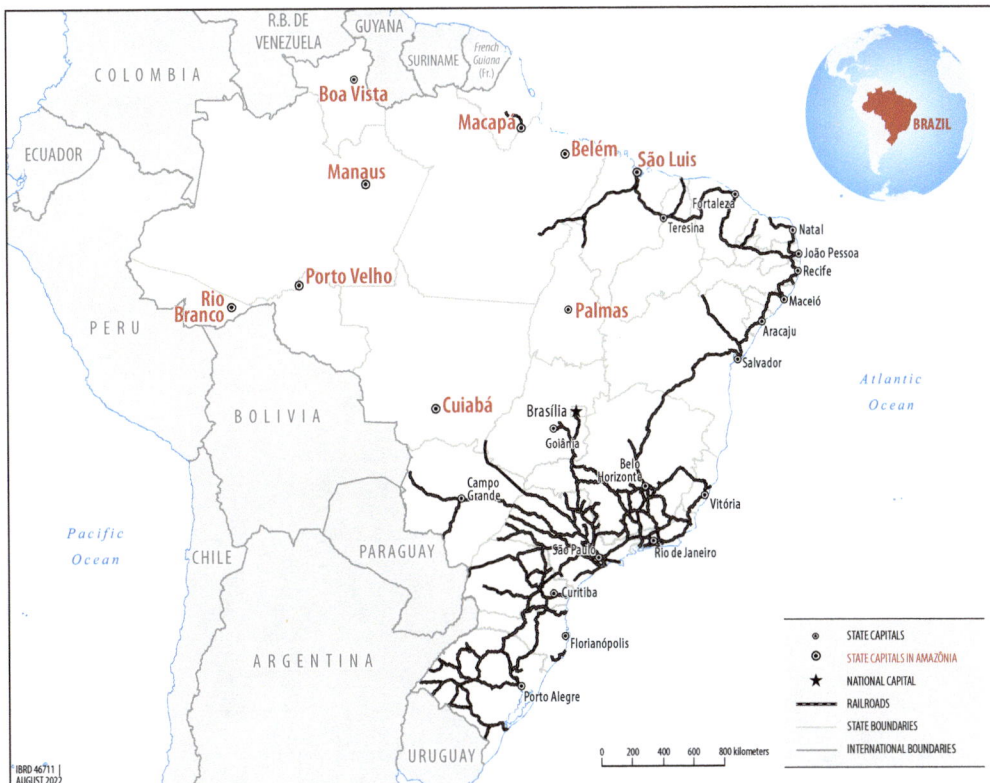

continued

MAP 1.1, *continued*

b. Paved and unpaved roads

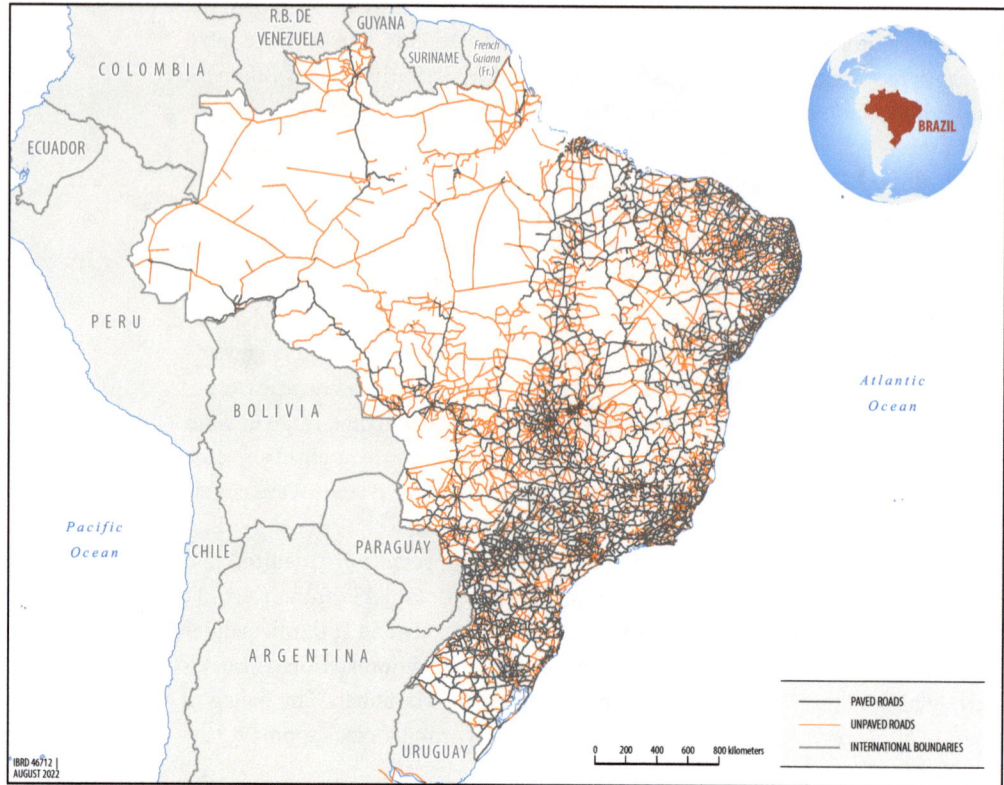

c. Navigable rivers and sea ports

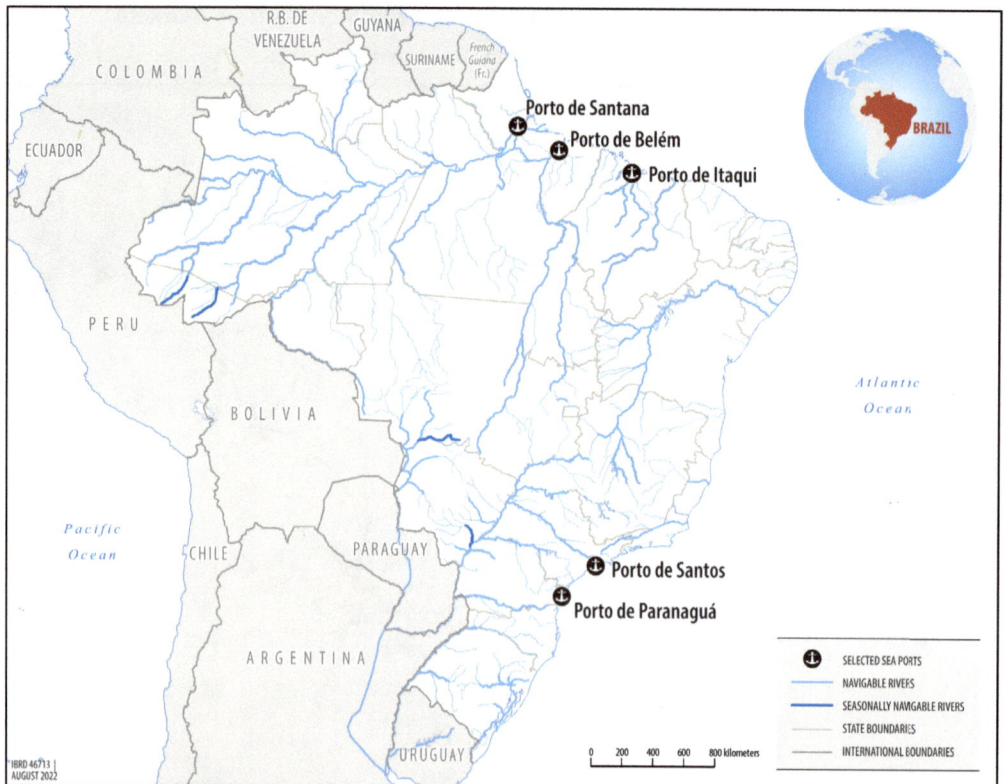

Sources: Modified from Souza-Rodrigues (2019), using National Plan for Logistics and Transport (PNLT) and National Institute for Space Research (INPE) data.

The role of mining and dams

The frontier economy increasingly included mining. The region is rich in highly demanded mineral resources—from iron ore and gold to "climate action" minerals (including copper and rare earth minerals), which offer the promise of clean energy technologies (wind, solar, and batteries) in the global transition to a net-zero carbon future. The world's largest iron ore deposit was discovered in the 1960s in southeastern Pará and exploited by the mining company Vale. The rail infrastructure required to export the Carajás ore brought some direct socioeconomic benefits to municipalities, but the growth of human settlement in large mining projects (such as the Carajás Mine and the Trombetas bauxite mine, also in Pará) and related infrastructure corridors also resulted in significant environmental damage.

Today, there is a strong commitment of private capital to more sustainable mining development. But the activities of artisanal or wildcat miners (*garimpeiros*) in more than 450 illegal mining sites (mainly gold) in Amazônia has resulted in extensive environmental degradation, at times within Indigenous areas and in some cases in violent conflict with Indigenous people. The modern *garimpeiros* are heavily mechanized and highly capitalized, getting a substantial part of their revenues from gold smuggling and money laundering.

Dams have also contributed to environmental destruction in Amazônia. Dams were erected in the Amazon basin to provide power to manufacturing industries associated with mining (for instance, to produce aluminum from the Trombetas bauxite mine) and to urban areas. The Belo Monte Dam in Pará, completed in 2019, was the latest controversial hydropower project. In the generally flat landscape of Amazônia, dams generate vast reservoirs and cause considerable damage. The Tucuruí Dam servicing Trombetas flooded 400,000 hectares of virgin forest and large tracts of Indigenous lands in 1987.[12] The Belo Monte Dam, feeding into Brazil's broader energy grid, has been associated with the displacement of 20,000 people and large losses in biodiversity.

Dams have also disrupted free-flowing rivers, which are essential for preventing erosion, maintaining the health of freshwater fish stocks, mitigating the impact of extreme floods and droughts, and supporting a wealth of biodiversity. Disrupting rivers' connectivity often diminishes or even eliminates these critical ecosystem services.

Amazônia's urbanization

As Amazônia developed, it became increasingly urbanized. Between 1960 and 2010, the population of Amazônia increased tenfold.[13] About three-quarters of Amazonians live in cities, a much higher percentage than in neighboring countries sharing the Amazon basin, and only somewhat below the Brazilian average. Urbanization has been a consequence of population growth and rural–urban migration, linked to agricultural transformation, the growth in urban jobs, and to the better amenities associated with towns and cities. Much of this was driven by the government's desire to settle Amazônia, and apart from some municipalities in the New Frontier, the government remains the largest formal employer (map 1.2).

Most Amazonians today live in Pará and in the New Frontier states (Rondônia, Mato Grosso, Tocantins, and Maranhão), and most poor Amazonians live in urban areas. Pará alone accounts for about 31 percent of the Amazonian population, with the states of the New Frontier—Mato Grosso, Maranhão, Rondônia, and Tocantins—accounting for another 45 percent, leaving just about 24 percent

MAP 1.2

Government is the largest formal employer in Amazônia, especially in the Colonial Frontier

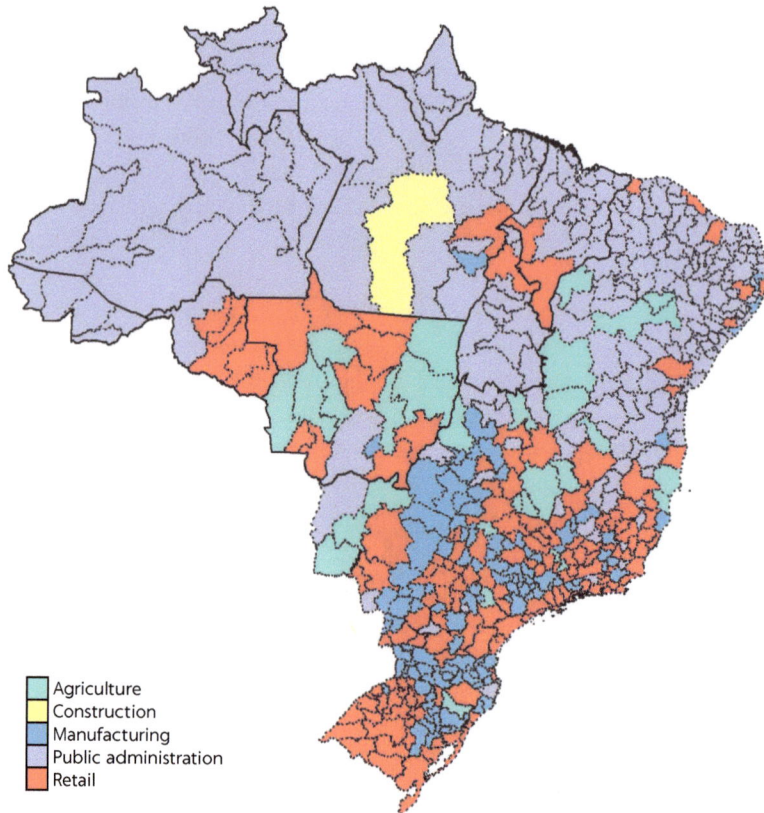

Agriculture
Construction
Manufacturing
Public administration
Retail

Source: World Bank, using the Registro Annual de Informações Sociais (RAIS) database of Brazil's Ministry of Labor, 2017 data.
Note: The map shows the dominant sector of formal employment, by immediate region (a group of municipalities in the same state).

to the vast areas of the Colonial Frontier including the states Acre, Amapá, Amazonas, and Roraima.[14] There are relatively few large cities within the Amazon rainforest, with Manaus standing out with about 2 million inhabitants (map 1.3). Most Amazonians live to the southeast of the Arc of Deforestation (that is, the deforested side). Because Amazônia is highly urbanized, most poor people live in towns and cities; Amazônia hosts 13 percent of Brazil's urban population but 25 percent of the urban poor.

History's lessons

History holds five main lessons for Amazônia:

- The long-standing goal of Brazilian governments to develop Amazônia economically remains intact, even though concerns about the environmental impacts of unsustainable development are rising in number and influence.
- Amazônia (especially the Amazon rainforest) harbors substantial natural wealth, but that wealth is not always easily appropriated by local people. Some medical advances in Europe, such as anesthetics, have been based on indigenous drugs. Coca has inspired multiple refreshments, including

MAP 1.3
MAP 1.3
Amazônia's system of cities

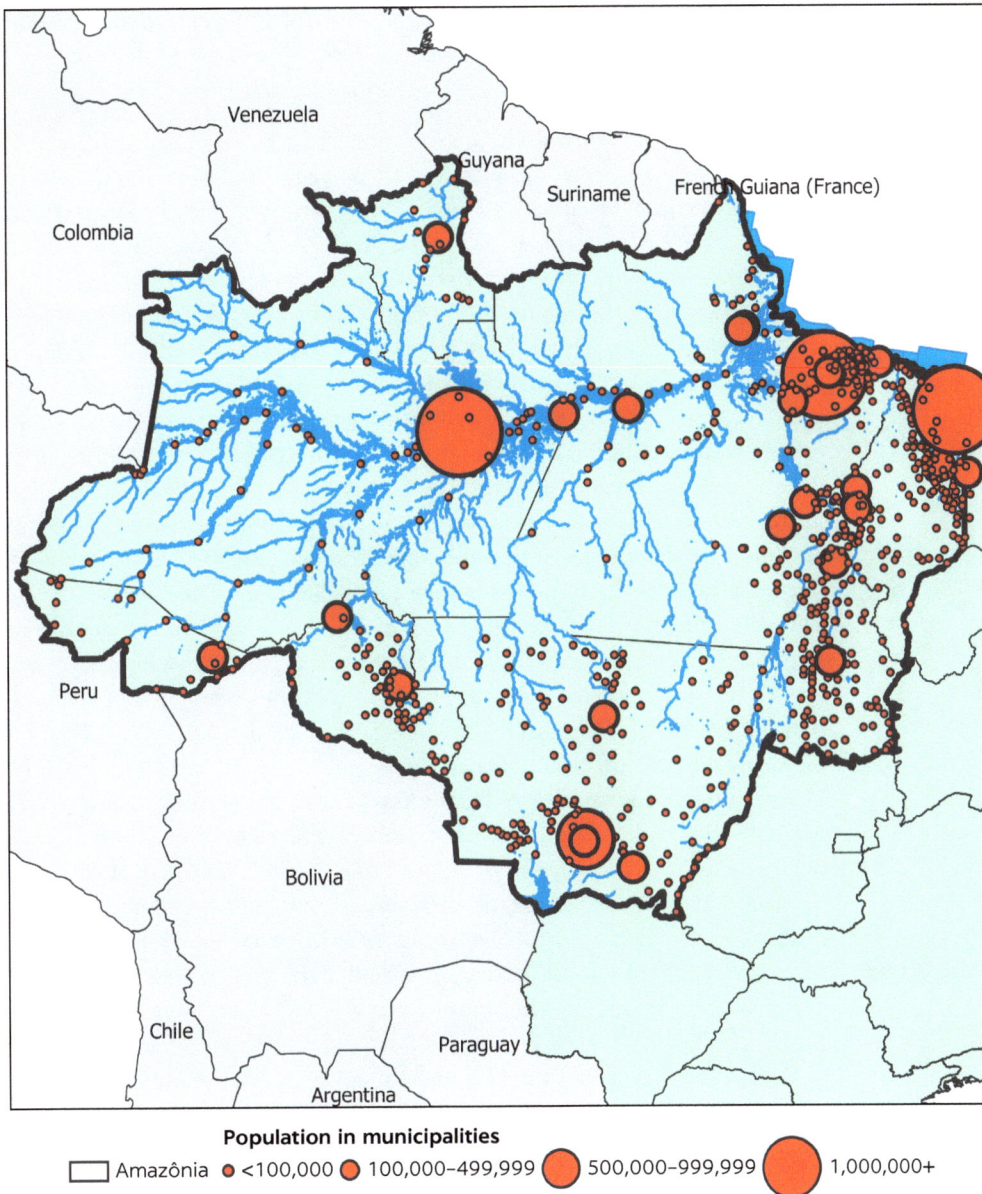

Population in municipalities

☐ Amazônia ● <100,000 ● 100,000–499,999 ● 500,000–999,999 ● 1,000,000+

Source: Sanchez Martinez et al. 2022.
Note: Bubbles indicate the cities' relative population sizes.

Coca-Cola, one of the most popular US products (although Coca-Cola no longer includes coca).

- Amazônia has struggled to commercialize its natural products at home, and cultivated production in other parts of the world has outcompeted native extractivist methods. Considered "biopiracy" by many Brazilians, such commercial cultivation includes quinine in India (to treat malarial fever), cocoa in West Africa, and rubber in southeast Asia.

- Amazônia retains its attraction for people who are trying to improve their condition in life, from farmers and *garimpeiros* to land speculators. At times, this results in conflict over land use and benefit sharing with communities that are more traditionally connected to the land, such as Indigenous people and *ribeirinhos*.

- Because settlements developed along rivers in the Colonial Frontier, the vast majority of towns and cities, especially in the Colonial Frontier, today can still be serviced through water transportation.

Agriculture on the frontier. Amazônia remains a frontier region, with socio-economic and environmental objectives often in conflict despite the challenges to agriculture in many areas, especially in the rainforest. Floodplains (*várzea*) make up about 3 percent of the Amazon territory, and these lands cannot be used for production other than extractivist types for most of the year.

Because trees in the rainforest store nutrients in their biomass rather than in the ground and because of quick degradation of soils, land in the Amazon rainforest is ill suited for most crops. However, some crops do well in Amazon soils and some technological innovation—such as certain types of grasses—have created better conditions for cattle (perhaps as a harbinger of agricultural innovation, such as previously opened up the Cerrado savanna). While there are many areas that are unsuitable for agriculture, the jury is still out on the extent of agricultural suitability of Amazonian soils, given current available technology (Soares-Filho et al. 2014; Souza-Rodrigues 2019; Brandão Jr. et al. 2020).

Cattle ranching has increasingly spread across Amazônia, in the Arc of Deforestation and further inland as well, such as in Roraima, whose savannas make it relatively suitable for cattle and later agricultural production.[15] Mining remains another challenge to natural forests, directly through *garimpeiros* and indirectly through infrastructure development.

Institutional capacity. Many institutions in Amazônia are still weak and thus less able to provide critical social and economic services or to counter illegal deforestation and other forms of lawlessness (Trajber Waisbich, Husek, and Santos 2022). Public service provision (from basic infrastructure to the quality of health and education services) lags considerably in Amazônia. Although there is some variance across states, and acknowledging the mature traditional governance systems, institutions in Amazônia tend to be weaker than in the rest of Brazil.

Poorly developed land markets, including large undesignated areas, leave room for *grilagem* (land grabbing), fuel violent conflict, and are a major enabler of illegal deforestation. Weak law enforcement also encourages the illegal timber business and fails to prevent violation of environmental regulations on private properties. And in recent years, the Latin American drug trade has made incursions into Amazônia, both benefiting from weak institutions and contributing to their erosion.

Institutions to protect Indigenous people and natural forests. The Brazilian government has made important advances in protecting Amazônia's natural lands and its traditional communities, but pressures persist. The Constitution of 1988 recognizes the rights of Indigenous communities, *quilombolas*, and *ribeirinhos*, but gaps remain in the protection of these rights. Large tracts of land in Amazônia have been declared to be Indigenous territories. In 1961, the vast Xingu Indigenous Park was created as the world's first area set aside solely for its Indigenous peoples and their environment (not a national park for visitors), and large additional tracts of land have since been designated for Indigenous groups.

In addition, Brazil has set aside other large areas of the Amazon biome as protected areas. The Tumucumaque National Park is one of the world's largest tropical forest parks, covering 70 percent of Amapá, Brazil's second least populous state. In 2004, Brazil launched the Action Plan for the Prevention and Control of Deforestation in the Legal Amazon (PPCDAm), which included near real-time satellite monitoring to curb illegal deforestation. In 2012, Brazil updated its landmark Forest Code, establishing minimum reserve areas of forested land of 80 percent in private areas in the Amazon biome (and lower minimums for other Amazonian biomes).[16] Under the Amazon Soy Moratorium, the private sector also committed not to grow soy on deforested Amazon land after 2006 or to purchase soy grown in such areas. However, these successes in curbing deforestation in the early 2000s have been outpaced by accelerating deforestation since about 2015. This memorandum shows that this reversal has been due to economic factors and a weakened policy environment.

THE VALUE OF THE AMAZON RAINFOREST: PUBLIC VERSUS PRIVATE WEALTH

There are many ways of thinking about the value of natural forests, some of which is private and some of which is public. Given the available data, this section focuses on the Amazon rainforest, which is not meant to dispute the important natural wealth of other biomes.

For Indigenous and other traditional communities, the value is linked inextricably to their way of life. In broader economic terms, the rainforest generates values that can be appropriated directly (private goods accruing to individuals) and indirectly (public goods, which are nonrival and nonexcludable,[17] such as carbon capture and storage, biodiversity, local climate impacts, and other ecosystem services)—with benefits that accrue to the global population rather than simply to a specific country or region.

The most important value aspects of the Amazon rainforest are *exploitation values* and *protection values*. Strand (2022) distinguishes between these two overriding concepts:

- *Exploitation values* are largely private values, harvested when the forest is cut down and its area and resources converted to other uses.
- *Protection values* are largely public values, gained from the forest area when its resources remain intact.

The rainforest's protection values

A conservative assessment of the total annual protection value of the Brazilian Amazon rainforest is US$317 billion a year (Strand 2022). This total includes three components: private use values, local and regional public-good values, and global public-good values. The total value is dominated by a global public-good value (carbon sequestration, biodiversity protection, and forest cover protection) of US$285 billion. In addition, US$12 billion are private values, and US$20 billion are local and regional public-good values (table 1.1).

Most of the total protection values are uncertain. Those presented in table 1.1 are calculated in a highly conservative way regarding key value parameters (such as the value of carbon and of possible biophysical impacts) and the exclusion of several important ecosystem values for which there are no reliable figures. This approach implies that the overall protection values are underestimated, perhaps greatly so.

TABLE 1.1 Assessed annual private, regional public, and global public protection values of the Brazilian Amazon rainforest total US$317 billion a year

US$, billions

EXPLOITATION VALUE[a]		PROTECTION VALUE[b]					
ALL PRIVATE (DIRECT USE)		PRIVATE VALUE (DIRECT USE)		REGIONAL PUBLIC VALUE (INDIRECT USE)		GLOBAL PUBLIC VALUE[c] (INDIRECT USE)	
Agriculture (crops or pasture)	25–75	Timber	1	Agriculture	7.5	Indirect use value	210
				Livestock	1.5	Carbon dioxide storage	210
				Soy, other agricultural products	2.5		
				Pollination	3.5		
		Nontimber	8.7	Nonagriculture	12.5	Option value	10
		Brazil nuts	1.8	Water regulation services (water and erosion)	8.7	Biodiversity	10
		Rubber	0.2				
		Other nontimber	6.7	Regional climate	2.3		
				Fire protection	1.5		
Timber values	10–15	Sustainable tourism	2.3			Existence values	65
						Biodiversity	35
						Forest cover	30
Mining	8						
Subtotal	**43–98**	**Subtotal**	**12**	**Subtotal**	**20**	**Subtotal**	**285**
TOTAL	43–98			317			

Source: Strand 2022.

Note: The estimated values cover the total Brazilian Amazon rainforest. "Direct use" refers to private goods whose value accrues to individuals. "Indirect use" refers to public goods whose value accrues to regional or global populations.

a. The "exploitation values" shown in this table are private values, harvested when the forest is cut down and its area and resources converted to other uses.

b. The "protection values" shown in this table include some private values but are largely public values, gained from the forest area when its resources remain intact.

c. Global "indirect use" values accrue to the global population; "option value" refers to the prospective value of pharmaceutical innovation from the harvest of the biosphere's genetic resources; and "existence values" are the values attached to having the resources available to current and future generations of humans.

Private protection values

The direct private protection values of the Amazon have been assessed at US$12 billion annually. Direct private protection values include activities that are considered sustainable, meaning that they intrude minimally on the forest and its sensitive ecosystem (Strand et al. 2018). These activities (assessed at US$1 billion a year) include timber produced through low-impact or reduced-impact logging techniques as well as harvesting selected trees in forest concession areas.

There are also important nontimber forest products. Table 1.1 assesses the annual value of two of them: Brazil nuts (US$1.8 billion) and rubber (US$200 million). Fish catches in the Amazon and its tributaries, valued at more (perhaps far more) than US$1 billion a year, are also included in this measure. The assessed annual joint value of these nontimber products is US$12 billion.

In addition, sustainable tourism is valued at US$2.3 billion for the regional population. Arguably, private protection values also accrue to tourists themselves and hence are of direct use even if not in monetary terms, and tourism can have important indirect ecological educational value as a nonassessed positive externality.

Public-good values

The public-good value of the Amazon is considerable and accrues to Brazil, the rest of South America, and the world. These values are appropriated indirectly and include both regional and global benefits. Regional benefits include indirect use values, while global benefits include indirect use values, option values, and existence values.

Regional public values. The regional public-good values represent benefits to humans in several indirect ways. They include specific climate effects for Brazil and neighboring countries. Amazon forest losses lead to changes in regional rainfall patterns ("flying rivers"),[18] affecting agricultural productivity across South America and hydropower output, which is essential for Brazil's electricity supply. These forest losses can also affect regional temperatures and the occurrence and severity of droughts. Maintaining forest cover also provides a range of other local and regional ecosystem services. It provides pollination services to local agriculture and water-regulating services by reducing flooding and droughts. And it reduces the risk of forest fires, which can affect adjacent lands.

In addition, there are regional (and potentially global) health benefits from maintaining the Amazon. Smoke from forest fires damages health, while the loss of forests can lead to increased insect prevalence and higher incidence of vector-borne diseases (box 1.2).

The overall value of these services is vast. Table 1.1 accounts for only the fraction of these services that can easily be measured, or about US$20 billion annually.

Global public values. The global public-good value dominates the overall value of the Amazon, especially carbon values. Most of the rainforest's global value is related to three aspects: storage of carbon (released when trees are cut down), biodiversity protection, and forest cover protection.

Carbon stock values make up the greatest share of measurable values for the Brazilian Amazon, representing at least US$7 trillion of their present stock value.[19] This in turn corresponds to an annualized carbon dioxide (CO_2) storage value of at least US$210 billion.[20]

Biodiversity protection, though difficult to assess precisely, represents another important global public value of the Amazon (box 1.3). One assessment approach is through global population sample surveys that ask people about their willingness to pay to maintain the Amazon's biodiversity as a global

---

BOX 1.2

Deforestation and pandemics: Possible connections

Connections exist between human-caused environmental degradation and epidemics and pandemics. Many pandemics are caused by viruses that are transmitted to humans from wildlife, especially rodents, birds, and bats.

Tropical forests are a rich source of pandemic-causing viruses, and deforestation and forest fragmentation bring people and wildlife into close contact.

Deforestation has been linked to more than 30 percent of new diseases reported since 1960, including Ebola in Africa, Nipah in Malaysia, and Hendra in Australia.

Two characteristics of the Amazon—a high diversity of wildlife virus hosts and rising deforestation rates—are common to hot spots for emerging diseases. Currently, the Amazon is still considered a low-spillover area, but this could change if deforestation is not controlled.

Source: Vale et al. 2021.

BOX 1.3

Biodiversity and ecosystem services of Amazônia's natural forests

The Amazon harbors exceptional biodiversity, with about 10 percent of total known global biodiversity and 25 percent of terrestrial biodiversity. It hosts about 40 percent of the world's remaining rainforest. Almost 80 percent of the Amazon biome is covered by evergreen forest, with smaller areas of flooded forests and swamps (or *várzea*), deciduous forest, and savanna. The Amazon basin contains the world's largest river system, and the Amazon River is the world's second longest river. The Amazon is home to about 40,000 plant species, over 2,500 species of freshwater fish, 1,300 species of birds, 427 species of mammals, 400 species of amphibians, and 370 species of reptiles, including many endemic and endangered plant and animal species (such as the jaguar, the Amazon River dolphin, and the giant pirarucu). The World Wide Fund for Nature (WWF)[a] estimates that about 90–95 percent of Amazon mammals are known but only 2–10 percent of its insects.

The Amazon provides vital ecosystem services, many of which are assessed in table 1.1. Brazilian law defines four categories of ecosystem services:

- *Ecosystem-related goods* such as water, food, and wood
- *Services to support life on earth*, such as nutrient cycling, pollination reduction, weed control, and biodiversity
- *Regulatory services* to maintain ecosystem processes, such as carbon sequestration, air regulation, and flood minimization
- *Cultural services* such as recreation, tourism, and cultural identity.

Amazônia covers parts of two other biomes—the Cerrado savanna and the Pantanal (an area of tropical wetlands and flooded grasslands)—where high biodiversity is also at risk because of deforestation. The Cerrado is the largest savanna region in South America, considered the richest in the world in biodiversity. It hosts more than 10,000 species of plants, almost half of them found nowhere else in the world. The WWF estimates that over half of its original vegetation has already been destroyed. The Pantanal is the world's largest wetland, with a unique, rich, but threatened ecosystem that extends into Brazil, Bolivia, and Paraguay. Although large areas of the Pantanal remain untouched, it is threatened by expanding human settlement, unsustainable farming practices, illegal mining, hydroelectric power plant construction, and unregulated tourism. Less than 10 percent of the biome is under protection.

The rapid loss of global biodiversity threatens people and economies. Biodiversity is declining at the fastest pace in human history (Brondizio et al. 2019).

Recent World Bank modeling suggests, under conservative assumptions, that a collapse in ecosystems could reduce global gross domestic product (GDP) by US$2.7 trillion by 2030 and that 1.6 billion people would be living in countries experiencing an associated GDP decline of 10–20 percent (Johnson et al. 2021). Although these effects would be concentrated in poor countries, Brazil could lose as much as 5 percent of its GDP in this conservative assessment.

This estimated loss does not account for potential spillovers to other sectors. For example, a collapse in ecosystem services could also ripple through the banking sector—which, in Brazil, could increase nonperforming loans by 9 percentage points (Calice, Diaz Kalan, and Miguel 2021). The potential economic multipliers linked to the destruction of ecosystem services are significant, further highlighting the urgency to act.

a. The organization's official name remains the World Wildlife Fund in Canada and the United States.
Sources: Brondizio et al. 2019; Johnson et al. 2021.

public good. Such values have been assessed for Brazil, North America, and beyond using Delphi methods (Siikamäki et al. 2019; Strand et al. 2018). Conservatively assessed, these studies estimate the value at a minimum of US$1 billion a year for Brazilians and US$5 billion a year for the populations of Canada and the United States for preventing the loss of 10 percent of the Amazon's biodiversity. Scaling these values up to the global population and for the value of all of the Amazon's biodiversity yields a plausible global value of at least US$35 billion a year.

Given the Amazon's unique biodiversity, substantial prospecting values (direct use and option values) associated with new pharmaceutical innovation based on genetic resources can also be harvested from the Amazon's biosphere. This total "option value" is assessed at US$10 billion a year.

Forest cover protection in itself—independent of its carbon stock and its biodiversity—is another important part of the Amazon's global value. Many estimates attach a high and increasing value to the Amazon rainforest owing to its large size and to maintaining this size for both current and future generations. This value derives in part from the Amazon's iconic status as the world's largest rainforest area. The protection value derived from a representative stated-preference survey of the North American population, plausibly scaled up to the global level, yields a total global valuation of at least US$30 billion a year (Siikamäki et al. 2019).

There is significant variation across the Amazon in private and public protection values. This variation reflects multiple areal differences in such factors as soil quality, microclimates, tree species and forest density, biodiversity, and areal access.

The rainforest's exploitation values

Values of alternative, exploitative land use for the Brazilian Amazon rainforest could also be significant. These exploitative-use values are realized when the rainforest is eliminated (deforested) and replaced with other activity, principally agriculture (pasture and cropland) and plantation forests (having much lower biodiversity value), as shown on the left side of table 1.1. Part of this value is also realized as the net value of timber extracted in land clearing.

The poor agricultural suitability of large areas of the Amazon limits the overall private value of Amazon land. This valuation exercise assumed that 20–35 percent of the Brazilian Amazon rainforest could be converted to high-productivity crop or grazing lands, with likely annual net returns of up to US$500–US$750 per hectare, for a total agricultural value of US$25–US$75 billion a year (Richards and VanWey 2015). This may be an overestimate, however: Souza-Rodrigues (2019) assesses the net value of much agricultural land in the Brazilian Amazon at below US$100 per hectare per year. Nonsustainable logging is assessed at a net annual value of US$10 billion. In addition, there is extensive mineral extraction activity in the Amazon that also puts some pressure on the rainforest. Its value is uncertain but has in recent years been around US$8 billion annually.

Protection values for the Brazilian Amazon heavily dominate exploitation values, suggesting that deforestation is an inefficient redistribution from public to private wealth. The total opportunity (exploitation) value of the same forest area, assessed much less conservatively, could total US$43–US$98 billion a year. This implies that the average protection value of the Brazilian Amazon far outweighs its average exploitation value, given today's knowledge. In this sense, converting Amazon land to exploitative use is an inefficient form of redistribution because less private value is created than public value is destroyed.[21]

Implications of the valuation exercise

Substantial further deforestation of the Amazon could magnify its protection values, further tilting the valuation exercise toward forest conservation. A recent surge in deforestation and broader land degradation may in fact have turned the Amazon rainforest into a net *emitter* of CO_2 (Qin et al. 2021).

BOX 1.4

A tipping point for the Amazon?

Tipping points are ecological shifts that may be irreversible. Ecosystems can withstand a certain amount of shock. Yet their resilience has boundaries, and a tipping point occurs when they lose integrity and transition into a different ecosystem or even die altogether (as with coral reefs). The speed of such is uncertain and can vary greatly. As summarized by Dasgupta (2021, 87), "It could take decades for a forest biome to tip over into savanna, whereas grasslands have been known to tip into shrubland in years, and garden ponds have been known to tip into a eutrophic state in a matter of hours."

Deforestation in the Amazon biome threatens the integrity of the rainforest, which may advance to a tipping point. A tipping point for the southern and eastern Amazon may be reached at a deforestation level of around 25 percent for the entire Brazilian Amazon, against today's deforestation of roughly 20 percent (Lovejoy and Nobre 2019; Nobre and Borma 2009).

Simulations indicate that climate change may accelerate the onset of such a tipping point and lead to serious Amazon dieback later in this century, given that Amazon protection is not a priority and climate change not sufficiently countered (Vergara and Scholz 2011). At what stage of deforestation this tipping point might be reached is, with today's scientific knowledge, highly uncertain. In light of such a risk, maintaining the Amazon ecosystem at or close to its current state is an unequivocally positive value calculation.

One of the potential unintended consequences from further deforestation (not accounted for in table 1.1) is related to reaching a "tipping point" for the Amazon, which would initiate a "dieback" process with much of the remaining Amazon rainforest transformed into savanna (box 1.4). Recent evidence suggests that about three-quarters of the Amazon has already lost resilience since the 2000s (Boulton, Lenton, and Boers 2022). Franklin and Pindyck (2018) show that, with tipping points, the marginal costs of further deforestation could then be several multiples of the levels in table 1.1. The resulting costs would include the loss of most of the estimated benefits; further costs related to serious regional and global climate impacts; and catastrophic biodiversity losses, even from relatively limited additional deforestation.

This valuation exercise suggests that preserving the value of the Amazon is welfare-optimal, but it also reveals that most of the value accrues to the global population outside South America rather than to Brazil. The protection values accruing to the people of Brazil could be lower than the exploitation values of the Amazon, at least for parts of the biome (table 1.1). As a result, there could be self-interest in Brazil and other Amazon countries to exploit parts of the rainforest for short-term economic gains, especially given Brazil's intrinsic challenges in generating economic growth. This self-interest clashes with Brazil's long-run protection interests, its climate commitments, and with the rest of the world's major interest in saving the Amazon.

THE NEXUS BETWEEN DEVELOPMENT AND FORESTS

From a historical perspective, the odds appear to be stacked against Amazônia's natural forests, with human expansion and economic development fundamentally altering natural landscapes across the globe (Ellis et al. 2021). Over the past 12,000 years, rangelands, croplands, and settlements spread across the globe, starting in Africa, Europe, the Middle East, and East Asia (annex 1A, map 1A.1).

Between AD 800 and AD 900, intensively used landscapes covered about 5 percent of the earth's land area; by 1700, this had increased to 10 percent. Land transformation accelerated after the Industrial Revolution, and between 1880 and 2017, intensively used areas expanded from 28 percent to 51 percent of the global land area (entirely wild areas had fallen to only 18 percent). European colonization spread technology—and the land use patterns it induced—to the Americas, including to Brazil.

Although Brazil was still mostly covered by woodlands around 1900, pasture and croplands moved rapidly inland from the more densely populated coastal areas. The two frontiers of Amazonian development, and especially the Arc of Deforestation, thus represent a continuation of a long evolution of human economies and pose a major threat to the survival of these precious ecosystems. Accordingly, decisive efforts are required to break this pattern.

The relationship between economic development and forests is complex and can result in the permanent destruction of ecosystems. Weak protection of Amazônia's natural forests enables illegal logging and agricultural expansion and is consistent with findings in the literature that "open access" of a natural resource—"where property rights over a resource stock are hard to define, difficult to enforce, or costly to administer"—can result in its decimation or extinction, especially when connected to global demand (Taylor and Brander 1998).[22]

Extensive agriculture reflects artificially low land prices: in the absence of effective forest governance, land in Amazônia is abundant and the land supply relatively elastic, making it a rational private economic choice to expand agriculture on the extensive margin (by converting natural forests into productive land). Economic growth then consumes natural capital—Amazônia's forests. Countries tend to deforest less as they become more developed, but destruction of natural ecosystems can be permanent, especially when tipping points are reached.

Brazil is still responsible for about one-third of global deforestation, largely linked to cattle ranching (Pendrill et al. 2019). Amazônia accounts for about 59 percent of Brazil's territory and about 80 percent of the country's deforestation, as deforestation in Brazil has increasingly shifted north—from the Cerrado to the Amazon (figure 1.3) and from the states of the New Frontier to the states of the Colonial Frontier.

Deforestation is now particularly strong in the state of Pará, and it has been increasing rapidly in Acre, Amazonas, Mato Grosso, and Rondônia. Amazônia is Brazil's deforestation hot spot. Deforestation is now lower elsewhere because large-scale deforestation has already occurred (including in northeastern states like Alagoas and Paraíba, the old and declining agricultural frontier, or the current agricultural heartlands in the south) (figure 1.4). In addition, some states are much more advanced in their structural transformation (like Brazil's economic centers Rio de Janeiro and São Paulo). In fact, some areas in the southeast of Brazil have recently experienced slight net reforestation.

Threats to natural forests can ultimately ease for various reasons. One is linked to the structural transformation associated with economic development: economic growth shifts from relatively land-intensive sectors (agriculture) to less land-intensive sectors (manufacturing and services) (Andrée et al. 2019). In this process, agricultural production may also become more capital intensive and efficient (supporting agricultural intensification). Another reason pertains to land availability: land scarcity may increase as deforestation depletes the stock of natural land or because natural-resource governance protects natural land

FIGURE 1.3

Deforestation is increasingly shifting from the Cerrado into the Amazon

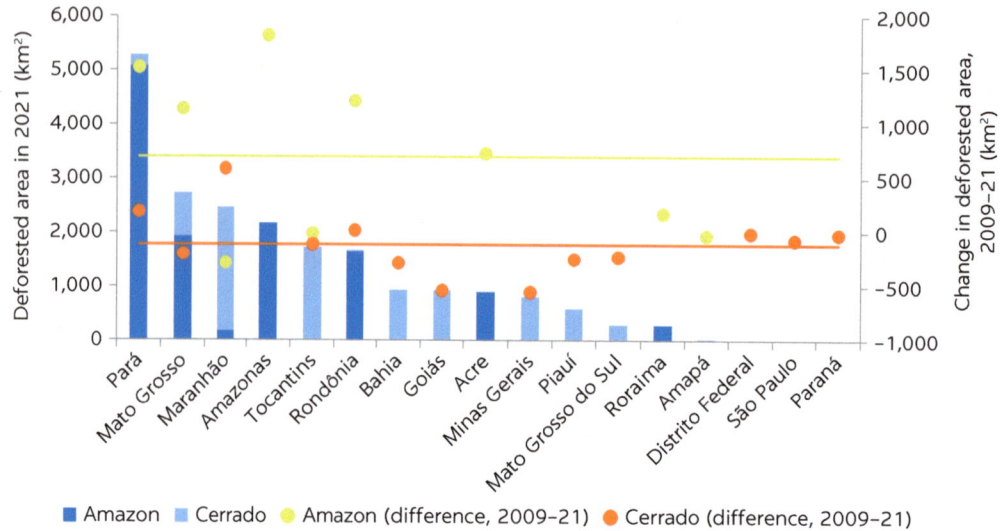

■ Amazon ■ Cerrado ● Amazon (difference, 2009–21) ● Cerrado (difference, 2009–21)

Sources: World Bank, using data from the Brazilian Project for Satellite Monitoring of Deforestation in the Legal Amazon (PRODES) of the National Institute for Space Research (INPE).
Note: The figure shows, in selected states and the Federal District, the extent of deforested area in 2021 (left axis) as well as the difference in that area between 2009 and 2021 (right axis). Green bars and dots indicate Brazilian states (or portions thereof) within the Amazon biome. Orange bars and dots indicate Brazilian states (or portions thereof) where deforestation occurred in the Cerrado (savanna) biome. km^2 = square kilometers.

FIGURE 1.4

Amazônia is Brazil's deforestation hot spot

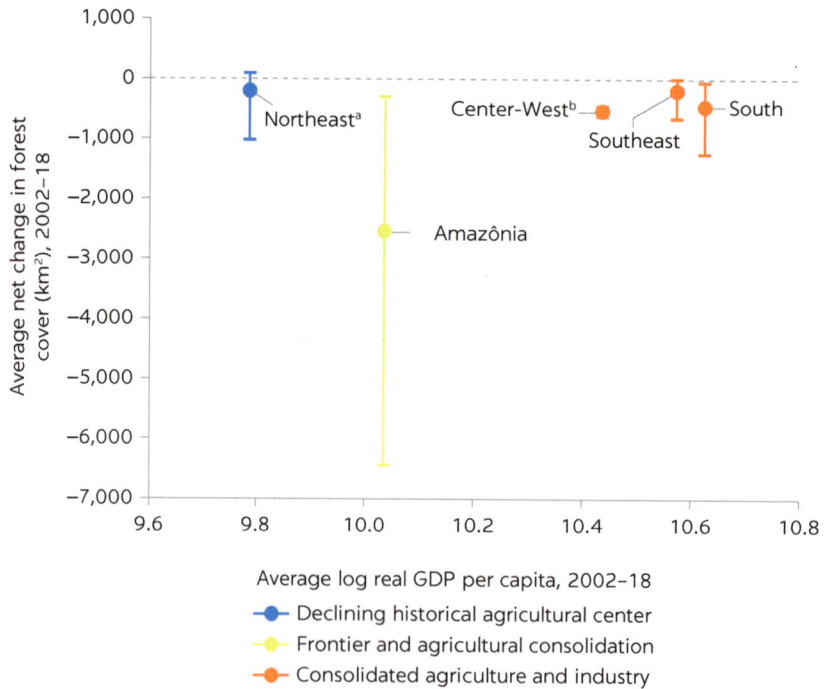

Average log real GDP per capita, 2002–18

● Declining historical agricultural center
● Frontier and agricultural consolidation
● Consolidated agriculture and industry

Sources: World Bank, using Brazilian Annual Land Use and Land Cover Mapping Project (MapBiomas) maps and Brazilian Institute of Geography and Statistics (IBGE) data.
Note: The figure covers all states in Brazil within their respective regions and biomes. Negative y-axis values reflect deforestation; positive values reflect reforestation. Dots indicate regional averages, and lines indicate regional maxima and minima.
a. Northeast excludes Maranhão (Amazônia).
b. Center-West excludes Mato Grosso (Amazônia).

from conversion to productive land. Governments may step up their efforts to protect the environment as the economic emphasis shifts from rural to urban sectors (structural transformation) and as citizens become more conscious of the need to protect ecosystems, not least because of accelerating climate change. A mix of economic and governance interventions is required to reconcile economic development with standing forests in Amazônia.

GROWTH MODELS AND LAND USE CHOICES

Deforestation is a rational private choice detrimental to public welfare. It is an inefficient form of redistribution from public to private wealth that is welfare-enhancing for certain private agents. Figure 1.5 lays out the private logic of deforestation. Land tenure status (especially linked to land designation) is an integral part of this logic and depends on whether the land is private or public—or still undesignated, which is characteristic of Amazônia as a frontier region. Land tenure affects private and public incentives, which are further conditioned by economic factors that shape decisions to clear forest for production.

In some cases, the distinctions are blurry. For example, traditional communities may have permission to produce sustainably on public lands like protected and Indigenous areas. This type of production tends not to be associated with deforestation and therefore falls outside the logic presented in figure 1.5.

FIGURE 1.5

The pernicious private logic of deforestation

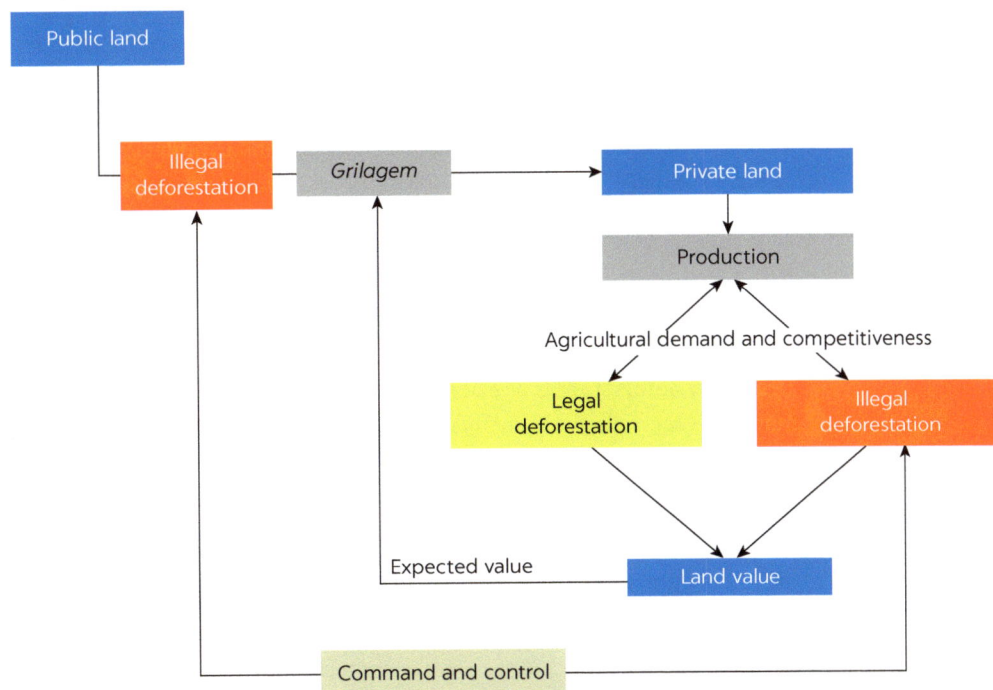

Source: World Bank.
Note: "Illegal deforestation" includes unauthorized logging in public lands (such as protected areas or Indigenous territories) and forest clearing as part of the *grilagem* (land grabbing) process. Illegal deforestation also occurs in private lands violating the Forest Code. "Legal deforestation" occurs in private lands within the limits of the Forest Code. Agricultural demand and competitiveness affect land use choices, land values (and expectations about future land values), and consequently incentives for *grilagem*. Command and control interventions aim to curb illegal deforestation. The figure does not account for legal logging, deforestation for infrastructure development, or legal forms of small-scale sustainable production in public lands.

The process of deforestation. Deforestation tends to be related to timber extraction, productive land use (mostly agriculture),[23] and *grilagem* (land grabbing). Deforestation is mostly illegal, but some is legal. The Forest Code allows private landowners in the Amazon biome to deforest up to 20 percent of their property—sometimes even more under formal exceptions. Less stringent limits apply in other biomes. Reduced-impact logging is allowed within concession areas and legal reserves. Construction of roads and other public infrastructure also involves legal deforestation, though the informal roads that spread out from legally constructed trunk roads often lead to illegal deforestation.

"Illegal deforestation" in figure 1.5 includes logging without permits (which often occurs on public land including Indigenous territories or protected areas); land clearing exceeding the limits of the Forest Code for agricultural use on private properties; and activities related to *grilagem* (which tends to be associated with public lands without clear designation).[24]

The pathways to deforestation can be intertwined. For example, where land is undesignated and forest protection weak, an individual or firm may hire loggers to extract the most valuable woods (mahogany and ipê, also called Brazilian walnut or lapacho). In addition to felling specific trees, heavy harvest and transport equipment used to reach the tree can destroy the surrounding ecosystem. The cash flow generated from selling the prized wood may finance the clearing of the remaining forest. The deforested land is then usually converted to pasture, populated with enough cattle to claim that the land is being used and eventually obtain a private title—in other words, *grilagem*.

Grilagem refers to taking possession of a parcel of undesignated land, typically with fake documentation, on the expectation that it will eventually get regularized and will be worth considerably more in the future.

Deforestation and degradation. Deforestation and broader forest degradation are also interlinked. Degradation is even more pervasive than deforestation, encompassing twice as much Amazon land between 2007 and 2016 (Gandour et al. 2021). Degradation can be caused by forest fires, and in protected areas it is often linked to illegal logging that damages the integrity of the ecosystem. This is often selective logging, which implies removing only the most valuable trees. Outside protected areas, forest degradation tends to be more explicitly linked to land use choices. Land degradation may "serve as an indicator that deforestation will soon occur in that region," showing that the two concepts are closely linked (Gandour et al. 2021).

Drivers of deforestation. Brazil has an ambitious environmental protection framework, especially for the Amazon biome, but economic forces, capacity gaps, and limited political will can undercut its effectiveness. Economic forces determine the demand for and the price of every product, and because land is an input to production, land use choices have economic drivers. As figure 1.5 indicates, as agricultural demand increases or farmers in Amazônia become more competitive (allowing them to take market share from other producers), their demand for land rises. This can result in legal or illegal deforestation on private land, especially if that is more cost-effective than intensifying agricultural production. When land demand exceeds supply, prices rise, creating further speculative incentives and fueling *grilagem*.

Brazil has made impressive progress in putting formal systems in place to protect Amazônia's forests, and figure 1.5 shows how enforcing them (command and control) would curb deforestation. Yet economic forces and weakening enforcement have contributed to a recent acceleration of deforestation in Amazônia. Stronger forest governance is needed as well as a more sustainable growth model.

Brazil's distorted and unsustainable growth model

Brazil remains an agricultural powerhouse, and primary production is still a pillar of its growth model. Yet the country needs to look beyond primary production for a more dynamic and less resource-intensive economy, creating better jobs.

Primary production includes extractives (minerals and mining) and agriculture (both crops and livestock). Although agriculture in Brazil is a relatively small percentage of overall GDP, roughly in line with Brazil's overall level of development, the sector has significant economic linkages, including agribusiness. When these linkages are considered, agriculture accounts, depending on the year, for over 20 percent of GDP, with significant job multipliers.[25]

Agriculture is one of the few competitive sectors in Brazil and the only one with an international market share of any considerable size over the past decades. Apart from extractives, Brazil's export basket is dominated by agricultural commodities, especially soy (figure 1.6). But this resource-intensive growth model has stopped delivering growth and does not create good jobs or significantly raise living standards for most Brazilians.

Many distortions undermine growth in Brazil and destroy its natural resources. Constraints to productivity exist in product and factor markets, many

FIGURE 1.6

Agricultural commodities dominate Brazil's export basket

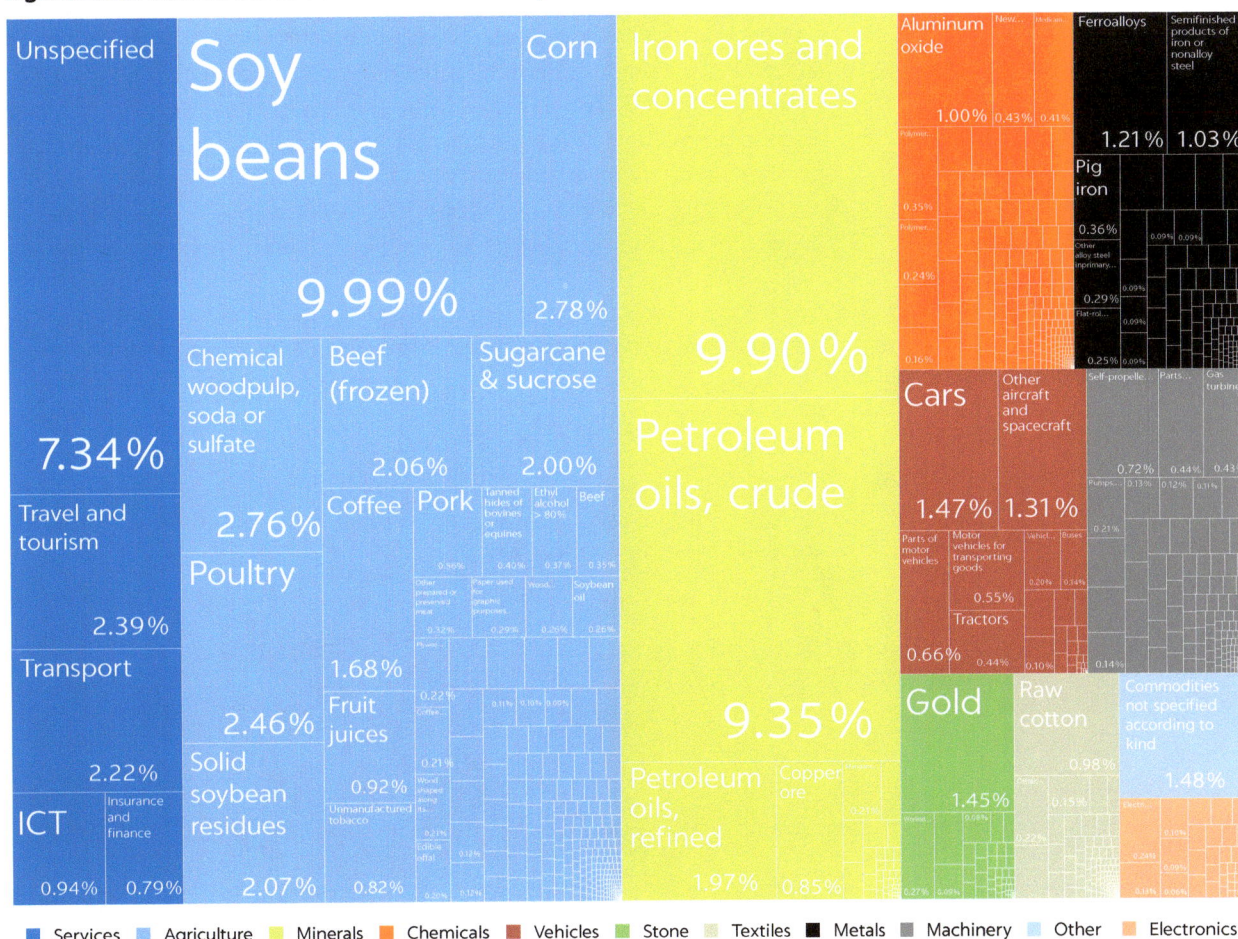

Source: Harvard University's Atlas of Economic Complexity research and data visualization tool (https://atlas.cid.harvard.edu/).
Note: The figure shows shares of total merchandise exports from Brazil in 2019. ICT = information and communication technology.

of which are described in Dutz (2018). Distortions are reflected in a high cost of doing business, known in Brazil as "Custo Brasil." This memorandum focuses on distortions in land, capital, labor, and product markets:

- *Land markets:* Incomplete land regularization undermines the ability of farmers without title to use their land efficiently. Ineffective forest protection is an implicit subsidy, as illegal deforestation redistributes income from the public (the public-good value of the standing forest) to private individuals.
- *Capital markets:* Earmarked credit distorts the efficient provision of credit, including in the agriculture sector.
- *Labor markets:* Low human capital and skill mismatches undermine structural transformation toward more productive activities and the rural-urban transition.
- *Product markets:* While promoting its agricultural exports, Brazil tends to shield its manufacturing and services sectors from competition. Industrial policy tools, like the tax and duty incentives for the Zona Franca de Manaus, attract companies to places where they would not otherwise be competitive (see the companion report to this memorandum, World Bank 2023b).

Land-intensive production has caused Brazil to expand agricultural land through deforestation, now especially in Amazônia. This model is not sustainable.

Sustainable growth accounts for the environmental externalities of economic activity. This is depicted in figure 1.7, which divides GDP into its components in a production function approach: total factor productivity (TFP), capital, labor, and land. The framework also adds inputs, which can be environmental like water or forest products—which may be shocked by climate change or other forms of destruction. Economic growth requires natural-resource inputs, and these can generate environmental costs by depleting finite natural resources and generating negative externalities (like GHG emissions). The smaller the increase in environmental costs and natural-resource extraction for a given

FIGURE 1.7

A sustainable and inclusive growth framework for this memorandum

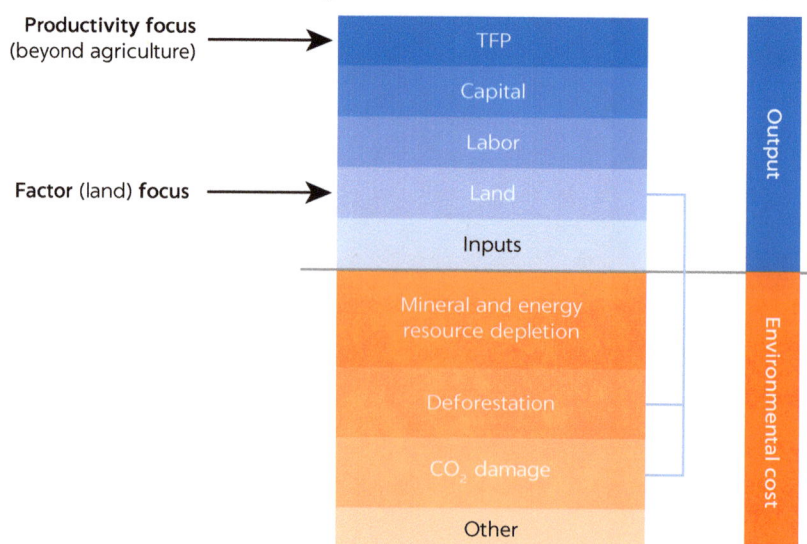

Source: World Bank.
Note: CO_2 = carbon dioxide; TFP = total factor productivity.

increase in GDP, the more sustainable the growth.[26] In figure 1.7, the connecting bracket (in blue) illustrates that a growth model with a foundation of land accumulation will by definition destroy forest wealth: it converts natural forests to productive use (deforestation) and releases CO_2 in the process.

This memorandum will focus on the importance of TFP (box 1.5) across the economy—that is, productivity gains *beyond* agriculture. Rebalancing economic development by more strongly supporting urban productivity will attenuate the competitiveness of primary production and help decouple economic development from deforestation.

As an aspiring member of the Organisation for Economic Co-operation and Development (OECD), Brazil will need to focus its growth model on productivity and diversify its exports. Although land accumulation provides some impetus for growth, Brazil is now too developed to propel itself to higher levels of development through agricultural frontier expansion, even if it still has a lot of natural land. Development tends to be associated with higher TFP growth relative to land accumulation, and Brazil has been lagging significantly in this regard (figure 1.8)—in part because it has a large amount of natural land, so it keeps converting it rather than fostering productivity.

Ultimately Brazil will need to change its growth model if it wants to become a high-income country, raising productivity in more advanced sectors, beyond primary commodities, and thus diversifying the economy and exports (box 1.6) and creating the foundation for good jobs and higher living standards. The same agenda applies to Amazônia more specifically.

BOX 1.5

What is productivity?

Total factor productivity (TFP) can be thought of as the efficiency of firms or economies in combining their workers, resources, tools, and inputs. It is the main driver of long-term economic development and generally arises from efficiency gains, either from a better allocation of factors of production or from innovation. It means doing more with less, thus also implying lower natural-resource use for a given level of output, making it an important component of sustainable growth.

Although TFP is the main theoretical measure in the analysis here, it is difficult to measure directly because it is residual. It also reflects economies of scale, variations in capacity utilization, and measurement errors. As noted in Loayza, Fajnzylber, and Calderón (2005, 20), "A failure to account for improvements in the quality composition of capital stocks or the labor force, for instance, will lead to an overestimation of the TFP component." Another limitation is that TFP, as an accounting measure, does not shed

light on the drivers underlying growth in TFP. Although most economists consider TFP to be a measure of technological change, it may also reflect externalities in many of the new growth models or even changes in the sectoral composition of output.[a] Lacking a reliable measure of TFP, economists sometime revert to labor productivity: the amount of output per worker.

TFP and labor productivity are closely related, since efficiency gains will raise both TFP and labor productivity. But the two measures can also diverge because labor productivity is affected by the intensity of use of the other factors of production. Two producers may thus have different labor productivities even though they have the same production technology, if, say, one uses capital much more intensively than the other. Where measures of TFP are incomplete, this chapter uses labor productivity or land productivity, depending on what is most appropriate, acknowledging the potential limitations.

a. For additional limitations of TFP, see Hsieh and Klenow (2010) and Klenow and Rodríguez-Clare (1997).

FIGURE 1.8

Achieving high-income status requires switching from land expansion to a focus on productivity, 1990–2016

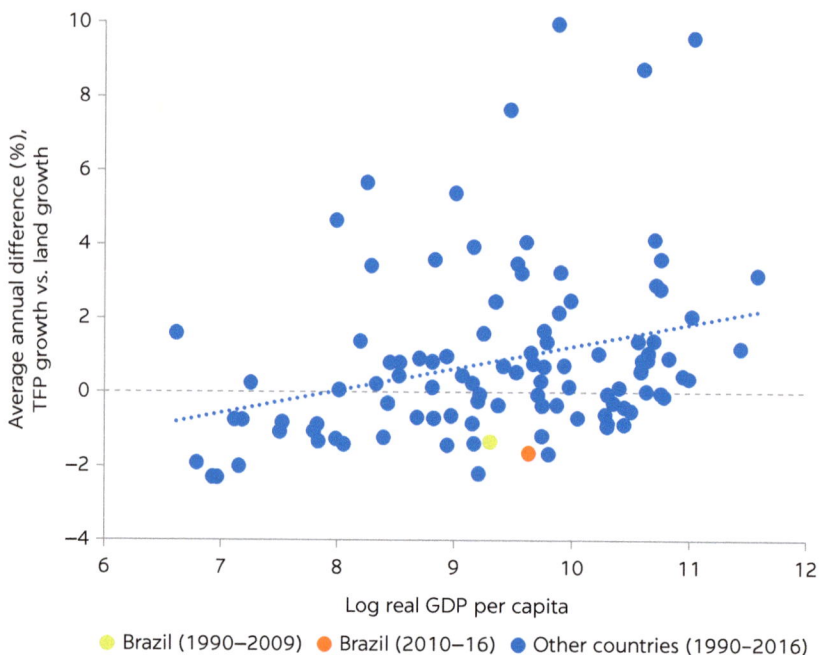

Sources: World Bank, based on Penn World Table 9.0 data from Feenstra, Inklaar, and Timmer 2015; and World Development Indicators Database.
Note: The x-axis represents the average log real GDP per capita, while the y-axis represents the percentage point difference between average TFP growth and average land growth. Brazil appears twice in the graph, one dot for 1990–2009 and the other dot for 2010–16. TFP = total factor productivity.

BOX 1.6

It's Apple, not soy, that helps make the United States one of the world's richest countries

Like Brazil, the United States is an agricultural power-house—also like Brazil, soy is the largest agricultural export of the United States. Unlike Brazil, the United States has been reforesting. The United States is the world's largest economy and sixth richest in gross domestic product (GDP) per capita. With about 1.5 times the population of Brazil, the United States' market share of global food production (8.9 percent) is about twice that of Brazil (4.6 percent). However, agriculture accounts for only 0.7 percent of US GDP, compared with 7 percent of Brazil's GDP, and it makes up a much smaller share of US exports than of Brazil's exports (figure B1.6.1).

Despite US agriculture's large relative size in world markets, agriculture sectors do not drive growth in the United States. Rather, US growth has been driven in large part by tech giants like Apple; high tech is an important part of US exports. In 2019, the value added of Apple alone (about US$41 billion) was equivalent to about a quarter of US agricultural value added. Apple and other Silicon Valley firms help make California a rich state: at US$2.8 trillion, California's GDP is about 1.5 times that of Brazil's.[a] Consistent with the framework for this memorandum, large productivity gains from across the economy—driven especially by high-tech sectors—have coincided with considerable reforestation in the United States (figure B1.6.2).

Brazil can become a much richer country, with an even larger agricultural market presence, without deforestation; and a larger preserved forest will contribute to this wealth. To achieve this economic growth, agriculture does not need to grow less; other

continued

Box 1.6, *continued*

FIGURE B1.6.1

Export composition in Brazil and the United States

a. Food exports, 2018

b. Total exports, 2018

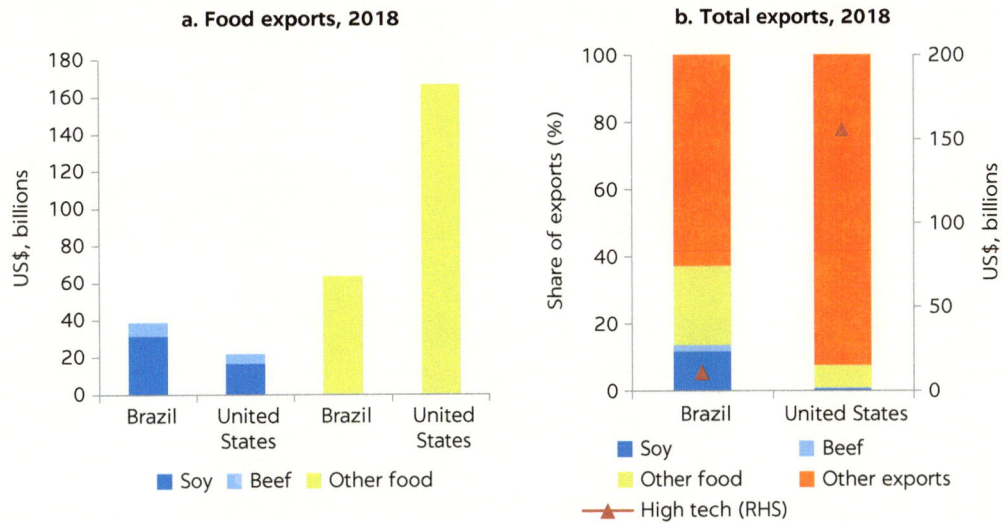

Sources: World Bank, based on Harvard University's Atlas of Economic Complexity research and data visualization tool (https://atlas.cid.harvard.edu/) and World Development Indicators Database.

FIGURE B1.6.2

Total factor productivity and forest cover in the United States

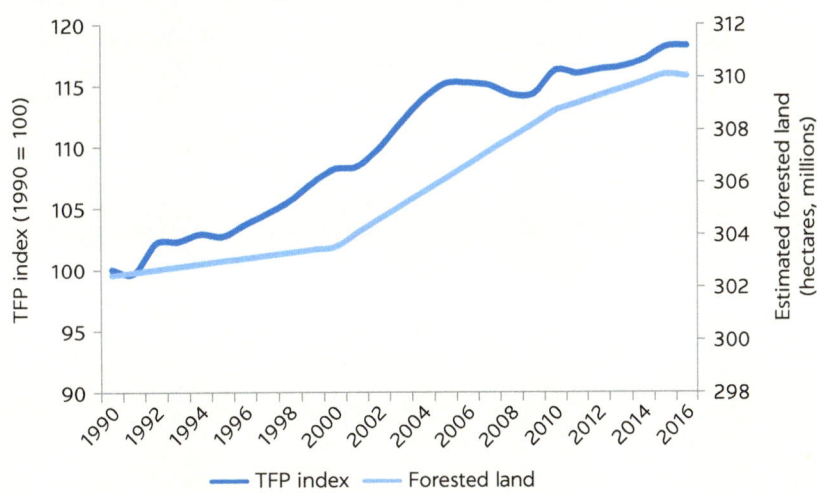

Sources: World Bank, based on Food and Agriculture Organization of the United Nations (FAO); Penn World Table 9.0 data from Feenstra, Inklaar, and Timmer 2015.
Note: TFP = total factor productivity.

sectors need to step up. At the global level, agricultural productivity gains are critical to meet global food demand more efficiently, including with less land. Brazil has been making progress in agricultural productivity. But while this can reduce deforestation in countries from which Brazil takes market share, it can enhance pressure on Brazilian forests, notably in Amazônia. A focus on productivity growth beyond

continued

Box 1.6, *continued*

agriculture would reduce this pressure, as it did in the United States.

Brazil already has a good foundation to build on. It boasts eight unicorns (start-ups quickly reaching a value of US$1 billion), trailing only the United States, China, India, and the United Kingdom.[b] Most Brazilian unicorns are in finance. In 2020, Brazil ranked 4th on the Global Innovation Index in Latin America (but only 62nd globally, of 131 economies) (Dutta, Lanvin, and Wunsch-Vincent 2020).

At the same time, Brazil remains isolated from global competition in nonprimary traded sectors like manufacturing. "Custo Brasil" (a reference to the high costs of doing business in Brazil) is emblematic of a protected economy that struggles to boost productivity. Addressing the productivity agenda will enable Brazil to eventually become an affluent country, with a competitive agricultural, manufacturing, and services base and vast natural forests.

a. Data for Brazil are from World Development Indicators, while California data are from Statistica: https://www.statista.com/statistics/248023/us-gross-domestic-product-gdp-by-state/.
b. See "Startups in Brazil: Statistics and Facts," Statista website: https://www.statista.com/topics/5281/startups-in-brazil/#topicHeader__wrapper.

Fostering development, fostering maturity

A new development approach would require a stronger focus on productivity and natural-resource governance. Richer, more mature economies have higher levels of productivity and tend to be propelled relatively more by urban sectors (figure 1.9). This memorandum will show that most Amazonian states still experience low economic maturity and exhibit high productivity gaps with the more mature parts of Brazil, implying even higher gaps with OECD countries. Low productivity results in high poverty—and this memorandum will look at ways to raise productivity and promote regional convergence of Amazônia.

FIGURE 1.9

A development framework accounting for economic and institutional maturity

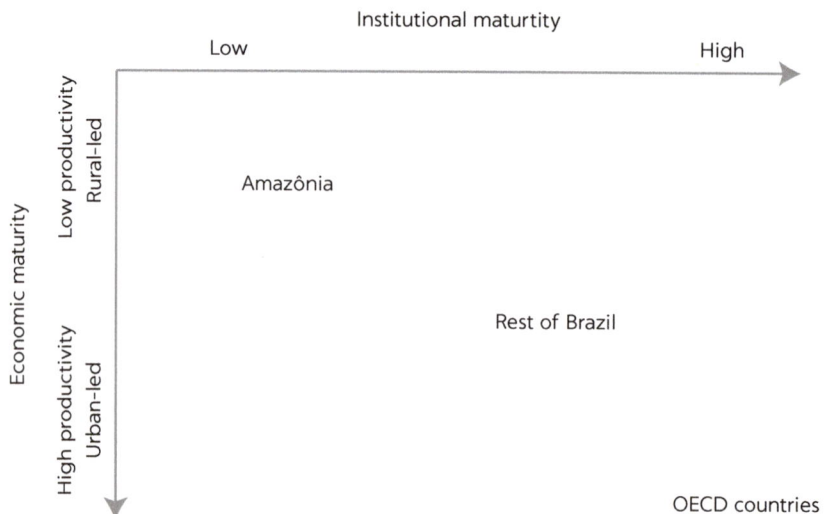

Source: World Bank.
Note: OECD = Organisation for Economic Co-operation and Development.

The maturing of the Amazonian frontier also requires stronger and more inclusive institutions to lay the foundations for social and economic development while protecting natural wealth. Of the complementarities, higher levels of development can also improve governance (North 1991), while stronger forest governance to limit land conversion through deforestation in Amazônia may release capital for urban sectors.

As Amazônia matures, economic growth will allow it to catch up with the rest of Brazil as regional convergence reduces spatial inequality across the country. Higher productivity, including in more urban sectors, and stronger institutions will help Brazil and Amazônia to also catch up with richer economies, such as OECD countries, further raising living standards. This memorandum also looks at financing that can support Amazônia's sustainable and inclusive transformation: conservation finance.

GOVERNMENT PRIORITIES FOR AMAZÔNIA

Reducing deforestation is essential to Brazil's meeting its NDC under the Paris Agreement. Agriculture, land use changes, and forests are by far the largest sources of GHG emissions in Brazil (figure 1.10). Accordingly, forest protection is a key component of Brazil's NDC. Zero illegal deforestation of the Amazon by 2030 was a goal under Brazil's original pledges regarding the Paris Agreement. When first submitted, these goals were among the most ambitious globally.

In the most recent update, during COP26, Brazil committed to zero illegal deforestation by 2028. Furthermore, at COP26, Brazil joined 140 countries to sign the Glasgow Leaders' Declaration on Forests and Land Use. Given the importance of land use change and forests in Brazil's net emissions, it will be

FIGURE 1.10

Agriculture and land use change and forestry are the largest sources of GHG emissions in Brazil

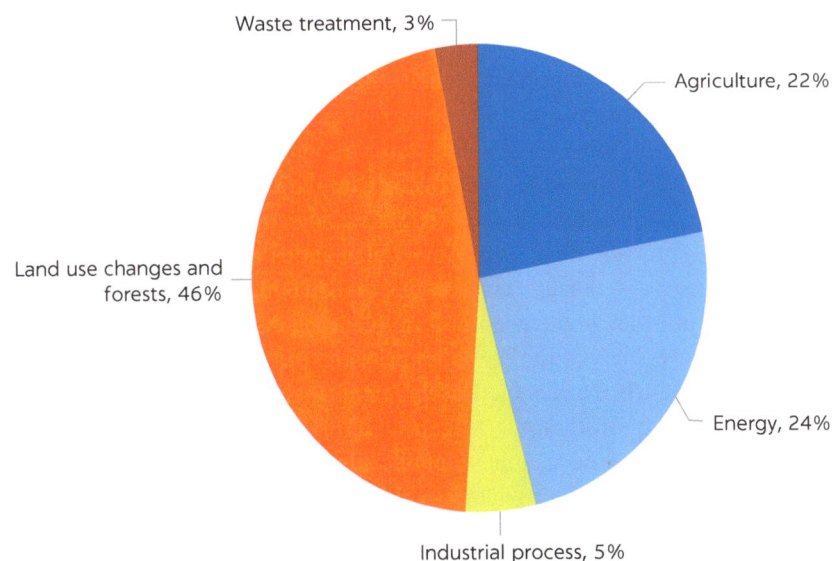

Source: Speranza, Romeiro, and Feder 2017.
Note: The chart shows the sources of gross Brazilian greenhouse gas (GHG) emissions in 2015, by estimated percentage share. GHG refers to carbon dioxide equivalent (CO_2e), calculated from global warming potential.

virtually impossible to meet Brazil's targets without a reduction in deforestation (World Bank 2023a).

The current federal strategy for development in Amazônia, and the Amazon biome particularly, is focused mainly on sustainable agriculture and ecosystem service payments. The environmental pillar of the current federal medium-term planning instrument—the four-year Multiannual Plan (Plano Plurianual, or PPA) for 2020–23—aims at reconciling economic growth and natural resource preservation through stronger enforcement of the Forest Code and through productivity improvements in more sustainable agricultural systems, including the Low-Carbon Agriculture (ABC) Plan[27] restoration of degraded land, cultivation of organic products, and mixed landscape and agroforestry production.

In addition to the medium-term PPA, the federal 2020 long-term National Strategy for Economic and Social Development for 2020–31 also promotes the introduction of payments for ecosystem services as one of the available tools to preserve biodiversity and reduce deforestation. In 2021, the federal Ministry of Environment launched the "Adopt-a-Park" program, which aims to attract financing from a broad set of stakeholders (including public and private entities and individuals) for forest protection but curtailed enforcement budgets for environmental protection, including for the main federal enforcement agency, the Brazilian Institute of the Environment and Renewable Natural Resources (IBAMA).

The federal government also has an agenda related to productivity. The long-awaited tax code reform, improvement in the business environment, increase in competitiveness, and market integration are all part of the Brazilian government's medium- and long-term growth agenda (federal 2020–23 PPA). These reforms are aligned with various country assessments, particularly with Dutz (2018), that call for institutional reforms and market integration as mechanisms for Brazil to realize its productivity promise.

Brazil's federal government provides considerable financial support to Amazonian states. The largest transfer from federal to state governments is the State Participation Fund (FPE), which accounts for around 85 percent of obligatory transfers from the federal government to states.[28] Less populous states, such as those in Amazônia, benefit the most.[29] The federal transfers are high not only in per capita terms but also represent a large share of the states' GDP. At the subnational level, some states earmark pooled resources from Brazil's state-level value added tax (Tax on Circulation of Goods and Services, or ICMS) to promote green policies (ICMS Ecológico).

The development priorities of Amazonian states are remarkably similar. Despite limited discretionary resources due to rigid budget laws and high public spending on personnel, the medium-term planning instruments (PPAs) of the Amazonian states indicate the key policy priorities of state governments. Taking into account the UN Sustainable Development Goals, the PPAs are structured around five common themes: citizen welfare, well-being, and inclusion; sustainable economic development; public administration; infrastructure and logistics; and science and technology (table 1.2).

In 2021, the Consortium of Amazon Governors launched the Green Recovery Plan for Amazônia to help the region emerge from the COVID-19 pandemic. The plan has four pillars: an end to illegal deforestation, sustainable productive development, green technologies and capabilities, and green infrastructure.

TABLE 1.2 Focus areas of 2020–23 multiannual plans for Amazonian states

STATE	FOCUS AREAS
Acre	(1) Institutional management, (2) citizenship and security, (3) economy and agribusiness, (4) infrastructure for development
Amazonas	(1) Quality of life, (2) sustainable development, (3) modernization of public management
Amapá	(1) Economic development, (2) social development, (3) infrastructure development, (4) security strengthening, (5) budget and finance strengthening
Maranhão	(1) Social injustices, (2) financial management and modernization of public management, (3) development for all, (4) infrastructure for logistics
Mato Grosso	(1) Quality of life, (2) sustainable development, (3) modern and efficient public management, (4) performance of all branches of government and autonomous units
Pará	(1) Just society, (2) smart growth, (3) dependable work, (4) active public management
Roraima	(1) Social inclusion, (2) sustainable growth, (3) efficiency and transparency in public management
Rondônia	(1) Social welfare, (2) sustainable competitiveness, (3) infrastructure for logistics, (4) modernization of public management
Tocantins	(1) Health; (2) education, science, and technology; (3) public security, social assistance, and human rights; (4) production factors; (5) infrastructure, regional development, and city network; (6) public management

Source: World Bank, compiled from Brazil's federal Multiannual Plan 2020–23.

On most issues, this memorandum is aligned with the priorities in the PPAs, although it calls for a stronger complementary emphasis on urban productivity than is evident in current government plans and programs. A new electoral term (at the federal and state level) starting in 2023 will provide further opportunities to promote sustainable and inclusive development in Brazil and in Amazônia specifically.

DEVELOPING AMAZÔNIA SUSTAINABLY AND INCLUSIVELY: THE LOGIC OF THIS MEMORANDUM

This memorandum builds on an existing knowledge foundation, including the value of Amazonian forests and their relevance for the climate, biodiversity, and the economy; the need for and practicalities of land and forest governance and Payments for Ecosystem Services (PES); and the role of the rural economy (including the bioeconomy) (figure 1.11). The memorandum enhances the existing knowledge, with a stronger focus on productivity and structural transformation and the role of urban economies, and discusses new potential avenues for conservation finance.

Brazil's model of factor accumulation and export-led agriculture has supported its development so far, but to eventually become a more affluent OECD country, Brazil needs higher productivity in sectors beyond agriculture—that is, sectors more associated with urban production. Financing is essential, and conservation finance should be availed for forest governance and the economic transition. Because such financing will pave the path toward a growth model that can reconcile economic development and natural forests, it is expected to also foster political will to protect forests, especially if such financing is conditioned on measurable reductions in deforestation.

FIGURE 1.11

The knowledge foundation and the original contributions of this economic memorandum

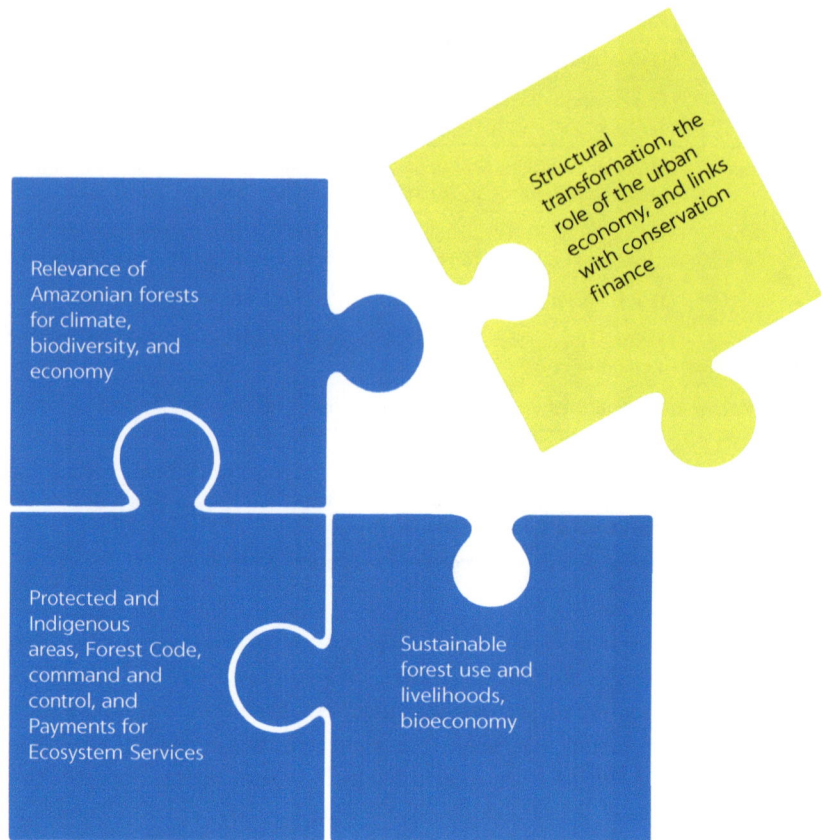

Source: World Bank.

Part I of this memorandum (chapters 2–4) focuses on poverty and inequality, on structural transformation and regional convergence, and on forests—and the interplay among them. Economic development is intended to benefit people, and the poor in particular. Chapter 2 provides the social context for this memorandum, providing an overview of the social landscape in Amazônia and the policies that can help raise household living standards while limiting inequality, through supply-side interventions (such as basic infrastructure services, human capital investments, or land regularization) and demand-side factors (such as the transition to a productivity-led growth model). Since demand-side factors are intimately linked to economic growth, chapter 3 develops this discussion further, investigating the global, national, and regional drivers of economic growth in Amazônia and how structural transformation has been occurring—particularly how economic forces have been shaping land use, notably deforestation. Chapter 4 then turns to institutions and financing aimed to control deforestation in Amazônia.

Part II (chapters 5–6) delves further into Amazônia's structural transformation from both rural and urban perspectives. Chapter 5 focuses on rural transformation showing that the transformation of agriculture will release labor for other economic activities. So that this process does not lead to widespread unemployment and entrenched poverty, the federal and subnational governments will need to identify paths to alternative employment, and the opportunities are likely to be in urban areas, especially in the longer term. Urbanization in Amazônia, though well under way, is far from complete. Cities in the region need to become hubs of productivity and job creation. Chapter 6 explores the urban space in Amazônia and identifies policies that can make towns and cities more conducive to doing business, and more competitive. It argues that towns and cities are a key part of Amazônia's sustainable and inclusive development story, but one that has not yet received enough attention. A companion report to this memorandum ("Urban Competitiveness in Brazil's State of Amazonas: A Green Growth Agenda," World Bank 2023b) zooms in on the state of Amazonas, and Manaus specifically, to explore policies that could support Amazonian urban productivity.

Part III (chapter 7) synthesizes the analysis, revisiting the delicate balancing act to develop Amazônia sustainably and inclusively. It reviews Amazonian development through a conservation lens to identify policy packages that can promote economic development and conserve natural forests in both the shorter and longer term.

ANNEX 1A: THE HUMAN IMPACT ON LAND USE ACROSS THE WORLD

MAP 1A.1

Land use change in an historical perspective

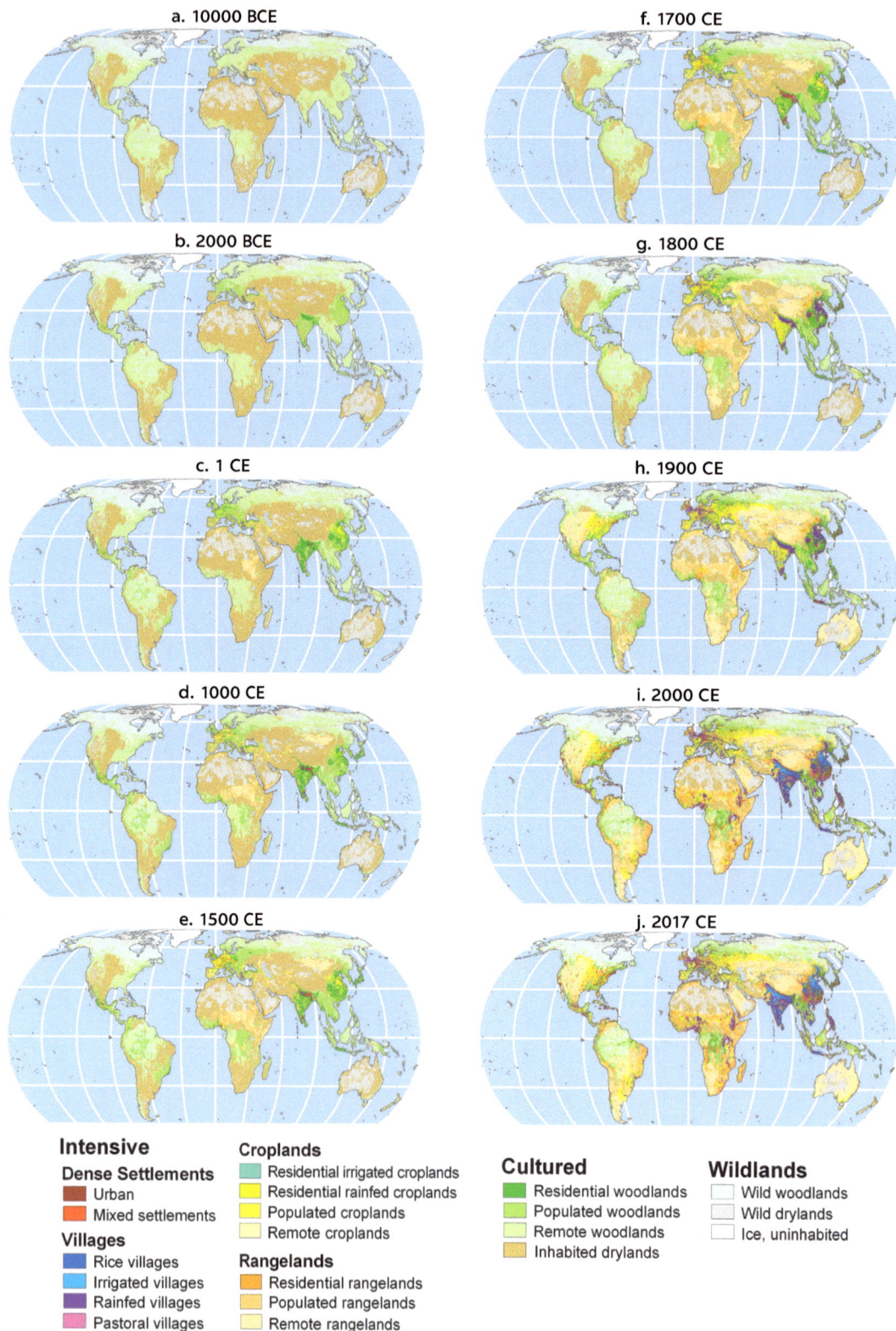

a. 10000 BCE

b. 2000 BCE

c. 1 CE

d. 1000 CE

e. 1500 CE

f. 1700 CE

g. 1800 CE

h. 1900 CE

i. 2000 CE

j. 2017 CE

Intensive

Dense Settlements
- Urban
- Mixed settlements

Villages
- Rice villages
- Irrigated villages
- Rainfed villages
- Pastoral villages

Croplands
- Residential irrigated croplands
- Residential rainfed croplands
- Populated croplands
- Remote croplands

Rangelands
- Residential rangelands
- Populated rangelands
- Remote rangelands

Cultured
- Residential woodlands
- Populated woodlands
- Remote woodlands
- Inhabited drylands

Wildlands
- Wild woodlands
- Wild drylands
- Ice, uninhabited

Source: Modified from Ellis et al. 2021.

NOTES

1. Calculations using Brazilian Institute of Geography and Statistics (IBGE) 2021 data.
2. According to some accounts, the Amazon River is the world's longest (Hemming 2009).
3. Latest available data for this memorandum are from 2018.
4. Poverty rates are calculated using the US$5.50 per day poverty line and the IGBE's Continuous National Household Sample Survey (PNAD) 2019 data.
5. Deforestation data from the Brazilian Project for Satellite Monitoring of Deforestation in the Legal Amazon (PRODES) of the National Institute for Space Research (INPE): http://terrabrasilis.dpi.inpe.br/app/dashboard/deforestation/biomes/legal_amazon/rates.
6. This section draws substantially on Hemming (2009) and was reviewed by the author.
7. Soils under temperate forests accumulate humus during fall and winter, whereas tropical rain forests grow constantly throughout the year: their horizontal root-and-litter mats recycle all falling nutrients back into the growing biomass. This recycling is more important than extracting nutrients from the soil. Soils under destroyed tropical forests are therefore weak and acidic, with exposed topsoil washed away by rains or baked hard in dry seasons.
8. Slightly more profitable products from Greater Pará were turtle oil, salted fish, and timber for shipbuilding.
9. This is further discussed in annex 3B of chapter 3.
10. This road was (controversially) supported by a World Bank loan.
11. Dirt roads are potholed and dusty in the dry season and often impassably muddy or slippery in the rainy season. With all-weather paving, the impact of roads increases hugely: logwood, cattle, and soybeans can be carried throughout the year, and sawmills and slaughterhouses are established all along them so that live animals do not need to be transported.
12. The devastation by dams in the Amazon is linked to the relatively flat landscape, resulting in vast reservoirs.
13. Calculations using IBGE census data from 1960 and 2010.
14. Calculations using IBGE 2021 data.
15. Cattle had already been introduced in Roraima in the 1800s.
16. This minimum can go down to 50 percent if relevant zoning is in place or if the municipality has over 50 percent protected areas.
17. These are the two qualities of a public good: "Nonrival" means that the goods do not decrease in supply as more people consume them, and "nonexcludable" means that the good is available to everyone.
18. See "The Flying Rivers Phenomenon," The Flying Rivers Project (website): http://riosvoadores.com.br/english/the-flying-rivers-phenomenon/.
19. Assuming a minimum average of 500 tons CO_2/hectare, 350 million hectares, and a global carbon price of US$40 per ton CO_2, is conservative at current prices.
20. The annualized carbon value is calculated at a 3 percent rate of return.
21. This does not take into account the regional variations in public and private values: in some areas, the private value from land conversion may exceed the public value, at least if negative externalities or unintended consequences are not taken fully into account.
22. For other "extinction equilibria," also see Clark (1973).
23. In this memorandum, agriculture includes both crop and livestock production.
24. Land is often cleared by burning forests, but not all forest fires are due to land clearing. Wildfires also occur, and climate change has made wildfires more common. This memorandum focuses on human causes of deforestation, and especially private decisions, acknowledging that human impacts can be amplified through wildfires.
25. Estimates are from "GDP of Agribusiness in Brazil" by the Center for Advanced Studies in Economics (CEPEA) and from Brazil's National Confederation of Agriculture and Livestock (CNA), https://www.cepea.esalq.usp.br/br/pib-do-agronegocio-brasileiro.aspx.
26. This concept is linked to the World Bank's work on the Changing Wealth of Nations, which describes growth as sustainable when, in the growth process, natural wealth is converted into other types of national wealth such as human or physical capital. In the framework of figure 1.7, adjusted net savings are GDP (plus factor income = gross national income), multiplied by the national savings rate, minus the environmental costs (plus human capital formation). According to this framework, growth is more sustainable the higher the adjusted net savings.
27. The "ABC Plan" refers to Brazil's Low-Carbon Agriculture Plan, which was updated in 2021 as "ABC+": the Brazilian Plan for Adaptation and Low Carbon Emission in Agriculture

(officially, "Brazilian Agricultural Policy for Climate Adaptation and Low Carbon Emission").

28. In 2020, the FPE amounted to R$74.4 billion (excluding the Fund for Maintenance and Development of Basic Education and Valuing Education Professionals, or FUNDEB), while other obligatory transfers amounted to R$12.3 billion.

29. According to the IBGE, the smallest state in the country in terms of population is Roraima, with just above 630,000 inhabitants. It is followed by Amapá (861,000 inhabitants) and then Acre (894,000 inhabitants). Tocantins and Rondônia have, respectively, 1.6 million and 1.8 million inhabitants.

REFERENCES

Andrée, B. P. J., P. Spencer, A. Chamorro, and H. Dogo. 2019. "Environment and Development Penalized Non-Parametric Inference of Global Trends in Deforestation, Pollution and Carbon." Policy Research Working Paper 8756, World Bank, Washington, DC.

Boulton, C. A., T. M. Lenton, and N. Boers. 2022. "Pronounced Loss of Amazon Rainforest Resilience since the Early 2000s." *Nature Climate Change* 12 (3): 271–78.

Brandão Jr., A., L. Rausch, A. P. Durán, C. Costa Jr., S. A. Spawn, and H. K. Gibbs. 2020. "Estimating the Potential for Conservation and Farming in the Amazon and Cerrado under Four Policy Scenarios." *Sustainability* 12 (3): 1277.

Brondizio, E. S., J. Settele, S. Díaz, and H. T. Ngo, eds. 2019. *Global Assessment Report on Biodiversity and Ecosystem Services.* Bonn: Intergovernmental Science-Policy Platform on Biodiversity and Ecosystem Services (IPBES).

Calice, Pietro, Federico Diaz Kalan, and Faruk Miguel. 2021. "Nature-Related Financial Risks in Brazil." Policy Research Working Paper 9759, World Bank, Washington, DC.

Charity, S., N. Dudley, D. Oliveira, and S. Stolton, eds. 2016. *Living Amazon Report 2016: A Regional Approach to Conservation in the Amazon.* Brasília and Quito: World Wildlife Fund Living Amazon Initiative.

Clark, C. W. 1973. "Profit Maximization and the Extinction of Animal Species." *Journal of Political Economy* 81 (4): 950–61.

Dasgupta, P. 2021. *The Economics of Biodiversity: The Dasgupta Review.* London: HM Treasury.

Dutta, S., B. Lanvin, and S. Wunsch-Vincent, eds. 2020. *The Global Innovation Index 2020: Who Will Finance Innovation?* Ithaca, Fontainebleu, and Geneva: Cornell University, INSEAD, and World Intellectual Property Organization.

Dutz, M. A. 2018. *Jobs and Growth: Brazil's Productivity Agenda.* International Development in Focus Series. Washington, DC: World Bank.

Ellis, E. C., N. Gauthier, K. Klein Goldewijk, R. B. Bird, N. Boivin, S. Díaz, D. Q. Fuller, et al. 2021. "People Have Shaped Most of Terrestrial Nature for at Least 12,000 Years." *PNAS* 118 (17): e2023483118.

Feenstra, R. C., R. Inklaar, and M. P. Timmer. 2015. "The Next Generation of the Penn World Table." *American Economic Review* 105 (10): 3150–82.

Franklin, S. L., and R. S. Pindyck. 2018. "Tropical Forests, Tipping Points, and the Social Cost of Deforestation." *Ecological Economics* 153: 161–71.

Gandour, C., D. Menezes, J. P. Vieira, and J. J. Assunção. 2021. "Forest Degradation in the Brazilian Amazon: Public Policy Must Target Phenomenon Related to Deforestation." Insight, March 9, Climate Policy Initiative, Rio de Janeiro.

Hemming, J. 2009. *Tree of Rivers: The Story of the Amazon.* New York: Thames & Hudson.

Hsieh, C.-T., and P. Klenow, 2010. "Development Accounting." *American Economic Journal: Macroeconomics* 2 (1): 207–23.

Johansen, B. E., ed. 1999. *The Encyclopedia of Native American Economic History.* Westport, CT: Greenwood Publishing Group.

Johnson, J. A., G. Ruta, U. Baldos, R. Cervigni, S. Chonabavashi, E. Corong, O. Gavryliuk, et al. 2021. "The Economic Case for Nature: A Global Earth-Economy Model to Assess Development Policy Pathways." Report, World Bank, Washington, DC.

Klenow, P., and A. Rodríguez-Clare. 1997. "The Neoclassical Revival in Growth Economics: Has It Gone Too Far?" In *NBER Macroeconomics Annual 12*, edited by B. S. Bernanke and J. Rotemberg, 73–114. Cambridge, MA: MIT Press.

Loayza, N., P. Fajnzylber, and C. Calderón. 2005. *Economic Growth in Latin America and the Caribbean: Stylized Facts, Explanations, and Forecasts*. Washington, DC: World Bank.

Lovejoy, T. E., and C. Nobre. 2018. "Amazon Tipping Point: Last Chance for Action." *Science Advances* 5 (12): eaba2949.

Nobre, C. A., and L. D. S. Borma. 2009. "Tipping Points for the Amazon Forest." *Current Opinion in Environmental Sustainability* 1 (1): 28–36.

North, D. C. 1991. "Institutions." *Journal of Economic Perspectives* 5 (1): 97–112.

Pendrill, F., U. M. Persson, J. Godar, and T. Kastner. 2019. "Deforestation Displaced: Trade in Forest-Risk Commodities and the Prospects for a Global Forest Transition." *Environmental Research Letters* 14 (5): 055003.

Qin, Y., X. Xiao, J.-P. Wigneron, P. Ciais, M. Brandt, L. Fan, X. Li, et al. 2021. "Carbon Loss from Forest Degradation Exceeds that from Deforestation in the Brazilian Amazon." *Nature Climate Change* 11 (5): 442–48.

Richards, P., and L. VanWey. 2015. "Where Deforestation Leads to Urbanization: How Resource Extraction Is Leading to Urban Growth in the Brazilian Amazon." *Annals of the Association of American Geographers* 105 (4): 806–23.

Sanchez Martinez, G., J. Paiva, G. L. de Paula, P. Moutinho, R. Castriota, and A. C. G. Costa. 2022. "Indigenous Peoples and Sustainable Development in the Brazilian Amazônia." Background note for this report, World Bank, Washington, DC.

Schetter, C., and M. Müller-Koné. 2021. "Frontiers' Violence: The Interplay of State of Exception, Frontier Habitus, and Organized Violence." *Political Geography* 87: 102370.

Siikamäki, J. V., A. Krupnick, J. Strand, and J. R. Vincent. 2019. "International Willingness to Pay for the Protection of the Amazon Rainforest." Policy Research Working Paper 8775, World Bank, Washington, DC.

Soares-Filho, B., R. Rajão, M. Macedo, A. Carneiro, W. Costa, M. Coe, H. Rodrigues, and A. Alencar. 2014. "Cracking Brazil's Forest Code." *Science* 344 (6182): 363–64.

Souza-Rodrigues, E. 2019. "Deforestation in the Amazon: A Unified Framework for Estimation and Policy Analysis." *Review of Economic Studies* 86 (6): 2713–44.

Speranza, J., V. Romeiro, and F. Feder. 2017. "Will Brazil Meet Its Climate Targets?" *Insights*, July 7. World Resources Institute, Washington, DC.

Strand, J. 2022. "Valuation of the Brazilian Amazon Rainforest." Background note for this report, World Bank, Washington, DC.

Strand, J., B. Soares-Filho, M. Heil Costa, U. Oliveira, S. C. Ribeiro, G. F. Pires, A. Oliveira, et al. 2018. "Spatially Explicit Valuation of the Brazilian Amazon Forest's Ecosystem Services." *Nature Sustainability* 1 (11): 657–64.

Taylor, M. S., and J. A. Brander. 1998. "International Trade and Open Access Renewable Resources: The Small Open Economy Case." *Canadian Journal of Economics* 30 (3): 526–52.

Trajber Waisbich, L., T. Husek, and V. Santos. 2022. "Territórios e Caminhos do Crime Ambiental na Amazônia Brasileira: Da floresta às demais cidades do país." Instituto Igarapé, Rio de Janeiro. https://igarape.org.br/wp-content/uploads/2022/07/2022-07-AE-territo-rios-e-caminho-do-crime-ambiental-amazonia-brasileira.pdf.

Vale, M. M., P. A. Marquet, D. Corcoran, C. A. de M. Scaramuzza, L. Hannah, A. Hart, J. Busch, A. Maass, P. Roehrdanz, and J. X. Velasco-Hernández. 2021. "Could a Future Pandemic Come from the Amazon?" Paper, Conservation International, Arlington, VA.

Vergara, W., and S. M. Scholz, eds. 2011. *Assessment of the Risk of Amazon Dieback*. World Bank Study. Washington, DC: World Bank.

World Bank. 2023a. *Brazil Country Climate and Development Report*. Washington, DC: World Bank.

World Bank. 2023b. "Urban Competitiveness in Brazil's State of Amazonas: A Green Growth Agenda." Companion paper for this report, World Bank, Washington, DC.

Sustainable, Inclusive Growth

2 People and Livelihoods in Amazônia

GABRIEL LARA IBARRA, ILDO LAUTHARTE, JORGE MUÑOZ,
CAMILLE BOURGUIGNON, ROVANE BATTAGLIN SCHWENGBER,
MICHAEL WEBER, MAREK HANUSCH, STELLA MENDES CARNEIRO,
CLAUDIA TUFANI, AND JOAQUIM BENTO DE SOUZA FERREIRA FILHO

KEY MESSAGES

- Amazônia has high levels of poverty. Inequality is lower than the Brazilian average but high by Latin American standards.
- Poverty rates are higher in rural areas, but most poor people in Amazônia live in cities.
- Afro-descendants, Indigenous people, and other traditional groups are overrepresented among the poor.
- There are significant public service gaps in Amazônia, especially for the poor, and rural Amazônia is particularly underserved.
- Household endowments, including human and financial capital, are low in Amazônia. Land distribution is highly uneven, and weak land tenure security disproportionately disadvantages the poor.
- Amazônia's slow structural transformation is reflected in sluggish labor markets, including low rural labor force participation and high urban unemployment.
- Competition over rural land and resources results in conflicts, often hurting Indigenous people.
- Urbanization rates are high in Amazônia, but cities do not provide sufficient good alternative jobs for former rural workers. Favela-like settlements have proliferated.
- A stronger focus on urban productivity in Amazônia's growth model is consistent both with protecting forests and raising welfare.
- Stronger productivity growth in the rest of Brazil can also raise incomes sustainably in Amazônia.
- *Policy implications:*
  - Investing in human capital, especially education, with an emphasis on teachers and on reskilling.
  - Improving basic service provision, especially water and sanitation, in both rural and urban areas.

– Strengthening land administration and tenure security, especially for rural settlers, Indigenous communities, and other traditional groups.
– Fostering financial inclusion.
– Complementing the social protection system with programs that take into account Amazônia's exceptional cultural and environmental wealth.
– Promoting rural sustainable livelihoods.
– Strengthening the emphasis on urban jobs and urban productivity.

RAISING LIVING STANDARDS IN AMAZÔNIA

Amazônia is one of Brazil's poorest regions. This chapter explores how to raise living standards in Amazônia. It provides an overview of Amazônia's poverty, inequality, service provision, and crime and conflict. The main emphasis, however, is on incomes. The chapter looks at broad channels and policy mechanisms to sustainably improve livelihoods in Amazônia, further refined in Part II (chapters 5–6) of this memorandum. The analysis in this chapter follows the logic of an asset-based framework that sees household income as a function of the following aspects (figure 2.1):

- The accumulated assets of a household include human capital, natural capital (generally land), and financial and physical assets.
- The income from these assets depends on the intensity of using them and the returns on the asset used. For example, being outside the labor force or being unemployed implies no income-generating utilization of human capital, whereas the salary of an individual when working reflects the returns from using the asset.
- When households have high asset endowments with high utilization rates and high returns, they tend to be more affluent.
- Transfers, another source of income, can be either monetary or in kind (such as food), from either inside or outside the country, and either private (remittances) or public (such as cash transfers from social programs).[1]

FIGURE 2.1

Generating income is a function of accumulating and using assets

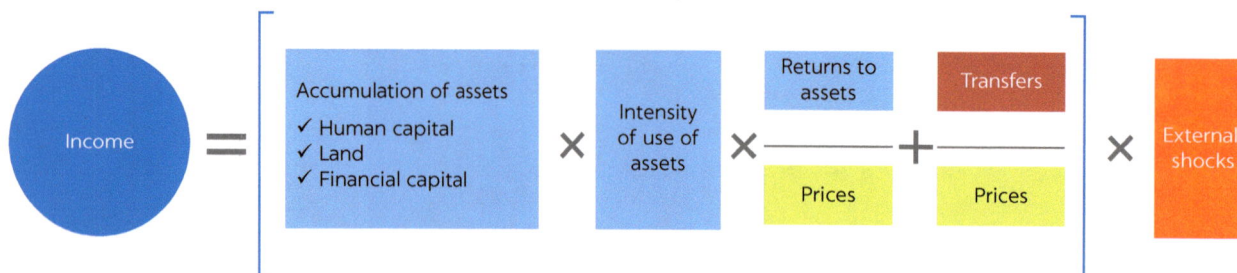

Source: Adapted from López-Calva and Rodríguez-Castelán 2016.

- To capture the purchasing power of a household, all sources of income are weighted by consumer prices. If prices increase faster than incomes, households lose purchasing power and become poorer—and vice versa.
- All sources of real income are weighted by the potential realization of shocks to households directly related to structural transformation or other sources (such as natural disasters).

Lower living standards in Amazônia reflect both lower income and less access to quality public services. Lower overall incomes are consistent with the notion of Amazônia as a lagging or frontier region. In a frontier region, the human, physical, and institutional foundations of modern economies still have to be built and developed. Some Amazonian states, especially in the New Frontier, are more advanced than others in basic infrastructure (logistics, schools, hospitals) and in providing adequate services (from teaching and policing to health care and water and sanitation). But living conditions and sanitation services are considerably worse in Amazônia than in the rest of the country, especially for the poor and rural populations. Adequate housing also remains a major concern.

Lower incomes are reflected in lower assets and returns, which tend to be much lower in Amazônia than in the rest of Brazil. In line with the framework in figure 2.1, figure 2.2 shows that total individual incomes in Amazônia are on average about 30 percent lower than incomes across the rest of Brazil, with 78 percent of the difference due to lower endowments, such as human capital. The gap is only slightly smaller when just urban areas are considered. However, for the poorest 40 percent in Amazônia, the gap is smaller: the poorest 40 percent of Amazonians tend to be only about 11 percent poorer than the poorest 40 percent in other parts of Brazil, when accounting for differences in prices. Although returns to these endowments (in wages, capital income, or rents) are, on average, lower in Amazônia than in the rest of Brazil, this is not the case for

FIGURE 2.2

Individual incomes in Amazônia are about 30 percent lower than in the rest of Brazil

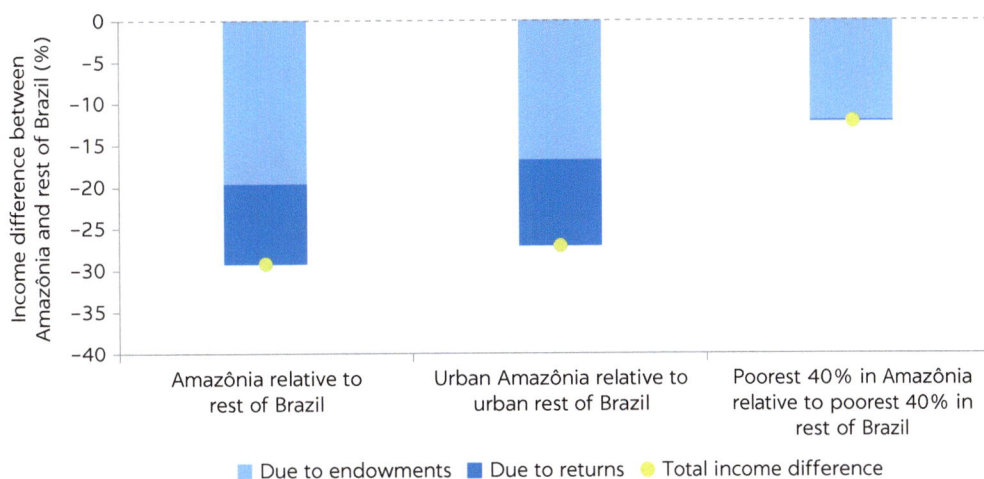

Source: World Bank, using Continuous National Household Sample Survey (PNADC) 2019 data.
Note: The figure follows the methodology in World Bank (2020). Data are further harmonized in the Socio-Economic Database for Latin America and the Caribbean (SEDLAC), which consists of country harmonized survey microdata (the PNADC in Brazil) jointly constructed by the Center for Distributive, Labor and Social Studies (CEDLAS) at the Universidad National de La Plata and the World Bank's Poverty Group for the Latin American and the Caribbean region. Incomes were adjusted at the state level and by metro, urban, and rural area using the Brazilian Institute of Geography and Statistics (IBGE) spatial deflators.

the poorest 40 percent, whose returns are comparable to returns of the poorest 40 percent in other parts of Brazil.

Building assets is critical, and generating good jobs, especially for poor Amazonians, remains a priority—particularly while the rest of Brazil is stagnant. Figure 2.2 points to strengthening individuals' endowments to allow them to raise their living standards to the levels elsewhere in Brazil. It also suggests that migrating to other parts of Brazil would not necessarily make those among the poorest 40 percent of Amazonians better off—unless economic growth and thus labor demand picked up in these regions. In the current scenario, poor Amazonians migrating to other parts of Brazil (perhaps not for income but for other reasons, such as amenities) might contribute to congestion without productivity, which tends to reduce welfare (Grover, Lall, and Maloney 2022). Policy can make poor Amazonians better off in two ways: (a) helping them build assets, especially by raising their human capital to enable them to find higher paying jobs in Amazônia or other parts of Brazil; and (b) fostering economic growth and thus jobs in Amazônia (chapters 3–6) and across Brazil.

Jobs are particularly central for reducing poverty, because labor income dominates all other forms of income in Amazônia, as in the rest of Brazil (table 2.1). Pensions are the most important source of nonlabor income for people who are not poor. Private transfers are small and public transfers substantial. Government programs like Bolsa Família and the Continuous Cash Benefit Program (BPC) have been important sources of nonlabor income for the poor across Brazil, representing about 17 percent of household income for the urban poor and 31 percent for the rural poor in Amazônia, slightly higher than the national average. Other nonlabor income, including capital gains, is concentrated among richer Brazilians and is relatively small, particularly in Amazônia.

Household endowments and economic growth reinforce each other. As chapter 3 shows, human capital is critical to support Amazônia's development, structural transformation, and convergence with more-developed regions. This chapter demonstrates that growth in Amazônia and Brazil also affects the returns to households' assets (with a focus on human capital and land). It also

TABLE 2.1 Household income per capita, by source, location, and poverty status, 2019

Brazilian reais

	BRAZIL				AMAZÔNIA			
	URBAN		RURAL		URBAN		RURAL	
VARIABLE	POOR	NONPOOR	POOR	NONPOOR	POOR	NONPOOR	POOR	NONPOOR
Total without imputed rent[a]	217	1,783	197	1,137	214	1,314	189	1,000
Labor income	154	1,309	113	698	151	1,012	107	621
Nonlabor income	63	474	84	439	63	302	82	379
Pensions	20	358	23	359	20	221	22	288
Private transfers	9	20	4	6	6	15	2	4
Other nonlabor income[b]	1	70	1	27	1	30	1	20
Public transfers[c]	33	27	56	47	36	36	58	68

Source: World Bank, using Socio-Economic Database for Latin America and the Caribbean (SEDLAC) 2019 data.
Note: "Poor" is defined as those living at or below the poverty line of US$5.50 per person per day, adjusted for purchasing power in 2011 prices.
a. "Total without imputed rent" refers to the full dataset without missing values filled in.
b. "Other nonlabor income" includes capital gains and other rents.
c. "Public transfers" include Bolsa Família; the Continuous Cash Benefit Program or Assistance Benefit (BPC or LOAS, respectively); and other social programs.

shows that a focus on balanced structural transformation can help raise household incomes inclusively and more sustainably. Echoing chapters 1 and 3, productivity growth in the rest of Brazil is important to raise welfare in Amazônia.

Amazônia exhibits idiosyncratic social fragilities not limited to its forests. It is a frontier region where modern and traditional worlds meet—and at times collide. This chapter pays close attention to Amazônia's Indigenous people and other traditional minorities whose livelihoods and, in some cases, centuries-old ways of life are threatened. These groups have often found ways to embrace opportunities associated with the region's structural transformation, but threats and conflicts need to be managed carefully.

The chapter is anchored in the logic of figure 2.1 and proceeds as follows: First, looking at income and living conditions more broadly, it canvasses the Amazonian population, with an emphasis on poverty and inequality, including for Indigenous people and other traditional minorities. Next, it unpacks the other components of the asset framework, looking first at labor, capital, and land. This analysis is followed by a discussion of prices and shocks and how transfers can help raise income while mitigating shocks. The chapter then explores how different growth models for Amazônia and Brazil affect the returns to human capital and land.

A SOCIAL CANVASS OF AMAZÔNIA

Poverty and inequality (a function of income in figure 2.1) are high in Amazônia, though inequality is slightly lower than for Brazil as a whole. Most poor people live in towns and cities, but poverty is deeper in rural areas. Amazônia has the largest Indigenous population in Brazil, though it makes up just 1.5 percent of Amazônia's population.

Poverty, inequality, and living conditions

Poverty and inequality

Amazônia is a poor region in Brazil, and inequality, although less extreme than in the rest of the country, is high. In the most recent period with comparable data (2012–19), Amazônia's annual average poverty rate was around 36 percent (using the World Bank's poverty line of US$5.50 per person per day, adjusted for purchasing power in 2011 prices), which exceeds Brazil's average of around 21 percent.

Current poverty rates vary across the Amazonian states, but except in Mato Grosso and Rondônia (the more advanced states of the New Frontier), they remain above the national average. Poverty is highest in Maranhão, at 46 percent in 2019. Although Amazônia is slightly less unequal than Brazil overall, income inequality is still high (figure 2.3).

The vast majority of Amazônia's poor live in cities, though poverty rates are higher in rural areas. Following the country's rapid urbanization, most Amazonians now live in urban areas (figure 2.4). In 1970, just over 3 million of Amazônia's 8 million residents, or 37 percent, lived in urban areas. By 2010, 72 percent of Amazônia's 24.3 million residents lived in cities, a share that rose to nearly 76 percent in 2019 (the latest estimate for Amazônia's population is about 28 million). While already quite urbanized, Amazônia is still somewhat less urban than Brazil as a whole.

Of the close to 10 million poor people in Amazônia in 2019, 6.5 million were urban residents, and 3.8 million were rural residents. But poverty rates are higher

FIGURE 2.3

Inequality is high in Brazil and Amazônia, even by Latin American standards

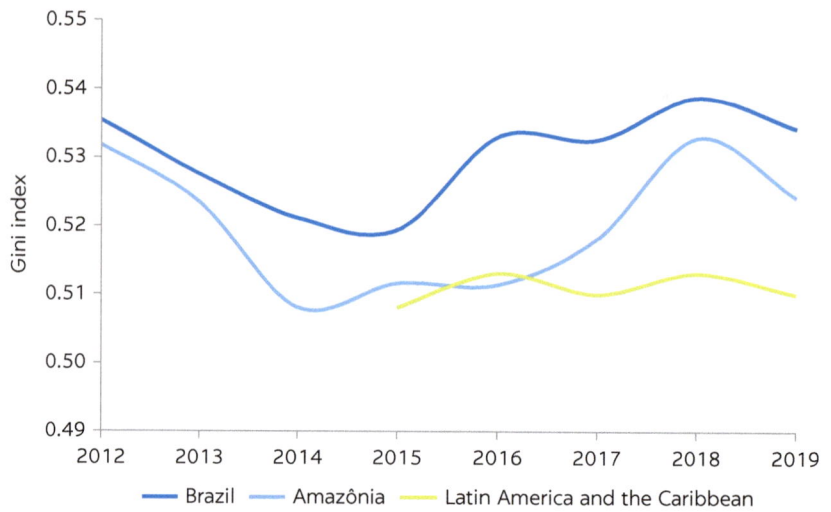

Sources: World Bank, using Socio-Economic Database for Latin America and the Caribbean (SEDLAC) data and the World Bank's LAC Equity Lab data-sharing platform.
Note: The Gini index measures the inequality of income (or consumption) distribution in an economy. A Gini value of 0.0 indicates perfect equality, and a value of 1.0 indicates perfect inequality.

FIGURE 2.4

The Amazonian population became increasingly urban, typified by Amazonas State

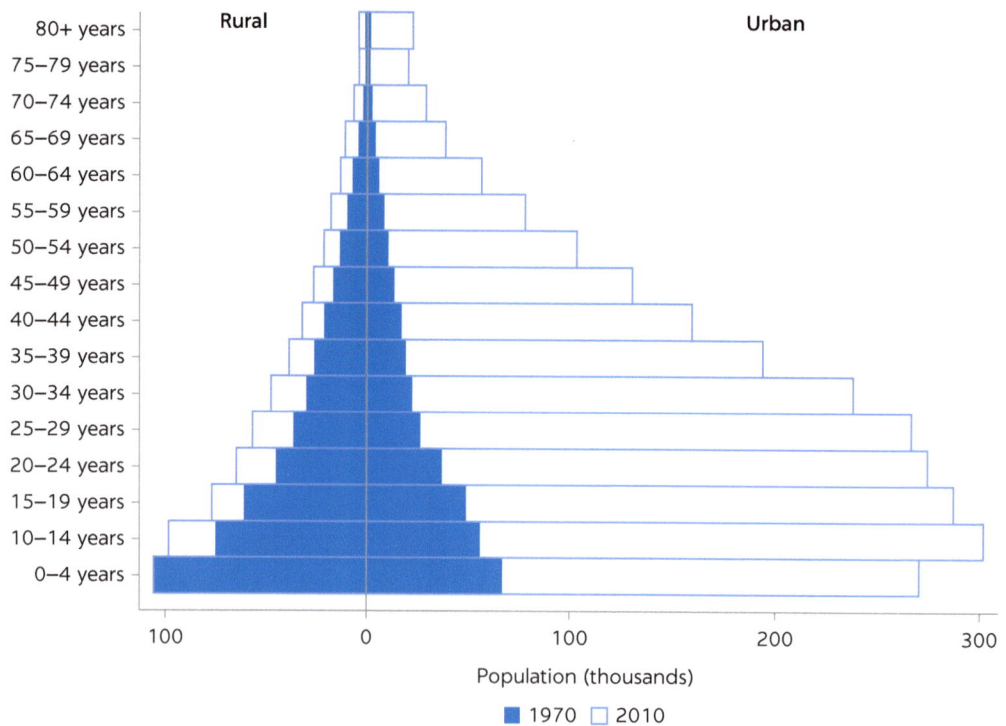

Source: World Bank, using the Brazilian Institute of Geography and Statistics (IBGE) Population Census data.
Note: The figure compares the population pyramid in Amazonas State between 1970 and 2010. The blue-shaded bars represent the population in 1970. White bars represent the population in 2010.

FIGURE 2.5
Most poor Amazonians live in towns and cities

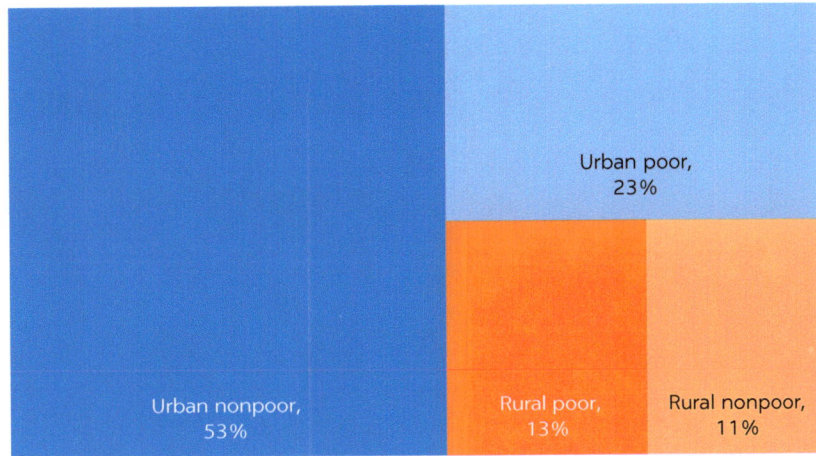

Sources: World Bank, using Socio-Economic Database for Latin America and the Caribbean (SEDLAC) and Continuous National Household Sample Survey (PNADC) 2019 data as of July 5, 2022 via Datalibweb Stata Package.
Note: The figure shows 2019 shares of Amazônia's population. "Poor" is defined as those living at or below the international poverty line of US$5.50 per person per day.

in rural areas, at 53 percent compared with 29 percent in urban areas (figure 2.5). Extreme poverty (less than US$1.90 per person per day) is also more prevalent in rural areas, at nearly 20 percent, compared with 6.3 percent in urban areas. The lower intensity of poverty in urban areas is a likely pull factor attracting rural inhabitants to cities, along with better amenities and health and education outcomes.

Poverty has a strong demographic component. Afro-Brazilians and *caboclos* (see chapter 1)[2] are overrepresented among rural residents and among the poor, constituting about 86 percent of the poor rural population in Amazônia (table 2.2). This is the case for fully Indigenous people, too. Female-headed households are also overrepresented among the urban poor, with 6 in 10 of those households headed by women, compared with less than 5 in 10 nonpoor urban households. By contrast, only around 5 in 10 rural households are headed by women. Finally, poorer households tend to be younger on average.

Living conditions

Living conditions and sanitation services are considerably worse in Amazônia than in the rest of the country, especially for the poor and rural populations, according to Continuous National Household Sample Survey (PNADC) 2019 data. For the urban nonpoor, differences in living conditions are small between Amazônia and Brazil overall, except for water connections (table 2.3). Poor urban dwellers in Amazônia, by contrast, face worse conditions than their richer neighbors and than poor urban dwellers in other parts of Brazil. There are clear advantages to living in cities, however, even for poor people, including near-universal access to electricity and relatively good sanitation.

Consistent with the notion of a frontier economy where both infrastructure and public service governance still need to mature, conditions are much worse in the rural areas of Amazônia, especially for poor households (and somewhat less so for the nonpoor). About 86 percent of the rural poor in Amazônia have no

TABLE 2.2 **Demographic characteristics of the Brazilian population, by location and poverty status, 2019**

	BRAZIL				AMAZÔNIA			
	URBAN		RURAL		URBAN		RURAL	
VARIABLE	POOR	NONPOOR	POOR	NONPOOR	POOR	NONPOOR	POOR	NONPOOR
Black or Pardo[a] (%)	74	51	79	59	84	75	86	79
Indigenous (%)	1	0	1	0	1	1	2	1
Average family size	4.5	3.4	4.7	3.3	5.0	3.7	5.2	3.6
Household head								
Male share (%)	39	52	63	68	39	51	68	73
Female share (%)	61	48	37	32	61	49	32	27
Mean age	41.7	49.2	41.7	52.1	42.0	48.2	41.4	51.5

Source: World Bank, using Socio-Economic Database for Latin America and the Caribbean (SEDLAC) data.
Note: "Poor" is defined as those living at or below the poverty line of US$5.50 per person per day.
a. "Pardo" refers to individuals who self-report as light-skinned Afro-Brazilians of mixed race.

TABLE 2.3 **Demographic and dwelling characteristics, by location and poverty status, 2019**

percent

	BRAZIL TOTAL				AMAZÔNIA			
	URBAN		RURAL		URBAN		RURAL	
DWELLING CHARACTERISTIC	POOR	NONPOOR	POOR	NONPOOR	POOR	NONPOOR	POOR	NONPOOR
Precarious materials	5	2	14	6	12	5	30	13
No water supply	4	1	42	29	7	2	46	27
No water network connection	10	4	59	59	22	18	65	67
No improved sanitation	2	0	26	8	4	1	34	14
Open defecation	2	0	25	6	7	1	46	18
No trash collection	3	1	72	54	7	2	86	79
No electricity access	0	0	2	1	0	0	5	2
No electricity network	0	0	6	2	0	0	16	8
No private bathrooms	3	0	26	7	8	1	48	20

Source: World Bank, using Continuous National Household Sample Survey (PNADC) 2019 data.
Note: "Poor" is defined those living at or below the poverty line of US$5.50 per person per day.

access to trash collection, 65 percent have no water connection, and 48 percent have no private bathroom. These differences illustrate the pull factors drawing people from rural to urban areas, amplifying the push factors experienced by agriculture workers affected by the rural structural transformation (chapter 3).

Population growth, informality, and unplanned urbanization underpin deficient water and sanitation services. Limited coverage and poor quality of water and sanitation services, combined with lower rates of wastewater collection, contribute to the spread of disease, affecting both health outcomes and labor productivity. Compared with the rest of Brazil, Amazônia has fewer revenues from sewer bills, worse water quality, lower density of connections per provider, shorter water networks, higher technical and commercial losses, and overall worse financial performance. The differences have widened since 2000. Accordingly, the states in Amazônia have proportionally more days lost to productivity (measured by disability-adjusted life years) from diarrhea and waterborne diseases than other states (excluding those in the Northeast region).

In rural areas, the persistence of unimproved water and sanitation services perpetuates the vicious cycle of poverty, inequality, and low productivity (Bernhofen, Dolan, and Borja-Vega 2022).

In both urban and rural areas, Indigenous people's access to sanitation services improved between 1991 and 2010, though a large gap remains between urban and rural residents (IBGE 2012). The share of the Indigenous population living in households with bathrooms jumped from 77 percent in 1991 to 92 percent in 2010 in urban areas and from 13 percent to 31 percent in rural areas. Still, the percentage of Indigenous-headed households without bathrooms was almost six times higher in Amazônia (36 percent) than in Brazil overall (6.6 percent) in 2010. These gaps are larger in the North region, where 71 percent of the households headed by Indigenous people had no access to private bathrooms compared with 22 percent of the households headed by non-Indigenous people (the highest gap in the country). The percentage of the Indigenous population residing in urban areas has also increased, from 24 percent in 1991 to 39 percent in 2010 (IBGE 2012).

Services in Amazônia's urban areas struggle to keep pace with the rate of urbanization, reflected in large informal, favela-like urban settlements. Even though urban areas provide much better public services than rural areas, they have difficulty absorbing a rapidly rising population and providing adequate housing opportunities and other services. Housing inadequacy can be proxied by the "housing deficit," a rough measure of the need for new homes in an area. The housing deficit is the number of "missing" houses—that is, the number of new houses that would be needed to end housing precariousness, which manifests in multiple families sharing single homes or too many people sharing single rooms. Housing deficits are higher in Amazônia than in the rest of Brazil (figure 2.6).

In addition, informal urban settlements (called "subnormal clusters"[3]) are common in Amazônia and more common in some Amazonian states than in the rest of Brazil. The number of urban residents living in such settlements ranges from about 2 percent of the households in Mato Grosso to 35 percent in Amazonas. These informal settlements are more prevalent in states with a sluggish economy and less prevalent in the faster-developing states on the New Frontier, as better economic opportunities there have translated into better housing (figure 2.7).

Crime and violence

Along with poverty and inequality, crime is high in Amazônia (chapter 5). In the larger Amazonian cities, violence is similar to that in other major urban centers in Brazil. It is linked to organized crime, drug trafficking, police corruption, smaller-scale armed robberies, and domestic violence. Amazônia is particularly vulnerable to drug traffickers, who enter the region at many porous locations along the frontier with neighboring countries en route to larger markets in other regions of Brazil and wealthy countries in other continents. The violence associated with these activities contributes to violent conflicts in the region (Chimeli and Soares 2017; Piva da Silva, Fraser, and Parry 2021). The Amazonian region is involved in drug production and large-scale distribution, while southeastern Brazilian cities are engaged in the consumption and small-scale distribution end of the drug trafficking trade (Paiva 2019).

The northern parts of Brazil, including most Amazonian states, had the highest homicide rates in 2018. The region's homicide rate has been rising

FIGURE 2.6

Urban housing deficits are higher in Amazônia than in the rest of Brazil, 2019

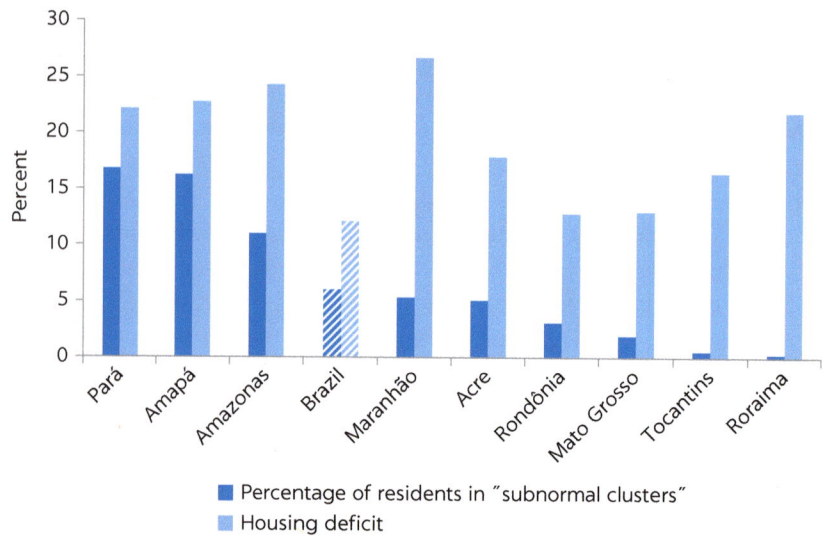

■ Percentage of residents in "subnormal clusters"
■ Housing deficit

Source: World Bank, using IBGE (2020a) data.
Note: The figure shows housing deficits in the nine states constituting Amazônia as well as in Brazil overall. The "housing deficit" refers to the total "missing" houses that would be needed to solve existing issues of housing affordability, which lead to several families sharing single homes, excessive burden of rent on wages, and excessive residents sharing single rooms. "Subnormal clusters" are informal urban settlements, defined as denser urban areas with at least 51 housing units lacking, in their majority, essential public services; occupying public or private land; and being characterized by a disorderly urban pattern (IBGE 2020a).

FIGURE 2.7

Informal settlements are more common in states with a sluggish economy, 2019

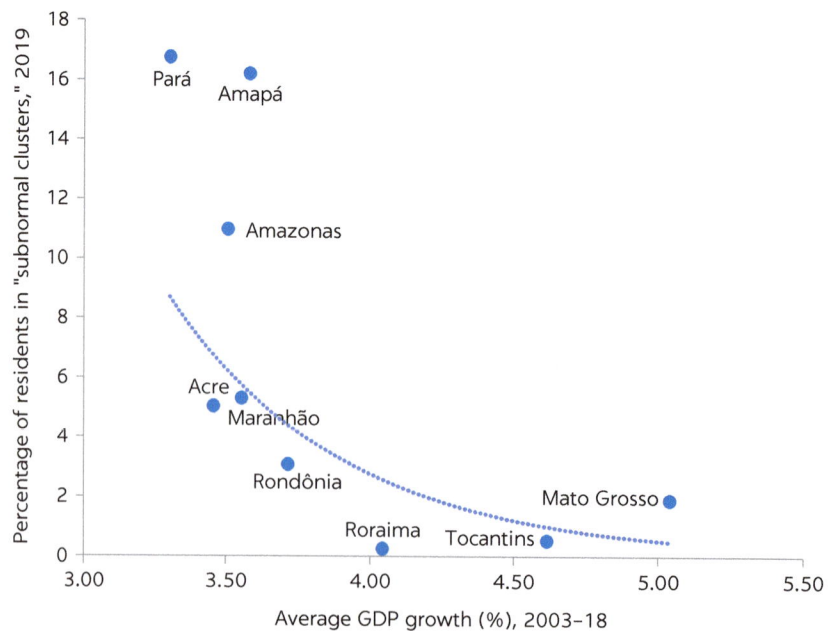

Sources: World Bank, using IBGE (2020a) and subnational accounts data.
Note: The figure shows the distribution of the nine Brazilian states constituting Amazônia in terms of the share of residents in subnormal clusters in relation to those states' 2003–18 GDP growth. "Subnormal clusters" are informal urban settlements, defined as denser urban areas with at least 51 housing units lacking, in their majority, essential public services; occupying public or private land; and being characterized by a disorderly urban pattern (IBGE 2020a).

since 2014, while the national average has remained fairly stable, according to the latest Institute of Applied Economic Research (Ipea) "Atlas da Violência" (Cequeira et al. 2020).[4] The Amazonian states with the highest homicide rates were Roraima (72 homicides per 100,000 inhabitants), Pará (53), and Amapá (51).[5] The Atlas suggests that Roraima's climbing homicide rates are spillovers from Venezuela's high homicide rate (81 per 100,000), and it relates Amapá's homicide rate to illegal migration and drug trafficking routes along French Guiana's borders with the state (Cequeira et al. 2020). Rondônia, Acre, Amazonas, and Roraima are the country's largest mass incarcerators (Jacarandá, Flores, and Feitoza 2019). Acre reportedly became the second most violent state in the country in 2017 in numbers of homicides and violent crimes, and its capital, Rio Branco, was the most violent in the country, at 87 homicides per 100,000 inhabitants (Jacarandá, Flores, and Feitoza 2019). There is some evidence from across Brazil that improving economic development outcomes could reduce crime as well (Baggio et al. 2019).

A focus on Indigenous people and other traditional communities

The income-generating potential of traditional communities in Brazil is not well documented. Because of the limited information, it is not straightforward to apply the asset framework to study the income-generating potential of Indigenous populations, *quilombolas* (descendants of fugitive African slaves), and other groups that reside in rural Amazônia.[6] This section briefly describes the size and spatial distribution of Indigenous populations, *quilombolas*, and other traditional communities.[7]

Indigenous populations

In 2010, Brazil's fewer than 900,000 Indigenous people inhabited all five regions of the country, with more than a third in Amazônia (IBGE 2010). About 58 percent of Indigenous people lived within Indigenous lands (95 percent of them in rural areas), and 42 percent lived outside the Indigenous lands (79 percent of them in urban areas). Those living within Indigenous lands were younger than those living outside them. Over a third of Indigenous people lived in urban areas, and about 380,000 lived in Amazônia, making it the region with the highest Indigenous population in Brazil though they constituted only 1.5 percent of the region's population (table 2.4). Amazonas has the largest Indigenous population in the country; its 167,000 Indigenous people account for 20 percent of the Indigenous people in Brazil and nearly 5 percent of the state population (IBGE 2010). About 80 percent of the Indigenous population live in rural areas and 20 percent in state capitals. Many Indigenous people move back and forth between urban and rural areas. Isolated Indigenous people constitute a separate Indigenous group that remains isolated from the broader society (box 2.1).

Quilombolas and other traditional communities

Quilombolas are not numerous in Amazônia (chapter 1). According to the Brazilian Institute of Geography and Statistics (IBGE), there are 5,972 *quilombola* localities in Brazil: 404 territories, 2,308 communities, and 3,260 regions (IBGE 2020b).[8] Only 15 percent of these localities (23 percent of the territories, 23 percent of the communities, and 7 percent of other regions) are in states in the North region, especially Pará; Amazonas accounts for 21 percent

TABLE 2.4 **Indigenous people in Amazônia**

STATE	INDIGENOUS POPULATION	INDIGENOUS POPULATION IN STATE CAPITAL	INDIGENOUS POPULATION OUTSIDE STATE CAPITAL	NON-INDIGENOUS POPULATION	TOTAL POPULATION	INDIGENOUS POPULATION AS SHARE OF TOTAL (%)
Acre	15,684	2,604	13,080	717,889	733,573	2.1
Amapá	7,333	1,341	5,992	662,139	669,472	1.0
Amazonas	167,079	41,181	125,898	3,316,933	3,484,012	4.8
Maranhão	34,305	5,967	28,338	6,539,023	6,573,328	0.5
Mato Grosso	43,114	6,469	36,645	2,990,462	3,033,576	1.4
Pará	38,207	10,989	27,218	7,541,230	7,579,437	1.1
Rondônia	13,618	3,168	10,450	1,546,826	1,560,444	0.9
Roraima	50,352	8,559	41,793	399,621	449,973	11.2
Tocantins	12,839	1,728	11,111	1,370,133	1,382,972	0.9
Total	**382,531**	**80,657**	**301,874**	**25,084,256**	**25,466,787**	**1.5**

Source: IBGE 2010.

BOX 2.1

Isolated Indigenous people

The Brazilian government recognizes 114 groups of Indigenous people who have chosen to live apart from other Indigenous and non-Indigenous groups, most of them in Amazônia. These groups range from hundreds of people to a few individual survivors. In the colonial past, they came in contact with segments of the national society—encounters often marked by violence, the spread of diseases, and even extermination. Later, the remaining members of these groups fled to refuge areas in remote and difficult-to-access locations. The decision to remain in isolation was also related to the desire to live under conditions that allow them to meet their social, material, and spiritual needs and to avoid engaging in social interactions that could trigger tensions or interethnic conflict.[a]

The Brazilian policy toward isolated Indigenous peoples is to avoid contact with them, except in cases of specific and clear-cut threats. This policy of non-contact has been in place since 1987, when the National Indian Foundation (FUNAI) created the Coordination of Isolated Indians (now the General Coordination of Isolated Indians and Recent Contact, CGIIRC) to safeguard the rights of isolated Indigenous people and those of recent contact. FUNAI is responsible for guaranteeing isolated people the full exercise of their freedom and their traditional ways of life without having to contact them.

When the presence of isolated Indigenous people is verified outside the boundaries of already demarcated Indigenous lands, FUNAI applies the legal provision of the "Restriction of Use" of the land to protect the area of occupation of isolated groups, restrict entry by others, and ensure the physical integrity of the Indigenous people while other protection actions and administrative procedures are being processed for the demarcation of the Indigenous land. Restriction of Use is supported by Article 7 of Decree 1775/96, Article 231 of the 1988 Federal Constitution and Article 1, item VII of Law No. 5371/67.

Source: Sanchez Martinez et al. 2022.
a. Among the isolated groups whose presence has been confirmed, only the Avá-Canoeiro live outside Amazônia.

of the northern *quilombola* localities. Many *quilombola* communities still wait to be officially recognized.

Traditional groups are well defined in Brazilian legislation. Presidential Decree 6040/2007 describes traditional people and communities as "culturally differentiated groups who recognize themselves as such, who hold their own forms of social organization, who occupy and use territories and natural resources as a condition for their cultural, social, religious, ancestral and economic reproduction, utilizing knowledge, innovations and practices generated and transmitted through tradition." It further defines traditional territories as "the spaces necessary for the cultural, social and economic reproduction of traditional people and communities, whether they are used permanently or temporarily" (Presidential Decree 6.040/2007, Article 3, §2). In addition, the Brazilian regulatory framework on the National System of Conservation Units allows the people of traditional communities to remain in territories of Sustainable Use Units and Extractive Reserves and to use resources sustainably (Law 9,985/2000).

A common set of characteristics defines the wide range of traditional populations and communities in Brazil (de Melo Lira and Rodrigues Chaves 2016; Gomes de Souza et al. 2020; Little 2018). Self-identification as members of a distinct cultural group and recognition of that identity by others is a critical element of traditional peoples' identity. They are also identified by the symbiotic relationship between their way of life and nature, and the use of renewable natural resources; the production and social reproduction of the group based on deep knowledge of natural cycles; and their dependence on various seasonal sources of income, which combine extractive activities, agriculture, and livestock, fishing, and handicrafts.

Traditional groups' economic organization centers around subsistence-oriented activities, though some may have engaged in the production of goods and have gained access to markets. Their productive systems tend to be based on a social division of labor according to gender roles. They rely on traditional systems to regulate access to terrestrial and natural resources based mainly on organizing the territory into spatial units for different but complementary economic activities. Consequently, their landscape is frequently marked by a combination of small family farms, with large areas of collective use for gathering, hunting, and pastoral activities. They own few financial assets, have little political representation or power, and are largely socially invisible. Their subsistence systems, characterized by sustainable use of the varied resources of the tropical forest and Amazon water courses, allow them considerable independence from foreign markets, even when they engage in activities essentially aimed at commercialization.

HUMAN CAPITAL

Human capital—the knowledge, skills, and health that people invest in and accumulate to realize their potential as productive members of society—is low in Amazônia. The World Bank's Human Capital Index (HCI) captures differences in human capital across countries or regions within a country. Based on indicators of health and education,[9] the HCI estimates that children born in Brazil today will realize only about 60 percent of their potential productivity if current health and education conditions prevail (World Bank 2022). The Northeast region and the states of Amazônia have the highest concentrations of municipalities with critically low human capital. In Amazônia, Mato Grosso, in the New Frontier, has by far the highest human capital (map 2.1). Education is the most important driver of the HCI gap in Amazônia, but challenges remain in health (figure 2.8).

Health

Gaps in health in Amazônia are consistent with its status as a frontier region, with weaker institutions and a less mature economic structure. Brazil's public health system, the Unified Health System (SUS), provides universal access to health services, but quality varies across states and regions, and between urban and rural areas. Less affluent—or less developed—states have higher infant mortality and lower life expectancy according to regression analysis for this memorandum. One contributing factor is inadequate sanitation services in poorer regions, where gaps persist in access to water and sanitation sectors.

MAP 2.1

Human capital is low in Amazônia, 2019

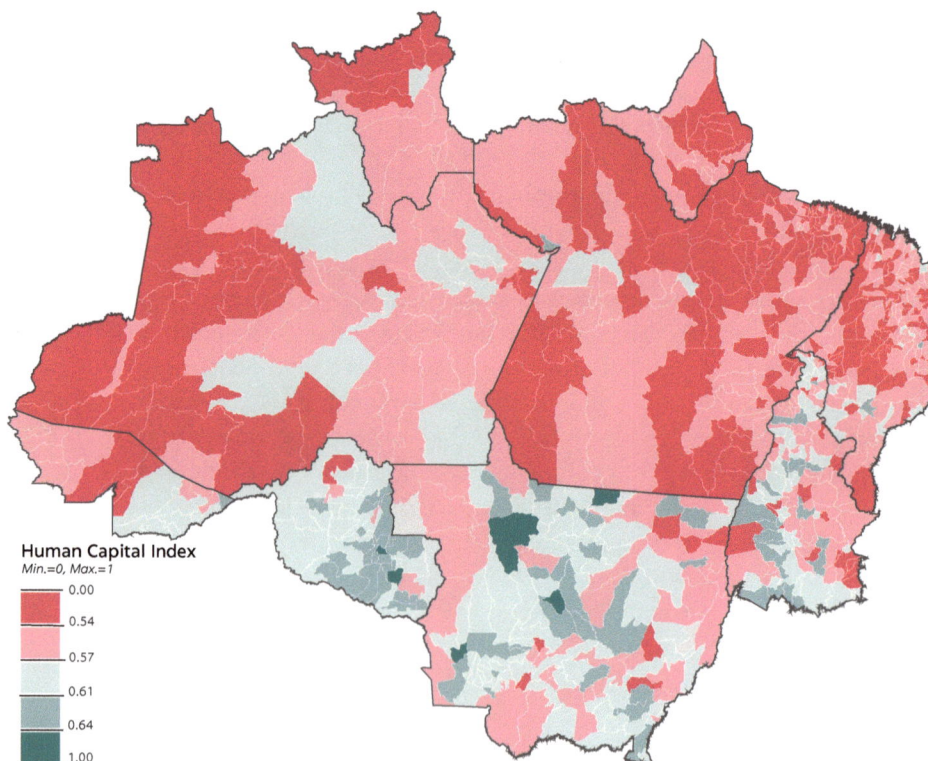

Human Capital Index
Min.=0, Max.=1

- 0.00
- 0.54
- 0.57
- 0.61
- 0.64
- 1.00

Source: World Bank 2022.
Note: The World Bank's Human Capital Index (HCI) benchmarks the key components of human capital across economies or across regions within an economy (https://www.worldbank.org/en/publication/human-capital). It is a summary measure of the amount of human capital that a child born today can expect to acquire by age 18, given the risks of poor health and poor education that prevail in the child's country. Ranging between 0 and 1, the HCI takes the value 1 only if a child born today can expect to achieve full health (no stunting as well as survival until at least age 60) and formal education potential (14 years of high-quality school by age 18). The score represents the difference between the prevailing conditions and the case where children enjoy full education and health during their lives. An HCI score of 0.57, for instance, indicates that the future earnings potential of children born today will be 57 percent of what it could have been achieved if the child had had access to full health and education.

FIGURE 2.8

Education is the widest human capital gap in Amazônia, 2019

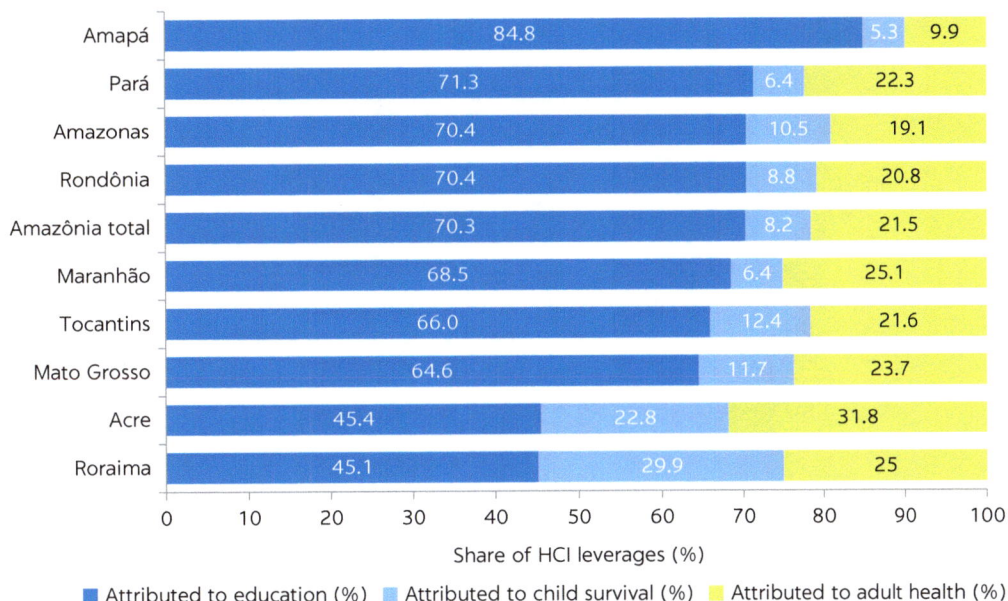

Source: World Bank 2022.
Note: The three components of human capital shown here are rates of child health (child survival at age 5 and no stunting); adult health (the likelihood, at age 15, of living to age 60); and education (learning-adjusted years of schooling, a measure that combines quantity and quality of schooling as a percentage of the expected number of years in school that a child achieves by age 18 if repetition and dropout remain unaltered across basic education). Amazônia comprises the nine listed states.

The COVID-19 pandemic exposed some of the weaknesses of health systems in Amazônia, many of which were overwhelmed by the pandemic. Preliminary data show that mortality in hospitals in the North region (which includes seven of the nine Amazonian states) was higher than in any other region of Brazil. In fact, mortality among intensive care unit admitted patients was 79 percent in the North (highest in the country), compared with Brazil's average of 55 percent. Overall, in-hospital mortality in the North was 50 percent (also the highest in the country), compared with 38 percent nationwide in Brazil. Although the population in the North tends to be younger than in other parts of Brazil, in-hospital mortality was higher in the North region across all age groups. Even before the pandemic, the North already had higher in-hospital mortality than other regions (Ranzani et al. 2021).

As in other parts of the country, the vulnerable population of Amazônia was the most affected by the pandemic. Early studies of the prevalence of SARS-CoV-2 antibodies in Brazil showed a rapid increase of SARS-CoV-2 seroprevalence in the North (and Northeast) regions, with seroprevalence being higher among those of Indigenous ancestry and those with low socioeconomic status (Hallal et al. 2020). A study carried out in Jurua Valley (interior of Amazonas State) showed that children from disadvantaged households (those that faced food insecurity) had their COVID-19 risk increased by 76 percent (Ferreira et al. 2022).

Another reason for poorer health outcomes in Amazônia is the region's sparser settlements. Because of economies of scale in health care provision, denser human settlements tend to have more efficient health services. A cross-country analysis found a significant and positive relationship between maternal health indicators and density measures, with a one-unit increase in the density score related to a 0.2 percent increase in coverage rates (Hanlon et al. 2012). In the Brazilian health care system, much of the inefficiency arises from the very small hospitals (almost 80 percent of Brazilian hospitals have fewer than 100 beds) that provide health services to small municipalities (World Bank 2017).

The least urbanized states in Amazônia struggle most to improve health indicators. Low density has a significant adverse impact on health outcomes in Brazil. On average, child survival rates are lower in municipalities in Amazônia, the country's least dense region, than in the rest of Brazil. Only the denser Amazonian municipalities have child survival rates comparable to those of other municipalities in Brazil (figure 2.9). In Acre and Roraima, two of the least urbanized and most remote states in Amazônia, low infant survival rates explain a considerable part of their human capital outcomes (see figure 2.8). In contrast, child survival explains only a small part of human capital performance in Amapá, the most urbanized state in the region.

Across Brazil, higher density at the state level is associated with higher life expectancy (figure 2.10); states in Amazônia have among the lowest life expectancy in Brazil. Jointly, these results provide some evidence that structural change and urbanization in Amazônia can also help improve health outcomes.

Education

Poor education is the most important constraint on building human capital in Amazônia (see figure 2.8). The education component of the HCI adjusts years of schooling by learning quality. In Brazil, when expected years of schooling (10–11 years) are adjusted for gaps in learning quality (based on proficiency data

FIGURE 2.9

Only denser Amazonian municipalities have child survival rates comparable to the rest of Brazil

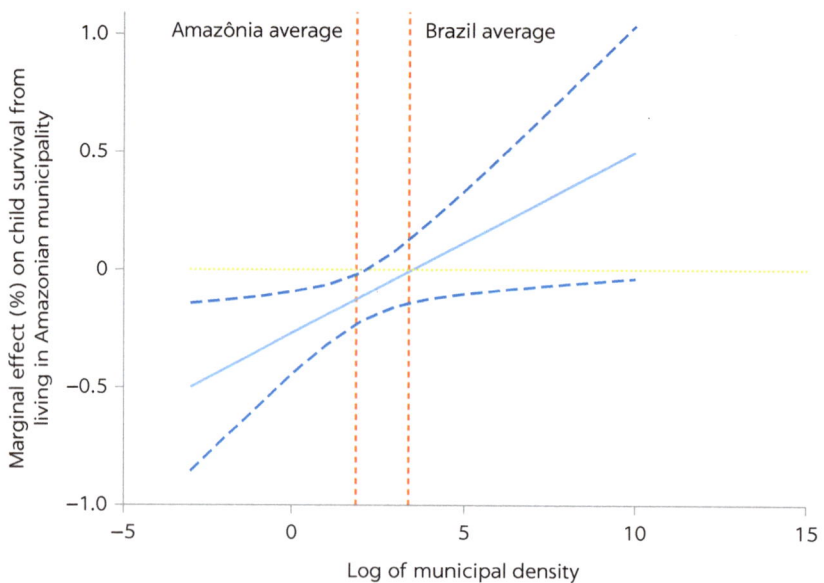

Sources: World Bank, using data from the Brazilian Institute of Geography and Statistics (IBGE) Territorial Areas database, IBGE Population Projections database, IBGE Population Estimates database, and Department of Informatics of the Unified Health System (DATASUS) database.
Note: Controls for GDP per capita. A control for health expenditure is statistically insignificant. Dashed blue lines represent 95 percent confidence intervals.

FIGURE 2.10

Across Brazil, life expectancy is associated with state density

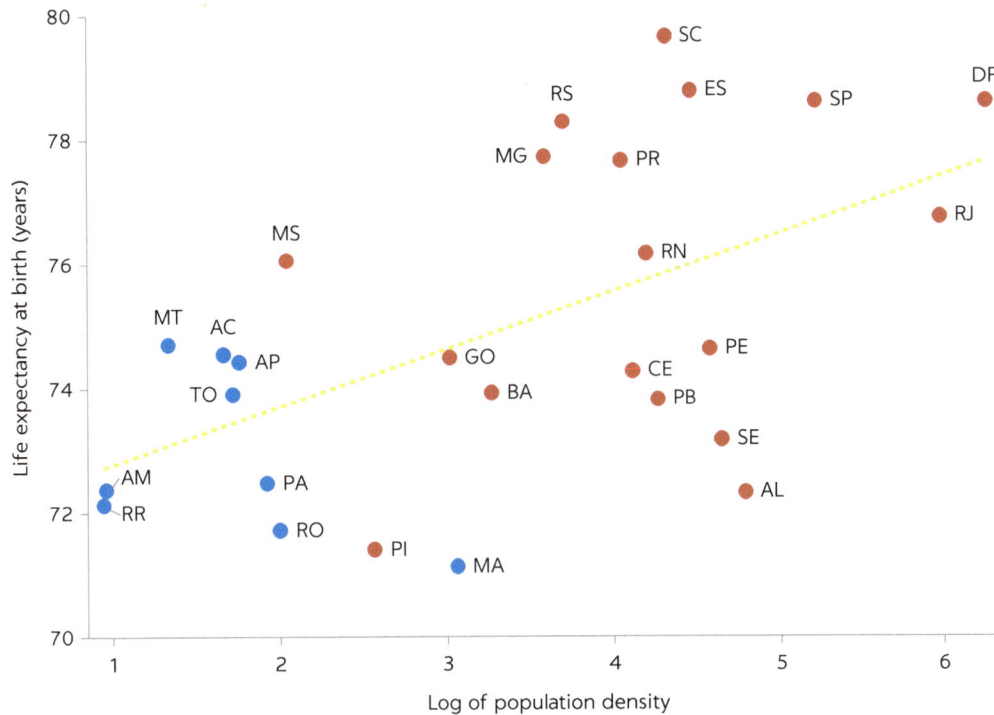

Sources: World Bank, using data from the Brazilian Institute of Geography and Statistics (IBGE) Population Estimates database, IBGE Territorial Areas database, and IBGE Population Projections database.
Note: Controls for GDP per capita. States are designated by two-letter abbreviations; Amazonian states are in blue.

from the National Learning Test, or SAEB), the learning-adjusted years of schooling fall to about 7–8 years. For instance, for cities in Maranhão that are within Amazônia, the 11 expected years of schooling drop to 6.6 years after adjusting for learning quality (World Bank 2022). The disruption to schooling due to COVID-19 has set back education in Brazil and Amazônia, and it may take many years to make up the losses (World Bank 2022).

There were meaningful gains in education among Indigenous groups between 1991 and 2010. According to IBGE census data, the illiteracy rate among Indigenous people ages 15 years and older fell from 51 percent in 1991 to 23 percent in 2010, though this was still much higher than the national average for non-Indigenous people, just under 10 percent. For Indigenous people, the illiteracy rate was higher in rural areas (33 percent) than in urban areas (12 percent) and higher among women (25 percent) than men (22 percent).

Education is crucial to the future quality of the region's labor force. The inequities in education, and human capital more generally, point to large potential limitations for sustainably improving labor productivity in Amazônia. Foundational skills, as measured by the learning poverty index—the percentage of 10-year-olds who cannot read and understand a short, age-appropriate paragraph—are lagging (figure 2.11) (World Bank 2019). Reading is important because learning to read fosters a readiness to learn.[10]

FIGURE 2.11
Learning poverty is high in Amazônia

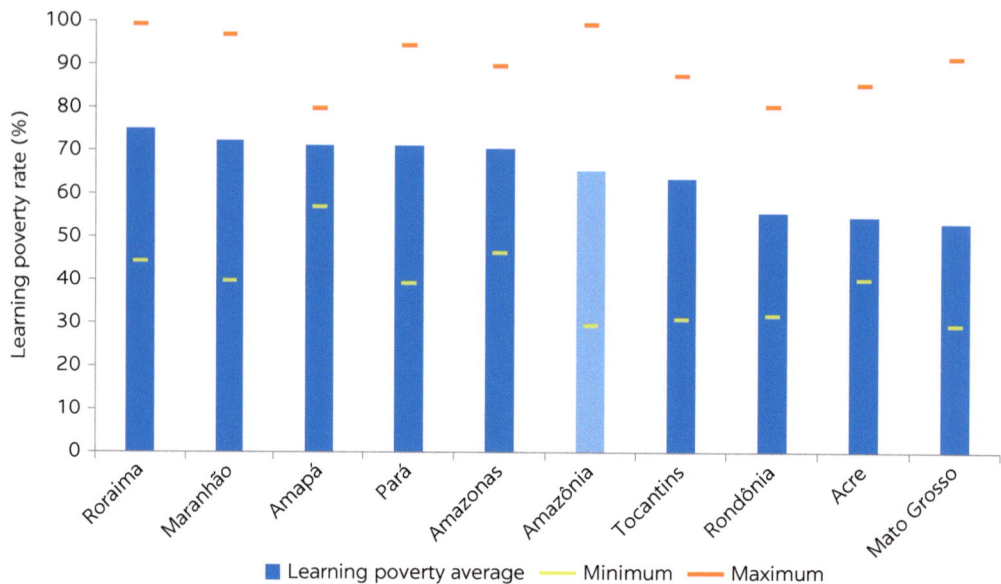

Source: World Bank, using data from the Brazilian Institute of Geography and Statistics (IBGE) Population Estimates 2019 data.
Note: Learning poverty is defined as the percentage of 10-year-old children who cannot read an age-appropriate paragraph. Amazônia comprises the nine states also shown, and its results are the average of the nine states. "Min" and "Max" refer to each state's municipalities with the lowest and highest learning poverty rates.

On average, 65 percent of children in Amazônia are in learning poverty, well above the Brazilian average of 48 percent. Differences within states are even larger than differences between states. Mato Grosso has the lowest learning poverty in Amazônia (29 percent), yet in one of its municipalities, 94 percent of 10-year-olds cannot read.

As with the health indicators, some education patterns are consistent with Amazônia's frontier status. States of the New Frontier—such as Mato Grosso, Rondônia, and Tocantins—have lower learning poverty rates than more remote states such as Roraima. Also like the health indicators, spatial density seems to matter for education outcomes, with more populous municipalities associated with better education outcomes (figure 2.12).

Improving the supply of human capital

Investing in teachers

High-quality teachers determine student achievement. So, policies that build the human capital of children today—to build the productivity of future workers—should focus on improving the quality of teaching. Teachers in Amazônia have several characteristics that reduce their effectiveness. And geographic isolation, small scale, and high transportation costs add to the difficulty of attracting more qualified teachers to municipalities and communities in Amazônia.

Amazonian municipalities have a lower share of teachers who have completed higher education than in the rest of Brazil, with larger gaps appearing at the lower-secondary level. In Amazônia, 86 percent of teachers have completed higher education, compared with 98 percent in other parts of the country.

FIGURE 2.12

In Amazônia, the worst performing schools are located in smaller municipalities

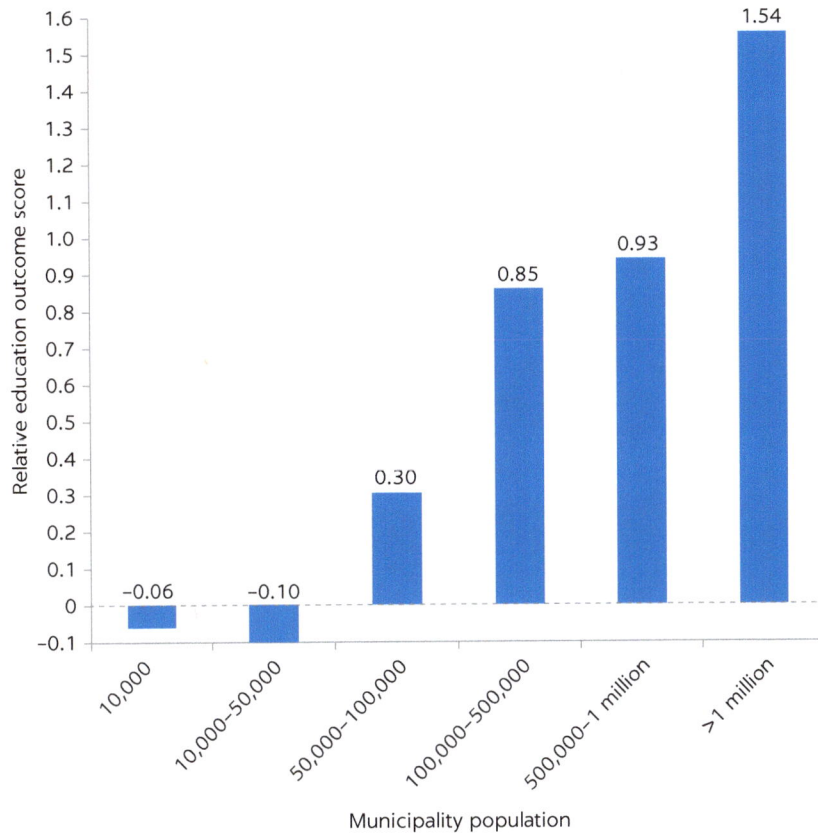

Sources: World Bank, using National Institute of Educational Studies Anísio Texeira (INEP) and Brazilian Institute of Geography and Statistics (IBGE) Population Estimates 2019 data.
Note: Education outcomes are normalized Basic Education Development Index (IDEB) scores (public network) within each state.

And the skills that teachers have acquired appear to be mismatched to their teaching: only 65 percent of primary education teachers and 42 percent of lower-secondary education teachers in Amazônia have a degree matched to the subject they are teaching. In the rest of Brazil, the respective shares are 76 percent and 70 percent (Lautharte, Mello, and Emmanuel 2022).

Amazônia has the highest percentage of teachers staying in their job for less than a year—and thus has more teachers with less experience. The typical teacher gets better at teaching in the first one to three years of teaching, after which the gains from experience tend to level out (Hanushek 2010; Staiger and Rockoff 2010). Thus the primary cost of teacher turnover is not the direct costs of hiring and firing but the loss in learning among students who are taught by a novice teacher rather than by a teacher with more experience (Staiger and Rockoff 2010). In Amazônia, about 14 percent of teachers have been in their job for less than a year, compared with 9 percent in the rest of Brazil (Lautharte, Mello, and Emmanuel 2022). While most teachers stay in the same school for two to four years—77 percent in Amazônia and 86 percent in the rest of Brazil—a non-negligible share of teachers in Amazônia did not work in their school long enough to acquire experience, to create bonds with the school and the students, or to learn from their experience in that specific environment. Thus, policies that increase teachers' tenure in the region might have a positive impact on student outcomes.

Poorer working conditions in Amazônia also affect teachers' ability to teach well. Schools in Amazônia have a shorter average school day than schools elsewhere in Brazil. Students in Amazônia receive 35–84 hours less instruction time per school year than students in the rest of Brazil. Gaps are largest at the lower-secondary education level. The average primary school class in Amazônia has 23.4 students, slightly fewer than in the rest of Brazil (24.1 students), while the average lower-secondary school has 27 students compared with 28.3 students in the rest of Brazil (Lautharte, Mello, and Emmanuel 2022). However, these average class sizes are larger than in countries with much higher student achievement. For example, the average class size in Organisation for Economic Co-operation and Development (OECD) countries is 21 students at the primary school level and 23 students at the lower-secondary level—3–5 fewer students than in Amazônia (OECD 2020).

And teachers may have low motivation to teach if they do not have the incentives. In Brazil, the average wage of a public basic education teacher is just 71 percent of the wage of a professional with a tertiary education. This gap is higher than in OECD countries, where teachers' wages at preprimary, primary, and general secondary levels of education are 80–94 percent of the earnings of an average tertiary-educated worker (OECD 2020). On an hourly basis, teachers with a tertiary degree earn more than other workers with a tertiary degree. But their total wages are lower because teachers are not commonly signed to full-time, 40-hour contracts; are not typically employed during school vacations; and are not properly paid for their work outside instruction time.

Higher average wages may encourage the most skilled individuals to become and remain a teacher. Policies that improve the attractiveness of teaching in public schools could increase teacher quality in Amazônia. Studies find that higher wages can induce individuals with higher academic skills to choose a teaching career (Chevalier, Dolton, and McIntosh 2007; Dolton 1990; Dolton and Makepeace 1993; Guarino et al. 2004; Han and Rossmiller 2004; Leigh 2012; Zibalza 1979). Higher wages are also associated with lower turnover and higher teacher retention in schools and in teaching (Boyd et al. 2008; Johnson, Berg, and Donaldson 2005).

But even if higher wages attract better-quality candidates to teaching, the evidence is inconclusive on whether higher wages by themselves improve student performance. There is no systematic relationship between teacher wage levels and measures of student proficiency or education outcomes (Podgursky 2011). One study in the state of São Paulo found that salary increases for incumbent teachers do not seem to affect their productivity and therefore do not affect student learning (Tavares and Ponczek 2018). However, and in line with the international literature, wage premiums of 24–36 percent for teachers in disadvantaged schools in the state of São Paulo significantly reduced teacher turnover (Camelo and Ponczek 2021). Although no direct effect was found on student test scores, lower teacher turnover improved the achievement of low-performing students (Camelo and Ponczek 2021).

These findings suggest that an increase in wages improves teaching quality only if accompanied by complementary interventions, such as autonomy for school managers to hire and dismiss teachers (Hanushek 2003;

Milanowski 2008). Overall, Amazônia should consider policies beyond higher wages that increase the attractiveness of teaching, such as better career progression plans, more time allocated to pedagogical planning, and support for struggling students.

Training and reskilling

Transitions of workers between sectors are very low in Amazônia—much lower than in the rest of Brazil—and education, training, and reskilling can enable greater worker adaptability. Mobility is especially low among agriculture workers in Amazônia (second only to public administration workers) as well as among informal sector workers, who are generally low skilled. Low mobility could imply that people cannot adapt to economic change and thus may end up unemployed, underemployed, or employed in the informal sector—which could impede the region's structural transformation. In addition, better education is associated with higher labor productivity, which in turn generates growth that draws demand across skill categories. Education must include basic education to lay the foundations but also needs to include higher levels of education and forms of lifelong learning to foster mobility.

Global trends—such as the rising role of technology, climate change, demographic shifts, urbanization, and the globalization of value chains—are transforming the nature of work and demand for skills in Brazil and across the world. To succeed in the twenty-first-century labor market, workers require a comprehensive skill set including cognitive, socioemotional, technical, digital, and green skills. The development of skills can contribute to structural transformation and economic growth by enhancing employability and labor productivity and helping Brazil become more competitive. The transformation of the labor market increases the urgency of ensuring that basic education systems and skill development systems are ready to meet the shifting demands of employers (Almeida and Packard 2018). Improving skill development services can enable the workforce to respond to the changing needs of increasingly dynamic labor markets, to transition to better jobs, and to become more productive as the economy evolves and grows.

Upskilling and reskilling workers, especially those most affected by structural change, requires lifelong learning strategies. As traditional approaches faltered during the COVID-19 pandemic and new skills were needed immediately, enterprises, workers, and governments took the initiative in upskilling and reskilling. Beyond technical and digital skills, workers need soft skills, such as socioemotional skills, time management, and occupational health and safety. The innovations adopted during the pandemic reveal several measures that can support workers in reskilling and upskilling across their career, such as investing in digital platforms, tools, and resources, including virtual reality and augmented reality; applying blended training methodologies; building the capacity of staff and teachers to design and deliver online training; and acquiring equipment and software for online training (ILO 2021).

Where supply and demand meet: Labor markets and jobs

The extent to which human capital is utilized and remunerated depends on both supply and demand factors. Chapter 3 focuses on demand-side factors—the drivers of economic performance that, in turn, requires labor. In the asset framework, these demand-side factors affect the utilization of labor through jobs and the returns to labor (earnings). Stronger growth would raise the demand for labor and boost returns, including for the poor (who currently have returns similar to those for poorer people in the rest of Brazil, as shown earlier in figure 2.2). Supply-side factors contribute to the formation of human capital, including health and education, which enhance labor productivity. There are also interactions between demand and supply factors: for example, human capital supports structural transformation, while the resulting higher level of development can encourage human capital formation (box 2.2).

BOX 2.2

Labor market developments and human capital formation

Labor market developments also affect education outcomes

There is ample evidence that parents' socioeconomic status predicts children's education performance (Black, Devereux, and Salvanes 2009; Lundborg and Majlesi 2018). Thus, as economies develop and economic opportunities for parents improve, that will also affect the learning outcomes of their children, in part mediated through expectations. If wages and opportunities are noticeably higher for workers with a better education, their children can also anticipate these higher returns from education and adapt their behavior accordingly by studying harder and staying in school. Conversely, weak labor markets can discourage student effort and lower their performance. Thus, although education policy—including investing in teachers, schools, and curriculum design—is critical for improving learning outcomes, there can also be a virtuous cycle between improving education and maturing economies, especially in the longer term.

Education effects observed during the construction of the Belo Monte Dam

The Belo Monte Dam in Pará received its construction license in June 2011, had its first turbine run in February 2016, and was completed in 2019. During construction, the region around the dam experienced substantial changes in population composition, its economy, and the provision of public services. Altamira, for example, absorbed more than 30,000 Belo Monte workers, many of them migrants who poured into the area between 2012 and 2015, swelling the population of Altamira from 77,439 in 2010 to 109,938 in 2016 (Lautharte, Mello, and Emmanuel 2022).

A study comparing exposed versus nonexposed municipalities found that the dam project was related to a drop in test scores for students in grade 5 of primary school and Portuguese scores in grade 9 of lower-secondary school in the municipalities directly affected by the dam construction (Lautharte, Mello, and Emmanuel 2022). Overall, the dam project was found to negatively affect student outcomes, being correlated with a 3–5 percentage point drop in standardized test scores in the exposed municipalities, using the National Learning Test (SAEB) scale, or around a 3–4 percent drop in baseline test scores. The dam project affected other education outcomes as well, with both repetition and dropout rates rising at all education levels.

Channels of adverse education outcomes from the Belo Monte Dam construction

For one, poorer people tend to be more liquidity-constrained, making them value current income opportunities (dam construction) over future income opportunities (associated with getting more education). In addition, the weak labor markets in Amazônia likely reduced the expected return from additional years of schooling compared with immediate income. And constraints further down the education value chain—notably bottlenecks in Brazil's university system—may make college wage premia appear unattainable, especially for low-income students.

All these factors are associated with families' socioeconomic circumstances. Thus, economic development, through its association with better job opportunities, will itself improve human capital through better education results. It also suggests that Amazônia's experience with boom-and-bust cycles can be a risk to human capital formation.

Labor force participation is low in Amazônia, especially among the poor and in rural areas. Unemployment is high, especially in urban areas. Labor markets offer fairly bleak prospects in Brazil and Amazônia, with relatively few or precarious employment options. Only just over half of the urban poor in Amazônia are employed or actively looking for work, lower than the country's average (table 2.5). Labor force participation among the poor is even lower in rural areas although in line with the rest of the country. As in much of Brazil, unemployment is high, especially in urban areas. In 2019, 29 percent of poor urban Amazonians were unemployed.

Unemployment is lower in rural areas, but many rural workers are engaged in precarious informal work. Self-employment is high among the poor in both urban and rural areas and is generally associated with informal activities. The number of formal workers subject to labor legislation (Consolidation of Labor Laws, or CLT) is low, especially among the poor. Public sector jobs are overrepresented in Amazônia, supporting salaries among the nonpoor. Agriculture and fishing tend to have the highest share of unskilled Amazonian workers (table 2.6).

The average job duration for wage workers in Amazônia (3.8 years) is shorter than in the rest of the country (4.8 years), and the average period of unemployment is slightly longer (1.2 years versus 1.1 years). These average duration rates, estimated from PNADC 2019 data, indicate higher labor turnover and less employment stability for workers in Amazônia and greater difficulty in finding a new job. Vulnerable workers suffer even more. For example, women with a secondary education have an average job duration of 3.2 years with an average unemployment spell of 1.6 years. During 2012–18, around 22 percent of wage workers spent less than a year in their current job, and 14 percent spent less than a quarter of a year.

Already weak, the labor market in Amazônia deteriorated after Brazil's deep recession in 2015/16. Since the beginning of the labor market crisis in 2015, labor force participation in rural areas of Amazônia has fallen by around 10 percentage points, from 65 percent to 55 percent, and unemployment has

TABLE 2.5 Labor market characteristics in Brazil and Amazônia, by location and poverty status, 2019

Percent

| | BRAZIL | | | | AMAZÔNIA | | | |
| | URBAN | | RURAL | | URBAN | | RURAL | |
LABOR FORCE CHARACTERISTIC	**POOR**	**NONPOOR**	**POOR**	**NONPOOR**	**POOR**	**NONPOOR**	**POOR**	**NONPOOR**
Labor force participation	54	66	46	55	51	65	46	54
Employer	0	5	0	3	1	4	0	3
Employee	39	64	35	49	39	61	26	44
Self-employed	22	21	34	35	29	25	44	40
Not salaried	2	1	14	8	3	1	22	10
Unemployed	37	9	17	5	29	9	9	4
Would like to work more	29	11	32	14	26	11	23	13
Public servant or military	1	9	1	5	1	12	1	6
Public sector (all)	2	13	3	9	3	18	3	12
CLT formal worker[a]	14	39	5	23	11	28	3	15

Source: World Bank, using Continuous National Household Sample Survey (PNADC) 2019 data.
Note: "Poor" is defined as those living at or below the poverty line of US$5.50 per person per day.
a. "CLT formal worker" refers to those subject to Brazil's labor legislation, Consolidation of Labor Laws (CLT).

risen (figure 2.13). From the first quarter of 2015 to the first quarter of 2017, the rural unemployment rate rose by about 5 percentage points and stabilized near the new level of 7 percent. Persistently high unemployment causes workers to become discouraged and to drop out of the labor force. Since the 2014 crisis, the discouragement rate in the rural areas of Amazônia soared by 8 percentage points, from 3 percent to 11 percent.

TABLE 2.6 Characteristics of workers in Amazônia, by sector, 2019

SECTOR	SHARE OF WORKERS (%)	MEDIAN AGE	EDUCATION LEVEL (%)	
			LESS THAN PRIMARY	COLLEGE OR MORE
Agriculture, hunting, and forestry	14.5	40	66	9
Fishing	2.2	38	80	5
Mining and quarrying	0.7	36	22	7
Manufacturing	7.3	37	37	8
Electricity, gas, and water supply	0.7	34	25	9
Construction	7.2	37	45	11
Wholesale and retail trade	21.0	34	23	10
Hotels and restaurants	5.7	37	33	11
Transport, storage, and communications	5.4	38	26	9
Financial intermediation	0.6	34	3	3
Real estate, renting, and business activities	5.4	36	14	7
Public administration and defense	6.6	41	10	4
Education	7.8	40	5	2
Health and social work	4.2	38	4	2
Other services[a]	4.6	34	19	11
Activities of private households	6.1	39	45	12

Source: World Bank, using Continuous National Household Sample Survey (PNADC) 2019 data.
a. "Other services" include community, social, and personal services.

FIGURE 2.13

Rural labor force participation has fallen in Amazônia and Brazil, 2012–20

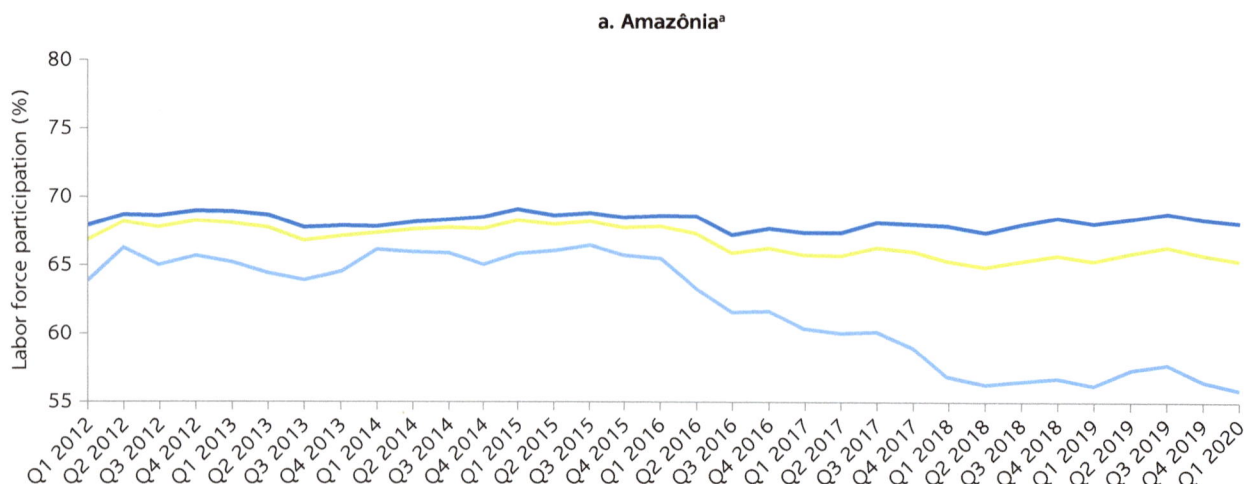

a. Amazônia[a]

continued

FIGURE 2.13, *continued*

b. Rest of Brazil

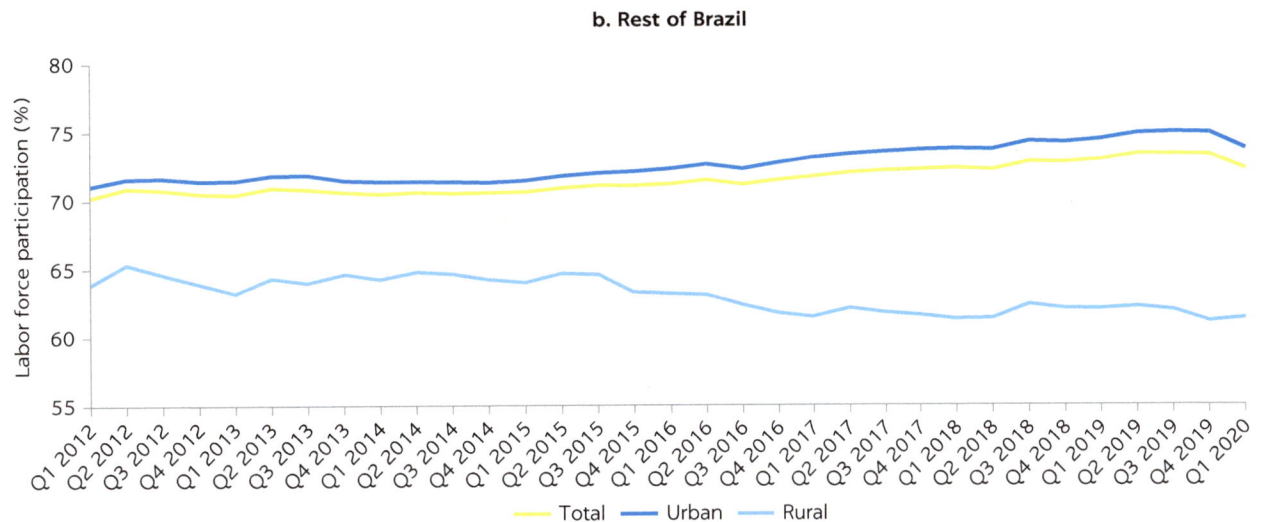

Source: World Bank, using Continuous National Household Sample Survey (PNADC) data.
Note: Rural labor force participation declined markedly during the 2015/16 recession and then stagnated.
a. Amazônia comprises nine Brazilian states: Acre, Amapá, Amazonas, Maranhão, Mato Grosso, Pará, Rondônia, Roraima, and Tocantins.

TABLE 2.7 **Returns to education in Brazil and Amazônia, 2019**

Dependent variable: Log (hourly wages)

VARIABLE	BRAZIL	AMAZÔNIA
Years of education	0.0666***	0.0679***
	(0.00137)	(0.00253)
Years of education * Urban	0.0219***	0.0104***
	(0.00141)	(0.00267)
Urban	−0.207***	−0.121***
	(0.0132)	(0.0260)
Male	0.186***	0.154***
	(0.00377)	(0.00937)
Afro-descendant	−0.115***	−0.101***
	(0.00357)	(0.00941)
Constant	0.261***	0.206***
	(0.0264)	(0.0446)
Number of observations	120,911	22,739
R-squared	0.436	0.437

Source: World Bank, using Continuous National Household Sample Survey (PNADC) 2019 data.
Note: Numbers in parentheses are standard errors. All regressions include state dummy variables, sector of employment dummy variables, and a quadratic of individual's age.
*** $p < 0.01$

Labor market returns to education are low, with higher skill premiums in urban areas. Overall, hourly wages increase at a similar rate for each additional year of education in rural Amazônia as in rural Brazil more broadly (table 2.7). Urban areas tend to be more skill intensive, and returns to education rise faster for each year of additional year of education. However, the effect is weaker for Amazônia than for Brazil overall. This reflects a relatively lower skills intensity of production in Amazônia than in Brazil and is consistent with labor markets in lagging regions, which tend to specialize in lower-skill economic activities.

Both improvements to human capital and a vibrant economy would improve labor income. Stronger growth in Amazônia would generate more demand for labor and improve labor market outcomes through higher employment and higher wages—especially if the right skills are in place, justifying higher wages and guarding against substitution of labor for capital.

LAND

Land in Amazônia is important as a productive asset, as a source of livelihoods, and as a natural resource providing ecological services. Especially for Indigenous people and other traditional communities, land has vital historical, cultural, and social value as well as economic value. While acknowledging these noneconomic dimensions of land, this memorandum focuses on the economic role of land, anchored in the asset-based framework.

Private land ownership in Amazônia is highly unequal (Claudino et al. 2014; Freitas and Giatti 2009; Lira, da Silva, and Pinto 2009; Oliveira 2008). For many decades, government efforts to increase access to land and economic opportunities outside major southern-central regions attracted large economic interests seeking to appropriate new forest and agricultural lands. As a result, most large-scale interventions ended up concentrating large estates (latifúndios) and resources (Hall 1987). Vulnerable residents, including Indigenous people, migrants, and peasants, countered with demands for agrarian reform, but it was never fully embraced by the Brazilian government and was implemented in a very controlled and selective manner. The formation of latifúndios reproduced on an expanded scale the historical patterns of agricultural occupation (Schmink and Wood 1992). In the asset-based framework, the highly unequal distribution of land helps explain poverty among small rural producers in Amazônia who had insecure access to land.

Disputes over land tenure and occupation continue, especially in rural areas. While most residents in Amazônia own a home, a lower share claim to own their land—and an even smaller share of people have a title formalizing land ownership (table 2.8). Although insecure tenure is also a problem in urban areas, it is particularly pronounced for the rural poor. Only 34 percent of the rural poor hold title to their land—much lower than for other groups in Amazônia and very low by Brazilian standards. It reflects the limited progress in land regularization in Amazônia (chapter 4). Competition over land also generates conflict, sometimes violent, including toward Indigenous and traditional people (chapters 1 and 4).

Land tenure insecurity affects farmers of all sizes in Amazônia, largely because of uncertainties about the reliability of land registries. Approximately 21 percent of Amazônia is recorded as privately owned or "appropriated" in the National Property Certification System (SNCI) and Land Management System (SiGeF) of the National Institute for Colonization and Agrarian Reform (INCRA). An unknown portion of the rights recorded in the land registries originated in errors or fraudulent entries. This occurred because large tracts of federal and state land are not registered and because many private land rights were registered at a time when parcels were not accurately surveyed, and land cadastres and registries were more loosely kept than today. Inaccuracies and fraud are typically uncovered when conflicts occur or when federal or state governments attempt to demarcate their land.

TABLE 2.8 **Characteristics of dwellings in Brazil and Amazônia, by location and poverty status**

percent

| | BRAZIL | | | | AMAZÔNIA | | | |
| | URBAN | | RURAL | | URBAN | | RURAL | |
DWELLING STATUS	POOR	NONPOOR	POOR	NONPOOR	POOR	NONPOOR	POOR	NONPOOR
Own dwelling	62	74	82	80	74	79	88	81
Own land	57	69	72	75	69	75	75	75
Have ownership title	46	67	44	60	52	66	34	49

Source: World Bank, using Continuous National Household Sample Survey (PNADC) 2019 data.
Note: "Poor" is defined as those living at or below the poverty line of US$5.50 per person per day.

Most of INCRA's 2,700 agrarian reform settlements in Amazônia, or *assentamentos*, were established since the 1970s as part of the government's development strategy for the Amazon and its broader land reform. The 41.8 million hectares in these settlements represent about 7.3 percent of Amazônia's territory[11] and are inhabited by 580,460 poor families, or about 2 percent of Amazônia's population (May et al. 2016). To qualify for land, the household must be "low income"—defined as not owning rural land, not being a shareholder of an agricultural enterprise, and not receiving income from nonagricultural activities of more than three times the minimum monthly wage or one minimum salary per capita when household income is considered.[12] In addition to being poor, an INCRA settlement beneficiary must meet multiple criteria such as being at least 18 years of age, being a Brazilian national, and not being a civil servant.

INCRA beneficiaries face various development challenges. The federal government has generally retained formal land ownership. A share of INCRA settlers received land use rights, but these were often temporary and have lapsed in most cases. This complicates the ability of low-income small farmers in agrarian reform settlements to obtain financing to improve their productivity and the ability of the local government to enforce environmental protection regulations and sustainable agriculture practices.[13] INCRA beneficiaries are also eligible for a federal loan program—the National Program to Strengthen Family Farming (PRONAF "A")—which provides small loans of up to R$25,000 at concessional interest rates of 0.5 percent with a 10-year repayment period (and a grace period of up to 3 years).[14] However, most poor, small farmers in Amazônia struggle to make a living, because their productivity is low, their market access is weak, and they are under increasing competitive pressures from more productive commercial farmers.

Indigenous people and other traditional communities also face tenure insecurity. Brazil has designated vast territories as Indigenous territories. The federal Northwest Region Integrated Development Program (Polonoroeste) of the 1980s—which aimed to open up Amazônia to settlement by paving an existing 1,500 kilometer dirt road from the densely populated south-central region into the Amazon and connecting a network of feeder and access roads cutting into the rainforest on both sides of the highway—provoked an international outcry for its adverse impacts on the environment and Indigenous people who lived there. Since then, the government has made large investments to support regularization of land tenure for Indigenous people and to establish conservation units. Between 1995 and 2004, the federal government set aside 38 million hectares of Indigenous land, or about a third of the Indigenous territories in the Amazon region, within the framework of the Indigenous Lands Project (World Bank 2007). Despite these achievements, numerous Indigenous people and other traditional communities still lack formal recognition of their land rights.[15]

Enforcing *quilombolas'* land rights remains a huge challenge. Under article 68 of the Transitional Constitutional Provisions Act of the Federal Constitution, *quilombola* settlements are recognized as property and the state must issue titles to the land. *Quilombola* territories are defined as "the lands occupied by remnants of quilomba communities and used to guarantee their physical, social, economic, and cultural reproduction." The common use of land by communities is another striking feature of these territories. The first land title award was not granted until November 1995, and since then only 186 *quilombola* territories have been titled, 52 of them only partially. Another 1,719 land-titling processes are pending; 44 percent of them have been open for more than 10 years.[16]

Strengthening land property rights, especially for the poor, requires systematic land regularization. This involves completing the identification and registration of federal and state land, reviewing and rectifying or canceling improperly registered land rights, and supporting land tenure regularization. In 2019, Pará Federal University, the Public Prosecutor's Office, and the State Court of Justice of Pará reviewed land registries in 10 municipalities in the state. Among other irregularities, they identified plots with up to 10 overlapping records and cases in which the registered areas were 10 times the size of the municipality (Chiavari, Lopes, and de Araujo 2020). An analysis of land records for Brazil found that overlapping land tenure records cover half the registered territory of Brazil and that one-sixth (16.5 percent) of land in the country has no official land tenure registration (Sparovek et al. 2019). The tenure uncertainty affects farmers' ability to improve production (through access to credit, for example) and creates ambiguity for the application of land use laws that could encourage *grilagem* (land grabbing).

The government needs to systematize its multiple land cadastres, registries, and other land information systems. The United Nations Global Geospatial Information Management (UN-GGIM) system offers detailed guidance to countries on adopting an Integrated Geospatial Information Framework. This could reduce fraud and disputes during the land regularization process. Brazil has the technical capacity to do this, but implementation requires sustained political will and institutional coordination across government levels. Land databases are not organized or coordinated, and the use of new technologies is still limited.

Some 22 agencies are involved in aspects of land tenure regularization, making it difficult to establish a single, shared source of information on land tenure. Increased coordination is required across agencies, including strong partnerships between the executive and judicial branches. There are encouraging experiences in this regard in Piauí and the other states of the MaToPiBa region (comprising Maranhão, Tocantins, Piauí, and Bahia).

There are land tenure regularization process in place. However, in recent years, there has been limited progress with formalization of the land tenure of small-scale farmers and traditional communities. Building on the positive experiences of large land tenure regularization programs in some states (such as Piauí and Pará), the federal government and state land agencies could simplify procedures, automate processes, decentralize implementation, and invest in systematic land tenure procedures, particularly in INCRA and in state agrarian reform settlements and traditional communities. Other important steps include investing in increasing productivity, access to market, stricter enforcement of land tenure and use regulations, and simpler, more accessible land dispute resolution mechanisms, such as arbitration, mediation, and other administrative procedures that keep disputes out of the slow, expensive, and often inaccessible court system.

Although systematic land regularization is critical to support rural incomes, additional measures are needed. Raising the competitiveness of small farmers requires complementary support for building their human capital and professional skills and for adopting sustainable farming methods. People in traditional groups and other poorer groups still use traditional extractivist production methods. Farmers pursuing these methods are at risk of being crowded out by economic competition, unless they can find niche markets that command a price premium for sustainable production (chapter 5). Also important for protecting rural livelihoods are social protection interventions and reskilling opportunities (chapter 5). And important issues are related to urban land (chapter 6).

Income from land partly depends on the growth model. The skewed distribution of land—and the gaps related to regularization that especially affect poor people—suggests that larger (or richer) landowners tend to gain more from land-based growth models in absolute terms (see later discussion).

FINANCIAL CAPITAL

Capital is highly concentrated in Brazil. In the past, wealth accumulation was related to land and real estate, owing partly to the country's agricultural growth model and partly to its use as a hedge against high inflation (Fandiño, Arretche, and Hanusch 2022). In more recent decades, however, Brazilian households have accumulated significant financial wealth as Brazil managed to tame inflation and develop its financial sector. Yet wealth is highly concentrated. The richest 1 percent of Brazilians are estimated to own almost half the country's household wealth, while about 70 percent of households have wealth of less than US$10,000 (CSRI 2019). Thus the Gini coefficient of wealth, at 0.85, is much higher than the income Gini shown in figure 2.3. Holders of financial assets, such as some kinds of corporate equity, benefit from artificially high returns because of protection policies that benefit specific companies, allowing them to charge monopoly rents (Dutz 2018).

There is suggestive evidence, based on limited data, that wealth inequality (and inequality in capital income) is also high in Amazônia—although it may be lower than in the rest of Brazil. In 2019, fewer than 4 percent of Amazonian households reported income from "rent and lease," and 1 percent reported income from "other sources"—including financial investments and savings accounts, according to PNADC 2019 data. Among poor Amazonian households, rent and lease accounts for less than 0.5 percent of income; for urban, nonpoor households, capital or rent income represents about 2 percent of income. Capital income is lower in Amazônia than elsewhere in Brazil, likely driven more by lower levels of assets than by lower returns. (Financial assets, at least, tend not to be geographically bound, providing room to equalize returns across regions.) The difference in income between richer and poorer households is lower in Amazônia than in the rest of the country, suggesting that wealth inequality may be high but lower than in the rest of Brazil.

Improving financial services in Amazônia may support capital and wealth generation and accumulation. The strengthening of Brazil's financial markets is reflected in the most recent Global Findex report showing financial account ownership jumping from 55 percent in 2011 to 70 percent in 2017 (Demirgüç-Kunt et al. 2018). Account ownership still lags among households in the bottom 40 percent, though the gap with the top 60 percent has narrowed. In 2017, 56 percent of the bottom 40 percent of households had a financial account compared with 79 percent of those in the top 60 percent. Better banking access has been accompanied by better access to credit, although access to credit is still unusual in lagging regions and among poorer households, with many entrepreneurs struggling to access finance. Innovations in financial services hold broad potential to advance financial inclusion in Amazônia, including in the more remote areas where banking costs are particularly high. Improving access to finance can also promote structural transformation (chapter 3).

Access to credit does not always build capital; it also stimulates consumption and may reduce savings and wealth formation. Credit, including credit cards, can help smooth consumption shocks. Credit card ownership is relatively high in Brazil: 27 percent of the population ages 15 and older—and 15 percent among people in the bottom 40 percent—owned a credit card in 2017, compared with 19 percent in upper-middle-income economies (Demirgüç-Kunt et al. 2018). Debit card ownership in Brazil, at 59 percent, is comparable to that in upper-middle-income economies, but it is much lower in Amazônia, at 42 percent, and among individuals in the bottom 40 percent in Brazil, at 43 percent. Data from other specialized surveys confirm that just under a quarter of households in Brazil use a credit card, but this is a less common instrument in Amazônia, especially among poorer households, where only 7 percent report using a credit card.

SHOCKS, PRICES, AND TRANSFERS

Households experience various shocks that affect income and welfare. Climate change is a potential source of macro shocks, as droughts, floods, extreme heat, and other natural disasters become more common. Such natural disasters reduce farmers' yields and can cause severe damage to housing and infrastructure in both rural and urban areas. Natural disasters can also result in deaths. Macro health risks include contagious diseases, and pandemics such as COVID-19. Among major economic risks are unemployment and individual terms-of-trade shocks, which can occur when structural transformation affects relative prices in ways that reduce the purchasing power of some households while raising it for others. Consider gains in agricultural productivity, which tend to result in lower food prices. Although lower prices benefit food consumers, they can harm producers who do not achieve productivity gains. Similarly, an inflow of unskilled rural migrants into urban areas can lower wages for unskilled workers if productivity does not rise and labor markets are weak, hurting unskilled workers while benefiting those who hire unskilled services (who tend to be more affluent).

Climate change threatens core sectors of the Amazonian economy, exacerbating variability in prices. Droughts, for instance, adversely affect two important sectors: (a) hydroelectric power, which generates nearly two-thirds of Brazil's electricity; and (b) agriculture, which has led the recovery from the economic contraction from the COVID-19 pandemic. Such goods can undermine the purchasing power of consumers through higher prices.

Nonmarket income is important for households as an income buffer against risks to market income. Private transfers are an important source of nonmarket household income (see table 2.1). Transfers from family or friends, such as remittances, are an important source of income for some households, allowing them to benefit from the market income earned by a household member in a more remote but more dynamic labor market. Although private transfers may be important for some households, they play a relatively minor role in the aggregate in Amazônia, especially among poorer households.

Brazil's public social assistance programs play a critical role in shock absorption. Unlike private transfers, public transfers are independent of the economic business cycle and thus are an important means of shock absorption. Importantly, public transfers can be countercyclical. During the COVID-19 pandemic, Brazil expanded its Bolsa Família cash transfer program and introduced a new temporary program to provide relief to households, the Auxílio Emergencial. In line with the higher level of poverty in Amazônia, public transfers are the most important source of nonmarket income for poor households in the region, even more than in the rest of Brazil (see table 2.1). In addition to cash transfers, pensions are particularly important in rural areas, reflecting both slightly higher pension payments under Brazil's rural pension system and an older population in rural areas. Among permanent social protection programs, Auxílio Brasil, previously known as Bolsa Família, is by far the most important program for Amazônia's poor.

Bolsa Família targeted low-income families, especially those with children under age 18.[17] The program provides a basic cash benefit to households that meet the maximum income eligibility criterion, with additional variable payments for families with children or nursing mothers. For almost 90 percent of beneficiary households, women are the direct recipients. The program also serves as a minimum income guarantee program for adults without children, including the self-employed who are ineligible for unemployment insurance.

Bolsa Família included a large share of the Indigenous population, although it could not mitigate all shocks Indigenous people face (box 2.3). As of April 2021, 75,178 Indigenous families in Amazônia received Bolsa Família transfers (representing 81 percent of the Indigenous families enrolled in Cadastro Único, the Unified Registry for social programs of the Brazilian government [see annex 2A, table 2A.1]). Delivery mechanisms were improved to make it easier to include Indigenous populations and members of other minority groups by adapting conditions of health and education to the cultural context of these groups.

Bolsa Família had positive medium-term impacts on human capital. It improved education outcomes, children's growth, food consumption, and diets, giving children in beneficiary families significantly higher chances of a life out of poverty (table 2.9). During 2016–18, more than 1 million families graduated out of Bolsa Família by moving above its income eligibility threshold (mainly by gaining labor market income). Most graduations happened because

BOX 2.3

Disruption to Indigenous people from the mining sector

In Brazil, there are no legal mining activities on Indigenous lands. Mining enterprises located within a 10-kilometer buffer zone of Indigenous lands have to follow an environmental licensing process that requires the participation of the National Indian Foundation (FUNAI), a study of the impact on Indigenous communities, and mitigation and compensation measures for any identified impacts. Nevertheless, mining activities, legal or illegal, can have negative spillovers into Indigenous territories, including pollution and deforestation.

Conflict can emerge with illegal miners in Indigenous lands or between Indigenous people and legal mining companies outside of Indigenous territories. Illegal mining in and around Indigenous lands often relies on some participation by Indigenous populations, and conflict is frequent. Conflict with legal mining companies was more common in the past, but problems remain even with current licensing requirements. For example, the first compensation agreements—developed in the 1980s, intermediated

by FUNAI, and involving about 90 villages and 12,500 Indigenous people—included both investments in infrastructure in health, education, transport, and other areas and cash transfers (Fernandes, Alamino, and Araujo 2014). To this day, there are still disagreements and conflicts between Indigenous people and mining companies related to the amounts transferred to the communities. Conflicts also occur because the compensation agreements can interfere, to some extent, with the functioning of their traditional systems.

Improvements are required to ensure that agreements respect traditional ways of life and reduce conflict. These should include measures to minimize adverse environmental and social impacts on natural habitats and traditional and vulnerable social groups, particularly Indigenous people living in voluntary isolation; meaningful consultation; free, prior, informed consent; culturally appropriate and accessible grievance redressing mechanisms; and fair systems for revenues and benefit sharing.

Source: Sanchez Martinez et al. 2022.

TABLE 2.9 **Impacts of Bolsa Família on education, employment, and health**

AREA	IMPACT
Education and labor market	• Reduction in school repetition rates • Improvements in progression rates • Increase in secondary school completion rates • Reduced time on domestic work for girls • Mixed outcomes, always small, in labor force participation and formal and informal work hours; stronger elasticity for women with children • Positive long-term effect on schooling and on formal labor market participation
Health and nutrition	• Positive effects on use of health services, particularly for prenatal care • Increased food consumption, improved children's anthropometric measures, and decreased anemia • Lower rates of under-5 mortality (reduction of 58 percent in mortality rates from malnutrition and 46 percent from diarrheal diseases) • Lower incidence of suicides and homicides and significant reductions in new cases of tuberculosis and leprosy • Significant enhancement in health outcomes among the poor in Brazil

Sources: Amaral and Monteiro 2013; Bastagli et al. 2019; Monteiro et al. 2014; Oliveira and Chagas 2020; Silva 2018; Simões and Soares 2012.

a family member found a formal job or children reached adult age, changing eligibility thresholds (Silva, Almeida, and Strokova 2015). Studies of the long-term effects of conditional cash transfers in Mexico (which has the world's oldest program) and in Brazil suggest that the impacts are lasting, especially in labor market outcomes, largely through increased chances of graduating from secondary education.

There are also complementary social protection programs in Amazônia that focus on fostering sustainable livelihoods and protecting traditional communities. The cash transfer program Bolsa Verde operated from 2011 to 2018 and covered all of Brazil. Reaching almost 50,000 beneficiaries in 2017, it covered federal conservation units, federal resettlement projects, and territories occupied by traditional populations. Beneficiaries had to be registered in Brazil's Cadastro Único, with income below the extreme poverty threshold of Bolsa Família (meaning that some beneficiaries could receive assistance from both programs). Payments amounted to R$300 quarterly—totaling R$1,200 per family per year for up to two years, which could be extended by another two years (Viana 2011). The transfers were conditional on participants' poverty status and their commitment to preserving ecosystems. The program focused on fostering sustainable livelihoods, including family farming, animal husbandry, extractivist activities, and agroforestry. The transfers helped reduce poverty and preserve traditional livelihoods and Amazônia's cultural richness.

Social programs, including conditional cash transfer programs, take on a particularly important role to maintain standards of living in traditional communities as Amazônia undergoes structural change, which will adversely affect the terms of trade of traditional producers as they are outcompeted by more productive producers (chapter 5) and as costs of services rise with economic development (chapter 3).

However, social protection programs may not be the most effective or appropriate tool to reduce deforestation. Although managing ecosystem services was a focus of Bolsa Verde, stemming deforestation specifically was not the primary objective. The program generally operated in areas with lower risk of deforestation, and reductions in deforestation due to the program were estimated to be small, at 3–5 percent (Wong et al. 2018). Amazonas introduced a similar program, Bolsa Floresta (with even smaller impacts on reducing deforestation, if any).

Targeting social programs to areas that are deforestation hot spots may help reduce illegal deforestation by limiting destitution that could fuel illegal behavior. Yet conditioning transfers on deforestation reduction would put beneficiaries, who tend to be among the most vulnerable communities, in direct conflict with illegal loggers, especially in a region where law enforcement is weak. To reduce deforestation, complementary activities are needed (chapter 7).

RETURNS TO HOUSEHOLD ASSETS

Amazônia's growth model (see chapters 1 and 3) affects the demand for household assets and therefore the returns to them. The growth model thus matters for household incomes and equity across households.

Agriculture is attractive because it has high job multipliers (figure 2.14) and generates many opportunities for Amazônia's unskilled workers. Catering to rising global agricultural demand improves household welfare across the country and income groups: simulations in table 2.10 suggest that rising global demand for agricultural goods raises real wages in a fairly inclusive way, especially given the still-high number of unskilled workers in the agriculture sector in Amazônia. At the same time, however, this model has been associated with the destruction of the forests of Amazônia. Yet, imposing stricter forest protection measures alone would result in relative welfare losses for wage earners and gains for landowners

FIGURE 2.14

Agriculture has high job multipliers

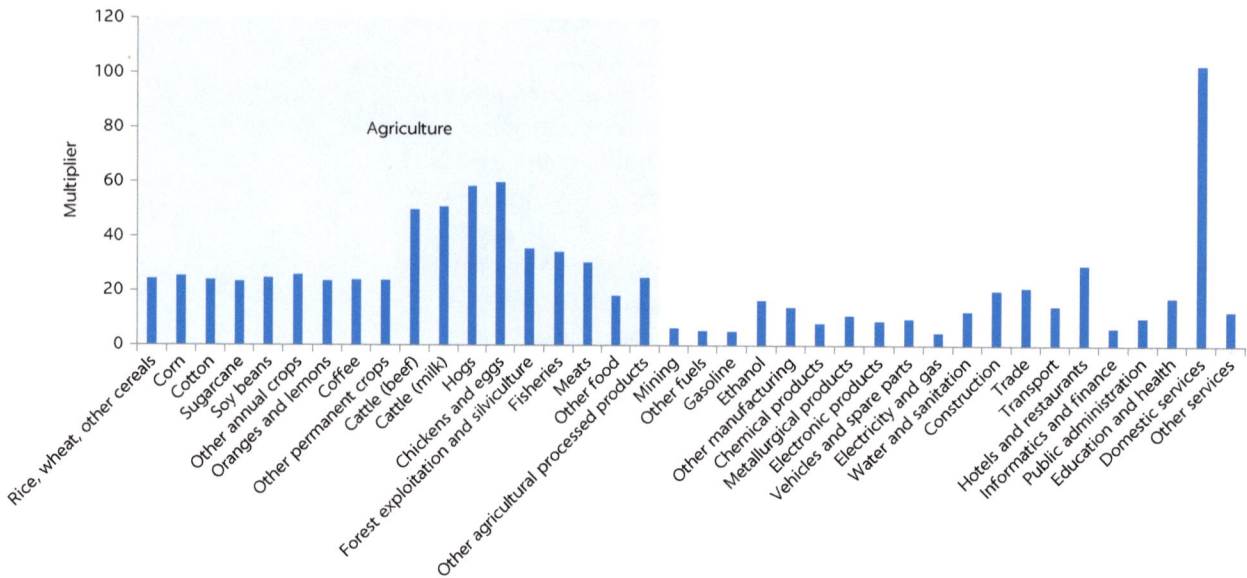

Source: World Bank, using an input-output model, with the same data used in Ferreira Filho and Hanusch 2022.
Note: The figure shows labor multipliers that represent the number of workers (labor creation) required for each R$1 million (2015 values) of final demand increase in each sector. The higher the multiplier, the bigger the effect on employment of an increase in the final demand of the sector. The blue box highlights agriculture sectors.

(at least without taking into account negative environmental impacts from forest loss on the poor). Policy actions that restrict the supply of land—by limiting the potential of converting natural forests to productive land—make agriculture more intensive, but they also raise production costs for farmers, reduce production and employment, and raise food prices, resulting in welfare losses for all workers (table 2.10). Simulations suggest that poor urban workers in other parts of Brazil (such as favela residents) suffer the largest welfare losses, mainly because of higher food prices, along with rural residents without access to land. In Amazônia, wages decline somewhat more in rural areas than in urban areas, reflecting the relative drop in agricultural employment as well as higher food prices.

Landowners in rural areas gain from these policies because restricting the supply of land raises land rents. Although this impact on land rents will offset some of the overall welfare losses of rural populations, who tend to have at least limited access to farmland, it will likely worsen inequality because land ownership is concentrated among a few more-affluent individuals.

Raising productivity within agriculture would enhance welfare but could also pose risks to forests, while changing the nature of rural livelihoods, as further discussed in chapters 3 and 5. Complementary policy interventions simultaneously fostering agricultural productivity, sustainable rural livelihoods, and forest protection would be mutually supportive, raising welfare while protecting forests (chapter 7).

Another complementary policy area that does not pose major risks to forests, while generating income opportunities where most Amazonians live, is urban productivity. Simulations suggest that productivity gains in urban sectors, proxied by manufacturing, raise income for both poor and nonpoor households in Amazônia, with positive welfare spillovers also for residents in other parts of

TABLE 2.10 Growth models, forest protection, and their distributional implications: Simulated cumulative impacts over 12 years

Percentages

LOCATION AND POVERTY STATUS	EXTERNAL AGRICULTURAL DEMAND (+0.5pp)	ENFORCING LOWER AMAZONIAN DEFORESTATION BY 1 Mha (CUMULATIVE)	TFP GROWTH IN AMAZONIAN MANUFACTURING (+0.5pp)	TFP GROWTH IN SOUTH AND SOUTHEAST OF BRAZIL (+0.5pp)
a. Return to labor (real wages)				
Rest of Brazil				
Rural nonpoor	2.2	−1.7	0.2	14.6
Rural poor	2.5	−1.9	0.5	7.0
Urban nonpoor	1.9	−1.4	0.1	19.6
Urban poor	2.2	−3.2	0.2	11.3
Amazônia				
Rural nonpoor	3.0	−2.8	5.2	3.7
Rural poor	2.8	−2.7	5.7	4.4
Urban nonpoor	3.0	−2.3	6.1	4.2
Urban poor	2.7	−2.3	6.0	4.5
b. Return to land (real land rents)				
Rest of Brazil	4.1	12.6	−0.1	−32.5
Amazônia	3.3	17.1	−8.4	−40.2

Sources: World Bank, using the computable general equilibrium (CGE) model of Ferreira Filho and Hanusch 2022, translated through microsimulations using National Household Sample Survey (PNAD) 2019 data.
Note: Assumes permanent percentage increases for external agricultural demand and in total factor productivity (TFP) scenarios and cumulative reduction in deforestation in the forest protection scenario. All values are relative to baseline. "Poor" is defined those living at or below the poverty line of US$5.50 per person per day. mha = million hectares; pp = percentage points.

Brazil (see table 2.10). Wages rise faster for poor workers than for nonpoor workers across the country (except for urban workers in Amazônia, where wage gains are similar across income groups). Complementary human capital investments would further help make growth inclusive.

Landowners experience losses under a more urban productivity-led growth model because land rents fall when urban productivity rises. Since land tends to be concentrated among the rich, this impact can help reduce inequality. Lower land rents also reflect lower competition for land, which may reduce pressure on Indigenous and traditional communities (box 2.4).

Finally, it is important to bear in mind that Amazônia is part of a broader Brazilian development story. Productivity gains in the rest of Brazil can enhance welfare in Amazônia, indicating that the productivity agenda is beneficial at both national and state levels. Productivity gains in other parts of Brazil (here, in table 2.10, focusing on the country's more dynamic states in the south and southeast) have large positive spillover effects for Amazônia—partly because of the small size of the Amazonian economy relative to the rest of Brazil. Wages rise through three channels as the productivity gains in the rest of the Brazil:

- *Stimulate demand for products* from all regions of the country, including Amazônia;
- *Reduce prices*, thus enhancing the purchasing power of consumers across the country; and
- *Boost labor demand* in other parts of Brazil, attracting workers away from the Amazonian states, thus reducing the labor supply there and raising wages across the country and income groups.

BOX 2.4

Growth models, land competition, conflict, and crime

Violent conflict in Amazônia—often related to land tenure and access to resources in rural and forested areas—frequently involves Indigenous groups and other traditional populations as well as, sometimes, landless peasants and environmental activists. In some regions of Amazônia, agroindustrial interests are behind the violence against these groups, many of whom are more directly dependent on preserved natural forests. Organized criminal networks connected to illegal wood extraction and its productive chains are often perpetrators of violence related to conflicts over land, deforestation, and natural resources in general.

A productivity-led growth model with an adequate urban focus could attenuate a source of crime and conflict by easing competition for land. When land rents are high, reflecting high demand for limited land, and especially when ownership is uncertain, violent conflict can erupt to eliminate competing claims. Higher land values can attract crime, especially in an environment with weak land administration (whereby criminals can essentially "steal" public land and sell it as private) and weak law enforcement. Illegal deforestation is also linked to money laundering (Fearnside 2017).

Reducing the real value of land can moderate the sources of conflict and crime by limiting competition over land. Groups most exposed to these types of conflict, especially Indigenous and traditional people, would thus gain from a more urban productivity-led growth model.

Source: Sanchez Martinez et al. 2022.

At the same time, land rents would fall across the country, attenuating one source of inequality in Amazônia and Brazil.

Productivity growth and structural transformation, across Brazil and in Amazônia specifically, can play a powerful role in strengthening sustainable and inclusive development in Amazônia. It can benefit people in rural and urban areas and, if well balanced, it can be consistent with protecting forests. Although this implies that the economic focus will increasingly shift to urban areas, policy will need to remain mindful that poverty rates in rural areas are very high. Chapter 5 will look more closely at how to promote sustainable livelihoods in rural areas.

CONCLUSIONS AND POLICY IMPLICATIONS

Human capital. Human capital is critical to facilitate structural transformation and ensure that it is inclusive. This chapter has shown that human capital is the most important asset of Amazonian households, especially poor households. The prospect of higher incomes may incentivize households to invest more in their human capital, further strengthening the virtuous cycle between human capital and structural transformation. Policy should focus both on the demand side (structural transformation, including strengthening urban productivity) and on the supply side (human capital).

Investing in teachers can have significant positive impacts on learning. Beyond basic education, policy should focus on continuous learning to prepare the labor force for the changing nature of work. Reskilling and technical assistance, especially for farming, will ensure that structural change brings more opportunities than disruption (chapter 5).

Services infrastructure. There is still a large unfinished agenda in meeting basic infrastructure service needs. Investments in the infrastructure and institutions for water and sanitation in rural and urban areas will be especially critical to raise living standards but also to help raise human capital by improving health outcomes.

Land regularization. Land is an important asset, especially in rural areas, and land regularization is a critical area for policy. Land security is low in Amazônia. Amazônia's rural poor are among the least tenure secure in Brazil, which disadvantages them economically and can lead to conflict. In rural areas, policy should focus on land regularization, strengthening land registries, arbitrating competing claims on land, and strengthening tenure rights—especially for rural settlers in *assentamentos* and Indigenous, *quilombola*, and other traditional rural communities.

Financial inclusion. Capital plays a limited role in household income, especially among the poor, and improving access to finance could help households make productive investments and smooth consumption. Limited access to finance is not unusual for lagging regions and poorer individuals. Although Brazil has made considerable progress in making financial services accessible, there is room for improvement. For farmers, clarity of tenure is critical to access credit. Improving access to consumer credit, including through credit cards and financial technology solutions, can increase financial inclusion and provide consumption smoothing opportunities—but such solutions can also reduce savings and thus the longer-term generation of wealth and financial buffers for families.

Social protection. Brazil's strong social protection system is critical for mitigating the disruptions associated with structural transformation. Amazônia has further scope for complementary systems that foster sustainable livelihoods and preserve the region's cultural wealth. Auxílio Brasil and the pension system are especially important for poorer households and can mitigate most economic shocks, including those emerging from the structural transformation process itself.

Complementary social protection systems can help preserve traditional livelihoods in rural areas, with a particular focus on maintaining Amazônia's cultural richness. To manage disruption for Indigenous and traditional people in Amazônia, it is important to recognize and strengthen their rights, include them in consultations on projects that affect them, and devise appropriate compensation mechanisms where needed.

Sustainable rural livelihoods. Given the high rates of rural poverty and the long time it takes for structural transformation to yield results, it will be critical for policy to support sustainable rural incomes (chapter 5).

Productivity beyond agriculture. A productivity-led growth model with a strong urban leg can be reconciled with inclusiveness and sustainability. The current extractive model benefits many poor households, but to reach higher levels of development, Brazil must focus more on productivity—and in sectors beyond agriculture. Increasing productivity in more-urban sectors, across Brazil and in Amazônia in particular, can improve livelihoods and foster inclusion, especially when coupled with human capital investments. The following chapters show that this model can also be reconciled with preserving natural lands in Amazônia in the longer term. Urban productivity thus forms part of an inclusive and a sustainable growth model (see chapter 6 and the companion report on urban competitiveness in the state of Amazonas, World Bank 2023).

ANNEX 2A: SUPPLEMENTARY INFORMATION ON INDIGENOUS PEOPLE IN BRAZIL'S SOCIAL PROTECTION SYSTEM

TABLE 2A.1 **Indigenous families in the Cadastro Único and share of Bolsa Família families, 2021**

AMAZONIAN STATES	NUMBER OF INDIGENOUS FAMILIES (CADASTRO UNICO)	NUMBER OF BF INDIGENOUS FAMILIES	SHARE OF FAMILIES RECEIVING BF (%)
Acre	4,826	4,238	88
Amapá	1,340	872	65
Amazonas	44,538	36,403	82
Maranhão	7,008	6,291	90
Mato Grosso	8,565	7,058	82
Pará	6,594	5,378	82
Rondônia	2,154	1,733	80
Roraima	14,781	10,796	73
Tocantins	2,880	2,409	84
Total	92,686	75,178	81

Source: Ministry of Citizenship's Consultation, Selection and Extraction of Information of the Unified Registry (CECAD) data from April 2021.
Note: BF = Bolsa Família; Cadastro Único = Unified Registry.

NOTES

1. The Auxílio Brasil program was launched in November 2021 to replace the widely known Bolsa Família program. It maintains several of the characteristics of Bolsa Família, including having income thresholds as eligibility criteria (R$200 for families with children) and a structure of benefits based on the household composition. Although conditionalities for Bolsa Família (school attendance and health checkups) were lifted because of the COVID-19 pandemic, it is expected that they will resume and be applied to the Auxílio Brasil beneficiaries in the future.
2. In recent years, Indigenous organizations have been claiming that the Pardo category includes individuals of Indigenous origin who do not live in their original communities and therefore represent a form of invisibility of the Indigenous presence in the society by the state.
3. "Subnormal clusters" are informal urban settlements, defined as denser urban areas with at least 51 housing units lacking, in its majority, essential public services, occupying public or private lands and are characterized by a disorderly urban pattern (IBGE 2020a).
4. The "Atlas da Violência 2020" report states that the war between the country's two largest criminal organizations (Primeiro Comando da Capital and Comando Vermelho) is largely responsible for the increase in homicides in recent years in the North and Northeast.
5. Other Amazonian states had the following rate of homicides per 100,000 inhabitants: Acre, 47.1; Amazonas, 37.8; and Rondônia, 27.1.
6. For some communities, there is little information available in surveys and censuses.
7. For a more detailed discussion, see the background note by Sanchez Martinez et al. (2022).
8. "Territories" are sites that are established via legislation; "communities" are defined as 15 or more *quilombola* individuals living in nearby areas; "regions" are defined as localities where *quilombola* individuals are established but the distance between households is greater than 50 meters (in general, they are more sparse communities).
9. These HCI indicators include rates of child health (child survival at age 5 and no stunting); adult health (the likelihood, at age 15, of living to age 60); and education (learning-adjusted years of schooling).
10. The learning poverty index combines two types of deprivations: the first is in schooling, and the second is in terms of learning. "Schooling-deprived" refers to a school-age child who is out of school. "Learning-deprived" refers to pupils at school who are performing below a minimum proficiency for reading (Azevedo 2020).

11. The settlements cover 33.6 million hectares in the Amazon biome.

12. National Institute for Colonization and Agrarian Reform (INCRA). 2019. "Normative Instruction No. 98, of December 30, 2019 [providing] for the selection process of benefi-ciary families of the National Agrarian Reform Program (PNRA)." Official Diary of the Union (12/31/2019), Edition 252, Section 1, p. 50 (accessed June 15, 2021) https://www.in.gov.br/en/web/dou/-/instrucao-normativa-n-98-de-30-de-dezembro-de-2019-236095812.

13. Approximately one-third of the region's agrarian reform settlements are in the state of Pará. As for the remaining settlements, they are mostly in Maranhão (808), Mato Grosso (549), Tocantins (378), and Rondônia (224), but also Acre (161), Amazonas (145), Roraima (67), and Amapá (54).

14. "Pronaf Agrarian Reform – Brazil Plant – Group A," Bank of Brazil (accessed on 15 June 2021) https://www.bb.com.br/pbb/pagina-inicial/agronegocios/agronegocio---produtos-e-servicos/pequeno-produtor/investir-em-sua-atividade/pronaf-reforma-agraria-planta-brasil-grupo-a#/.

15. For instance, over 350 *quilombola* communities are registered with the Palmares Cultural Foundation, but less than half have a land tenure regularization process opened with INCRA, and only a handful had their land regularized. Many of these pending land tenure regularization requests were filled over a decade ago, reflecting both the complexity of the land tenure regularization process and INCRA's limited capacity.

16. "Quilombolas Communities in Brazil," São Paulo Pro-Indian Commission (CPI-SP) website: https://cpisp.org.br/direitosquilombolas/observatorio-terras-quilombolas/quilombolas-communities-in-brazil/.

17. Bolsa Família has been subsumed under Auxílio Brasil.

REFERENCES

Almeida, R., and T. Packard. 2018. *Skills and Jobs in Brazil: An Agenda for Youth.* International Development in Focus Series. Washington, DC: World Bank.

Amaral, E. F. L., and V. P. Monteiro. 2013. "Avaliação de impacto das condicionalidades de educação do Programa Bolsa Família (2005 e 2009)." *Dados* 56 (3): 531–70.

Azevedo, J. P. 2020. "Simulating the Potential Impacts of COVID-19 School Closures on Schooling and Learning Outcomes: A Set of Global Estimates." Policy Research Working Paper 9284, World Bank, Washington, DC.

Baggio, I. S., P. H. B. de Barros, A. L. Stege, and C. M. de Almeida Tupich Hilgemberg. 2019. "Economic Development and Crime in Brazil: A Multivariate and Spatial Analysis." *Revista Brasileira de Estudos Regionais e Urbanos* 13 (1): 1–22.

Bastagli, F., J. Hagen-Zanker, L. Harman, V. Barca, G. Sturge, and T. Schmidt. 2019. "The Impact of Cash Transfers: A Review of the Evidence from Low- and Middle-Income Countries." *Journal of Social Policy* 48 (3): 569–94.

Bernhofen, M., F. Dolan, and C. Borja-Vega. 2022. "Water in the Brazilian Amazon." Background note for this report, World Bank, Washington, DC.

Black, S. E., P. J. Devereux, and K. G. Salvanes. 2009. "Like Father, Like Son? A Note on the Intergenerational Transmission of IQ Scores." *Economics Letters* 105 (1): 138–40.

Boyd, D., H. Lankford, S. Loeb, J. Rockoff, and J. Wyckoff. 2008. "The Narrowing Gap in New York City Teacher Qualifications and Its Implications for Student Achievement in High-Poverty Schools." Working Paper 14021, National Bureau of Economic Research, Cambridge, MA.

Camelo, R., and V. Ponczek. 2021. "Teacher Turnover and Financial Incentives in Underprivileged Schools: Evidence from a Compensation Policy in a Developing Country." *Economics of Education Review* 80: 102067.

Cequeira, D., S. Bueno, P. P. Alves, R. S. de Lima, E. R. A. da Silva, H. Ferreira, A. Pimentel, et al. 2020. "Atlas da Violência 2020." Annual statistical report, Institute of Applied Economic Research (Ipea), Brasília.

Chevalier, A., P. Dolton, and S. McIntosh. 2007. "Recruiting and Retaining Teachers in the UK: An Analysis of Graduate Occupation Choice from the 1960s to the 1990s." *Economica* 74 (293): 69–96.

Chiavari, J., C. L. Lopes, and J. N. de Araujo. 2020. "Panorama dos Direitos de Propriedade no Brasil Rural." Report, Climate Policy Initiative, Rio de Janeiro.

Chimeli, A. B., and R. R. Soares. 2017. "The Use of Violence in Illegal Markets: Evidence from Mahogany Trade in the Brazilian Amazon." *American Economic Journal: Applied Economics* 9 (4): 30–57.

Claudino, L. S. D., P.-C. Rene, L. A. F. Darnet, and I. Gehlen. 2014. "Desiguais desde a chegada, mas a distância aumenta: a ampliação das desigualdades sociais numa área de fronteira na Amazônia brasileira." *Revista Ensambles* 1: 83–98.

CSRI (Credit Suisse Research Institute). 2019. "Global Wealth Report 2019." Annual analytical report, CSRI, Zurich.

de Melo Lira, T., and M. d. P. S. Rodrigues Chaves. 2016. "Comunidades Ribeirinhas na Amazônia: organização sociocultural e política." *Interações* 17 (1). doi:10.20435/1518-70122016107.

Demirgüç-Kunt, A., L. Klapper, D. Singer, S. Ansar, and J. Hess. 2018. *The Global Findex Database 2017: Measuring Financial Inclusion and the Fintech Revolution.* Washington, DC: World Bank.

Dolton, P. J. 1990. "The Economics of UK Teacher Supply: The Graduate's Decision." *Economic Journal* 100 (400): 91–104.

Dolton, P. J., and G. H. Makepeace. 1993. "Female Labour Force Participation and the Choice of Occupation: The Supply of Teachers." *European Economic Review* 37 (7): 1393–411.

Dutz, M. A. 2018. *Jobs and Growth: Brazil's Productivity Agenda.* International Development in Focus Series. Washington, DC: World Bank.

Fandiño, P., M. Arretche, and M. Hanusch. 2022. "A Genesis of Poverty and Inequality in Brazil." World Bank, Washington, DC.

Fearnside, P. 2017. "Deforestation of the Brazilian Amazon." In *Oxford Research Encyclopedia of Environmental Science*, edited by H. H. Shugart. Oxford: Oxford University Press.

Fernandes, F. R. C., R. C. J. Alamino, and E. R. Araujo. 2014. *Recursos minerais e comunidade: impactos humanos, socioambientais e econômicos.* Rio de Janeiro: Mineral Technology Center (CETEM), Ministry of Science, Technology and Innovation (MCTI).

Ferreira, M. U., I. Giacomini, P. M. Sato, B. H. Lourenço, V. C. Nicolete, L. F. Buss, A. Matijasevich, M. C. Castro, and M. A. Cardoso. 2022. "SARS-CoV-2 Seropositivity and COVID-19 among 5 Years-Old Amazonian Children and Their Association with Poverty and Food Insecurity." *PLoS Neglected Tropical Diseases* 16 (7): e0010580.

Ferreira Filho, J. B. S., and M. Hanusch. 2022. "A Macroeconomic Perspective of Structural Deforestation in Brazil's Legal Amazon." Policy Research Working Paper 10162, World Bank, Washington, DC.

Freitas, C. M. de, and L. L. Giatti. 2009. "Environmental Sustainability and Health Indicators in the Legal Amazonia, Brazil." *Cadernos de Saúde Pública* 25 (6): 1251–66.

Gomes de Souza, D., F. P. de Oliveira, R. da Silveira Santos, G. B. de Moura Ferreira, E. J. dos Santos Silva, and G. da Silva Silva. 2020 "Sistema de produção em comunidades tradicionais na costa amazônica brasileira." *Brazilian Journal of Development* 6 (1): 3688–704.

Grover, A., S. V. Lall, and W. F. Maloney. 2022. *Place, Productivity, and Prosperity: Revisiting Spatially Targeted Policies for Regional Development.* Washington, DC: World Bank.

Guarino, C. M., L. Santibanez, G. A. Daley, and D. J. Brewer. 2004. "A Review of the Research Literature on Teacher Recruitment and Retention." Technical report, RAND Corporation, Santa Monica, CA.

Hall, A. 1987. "Agrarian Crisis in Brazilian Amazonia: The Grande Carajas Programme." *Journal of Development Studies* 23 (4): 522–52.

Hallal, P. C., F. P. Hartwig, B. L. Horta, M. F. Silveira, C. J. Struchiner, L. P. Vidaletti, N. A. Neumann, et al. 2020. "SARS-CoV-2 Antibody Prevalence in Brazil: Results from Two Successive Nationwide Serological Household Surveys." *The Lancet Global Health* 8 (11): e1390–98.

Han, Y.-K., and R. A. Rossmiller. 2004. "How Does Money Affect Teachers' Career Choices? Evidence from NLS-72." *Journal of Education Finance* 30 (1): 79–100.

Hanlon, M., R. Burstein, S. H. Masters, and R. Zhang. 2012. "Exploring the Relationship between Population Density and Maternal Health Coverage." *BMC Health Services Research* 12 (1): 416.

Hanushek, E. 2003. "The Failure of Input-Based Schooling Policies." *Economic Journal* 113 (485): 64–98.

Hanushek, E. 2010. "The Economic Value of Higher Teacher Quality." *Economics of Education Review* 30 (3): 466–79.

IBGE (Brazilian Institute of Geography and Statistics). 2010. *Censo Demográfico 2010.* Rio de Janeiro: IBGE.

IBGE (Brazilian Institute of Geography and Statistics). 2011. *Censo Demográfico 2010: Aglomerados Subnormais.* Rio de Janeiro: IBGE.

IBGE (Brazilian Institute of Geography and Statistics). 2012. "Os indígenas no Censo Demográfico 2010: primeiras considerações com base no quesito cor ou raça." Report, IBGE, Rio de Janeiro.

IBGE (Brazilian Institute of Geography and Statistics). 2020a. "Aglomerados subnormais 2019: Classificação preliminar e informações de saúde para o enfrentamento à COVID-19." Report, IBGE, Rio de Janeiro.

IBGE (Brazilian Institute of Geography and Statistics). 2020b. "Base de Informações Geográficas e Estatísticas sobre os indígenas e quilombolas para enfrentamento à COVID-19: Notas técnicas." Report, IBGE, Rio de Janeiro.

ILO (International Labour Organization). 2021. *Skilling, Upskilling and Reskilling of Employees, Apprentices & Interns during the COVID-19 Pandemic: Findings from a Global Survey of Enterprises.* Geneva: International Labour Office.

Jacarandá, R., L. Flores, and M. Feitoza. 2019. "O encarceramento em massa e o aumento da violência nos estados da Amazônia Ocidental, 2005–2017: Análise e perspectivas." *Revista de Direito da Cidade* 11 (3): 636–63. doi:10.12957/rdc.2019.44025.

Johnson, S. M., J. H. Berg, and M. L. Donaldson. 2005. *Who Stays in Teaching and Why: A Review of the Literature on Teacher Retention.* Washington, DC: NRTA.

Lautharte, I., U. Mello, and L. Emmanuel. 2022. "Education as a Leverage for Future Skills in the Amazon." Background note for this report, Washington, DC.

Leigh, A. 2012. "Teacher Pay and Teacher Aptitude." *Economics of Education Review* 31 (3): 41–53.

Lira, S. R. B. de, M. L. M. da Silva, and R. S. Pinto. 2009. "Desigualdade e heterogeneidade no desenvolvimento da Amazônia no século XXI." *Nova Economia* 19 (1): 153–84.

Little, P. E. 2018. "Territórios Sociais e Povos Tradicionais no Brasil: Por uma Antropologia da Territorialidade." *Anuário Antropológico* 28 (1): 251–90.

López-Calva, L. F., and C. Rodríguez-Castelán. 2016. "Pro-Growth Equity: A Policy Framework for the Twin Goals." Policy Research Working Paper 7897, World Bank, Washington, DC.

Lundborg, P., and K. Majlesi. 2018. "Intergenerational Transmission of Human Capital: Is It a One-Way Street?" *Journal of Health Economics* 57: 206–20.

May, P. H., M. F. Gebara, L. Muccillo de Barcellos, M. Benicio Rizek, and B. Millikan. 2016. *The Context of REDD+ in Brazil: Drivers, Actors and Institutions.* 3rd edition. Bogor Barat, Indonesia: Center for International Forestry Research.

Milanowski, A. 2008. "Do Teacher Pay Levels Matter?" Paper, Consortium for Policy Research in Education, University of Wisconsin-Madison.

Monteiro, F., S. T. Schmidt, I. B. Costa, C. C. B. Almeida, and N. S. Matuda. 2014. "Bolsa Família: Food and Nutrition Insecurity of Children under Five Years of Age." *Ciencia & Saude Coletiva* 19 (5): 1347–58.

OECD (Organisation for Economic Co-operation and Development). 2020. *Education at a Glance 2020: Education Indicators.* Paris: OECD Publishing.

Oliveira, G. L., and A. L. S. Chagas. 2020. "Long-Term Effects of CCTs on Children: The Brazilian Case." Doctoral dissertation, University of São Paulo.

Oliveira, J. A. P. de. 2008. "Property Rights, Land Conflicts, and Deforestation in the Eastern Amazon." *Forest Policy and Economics* 10 (5): 303–15.

Paiva, L. F. S. 2019. "The Dynamics of the Illegal Cocaine Market in the Triple Border between Brazil, Peru, and Colombia." *Revista Brasileira de Ciências Sociais* 34 (99). doi:10.1590/349902/2019.

Piva da Silva, M., J. A. Fraser, and L. Parry. 2021. "Capability Failures and Corrosive Disadvantage in a Violent Rainforest Metropolis." *Geographical Review*. Published ahead of print, doi:10.1080/00167428.2021.1890995.

Podgursky, M. 2011. "Teacher Compensation and Collective Bargaining." In *Handbook of the Economics of Education*, Vol. 3, edited by E. A. Hanushek, S. Machin, and L. Woessmann, 279–313. Amsterdam: Elsevier.

Ranzani, O. T., L. S. L. Bastos, J. G. M. Gelli, J. F. Marchesi, F. Baião, S. Hamacher, and F. A. Bozza. 2021. "Characterisation of the First 250 000 Hospital Admissions for COVID-19 in Brazil: A Retrospective Analysis of Nationwide Data." *The Lancet Respiratory Medicine* 9 (4): 407–18.

Sanchez Martinez, G., J. Paiva, G. L. de Paula, P. Moutinho, R. Castriota, and A. C. G. Costa. 2022. "Indigenous Peoples and Sustainable Development in the Brazilian Amazônia." Background note for this report, World Bank, Washington, DC.

Schmink, M., and C. H. Wood. 1992. *Contested Frontiers in Amazonia*. New York: Columbia University Press.

Silva, J., R. Almeida, and V. Strokova. 2015. *Sustaining Employment and Wage Gains in Brazil: A Skills and Jobs Agenda*. Washington, DC: World Bank.

Silva, T. F. 2018. *Bolsa Família 15 Anos (2003–2018)*. Brasília: National School of Public Administration (Enap).

Simões, P., and R. B. Soares. 2012. "Efeitos do Programa Bolsa Família na fecundidade das beneficiárias." *Revista Brasileira de economia* 66 (4): 445–68.

Sparovek, G., B. P. Reydon, L. F. Guedes Pinto, V. Faria, F. L. Mazzaro de Freitas, C. Azevedo-Ramos, T. Gardner, C. Hamamura, R. Rajão, F. Cerignoni, G. Pansani Siqueira, T. Carvalho, A. Alencar, and V. Ribeiro. 2019. "Who Owns Brazilian Lands?" *Land Use Policy* 87: 104062.

Staiger, D. O., and J. E. Rockoff. 2010. "Searching for Effective Teachers with Imperfect Information." *Journal of Economic Perspectives* 24 (3): 97–118.

Tavares, P., and V. Ponczek. 2018. "Teacher Pay and Student Performance: Evidence from Brazil." *Brazilian Review of Econometrics* 3 (2): 197–219.

Viana, V. 2011. "Bolsa Floresta and Bolsa Verde: Similarities, Differences, and Challenges." Article, Soluções para a Sustentabilidade na Amazônia, Fundação Amazônia Sustentável, Manaus.

Wong, P. Y., T. Harding, K. Kuralbayeva, L. O. Anderson, and A. M. Pessoa. 2018. "Pay for Performance and Deforestation: Evidence from Brazil." http://barrett.dyson.cornell.edu/NEUDC/paper_366.pdf.

World Bank. 2007. "Implementation Completion and Results Report on a Grant in the Amount of US$2.1 Million to the Federative Republic of Brazil for the Indigenous Lands Project (Pilot Program to Conserve the Brazilian Rain Forest)." Report No. ICR0000338, World Bank, Washington, DC.

World Bank. 2017. "A Fair Adjustment: Efficiency and Equity of Public Spending in Brazil." Brazil Public Expenditure Review, World Bank, Washington, DC.

World Bank. 2019. "Ending Learning Poverty: What Will It Take?" Report, World Bank, Washington, DC.

World Bank. 2020. *Convergence: Five Critical Steps toward Integrating Lagging and Leading Areas in the Middle East and North Africa*. Washington, DC: World Bank.

World Bank. 2022. "Brazil Human Capital Review: Investing in People." Report 173246, World Bank, Washington, DC.

World Bank. 2023. "Urban Competitiveness in Brazil's State of Amazonas: A Green Growth Agenda." Companion paper for this report, World Bank, Washington, DC.

Zibalza, A. 1979. "The Determinants of Teacher Supply." *Review of Economic Studies* 46 (1): 131–47.

3 Economic Growth and Land Use

MAREK HANUSCH, GABRIEL ZAOURAK, JOAQUIM BENTO DE SOUZA FERREIRA FILHO, AND DIOGO BARDAL

KEY MESSAGES

- Brazil continues with its model of factor accumulation (labor, capital, and land), which has helped it attain upper-middle-income status. Yet Brazil struggles to raise productivity.
- Agriculture is one of the few sectors in Brazil that is competitive and has experienced productivity gains.[1]
- To reach the higher levels of development of Organisation for Economic Co-operation and Development (OECD) countries, Brazil cannot rely on primary export sectors like agriculture alone but requires urban sectors like manufacturing and services to step up, raising their productivity.
- Higher growth in more advanced regions of Brazil would lift up lagging regions such as Amazônia by raising demand for Amazonian products, while internal migration would allow Amazonians to benefit from job opportunities across the country.
- Regional convergence implies that incomes in lagging economies, such as Amazônia, can catch up with incomes in more developed ones. This requires structural transformation.
- Structural transformation across Amazonian states has been uneven. In some, it has barely begun; in others, it has been overly focused on agriculture. Amazonas is at risk of regressing into extensive agriculture.
- Macroeconomic factors affect land use. Weak forest governance, strong global commodity demand, and unbalanced structural transformation in Amazônia combine to drive deforestation.
- A productivity focus beyond primary sectors would balance Amazônia's structural transformation, promote its convergence, and attenuate macroeconomic pressures on natural forests.

- *Policy implications:*
  - Fostering productivity-led growth across Brazil, and supporting export diversification into more urban sectors. This effort includes tackling "Custo Brasil."
  - Strengthening the foundation of Amazônia's regional convergence by improving logistics (especially water transportation, where possible); economic infrastructure (like energy and digital connectivity); and the business environment and institutions (from the education system to law enforcement).
  - Strengthening institutions for forest protections (as discussed in chapter 4).

SHIFTING THE GROWTH MODEL

As a lagging economy, Amazônia has significant potential for economic growth, allowing it to catch up with other parts of Brazil and eventually with the rest of the world. This is regional convergence (figure 3.1).

Chapter 1 discussed how Amazônia, a lagging frontier region, developed as economic activity expanded into its natural forests. This expansion occurred initially along the large rivers (the Colonial Frontier) and, more recently, mostly along the southeastern parts of Amazônia largely synonymous with the Arc of Deforestation (as illustrated in box 1.1). Chapter 2 showed that economic development has been uneven across Amazônia, with higher poverty across many states and urban areas struggling to deliver on their promise of better lives.

FIGURE 3.1

Economic growth and land use change in Amazônia

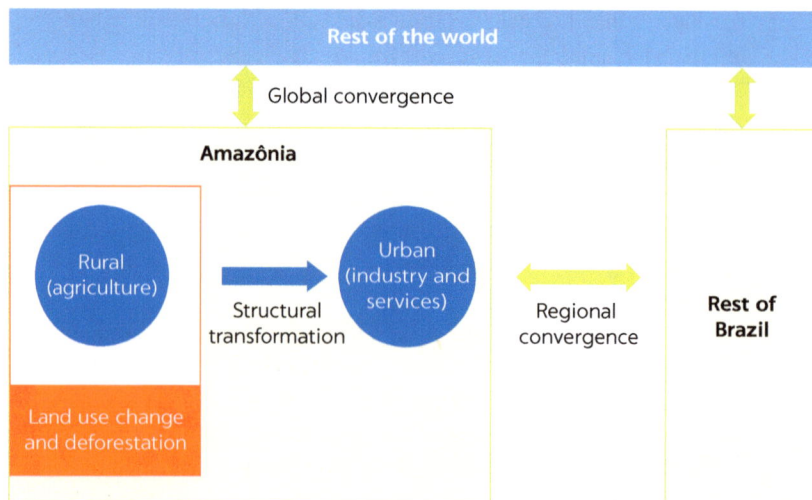

Source: World Bank.
Note: Amazônia comprises nine Brazilian states: Acre, Amapá, Amazonas, Maranhão, Mato Grosso, Pará, Rondônia, Roraima, and Tocantins.

Building on the insights in chapter 2, this chapter explores how poor, lagging economies like Amazônia can converge with more advanced economies through productivity-led growth and balanced structural transformation, including both rural and urban sectors. This will not only raise income and generate jobs, but it also matters for land use decisions and deforestation in Amazônia. This chapter highlights that a shift in the growth model, both in Brazil and Amazônia, is needed for more sustainable and inclusive development in Amazônia.

In principle, being an integral part of the Brazilian economy can be an opportunity to raise incomes for Amazonians. Amazônia is small, accounting for less than 10 percent of national gross domestic product (GDP) and about 13 percent of Brazil's population. This means that the rest of Brazil, especially the more developed parts, can be a large market for Amazonian products and a large labor market for workers seeking opportunities outside of Amazônia or to attract needed skills into Amazônia. Although frictions do exist between Brazilian states—most notably differential tax structures (Mello 2008)—and internal migration in Brazil could be more fluid, goods, capital, and labor can still flow relatively freely (Grover, Lall, and Maloney 2022). Amazônia certainly is in a more advantageous position than small countries trying to catch up with the world when limited by tariffs and immigration controls.

Yet Brazil's growth model provides little uplift to Amazônia, while intensifying pressure on its natural forests. Selling into growing markets is easier than selling into sluggish markets. Although Brazil has become an upper-middle-income country, its growth model of factor accumulation is reaching the point of exhaustion. With a low savings rate and an aging population, Brazil needs to boost its productivity to reach higher income levels, yet it has been struggling to do so (Dutz 2018). Growth of the Brazilian economy has been disappointing since 2015—the end of the last commodity supercycle. Relying on commodity exports instead of productivity across the economy puts pressure on Amazonian natural lands as the agricultural frontier, the Arc of Deforestation, moves deeper into Amazônia. Some Amazonian states, like Mato Grosso, have raised their GDP through this process but at a large cost associated with the destruction of the ecosystem services from natural forests.

Within Amazônia, unbalanced structural transformation is not only a social problem but also an environmental one. In a frontier where institutions—including forest governance—are weak, strong commodity demand and an increasingly competitive agricultural sector raise the demand for land, causing deforestation (see chapter 1, figure 1.5). This chapter will show that structural transformation needs to balance rural and urban productivity gains if Amazônia is to reach higher levels of development to reduce poverty and converge with other parts of Brazil while also limiting macroeconomic pressures on natural forests.

This chapter identifies broad policy reform areas for Amazônia that promote economic growth in a more sustainable way. To this end, it first presents the limits of Brazil's growth model, followed by a review of Amazônia's structural transformation experience to date. These insights motivate a discussion of macroeconomic impacts on land use, including deforestation, highlighting the role of productivity for growth and forests. The chapter then surveys implications for policies aimed at overcoming core development challenges in a sensitive ecosystem, ranging from the business climate to logistics and institutions (further unpacked in chapters 5 and 6 and the companion report to this memorandum, World Bank 2023b). Whereas this chapter focuses on longer-term development issues, chapter 4 will focus on how to protect Amazônia's natural wealth—its forests—in the shorter term, by strengthening forest protection systems.

ECONOMIC GROWTH IN BRAZIL

After years of macroeconomic volatility and imbalances, structural reforms and favorable external conditions in the 1990s and 2000s helped stabilize Brazil's economy. Like many other Latin American countries, Brazil pursued industrialization through import substitution since the 1930s. Though initially successful in the 1950s and 1960s (figure 3.2), this pursuit generated severe economic distortions.

Reforms and the commodity supercycle

After the "lost decade" of 1981–92—with a debt crisis, hyperinflation, political instability, and dismal growth—Brazil undertook liberalizing reforms, including opening to trade in the 1990s and implementing a set of macroeconomic measures known as the Plano Real ("Real Plan"). Following previous failed attempts to tame inflation, the Plano Real finally succeeded in 1995.[2] After a series of emerging markets crises in 1997–98, Brazil eventually also opted to let its exchange rate float under an inflation-targeting regime and introduced the Fiscal Responsibility Law in 2000. These three policies were the key pillars of Brazil's economic growth in the 2000s. But despite better economic performance in the 2000s, growth still remained too low for the country to catch up with more advanced economies like the United States or peer economies like Malaysia, Mexico, or the Republic of Korea (figure 3.3).

Fading tailwinds

Stabilization policies paid substantial growth dividends in the late 1990s and early 2000s (figure 3.4) as the commodity price supercycle of the 2000s provided significant economic uplift to Brazil (see figure 3.2), a major

FIGURE 3.2

Brazil's stop-go economic growth cycles and its declining trend in growth

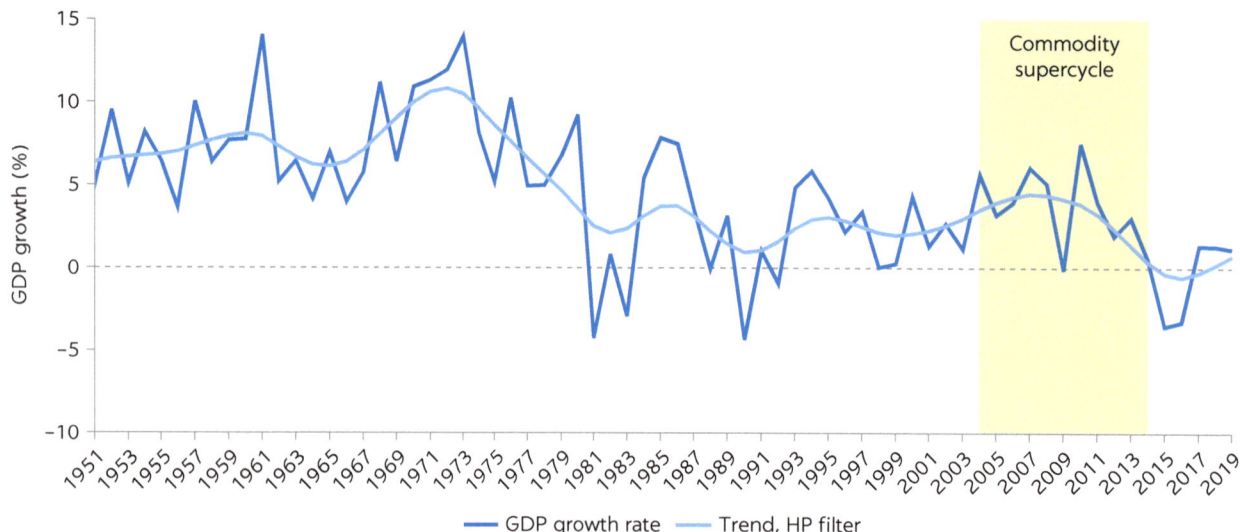

Source: World Bank, using Penn World Table 10.0 data from Feenstra, Inklaar, and Timmer 2015.
Note: Growth trend calculated using the Hodrick-Prescott (HP) filter.

FIGURE 3.3

Brazil's catching-up process has stagnated while its peers' incomes have been converging

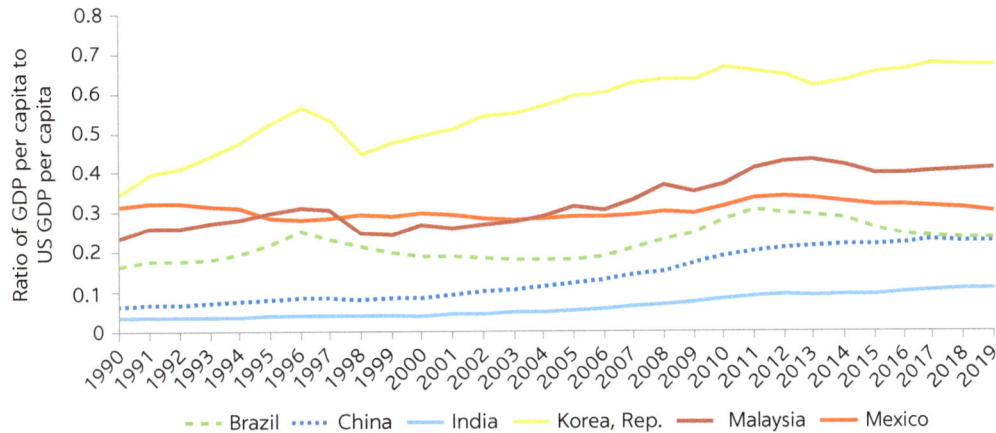

Source: World Bank, using World Table 10.0 data from Feenstra, Inklaar, and Timmer 2015.
Note: Calculations are based on output-side real GDP at chained purchasing power parity (in 2017 US$, millions). GDP = gross domestic product.

FIGURE 3.4

Key growth drivers in Brazil, 1997–2019

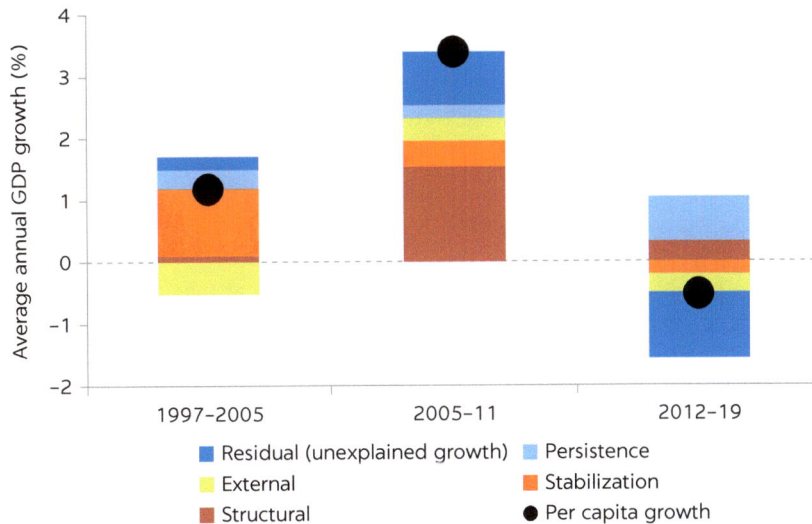

Source: World Bank, based on Araujo et al. (2014).
Note: The figure shows the average annual GDP growth rate for each period (black circle) and a decomposition of the relative drivers of growth in the same respective period. GDP = gross domestic product.

commodity exporter. The impact was reflected directly in such external drivers of growth as terms of trade and export commodity prices. It was also reflected indirectly in structural drivers of growth: better terms of trade improved business and household balance sheets, which, along with financial sector reforms, supported an expansion in credit (figure 3.5).

When the commodity price supercycle ended in 2015, the economy slid back into a period of weakness. The main driver of Brazil's (low) growth over 2012–19

FIGURE 3.5

Structural drivers of growth in Brazil, 1997–2019

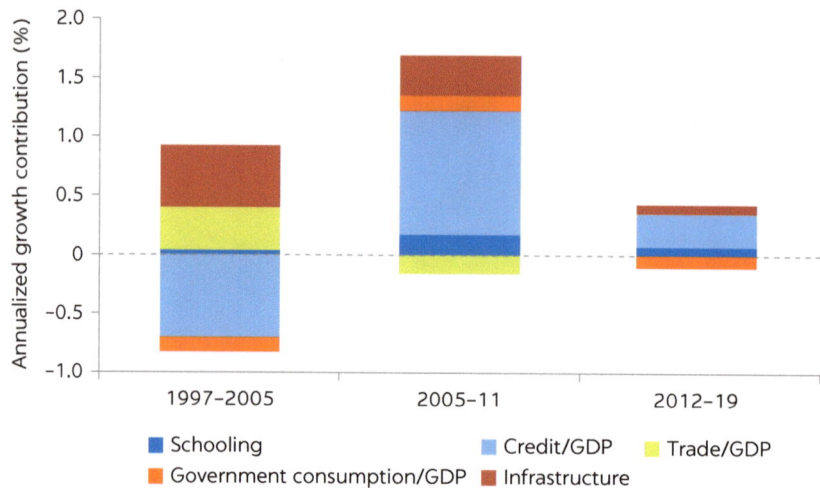

Source: World Bank, based on Araujo et al. (2014).
Note: The decomposition shows relative contributions of several drivers of structural growth in three successive periods.

was the legacy of previous structural reforms, together with tailwinds from the commodities supercycle (figure 3.4). Since 2015, Brazil has been hit by two recessions: (a) in 2015/16, caused by the end of the commodity cycle, macroeconomic imbalances and structural weaknesses, and a corruption scandal (the Lava Jato affair [World Bank 2016]); and (b) in 2020/21, caused by the COVID-19 pandemic.

The productivity problem

As tailwinds abated, Brazil struggled to switch its growth model from factor accumulation to productivity. Accumulating factors of production by expanding the labor force, accumulating capital (such as buildings, machines, and infrastructure), and expanding productive land is common at the early stages of a country's development.

In Brazil, expansion of the workforce has been a main driver of economic growth (figure 3.6), contributing more to growth than in peer countries and regions (figure 3.7). Labor adjusted for education played an even more prominent role. Even though starting from a low initial level and with many gaps remaining, this success points to the achievements of the Brazilian education system in raising average years of schooling (though quality remains low). Capital accumulation also contributed to Brazil's growth, though less than in East Asia because of lower savings rates. Converting natural land into productive land, mainly for agriculture, also contributed to growth.[3]

Why is Brazil lagging the faster progress of its middle-income peers in closing the income per capita gap with richer countries? It is due to its unsuccessful struggle to raise productivity. Although the country still has scope to benefit from factor accumulation through further improvements in education (labor) and savings rates (capital), the main obstacle to growth is low and even negative total factor productivity (TFP) growth.

FIGURE 3.6

Labor, adjusted for education, is the main driver of growth

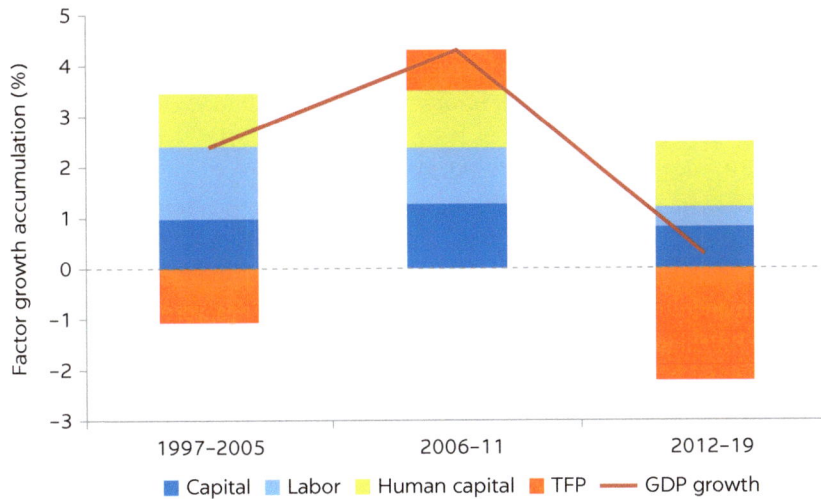

Source: World Bank, using Penn World Table 10.0 data from Feenstra, Inklaar, and Timmer 2015.
Note: Human capital = education and health; TFP = total factor productivity.

FIGURE 3.7

Brazil's productivity performance is poor among its peers

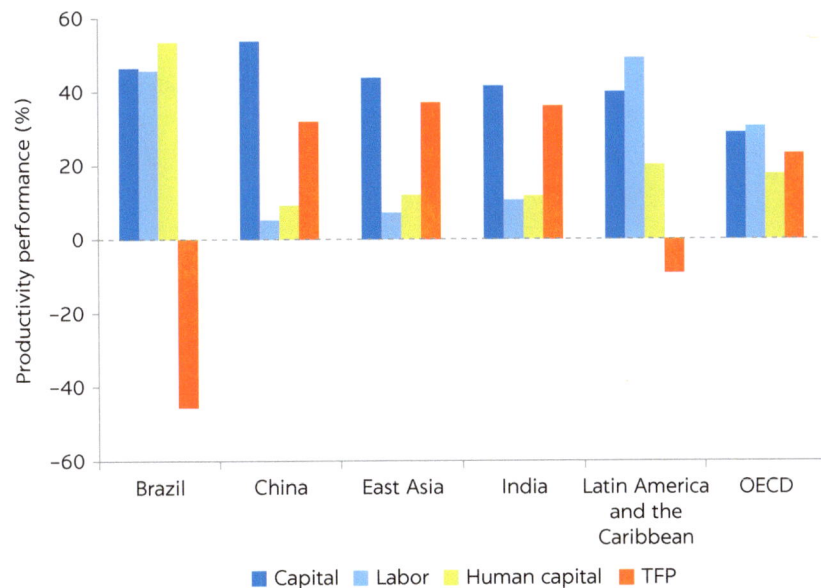

Source: World Bank, using Penn World Table 10.0 data from Feenstra, Inklaar, and Timmer 2015.
Note: "East Asia" includes China and "Latin America and the Caribbean" includes Brazil. "Human capital" includes education and health. OECD = Organisation for Economic Co-operation and Development; TFP = total factor productivity.

Except during the commodity supercycle in the 2000s, when productivity improved, TFP growth has been negative (figure 3.6), with growth driven mainly by factor accumulation. Productivity has been low in Brazil, even by Latin America's lackluster standards (figure 3.7), but productivity has been the key driver of economic growth in countries including China, India, and members of the OECD. Higher productivity holds the key to continued development in Brazil.

Brazil's agricultural engine of growth

Agriculture is the main driver of productivity in Brazil, while manufacturing productivity growth has been negative. Between 1996 and 2020, labor productivity (sectoral TFP estimates are unavailable) in agriculture grew by an average 6 percent annually (figure 3.8). Sectoral TFP estimates for Brazilian agriculture alone are available from Gasques, Bacchi, and Bastos (2018), who peg agricultural TFP growth between 2000 and 2016 at 3.2 percent.

There are many reasons for the success of Brazilian agriculture, including the migration to Brazil, especially to the south, of farmers from other parts of the world (notably Europe) (Luna and Klein 2014) and the substantial investments in research and development (R&D) by Brazilian universities, research institutes, and the Brazilian Agricultural Research Corporation (Embrapa). According to the International Food Policy Research Institute's 2016 "Agricultural R&D Indicators Factsheet," "Brazil's agriculture research system is by far the region's largest, in terms of both research capacity and spending" (Flaherty et al. 2016). Chapter 5 looks at the professionalization of farming in Amazônia, where overall productivity rises because the more-productive farmers crowd out the less-productive ones.

Growth in labor productivity across sectors between 1996 and 2021 was positive (though modest) overall and, beyond primary sectors, mostly in nontraded sectors like utilities, finance, and real estate. Productivity gains were strongly negative in manufacturing. Despite some trade liberalization measures in the 1990s, Brazil has not overcome its legacy of import substitution industrialization. Its industrial sectors, protected by high trade barriers, are not internationally competitive.[4]

Brazil has been benefiting from rising global food demand, and agricultural productivity allowed it to gain global market share. Although the rate of global population growth is declining, the world's population is still growing and expected

FIGURE 3.8

Agriculture experienced the highest labor productivity gains in Brazil while manufacturing productivity fell, 1996–2021

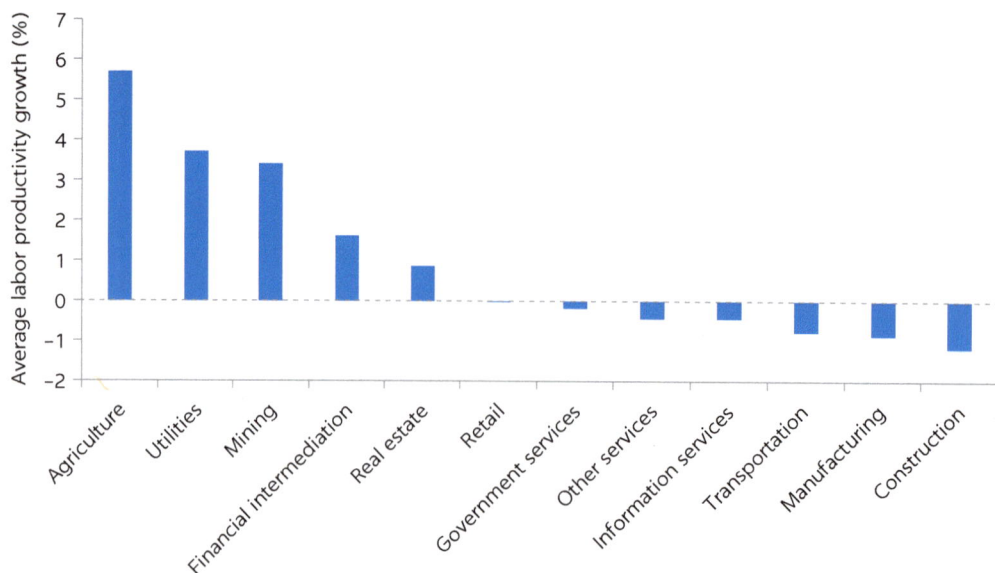

Source: Regis Bonelli Productivity Observatory database, Brazilian Institute of Economics (IBRE) of Fundação Getulio Vargas (FGV IBRE).

to exceed 10 billion by 2050 (figure 3.9), and Brazil continues to help meet the associated rising food demand. Beyond the productivity gains of agriculture itself, the sector's external competitiveness may be further boosted by other sectors. Productivity gains in certain nontraded sectors and productivity losses in traditionally traded sectors such as manufacturing[5] can augment the relative external competitiveness of agriculture (and mining).

While Brazilian agriculture enhanced its market share, other sectors have struggled. Even though agriculture's share in the Brazilian economy is small, export-led agriculture, supported by agricultural productivity and strong global food demand, is a key pillar of Brazil's growth model. Excluding agribusiness, agriculture itself accounts for only about 7 percent or less of Brazil's GDP,[6] yet it dominates the country's exports (chapter 1), allowing Brazil to gain market share in global food markets (figure 3.10). By contrast, Brazil lags peers in medium- and high-tech exports, reflecting the relative weakness and lack of competitiveness of its manufacturing sector. While Brazil's labor productivity in agriculture has managed to keep pace with that of its large peers, including China and India, Brazil has been hugely outperformed in industry and services.[7]

Brazil's difficulty in raising productivity in nonprimary sectors undermines the prospects for future prosperity. Its growth model hence provides a poor foundation for generating good jobs across the country, including in Amazônia. Agriculture is now too small to propel Brazil's growth, so urban sectors need to step up to enable future growth.

Although Brazil created many new jobs in the 2000s, the labor market has softened in recent years. Productivity growth is critical to revive the labor market and create good jobs beyond the low-productivity services and informal sectors (Dutz 2018; World Bank 2016). Low growth across Brazil, especially in what should be its growth centers—the big cities in the Southeast region, like Rio de Janeiro and São Paulo—provides little impetus for growth in more lagging regions such as Amazônia. Higher productivity will be critical for creating economic opportunities in Brazil's precarious urban settlements (notably favelas)

FIGURE 3.9

Global population is set to approach 10 billion by 2050, but population growth is slowing

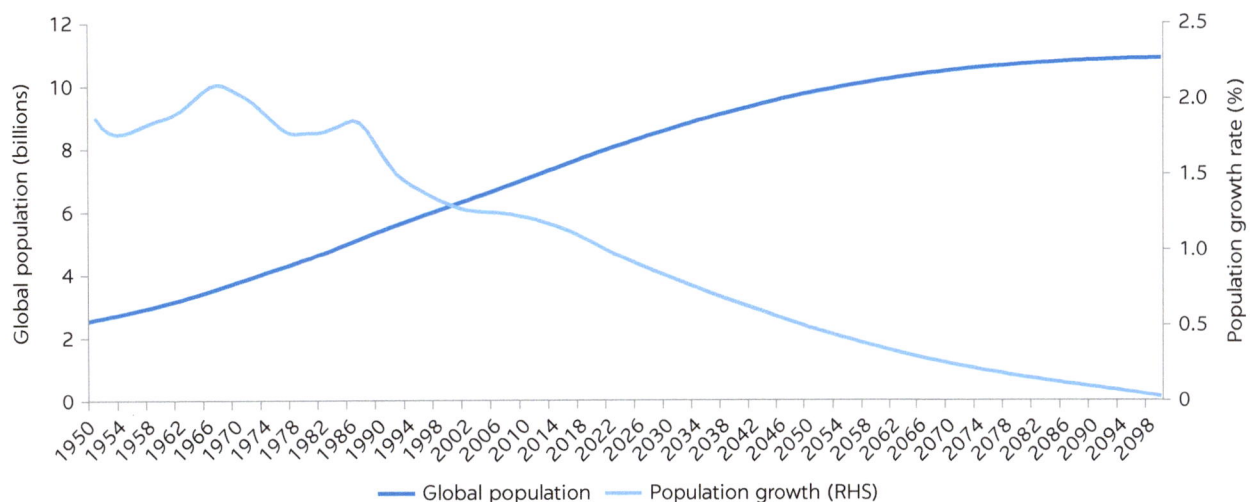

Source: UN DESA 2022.
Note: The medium scenario is used for the projections starting in 2022.

FIGURE 3.10

Brazil's agriculture has doubled its global export share

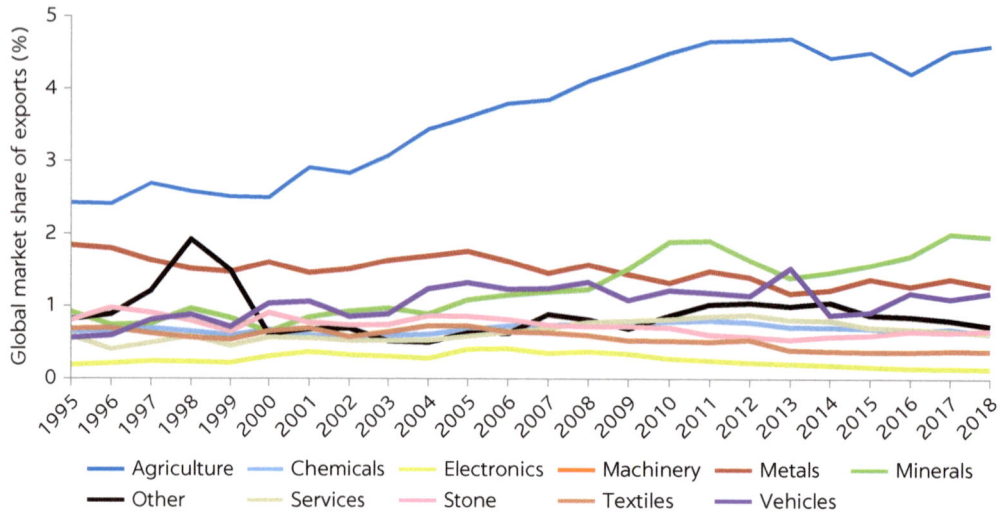

Source: Harvard University's Atlas of Economic Complexity research and data visualization tool (https://atlas.cid.harvard.edu/).

and thus for reducing poverty, both in Brazil more broadly and Amazônia specifically, while taking pressure off the agricultural frontier in Amazônia. Brazil's broader productivity agenda is explored in Dutz (2018).[8]

STRUCTURAL TRANSFORMATION AND REGIONAL CONVERGENCE IN AMAZÔNIA

Structural transformation is an integral part of development and convergence with more-advanced economies.[9] Structural transformation is driven by at least two factors: (a) exogenous changes across sectors, including productivity differentials between sectors; and (b) changes in consumer preferences (beyond food to other goods and services) as countries get richer.

As economies grow and human capital and institutions improve, the employment share and nominal value-added share of agriculture tends to decline while those of services and industry—referred to here as the "urban" sectors—rise. For industry, these shares rise in the early stages of development, reach a peak, and then decline as the economy grows and services become increasingly important. In Brazil, education has played an important role in facilitating the structural transformation process (Porzio, Ross, and Santangelo 2020). This section focuses on labor productivity, which, in the structural transformation discussion, is particularly driven by TFP and investment.

Principles of structural transformation and regional convergence

Structural transformation tends initially to be driven by agriculture. In poorer countries and regions, most people live in rural areas, off the land. Better access to markets often sets structural transformation in motion as the most productive farmers—able to compete in newly accessed markets—crowd out less productive ones (chapter 5). Agriculture declines in the shares of value added, consumption, and employment relative to manufacturing and services in part because of agricultural productivity gains and the relatively low demand elasticity for food products.[10] As agriculture becomes more productive and efficient, less labor is needed to produce the same output and agricultural wages rise, which releases labor from agriculture and contributes to rural–urban migration and rising urbanization.

In the early stages of structural transformation, urban areas tend to be relatively cheap. For tradable sectors in urban areas (mainly manufacturing) to be competitive, wages have to be relatively low. In turn, other prices in urban areas are generally also low, including land and nontradables (mainly services). The influx of rural labor into cities puts downward pressure on urban wages, supporting the competitiveness of tradable sectors. In theory, these processes, by lowering production costs, allow urban sectors to compete in global markets, attracting lower-skill manufacturing production to poorer countries and regions. As the manufacturing sector grows and becomes more productive, wages rise.

As long as urban productivity grows along with wages, higher manufacturing wages do not undermine the competitiveness of urban production and urban sectors can continue to grow. As manufacturing productivity and wages grow, nontradable prices in urban areas will catch up, leading to rising wages in both tradable and nontradable sectors (the Balassa-Samuelson effect [Balassa 1964; Samuelson 1964]).[11] There is evidence of this process in Brazil: on average, rents are 110 percent higher in São Paulo than in the capital cities in Amazônia. Similarly, consumer price indexes, including rents, are about 17 percent higher in São Paulo than in Manaus and 21 percent higher than in Belém (table 3.1).

Structural transformation implies higher urbanization accompanied by rising welfare in both rural and urban areas. Wages rise in rural areas because of gains in agricultural labor productivity as well as a smaller labor supply as rural workers move to urban areas. In cities, relatively low wages in manufacturing attract capital from other regions, boosting labor productivity through investment and associated TFP. Urban productivity can further support urban growth owing to agglomeration economies. These emerge, for example, because more people share infrastructure more efficiently, because of better matching of jobs and job-seekers in labor markets, or because of innovation and better diffusion of new ideas. This would then raise wages, and thus welfare, in both tradable and nontradable sectors in rural and urban areas through the Balassa-Samuelson effect. Removing distortions to attract investment that drives structural transformation and regional convergence is thus critical.

TABLE 3.1 **Percentage difference between prices in São Paulo and capital cities in Amazônia, 2021**

PRICE METRIC	MANAUS	BELÉM	CUIABÁ	SÃO LUIS	MACAPÁ	BOA VISTA	PORTO VELHO	PALMAS	RIO BRANCO
Consumer price index (CPI)	5.5	11.6	—	—	—	—	—	—	—
CPI including rent	17.1	21.3	—	—	—	—	—	—	—
Rent prices	69.3	60.6	90.6	123.6	102.7	141.2	201.5	212.0	182.3
Restaurant prices	42.8	30.6	32.3	21.4	81.1	38.1	—	45.0	—
Groceries	5.0	17.4	12.0	10.7	—	7.7	23.7	—	0.6

Sources: Numbeo.com cost of living database and World Bank.
Note: Amazônia comprises nine Brazilian states (capital cities in parentheses): Acre (Rio Branco), Amapá (Macapá), Amazonas (Manaus), Maranhão (São Luis), Mato Grosso (Cuiabá), Pará (Belém), Rondônia (Porto Velho), Roraima (Boa Vista), and Tocantins (Palmas). — = not available.

Agriculture-led structural transformation in Amazônia

Amazônia's structural transformation is led by agriculture, while industry and services tend to underperform. Between 2012 and 2018, all of Brazil's states experienced a substantial reallocation of employment shares from agriculture to other sectors (see annex 3A). In Amazônia, all these employment gains accrued to services, rather than manufacturing, with the employment share of manufacturing even declining.

Structural change contributed to aggregate labor productivity growth between 2012 and 2018 for most Amazonian states, but the rate of increase was slowed by the shift from agriculture directly into low-productivity services. The reallocation of labor from agriculture to nonagriculture sectors between 2012 and 2018 enhanced productivity in Amazônia, except in Amazonas and Mato Grosso (table 3.2). Structural change accounted for nearly one-third of aggregate productivity growth in Maranhão and for almost 15 percent of labor productivity growth in Tocantins. For these states, this is in line with the broader Brazilian experience with structural change contributing positively to productivity growth (Dutz 2018). However, because most low-skilled workers reallocated from agriculture to low-productivity services, gains from structural change were modest, limiting opportunities for the creation of good jobs.

Productivity gains within agriculture have been substantial in Amazônia, especially in states with better market access. Gains in industry and services have been much weaker. Between 2012 and 2018, labor productivity gains were stronger within sectors than structural change across sectors (figure 3.11), which can be linked to better market access for agriculture. In the rest of Brazil, the within-sector component of labor productivity growth was a drag on productivity growth, but in Amazônia it accounted for almost 70 percent of the increase in labor productivity.

The within-sector productivity gains tended to be strongest in the states of the Arc of Deforestation, driven—with the exception of Mato Grosso—mainly by agriculture (figure 3.12). These states tend to be better connected to transport infrastructure (chapter 1). Productivity gains linked to market access are

TABLE 3.2 **Components of labor productivity growth in Amazonian states, 2012–18**

Percentage points

STATE	STRUCTURAL CHANGE COMPONENT	WITHIN-SECTOR COMPONENT	PRODUCTIVITY GROWTH
Amazonas	−0.23	−0.47	−0.70
Amapá	−0.05	−0.31	−0.22
Roraima	0.00	−0.17	−0.13
Rondônia	0.03	−0.10	−0.05
Pará	0.05	−0.02	−0.02
Acre	0.08	−0.09	0.02
Tocantins	0.09	0.56	0.65
Mato Grosso	0.11	0.86	0.81
Maranhão	0.27	0.66	0.93

Source: World Bank, using Brazilian Institute of Geography and Statistics (IBGE) data.
Note: Labor productivity is defined as the ratio of output to employment.

FIGURE 3.11

Many New Frontier states in Amazônia underwent significant structural transformation, 2012–18

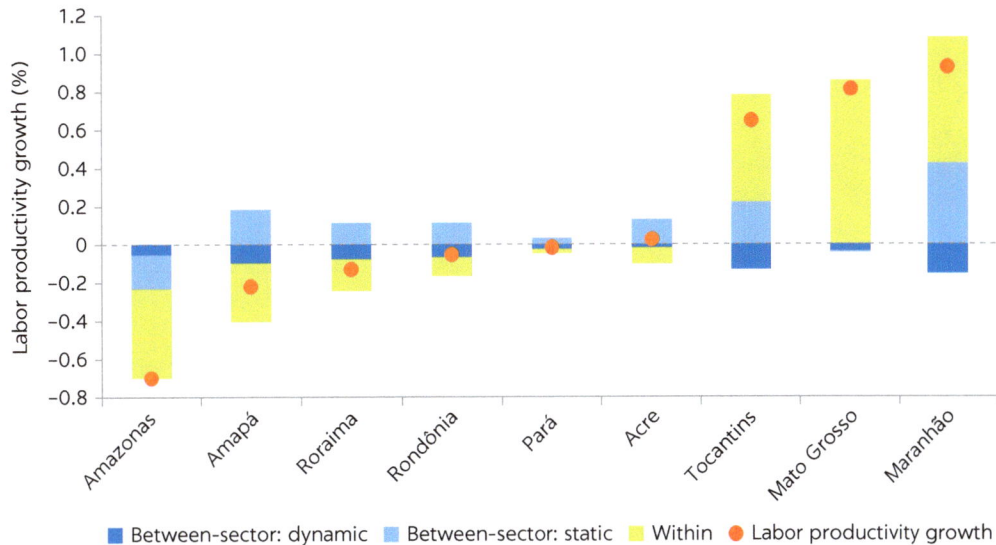

■ Between-sector: dynamic   ■ Between-sector: static   ■ Within   ● Labor productivity growth

Source: World Bank, using Brazilian Institute of Geography and Statistics (IBGE) data.
Note: The figure decomposes the total gains in labor productivity (the ratio of output to employment) from agriculture, industry, and services into within-sector gains and between-sector gains using the average values for 2012–18. Black dots represent the overall productivity growth (the sum of contributions for each bar). "New Frontier" states (as further discussed in chapter 1, box 1.1) include Maranhão, Mato Grosso, Rondônia, and Tocantins. "Dynamic" between-sector gains represent the extent to which workers move to sectors with higher productivity growth. "Static" between-sector gains represent the extent to which workers move to sectors with higher productivity levels. "Within" represents productivity gains within individual sectors.

FIGURE 3.12

In most Amazonian states, average annual within-sector labor productivity gains have been particularly strong in agriculture, 2012–18

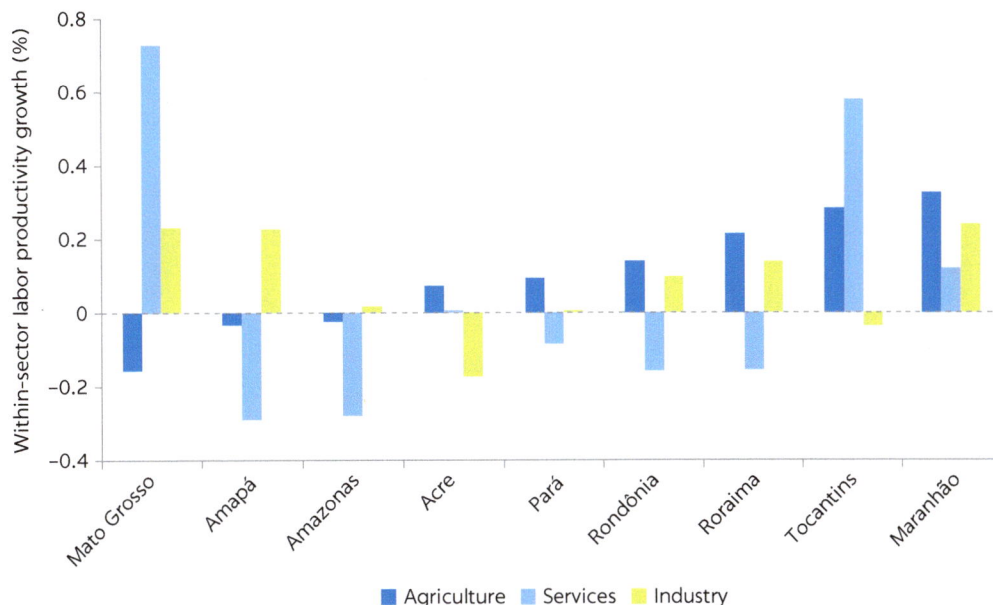

■ Agriculture   ■ Services   ■ Industry

Source: World Bank, using Brazilian Institute of Geography and Statistics (IBGE) data.
Note: Labor productivity is defined as the ratio of output to employment.

consistent with professional commercial farmers expanding relative to less productive farmers, as discussed in chapter 5. Consistent with its relatively advanced level of structural transformation, labor productivity gains were relatively high in industry and services in Mato Grosso. In most other states, productivity in industry was mixed, and labor productivity growth in services was stagnant or declined.

Weak structural transformation in many parts of Amazônia is likely a consequence of deep-seated competitiveness challenges. As manufacturing tends to be a traded sector, the shift from manufacturing into services in essence represents a shift from tradables into nontradables—in other words, from sectors that need to compete in markets to sectors that are much more localized and thus sheltered. This can contribute to premature deindustrialization (box 3.1).

Figure 3.13 shows the relative decline in external competitiveness for Brazil and most of the Amazonian states between 2004–16 and 2017–19. Consistent with the analysis in this chapter, most agricultural states in the

Premature deindustrialization and the unfulfilled promise of cities for better lives

Manufacturing has been underperforming, and there are signs of premature deindustrialization. Manufacturing has been losing employment shares in most of Amazônia (see table 3A.3 in the annex).[a] While this is a broader Brazilian phenomenon (Silva and Alencar Nääs 2020), it poses a larger problem for Amazônia because it is a lagging region. The decline in manufacturing is a sign of premature deindustrialization in a lagging region whose convergence would still be expected to be supported by manufacturing (Rodrik 2013). In premature deindustrialization, labor moves away from manufacturing into lower productivity growth sectors, usually services, reducing overall productivity growth. This has negative consequences for real income growth and standards of living.

Several factors could be contributing to this premature deindustrialization, though they are difficult to identify clearly. Barriers to the reallocation of resources from agriculture to manufacturing might be one factor. As shown in chapter 1, there is an unbalanced policy focus toward rural areas in Amazônia, which can work against the logic of structural transformation. This explanation would be consistent with the pattern of structural change in table 3.3. More broadly, across Latin America, and Brazil particularly, constraints to

convergence have been associated with the level of human capital, financial market inefficiencies, regulatory distortions, and the low quality and quantity of infrastructure (Araujo et al. 2014; Dutz 2018).

Premature deindustrialization, or more generally the inability to raise incomes in sectors beyond agriculture, limits the ability of cities to generate good jobs. As agriculture released labor and structural transformation raised incomes in Amazônia, urbanization rates increased (figure B3.1.1, panel a). Yet Amazonian cities are unlikely to see incomes that match their urbanization rates, a broader Brazilian problem figure B3.1.1, panel b). This reflects the fact that urban sectors underdeliver on their economic development potential. Amazonian states' premature deindustrialization suggests that cities underdeliver on their potential because they absorb labor mostly into lower-productivity services rather than manufacturing.

This is not unusual in Brazil, where low productivity in manufacturing is a national phenomenon. It implies not that urbanization should be reversed but that economic development should rise to the commensurate level of urbanization, which requires higher urban productivity.

continued

Box 3.1, *continued*

Urbanization in relation to development levels in Brazil and the world

a. Urbanization rate and real GDP per capita, 2010[a]

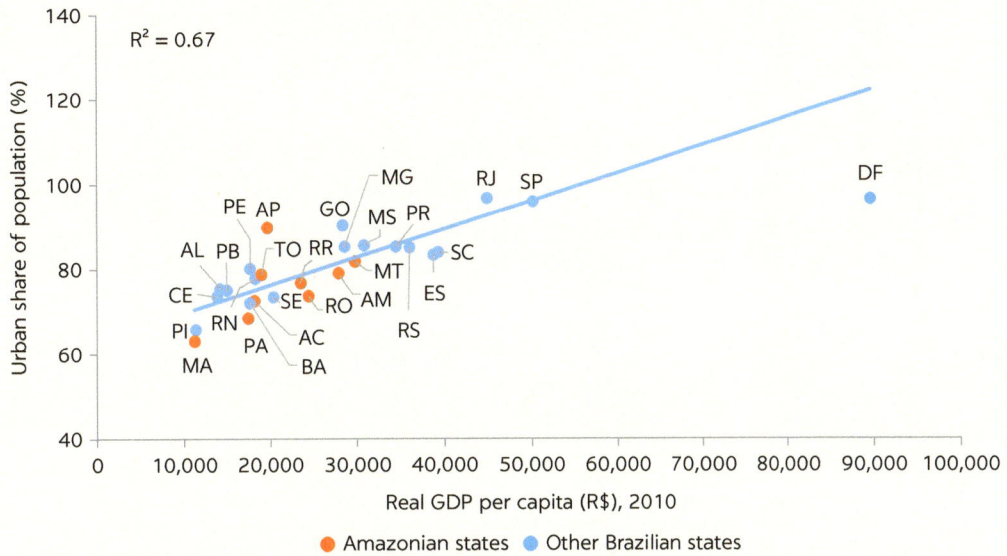

$R^2 = 0.67$

Urban share of population (%)

Real GDP per capita (R$), 2010

● Amazonian states   ● Other Brazilian states

b. Urban share of population and GDP per capita, 1990–2019

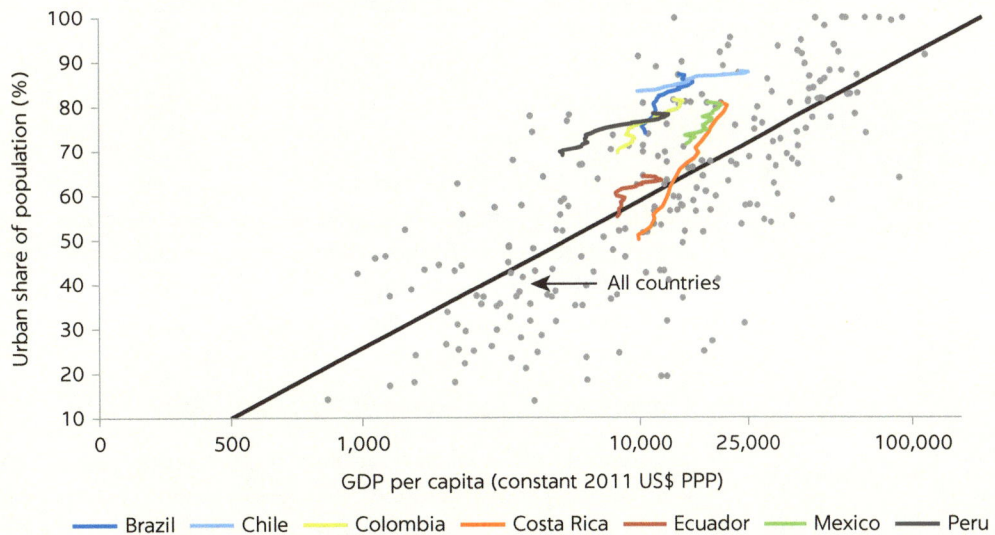

Urban share of population (%)

All countries

GDP per capita (constant 2011 US$ PPP)

━━ Brazil   ━━ Chile   ━━ Colombia   ━━ Costa Rica   ━━ Ecuador   ━━ Mexico   ━━ Peru

Sources: World Bank, using Brazilian Institute of Geography and Statistics (IBGE) and World Development Indicators data.
Note: PPP = purchasing power parity.
a. "Urbanization" is defined as the percentage of the population living in urban areas. Data are from 2010. The nine Amazonian states are in green, designated by abbreviation: Acre (AC), Amapá (AP), Amazonas (AM), Maranhão (MA), Mato Grosso (MT), Pará (PA), Rondônia (RO), Roraima (RR), and Tocantins (TO). Line does not include the Federal District (DF).
b. Colored lines indicate annual changes for selected Latin American countries.

---

a. Acre actually showed a marginal increase of 0.2 percent in the employment share of industry, and Mato Grosso increase the share of employment in agriculture by 0.2 percent.

FIGURE 3.13

External competitiveness is high or rising in many states of the New Frontier and slipped in other parts of Amazônia and the rest of Brazil, 2004–16 and 2017–19

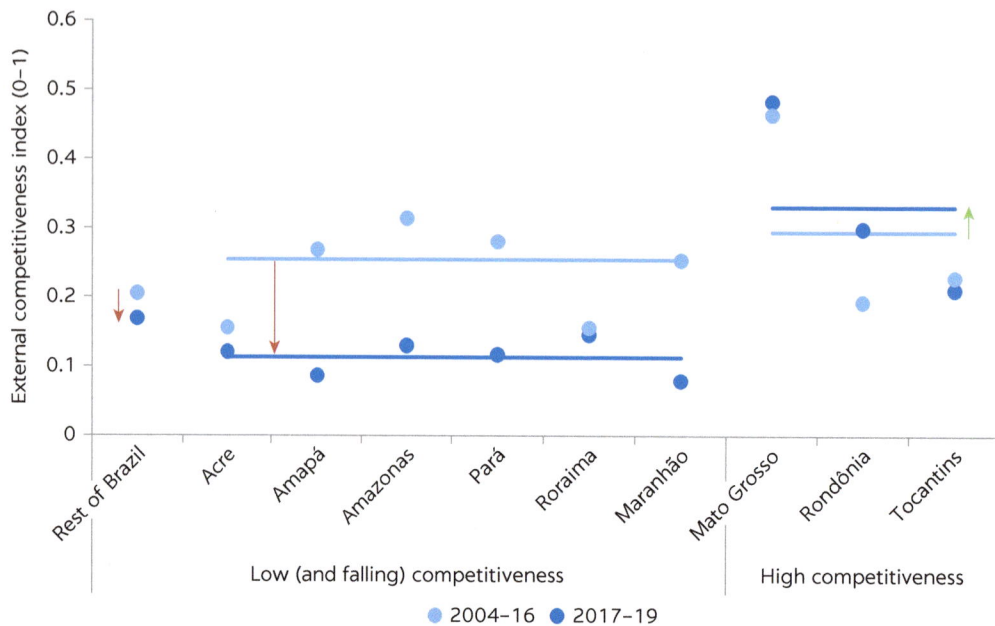

Source: World Bank, based on data from the Brazil Secretariat for International Trade, Ministry of Economy.
Note: External competitiveness is proxied by an estimate of the comparative advantage of Amazonian states relative to each other and to the rest of Brazil. The "New Frontier" states of Amazônia include Maranhão, Mato Grosso, Rondônia, and Tocantins. Higher values indicate higher competitiveness. Horizontal light blue lines represent the 2004–16 annual average index score of a group of states, and the horizontal dark blue lines, the average 2017–19 score. Arrows designate the trend in each group between the two periods—either downward (red arrows) or upward (green arrow).

Amazonian New Frontier (Mato Grosso, Rondônia, and Tocantins) increased or maintained their external competitiveness, while states on the Colonial Frontier tended to lose competitiveness. (The companion report to this memorandum [World Bank 2023b] looks at ways for industrial sectors to regain external competitiveness, focusing on the state of Amazonas.)

Regional convergence of Amazonian states

Despite challenges to Amazônia's structural transformation, there has been some regional convergence, especially in the more advanced agricultural states. Between 2002 and 2018, there were negative correlations between initial (2002) productivity and GDP per capita and growth rates across states in Brazil (figure 3.14, panel a and panel b, respectively). This indicates that, consistent with structural transformation, there has been some convergence across the country in labor productivity and income. Convergence in GDP per capita has been particularly strong in the Amazonian states that experienced strong structural transformation in agriculture, notably Mato Grosso and Tocantins, states in the New Frontier. With poverty widespread among the Amazonian states, closing productivity gaps could advance a broader convergence of Amazonian states with Brazil's more developed regions or states.

FIGURE 3.14

Both labor productivity and GDP per capita are converging across states, 2002–18

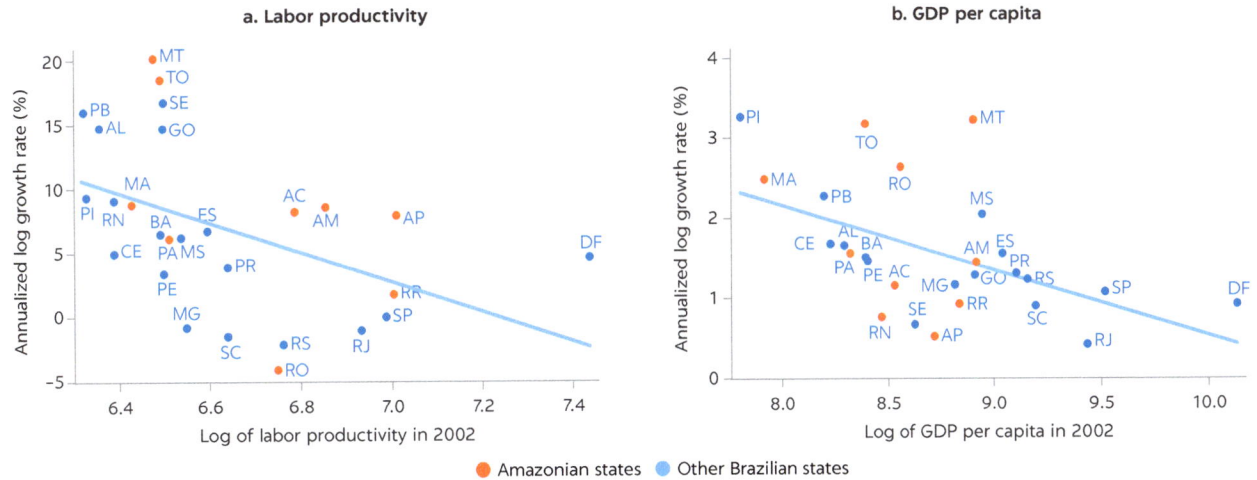

a. Labor productivity

b. GDP per capita

● Amazonian states ● Other Brazilian states

Sources: World Bank, based on Annual Social Information Report (RAIS) data (panel a) and regional accounts and population numbers by the Brazilian Institute of Geography and Statistics (IBGE) (panel b).
Note: Labor productivity is defined as the ratio of the wage bill to employment. The negatively sloped curve indicates that states with lower initial values grew faster on average, allowing them to catch up. RAIS data are used here for longer comparable time series but only include formal sector labor. Brazilian states in the plot are designated by their two-digit code. GDP = gross domestic product.

OPPORTUNITIES FOR ACCELERATING REGIONAL CONVERGENCE IN AMAZÔNIA

Prospect of higher productivity growth in Amazônia

Lagging economies can catch up by closing productivity gaps, and Amazônia's regional convergence does not depend on using its natural wealth. To foster convergence, lagging states need to level the playing field by investing in the foundations for growth and strengthening markets, and by enabling citizens to move to where the opportunities are. In many states, especially in the New Frontier, this has helped agriculture catch up—although at a significant cost to Amazonian forests. As a more sustainable alternative, the bioeconomy has been identified as a driver of growth. However, in principle, regional convergence does not require any natural wealth. Closing productivity gaps in more urban sectors in particular could promote faster and sustainable convergence of Amazonian states with the rest of Brazil.

In agriculture, Mato Grosso has almost closed its productivity gap with Brazil's best performer. Figure 3.15, panel a, shows the gaps in labor productivity between Amazonian states and Mato Grosso do Sul, the state with the best performance in 2017. Productivity gaps are smaller for states of the New Frontier—Mato Grosso, Rondônia, and Tocantins—which have dramatically improved their market access over the last decades than for the more remote states of the Colonial Frontier—Acre, Amapá, and Roraima (see chapter 5). This is consistent with the notion that market access has allowed agriculture in the New Frontier states to converge, to varying degrees, with the more advanced agricultural states across Brazil. This convergence in labor productivity has been led by Mato Grosso, followed by Amazonas and Pará, and trailed by the most lagging states.

There is considerable potential for states in Amazônia to catch up in manufacturing. Except for Amazonas, states in Amazônia have large labor

FIGURE 3.15

Amazônia's labor productivity gaps are generally wide

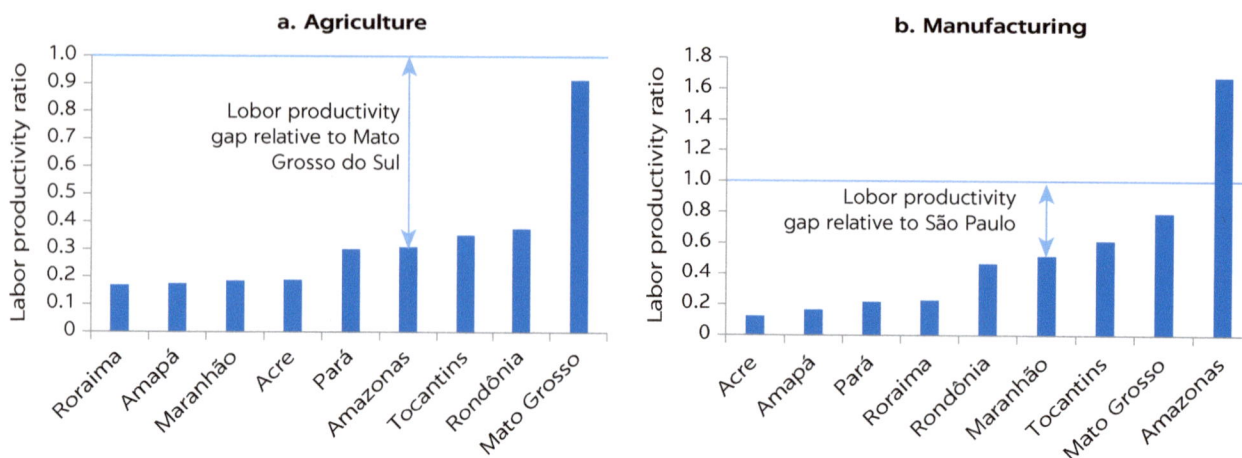

Sources: World Bank, using Brazilian Institute of Geography and Statistics (IBGE) subnational accounts and Agricultural Census (panel a) and sectoral employment series (panel b) data.

Note: Labor productivity is defined as the ratio of output to employment.

productivity gaps with São Paulo, Brazil's economic center (figure 3.15, panel b). Even Mato Grosso, the Amazonian state with the strongest convergence performance in agriculture, has a large labor productivity gap in manufacturing with São Paulo, with productivity about 20 percent lower. Generally, states in the New Frontier had lower productivity gaps in manufacturing than states on the Colonial Frontier (except Amazonas), consistent with a more advanced level of structural transformation.

Even Amazonas has significant room to catch up in manufacturing. Removing distortions from tax incentives will be important. Figure 3.15, panel b, suggests that its labor productivity is higher than in São Paulo. Rather than indicating that Amazonas is more efficient than São Paulo, it points at distortions. Using average wages as an alternative measure of labor productivity reveals that Amazonas is less productive than São Paulo. Amazonas' apparently good showing reflects very high capital intensity, a consequence of fiscal incentives that lower the cost of machinery and inputs relative to the cost of labor, which receives no incentives. So, the high productivity in figure 3.15, panel b, is more likely to reflect distortions than higher productivity. Low average wages suggest that there is catch-up potential for manufacturing in Amazonas as well.

Manufacturing has greater potential for productivity growth than other sectors, however, realizing that potential requires policy measures to stem the decline in competitiveness. Focusing policy on preventing premature deindustrialization would help reverse the employment decline. This would accelerate regional convergence since most manufacturing activities are tradable and thus tend to have a near-automatic propensity to raise labor productivity, which accounts for their higher productivity growth over time (Rodrik 2013). In other words, rising employment in manufacturing accelerates the catch-up process, while declining employment hampers convergence.

Increasing productivity in services, the largest employer, would support Amazônia's convergence. In 2018, services accounted for almost 50 percent of employment in Amazônia, by far the largest sector. Growth in service sector productivity could therefore have a large impact on aggregate productivity. Because services are inputs to the production of goods (embodied services) and are also provided to customers bundled with goods (embedded services), raising productivity in the services sector could also raise productivity in the other sectors of the economy. Raising the productivity and quality of crucial services—such as finance, logistics, and professional services—is thus increasingly important to convergence.

Modern traded services provide new opportunities for productivity convergence, but convergence is harder for nontradable services. Historically, manufacturing was the preferred sector for driving growth because of its ability to address competitive pressures by improving efficiency and its ability to increase demand by exporting to global markets. These characteristics were not relevant to services, which were largely viewed as nontradable, with low scale and low productivity. Today, however, the evolution of the internet, digitalization, and electronic storage is enabling the rapid increase in cross-border trade in services. This opens opportunities for developing countries and individual states to achieve service-led growth, especially for economies that have already made some progress on development, with a strong human capital foundation.[12] The spread of productivity-enhancing characteristics in services, including in low- and middle-income countries, expands the range of activities that will likely have positive spillovers for development (Ghani and Kharas 2010). And tradable services like telecommunications, logistics, finance, information technology, as well as professional and other business services, can support regional convergence.[13] Like manufacturing, these services benefit from technological advances, specialization through economies of scale, agglomeration, network effects, and division of labor.

Toward more balanced structural transformation

As in the rest of Brazil, agriculture is a growth pillar in many parts of Amazônia, while urban performance is lagging. Mato Grosso is the most advanced Amazonian state, with an internationally competitive export sector focused on agriculture. In a sense, this makes it a role model in Amazônia. Amazonas, the only Amazonian state with an economy based mostly on urban sectors and manufacturing (the Zona Franca de Manaus), suffers the consequences of the stagnant Brazilian economy, and its poor urban productivity performance puts it at risk of slipping into extensive agriculture. Many poorer Amazonian states focus on agriculture and largely for the local market (especially beef). As their structural transformation advances, they are likely to follow the model of Mato Grosso.

A stronger focus on productivity in Amazônia and across Brazil, beyond agriculture, would raise incomes and could also foster greater social and economic cohesion. For example, chapter 2 showed how Amazonian workers would gain from a more productivity-focused growth model with a stronger urban focus, while reducing a source of inequality, linked to the skewed distribution of land ownership. A greater focus on productivity across the economy could also integrate Brazilian value chains with each other and, increasingly, the world. This would not only allow Brazil to move up the value chain but also help align business cycles across the country, strengthening national economic cohesion. This is important in a currency union, making federal policies (from fiscal to monetary to structural policies) much more effective. Shifting the growth model toward balanced productivity gains, including a stronger urban productivity performance, is a joint agenda for Amazônia and the rest of Brazil. It would generate inclusive growth—and this growth would also be more environmentally sustainable, as will be discussed in the following sections.

LAND USE IMPACTS

How external agricultural demand affects Amazonian deforestation

Brazil's current growth model, partly based on export-led agriculture, is land hungry and drives deforestation especially in the states of the Arc of Deforestation (see box 1.1 in chapter 1). General equilibrium simulations suggest that growth in external agricultural demand, from a GDP perspective, particularly benefits states like Maranhão, Pará, Rondônia, and Tocantins, at the cost of higher deforestation (figure 3.16). The more remote states (generally in the Colonial Frontier) are less agriculturally advanced and thus see a more modest acceleration in deforestation. Mato Grosso has a more developed agricultural market, and much deforestation has already occurred in the past, so rising agricultural demand raises GDP substantially but now causes less deforestation than in other states in the Arc of Deforestation. Amazonas, as a more manufacturing-focused,

FIGURE 3.16

Higher external agricultural demand fuels deforestation

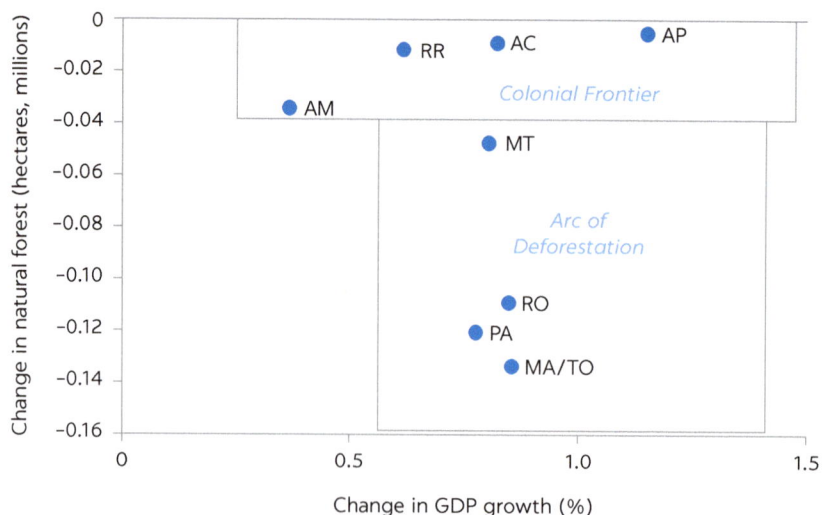

Source: World Bank, based on the computable general equilibrium (CGE) model in Ferreira Filho and Hanusch (2022).
Note: The figure shows changes from the baseline projection of the economy and land use over a 12-year period. The impacts are the cumulative deviations from the baseline in percent. The nine Amazonian states are designated by abbreviation: Acre (AC), Amapá (AP), Amazonas (AM), Maranhão (MA), Mato Grosso (MT), Pará (PA), Rondônia (RO), Roraima (RR), and Tocantins (TO). Pará is part of both the Colonial Frontier and the Arc of Deforestation in the New Frontier. MA/TO is Maranhão and Tocantins and also includes Piauí in the modeling (which is not part of Amazônia). For details on the Colonial Frontier, New Frontier, and Arc of Deforestation, see chapter 1, box 1.1.

domestically oriented state, experiences increasing encroachment by the Arc of Deforestation in this simulation, at a relatively modest economic benefit. Although the other states in the Colonial Frontier deforest only a little more, their economies expand as they increase their sales to states that benefit more directly from higher external agricultural demand.

How external competitiveness and productivity affect Amazonian deforestation

Amazonian deforestation is also closely linked to Brazil's external competitiveness. The literature has well documented that macroeconomic factors explain deforestation, such as agricultural and timber prices or the real effective exchange rate (REER) (for example, Arcand, Guillaumont, and Guillaumont Jeanneney 2008). The REER is the trade-weighted nominal exchange rate between trade partners, accounting for relative price differentials across them. It is thus a measure of a country's external competitiveness. Between about 2004 and 2015, there appeared to be a decoupling between commodity prices and Amazonian deforestation (see, for example, Assunção, Gandour, and Rocha 2015); however, the relationship between the REER and Amazonian deforestation remained strong (figure 3.17a).

Since agriculture is one of Brazil's most important export sectors, external competitiveness impacts demand for land and therefore deforestation. Higher external competitiveness—that is, a depreciated REER—raises global demand for Brazilian commodities and thus for agricultural land, putting upward pressure on real land prices across Brazil (figure 3.17, panel b). Although higher demand for land raises land prices, recent empirical evidence (Instituto Escolhas 2022), demonstrates that the expanded land supply from deforestation reduces land prices. This reinforces the point that in Brazil's resource-intensive growth model, deforestation is a means to expand agricultural

FIGURE 3.17

Real depreciation raises Amazonian deforestation and land prices across Brazil

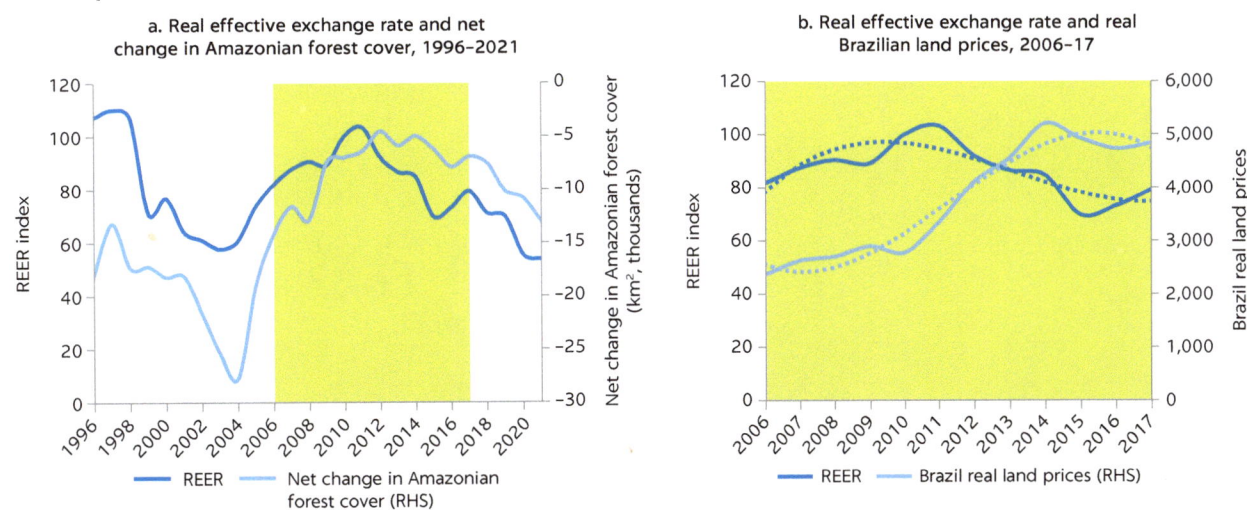

Sources: World Bank, based on data from the National Institute for Space Research (INPE) Project for Satellite Monitoring of Deforestation in the Legal Amazon (PRODES), World Development Indicators Database, and Instituto Escolhas (2022).
Note: The real effective exchange rate (REER) is the trade-weighted nominal exchange rate between trade partners, accounting for relative price differentials across them. Decreases in REER index values indicate depreciation, and increases indicate appreciation. The shaded box in panel a indicates the identical period in panel b. km² = square kilometers.

production through cheap land. Accordingly, the more land prices rise the higher are the incentives to deforest.

Productivity determines external competitiveness in the long-term. Higher Brazilian productivity reduces Amazonian deforestation through three channels. Since productivity is the main long-term determinant of the REER, there is also a strong relationship between productivity and deforestation (figure 3.18). When productivity increases across the Brazilian economy it reduces Amazonian deforestation through impacts on prices, wages, and factor substitutions:

- *Prices.* Much of the adjustment in the REER is driven by the nominal exchange rate. A nominal appreciation reduces the global price of primary goods in local currency terms, thus lowering incentives for farmers to convert forest into productive land.
- *Wages.* Productivity raises real wages across the economy (the Balassa-Samuelson effect). Higher wage costs reduce the profitability of farmers (potentially crowding out the least productive ones) and, jointly with the price effect lower demand for land and thus deforestation.[14] This is reflected in the relationship between Brazilian unit labor costs and Amazonian deforestation (figure 3.19).
- *Factor substitution.* To remain competitive under conditions of lower commodity prices and higher wage costs, farmers substitute away from labor into machinery and inputs (like fertilizer), whose price has fallen either directly from productivity gains or from a cheaper cost of import associated with a stronger exchange rate. The price of land may also have fallen, depending on the extent to which productivity derived from agriculture or other sectors. If land prices fall, the net substitution effect on deforestation is ambiguous. This is further discussed below.

FIGURE 3.18

Brazil's productivity is associated with three-quarters of Amazônia's deforestation, 1996–2019

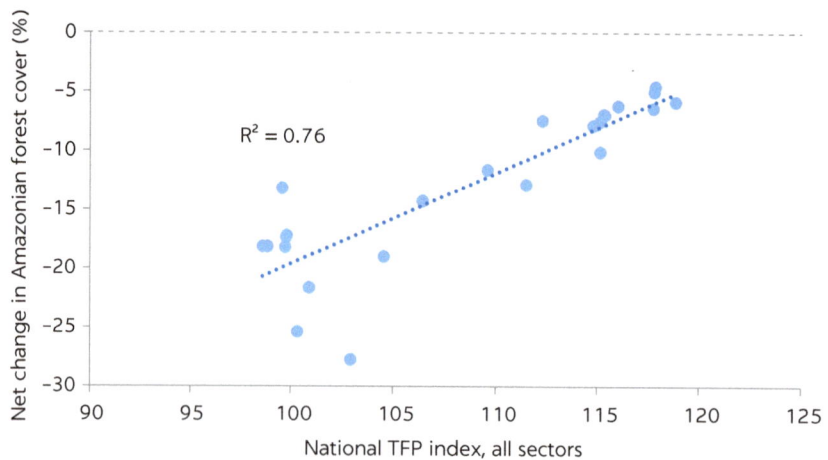

Sources: World Bank, using data from the National Institute for Space Research (INPE) Project for Satellite Monitoring of Deforestation in the Legal Amazon (PRODES) and Fundação Getulio Vargas (FGV).
Note: Each point in the scatterplot represents one year in the 1996–2019 period. The higher the productivity, the lower the rate of deforestation. TFP = total factor productivity. km² = square kilometers.

FIGURE 3.19

Amazônia's deforestation tracks Brazil's unit labor costs

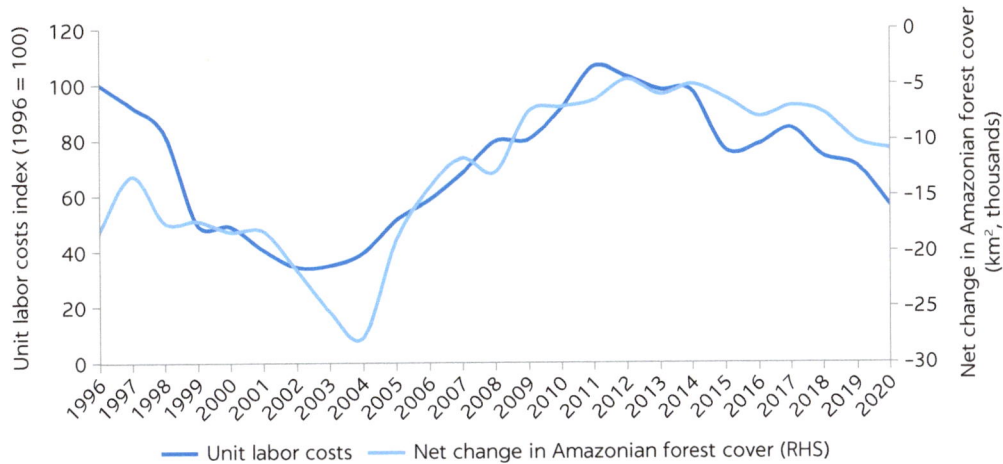

Sources: World Bank, using data from the National Institute for Space Research (INPE) Project for Satellite Monitoring of Deforestation in the Legal Amazon (PRODES) and Central Bank of Brazil. km² = square kilometers.

Amazonian deforestation accelerated when the commodities supercycle ended. Brazil's REER appreciation in the 2000s was a consequence of higher productivity from structural reforms and a positive terms-of-trade shock during the commodity supercycle, which mimicked an increase in TFP by boosting aggregate demand, capacity utilization of factories, and demand for labor. This resulted in higher real wages for workers, enhancing Brazil's purchasing power relative to that of its trading partners, leading to an appreciation of the REER. As the structural reform agenda stalled and the supercycle ended in 2015, productivity deteriorated and the REER depreciated, while Amazonian deforestation picked up again.

Land use impacts from a Brazilian growth model anchored in productivity

Brazil's national productivity agenda matters for Amazonian forests. Amazônia's economy is small compared to Brazil's, so what happens across the country has a large impact on Brazil's macroeconomic aggregates and thus also affects the Amazônia economy. Table 3.3 illustrates this point by only focusing on Brazilian productivity gains *outside* Amazônia (focusing here in the South and Southeast regions as the economic centers of the country).[15] The general equilibrium simulations show that this would not only raise GDP and consumption in Amazônia, as discussed earlier, but also lower Amazonian deforestation. This stands in stark contrast with a growth model catering to increasing external agricultural demand: the simulations suggest that an annual 0.5 percentage point productivity gain in the rest of Brazil over 12 years would raise Amazonian GDP by 0.5 percent and save 1.9 million hectares of Brazilian natural forests (0.8 million of which is in Amazônia), while an annual 0.5 percentage point increase in external agricultural demand over 12 years would raise Amazonian GDP by 0.8 percent while destroying another

TABLE 3.3 Cumulative sectoral impacts of annual 0.5 percentage point productivity gains on GDP, land rents, deforestation, and net GHG emissions over 12 years

SECTOR WITH 0.5 PP PRODUCTIVITY GAIN	GDP (%)	LAND RENTS (%)	AMAZÔNIA FORESTED LAND (HECTARES, MILLIONS)	AMAZÔNIA CARBON DIOXIDE (GIGAGRAMS)	ALL OF BRAZIL FORESTED LAND (HECTARES, MILLIONS)	ALL OF BRAZIL CARBON DIOXIDE (GIGAGRAMS)
Agricultural external demand	0.8	6.0	−0.4	13,049	−1.0	29,192
TFP Brazil South and Southeast	0.5	−40.6	0.8	−56,605	1.9	−90,420
TFP Brazil						
Agriculture	1.8	0.0	0.3	4,193	0.8	18,221
Manufacturing	3.9	−24.9	0.8	−33,486	1.9	−67,833
Mining	0.3	−1.2	0.1	−2,834	0.2	−650
Services	9.1	−10.5	−0.1	−6,637	−0.1	3,085
TFP Amazônia						
Agriculture	2.1	10.3	−0.5	32,282	−0.1	15,004
Manufacturing	3.8	−8.1	0.6	−16,310	0.4	−14,350
Mining	0.2	0.9	0.0	−693	0.0	−708
Services	9.8	−5.9	0.4	−14,211	0.2	−8,372

Source: Ferreira Filho and Hanusch 2022.
Note: Green shading indicates lower deforestation (higher forested land) and emissions, and red shading indicates higher amounts. Greenhouse gas (GHG) emissions are in carbon dioxide equivalents (CO_2e). Does not account for certain indirect effects, such as the potential impacts of more productive mines on infrastructure development and associated deforestation. pp = percentage points; TFP = total factor productivity.

1 million hectares of natural forests across Brazil (0.4 million of which is in Amazônia).

Increasing the productivity of non-land-intensive tradable sectors, like manufacturing, across Brazil would improve welfare and lower deforestation in Amazônia and the rest of the country.[16] Table 3.3 shows that higher productivity in manufacturing across all of Brazil's 27 states would also have large positive impacts on GDP and forest conservation. Figure 3.20 unpacks the modeled results, showing that the increase in national manufacturing TFP appreciates the Brazilian real in real terms as manufacturing prices fall relative to nontraded (services) prices and wages rise, improving welfare (figure 3.20). Yet higher wages also reduce the competitiveness of primary commodities. Global commodity prices fall in local currency terms. The net effect is less deforestation, both in Amazônia and in the rest of Brazil. Assuming that Amazonian deforestation continues at its five-year average (2016–20), the simulations for this memorandum suggest that a modest annual 0.5 percentage point increase in Brazilian manufacturing GDP would cause deforestation to fall by half by 2050 and stop entirely by 2078 (figure 3.21). Deforestation would stop even sooner with stronger TFP growth. This also has positive net effects on lowering Brazil's greenhouse gas emissions and protecting biodiversity (box 3.2).

Productivity gains in agriculture across Brazil could reduce deforestation, but the story is nuanced. Agricultural productivity reduces deforestation globally but can increase it locally. Box 3.3 lays out the mechanisms through which agricultural productivity affects incentives to convert natural land into productive land for agriculture. As table 3.3 suggests, the Borlaug effect (agricultural productivity reduces deforestation) would hold at the national level. The table also

FIGURE 3.20

Impacts from an increase in Brazilian manufacturing TFP are similar to those of the commodity supercycle

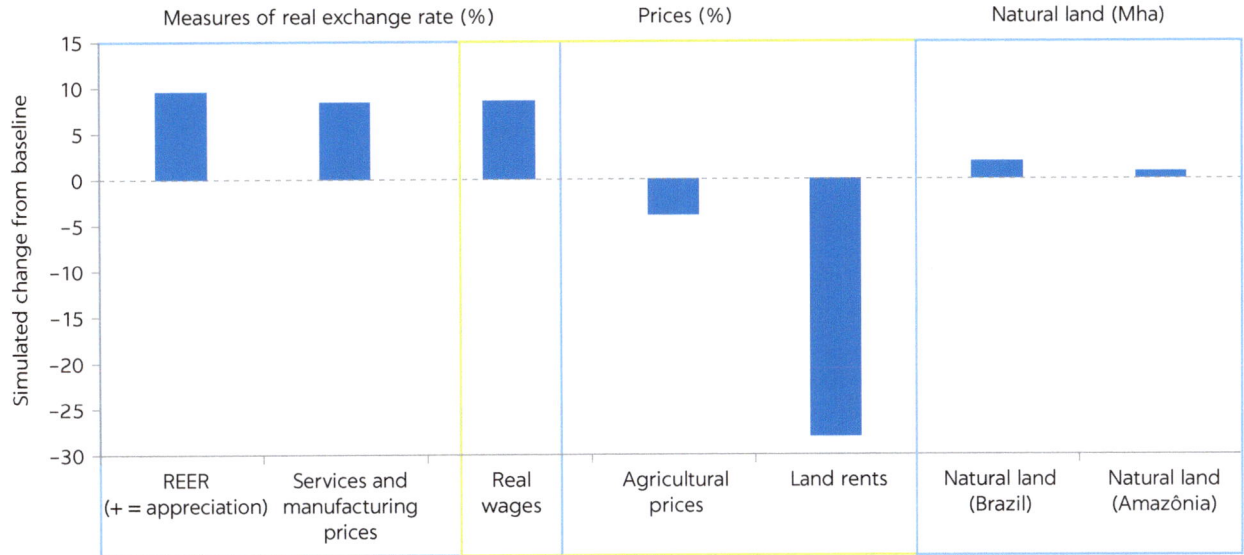

Source: Ferreira Filho and Hanusch 2022.
Note: The figure is a projection of the economy and land use into the future. It applies the Brazilian manufacturing total factor productivity (TFP) scenario from table 3.3. Mha = millions of hectares.

FIGURE 3.21

Simulated forest cover in Amazônia following an increase in Brazilian manufacturing TFP

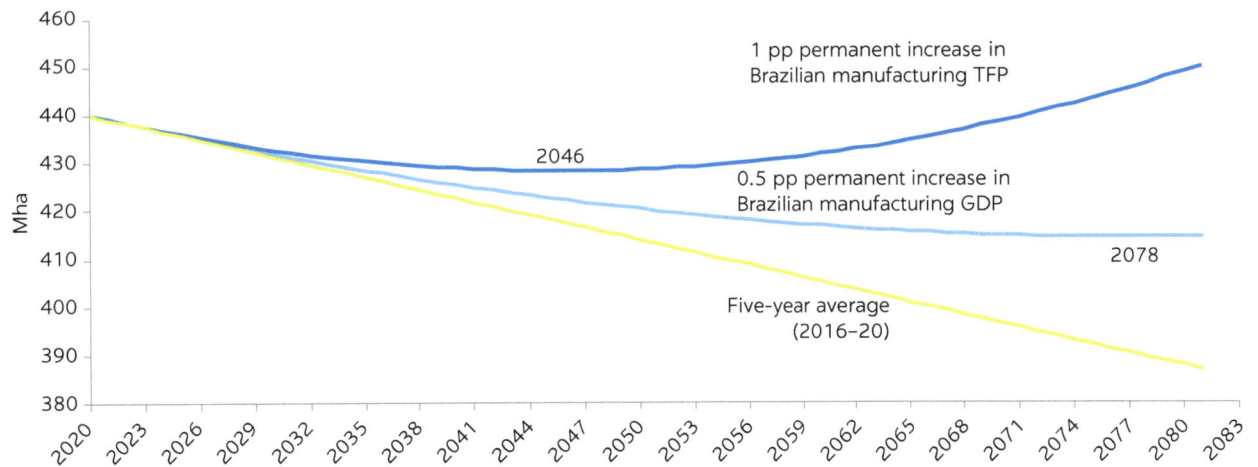

Source: World Bank, based on Ferreira Filho and Hanusch 2022.
Note: The simulation assumes the average deforestation rate of 2016–20 in the baseline. It applies the Brazilian manufacturing total factor productivity (TFP) scenario from table 3.3 and adds a scenario of 1 percentage point gain in manufacturing TFP. Mha = millions of hectares; pp = percentage points.

suggests that in Amazônia the Jevons effect would hold, where agricultural productivity gains lead to higher deforestation.[17] This is because productivity gains greater than the national average in Amazônia would give the region a relative advantage, taking some market share from the rest of Brazil, as further discussed below. The simulations suggest that productivity gains across the country would reduce deforestation for two reasons: First, a national increase in agricultural TFP would have a large impact on Brazil's REER, disproportionately driven by

BOX 3.2

Through its impact on deforestation, productivity can also lower greenhouse gas emissions and protect biodiversity

Land use changes and production structures affect greenhouse gas (GHG) emissions, and productivity affects both net emissions and the preservation of biodiversity. Productivity growth in manufacturing reduces GHG emissions the most, as lower net emissions from land use outweigh any acceleration in industrial emissions—which are relatively low in Brazil due to the country's reliance on green energy like hydropower. If Brazil were to permanently raise TFP in manufacturing by 0.5 percentage points per year, simulations suggest that the country could reduce total GHG emissions by 67,833 gigagrams of CO_2 equivalent relative to the baseline over 12 years (see table 3.3). At a carbon price of US$40 per ton of CO_2 discussed in chapter 1, this is equivalent to about US$10 billion.[a]

The calculation is more complex for the effects on biodiversity. At the conservative estimates of existence and option values for the Amazon biome alone, described in chapter 1, the 800,000 hectares of preserved forest would be valued at US$3.9 billion within 10 years.[b] Raising agricultural productivity at the national level would not reduce GHG emissions because lower deforestation would not be sufficient to offset the direct emissions associated with agricultural production (especially livestock production), though lower deforestation (see table 3.3) would preserve some biodiversity. Within Amazônia, however, higher agricultural productivity would likely increase deforestation and thus raise net GHG emissions while reducing biodiversity.

a. One ton of carbon holds 3.67 tons of CO_2; hence 68 million tons of carbon = 68 times 3.67 tons of CO_2. At a carbon price of US$40 per ton, the total value is about US$10 billion, given no discounting of future carbon saving benefit.
b. US$45 billion for the entire Amazon or US$4,286 of underlying value per hectare at a 3 percent discount.

BOX 3.3

The impact of agricultural productivity on deforestation—Jevons or Borlaug

The Jevons effect suggests that agricultural productivity would increase deforestation

Higher agricultural productivity may increase or reduce deforestation. In 1866, William Stanley Jevons found that improved technology in coal production would likely increase the use of coal—a counterintuitive finding, since greater efficiency was associated with lower input use—giving rise to the "Jevons paradox" in environmental economics. It suggests that more productive agriculture will increase the use of inputs, including land, giving rise to more deforestation: Higher productivity allows farmers to serve a larger market, increasing their demand for productive land.

The Borlaug effect suggests that agricultural productivity would reduce deforestation

Norman Borlaug suggested in 2002 that more productive farmers would meet the same demand with fewer inputs. There would then be no paradox because higher productivity would lead to lower input use, including land, thus also reducing deforestation.

The elasticity of agricultural demand strongly affects the relationship

Hertel (2012) reconciled this debate: If agricultural demand is inelastic, an increase in production would reduce prices, reducing agricultural output, and so inputs and production would increase only slightly.

continued

Box 3.3, *continued*

If demand is elastic, prices would be stable, and farmers would gain from producing more, using more land, and putting pressure on forests. Local markets tend to have more inelastic demand than global markets (chapter 5). So, the Jevons effect is more likely when farmers have access to international markets, leading to more deforestation. The closer Amazonian farmers are to roads, the more likely their productivity gains will result in deforestation (states of the Arc of Deforestation have a relatively high road density).

The elasticity of land supply is also important

If the price of land increases steeply with demand for land (supply is inelastic), intensifying the use of existing land is cheaper for farmers than acquiring new land. Increased agricultural productivity then leads to intensification of farming rather than forest conversion. Land supply tends to be more inelastic when land markets are consolidated. In Amazônia, as a frontier region with outstanding land regularization issues, the land supply is relatively elastic, suggesting that agricultural productivity gains in Amazônia are likely to increase deforestation.

There is currently no consensus on the extent to which the Jevons effect holds in Amazônia. Modeling for this memorandum suggests that it does hold.[a] At a minimum, it is a risk that policy makers need to be mindful of when fostering agricultural productivity in Amazônia: effective land and forest governance will render the land supply more inelastic and thus contain the Jevons effect.

Sources: Borlaug 2002; Hertel 2012; Jevons 1866.
a. Alternative findings on the strength of the Jevons effect in Brazil and Amazônia include Szerman et al. (2022) and Cattaneo (2005).

other parts of the country, given the small relative size of Amazônia. Second, the land supply in the rest of Brazil is more inelastic than in Amazônia, so deforestation pressures would be contained at the national level.[18]

Productivity gains across Brazilian service sectors can also reduce deforestation pressures, though the mechanism is more complex. At the national level, higher productivity in services overall does not reduce deforestation because most services are nontraded and thus have a lower direct impact on the real exchange rate (see table 3.3). In fact, a productivity gain in services may depreciate the real exchange rate because the associated income gain will boost import demand without a sizable offsetting increase in exports. There is significant diversity in services, however. They are often complements to traded sectors like manufacturing and can thus have indirect positive competitiveness effects. For example, isolating the impact for the transport sector alone shows that an overall increase in Brazilian transport service productivity would decrease deforestation by improving the external competitiveness of traded goods.[19] And some service are traded (like tourism or call centers), and the macroeconomic impacts of their productivity increases would reduce deforestation. The conclusion, then, is that productivity gains in non-land-intensive activities like manufacturing and some service sectors that tend to be concentrated in cities, have positive macroeconomic impacts on Brazil's forests.

Absent another boom in minerals and metals prices, the macroeconomic impacts of mining on deforestation are small—unless new mining infrastructure disrupts Amazonian landscapes. Mining, an important but relatively small sector in Brazil, would require very large productivity gains—or a surge in external demand as occurred during the last commodity supercycle—for the sector to have macroeconomic impacts on Brazil's agricultural competitiveness and land use. The infrastructure and human settlements associated with new mines, or the expansion of mines, is more likely than productivity gains in mining to have adverse impacts on the forest.

Overall, Brazil's global convergence would help raise incomes and conserve natural forests—yet further divergence would be a major threat to Amazonian natural forests.[20] Higher productivity will help Brazil catch up with more developed countries and table 3.3 suggests that this will help reduce deforestation pressures, especially if they are balanced across the country and across sectors. Given Brazil's historical productivity performance, especially relative to other countries, there is a significant risk of Brazil's global *divergence*. In this case, the results of this discussion would be inverted and pressure on Brazil's forests, including in Amazônia, would *increase*. This adds to the urgency to both reinvigorate Brazil's productivity agenda while doubling down on institutions to protect its natural forests.

Land use impacts from a productivity-led growth model for Amazônia—with a stronger urban leg

Slow and unbalanced structural transformation in Amazônia focused overly on agricultural productivity growth limits development potential and forest conservation. This chapter has shown that although structural transformation has been ongoing in Amazônia, it has been happening at different speeds and with significant imbalances, notably much more progress on productivity in agriculture than in manufacturing and services, which are generally associated with urban production. The simulations of table 3.3 suggest that in Amazônia the Jevons effect would hold. Figure 3.22 breaks down the simulation results of table 3.3 for Mato Grosso to show how boosting agricultural productivity there would increase deforestation in the state while reducing it in all other states of Amazônia. Chapter 5 traces in more detail how the development of agricultural markets on the Amazonian frontier is associated with social and environmental disruption, including deforestation.

Strengthening the urban leg of structural transformation, including manufacturing and services, can have a significant impact on forest preservation in Amazônia. Both nationally and in Amazônia, raising manufacturing TFP has the biggest sectoral impact on preserving Amazonian natural land and other natural lands in Brazil while reducing net GHG emissions (see table 3.3). In Amazônia, productivity gains in services would also on average reduce deforestation (figure 3.23). Both manufacturing and (advanced) services tend to be associated with urban growth.

Urban productivity growth would reduce pressure on rural land prices and thus incentives for deforestation, while potentially creating more conducive conditions for environmental protection. The relationship between urban productivity and deforestation is intuitive: land is not an important input to manufacturing production or services, and a TFP increase in these sectors will reduce the relative competitiveness of agriculture, a land-intensive sector. Accordingly, agricultural demand will decline overall, causing rural land prices to fall relative to the baseline, dampening incentives to clear land and speculative motives associated with *grilagem* (land grabbing). As urban incomes become an alternative to rural, land-intensive, production, opposition to designating areas for

FIGURE 3.22

Without more effective forest governance, boosting agricultural productivity in Mato Grosso could increase deforestation there—but reduce it in the rest of Amazônia

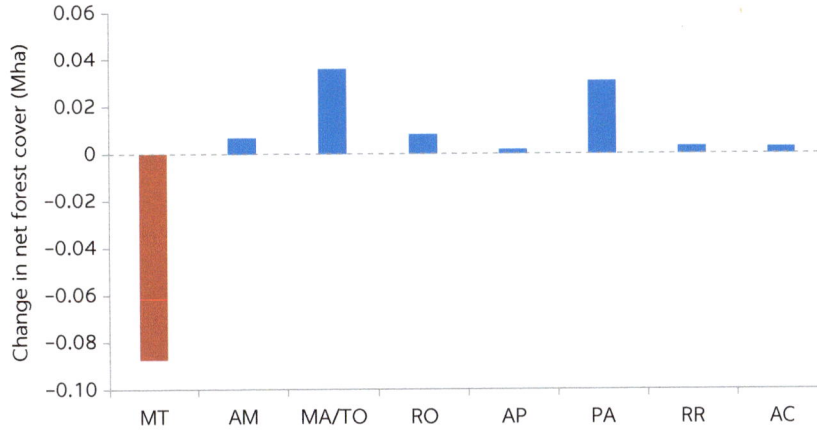

Source: World Bank, based on Ferreira Filho and Hanusch 2022.
Note: The figure shows the cumulative 12-year impacts of an annual 0.5 percentage point increase in agricultural total factor productivity (TFP) in Mato Grosso (red bar) on net forest cover in the nine states of Amazônia: Acre (AC), Amapá (AP), Amazonas (AM), Mato Grosso (MT), Pará (PA), Rondônia (RO), Roraima (RR), and Maranhão and Tocantins (MA/TO) (includes Piauí in the modeling, which is not part of Amazônia). Mha = millions of hectares.

FIGURE 3.23

Higher manufacturing and services productivity in Amazônia would reduce Amazonian deforestation

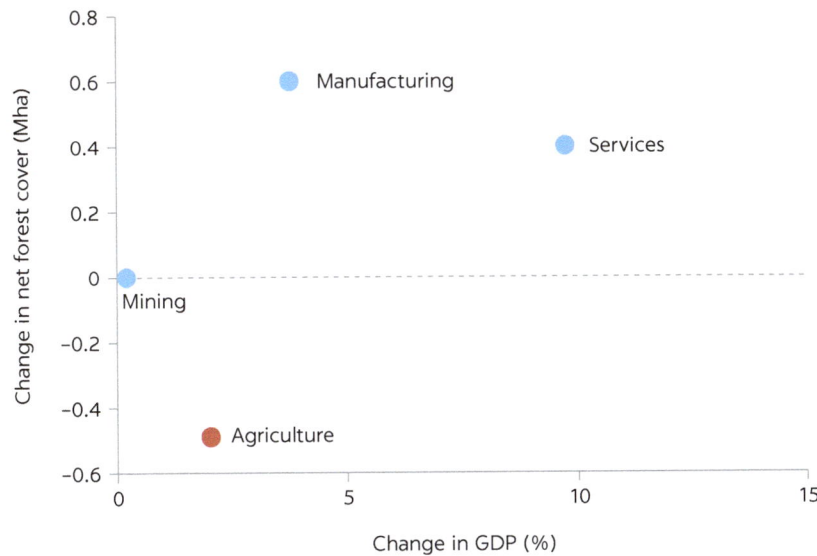

Source: World Bank.
Note: The figure is a representation of the values given in table 3.3. Mha = millions of hectares.

environmental preservation as protected areas or Indigenous lands could be expected to ease.

Sustainable development in Amazônia requires a growth model focused on more balanced urban and rural productivity growth. Structural transformation in less developed regions tends to be propelled by agricultural productivity growth. An exclusively urban focus is thus unrealistic. Worse, table 3.3 shows that it would reduce agricultural output in Amazônia, which could be picked up by other regions of the world where natural lands are also under pressure, merely displacing the deforestation. In addition, the reduction of the price of land relative to wages would boost incentives to use relatively more land, resulting in less agriculture overall but higher land intensity—land productivity would fall, and agriculture would become more extensive in relative terms.

A simultaneous increase in productivity in agriculture and manufacturing would, relative to business as usual, raise agricultural output and land productivity (resulting in the intensification of agriculture) and limit pressure on land rents (reducing incentives for *grilagem*) while maintaining more natural forests (see table 3.4). A growth model focused more on urban productivity is thus an important complement to agricultural productivity growth. It is a better fit for Amazônia than a model focused on extensive agriculture and will make the region more prosperous with lower loss of natural wealth.

To support Amazônia's structural transformation, the bioeconomy can be a further important complement (box 3.4). Chapter 4 will show how effective forest governance will need to accompany the structural transformation process to further minimize the loss of natural forest and intensify agriculture. Policy packages focusing on rural and urban productivity, sustainable rural livelihoods, and effective institutions are further discussed in chapter 7.

TABLE 3.4 Cumulative impacts of sectoral productivity increases on agricultural output, land productivity, land rents, wages, and deforestation in Amazônia over 12 years

| SECTOR | OUTPUT | | LAND PRODUCTIVITY | | LAND RENTS | | WAGES (RELATIVE TO ALL OF BRAZIL) (%) | FORESTED LAND IN AMAZÔNIA (Mha) |
	CATTLE (%)	SOY (%)	PASTURE (%)	CROPS (%)	PASTURE (%)	CROPS (%)		
Agriculture	8.87	9.73	8.15	8.07	11.62	12.56	1.70	−0.54
Manufacturing	−3.61	−3.06	−2.93	−2.59	−8.59	−9.29	5.11	0.54
Agriculture and manufacturing	4.95	6.53	5.00	5.35	1.89	2.30	6.89	0.02

Source: Ferreira Filho and Hanusch 2022.
Note: The table shows the impact of an annual 0.5 percentage point increase in total factor productivity, by sector, relative to the baseline in percent for all variables except forested land, which is expressed in millions of hectares (Mha). Deforestation is represented by a fall in forested land.

BOX 3.4

The macroeconomics of the bioeconomy

Fostering sustainable production can reduce deforestation by providing alternative rural livelihoods. Less productive, mostly smaller farmers can be a source of deforestation when they come under competitive pressures (chapter 5).[a] Structural transformation in rural areas implies that more productive farmers will crowd out unproductive farmers who, lacking alternative options, might engage in illegal deforestation—in addition to rising food demand, this could be one explanation for the deforestation observed in *assentamentos*. The ability to switch economic activities between sectors is important to reduce deforestation (Porcher and Hanusch 2022), but in practice, switching professions is difficult. It is easier, however, to transition between related disciplines. Promoting alternative sustainable income options in rural areas is an important complementary strategy to a broader strategy of facilitating structural transformation by preparing populations for urban jobs.

continued

Box 3.4, *continued*

A focus on the bioeconomy can help reduce deforestation, but there are also limitations. Amazônia may have an absolute advantage in bioeconomy products (but Amazônia also has a history of falling victim to "biopiracy," see chapter 1). Although creating alternative employment options linked to sustainable production can reduce deforestation, it is unlikely to affect macroeconomic pressures that lead to deforestation because it tends to be very small (see annex 3B for examples from açai and cocoa). There are also important global equity implications given poorer parts of the world. Amazônia will be competing with very poor countries, for example, West African producers in the case of cocoa.

Effective governance is critical to limit unintended consequences from rural supply chains, including the bioeconomy. Strong urban-rural links exist in sectors such as agribusiness, the bioeconomy, and others (for example, auto producers have been associated with inadvertently causing deforestation through their demand for leather). Porcher and Hanusch (2022) demonstrate that where manufacturing has pronounced agricultural (or bioeconomy) value chains, the higher competitiveness resulting from productivity gains increases demand for all inputs, including primary commodities. This raises demand for land and can fuel deforestation even if productivity gains occur in manufacturing, generally considered an urban sector. The net impact is ambiguous as higher manufacturing productivity tends to reduce deforestation while higher demand for rural commodities tends to increase it. Strong forest governance as well as effective sustainability measures across supply chains will be critical to avoid such unintended consequences.

a. They can be a source of deforestation through "subsistence" deforestation to increase pasture areas or by leasing land to large landowners.

AN ENABLING ENVIRONMENT FOR GROWTH AND REGIONAL CONVERGENCE

Leveling the playing field and strengthening endowments can help Amazônia close its productivity gaps and converge with the rest of Brazil. Its development requires federal interventions that will affect all states, such as opening Brazil to trade or reducing the national "Custo Brasil" along with state-specific interventions. Increasing connectivity and market access are critical for regional convergence but harbor risks for Amazônia's forests. Other important reform areas include a conducive business environment, adequate economic infrastructure, and institutions. Some of the policies that can support development in the Amazonian states are described below and in later chapters. A strong human capital foundation is critical, as is access to finance. These were already discussed in chapter 2.

Investment needs are high in a frontier region, since economic infrastructure still needs to be developed. Public investment in Amazonian states is higher, on average, than the nationwide average (relative to net current revenues), though there are large differences across states (see annex 3C). As this memorandum shows, significant investment needs remain, however, including in economic infrastructure (like electricity or digital connectivity) and social infrastructure (like water and sanitation). Where needs exceed the means, prioritization is critical. For example, evidence suggests that strengthening road connectivity across Brazil's urban hubs (especially along the coast) will yield higher welfare gains across the country, including Amazônia, than building new rural roads into Amazônia (Gorton and Ianchovichina 2021).

Increase connectivity and market access

Any economy needs logistics to thrive, but transport is a contentious issue in Amazônia's natural forests. Rural roads are particularly harmful to forests, as trunk roads lead to networks of smaller, sometimes informal roads and often pave the way for illegal logging (Soares-Filho et al. 2004). But in principle, any lowering of transport costs can cause deforestation by generating new market opportunities for extensive farming and logging (Bragança, Araújo, and Assunção 2020; Porcher and Hanusch 2022). This is why it is important to carefully consider where these investments are to be undertaken: lower transport costs tend to be less harmful to forests in more mature markets, where the supply of land is already more inelastic. Accordingly, logistics can be particularly harmful to forests in the least developed frontier regions of Amazônia (Weinhold and Reis 2008). To reduce the impact of transport infrastructure on ecosystems, it is important to package them with other interventions, including strong environmental protection policies (as discussed in the next chapter) and investments in urban productivity (as discussed in this chapter, chapter 6, and World Bank 2023b).

Waterways and rail are likely to cause less immediate deforestation than rural roads, and because they connect many cities especially in the Amazon biome, they are consistent with the call for a greater economic role for urban areas. Chapter 1 has shown how deforestation tends to be much more prevalent in the New Frontier, which developed around roads. Waterways, along which the Colonial Frontier developed, are much less associated with deforestation, on the other hand. The Amazon is the world's largest basin, making water transport a cost-competitive alternative to rural roads for cargo (see annex 3A) in the Colonial Frontier (although water transport can still be disruptive to river biodiversity). For areas that are not as easily accessible by water, rail may be a better alternative than roads. One reason why both modes of transport are associated with lower deforestation than roads is because they have fewer stops (thus making it more difficult to deforest along the way) and have better and more centralized systems for monitoring cargo. Air transport has perhaps the lowest impact on deforestation and is the preferred mode of transport for individuals and fresh produce, though it is associated with high GHG emissions (this may change as cleaner jet fuels are developed).

Enabling migration across Brazil is important to support structural transformation, regional convergence, and forest conservation (box 3.5). Transport costs are one factor impacting migration, highlighting that the transportation sector does not only matter for freight but for passenger travel, too.

Improve the business environment

Reducing the Custo Brasil is critical but has been politically challenging as governments have used various policy tools to compensate firms. High costs result from multiple impediments to doing business, including inefficient financial markets, complex and burdensome tax and administrative rules, and operating in a context where regulations change frequently. These costs reduce the competitiveness of firms, weaken incentives to innovate, and favor rent-seeking behavior. Government attempts to compensate firms for the high costs, through interventions in product and input markets, have generated more misallocations of resources (as in the Zona Franca de Manaus) and may even have reduced competition. Governments have introduced high import barriers, local content

BOX 3.5

Migration, welfare, and forests

Migration is important to unlock the gains from productivity. Amazônia need not necessarily attract workers to become richer. Table B3.5.1 illustrates this for Mato Grosso, as Amazônia's leading agricultural exporter, and for Amazonas as its main manufacturer. It shows that both states will raise their gross domestic product (GDP) and attract labor when Amazônia experiences productivity gains. However, states do not require larger populations to develop: GDP increases in table B3.5.1 along *out*-migration in Amazonas under scenarios focused on higher external agricultural demand and total factor productivity (TFP) in other parts of Brazil. Mato Grosso experiences in-migration when benefiting from higher agricultural demand but, similarly, out-migration when productivity rises in the rest of Brazil. Making Amazonians better off requires allowing them to migrate to where the opportunities are—and higher human capital will broaden opportunities (chapter 2).

Skills and migration matter for Amazônia's sustainable and inclusive development. Schools must prepare future workers for the right jobs—most of these will be urban, so even rural populations should be prepared for urban jobs. Farmers who come under economic pressures without having alternative employment options have incentives to maintain their purchasing power by illegally infringing on the forest (Porcher and Hanusch 2022).

In urban areas, skills are needed to drive urban productivity growth, and this will require some skilled in-migration. Although in-migration would increase the population in towns and cities, it would not necessarily cause greater deforestation if productivity gains from migration are sizable, urban sprawl is controlled, and transport costs are low enough to service some additional urban agricultural demand from elsewhere (Porcher and Hanusch 2022). While creating skills in Amazônia is important, raising education levels across the whole country is essential to reduce incentives for unemployed and unskilled Brazilians from other parts of the country to migrate to Amazônia to seek opportunities in rural areas—for example, linked to *grilagem* (land grabbing) or *garimpo* (wildcat mining)—that could result in deforestation and conflict (Porcher and Hanusch 2022). Rather, skills raising productivity across Brazil would also raise welfare and lower deforestation in Amazônia.

TABLE B3.5.1 Cumulative impacts of an annual 0.5 percentage point increase in TFP and external agricultural demand over 12 years

SIMULATION	AMAZONAS	MATO GROSSO
TFP increase in Amazônia		
GDP (%)	19.31	14.88
Migration (%)	56.27	34.10
Increase in agricultural demand		
GDP (%)	0.37	0.80
Migration (%)	−3.98	7.75
TFP increase in south and southeast Brazil		
GDP (%)	0.56	−0.47
Migration (%)	−5.61	−43.79

Source: World Bank, based on Ferreira Filho and Hanusch 2022.
Note: GDP = gross domestic product; TFP = total factor productivity.

requirements, differential tax rates and tax exemptions, credit subsidies, and other measures to benefit specific industries, regions, and often particular firms (Dutz 2018).

Regulations for conducting business are a large component of Custo Brasil, and differences in regulations across states in Amazônia point to opportunities to boost productivity growth. A subnational Doing Business study for Brazil found examples of best performance in states at all income levels, sizes, and regions. Amazônia scores close to the Brazilian average, but with important variations across states (see annex 3A). For example, over the five indicators studied, the average scores for Roraima and Tocantins are above the Brazilian average (Roraima ranks second only to São Paulo). In addition, while richer states in the Southeast region perform on average above the mean, good performers can also be found in Amazônia. For example, it is easiest to start a business in Pará, thanks to the successful local implementation of Redesim, a national initiative to integrate and digitalize business registration. Similarly, Roraima is the best state to obtain construction permits in a timely manner (an average of 179.5 days). But the region also has some of the worst performers: Acre and Amapá rank in the lowest decile for registering property, and Maranhão is at the bottom of the distribution for dealing with construction permits. Although some Amazonian states are the best performers on some indicators, they are bad performers on others—sometimes even the worst. For example, while it is easy to start a business in Pará, it is the most challenging state for paying taxes because of the large number of payments required and the time it takes to comply. Improving the regulatory environment in Amazônia will be critical for productivity.

Make energy more efficient and reliable

The states in Amazônia are dependent on inefficient, unreliable, and often polluting sources of energy. While hydropower, which has a low carbon footprint, is the main source of power nationally, inefficient, greenhouse gas–emitting thermal plants are the main source of power for some Amazonian states (Vagliasindi 2022). Electricity is distributed through a combination of grid-connected and isolated systems, and gaps in access are common. Utilities are characterized by high losses, poor management, and a lack of commercial discipline, all exacerbated by political interference from local authorities.

Access to electricity is low, and quality and reliability create challenges for many firms. Despite good progress under the Luz para Todos (Lights for All) program, the goal of providing electricity access to the entire population has not been achieved, and the program has been extended until 2022 (see annex 3A). The poor quality of electricity services affects both households and firms and is a drag on the productivity of firms (see annex 3A). A World Bank Enterprise Survey in 2009, asking firms to quantify the cost of sales forgone because of power outages, found losses of about 5 percent of sales for Amazonas, considerably higher than the national average of 3 percent. After discounting the value of the losses among all enterprises that reported power outages, the percentage declined to around 1.2 percent, still twice the national average, but after discounting the losses among all firms surveyed, Amazonas's loss is below the national average. However, these are likely underestimations that do not take into account firms' coping mechanisms to maintain an uninterrupted power supply, such as owning their own generator. The enterprise survey found that about 18 percent of firms in Amazonas own a generator, one of the highest percentages in Brazil. Productivity losses from inadequate electricity are estimated to be high.[21]

Strengthen institutions

Stronger institutions are critical to support Amazônia's regional convergence. Institutions are discussed across this memorandum. They are fundamental to improve human capital and basic infrastructure (chapter 2), both of which are important to generate productivity and enable structural transformation. They are also required for high-quality, well-prioritized public investments in economic infrastructure. They are needed to enforce contracts and to guarantee the safety of people and properties—but law enforcement is a challenge in Amazônia, with adverse impacts for people, firms, and forests. The next chapter looks more closely at institutions, with a particular focus on institutions focused on forest conservation (see the annex of chapter 4 for a broader look at institutions in Amazônia).

CONCLUSIONS AND POLICY IMPLICATIONS

To reach higher levels of development, Brazil must transition from a model based on factor accumulation and natural resource extraction to a productivity-led model, including higher productivity in urban sectors. Agriculture, one of Brazil's few competitive sectors, is too small to raise income per capita in the future, and the shifting agricultural frontier, a reflection of the current growth model, is causing large-scale deforestation. Boosting productivity growth beyond agriculture, in manufacturing and services, calls for accelerating Brazil's broader productivity agenda to make the country more competitive and generate economic growth and demand for labor, thus helping create good jobs (chapter 2). This includes reducing Custo Brasil and fostering competition. One way of achieving this is by opening markets to greater foreign competition, attracting foreign direct investment into services and slowly reducing tariffs to expose Brazil's heavily protected manufacturing sectors more to external competitors (World Bank 2023a).

A productivity-led growth model for Brazil would also benefit Amazônia. Low growth across Brazil, especially in the most developed parts of the country, also reduces growth prospects in lagging regions and impedes their structural transformation.

In Amazônia, many cross-cutting policies are needed, from human capital to access to finance, a regulatory environment conducive to doing business, reliable and affordable energy, and a strong rule of law. As a remote region, Amazônia will also require better connectivity, yet transport infrastructure needs to be carefully designed to avoid impacts on the region's ecosystems. Except perhaps for aviation, this holds for all modes of transport, in particular however for rural roads.

Faster but more balanced structural transformation would enable Amazônia to catch up with the rest of the country, and this and the next chapter show that this can occur with lower pressures on the region's natural forests. Lagging areas, with large gaps in labor productivity, have substantial potential for growth.

In Amazônia that potential could be realized by focusing more on productivity in the urban sectors of manufacturing and advanced services, where productivity gains are driven by agglomeration, network effects, and specialization, among others (see chapter 6 and World Bank 2023b). Urban areas are more likely than rural areas to attract people with the critical skills needed for competitive manufacturing and high-productivity services and are also more likely to generate higher-level skills. The current heavy policy emphasis on developing rural production to the relative neglect of urban productivity may be contributing to premature deindustrialization and accelerating deforestation.

This does not diminish the need for agricultural productivity gains in Amazônia but calls for a rebalancing to add a stronger complementary focus on urban productivity, coupled with strong institutions for forest protection (see next chapter)—different policy measures are complementary, as further elaborated in chapter 7. Annex 3C provides some implications from this chapter for sustainable private investment in Amazônia.

ANNEX 3A: SELECTED INDICATORS OF AMAZÔNIA'S BUSINESS ENVIRONMENT

Trade tariffs

Brazil's average trade tariffs outstrip its peers and high-income countries

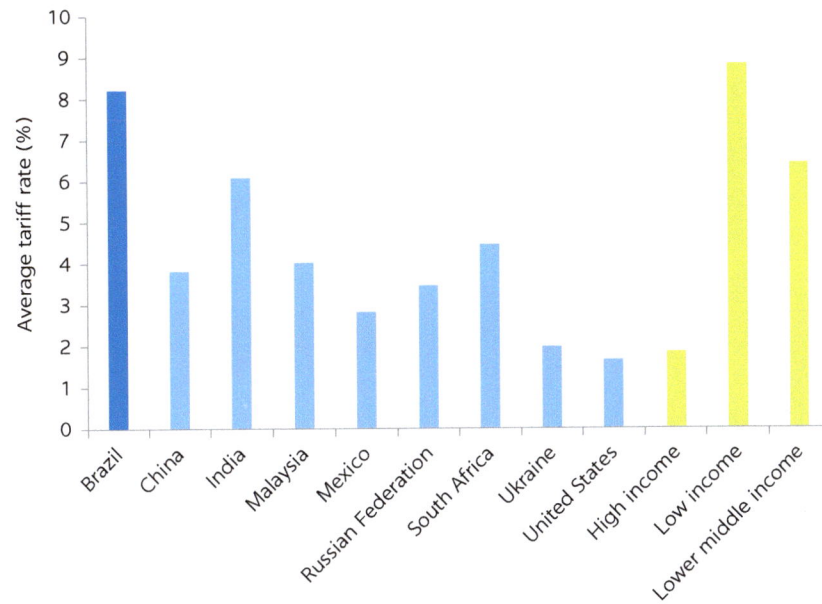

Source: World Development Indicators Database.

Public investment

FIGURE 3A.2

Public investment in most Amazonian states is above the national average

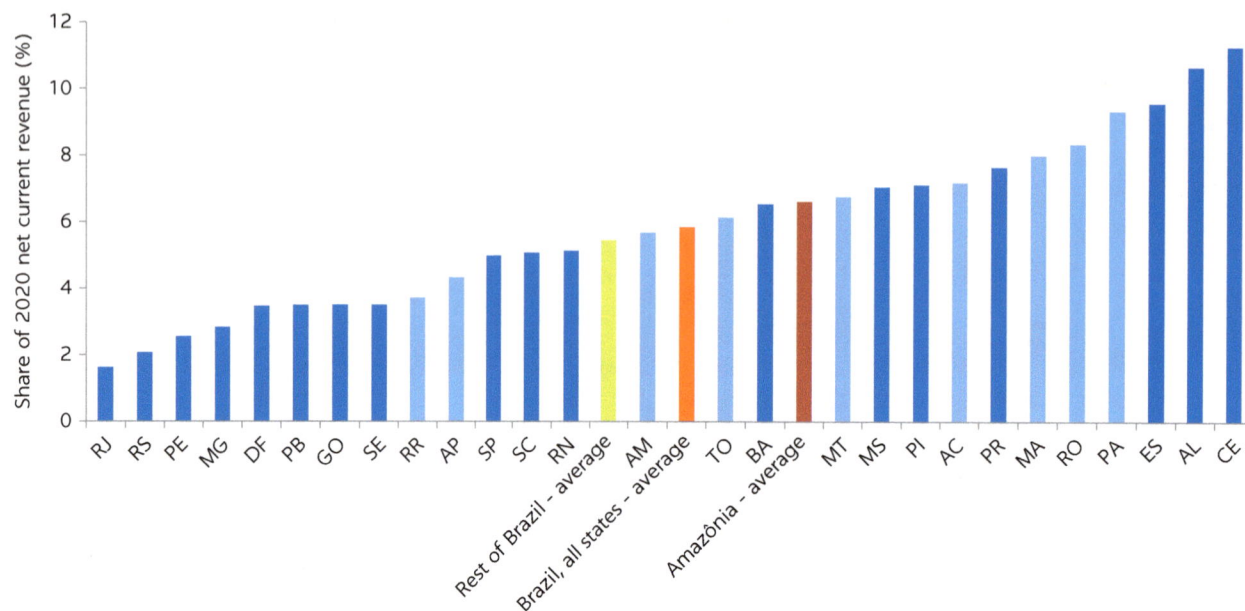

Source: Federal Treasury.
Note: The figure shows the level of public investment in each Brazilian state, as a percentage of net current revenues in 2020. "Amazônia" (red bar) comprises nine Brazilian states: Acre (AC), Amapá (AP), Amazonas (AM), Maranhão (MA), Mato Grosso (MT), Pará (PA), Rondônia (RO), Roraima (RR), and Tocantins (TO). Light blue bars designate the individual Amazônian states. "Brazil, all states" (orange bar) includes all Brazilian states. "Rest of Brazil" (green bar) includes all Brazilian states except those in Amazônia.

Regulatory environment

TABLE 3A.1 Subnational Doing Business indicators, ranking by Amazonian state

Ranking among 27 Brazilian states

STATE	COST OF STARTING A BUSINESS	CONSTRUCTION PERMITS	REGISTERING PROPERTY	PAYING TAXES	ENFORCING CONTRACTS
Acre	24	11	25	22	6
Amapá	19	21	27	5	13
Amazonas	18	14	8	7	15
Maranhão	5	27	20	10	7
Mato Grosso	21	17	16	16	14
Pará	1	24	9	27	24
Rondônia	10	23	17	2	4
Roraima	25	1	10	18	5
Tocantins	23	5	13	15	9

Source: World Bank 2021.
Note: Red shading indicates performance in the lowest decile and green shading, performance in the highest decile.

Electricity

FIGURE 3A.3

Electrification rates are low in some states of Amazônia

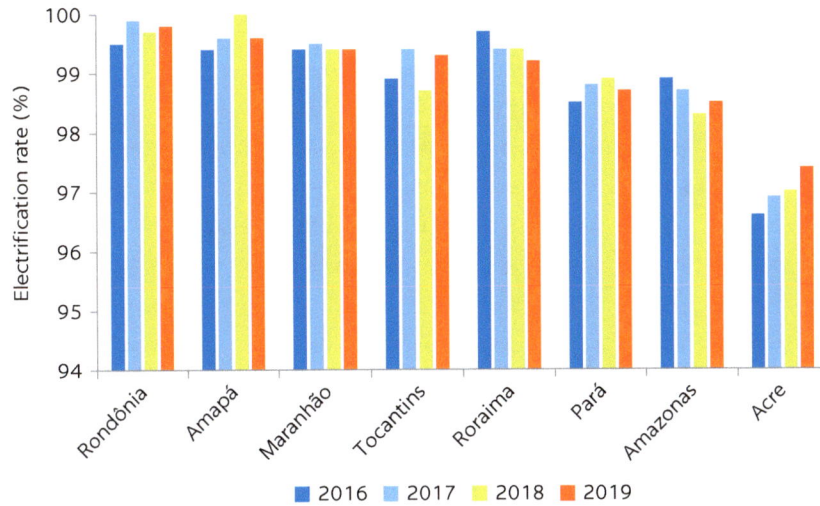

Source: Luz Para Todos ("Light for All") program, federal government of Brazil.

MAP 3A.1

Power outages drag down the productivity of firms

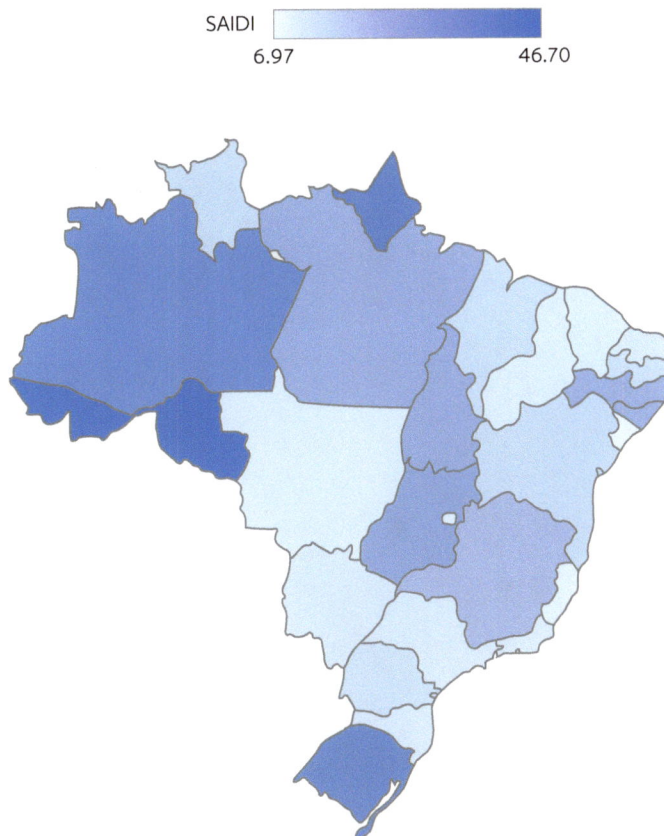

Source: Vagliasindi 2022.
Note: SAIDI = average duration of system interruptions (minutes).

Transport

TABLE 3A.2 Transport costs, by mode of transportation for Amazonian states

Freight + insurance + other costs as a percentage of product value

STATE	ALL MODES		WATER		ROAD		PLANE		RAIL		MULTIMODAL	
	OUT	IN	OUT	IN	OUT	IN	OUT	IN	OUT	IN	OUT	IN
Acre	8.76	8.65	12.68	9.77	8.69	8.58	3.94	17.72	—	—	—	17.10
Amapá	4.75	8.24	2.29	4.77	9.07	8.68	14.39	14.51	—	0.54	—	24.10
Amazonas	8.30	8.93	2.14	6.21	8.90	9.08	9.27	14.53	—	0.32	4.26	10.54
Maranhão	9.28	9.47	7.47	8.33	9.31	9.43	5.58	17.86	6.58	25.72	—	16.08
Mato Grosso	10.11	9.19	—	1.67	10.12	9.19	31.11	15.28	19.67	10.86	25.64	20.47
Pará	8.47	9.85	5.17	15.70	8.60	9.96	10.10	16.39	—	1.71	5.34	18.14
Rondônia	5.32	8.32	3.41	14.10	5.70	8.29	8.14	19.77	—	—	1.04	27.01
Roraima	5.89	6.25	—	3.42	5.92	6.13	7.78	15.93	—	0.55	—	11.52
Tocantins	6.91	7.74	—	3.96	6.97	7.73	9.88	15.45	5.56	5.60	—	10.59
Rest of Brazil	7.96	7.91	6.92	4.90	8.00	7.97	13.78	13.55	3.17	3.15	10.93	10.33
Brazil	8.07		5.62		8.07		13.69		4.07		10.82	

Source: Electronic bill of lading data, Arquivei.
Note: — = not available.

Brazilian comparative productivity performance

FIGURE 3A.4

Brazil's labor productivity industry and services has barely moved between 1994 and 2018

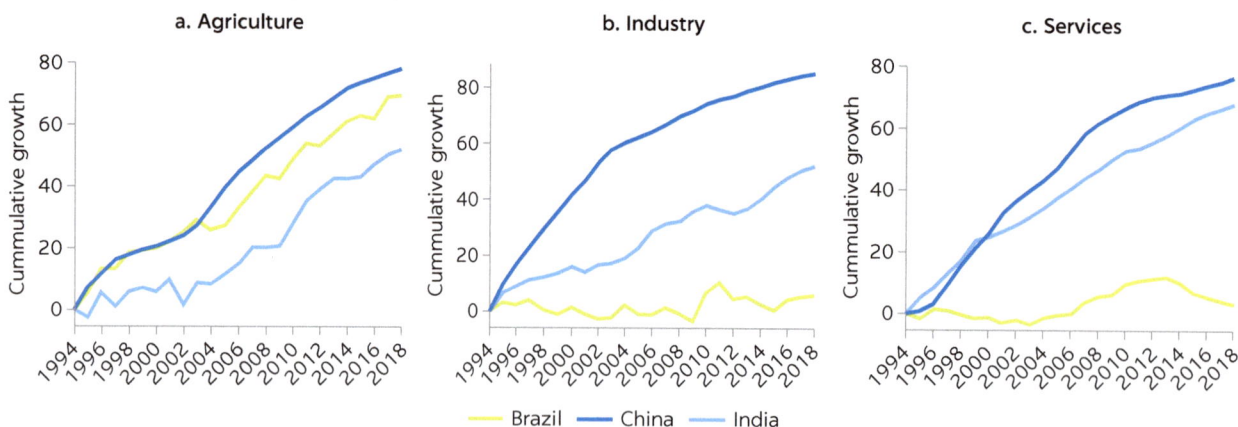

Source: World Bank.
Note: Cumulative index, 1994 = 0.

Amazonian sectoral structure of employment

TABLE 3A.3 Sectoral shares of employment in Amazonian states, 2012 and 2018

Share of total employment (%)

STATE	AGRICULTURE		INDUSTRY		MANUFACTURING		SERVICES	
	2012	2018	2012	2018	2012	2018	2012	2018
Acre	18	13	15	15	4	5	67	72
Amapá	9	7	18	13	4	2	73	80
Amazonas	19	17	21	17	8	6	60	67
Maranhão	29	17	16	14	3	3	55	69
Mato Grosso	17	17	19	18	7	7	64	65
Pará	19	15	21	19	7	7	60	65
Rondônia	24	23	19	15	6	5	57	62
Roraima	10	8	16	14	4	3	73	78
Tocantins	18	15	17	14	5	3	64	72
Amazônia	18	15	20	17	5	4	64	68

Source: World Bank, using Brazilian Institute of Geography and Statistics (IBGE) data.
Note: "Industry" sector includes manufacturing, mining, construction, and utilities.

ANNEX 3B: AÇAI AND COCOA IN AMAZÔNIA: CONSERVATION AND GLOBAL EQUITY

Cocoa and açai are sought-after commodities. Cocoa is native to Latin America, including to areas in Brazil such as parts of Amazônia. During the European conquest of Latin America, "chocolate mania" spread across Europe from the 1500s onward, and plantations emerged in Brazil. Colonists also brought cocoa from Latin America to West Africa. Today, cocoa is an important export product of Ghana and Côte d'Ivoire, even though the bulk of value addition and chocolate production is in Europe and other high-income countries. Açai is also a native Amazon fruit, and "açai mania" has recently been sweeping parts of the United States and Europe, mostly in lightly processed forms in powders, drinks, and sorbets.

Both fruits are popularly considered to play a role in conserving Amazonian forests (especially the Amazon), but significant market demand may be met by monocultures. Because açai already grows in the wild in the Amazon, accelerating Brazilian and international demand is considered an opportunity for selected rural communities to improve their incomes using sustainable (extractivist) methods. But in view of increasing demand, large commercial açai producers have entered the market, planting açai as a monoculture, especially in states like Pará, with lower biodiversity value than extractivism.

Commercial cocoa production is currently limited in Amazônia, but there is increasing interest by multinationals to diversify their sources of cocoa beans, mainly instigated by environmental concerns such as climate change (and its impact on growing conditions in cocoa-growing areas in West Africa) as well as social concerns such as child labor, also linked to West African supplies. From a biophysical point of view, cocoa is considered suitable for sustainable production in integrated landscapes. However, the agricultural transformation process in Amazônia is likely to first move toward crop specialization and monocultures (also see chapter 5). Demand for products processed from sustainably produced cocoa remains limited to small niche markets. While there is room for some production catering to these markets, it is unlikely to have a large impact on shaping Amazonian landscapes.

Forest product outputs are too small to outcompete less sustainable production systems at the macro level. Resolving a land-based problem (deforestation) linked to a land-based activity (agriculture) with a land-based solution (more sustainable production) may appear intuitively attractive, but it is not straightforward. First, the economic importance of cocoa and açai is relatively small in Brazil and in Amazônia, accounting for 0.6 percent (cocoa) and 1.6 percent (açai) of Amazônia's agricultural GDP. Since both crops are also too small to appear in official input–output matrices, table 3B.1 shows the effects of an annual 0.5 percentage point increase in TFP for forest products (including rubber, Brazil nuts, cocoa, açai, and timber). The economic intuition is comparable to that of the earlier discussion of intersectoral dynamics in this chapter: an increase in TFP for forest products results in a competitiveness boost that leaves other products relatively less competitive, including soybean and cattle. Accordingly, the amount of land under pastures and crops decreases, as does deforestation (table 3B.1). There are, however, some important limitations to these results.

TABLE 3B.1 Cumulative impacts of annual 0.5 percentage point increase in TFP in manufacturing and forest products in Amazônia over 12 years

	LAND AREA (Mha)				LAND RENT (%)	WELFARE (%)
SECTOR	**NATIVE FOREST**	**AGROFORESTRY**	**PASTURE**	**CROPS**		
Manufacturing	0.500	−0.003	−0.46	−0.075	−8.1	5.8
Forest products	0.007	0.012	−0.01	−0.005	0.6	0.1

Source: World Bank, based on Ferreira-Filho and Hanusch 2022.
Note: The estimates assume a 0.5 percentage point permanent increase in sectoral total factor productivity (TFP) relative to the baseline. Mha = millions of hectares.

The small size of markets for forest products means that their macroeconomic impact is negligible barring outsized growth. In addition, expansion of any agricultural commodity will raise both the value added of land and competition for land, leading to higher land rents, which can stimulate *grilagem.*

Important global equity considerations need to be weighed against the limited potential of forest products to stem large-scale deforestation in Amazônia. The market for agroforestry products is small. For example, the world cocoa bean market has a value of about US$8 billion a year compared with US$56 billion for soybeans. Even a large increase in Brazilian output would be too small for aggregate effects across the broader domestic economy, but if large enough relative to the world cocoa market, such an increase could reduce prices in the world market. That would crowd out less productive producers in Brazil (including extractivist producers, unless they cater to niche markets) and in African countries, notably Côte d'Ivoire and Ghana or Cameroon, countries that are much poorer than Brazil (figure 3B.1). More than half of Ivorian producers are estimated to be living below the poverty line already (World Bank 2019). The global and local net impact on employment is likely to be negative as any large-scale expansion of cocoa production in Brazil is likely to be much more capital intensive than in West Africa, although higher labor productivity associated with greater capital intensity would likely raise wages of those employed in the sector.

Chapter 5 shows how the rural bioeconomy can help reduce deforestation by providing alternative, more sustainable, livelihoods for less productive farmers—in other words, not by altering macroeconomic forces but by overcoming frictions in the transition across jobs. This will not require outsized gains in bioeconomy production.

Beyond this, and recognizing remaining risks, graduating from merely producing primary products to processing them could result in lower pressures on deforestation. For example, Ivorian cocoa shows how processing primary commodities generates much more value than producing the raw commodity itself (figure 3B.2). For Brazil, this highlights the potential role of agribusiness and the urban bioeconomy (which tends to be more focused on processing). Brazil already has many capabilities further down the value chain, consistent with its upper-middle-income level, which it could further build on. However, it is important to bear in mind that rural value chains in manufacturing will generate demand for land, which can fuel deforestation (Porcher and Hanusch 2022).

FIGURE 3B.1

Brazil's share of global cocoa exports is minuscule

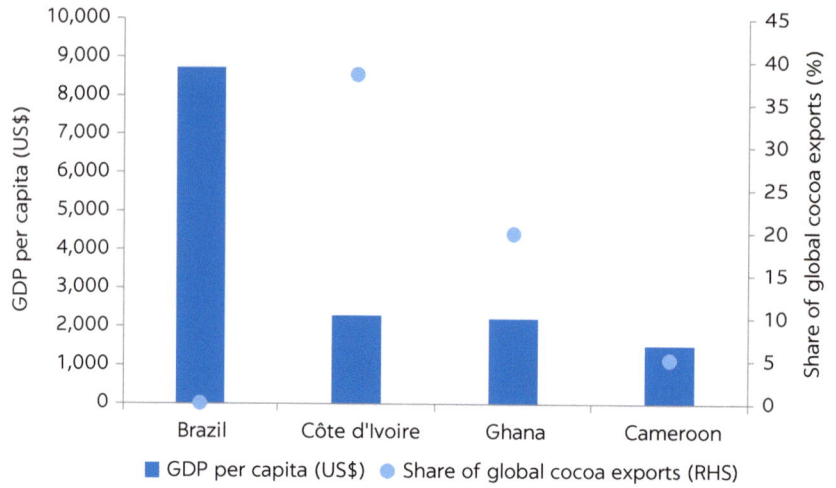

Sources: World Bank, using the World Development Indicators Database and Harvard University's Atlas of Economic Complexity data (https://atlas.cid.harvard.edu/).

FIGURE 3B.2

Cocoa producers in Côte d'Ivoire get a small share of the total value added

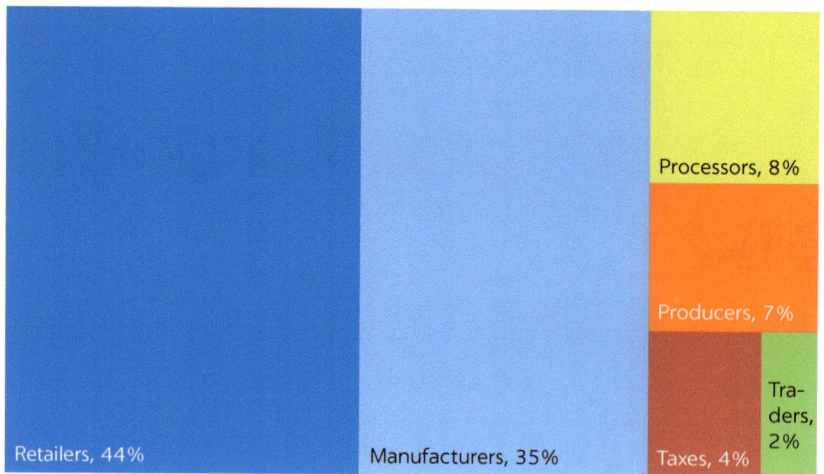

Source: World Bank 2019.

ANNEX 3C: SUSTAINABLE DEVELOPMENT IN AMAZÔNIA: SOME IMPLICATIONS FOR INVESTORS

A coherent investment strategy in Amazônia should seek additionality of investment in multiple sectors to reduce deforestation pressures. It can do this by carefully focusing on productivity gains and the consolidation of sustainable supply chains in each industry. A portfolio approach is important for a climate change strategy, where projects in multiple sectors across Brazil are to be financed with a clear linkage to the impact of those projects on land use change. Investments in productivity will diversify the economy into higher value-added sectors and away from extensive agriculture, reducing deforestation. This should be complemented by other sustainable activities, such as nature-based solutions and climate smart techniques (World Bank 2016). Sovereign environmental, social, and governance (ESG) indicators can serve as a possible reference to guide such a portfolio approach on the national level. In addition to environmental sustainability, they can include poverty rates, government effectiveness, and access to electricity and education.

Some activities may have small aggregate economic impacts while still being important for rural communities. Extractivism, for example, has limited productivity potential but important links with poverty reduction and cultural diversity. It does not cause deforestation—yet it is also too small to reduce broader deforestation pressures markedly. Conservation promotes sustainable land use, yet this memorandum has shown that promoting sustainable production may still cause deforestation, indirectly, by raising the demand for land which can fuel *grilagem* (land grabbing). Weighing economic and environmental impacts, extensive agriculture is at the other extreme. Sectors like soy and cattle, which tend to be associated with extensive production, have more sizable growth potential, and since they are relatively labor-intensive, they could also reduce poverty. But they have also been causing large-scale deforestation. This memorandum suggests that Amazônia should move from a growth model focused on extensive agriculture to one based more on urban productivity, with the bioeconomy, despite the risks, an important sector for rural livelihoods and longer-term transitions implicit in structural transformation. It also sheds light on important linkages between sectors, where productivity gains in the processing industry may have indirect impacts on land use through agricultural value chains.

Investing in innovation is critical to raise productivity. Investments in research and development (R&D) will have a large impact on longer-term growth and poverty reduction. Brazil has considerable strength in agricultural research (notably through Embrapa). To help diversify the economy and reduce macroeconomic pressures on natural forests, effective R&D will also be needed in sectors beyond agriculture. Investments in infrastructure and the financial sector can support productivity, while the financial sector also has a critical role in providing resources for sustainable production and the protection against risks. Yet by fostering production they can also generate demand for more land and raise pressures on forests.

Table 3C.1 summarizes some of the insights for individual sectors from across this memorandum that could support decisions about sustainable private investments into Amazônia with a focus on potential direct and indirect impacts on deforestation.

TABLE 3C.1 Some pointers for sustainable private investment in Amazônia, by sector

SECTOR	ROLE	IMPACT	RISKS
Agriculture			
Annual crops and livestock	Encourage intensification of production: integrated landscapes (crop-livestock or ideally crop-livestock-forestry), mixtures of improved grasses with nitrogen-fixing legume species, and so on	Increase output of existing agricultural land (land productivity), thus reducing pressure to convert natural lands	If supported by concessional credit, incentives to expand production could partly offset intensification incentives
Crops	Encourage crop integration	Increase integration of different crops, increasing soil coverage, and growing in each other's shade	Potential slippery slope into monocultures with lower carbon and biodiversity benefits when support ends
Agribusiness	Raise the productivity of agribusiness	Raising TFP in manufacturing reduces the competitiveness of land-intensive sectors, reducing deforestation	Resulting input demand in agribusiness will increase agricultural demand, which can offset the forest-saving effects from productivity
Forestry			
Extractivist nontimber forest products	Encourage aggregation and product differentiation: Help generate scale (as through cooperatives) and help tap niche markets through niche product labels	Extractivist production is highly sustainable, but producers are small with limited market access. Aggregation and access to processing would allow them to cater to niche value chains	Growth constrained by size of the niche market. If price premia are not sufficient to guarantee profitability, risk of slipping into less sustainable production
Timber products and sustainable forestry	Encourage legal logging through forest concessions and certified planted forests	Forest management through selective harvesting of trees can generate income while maintaining remaining biodiversity	Competition from illegal logging is likely to make this sector uncompetitive until deforestation pressures are contained
Manufacturing and trade			
Other manufacturing and trade services (not sourcing from primary value chains)	Raise the productivity of manufacturing and trade services	Raising TFP in manufacturing reduces the competitiveness of land-intensive sectors, reducing deforestation	Low deforestation risks but other potential environmental risks, such as pollution
Infrastructure			
Network services like electricity, green buildings, and municipal services	Raise the productivity of urban areas, manufacturing, and services	Better infrastructure and connectivity will also raise the competitiveness of manufacturing and services in cities	To the extent that this infrastructure also raises the productivity of agriculture, could increase localized deforestation
Transport and logistics	Raise the productivity of urban areas, manufacturing, and services	Can help mature agricultural areas become more competitive, without the need to expand agriculture and livestock at the frontier	Generating market access in less mature rural markets can generate deforestation

continued

TABLE 3C.1, *continued*

SECTOR	ROLE	IMPACT	RISKS
Finance			
Micro, small, and medium enterprises (MSMEs)	Increase investment and productivity of MSMEs	By reducing the MSME financing gap, the financial sector fosters innovation (productivity) and sustainable supply chains in cities (including the bioeconomy); insurance is also key to protect against shocks	Deforestation risks if supported MSMEs or their ecosystems operate in primary value chains
Rural credit	Enhancing economic and environmental performance of farmers	Rural credit can support farmers while enhancing the tracking of environmental performance variables and link financing to environmental compliance. It can also help unproductive farmers switch into alternative and sustainable methods, and it can finance climate risk insurance	Rural credit raising the competitiveness of agriculture can fuel deforestation. Tracking can only reduce deforestation of borrowers *directly* but not address deforestation linked to credit *indirectly* fueling demand across rural land markets

Sources: World Bank and International Finance Corporation (IFC).
Note: TFP = total factor productivity.

NOTES

1. "Agriculture" in this memorandum includes crop and livestock production.
2. The main component of the Plano Real was the creation of the *real*, which was originally tied to the price of the dollar.
3. Because land is an omitted factor in the accounting equation, it is included in the total factor productivity (TFP) measures. Natural land expansion had a positive contribution to growth, implying that the actual productivity performance is even lower than what is observed in figure 3.6.
4. For a comparison of Brazil's average trade tariffs with those of selected peer and high-income countries, see annex 3A, figure 3A.1.
5. This is linked to the Balassa-Samuelson effect, further discussed in the next section.
6. Agriculture's 7 percent share of Brazil's GDP is based on 2020 data. In 2019, agriculture made up only 4.3 percent of GDP. The difference is largely due to the strong performance of agriculture and the weak performance of nonagricultural sectors during the COVID-19 crisis.
7. For a comparison of Brazil's labor productivity with that of China and India, by major sector, see annex 3A, figure 3A.4.
8. Regular research on productivity in Brazil is conducted, for example, by the Regis Bonelli Productivity Observatory at the Brazilian Institute of Economics (IBRE) of Fundação Getulio Vargas (FGV IBRE): https://ibre.fgv.br/observatorio-produtividade.
9. Structural transformation typically holds for both high-income countries and for low- to middle-income countries. See Beylis et al. (2020). Also, see Kuznets (1973) and Herrendorf, Rogerson, and Valentinyi (2014).
10. Relatively inelastic food demand means that higher income does not generate much additional demand for food products.
11. Evidence for the Balassa-Samuelson effect at the Brazil level can be found in OECD (2004) and Goda and Priewe (2000).
12. At early stages of development, countries or regions tend to move to what is called "traditional services," which are nontradable, including transportation, travel, and construction. As they continue the development process, there is a shift toward modern or nontraditional services (Duarte and Restuccia 2010, 2016, 2018). Among these services economists typically include information and communications technology (ICT), financial and insurance services, and health and other business services, that are mostly professional services (such

as consulting and architecture). A feature of these services is that in general they are more intensive in high-skill labor, and this implies that they are important to generate high-wage jobs that allow the absorption of highly skilled workers.

13. Enache, Ghani, and O'Connell (2016) and Kinfemichael and Morshed (2016) find that telecommunications, finance, information technology, and professional services are among them.

14. Araujo, Combes, and Féres (2018) provide evidence that when wages rise in other parts of the economy, this increases the opportunity cost of farming and lowers Amazonian deforestation.

15. These simulations do not include a cost for higher productivity; they thus best reflect regulatory reforms. Where investment is required for productivity, the source of financing matters. Simulations suggest that an increase in investment financed with foreign direct investment (FDI) will be particularly beneficial for natural forests, as FDI further appreciates the REER. Investment financed with domestic savings would have a smaller impact on the real exchange rate than FDI, but given the implicit shift from consumption to capital, it could reduce national agricultural demand and thus also lessen pressure on forests, although the effects are more ambiguous than in an external financing scenario: the forest-saving impact will depend on how much productivity the investment generates.

16. Related to this, Gorton and Ianchovichina (2021) show that improving connectivity across Brazil's coastal urban hubs is welfare-enhancing relative to building rural roads, including into Amazônia.

17. This is consistent with the findings of Cattaneo (2005).

18. This assessment is consistent with the notion that promoting agriculture outside of Amazônia can reduce Amazonian deforestation, as highlighted by Catteneo (2008).

19. Reducing transport costs for Amazonian agriculture alone would likely increase deforestation by making Amazonian farmers more competitive, without offsetting effects.

20. This is consistent with recent empirical evidence in Assa (2021).

21. Firm-level regressions in Vagliasindi (2022) suggest potentially high firm losses from power outages; productivity losses are also potentially very high. The marginal impact of an increase in the duration of power outages on sale losses is significantly higher in Amazonas than elsewhere in Brazil, a result that holds even after controlling for state and sectoral fixed effects. Many studies find that power outages are a major constraint on firm productivity in developing countries. One study found that eliminating outages generates increases in aggregate output per worker on the order of 20 percent.

REFERENCES

Araujo, C., J.-L. Combes, and J. G. Féres. 2018. "Determinants of Amazon Deforestation: The Roll of Off-Farm Income." *Environment and Development Economics* 24 (2): 138–56.

Araujo, J. T., M. Brueckner, M. Clavijo, E. Vostroknutova, and K. M. Wacker. 2014. "Benchmarking the Determinants of Economic Growth in Latin America and the Caribbean." Report 91015-LAC, World Bank, Washington, DC.

Arcand, J.-L., P. Guillaumont, and S. Guillaumont Jeanneney. 2008. "Deforestation and the Real Exchange Rate." *Journal of Development Economics* 86 (2): 242–62.

Assa, B. S. K. 2021. "The Deforestation–Income Relationship: Evidence of Deforestation Convergence across Developing Countries." *Environment and Development Economics* 26 (2): 131–50.

Assunção, J., C. Gandour, and R. Rocha. 2015. "Deforestation Slowdown in the Brazilian Amazon: Prices or Policies?" *Environment and Development Economics* 20 (6): 697–722.

Balassa, B. 1964. "The Purchasing-power Parity Doctrine: A Reappraisal." *Journal of Political Economy* 72 (6): 584–96.

Beylis, G., R. Fattal-Jaef, M. Morris, A. R. Sebastian, and R. Sinha. 2020. *Going Viral: COVID-19 and the Accelerated Transformation of Jobs in Latin America and the Caribbean.* Washington, DC: World Bank.

Borlaug, N. 2002. "Feeding a World of 10 Billion People: The Miracle Ahead." *In Vitro Cellular & Developmental Biology - Plant* 38 (2): 221–28.

Bragança, A., R. Araújo, and J. Assunção. 2020. "Measuring the Indirect Effects of Transportation Infrastructure in the Amazon." White paper (October), Climate Policy Initiative, Washington, DC.

Cattaneo, A. 2005. "Inter-regional Innovation in Brazilian Agriculture and Deforestation in the Amazon: Income and Environment in the Balance." *Environment and Development Economics* 10 (4): 485–511.

Cattaneo, A. 2008. "Regional Comparative Advantage, Location of Agriculture, and Deforestation in Brazil." *Journal of Sustainable Forestry* 27 (1–2): 25–42.

Duarte, M., and D. Restuccia. 2010. "The Role of the Structural Transformation in Aggregate Productivity." *Quarterly Journal of Economics* 125 (1): 129–73.

Duarte, M., and D. Restuccia. 2016. "Relative Prices and Sectoral Productivity." Working Paper tecipa-555, University of Toronto, Department of Economics.

Duarte, M., and D. Restuccia. 2018. "Relative Prices and Sectoral Productivity." Working Paper, National Bureau of Economic Research, Cambridge, MA.

Dutz, M. A. 2018. *Jobs and Growth: Brazil's Productivity Agenda*. International Development in Focus Series. Washington, DC: World Bank.

Enache, M., E. Ghani, and S. O'Connell. 2016. "Structural Transformation in Africa: A Historical View." Policy Research Working Paper 7743, World Bank, Washington, DC.

Feenstra, R. C., R. Inklaar, and M. P. Timmer. 2015. "The Next Generation of the Penn World Table." *American Economic Review* 105 (10): 3150–82.

Ferreira Filho, J. B. S., and M. Hanusch. 2022. "A Macroeconomic Perspective of Structural Deforestation in Brazil's Legal Amazon." Policy Research Working Paper 10162, World Bank, Washington, DC.

Flaherty, K., R. do Carmo Nascimento Guidicci, D. A. P. Torres, G. L. Vedovoto, A. F. D Ávila, and S. Perez. 2016. "Agricultural R&D Indicators Factsheet, April 2016: Brazil." Country factsheet, International Food Policy Research Institute (IFPRI), Washington, DC.

Gasques, J. G., M. R. P. Bacchi, and E. T. Bastos. 2018. *Crescimento e Produtividade da Agricultura Brasileira de 1975 a 2016*. Carta de Conjuntura 38. Brasília: Instituto de Pesquisa Econômica Aplicada.

Gasques, J. G., M. R. Piedade, and E. T. Bastos. 2018. "Crescimento e Produtividade da Agricultura Brasileira de 1975 a 2016." Carta de Conjuntura 38. Institute of Applied Economic Research (Ipea), Brasília.

Ghani, E., and H. Kharas. 2010. "The Service Revolution." Economic Premise 14, World Bank, Washington, DC.

Goda, T., and J. Priewe. 2020. "Determinants of Real Exchange Rate Movements in 15 Emerging Market Economies." *Brazilian Journal of Political Economy* 40 (2). doi:10.1590/0101-31572020-3072.

Gorton, N., and E. Ianchovichina. 2021. "Trade Networks in Latin America: Spatial Inefficiencies and Optimal Expansions." Policy Research Working Paper 9843, World Bank, Washington, DC.

Grover, A., S. V. Lall, and W. F. Maloney. 2022. *Place, Productivity, and Prosperity: Revisiting Spatially Targeted Policies for Regional Development*. Washington, DC: World Bank.

Herrendorf, B., R. Rogerson, and A. Valentinyi. 2014. "Growth and Structural Transformation." In *Handbook of Economic Growth, Vol. 2B*, edited by P. Aghion and S. Durlauf, 855–941. Amsterdam: Elsevier.

Hertel, T. W. 2012. "Implications of Agricultural Productivity for Global Cropland Use and GHG Emissions: Borlaug vs. Jevons." GTAP Working Paper 69, Center for Global Trade Analysis, Purdue University, West Lafayette, IN.

Instituto Escolhas. 2022. "Como o agro brasileiro se beneficia do desmatamento?" Final report, Instituto Escolhas [Choices Institute], São Paulo. https://www.escolhas.org/wp-content/uploads/Relat%C3%B3rio-Final_AgroDesmatamento.pdf.

Jevons, W. S. 1866. "VII." In *The Coal Question*. 2nd ed. London: Macmillan and Company.

Kinfemichael, B., and A. M. Morshed. 2016. "Convergence of Labor Productivity Across the US States." *Economic Modelling* 76 (C): 270–80.

Kuznets, S. 1973. "Modern Economic Growth: Findings and Reflections." *American Economic Review* 63 (3): 247–58.

Luna, F. V., and H. S. Klein. 2014. The Economic and Social History of Brazil Since 1889. Cambridge, UK: Cambridge University Press.

Mello, L. R. de. 2008. "The Brazilian 'Tax War:' The Case of Value-Added Tax Competition among the States." *Public Finance Review* 36 (2): 169–93.

OECD (Organisation for Economic Co-operation and Development). 2004. *Trade and Competitiveness in Argentina, Brazil and Chile: Not as Easy as A-B-C.* Paris: OECD Publishing.

Porcher, C., and M. Hanusch. 2022. "A Model of Amazon Deforestation, Trade, and Labor Market Dynamics." Policy Research Working Paper 10163, World Bank, Washington, DC.

Porzio, T., F. Ross, and G. Santangelo. 2020. "The Human Side of Structural Transformation." Working Paper. Warwick Economics Research Papers Series (WERPS), University of Warwick, Coventry, UK.

Rodrik, D. 2013. "Unconditional Convergence in Manufacturing." *Quarterly Journal of Economics* 128 (1): 165–204.

Samuelson, P. A. 1964. "Theoretical Notes on Trade Problems." *Review of Economics and Statistics* 46 (2): 145–54.

Silva, A. V. da, and I. de Alencar Nääs. 2020. "Deindustrialization: A View of the Brazilian Economy." *Research, Society and Development* 9 (12): e6591210494.

Soares-Filho, B., A. Alencar, D. Nepstad, G. Cerqueira, M. del C. Vera Diaz, S. Rivero, L. Solorzano, and E. Voll. 2004. "Simulating the Response of Land-Cover Changes to Road Paving and Governance along a Major Amazon Highway: The Santarem-Cuiaba Corridor." *Global Change Biology* 10 (5): 745–64.

Szerman, D., J. Assunção, M. Lipscomb, and A. Mushfiq Mobarak. 2022. "Agricultural Productivity and Deforestation: Evidence from Brazil." Discussion Paper 1091, Economic Growth Center, Yale University, New Haven, CT.

UN DESA (United Nations Department of Economic and Social Affairs). 2022. *World Population Prospects 2022: Summary of Results.* New York: United Nations.

Vagliasindi, M. 2022. "Key Challenges and Opportunities in the Power Sector of the State of Amazonas." Background note for this report, World Bank, Washington, DC.

Weinhold, D., and E. Reis. 2008. "Transportation Costs and the Spatial Distribution of Land Use in the Brazilian Amazon." *Global Environmental Change* 18 (1): 54–68.

World Bank. 2016. "Retaking the Path to Inclusion, Growth and Sustainability: Brazil Systematic Country Diagnostic." Report 106569, World Bank, Washington, DC.

World Bank. 2019. "Au pays du cacao: Comment transformer la Cote d'Ivoire" [In the Land of Cocoa: How to Transform Cote d'Ivoire]. Report 138517, World Bank, Washington, DC.

World Bank. 2021. "Subnational Doing Business in Brazil 2021: Comparing Business Regulation for Domestic Firms in 27 Brazilian Locations with 190 Other Economies." Report, World Bank, Washington, DC.

World Bank. 2023a. *Brazil Country Climate and Development Report.* Washington, DC: World Bank.

World Bank. 2023b. "Urban Competitiveness in Brazil's State of Amazonas: A Green Growth Agenda." Companion paper for this report, World Bank, Washington, DC.

4 Institutions and Finance for Conservation

JORGE MUÑOZ, CAMILLE BOURGUIGNON, LUIS DIEGO HERRERA GARCIA, MAREK HANUSCH, ERIC ARIAS, FABIANO SILVIO COLBANO, ALEXANDRE KOSSOY, BRYAN GURHY, DIETER WANG, JON STRAND, RAFAEL AMARAL ORNELAS, CLAUDIA TUFANI, AND GUIDO PENIDO

KEY MESSAGES

- Strong institutions are critical for sustainable and inclusive development in Amazônia to counter the natural resource curse.
- Given the region's exceptional natural wealth, good governance for forests is critical.
- The rural tax and credit systems encourage extensive agriculture.
- Brazil has put in place systems to protect its forests by
  - Designating large areas as protected areas or Indigenous territories
  - Updating its Forest Code and introducing the Rural Environmental Cadastre
  - Generating systems for farmers to become compliant with the Forest Code
  - Blacklisting municipalities with high deforestation rates
  - Supporting law enforcement with real-time satellite monitoring (command and control).
- Lowering deforestation requires action from both the private and public sectors.
- Land regularization remains an unfinished agenda, and law enforcement has recently weakened.
- It is critical to strengthen the political will to enforce environmental protection laws in Amazônia.
- Conservation finance, from public or market-based resources, can generate resources and political will for more sustainable and inclusive development in Amazônia.

- *Policy implications:*
  - Reforming the rural credit system and the rural land tax.
  - Designating public lands, regularizing tenure, and enforcing environmental law.
  - Strengthening private sector corporate governance and encouraging deforestation-free value chains.
  - Bolstering forest protection with performance-linked conservation finance.

PROTECTING NATURAL WEALTH, FINANCING SUSTAINABLE AND INCLUSIVE GROWTH

As it develops, Amazônia must protect its natural wealth. Amazônia has exceptional natural capital (chapter 1), which sets it apart from other lagging regions. The previous chapter shows how economic factors drive deforestation. Given the current development trajectory, forests in Amazônia—and Brazil more broadly—are under significant threat. Tipping points, although uncertain, risk amplifying the economic costs from continued deforestation for Amazônia, Brazil, South America, and the world. It is thus paramount to counter the economic forces that are destroying Amazonian forests by creating strong institutions, backed by adequate financing. This subject is the focus of this chapter.

Despite their rich traditional institutions, frontier regions tend to have weak modern institutions requiring the systems governing them to develop and mature. In addition, since frontier regions tend to emerge in pursuit of natural resource wealth, governance may be undermined by the natural resource curse, where the extraction of natural rents undermines effective democratic institutions (Auty 1993). In Amazônia, natural rent extraction includes *garimpo* (wildcat mining), *grilagem* (land grabbing), and deforestation. In light of these forces, strengthening institutions in Amazônia requires extra effort.

Strengthening forest protection forms part of a broader need for institution building. Institutional gaps cut across many sectors in Amazônia (see annex 4A), and this memorandum points to many areas where strong institutions are required, from better health and education systems to adequate basic and economic infrastructure services. Strengthening institutions to protect Amazônia's forests does not need to occur at the expense of other institutions, but it can be complementary: a state that can effectively assert its authority in one area will be more credible in others, too, while capacity may develop across sectors.

Strong forest protection is a central piece of Amazonian development solutions. First, as chapter 1 showed, deforestation is an inefficient form of redistribution, destroying large amounts of public wealth. It is an inefficient subsidy that favors resource-intensive production. Second, effective forest protection is complementary to balanced structural transformation. Chapter 3 showed that an elastic supply of land associated with lax forest protection can result in unintended consequences from investments in agriculture, potentially harming forests when demand for rural land rises. Conversely, effective forest protection can support agricultural intensification.

This chapter focuses on public and private governance for forest protection and conservation finance.[1] Protecting Amazônia is a shared agenda between the public and private sectors. And although Amazonian forests belong to Brazil, they provide ecosystem services beyond Brazil's borders. This chapter discusses financing solutions for sustainable and inclusive development in Brazil that include domestic and external resources. Strong institutions coupled with adequate—ideally performance-based—financing linked to verifiable deforestation control are critical to address the urgency posed by deforestation. They complement parallel interventions to foster inclusive growth in Amazônia.

INSTITUTIONS ENCOURAGING EXTENSIVE AGRICULTURE

Multiple policies, perhaps inadvertently, encourage the private accumulation of land in Amazônia. Chief among these are rural credit policies and the structure of the rural land tax, the Imposto sobre a Propriedade Territorial Rural (ITR).

Rural credit

Rural credit is among Brazil's primary fiscal instruments to bolster agriculture, whose expansion drives deforestation.[2] Richer countries tend to subsidize agriculture more than poorer countries do (figure 4.1). Such subsidies are consistent with more advanced levels of development, where rising wages weaken the competitiveness of agriculture, and fiscal support (or trade protection) is needed

FIGURE 4.1

Richer countries tend to subsidize agriculture more than poorer countries

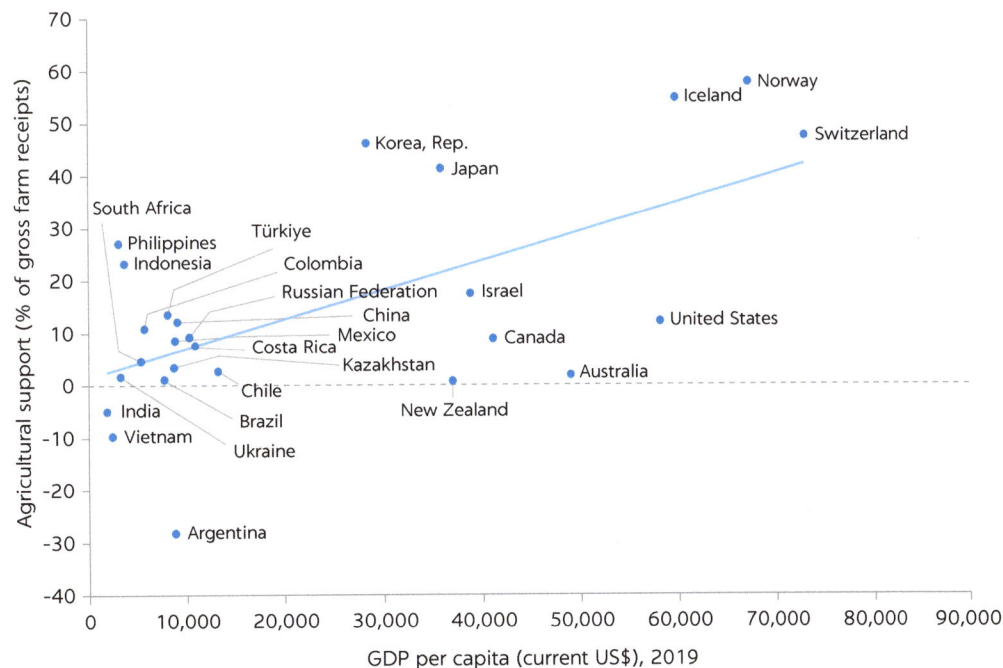

Source: World Bank, using Organisation for Economic Co-operation and Development 2019 agricultural support indicator data.
Note: Agricultural support is defined as the annual monetary value of gross transfers to agriculture from consumers and taxpayers arising from government policies that support agriculture, regardless of their objectives and economic impacts.

to maintain some national production (while richer countries also tend to shift from output subsidies to subsidies for environmental services). Brazil's subsidies are relatively low, reflecting the country's less advanced structural transformation compared with that of higher-income countries and its higher relative agricultural competitiveness. Even so, agriculture is one of the most subsidized sectors in the country, receiving fiscal support totaling about 0.35 percent of gross domestic product (GDP). Most of the subsidies take the form of interest subsidies on rural credit (the Plano Safra [Harvest Plan] and the National Program to Strengthen Family Farming [PRONAF]); indirect subsidies are provided through Constitutional Funds. The support programs are fragmented, undermining their efficiency. Moreover, interest rate subsidies benefit mostly large farmers, and the substantial amount of fiscal resources dedicated to them would be better spent through other types of support for agricultural finance, including partial credit guarantees and agriculture insurance.

Brazil's subsidy regime encourages deforestation by inflating demand for agricultural land and by creating distortions that reduce productivity across the economy.[3] Most of the credit subsidies under Plano Safra support cattle ranching in Amazônia's Colonial Frontier (described in chapter 1) and crop production in the New Frontier (figure 4.2). Following the logic of figure 1.5 in chapter 1, subsidizing agriculture increases the demand for productive land, which increases deforestation. More indirectly, earmarking credit for agriculture constrains productivity by reducing the financial resources available for other, potentially more productive sectors (Calice and Kalan 2022)—as chapter 3 shows, reducing the productivity of the overall economy can also foster deforestation. Thus, there are direct and indirect ways in which the current rural credit system fuels deforestation.

FIGURE 4.2

Relatively higher credit subsidies tend to be allocated to cattle in Amazônia's states of the Colonial Frontier

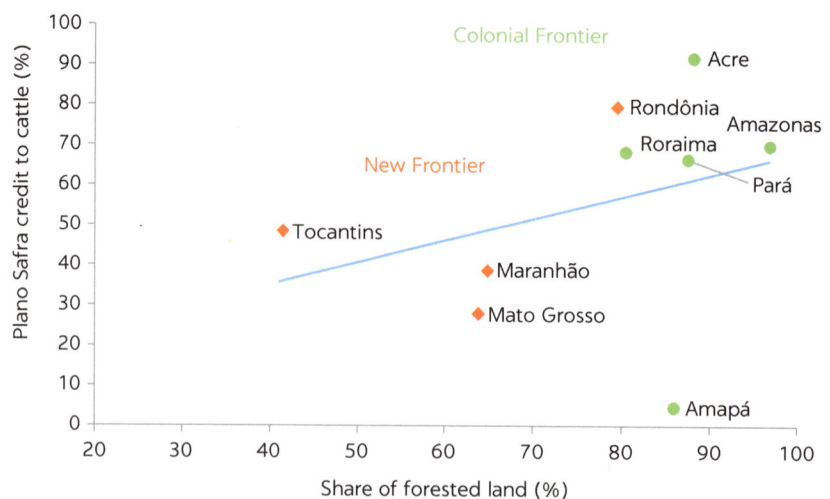

Source: World Bank, using Ministry of Agriculture data and World Bank forested land data from the Hidden Dimensions of Poverty dataset.
Note: Plano Safra (Harvest Plan) provides interest subsidies on rural credit. Cattle tends to receive higher subsidies in the states of the Colonial Frontier (where forest cover is still relatively high), while crops tend to receive higher subsidies in the states of the New Frontier (which already experienced high levels of deforestation while also exhibiting more suitable soils for crop production).

Although Brazil has rural credit programs to promote sustainable farming, such as the ABC Plan (Low-Carbon Agriculture Plan, further discussed in chapter 5), they tend to be less attractive than the standard programs like Plano Safra.

An innovative financial sector policy in 2008 mitigated some of the direct pressures on deforestation implicit in subsidized credit. In Amazônia states with large remaining natural forest cover, the main rural credit program, Plano Safra, tends to support cattle ranching, which is strongly associated with deforestation. To limit this risk, the Central Bank of Brazil made concessional credit in Amazônia conditional on compliance with legal titling requirements and certain environmental regulations (Resolution 3545 of 2008). This powerful and innovative policy reduced deforestation, but persistent uncertainty of tenure limited its effectiveness (Assunção et al. 2020).

Rural land taxes

Another important rural policy is the ITR, a progressive land tax that is intended to raise both revenue and land productivity but has had limited effectiveness. Assessed progressively at rates ranging from 0.03 percent to 20 percent, the tax is based on the area and value of the land as well as on the degree of use (productive area as a percentage of total area) (IPAM 2016; Fendrich et al. 2022). The taxable area does not include legal reserves or other conservation areas or set-asides. In Amazônia, small-scale farms under 100 hectares are exempt from the ITR,[4] as are all settlement farmers with just one property under 100 hectares. Why the modest effect? Municipalities are allowed to collect the ITR, but collection efforts have been weak—partly because the return on collection is low (ITR rates are low) and partly because municipalities want to encourage agriculture and ranching to foster economic development in their jurisdiction. Another complication is that landowners self-assess the key variables for calculating the ITR and often underestimate their tax responsibilities.

Although intended to boost land productivity, the ITR encourages deforestation in practice. Land taxes are often used to preserve natural land (World Bank 2021), but they have the opposite effect in Brazil.[5] The progressive nature of the ITR is supposed to reward more intensive use of land, but the values defining intensive land use (especially for cattle ranching) are unambitious and have not been adjusted for years. Even quite extensive cattle ranching can be consistent with the lowest ITR tax bracket. In addition, while the taxable property size excludes forested land, the ITR rate considers the whole property size, irrespective of whether the land is forested. Thus, landowners have an incentive to produce on as much of their land as possible to justify the size of their holdings. But since they can achieve this productivity with relatively low-productivity ranching, the overall impact is to reduce forested area for extensive land use—thus the ITR's design and implicit rates and quotas generate incentives for deforestation.

LAND REGULARIZATION AND FOREST GOVERNANCE

Deforestation decelerated and environmental protection policies tightened in Brazil in the 2000s, especially in the Amazon biome. The Amazon Region Protected Areas Program, launched in 2002, created 60 million hectares of protected area. In 2004 the government adopted the Action Plan for the Prevention and Control of Deforestation in the Legal Amazon (PPCDAm), which initially focused on land tenure and territorial planning, sustainable production, and environmental monitoring and control. In addition, law enforcement was stepped up through remote-sensing monitoring, including the Real-Time Deforestation Detection System (DETER). Since 2009, targeted enforcement has increased in priority (blacklisted) municipalities (Assunção and Rocha 2019; Sills et al. 2020; Soares-Filho et al. 2014). In 2012 Brazil updated its 1965 Forest Code and introduced the Rural Environmental Cadastre (Cadastro Ambiental Rural, CAR), an innovative database and environmental management tool. Although the updated Forest Code offered a special regime for landowners who had illegally deforested before 2008, it also provided tools to curb illegal deforestation on private lands going forward. And voluntary private sector initiatives in the agricultural value chain also sought to reduce deforestation. While all of these considerable efforts are credited with reducing deforestation during the 2000s,[6] they failed to prevent the acceleration in deforestation that began in 2015. Accelerating land regularization, enforcing existing environmental protection laws (command and control), and adequately financing sustainable policy interventions (conservation finance) are paramount to reversing this trend.

Land regularization remains an unfinished area of policy reform. The tenure status of much of the land in Amazônia is still unknown. Regularizing land tenure in Amazônia has been on the agenda since Brazil became a republic in 1889, and lands, which were no longer royal property, were transferred to de facto government ownership (Chiavari, Lopes, and de Araujo 2020a, 2020b). Federal and state governments have made headway in regularizing land in Amazônia. About 42 percent of land is designated as protected areas and Indigenous lands (both officially public lands) and 29 percent is designated as private lands, but another 29 percent or so remains undesignated (table 4.1) (Brito et al. 2021). These areas are awaiting designation as conservation units,[7] Indigenous lands, agrarian reform settlements (*assentamentos*), land eligible for tenure regularization, or some other category of tenure. Undesignated public lands (and lands without destination) encompass an estimated 140 million hectares,[8] of which around a third are public forest lands not allocated by the federal or state governments to a specific tenure status (the so-called undesignated public forest). Around 11.6 million hectares of undesignated public forest had been claimed as "private property" as of 2020, even though these lands are public by law (Azevedo et al. 2020).

Undesignated lands are the main deforestation hot spots, followed by private lands (figure 4.3). The financial benefits associated with *grilagem* (or, more broadly, with any real estate speculation) are a major driver of deforestation (Miranda et al. 2019). *Grilagem* is easier in areas where private agents can exploit legal uncertainty around land designation (Azevedo et al. 2020). Private properties are the second largest hot spot for deforestation along both the Colonial and New Frontiers. Currently, *assentamentos* are responsible for about a quarter of all deforestation. Farmers outside those settlements (mainly within the Arc of Deforestation) are responsible for about a third of deforestation. Finally, mining and its associated infrastructure and human settlements are responsible for an estimated 10 percent of deforestation, including indirect effects (Sonter et al. 2017). Deforestation—generally perpetrated by outsiders—occurs less often in protected and Indigenous territories, although it has been increasing recently (figure 4.4).

TABLE 4.1 **Land tenure in Amazônia**

STATE	TOTAL AREA (Mha)	AREA WITH DESIGNATION (% OF TOTAL)					TOTAL AREA WITH DESIGNATION	AREA WITHOUT DESIGNATION (% OF TOTAL)
		PROTECTED AREAS[a]	INDIGENOUS TERRITORIES (INCLUDING *QUILOMBOLAS*)	AGRARIAN REFORM SETTLEMENTS (*ASSENTAMENTOS*)	AREAS PRIVATELY OWNED[b]	OTHER AREAS[c]		
Acre	16.4	32.0	15.0	11.0	14.0	0	72.0	28.0
Amapá	14.2	62.5	8.5	8.0	3.0	0	82.0	18.0
Amazonas	155.9	24.0	29.5	5.5	3.0	0.5	62.5	37.5
Maranhão[d]	26.1	6.0	9.0	11.0	30.0	0	56.0	44.0
Mato Grosso	90.3	2.5	16.5	5.0	65.5	0	89.5	10.5
Pará	124.6	23.0	25.0	11.0	10.5	3.5	73.0	27.0
Rondônia	23.8	21.5	21.0	17.5	13.0	0	73.0	27.0
Roraima	22.4	8.5	46.0	5.5	5.0	1.0	66.0	34.0
Tocantins	27.7	4.0	9.5	4.0	48.5	0	66.0	34.0
Amazônia (total)	501.5	18.5	23.1	7.8	21.0	1.0	71.4	28.6
Country mass equivalent (approximate)	European Union + Japan + Uruguay + Ecuador	France + Germany	Colombia	Paraguay	Chile + Italy	Costa Rica	India + Malaysia	Norway + Sweden + Finland

Source: Brito et al. 2021.

Note: Mha = million hectares.

a. Exclusive of environmental protection areas.

b. Due to differences in methodology and complementary sources, the Imazon (Amazon Institute of People and the Environment) estimate of 105.1 million hectares in private lands differs from the IPAM (Amazon Environmental Research Institute) estimate of 92 million hectares.

c. Including military areas and public forests. In the Imazon estimates, public forests include areas reserved for forest concessions or communities but not designated yet (such as two large areas in Pará).

d. Includes only municipalities that are part of Amazônia.

FIGURE 4.3

More deforestation occurs on undesignated lands, 2007–18

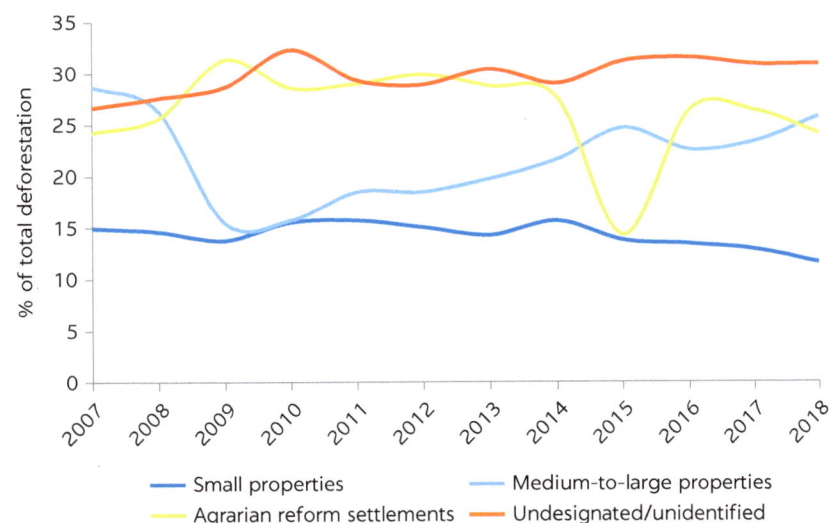

Source: World Bank, using data from Gandour et al. 2021.
Note: Small, medium, and large properties = private farms; agrarian reform settlements = *assentamentos*; undesignated/unidentified = areas awaiting designation as conservation units, Indigenous lands, agrarian reform settlements, land eligible for tenure regularization, or some other category of tenure.

FIGURE 4.4

Deforestation recently rose in protected areas and Indigenous territories in Amazônia, 2008–21

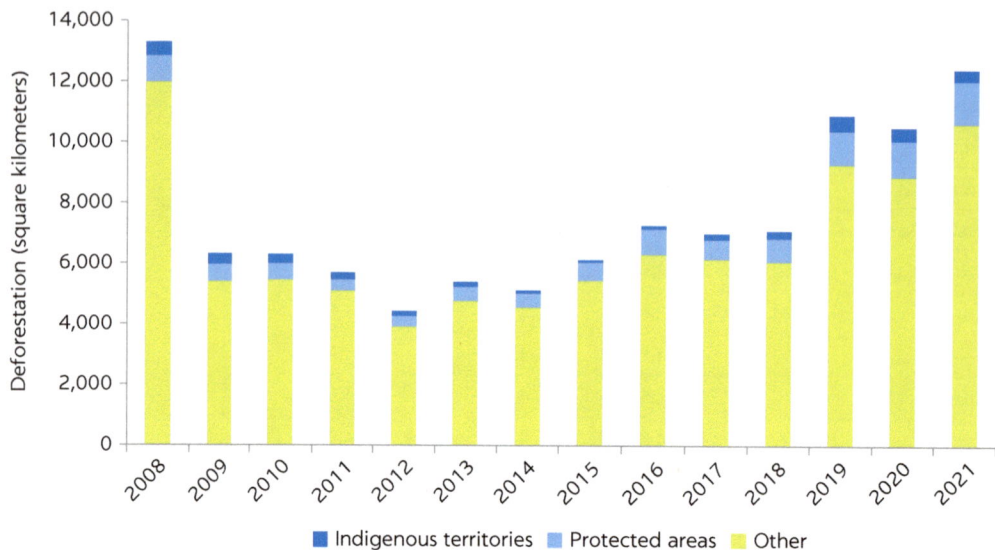

Source: World Bank, using data from the National Institute for Space Research (INPE) Project for Satellite Monitoring of Deforestation in the Legal Amazon (PRODES).

The large tracts of undesignated and unregistered public lands are one reason for the difficulty of determining land tenure in Amazônia. Other reasons are the existence of multiple mechanisms for acquiring rights over public lands (legally or not) and the coexistence of multiple unconnected cadastres and registries. Land registries administered by public notaries are not fully reliable either, even though they should serve as the primary proof of land ownership. The registration of a dozen different categories of land tenure is handled by at least five different federal entities, which do not coordinate with the multiple state and municipal agencies that have overlapping mandates and manage separate disconnected databases. At least 22 federal and state entities have mandates to regularize lands in Amazônia (Brito et al. 2021). Moreover, Amazonian states handle approval of regularized lands in different ways, some requiring approval of the legislative assembly for large tracts, which vary in size from as small as 100 hectares and larger in Acre to 2,500 hectares and larger in Amapá and Roraima, which also require national congressional approval.

Indigenous lands and protected areas

Large parts of Amazônia have been regularized in recent years, including large areas designated for traditional ways of life and environmental protection. Approximately 23 percent of Amazônia is legally registered as Indigenous land (an area roughly comparable in size to Colombia), and an additional 18.5 percent has been declared by federal or state governments as protected areas (equivalent to the joint area of France and Germany). Most of these areas were created in the 1980s, as social and environmental concerns mounted, although some were created in the 1990s and 2000s. States can create their own protected areas as long as they align with predetermined objectives and principles (for example, Amazonas State has created several protected areas).

Under certain conditions, protected areas allow some limited forms of economic activity. Category I areas do not allow for productive use except for sustainable tourism; category II areas allow for sustainable use of local communities and forest dwellers or, in some areas, for sustainable use through concessions (ensuring that such uses do not encroach on areas used by local communities).

Indigenous territories and protected areas are associated with less deforestation, so expanding them could protect larger areas from deforestation. Indigenous territories often have more limited agricultural potential, and many are in remote areas, thus reducing economic incentives for outsiders to encroach on them (deforestation tends to be higher in Indigenous territories that are closer to the Arc of Deforestation agricultural frontier) (FAO and FILAC 2021). Even though stronger protections make *grilagem* more difficult in Indigenous territories, the CAR has sometimes illegally been abused to claim Indigenous land (Sanchez Martinez et al. 2022).[9] Indigenous people themselves are not associated with deforestation; they have been applying traditional knowledge over millennia and sustainably managing their environment (Sanchez Martinez et al. 2022). Strengthening and enforcing the land rights of Indigenous populations and other traditional communities with strong links to the earth would thus reduce deforestation in those areas, in addition to protecting traditional livelihoods and protecting these communities from conflicts over land (chapters 2 and 5). Various Indigenous groups still await the legal recognition of their rights to land.

Like Indigenous territories, deforestation tends to be lower in protected areas, and, like with Indigenous territories, deforestation in protected areas is greater in areas that have better market access, notably areas within the Arc of Deforestation, like Triunfo do Xingu or Jaci-Paraná.

While deforestation is lower in protected areas, it is greater in unprotected forest areas (Assunção and Gandour 2020; Assunção, Gandour, and Rocha, forthcoming; Herrera, Pfaff, and Robalino 2019). Grabbing federal land and lands with clear tenure status is more difficult than grabbing undesignated public land, especially if that land belongs to the state government. Federal government agencies are generally more effective at enforcing environmental protection laws than the states. This situation can occur because government agencies are more efficient and capable, but it is more likely because of weaker incentives to enforce the law in state agencies. Although *grileiros* (land grabbers) are more likely to avoid protected areas and seek the path of least resistance in undesignated land and land with weak protection, protected areas are still at risk. The integrity of existing protected areas is threatened by proposals to downsize, downgrade, and degazette (remove official status from) them (Chiavari et al. 2020b). Keles et al. (2020) report 30 degazettements and 21 downsizings of protected areas between 2006 and 2015, generally for economic reasons. As the region develops and demand for land grows, protected areas are increasingly being threatened by a watering down of environmental protection laws and weak enforcement of existing laws.

Private lands

Uncertainty over ownership of private land can lead to deforestation. Many farmers in *assentamentos* still have not received ownership title for land that the government has designated to them (in some cases as far back as the 1970s). The lack of land title generates legal uncertainty, limits economic opportunities, and creates difficulties in enforcing environmental protection laws. Lack of title can be associated with deforestation, although incentives for deforestation may differ between poorer farmers (many of them living in *assentamentos*) and more commercially oriented farmers. Chapter 5 argues that, whereas rural settlers may be more likely to expand their production into adjacent territory (which may be public or undesignated land), larger farmers often deforest either directly—legally or illegally—or indirectly by legally bidding up land prices, which creates incentives to deforest elsewhere (especially in undesignated areas).

Brazil's Forest Code clarifies the boundaries of legal deforestation in private lands and establishes the CAR, a rural environmental registry. The Forest Code stipulates that only 20 percent of private land in the Amazon biome can be legally cleared, with some exceptions (and less stringent limits apply to other biomes). The CAR is critical for enforcing the Forest Code, as landowners are required to register their property boundaries and demarcate protected areas. These maps of land parcels can then be overlaid with satellite images to check compliance with the preservation requirements. However, the Forest Code and the CAR have been criticized for two reasons: For one, in the case of untitled properties, the CAR often serves as a smokescreen to claim illegal ownership of Indigenous, protected, or undesignated territories. For another, the natural-reserve requirements of the Forest Code still fragment the natural landscape across adjacent private territories, undermining the integrity of the forest.

The Forest Code provides for a trading system for Environmental Reserve Quotas (Cotas de Reserva Ambiental, CRAs) to enhance compliance and possibly to generate incentives for discouraging legal deforestation. In the CRA market, a landowner who maintains natural forest cover above the legal threshold can sell the quotas to another landowner in the same biome and state whose natural forest cover is in deficit if the excess deforestation occurred before 2008. The system applies across Brazil and could reduce the cost of environmental compliance for farmers with native vegetation deficits. The system can also optimize land use where clearing land with higher agricultural potential can be offset by setting aside more conservation lands with lower agricultural potential (but not necessarily lower biodiversity or climate value). This process can also result in larger contiguous forested units on land less suitable for agriculture and thus reduce fragmentation of natural landscapes. Soares-Filho et al. (2016) estimate that the main demand for CRAs could come from Mato Grosso, Mato Grosso do Sul, Paraná, and São Paulo, while supply could originate mostly from Amazonas and Pará, thus generating opportunities to lower legal deforestation, especially in states of the Amazon biome.

There are, however, limits to the effectiveness of CRAs. The system depends on secure land tenure for both surplus and deficit areas, robust monitoring and effective enforcement of areas demarcated for protection, and reasonably low transaction costs to run the trading system (May 2015). Outstanding issues regarding the security of tenure and weakening of monitoring and enforcement, especially in recent years, thus undermine the viability of CRAs. In addition, the supply of available forested land in some states and biomes may drive the price of CRAs to zero, all but eliminating them as a conservation incentive (Rajão and Soares-Filho 2015).[10] The price could be increased by restricting eligible land under the CRA system to areas under high risk of deforestation or by using additional systems to pay for ecosystem services.

Land restoration in Amazônia

Degraded land can be rendered productive, which could reduce deforestation, especially if complemented with productivity investments. About 25 percent of Amazonian land is degraded, and some of it could be restored (Center for Strategic Studies and Management 2016). Restoring land for productive use would increase the supply of land, attenuating competition for land and lowering its price, thus reducing the incentives for *grilagem* (land grabbing) and deforestation—while generating ecosystem services that are higher on agricultural land than on degraded soils.

While land restoration would reduce the incentives to engage in deforestation, it could also make agriculture somewhat more extensive because the price of land would fall relative to that of other factors of production. Land restoration should therefore be coupled with on-farm investments in productivity.

Public incentives for land restoration will be more effective when land and forest governance is strong. In most cases, land restoration will require some public financial support to be commercially viable. Porcher and Hanusch (2022) show that such support could create an expectation of future subsidies for restoring degraded lands, creating perverse incentives for farmers to let land degrade deliberately. Because this decision would lower the supply of usable agricultural land, it would raise the price of land and thus deforestation.[a]

Restoring degraded lands to forests will unambiguously increase the forest stock. Since degraded land is not part of the supply of land, turning it into natural forests (without productive use) would not affect land values, eliminating even indirect effects on deforestation.

a. Through general equilibrium effects, actions in one area can affect incentives in other areas through prices that govern the broader land market.

Restoring degraded lands may reduce deforestation pressures by increasing the supply of land. To be effective, such policies need to take into account private incentives and the credibility of forest protection (box 4.1). When forest protection is ineffective, restoring degraded land back to forests, rather than to productive land, can increase the stock of forests with less scope for unintended consequences.

Undesignated lands

Most undesignated land in Amazônia is in the vast states of Amazonas and Pará (figure 4.5). Undesignated land or land of uncertain ownership makes up almost 38 percent of the territory in Amazonas and 27 percent in Pará. These areas had the highest rate of deforestation in 2020 (Pará) and one of the highest rates of acceleration in deforestation (Amazonas). Undesignated areas in Amazônia remain vast (table 4.1).

Grilagem is easier in undesignated areas, which are thus a major hot spot of deforestation. Different procedures at the federal and state levels for regularizing public lands as private and differential access to information and public entities lead to asymmetric access to land, create gaps between low current land values and high future expected land values, and stimulate land market segmentation and *grilagem*. On average, when regularizing public lands, states charge private agents 15 percent of the market value while the federal government charges 26 percent. Tocantins charges the least, an average of only R$4 per hectare (figure 4.6)—and as little as R$1 for small parcels of under four fiscal modules.[11] Pará charges the most, an average of R$789 per hectare, but still only

FIGURE 4.5

Amazonas and Pará account for almost two-thirds of the undesignated land in Amazônia, 2019

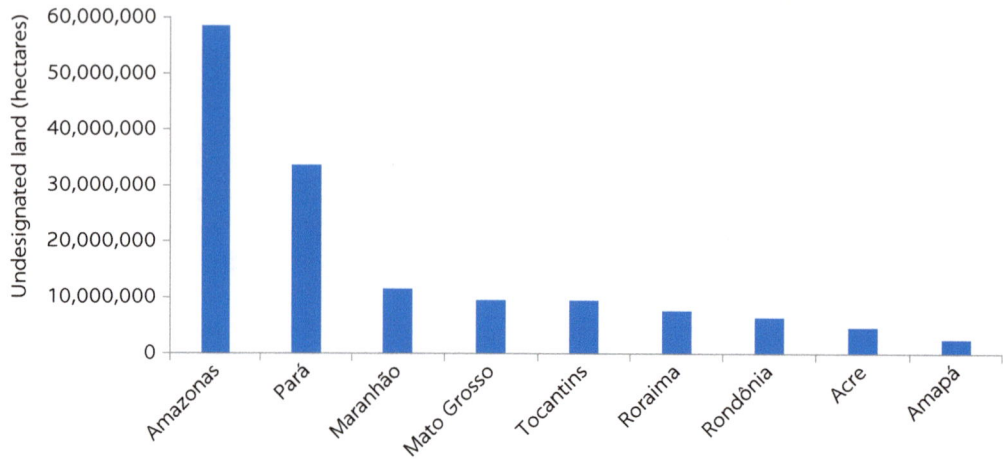

Source: World Bank.
Note: This figure depicts the data in table 4.1. "Undesignated land" refers to public land awaiting designation as conservation units, Indigenous lands, agrarian reform settlements, land eligible for tenure regularization, or some other category of tenure.

FIGURE 4.6

There are significant implicit discounts in land regularization in Amazônia, 2019

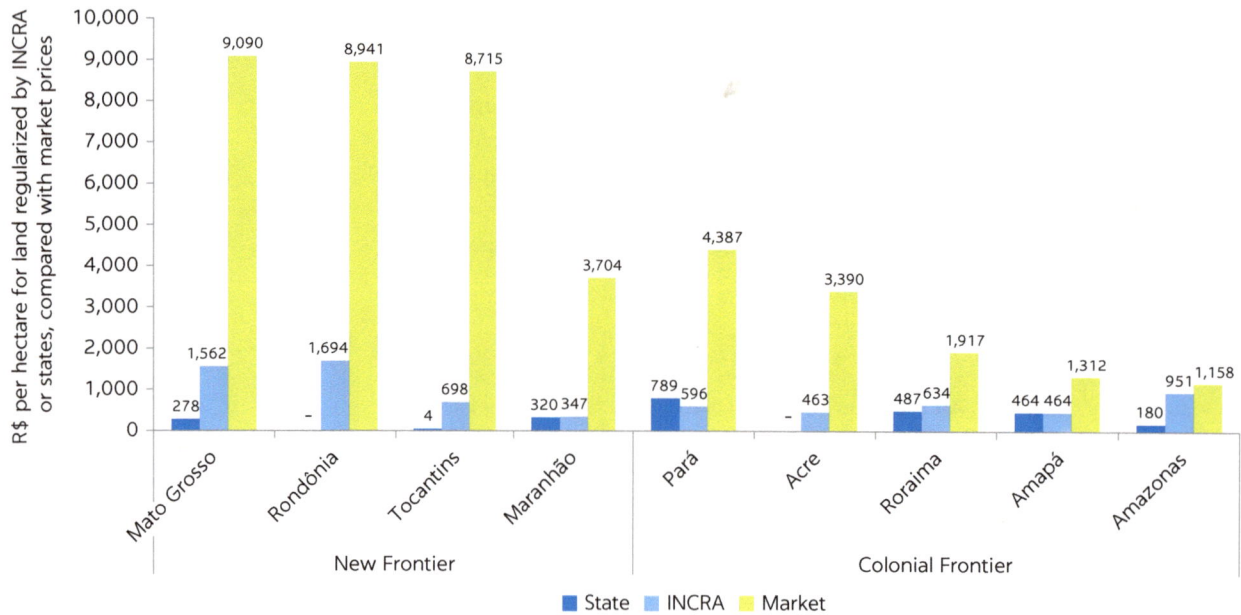

Source: Brito et al. 2021.
Note: The figure compares values (in reais per hectare) of land regularized by the National Institute for Colonization and Agrarian Reform (INCRA) or states with market prices. The comparison between average market values per hectare and bare land values is used as a basis for land sales by Amazonian state and state governments. Note that market prices for land are much higher in the states of the New Frontier, which are more developed agriculturally (see chapters 3 and 5). – = data not available.

18 percent of the average market value (R\$4,387). In Pará, the difference between land market values and state charges for some 8,053 properties that could be regularized under the Instituto de Terras do Pará is estimated at R\$9 billion (Brito et al. 2021). If the federal government were to regularize the 19.6 million hectares of undesignated lands in Amazônia using the current values allowed by

law, the estimated subsidy for the persons or entities obtaining land titles would amount to between R$62 billion and R$88 billion, which is equivalent to about one-quarter of the market capitalization of Petrobras in 2019.

The conflicts over appropriate land use (production or conservation) that arise in undesignated lands can be linked to the dominant extractive agricultural growth model. Federal and state policies create implicit incentives for *grilagem* with the aim of eventually regularizing the land (Brito et al. 2021). Since the 1850s, tenure regularization programs have been characterized by shifting cutoff dates. Under the federal land tenure regularization program Terra Legal, which provided squatters with legal title to the land they occupy, cutoff years shifted from 2004 to 2009 and then to 2011; although the program was discontinued in 2019, discussions about legalizing claims continue to this day (Stabile et al. 2019). This experience suggests to potential *grileiros* that, if they wait, they will eventually attain legal title to the land, thus casting the legality of any associated deforestation into a gray area. The large gap between the market value of land and the price paid under regularization in figure 4.6 is another incentive for *grilagem*. These implicit incentives are particularly high in states within the Arc of Deforestation (states of the New Frontier and Pará), which tend to be more advanced in their agricultural development (chapters 3 and 5). This implicit subsidization of private land uses is consistent with a growth model based on land accumulation (chapter 3). Under this model, the costs associated with land intensification can make a simultaneous focus on agriculture-driven development and forest protection appear contradictory.

PRIVATE SECTOR COMMITMENTS TO REDUCING DEFORESTATION

Zero-deforestation agreements

The Amazon Soy Moratorium of 2006 was one of the first large voluntary private sector commitments to zero deforestation in the tropics. Companies accounting for about 90 percent of the soy produced in Amazônia committed not to purchase soy grown on Amazon land deforested after 2006 (later revised to 2008) and also blacklisted farmers who ignored minimum labor standards. This landmark effort was in response to rising public concern with protecting the natural wealth of the Amazon rainforest. Three years later, the Amazon Soy Moratorium was followed by the Zero Deforestation Cattle Agreement (also known as G4).

The jury is still out on whether private sector commitments to reducing deforestation linked to soy or cattle are effective or whether they merely displace deforestation. There is evidence that these agreements led to behavioral changes among signature parties. For example, JBS, the world's largest beef processor, introduced stricter procurement rules and tracking systems, increasing the likelihood of blocking the purchase of cattle raised on recently deforested lands (Gibbs 2015). Yet compliance was low (Azevedo, Stabile, and Reis 2015), and these agreements displaced production into the Cerrado (Moffette and Gibbs 2021). Thus, while the agreements may have reduced deforestation in the Amazon, they likely increased deforestation in other important biomes.

Loopholes continue to limit the effectiveness of such moratoria. For example, although Brazil's System of Identification and Certification of Bovine and Bubaline Origin records cattle and buffalo born in Brazil (or imported), only exporters are required to join it, even though most beef is sold into the Brazilian market. And although the Animal Identification Document System tracks animals from birth to death, only their last property is recorded, making it impossible to identify indirect suppliers. Cattle from illegally deforested areas thus can still enter the system unnoticed (Proforest 2021).

With the required systems in place, it would be important to enforce deforestation-free standards across the value chain, with roles for off-takers, consumers, and governments. For example, while many of the larger meat packers have agreed to purchase cattle from deforestation-free sources using purchase control systems, smaller slaughterhouses have been reluctant to join such agreements. Credible sustainability labels could also inform consumer choices, although uncertainty remains over the strength of consumer pressure in Brazil. With sufficient political will, governments could create incentives to join sustainability certification schemes by discounting tax obligations for certified beef, offset by fees on uncertified beef ("feebates") (World Bank 2021). Developing credible certification systems would reduce deforestation by cleaning up the value chain.

Environmental, social, and governance (ESG)

Environmental, social, and governance (ESG) investing is becoming a tenet of the asset management world, and more investors are assessing the impact of their investment decisions on the wider society. In particular, deforestation has been a headline issue for many European institutional investors since 2020 (Cavallito 2021). In principle, ESG issues are relevant at both the corporate and the sovereign levels; for example, many foreign investors active in the Brazilian equity market focus on both direct and indirect links to deforestation when devising their investment mandates. As a result, corporate disclosure and governance are increasingly important for Brazilian companies. Local investors have historically focused more on the short term, but they, too, are thinking more about how to improve their engagement with companies, especially regarding governance and other ESG-related issues.

Companies operating in Amazônia employ a variety of ESG standards to guide their operations and signal their sustainability commitments to the market. Among the most common are disclosure standards (for example, the Global Reporting Initiative and the Sustainability Accounting Standards Board); reports based on questionnaires (Carbon Disclosure Ratings); leveraged information reports (Green Rankings); certifications (the International Council of Mining and Metals, or ICMM); sectoral or geographic commitments (as for the Amazon Soy Moratorium and the Zero Deforestation Cattle Agreement); and ad hoc internal company policies. While these standards have the common objective of advancing sustainability practices, they operate through different methodologies. Questionnaires and leverage information reports are usually used to evaluate companies' ESG practices through rankings and reports, while reporting frameworks, certifications, and compliance agreements offer voluntary guidance for firms that decide to engage with ESG practices. Another difference is that the agreements can be either unilateral or bilateral. In the first case (compliance agreements, reporting frameworks), the company takes advantage of guidance concerning ESG practices to implement its policies. In the second case, the institution that developed the ESG framework assumes a public commitment to disclose the firm's position on ESG practices.

In the agriculture sector, companies with a well-developed environmental and social management system (ESMS) tend to give priority to practices related to reforestation and zero-deforestation commitment programs, support to small farmers, and control over greenhouse gas (GHG) emissions and supply chain traceability (although sometimes they do not include indirect suppliers). Certifications and compliance agreements are widely used due to the high specificity of commodities connected to the activity of private companies operating in the region. Agreements such as the Amazon Soy Moratorium and Zero-Deforestation Cattle Agreement or the Roundtable for Responsible Soy and the Rainforest Alliance certification are widely adopted and ensure, among others, that products respect animal welfare and do not originate from illegally deforested areas.

In the mining sector, companies with robust ESG practices exceed national and international standards with activities that include using the latest technologies, engaging with surrounding communities, and protecting and restoring biodiversity. For instance, some companies operating in Amazônia have made voluntary commitments to responsible mining and joined initiatives such as the Aluminum Stewardship Initiative and the ICMM. These initiatives have also established corporate guidelines and policies that align with voluntary commitments and are directing investment linked to corporate social responsibility to local initiatives to address the social, environmental, and economic impacts of mining. Projects include, but are not limited to, the environmental rehabilitation of closed sites, partnerships with local governments, and charitable donations.

In the infrastructure sector, companies focus more on internal mitigation mechanisms for GHG emissions, recycling, and water management. Given the big impact of their activities, especially when working close to communities, they often prioritize community development projects (also through their nonprofit institutes) close to their sites of operations. Lead industries in this sector adopt the Global Reporting Initiative standards.

Whereas some companies demonstrate minimum compliance with national legislation and limited ESG practices, others go beyond compliance by working to minimize business risks and, in some cases, by acting as front-runners among peers to lead long-run value creation. Overall, companies with higher exposure to international markets and thereby to stakeholders from high-income markets, tend to have more robust ESMSs. These practices often include reporting aligned with international standards (as for the Global Reporting Initative or the United Nations Global Compact), sectoral and geographic-based certifications, and involvement in sector-specific international organizations dedicated to strengthening ESG performance in given activities. The International Finance Corporation's Performance Standards and the World Bank Group's Environmental and Social Framework also provide a comprehensive set of principles and environmental and social requirements and standards for financial and nonfinancial institutions. These standards can be adopted for Amazônia and even enhanced in some cases, especially for large infrastructure projects. One of the main characteristics is that they are, by default, "beyond compliance" with local laws and regulations.[12]

Good corporate governance is thus critical for Amazônia's development. Corporate governance systems need to engage with stakeholders and increase transparency over their business decisions. Especially among smaller enterprises with generally weaker corporate governance, boosting corporate governance practices could have the most impact on innovation, productivity growth, and sustainable conduct. Business associations and institutions like the Brazilian Support Service for Micro and Small Enterprises (SEBRAE) have a role to play in disseminating corporate governance standards adapted for small and medium enterprises and family companies.

Good corporate and public sector governance are complements. Governments should encourage the adoption of and compliance with ESG standards, both to support more sustainable and inclusive development for citizens and to generate a level playing field for firms, ensuring that unsustainable practices do not undercut sustainable ones. In addition, private action can generate externalities that are difficult to control at the firm level. For example, a sustainable investment in a rural area may indirectly cause deforestation outside the firm's property if it raises demand for land. Strong forest governance across Amazônia is needed to control such unintended consequences.

COMMAND AND CONTROL

Brazil has exemplary systems for controlling Amazonian deforestation, at least in principle. Enforcing them means "command and control." *Grilagem* and illegal deforestation are the main drivers of deforestation in Amazônia and reflect weak law enforcement. The recent acceleration of deforestation shows that law enforcement has weakened. Apart from recent political rhetoric, one indicator of weaker enforcement is a decline in the number of environmental infraction notices issued. Such notices tend to be highly correlated with Amazonian deforestation, but this relationship broke down in 2019, with deforestation increasing and infraction notices falling (OECD 2021).

Evidence points to the effectiveness of various measures, including blacklisting of municipalities and satellite-supported law enforcement. The blacklisting of municipalities that are major deforestation hot spots has been shown to reduce deforestation significantly (West and Fearnside 2021). Blacklisting holds particular potential given that deforestation is concentrated in a dozen municipalities in the Arc of Deforestation. Satellite monitoring is another important tool. DETER is a satellite-based monitoring system that delivers real-time deforestation alerts for the Brazilian Amazon. This cutting-edge tool is at Brazil's disposal and has the potential to be adopted in other countries with deforestation problems. Assunção and Rocha (2019) provide evidence that blacklisting, when implemented resolutely and combining satellite monitoring with on-the-ground law enforcement, can be effective. Their results suggest that reducing command and control effort by half raises municipal deforestation rates by 44 percent. Political will is required for effective implementation.

THE POLITICAL ECONOMY OF FOREST GOVERNANCE: GENERATING THE POLITICAL WILL FOR ENFORCEMENT

The implications for public and private welfare associated with different land uses have critical political economy implications for protecting Amazônia's forests. Environmental protection is, at its core, a political decision concerning an implicit form of redistribution across individuals, administrative units, and generations. For this fundamental reason, deforestation can be difficult to control, and factors such as incentives linked to macroeconomic developments (chapter 3) and electoral incentives can undercut the effectiveness of environmental protection laws and institutions.

Deforestation in Amazônia is an example of the tragedy of the commons, with concentrated private benefits on one side and diffused public costs on the other (Hardin 1968). Preserving forests in the Arc of Deforestation costs local communities an estimated US$979 per hectare annually in forgone agricultural income (de Figueiredo Silva, Fulginiti, and Perrin 2019). Further evidence suggests that households that deforested more than the Forest Code allowed were richer than those who did not (Schons 2019). Farmers who complied with the Forest Code lost an estimated US$4 billion annually in forgone income (Souza-Rodrigues 2019). These empirical results are consistent with the general equilibrium modeling presented in chapter 2. Perceived trade-offs between private and public benefits make for complex politics.

The effectiveness of forest governance depends on political preferences. Political and ideological trends, along with the commitment of the international community, can shape the political economy of deforestation. The recent acceleration in Amazonian deforestation is consistent with an ideological preference for the private exploitation values of Amazônia's forests—unless the public value is monetized. A preference for private exploitation is evident in smaller budgets, not only for environmental enforcement agencies, notably the Brazilian Institute of Environment and Natural Resources (IBAMA), but also for the prevention and control of forest fires. At the same time, Congress recently has been working to reduce environmental safeguards. To monetize the public value of the forest, the federal government launched the Floresta+ Program in 2020. In 2021 negotiations between Brazil and the United States focused on financial compensation in return for lower illegal deforestation, and high-income countries pledged resources to support a global reduction in deforestation under the United Nations Framework Climate Change Convention in Glasgow (COP26). Yet there have been important setbacks in monetizing the public-good value of the Amazon (the Brazilian biome which most attention focuses on). In light of accelerating deforestation, the Amazon Fund, financed mainly by Germany and Norway, was suspended.

There is also evidence that the federal government systematically overdesignated protected areas in municipalities controlled by opposition parties relative to municipalities controlled by the ruling party (Mangonnet, Kopas, and Urpelainen 2022), highlighting the political payoffs of higher protection rewarded at the federal level (benefiting the ruling party) but punished by voters at the local level (hurting the opposition party). At the state level, forest governance has often fallen victim to electoral politics, helping to explain why forest governance tends to be stronger in federal jurisdictions. Decision-making at the local level tends to give less weight to the benefits to individuals outside the locality (Besley and Coate 2003; Sigman 2005). For this reason, federal agencies (representing all Brazilian citizens) tend to be more effective at reducing deforestation than state agencies (representing citizens of the state), and deforestation tends to be lower on federal lands, such as Indigenous lands and protected areas (Herrera, Pfaff, and Robalino 2019).

Finally, there is evidence that deforestation rates increase 8–10 percent in election years when an incumbent mayor runs for reelection, an amount equivalent to 4 percent of the total forest area lost since the 2004 elections (Pailler 2018).

These examples highlight how perceived private-public trade-offs in environmental protection can create political economy dynamics that tip the balance against public welfare and lead to more deforestation; durable and effective regimes have not yet been established for the enforcement of zero illegal deforestation.

Especially at the municipal level, additional frictions arise, including capacity constraints (Abers, Oliveira, and Pereira 2017). The finding that strengthening the capacity of some municipalities to monitor and enforce the law tends to reduce deforestation—displacing it to municipalities without such support—suggests that more municipalities may require capacity support than resources allow (Slough and Urpelainen 2018). Already low capacity and weak institutions in Amazônia are being corroded further by criminal networks, fueling deforestation (Human Rights Watch 2019).

Finally, policy in Brazil often lacks credibility, making it less effective (World Bank 2023a). Albuquerque Sant'Anna and Costa (2021), looking at the politics of the 2012 update of the Forest Code, find that active lobbying by rural producers resulted in amnesty for illegal deforestation under the 1965 Forest Code. They argue that this success signaled that environmental laws could be circumvented, encouraging poor compliance with the Forest Code's provisions for private land. A similar logic applies to the shifting timelines in land regularization, which undermine the credibility of the authorities and indirectly encourage *grilagem*.

Support for environmental protection is often a weak political equilibrium that can be eroded by economic factors, which helps to explain the recent increase in deforestation. Despite efforts over many years to strengthen the laws and institutions to protect the Amazonian forests, and especially the Amazon, deforestation has accelerated as the macroeconomic environment turned less benign (chapter 3). Although systems for forest governance are formally in place, their effectiveness and actual engagement require strengthening. Conservation finance can play an important role in this.

CONSERVATION FINANCE

Conservation finance can avail resources for forest protection and sustainable, inclusive development and align political will. The positive externality associated with forests can justify the mobilization of public resources (box 4.2). Market-based financing can leverage private sector resources, potentially cofinanced with public sources.

Financing sources

Government revenue is the first source of financing for a country's conservation efforts. Conservation in Brazil is financed by the federal, state, and municipal budgets. For example, the ABC Plan is financed by the federal government, and Bolsa Floresta is financed through the Amazonas state budget—that is, by the state's own taxes and other sources of state revenue, such as federal transfers, grants, or loans. Land regularization and law enforcement are also budget items. Conservation financing can also happen across units of government. For example, the Ecological Tax on the Circulation of Goods and Services (ICMS Ecológico) to promote green policies is a portion of state sales taxes for

Conservation finance and incentives for sustainable behavior

Monetizing Amazonian forests' ecosystem services would generate incentives to conserve natural forests. Macroeconomic deforestation pressures may decline in the longer term, as Brazil transitions to a model of productivity-led growth beyond agriculture and as consumer preferences and the global trade infrastructure increasingly focus on models of sustainable production. Yet the immediate damage of deforesting a millennia-old ecosystem under the existing growth model is hard to undo, and tipping points may accelerate the destruction of these systems.

Perceived trade-offs between economic and environmental objectives will be strong until macroeconomic and other forces become more benign. Financing conservation efforts—including regulatory, fiscal, and structural reforms—can tilt the balance from private to public welfare by changing the incentives of actors with agency in Amazônia. The sooner macro forces become more benign, the sooner such financing needs will diminish. In other words, drawing on the findings of chapter 3, progress in transitioning to a more producitivty-led growth model for Brazil and Amazônia can lower the lifetime financial cost of protecting Amazonian natural forests.

Payments for ecosystem services

Wunder (2014) argues that payments for ecosystem services (PESs) should be voluntary transactions between service users (liable for the payment) and providers of the ecosystem services (who receive the payment), conditional on agreed-upon rules governing the management of natural resources.[a] Wunder adds that PESs should, ideally, be paid for off-site services to account for externalities that cannot be internalized directly by the legal owner of the ecosystem in question. This chapter uses a broader definition of conservation finance, with the main requirement being that the motivation for payments be linked to conservation and the provision of ecosystem services. The classification here includes cases where there are clearly identifiable users and providers (as in PESs) but also where this connection is less straightforward (as when investments in productivity reduce the macroeconomic pressures on natural forests).

Monetizing positive externalities

Financial incentives may reward a continuation of behavior. This first interpretation of conservation finance applies to cases where, through such ecosystem services, an activity simultaneously brings private benefits to an individual while generating positive externalities for society (figure B4.2.1). Programs like Bolsa Verde and Bolsa Floresta fall in this category, as beneficiaries receive cash transfers for the positive biodiversity benefits that result from their sustainable ways of life and their contribution to good forest governance. In this case, the incentives of the program sponsor or donor and the beneficiary tend to be

FIGURE B4.2.1

Conceptualizing financial incentives for conservation

Monetizing positive externalities
  ✓ Incentives are aligned
  ✓ Positive externalities of private action at no cost
  ✓ Reward behavior

Cost sharing
  ✓ Incentives are (in principle) compatible
  ✓ Positive externalities from private action at a cost (cobenefits)
  ✓ Enable behavior

Compensation for forgone welfare
  ✓ Incentives are incompatible
  ✓ Negative externalities from private action
  ✓ Reward a change in behavior

continued

Box 4.2, *continued*

generally aligned—that is, for sustainable livelihoods. This form of payment can be associated with social protection policies, as they would focus especially on poorer communities. They can gain further relevance if structural change threatens sustainable livelihoods (chapters 2 and 5).

Cost sharing

A second interpretation relates to cost sharing. Private and public incentives are compatible in principle, at least in part, and positive externalities could be enhanced through cost sharing (related to the notion of shared benefits, where some of the benefits go to the private party responsible for deforestation). An example is subsidized credit, like the Low-Carbon Agriculture (ABC) Plan. Farmers would adopt production models that, for example, yield higher biodiversity benefits and where society cofinances the additional producer costs associated with these production models. Another example is public support for land restoration. In these cases, public resources would support positive externalities, namely higher ecosystem services. Supporting more balanced structural transformation in Amazônia and in Brazil more broadly would also eventually enable benign changes in behavior, as it would lower the demand for further expansion of farmland or pasture.

Compensating for forgone welfare

Under a third interpretation, private incentives are incompatible with the public good, and financial compensation is provided for welfare forgone from a change in behavior. Payments are made where the incentives between donors and beneficiaries are misaligned because private action increases individual welfare but reduces society's welfare—as in the case of legal deforestation on private properties. Here, a donor could compensate a beneficiary for the welfare loss associated with a change in behavior

(avoiding legal deforestation). Another example is raising the Imposto sobre a Propriedade Territorial Rural (ITR) rural land tax to intensify agricultural production, while recycling the revenue back to farmers (although this payment would only partially compensate for incurred losses without additional funding).

Focusing on governments in an environment marked by illegality

Conservation finance should not be used to incentivize individuals to comply with the law, but it can be used to support governments in enforcing the law. Most Amazonian deforestation is illegal and penalties can change individual behavior. According to the polluter pays principle, agents causing illegal deforestation ought to be prosecuted and punished.[b] In principle, fines would be preventive and reflect the environmental cost. While these environmental costs can be very large and hard to determine, they should be high enough to deter illegal behavior. The fact that illegal deforestation in Amazônia continues suggests that the sanctions for perpetrators are too low or that the law is not sufficiently enforced. Governments could raise revenue through adequate fines and through conservation finance if fines translate into a change in behavior, reducing deforestation.

Conservation finance for governments to enforce the law can be justified under all the approaches listed in figure B4.2.1, as they reward behavior (protecting natural capital); share costs (of regularizing land tenure, engaging in command and control, or fostering productivity and diversifing the economy beyond commodities); and generate political will by compensating for discontinuing growth models based on extensive agriculture. In principle, conservation finance could be available for all entities that have an impact on forest protection and development, including the federal, state, and municipal layers of government.

a. After seven years of deliberations, in 2021 the Brazilian Congress created a National Program for Payment for Ecosystem Services. By creating a legal framework for contracts between providers and buyers of ecosystem services, the law fills a legal gap long considered a hindrance to the more widespread use of PESs in Brazil. The law also establishes that payments for such services are voluntary, that the seller (and buyer) can be either public or private, and that payments can take several forms, including money, green bonds, and in-kind payments.

b. For further discussion of payments and their relationship with the polluter pays principle in this context, see Börner et al. 2017; Engel, Pagiola, and Wunder 2008; Mauerhofer, Hubacek, and Coleby 2013; and Wunder et al. 2020.

municipalities earmarked for performance-based environmental outcomes, including deforestation control. ("Blacklisting" municipalities for not upholding environmental standards can also be effective, a stick rather than a carrot.) It will be critical to ensure that policies for sustainable and inclusive development in Amazônia are adequately resourced (box 4.3), which can include generating new revenue or reallocating expenditures.

Taxes can finance conservation efforts or change behavior by directly altering incentives. For example, reforming the ITR rural land tax could reduce deforestation by raising the cost of land and thus encouraging agricultural intensification. Souza-Rodrigues (2019) estimates that an annual land tax of

---

BOX 4.3

Public finance for Amazônia

Public finances are strained at the federal level, leaving little room for additional support for Amazônia, whether for economic development or for conservation. In 2021, general government gross public debt stood at 80.3 percent of GDP. These levels are high but do not yet threaten debt sustainability. Yet they do call for further fiscal consolidation, in line with the fiscal anchor. Doing so will require significant spending discipline at the federal level, including the need to limit transfers to state governments, envisaged as part of several constitutional amendments currently discussed in Congress. It puts an even stronger onus on the public finances of Amazonian states, including prioritizing the right spending in the present and maintaining stable public finances in the future. Constrained budget envelopes further motivate the need to attract potential conservation payments from abroad to support the environmental protection effort.

Overall, Amazonian states are in a relatively better fiscal position than other Brazilian states. They receive a relatively large share of the federal transfers under the State Participation Fund (FPE). These transfers insulate their revenues somewhat from state-level economic shocks. During the COVID-19 pandemic, federal support benefited Amazonian states disproportionally. Overall, these relatively strong subnational finances are reflected in their shadow credit ratings, which are maintained by the federal Treasury, with a score of A for three Amazonian states and a score of B for another three (on a scale from A to D) in early 2022.[a]

The wage bill poses the biggest challenge to public finances and fiscal space for development interventions. Pensions absorb about 27 percent of net current revenues across Brazil, compared with the relatively "young" Amazonian states, which spend only about 15 percent on pensions. Yet lower pension liabilities do not translate into higher investment in Amazônia; instead, they translate into higher wage bills and lower borrowing for investments: the average wage bill stands at about 43 percent of net current revenue in Amazônia, compared with only 36 percent in other Brazilian states. Other current expenditures are slightly lower in Amazônia than in the rest of Brazil. Yet overall, only about 8 percent of net current revenues remain for investment—less than 2 percentage points higher than for other Brazilian states.

While there is some room to raise additional revenue, especially at the state level, reprioritizing spending is another avenue to aligning state budgets with shifting development priorities. At the federal level, revenues already are relatively high in Brazil, leaving limited scope to raise taxes (a carbon tax could raise some revenue but could be redirected to cut other taxes). There is more room at the subnational level. Raising tax rates would generate fiscal space and somewhat reduce dependence on federal transfers. This effort could include higher state-level sales taxes (the ICMS), greater parts of which could be devoted to environmental developmental expenditures (like the ICMS Ecológico).

On the spending side, there are significant rigidities in Brazilian budgets across levels of government. At the state level, for example, 37 percent of revenue is earmarked for health and education spending. The space for discretionary spending tends to be low. But there may be scope for reprioritization. At the federal

continued

Box 4.3, *continued*

level, reprioritization could include a shift in priorities in the provision of rural credit or a change in the way Amazônia's special economic zones (notably the Zona Franca de Manaus; see World Bank 2023b) are supported. At the state level, the Multiannual Plans (Planos Purianual, PPAs) need to avoid neglecting urban productivity growth relative to rural investments.

Municipalities also need to strengthen their public finances to be able to deliver on their policy priorities. Although Amazonian states perform relatively well compared with other Brazilian states, municipal public accounts in Amazônia are much poorer than in the rest of Brazil, except for municipalities in Mato

Grosso and Rondônia. Many municipalities in Amazônia face large development needs coupled with vast territories that require basic services. For example, the municipality of Altamira in Pará covers about 160,000 square kilometers (it is bigger than Tunisia). And most municipalities depend heavily on government transfers. But there is room to raise municipal revenue, for example, by improving collection of the Imposto sobre a Propriedade Territorial Rural (ITR) rural land tax or, in more urban areas, the Imposto Predial e Territorial Urbano (IPTU), the urban property tax. Just as for states, municipalities also need to reprioritize spending and improve efficiency.

a. See the "Payment Capacity (CAPAG), Cities and Municipalities" data on the National Treasury website: https://www.tesourotransparente .gov.br/temas/estados-e-municipios/capacidade-de-pagamento-capag/#item-visualizacao.

US$42.50 per hectare would induce farmers to use only 20 percent of their land, thus achieving goals consistent with the Forest Code. Under the proposed scheme, the additional tax revenue would be returned to farmers through a federal transfer, since the main purpose of the tax is to change the relative price of land rather than to raise new revenue. In fact, recycled revenue would still leave an annual estimated welfare loss for farmers of about US$479 million, which could require additional compensation that would need to be financed from other sources. The "feebate" tax instruments could reduce deforestation in a revenue-neutral way by providing rebates to producers who can prove sustainable sourcing while penalizing producers who cannot.

A carbon tax could reduce deforestation while simultaneously raising revenues for conservation and complementary policies. A comprehensive carbon tax set at a (highly conservative) level of US$18.50 per ton of carbon dioxide (CO_2) could essentially eliminate all agricultural land in Amazônia (Souza-Roridgues 2019). A carbon-pricing system could be designed in a way that helps to meet Brazil's Nationally Determined Contribution (NDC) in an equitable way if the proceeds are used to cushion the impact on low-income households (Souza-Roridgues 2019). Alternatively, the proceeds could be invested in productivity-enhancing measures, focusing on non-land-intensive sectors (many of which are urban).

International conservation finance is another potential source of funding. It includes bilateral financing sources, such as the (currently discontinued) Amazon Fund financed by Norway and Germany, and multilateral financing sources, such as the Forest Investment Program under the Climate Investment Funds, the Green Climate Fund, the Amazon Sustainable Landscapes Program of the Global Environment Facility, or the Inter-American Development Bank's Amazon Initiative (covering the whole Amazon biome).[13] A very large fraction of the total value of Amazônia's forests is held by the global community and not by the Brazilian government or people; for this reason, much of the finance could come from international sources. Under COP26, Brazil, alongside more than 100 other countries, signed a pledge to stop deforestation by 2030—an intention supported by a promise of US$19.2 billion in public and private funding.

Different mechanisms can ensure that the spending of international public resources achieves its intended purpose. In an output- or results-based system (using results-based finance), payments are made based on results (comparable to ICMS Ecológico). In theory, results-based finance has the strongest impact on behavior because it links disbursement directly to results. Traditionally, however, donors have used input-based systems more often because these systems are easier to monitor and provide greater predictability of disbursements to the beneficiary. The main weakness of input-based systems is that it is impossible in practice to know, at the time of disbursement, whether or not the required reduction in deforestation will be achieved.

Conservation finance could come from private sector initiatives such as corporate social responsibility initiatives, corporate philanthropy, royalties, and impact investment. Various private funds are also used to raise environmental sustainability and reduce deforestation—most recently, the US$1 billion (global) LEAF initiative put forward by Amazon, Boston Consulting Group, McKinsey, Unilever, Salesforce, Airbnb, GSK, and Nestlé. The Group of Institutes, Foundations and Companies (GIFE), the association for Brazilian foundations and social investors, has mapped 932 projects and 133 organizations actively engaged in social private investment in both urban and rural areas of Amazônia. The Rainforest Business School and the Laboratórios Criativos da Amazônia are financed through a private nonprofit initiative (Arapyaú). Financial Compensation for the Exploitation of Mineral Resources (mineral royalties or CFEM) are significant and could also help to finance conservation payments (chapter 5). Private sector commitments that potentially reduce commercial profitability (an implicit, self-imposed tax) can also be included, such as the Amazon Soy Moratorium and the Zero-Deforestation Cattle Agreement.

Voluntary donations can be mobilized more broadly through programs like nongovernmental organization–led programs or the Adopt a Park Program,[14] leveraging the considerable global willingness to contribute to the conservation of Amazônia.

Finance instruments

A broad range of instruments exists for conservation finance. Drawing on the Organisation for Economic Co-operation and Development (OECD) taxonomy for biodiversity finance, such instruments include grants, subsidies and transfers, concessional debt, commercial debt, equity and own funds, PESs, and various forms of offsets (OECD 2020), all of which can support activities to support sustainable development in Amazônia.

Market-based instruments for conservation finance can be grouped into four broad categories: debt instruments, equity instruments, hybrid instruments, and carbon credits. They can all help to finance sustainable development, as long as the activities they support can credibly demonstrate that they have positive environmental or climate impacts. Some of the measures can have direct targets related to deforestation, and some could have intermediate targets consistent with fostering lower deforestation in the longer term (like productivity, as per chapter 3) and other ESG criteria (related not only to deforestation but potentially also to other environmental and social criteria).

The design of market-based financing solutions focused on impact is in a nascent stage of development: private sector projects linked to nature-based solutions often suffer from low financial viability. Even though some projects in Latin America and the Caribbean have secured funding and become financially viable in the long term, about 60 percent are still actively seeking financial support (Ozment et al. 2021). The majority of such projects rely on grant financing, and none of the projects has yet tapped into private investments. The main reasons tend to include the small scale of possible investments and unattractive risk-return profiles, both financially and environmentally (Rode et al. 2019).

The following are some possible market-based financing solutions:

- *Green and sustainable bonds or loans.* Such instruments, known as labeled or use-of-proceeds bonds, could be issued at either the sovereign or subsovereign level. They are created to fund projects that have positive environmental or climate benefits. Most are green "use-of-proceeds" or asset-linked bonds, whereby proceeds from these bonds are earmarked for green projects but backed by the issuer's entire balance sheet.[15] In the case of Amazônia, proceeds could focus on financing forest governance and sustainable economic growth. Given constraints on the ability of Brazilian states to issue bonds, green bonds issued at the federal level, with the explicit intent of supporting Amazônia's sustainable development, could be more effective.

- *Sustainability-linked bonds (SLBs) or key performance indicators (KPI)–linked bonds.* These bonds could also be a viable alternative to use-of-proceeds bonds (Wang, Gurhy, and Hanusch 2022). They are any type of bond instrument for which the financial or structural characteristics vary depending on whether the issuer achieves predefined sustainability or ESG objectives. In that sense, issuers are committing explicitly (in the bond documentation) to future improvements in sustainability outcomes within a predefined timeline. SLBs are a forward-looking performance-based instrument and thus require clearly measurable performance targets (ICMA 2020). They could, in principle, be issued by both public and private entities.

- *Carbon credits.* Such credits leverage a mechanism that allows internalizing the social cost associated with the externality of GHG emissions by structuring carbon credits and selling them into (voluntary or compliance) carbon markets. Trading of Internationally Traded Mitigation Outcomes (ITMOs) under Article 6 of the Paris Agreement could provide incentives to reduce or eliminate deforestation in Brazil (World Bank 2023a)—if carbon emissions could be reduced substantially below Brazil's NDC target and if the ITMO price were sufficiently high. Combined with project finance products, having access to such finance can overcome investment barriers and generate significant resources for project capital expenditures. Carbon credits can complement international development finance (box 4.4).

- *International development finance.* In addition to traditional official development assistance, blended finance has gained popularity in recent years. Combining public and private funding has directed significant investment to issues related to the Sustainable Development Goals. Public entities, such as multilateral development banks, philanthropic capital, or development and climate finance institutions, lower the barriers for private capital to enter markets that would otherwise have been inaccessible or too risky. To overcome these barriers, entities—such as the Adaptation Fund, Green Climate Fund, Global Environment Facility, or Climate Investment Funds—mobilize additional private capital through concessional financing instruments

BOX 4.4

Brazil's experience with carbon pricing at the project level

For carbon pricing to work, it is necessary to consider solutions to monetize future carbon credit receivables, as with the financial structure developed by Rabobank International Brazil in 2000. The World Bank signed an Emission Reductions Purchase Agreement (ERPA) with a Brazilian company, Plantar. Under the contract, the World Bank would pay for the carbon credits that Plantar produced and delivered. However, Plantar did not have the resources to develop the projects that would generate the credits. So, Rabobank International Brazil advanced the resources that Plantar needed to get the project off the ground in exchange for the proceeds of the ERPA. Once the credits were generated, the World Bank paid Rabobank for the credits, reducing the outstanding debt from Plantar with Rabobank.

(capital or technical assistance grants, guarantees, first- or second-loss policies, or interest rate subsidies). These mechanisms help to derisk novel instruments at the design stage. They include capital market instruments issued to develop capacity, subsidize high operating costs (at least initially), and reduce risk (box 4.4). The payment for environmental services can also take the form of a collateral or a guarantee that would derisk a project.

- *Domestic development finance.* Local development banks, strategic investment funds, sovereign wealth funds, or state pension funds can also make debt or equity coinvestments. Such investors are often well placed to invest in sustainable projects, and their involvement could catalyze other private sector capital through structured funds or guarantees. Structured funds, such as Credit Rights Investment Funds (Fundos de Investimento em Direitos Creditórios, FIDCs), are flexible enough to explore credit enhancement, risk mitigation, and blended finance and thus are particularly important for operating in the region. They also allow for the aggregation of a small and medium enterprise portfolio, smaller infrastructure projects (such as small solar), and investment in sustainable supply chains (aggregating cooperatives and smallholders).
- *Venture capital and private equity funds.* All companies require a functionable business ecosystem that can channel resources to innovative businesses that come from primary research and development, which is where typical sustainable projects can start and gain scale. Given the emergence of new asset classes related to environmental preservation, these markets have an essential role.

Carbon credits hold significant potential and could be linked to a broader reform of Brazil's approach to carbon pricing. Under the Partnership for Market Readiness, the Brazilian Ministry of Economy, with support from the World Bank, explored options for Brazil to decarbonize by developing a regulated domestic emissions trading system (ETS), also known as a carbon market.[16] Such a system could help Brazil to achieve its NDCs, supporting welfare if complemented with carbon credits, including forest offsets (and other measures, such as revenue recycling to cut labor taxes or to provide additional social transfers). Brazil has recently been advancing toward the adoption of an ETS through legislative and executive action (World Bank 2023a).

Brazil already has experience selling carbon credits in international markets. In fact, it used to be the third largest country in the number of projects and fourth largest in the sale of credits globally. The World Bank–backed BioCF (Bio Carbon Fund) successfully supported two projects generating forest-based credits in

Brazil (reforestation): the Brazil AES Tietê project in the state of São Paulo and the Plantar project in Minas Gerais (box 4.4). Today, buyers primarily include companies aiming to meet their own, voluntary decarbonization goals, both in Brazil and abroad. The Carbon Offsetting and Reduction Scheme for International Aviation (CORSIA) is a key potential source of demand for Brazilian forest offsets, as will likely be the international carbon markets structured under Article 6 of the Paris Agreement. Unlike voluntary markets, many compliance markets apply stricter standards and historically have not accepted forest credits. But this reality has been changing quickly, since robust methodologies have been developed for the issuance of forest offsets and are being successfully applied. And forest offsets are expected to enjoy further tailwinds following COP26.

Forest offsets need to be a fundamental component of a Brazilian ETS, generating a domestic compliance market.[17] Under the Partnership for Market Readiness, modeling and consultations have shown that a Brazilian ETS would be much more viable in Brazil if it allowed forest offsets. With deforestation among the main sources of Brazil's net emissions, a carbon price excluding the land use, land change, and forestry sector would put a disproportionate burden on other sectors, notably energy and manufacturing, resulting in a politically hard-to-justify carbon price. It would run counter to the need to diversify the economy into more urban sectors. Including forest offsets in a Brazilian ETS would significantly improve welfare impacts from carbon pricing and ensure that the adjustment does not come at the expense of urban sectors.[18] Modeling under the Partnership for Market Readiness also has looked at afforestation and reforestation, but in principle forest offsets could also be issued for avoided deforestation.

Forest offsets could be issued by subnational governments in return for a reduction in deforestation. Recent updates to Article 6 of the Paris Agreement, which defines the basis and creates mechanisms for implementing the international carbon markets, might generate new opportunities for issuing credits based on avoided deforestation. And under Article 6.2, which allows mitigation outcomes to be traded directly between parties, jurisdictional approaches based on avoided deforestation could become eligible. The 2020 REDD+ Environmental Excellence Standard (TREES) under the Architecture for REDD+ Transactions (ART) Program provides opportunities to issue credits for reducing emissions at the state level (with the aim being to move to a national system by 2030) (see ART 2020). TREES requires that there be no leakage in deforestation to neighboring jurisdictions (yet mechanisms to detect leakage are currently limited). This risk could be reduced if all Amazonian states join the program, perhaps coordinated by groupings like the National Council for the Legal Amazon. Eventually, all Brazilian states would join in reducing deforestation leakage across the country.

Applying conservation finance instruments to reduce deforestation in Amazônia

Conservation finance can reduce deforestation in Amazônia in several ways, focusing on government efforts to tackle illegal deforestation. Since most deforestation in Amazônia is illegal, governments play a particularly important role in controlling it (box 4.2), making conservation finance highly relevant to governments (box 4.5). Although the main focus should be on Amazonian governments, the federal government also plays an important role in forest protection while economic opportunities across Brazil have positive externalities for sustainable development in Amazônia. Various levels of government have a role to play (and

Developing conservation finance for Amazonian governments

Calculating avoided deforestation

To be eligible for conservation finance, Amazonian governments would need to prove that they reduce deforestation. In principle, macroeconomic indicators could be used to establish a counterfactual for calculating avoided deforestation.[a] In Brazil's context, macroeconomic factors, such as global commodity prices or the real effective exchange rate (REER), are important drivers of deforestation (figure B4.5.1). With more refinement,[b] an index based on these insights could serve as a baseline (forest at risk of deforestation) for evaluating policy efforts to reduce deforestation. Schematically, avoided deforestation would be the area below "estimated deforestation" and above "actual deforestation" (the green area in figure B4.5.2). Stepping up conservation efforts to avoid deforestation will slow down the deforestation process.

Slowing deforestation and rendering conservation permanent

Governments would obtain financing for slowing deforestation, thus conserving a larger stock of natural forest. Avoided deforestation will become permanent if deforestation pressures fall as Brazil and Amazônia change their growth model and both economies and institutions mature (the downward trend in estimated deforestation in figure B4.5.2).

Alternatively, the potential life span of such an incentive mechanism would be determined by the overall area of natural forest in Amazônia, which is the potential total forest area that could ever be at risk of deforestation.

The agricultural frontier moves into Amazonian forests in a business-as-usual scenario, resulting in an area of lost natural forest (figure B4.5.3, panel a). If deforestation is slowed down by policy, the frontier

FIGURE B4.5.1

Estimating "forest at risk" in Amazônia using macroeconomic variables and accounting for policy action to reduce deforestation

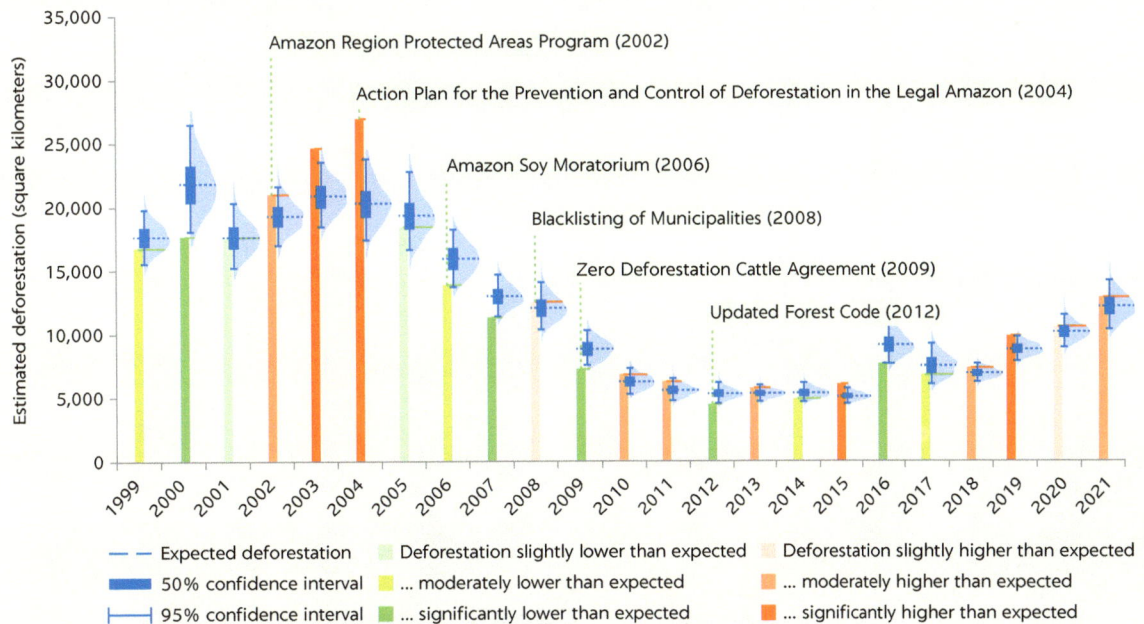

Source: Wang, Gurhy, and Hanusch 2022.
Note: The green and red bars show the level of observed deforestation, and the blue dashed horizontal lines show the estimated level of deforestation with bootstrapped confidence intervals. The model uses lagged commodity prices and the lagged real effective exchange rate, which were identified as the most important predictors using regularization methods. The flags show how various policy interventions coincided with statistically significantly lower levels of deforestation, which can be attributed to policy effectiveness.

continued

Box 4.5, *continued*

FIGURE B4.5.2

Illustrating conservation finance to protect "forest at risk" using a macroeconomic deforestation index

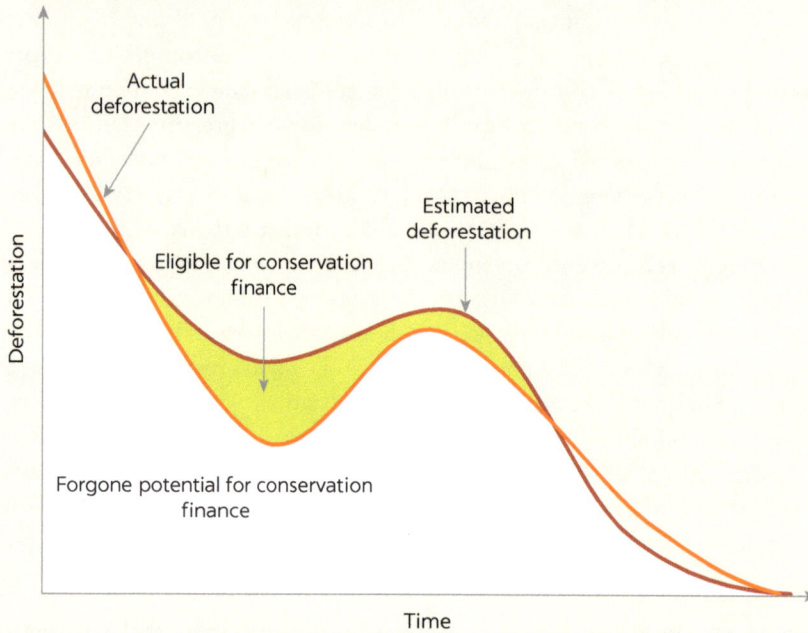

Source: World Bank.
Note: The red line (estimated deforestation) represents the forest at risk estimated using an economic model (like the blue dashed horizontal lines in figure B4.5.1). It is the maximum amount of forest eligible for conservation finance each year if the government avoids the loss of all forest at risk. "Avoided deforestation" is the forest area below the estimated forest at risk (the red line) and above the level of observed "actual deforestation" (the orange line). Higher levels of avoided deforestation attract more conservation finance.

FIGURE B4.5.3

Slowing the Arc of Deforestation

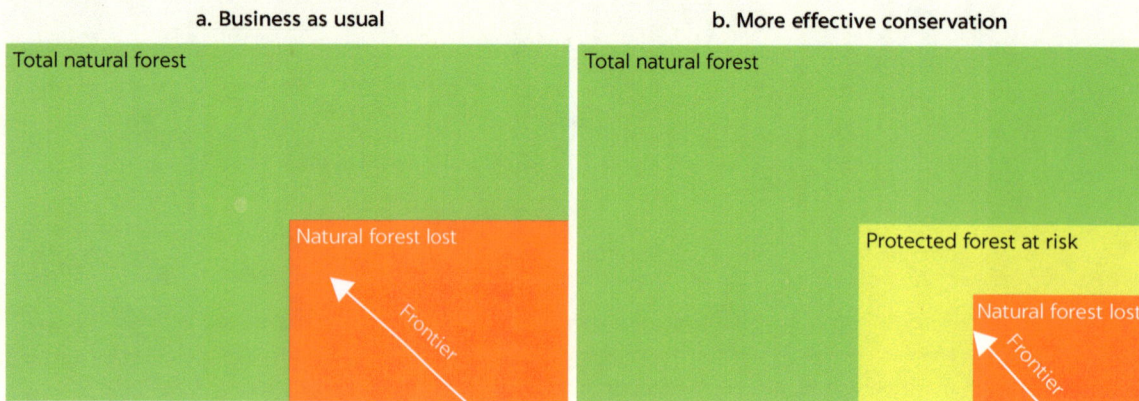

Source: World Bank.
Note: If conservation finance rewards higher levels of avoided deforestation, it will slow down the advance of the Arc of Deforestation (the agricultural frontier). Permanently avoided deforestation will be forest that the Arc of Deforestation never reaches, that is, forest that would be at risk under a business-as-usual scenario without conservation finance.

continued

Box 4.5, *continued*

does not reach the more interior parts of the natural forest, eventually rendering it permanently protected (figure B4.5.3, panel b). This permanently protected area is equivalent to the total area of forest at risk that was effectively protected each year.

Because slowing deforestation will result in some forest area being permanently protected (the frontier will never reach it), annual outcomes in effectively avoiding deforestation relative to the counterfactual could be eligible for conservation finance since slowing (and eventually stopping) deforestation will help to protect forests permanently.

Setting up buffers

A buffer could protect against policy reversals and other pressures on forests, including natural disasters. Following common practice in carbon markets for forest credits, a buffer should be set up to make buyers more inclined to purchase credits. This buffer would serve as a type of insurance—say, against reversals in government policy toward conservation or natural shocks that destroy forests (such as natural forest fires or a forest tipping point), reducing the risk that such events will erase past gains in forest protection.

Generating political will

The proposed mechanism would provide incentives for governments to implement policies with large verifiable conservation impacts. Governments would then have an incentive to implement ambitious policies that could reduce actual deforestation fairly quickly—for example, by designating outstanding (uncontested) undesignated areas as protected or Indigenous territories, stepping up command and control efforts, reforming and increasing the Imposto sobre a Propriedade Territorial Rural (ITR) rural land tax, or strengthening the foundations for value chain tracing—to maximize the amount of forest protected and the associated financing.

Donor financing

Donor financing is one potential source of financing such a mechanism. For example, the Amazon Fund deploys performance-based financing modalities using a different counterfactual mechanism. Donor-based financing could have significant potential to develop "proof of concept" for the proposed mechanism.

Sustainability-linked bonds

Sustainability-linked bonds (SLBs) are one source of conservation financing under the proposed mechanism (Wang, Gurhy, and Hanusch 2022). They could be linked to conservation outcomes such as protecting "forest at risk" with, say, lower coupon payments linked to effective protection of "forest at risk" (or higher coupons if performance is not achieved). A rigorous model to illustrate targets and avoided deforestation would be particularly attractive to investors, as it would support instrument pricing, strengthen investor due diligence, and provide the basis for a robust key performance indicator that triggers possible rewards or punishments for the SLB issuer (Flugge, Mok, and Stewart 2021). Such modeling could help to make SLB instruments more saleable and avoid some of the "green-washing" accusations that have affected SLB instruments to date (Hay 2021). Relatively easy to implement, they could be a first step toward more complicated systems such as forest carbon credits.

Carbon credits

Carbon credits, another potential source of funding, could result in significant revenue—depending on how carbon markets develop (for a related discussion, see Nepstad et al. 2022). In 2020 the average global price for forest credits was US$3.80 under the Reducing Emissions from Deforestation and Forest Degradation (REDD) program of the United Nations. The modeling for the Partnership for Market Readiness yielded forest offsets trading at US$8.40 per avoided ton of carbon dioxide (CO_2) under a Brazilian emissions trading scheme (World Bank 2021), and prices are likely to rise over time. Assuming that actual deforestation reflected all predicted "forest at risk" in 2020, the counterfactual of zero deforestation could then have resulted in revenue equivalent to US$1.8 billion with a price of US$3.80 or US$20.6 billion if applying a price of US$40.[c] This amount would be equivalent to a range of 1–12 percent of Amazonian gross domestic product (GDP) and 0.1–1.4 percent of Brazilian GDP. (By way of

continued

Box 4.5, *continued*

comparison, fiscal incentives to the Zona Franca de Manaus amount to about 0.4 percent of national GDP.)

This scenario assumes that demand exists for such credits and that a carbon market develops. Eventually, it could also be linked to generating larger markets for private issues of forest offsets under "CRA [Environmental Reserve Quota] Carbono" to address the current demand shortfall under the existing CRA scheme.

Timing matters: Carbon prices may rise and "forest at risk" may fall

If linked to carbon markets, potential financing would rise as carbon prices increase but fall as Brazil develops. Partly depending on the pace of Brazilian and global decarbonization, carbon prices are likely to rise, which would increase the value of forest credits and generate more revenue for sustainable development in Amazônia. As Amazônia and Brazil more broadly develop, pressures on the forest may decline (chapter 3), thus limiting the area of "forest at risk" and eventually eliminating opportunities for governments to obtain credits for curbing deforestation (as reflected in the downward trend in figure B4.5.2).

Limited perverse incentives for development

Since conservation financing would not necessarily be available indefinitely, Amazonian governments have additional incentives to use conservation financing to accelerate sustainable development. In theory, governments could deliberately retard economic development to maximize "forest at risk" and thus conservation revenue. This scenario is unlikely in the longer term, however, as conservation revenue will not yield the same benefits in a more developed economy. In addition, productivity gains in other parts of Brazil will reduce "forest at risk" on the Amazonian frontier (chapter 3). It is therefore more likely that governments eligible for conservation financing in Amazônia would invest their resources in sustainable economic development.

a. Discussions on predicting deforestation to identify possible payments under the Reducing Emissions from Deforestation and Forest Degradation (REDD) Program were prominent, for example, when the Bali Action Plan was drawn up as part of COP13, yet at the time it proved difficult to find suitable indexes. See Angelsen (2008).

b. In principle, this refinement could also include variables that capture global policy efforts to reduce deforestation. Arcand, Guillaumont, and Guillaumont Jeanneney (2008), among others, offer a similar modeling effort. If used to reward governments for protecting forests, the challenge will be to disentangle the extent to which the indicators predict production choices versus political will to protect forests.

c. A price of US$40 underlies the valuation exercise of table 1.1 in chapter 1.

potential opportunities for financing). Once forest governance is strengthened, conservation finance to the private sector directly focused on forest protection will become more efficient because the risk of deforestation leakage will be reduced (chapter 7). Conservation finance could help to address deforestation in Amazônia through a sequencing or a mix of conservation finance instruments.

CONCLUSIONS AND POLICY IMPLICATIONS

Effective natural capital governance rests on strong institutions and strong enforcement. Protecting Amazônia's forests requires a reform of institutions that currently promote extensive agriculture (rural credit and the ITR rural land tax), regularizing lands and enforcing existing laws against illegal deforestation and *grilagem*—that is, command and control. Fostering sustainable value chains is critical, and private investment is needed, supported by good corporate governance. Conservation financing should be leveraged to support efforts to protect forests while laying the foundations for more sustainable and inclusive development in Amazônia.

Rural credit

Rural credit needs to favor productivity and sustainability.[19] By favoring large farmers, who can borrow in private markets, rural credit policies provide an implicit advantage to agriculture—a land-intensive sector—over other sectors. It does so inefficiently, owing to both the fragmentation of credit programs and the distortions arising from credit earmarking, which reduce productivity. Central bank regulations to reduce the direct impact of rural credit on deforestation are an important advance. To better reconcile agricultural growth with environmental and fiscal sustainability, the government should consider the following:

- Focus fiscal support on smaller, productive farmers, with a greater emphasis on fostering resilience (through insurance) and sustainable practices rather than just production. For less productive small farmers, social protection programs are more helpful than credit (chapter 5).
- Revise subsidies or incentives to lending programs for large farms, targeting subsidies and incentives exclusively to programs that contribute clearly to public goods, including low-carbon agriculture and agroforestry methods (chapter 5).
- Revise programs for midsize farmers based on analyses of current market conditions and gradually phase out quotas and interest rate caps.
- Remove quotas and interest rate caps for loans to large farmers to avoid distorting competition.
- Possibly reallocate some of the budget for rural development to urban development, which plays a critical complementary role in rural transformation.
- Because increasing demand for land causes deforestation and any credit system that incentivizes more production will generate demand for land, reforming the rural credit system by reallocating the existing budget is likely to have a large impact on reducing deforestation.

Land taxes

Updating the ITR rural land tax to avoid perverse incentives for deforestation can be done in four ways (IPAM 2016). First, municipalities should adjust their stocking rates to reflect realistic levels of productivity, associating lower tax rates with much higher levels of ranching productivity. This adjustment would affect the tax burden with respect to the productive taxable area (which notably excludes forests). Second, the definition of total property size (which includes forests) for ITR calculations should be updated. Both the productive taxable area and the total property area should be net of forests to reduce deforestation incentives. Third, the ITR and the CAR systems should be better integrated to ensure that environmental protection areas are respected. Fourth, for tax rates to meet their intended objectives, self-declaration by owners ought to be replaced by an independent assessment.

Raising the ITR rate could reduce deforestation pressures, while policy could mitigate associated welfare losses. Souza-Rodrigues (2019) shows for the Amazon biome that reforming the ITR could yield similar conservation outcomes as the 80 percent reserve requirement under the Forest Code, if a uniform ITR were set at US$42.50 per hectare of agricultural land per year. Souza-Rodrigues estimates that doing so would preserve 80 percent of the natural forest in the Amazon because farmers would make their land more productive to minimize their statutory tax burden. This system would be efficient, Souza-Rodrigues argues, because more productive farmers would produce beyond the 80 percent limit on their properties (since they can afford the higher associated tax implication) while less productive farmers would find it economical to convert less natural land to farming. Land tax revenue could be used for compensation payments to ensure that the accompanying environmental protection is a political equilibrium and to invest in productivity-enhancing measures.

Land regularization

Tenure security affects both welfare and forest protection—in particular, land regularization should be prioritized as a public investment in an essential public good. For example, clarity in land tenure is important to allow an effective and fair conditioning of credit on compliance with forest protection laws. It is also important for accountability, as uncertain land tenure creates gray areas for law enforcement agencies concerning breaches of environmental protection laws.

Completing the designation of undesignated public rural lands is critical. Undesignated areas continue to be deforestation hot spots. In the states of Amazônia, they may reflect an implicit policy preference for agricultural development. The policy focus favoring agricultural production—combined with incomplete or unreliable information on tenure and ineffective land administration institutions—creates strong expectations that rural land prices will rise, incentivizing *grilagem* for speculative purposes. Focusing more strongly on urban development, by reducing pressure on rural land prices, could discourage land speculation while providing alternative, nonagricultural, nonrural income opportunities, ideally supported by conservation finance. This focus could generate political will toward designating more undesignated land as protected areas or Indigenous lands, thus preserving more forest while having a smaller negative impact on welfare.

To be effective, land regularization should begin with identifying and clarifying the intention for undesignated areas. The government should identify and complete the designation, mapping, demarcation, and registration of all federal and state proposed protected areas, Indigenous people's lands, agrarian reform settlements, and other public land categories, which would raise the expected legal cost of *grilagem* and prevent these lands from falling into the hands of private agents. Brazil would benefit from having an open discussion of the disposition of the approximately 140 million hectares of undesignated lands in Amazônia. Protection is more likely to succeed if the Amazonian states shift their development focus from land-based activities to higher value added, especially urban, activities and if their fiscal transfers depend on progress with this activity.

Second, federal and state governments should prioritize land regularization and integrate land tenure and environmental regularization. Both federal and state land adjudication entities should reduce the gap between the low (private) cost of access and the high (social) value of undesignated public lands. For equity reasons, land parcels below a certain threshold (such as four fiscal modules) should be exempted. This exemption can be achieved by adjusting statutory adjudication values closer to market values, assessing higher penalties for illegal deforestation on all public lands, halting changes to the cutoff year for valid unregularized tenure claims, and opening access to information on land tenure and market transactions to all public and private agents. In strengthening land administration and environmental institutions, federal and state governments should integrate land tenure and environmental regularization, giving special attention to equity. Because deforestation rates are two to three times higher in areas without land tenure regularization, regularization should start with small-scale farmers in INCRA agrarian reform settlements (Chiavari and Lopes 2019). That process would require updating the environmental cadastre system (SICAR) by obtaining the mandatory data for properties in INCRA's land reform settlements, enrolling properties in the SICAR, and verifying the environmental compliance of enrolled properties. Confirming environmental compliance will improve the legal security of smallholder families in agrarian settlements and rehabilitate the public image of rural settlers as the main group responsible for deforestation in Amazônia.

Third, under the leadership of the federal government, Brazil should mandate the interoperability and integration of its multiple land cadastres, registries, and other land information systems. The United Nations Global Geospatial Information Management (UN-GGIM) system provides countries with detailed guidance on adopting an Integrated Geospatial Information Framework (IGIF). Brazil has the technical capacity, but sustained political will and institutional coordination across multiple levels of government are also required.

Fourth, the government should invest in more accessible and simpler dispute resolution mechanisms and stricter enforcement of land tenure and land use regulations. Simple, alternative mechanisms for addressing disputes, such as arbitration, mediation, and other administrative procedures, can keep disputes out of the expensive, slow-moving, and often inaccessible court system. Enforcement should focus on credible penalties for illegal occupation and deforestation of land, falsification of documentation, tax evasion, and registration of nonregularized land parcels in CAR (or other entities) as a means of claiming ownership.

Compliance with forest laws

To strengthen compliance with the Forest Code, operationalizing the CRA market will be important. Doing so would provide for an efficient system to achieve core objectives of the Forest Code, generating financial incentives for higher forest cover in many parts of Amazônia.

Compliance with the law can be further enhanced by strengthening enforcement agencies and targeting resources. In some cases, weak enforcement is due to institutional capacity constraints, including inadequate resourcing and training of law enforcement agents and overlapping mandates. These shortcomings can be addressed through better resourcing, capacity training, and interagency collaboration. Recently, resources allocated to Brazilian forest law enforcement have been cut drastically. It is imperative that this development be reversed. Ideally, these efforts should extend beyond Brazil's borders to achieve a regional approach to Amazonian protection. Prioritizing municipalities with the highest deforestation rates can reduce deforestation more efficiently, while guarding against the danger that deforestation will be displaced to other areas. Conservation finance could help to shoulder associated costs and generate political will for better enforcement. Good enforcement at the state and local level also depends on incentives to enforce. These incentives will be improved if states' fiscal revenues are dependent on such enforcement.

ESG and sustainable value chains

Strong ESG needs to underlie private investment in Amazônia. Attracting firms with high environmental corporate governance policies to a region marked by high illegality also requires strong, verifiable, and enforceable sustainability standards. Effective ESG systems not only are a moral obligation for firms but also are increasingly demanded by financiers.

The government should close loopholes in monitoring the beef supply chain and increase incentives to adopt sustainable standards. Beef is a key sector linked to Amazonian deforestation. Monitoring and tracing systems to ensure that beef does not originate in illegally deforested areas must include indirect suppliers. To increase confidence in the monitoring system, data should be publicly available (while properly accounting for confidentiality requirements). Off-takers, including small and medium slaughterhouses, should be encouraged to join purchase control systems, and all meat packers should use harmonized purchase criteria. Fiscal policy can create incentives to join deforestation-free value chains by providing rebates to certified suppliers and equalizing the revenue shortfall through higher taxes on noncertified beef.

Conservation finance

Conservation finance should support sustainable and inclusive development in Amazônia. It can come from public resources or be market based; it can be domestic or international. Accelerating momentum in Brazilian and global climate finance provides potential for new solutions to stopping deforestation, especially if it is performance based. The trading mechanisms under Article 6 of the Paris Agreement open up large potential revenues for Brazil if deforestation in Amazônia can be contained. Such financing should support efforts to protect forests while laying the foundations for development. Chapters 3 and 5 show that this effort requires investments in balanced structural transformation and more sustainable methods of production in Amazônia.

Conservation finance could also be deployed to increase forest cover in Brazil by incentivizing private landowners to maintain more than the legally mandated forest stock on their properties. It could also cofinance the restoration of degraded lands. The efficiency of such investments is likely to rise as broader deforestation pressures are controlled (as further discussed in chapter 7).

ANNEX 4A: A BROADER LOOK AT INSTITUTIONAL GAPS IN AMAZÔNIA

Governance challenges are particularly pronounced in frontier regions, ranging from relatively large gaps in public services and a relatively high tolerance for illegal activities, encouraged by a sense of impunity associated with a weak state. The PPAs in most Amazonian states thus rightly prioritize improving governance (chapter 1). Strengthening governance in Amazônia, for both its forests and people, is critical for enabling the state to play its role.

Current constraints can be a consequence of budget limitations and of how effectively and efficiently the public administration functions. In Amazônia, these constraints are exacerbated by the vastness of the territory, requiring a relatively high outlay of resources to police and monitor the territory, while providing services to remote communities. Human capital is lower in Amazônia, affecting the quality of civil servants whom local administrations can hire, and affecting the quality of health and education. Poor service delivery is linked not only to limited budgets but also to weak governance, including for garbage,

FIGURE 4A.1

Amazônia exhibits significant gaps in governance of municipal services, 2021

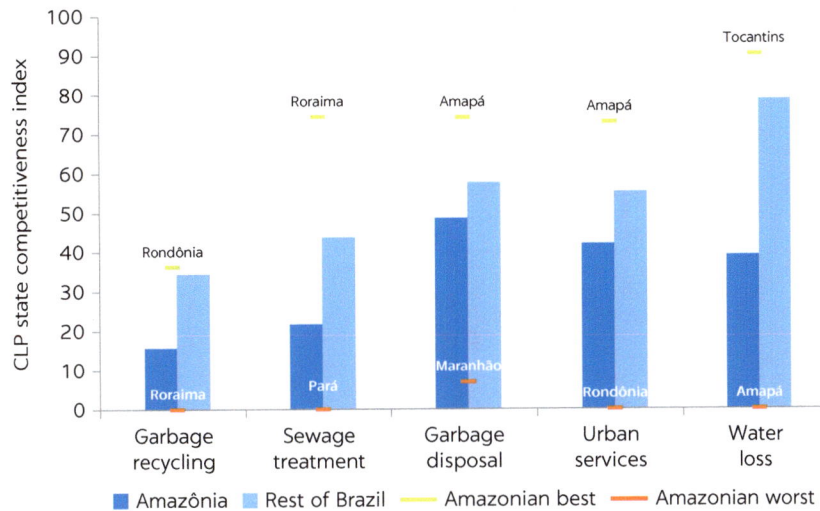

Source: World Bank, based on 2021 state competitiveness rankings by the Public Leadership Center (Centro de Liderança Pública, CLP).

sewage, water management, and urban services, albeit with significant variance in performance across Amazônia (figure 4A.1).

Public sector efficiency is low in Amazônia. The Public Leadership Center (Centro de Liderança Pública, or CLP) indicator for public efficiency looks at public sector efficiency and productivity in several core areas, including cost of central state government, cost of judiciary and legislature, judiciary case load delays, public sector transparency, quality of fiscal data and reporting, and availability and quality of digital public services.[20] Amazônia tends to rank low, with several states occupying the lowest five to six places. The central state machinery is much costlier in these states than the national average: Amapá and Roraima spend nearly 3 percent of GDP on the central administration, while an efficient state such as Paraná in Brazil's South region spends less than 0.2 percent. Except for Amazonas, all states in the group spend more than 1 percent of their GDP on the judiciary, while most other states spend around 0.5 percent on average. The overall spending on personnel is comparable to that of other states, meaning that wages in the judiciary may crowd out other important services. Despite efforts to strengthen it and considerable variance across states, the judiciary still tends to be weaker in Amazônia than in other parts of Brazil (figure 4A.2).

Enforcing the law is a challenge in Amazônia, making it difficult to reduce all types of crime, from drug trafficking to murder to illegal deforestation. The Amazonian frontier is marked by high illegality, weak rule of law, and generally lower levels of personal safety and property security. The magnitude of the challenge explains why states spend such a large share of their budgets on the judiciary. But the budgetary outlay is still insufficient to assert the law, and there is evidence that organized crime corrodes institutions in Amazônia. This situation highlights the challenge of enforcing the law, including but not limited to environmental protection laws.

Adequate resourcing and the ability to execute budgets properly matter. Amazônia's states receive significant equalization transfers from the federal

FIGURE 4A.2

The rule of law also tends to be weaker in Amazônia, 2021

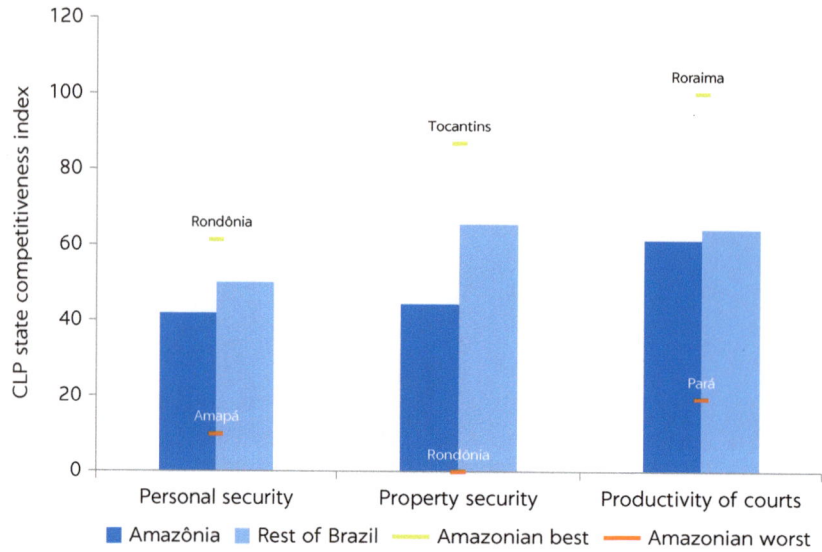

Source: World Bank, based on 2021 state competitiveness rankings by the Public Leadership Center (Centro de Liderança Pública, CLP).

government, somewhat reflective of their significant development needs. Within the budget constraints, the quality of spending is critical and largely within the purview of the subnational governments. But budget implementation is a big issue. Budget planning and management are weaker in Amazônia than in the rest of Brazil, reflected in budget execution that, on average, is 5.5 percent lower in these states than the national average (83 percent vs. 88.5 percent). Hence the need to build capacity in implementing ministries.

Sound public investment management (PIM) is critical when resources are scarce and requires a particularly strong emphasis on environmental safeguards in Amazônia's delicate ecosystem. Brazil has a complex and fragmented PIM system, common to many federal countries, with many actors and modalities for financing and executing public investment, including the federal government, subnational governments, state-owned enterprises, public development banks, concessionaires, and extrabudgetary funds. This fragmentation leads to a lack of uniform practices and approaches. Few Brazilian states have modern PIM systems. Instead, sectors and institutions have their own systems and manuals for project preparation, resulting in significant variation in the quality of investment projects and complicating comparisons between alternative investment projects. Political considerations and lobbying can affect project selection and, combined with uncertain funding, uneven project management, and a lack of capacity at the subnational level, and some spending ministries contribute to weak project execution, cost overruns, construction delays, and poor-quality infrastructure. Environmental standards are still weak in most subnational PIM systems.

Amazonian states are slow adopters of digital public services. Except for Amapá, all Amazonian states score below the national average on digital maturity, as measured by the Brazilian Association of State and Public ICT Entities (ABEP-TIC).[21] Most states lack an interoperability platform, leaving institutions to develop their own applications and systems without planning for the exchange or use of existing data. While most states have digital services platforms, they lack unique login capabilities and mostly redirect users to other websites, each with its own backend system, login, registry, and verification requirements. The result is a complex web of systems that users must navigate to access services. Most digital public services are simple information services, including the ability to download various forms and legislation. Few states have complex end-to-end digital services that require payment or document signatures. As a result, many users express confusion and dissatisfaction with digital services. Only Amapá has systems in place for user feedback, and only Rondônia has passed regulations to implement federal legislation on simplifying public services, an essential element for the rollout of simplified digital services.

NOTES

1. Interventions related to land regularization and law enforcement are described in figure 1.5 in chapter 1 illustrating the deforestation process.
2. This section draws on Calice and Kalan (2022).
3. Exceptions include credit for sustainable production, such as through the Low-Carbon Agriculture (ABC) Plan.
4. The size of farm exempt from the ITR by region, but is as small as 30 hectares in the majority of Brazil.
5. For recent proposals to reform the ITR, see Instituto Escolhas (2019) and Fendrich et al. (2022).
6. For a summary of the evidence, see the Climate Policy Initiative's "Evidence Pack" platform for viewing academic research (updated July 21, 2021): https://www.climatepolicyinitiative.org/dataviz/evidence-pack/.
7. Conservation units include units for sustainable use and those for preservation. While the first category allows for activities such as extractivism and human settlement (under specific conditions), the second does not allow for direct use of the unit's resources. Only activities such as research or ecotourism (sightseeing) are allowed in conservation units that are destinated for protection.
8. Estimates of undesignated lands vary by source, timing of data, and methodology. Based on National Institute for Colonization and Agrarian Reform (INCRA) data (2021 for private lands; 2020 for *quilombola* and INCRA settlements), the Amazon Institute of People and the Environment (Imazon) estimates 143.6 million hectares of undesignated lands. Excluding area covered with water (5.7 million hectares in Amazônia), the Amazon Environmental Research Institute (IPAM) (using 2021 CAR data, 2021 INCRA private lands data, 2020 INCRA settlements data, and 2019 National Register of Public Forests [CNPF] data) estimates 139.9 million hectares of undesignated lands. Both INCRA and IPAM agree on total land in Amazônia of 501.5 million hectares.
9. The CAR was designed to improve compliance with the Forest Code.
10. A "CRA Carbono" could solve this issue since global demand for forest offsets should grow significantly in the next decade. It would, however, make it more costly for noncompliers to resolve their status.
11. Fiscal modules are a unit of measure, in hectares, whose value is fixed by INCRA for each municipality, taking into account (a) the type of production prevalent in the municipality (horticulture, permanent culture, temporary culture, livestock, or forestry); (b) the income obtained in the predominant type of production; (c) other production in the municipality that, although not predominant, is substantial in terms of income or area used; and (d) the concept of "family ownership." The size of a fiscal module varies according to the municipality where the property is located. The value of the fiscal module in Brazil ranges from 5 hectares to 110 hectares.
12. In an initiative led by the International Finance Corporation and the Center for Sustainability Studies (FGVces) in 2017, the two institutions carried out a wide consultation process for governments, the private sector, and civil society to discuss a voluntary set of environmental and social guidelines for investments in large infrastructure projects.

Often there is a disconnect between commitments and on-ground implementation and monitoring of practices. Many companies gave high priority to their involvement with surrounding communities, given the economic drawbacks that may arise from potential disruption, and to the receipt of sustainability certifications for their products, when addressing the impact of consumer behavior.

13. For a list of donor funding for Amazon conservation and sustainable management, see the data dashboard of the World Bank's Amazon Sustainable Landscapes program: https://spatialagent.org/FundingAmazonConservation/datatool.html.

14. Among the various programs and initiatives is the Rock in Rio music festival's Amazon Live initiative.

15. There have also been green "use-of-proceeds" revenue bonds, green project bonds, and green securitized bonds. See "Explaining Green Bonds," Climate Bonds Initiative website: https://www.climatebonds.net/market/explaining-green-bonds.

16. The World Bank concluded its support to the Brazilian Ministry of Economy under the Partnership for Market Readiness in 2020.

17. In theory, forest offsets could also work under a carbon tax, but stakeholders consulted as part of the Partnership for Market Readiness in Brazil said that they prefer the ETS.

18. Under the program, the adoption of an ETS applicable to static combustion and industrial processes, covering approximately 20 percent of the Brazilian GHG emissions, would allow Brazil to comply with its NDCs in 2030 with a cost reduction of US$30 billion and a 2.2 percent increase in GDP relative to other abatement measures.

19. These recommendations are elaborated further in Calice and Kalan (2022).

20. The Centro de Lideranca Publica (CLP) is an independent research institution that ranks Brazilian states on their performance on a range of public policy topics including environmental sustainability, human capital, education, public sector performance, infrastructure quality, innovation, market potential, fiscal management, public security, and social development (poverty, health, access to sanitation).

21. See the ABEP-TIC Index of Digital Public Services Offered by State and District Governments: https://www.abep-tic.org.br/indice-abep-de-oferta-de-servicos.

REFERENCES

Abers, R., M. Oliveira, and A. Pereira. 2017. "Inclusive Development and the Asymmetric State: Big Projects and Local Communities in the Brazilian Amazon." *Journal of Development Studies* 53 (6): 1–16.

Albuquerque Sant'Anna, A., and L. Costa. 2021. "Environmental Regulation and Bail Outs under Weak State Capacity: Deforestation in the Brazilian Amazon." *Ecological Economics* 186 (August): 107071.

Angelsen, A., ed. 2008. *Moving Ahead with REDD: Issues, Options, and Implications*. Bogor, Indonesia: Center for International Forestry Research.

Arcand, J.-L., P. Guillaumont, and S. Guillaumont Jeanneney. 2008. "Deforestation and the Real Exchange Rate." *Journal of Development Economics* 86 (2): 242–62.

ART (Architecture for REDD+ Transactions). 2020. *The REDD+ Environmental Excellence Standard (Trees)*. Arlington, VA: ART Secretariat. https://www.artredd.org/wp-content/uploads/2020/04/TREES-v1-February-2020-FINAL.pdf.

Assunção, J., and C. Gandour. 2020. "Protected Territories, though Critical, Are Not Enough to Slow Amazon Deforestation: Brazil Requires Coordinated and Targeted Conservation Policies." Policy Brief, Climate Policy Initiative, Rio de Janeiro.

Assunção, J., C. Gandour, and R. Rocha. Forthcoming. "DETERring Deforestation in the Brazilian Amazon: Environmental Monitoring and Law Enforcement." *American Economic Journal: Applied Economics*. https://www.aeaweb.org/articles?id=10.1257/app.20200196.

Assunção, J., C. Grandour, R. Rocha, and R. Rocha. 2020. "The Effect of Rural Credit on Deforestation: Evidence from the Brazilian Amazon." *Economic Journal* 130 (626): 290–330.

Assunção, J., and R. Rocha. 2019. "Getting Greener by Going Black: The Effect of Blacklisting Municipalities on Amazon Deforestation." *Environment and Development Economics* 24 (2): 115–37.

Auty, R. 1993. *Sustaining Development in Mineral Economies: The Resource Curse Thesis.* Abingdon-on-Thames: Routledge.

Azevedo, A. A., M. C. C. Stabile, and T. N. P. Reis. 2015. "Commodity Production in Brazil: Combining Zero Deforestation and Zero Illegality." *Elementa: Science of the Anthropocene* 3: 3: 000076. doi:10.12952/journal.elementa.000076.

Azevedo, J. P., A. Hasan, D. Goldemberg, S. A. Iqbal, and K. Geven. 2020. "Simulating the Potential Impacts of COVID-19 School Closures on Schooling and Learning Outcomes: A Set of Global Estimates." Policy Research Working Paper 9284, World Bank, Washington, DC.

Besley, T., and S. Coate. 2003. "Centralized versus Decentralized Provision of Local Public Goods: A Political Economy Approach." *Journal of Public Economics* 87 (12): 2611–37.

Börner, J., K. Baylis, E. Corbera, D. Ezzine-de-Blas, J. Honey-Roses, U. M. Persson, and S. Wunder. 2017. "The Effectiveness of Payments for Environmental Services." *World Development* 96 (August): 359–74.

Brito, B., J. Almeida, P. Gomes, and R. Salomão. 2021. *Dez fatos essenciais sobre regularização fundiária na Amazônia legal.* Belém, Brazil: Imazon.

Calice, P., and F. D. Kalan. 2022. "Sustainable, Inclusive Growth: Rural Finance in the North Region." Background note for this report, World Bank, Washington, DC.

Cavallito, M. 2021. "Financial Firms Put Pressure on Bolsonaro: 'Brazil Must Save the Amazon.'" Re Soil Foundation, August 16.

Center for Strategic Studies and Management. 2016. *Land Degradation and Neutrality: Implications for Brazil.* Brasília: Center for Strategic Studies and Management.

Chiavari, J., and C. L. Lopes. 2019. "Onde Estamos na Implementação do Código Florestal." Report, Climate Policy Initiative, Pontifical Catholic University of Rio de Janeiro.

Chiavari, J., C. L. Lopes, and J. N. de Araujo. 2020a. *Onde estamos na implementação do Código Florestal? Radiografia do CAR e do PRA nos estados brasileiros.* Rio de Janeiro: Climate Policy Initiative.

Chiavari, J., C. L. Lopes, and J. N. de Araujo. 2020b. *Panorama dos direitos de propriedade no Brasil.* Rio de Janeiro: Climate Policy Initiative.

de Figueiredo Silva, F., L. Fulginiti, and R. Perrin. 2019. "The Cost of Forest Preservation in the Brazilian Amazon: The 'Arc of Deforestation'." *Journal of Agricultural and Resource Economics* 44 (3): 497–512.

Engel, S., S. Pagiola, and S. Wunder. 2008. "Designing Payments for Environmental Services in Theory and Practice: An Overview of the Issues." *Ecological Economics* 65 (4): 663–74.

FAO (Food and Agricultural Organization of the United Nations) and FILAC (Fund of the Development of the Indigenous Peoples of Latin America and the Caribbean). 2021. *Forest Governance by Indigenous and Tribal Peoples. An Opportunity for Climate Action in Latin America and the Caribbean.* Santiago: FAO and FILAC. doi:10.4060/cb2953en.

Fendrich, A. N., A. Barretto, G. Sparovek, G. W. Gianetti, J. da Luz Ferreira, C. F. M. de Souza Filho, B. Appy, C. M. Guedes de Guedes, and S. Leitão. 2022. "Taxation Aiming Environmental Protection: The Case of Brazilian Rural Land Tax." *Land Use Policy* 119: 106164.

Flugge, M. L., R. C. K. Mok, and F. E. Stewart. 2021. "Striking the Right Note: Key Performance Indicators for Sovereign Sustainability-Linked Bonds." World Bank, Washington, DC.

Gandour, C., D. Menezes, J. P. Vieira, and J. J. Assunção. 2021. "Forest Degradation in the Brazilian Amazon: Public Policy Must Target Phenomenon Related to Deforestation." Insight report, Climate Policy Initiative, Pontifical Catholic University of Rio de Janeiro.

Gibbs, H. K. 2015. "Did Ranchers and Slaughterhouses Respond to Zero Deforestation Agreements in the Brazilian Amazon?" *Conservation Letters* 9 (1): 32–42.

Hardin, G. 1968. "The Tragedy of the Commons." *Science* 162 (3859): 1243–48.

Hay, J. 2021. "Greenwashing Is in the Mouth of the Investor." *GlobalCapital Securitization,* June 24.

Herrera, D., A. Pfaff, and J. Robalino. 2019. "Impacts of Protected Areas Vary with the Level of Government: Comparing Avoided Deforestation across Agencies in the Brazilian Amazon." *Proceedings of the National Academy of Sciences* 116 (30): 14916–25.

Human Rights Watch. 2019. *World Report 2019.* New York: Seven Stories Press.

ICMA (International Capital Market Association). 2020. "Sustainability-Linked Bond Principles: Voluntary Process Guidelines, June 2020." ICMA, Paris.

Instituto Escolhas. 2019. *Imposto territorial rural: Justiça tributária e incentivos ambientais*. São Paulo: Instituto Escolhas.

IPAM (Amazon Environmental Research Institute). 2016. "O imposto territorial rural: Como forma de induzir boas práticas ambientais." Report, IPAM, Brasília.

Keles, D., P. Delacote, A. Pfaff, S. Qin, and M. B. Mascia. 2020. "What Drives the Erasure of Protected Areas? Evidence from across the Brazilian Amazon." *Ecological Economics* 176 (October): 106733.

Mangonnet, J., J. Kopas, and J. Urpelainen. 2022. "Playing Politics with Environmental Protection: The Political Economy of Designating Protected Areas." *Journal of Politics* 84 (3). doi:10.1086/718978.

Mauerhofer, V., K. Hubacek, and A. Coleby. 2013. "From Polluter Pays to Provider Gets: Distribution of Rights and Costs under Payments for Ecosystem Services." *Ecology and Society* 18 (4): 41.

May, P. 2015. *Tourism's Contribution to Forest Benefits in the Amazon Basin*. Washington, DC: World Bank.

Miranda, J., J. Börner, M. Kalkuhl, and B. Soares-Filho. 2019. "Land Speculation and Conservation Policy Leakage in Brazil." *Environmental Research Letters* 14 (4): 045006.

Moffette, F., and H. K. Gibbs. 2021. "Agricultural Displacement and Deforestation Leakage in the Brazilian Amazônia." *Land Economics* 97 (1): 155–79.

Nepstad, D., M. de los Rios, R. Seroa da Motta, C. Dihl Prolo, M. Warren, C. Stickler, J. Ardila, L. Lopes, T. Bezerra, and J. Shimada. 2022. "The New Carbon Market and the Brazilian Amazon." Policy Brief, Earth Innovation Institute, San Francisco, CA.

OECD (Organisation for Economic Co-operation and Development). 2020. "A Comprehensive Overview of Global Biodiversity Finance." Final Report, OECD, Paris.

OECD (Organisation for Economic Co-operation and Development). 2021. "Evaluating Brazil's Progress in Implementing Environmental Performance Review Recommendations and Promoting Its Alignment with OECD Core Acquis on the Environment." Report, OECD, Paris.

Ozment, S., M. Gonzalez, A. Schumacher, E. Oliver, G. Morales, T. Gartner, M. Silva, A. Grünwaldt, and G. Watson. 2021. *Nature-Based Solutions in Latin America and the Caribbean: Regional Status and Priorities for Growth*. Washington, DC: Inter-American Development Bank and World Resources Institute.

Pailler, S. 2018. "Re-election Incentives and Deforestation Cycles in the Brazilian Amazon." *Journal of Environmental Economics and Management* 88 (March): 345–65.

Porcher, C., and M. Hanusch. 2022. "A Model of Amazon Deforestation, Trade, and Labor Market Dynamics." Policy Research Working Paper 10163, World Bank, Washington, DC.

Proforest. 2021. "Beef Traceability in Brazil." Report prepared for the International Finance Corporation, Washington, DC.

Rajão, R., and B. Soares-Filho. 2015. *Cotas de reserva ambiental (CRA): Potencial e viabilidade econômica do mercado no Brasil*. Belo Horizonte, Brazil: Center for Remote Sensing of the Federal University of Minas Gerais.

Rode, J., A. Pinzon, M. C. C. Stabile, J. Pirker, S. Bauch, A. Iribarrem, P. Sammon, et al. 2019. "Why 'Blended Finance' Could Help Transitions to Sustainable Landscapes: Lessons from the Unlocking Forest Finance Project." *Ecosystem Services* 37 (June): 100917.

Sanchez Martinez, G., J. Paiva, G. L. de Paula, P. Moutinho, R. Castriota, and A. C. G. Costa. 2022. "Indigenous Peoples and Sustainable Development in the Brazilian Amazônia." Background note for this report, World Bank, Washington, DC.

Schons, S. 2019. "Smallholder Land Clearing and the Forest Code in the Brazilian Amazon." *Environment and Development Economics* 24 (2): 1–23.

Sigman, H. 2005. "Transboundary Spillovers and Decentralization of Environmental Policies." *Journal of Environmental Economics and Management* 50 (1): 82–101.

Sills, E., A. Pfaff, L. Andrade, J. Kirkpatrick, and R. Dickson. 2020. "Investing in Local Capacity to Respond to a Federal Environmental Mandate: Forest & Economic Impacts of the Green Municipality Program in the Brazilian Amazon." *World Development* 129 (May): 104891.

Slough, T., and J. Urpelainen. 2018. "Public Policy under Limited State Capacity: Evidence from Deforestation Control in the Brazilian Amazon." Unpublished technical report.

Soares-Filho, B., R. Rajão, M. Macedo, A. Carneiro, W. Costa, M. Coe, H. Rodrigues, and A. Alencar. 2014. "Cracking Brazil's Forest Code." *Science* 344 (6182): 363–64.

Soares-Filho, B., R. Rajão, F. Merry, H. Rodrigues, J. Davis, L. Lima, M. Macedo, M. Coe, A. Carneiro, and L. Santiago. 2016. "Brazil's Market for Trading Forest Certificates." *PLOS ONE* 11 (4): e0152311.

Sonter, L. J., D. Herrera, D. J. Barrett, G. L. Galford, C. J. Moran, and B. S. Soares-Filho. 2017. "Mining Drives Extensive Deforestation in the Brazilian Amazon." *Nature Communications* 8 (1): 1013.

Souza-Rodrigues, E. 2019. "Deforestation in the Amazon: A Unified Framework for Estimation and Policy Analysis." *Review of Economic Studies* 86 (6): 2713–44.

Stabile, M. C. C., A. L. Guimarães, D. S. Silva, V. Ribeiro, M. N. Macedo, M. T. Coe, E. Pinto, P. Moutinho, and A. Alencar. 2019. "Solving Brazil's Land Use Puzzle: Increasing Production and Slowing Amazon Deforestation." *Land Use Policy* 91 (February): 104362.

Wang, D., B. Gurhy, and M. Hanusch. 2022. "Could Sustainability-Linked Bonds Incentivize Lower Deforestation in Brazil's Legal Amazon?" Background note for this report, World Bank, Washington, DC.

West, T. A. P., and P. Fearnside. 2021. "Brazil's Conservation Reform and the Reduction of Deforestation in Amazonia." *Land Use Policy* 100 (January): 105072.

World Bank. 2021. *Designing Fiscal Instruments for Sustainable Forests*. Washington, DC: World Bank.

World Bank. 2023a. *Brazil Country Climate and Development Report*. Washington, DC: World Bank.

World Bank. 2023b. "Urban Competitiveness in Brazil's State of Amazonas: A Green Growth Agenda." Companion paper for this report, World Bank, Washington, DC.

Wunder, S. 2014. "Revisiting the Concept of Payments for Environmental Services." *Ecological Economics* 117 (September): 234–43.

Wunder, S., J. Börner, D. Ezzine-de-Blas, S. Feder, and S. Pagiola. 2020. "Payments for Environmental Services: Past Performance and Pending Potentials." *Annual Review of Resource Economics* 12 (1): 209–34.

Rural and Urban Development

5 Rural Transformation and Diversification in Amazônia

HANS JANSEN, MAREK HANUSCH, GIOVANI WILLIAM GIANETTI,
FRANK MERRY, ADAUTO BRASILINO ROCHA JUNIOR,
CLAUDIA TUFANI, AND DANIELE LA PORTA

KEY MESSAGES

- Rural transformation in Amazônia is driven primarily by improved access to markets and increasing demand for agricultural products. While rural transformation raises incomes overall, it also causes social and environmental disruption.
- Competitive pressures intensify agricultural production on commercial farms and crowd out smaller, more traditional, and less productive farms.
- Deforestation increases as agriculture demands more land—which is relatively cheap in frontier regions such as Amazônia—and poorer farmers seek to maintain their standard of living. Deforestation also increases land degradation.
- Cattle ranching and certain crops are the main drivers of deforestation. There is potential for more sustainable production systems, but their adoption is currently limited in frontier economies. Support for climate-smart and greener practices in agriculture is therefore critical for sustainable rural development in Amazônia.
- Diversification options (like agroforestry) exist in rural Amazônia, but their adoption requires more developed markets in the region.
- Cities will need to absorb much of the labor that leaves rural areas during periods of structural transformation.
- *Policy actions:*
  - Supporting smaller farmers in moving into higher-value-added agriculture using climate-smart production technologies.
  - Supporting private sector initiatives in agribusiness aimed at sourcing from zero-deforestation production only.
  - Improving tenure security and strengthening command and control (see also chapter 4).

- Creating an enabling environment for productivity growth in non-land-intensive rural activities (like fisheries and aquaculture).
- Educating and retraining small farmers and rural laborers and enable rural-urban transitions (see also chapter 2).
- Expanding social protection, including protection linked to ecosystem services (see also chapter 2).

GROWTH, DISRUPTION, AND RESILIENCE IN RURAL AMAZÔNIA

Rural transformation will contribute to long-term prosperity in Amazônia, but it will also cause disruption, which policy needs to manage. As discussed in chapters 2 and 3, structural transformation from agriculture into manufacturing and services and increasing urbanization are part of long-term economic development. This transformation will raise incomes over time but also cause social and cultural disruption. Chapter 3 also showed that balancing careful management of economic transformation in rural areas (including increases in both agricultural and nonagricultural productivity) with higher productivity in urban areas is required to absorb rural labor and will eventually support more favorable land dynamics while reducing pressure on natural forests. Rural transformation thus has a major impact on nature and livelihoods in Amazônia. This chapter explores how rural transformation affects rural areas and investigates how a policy that combines environmental protection, support for climate-smart practices in agriculture,[1] and social protection can shape the transformation process and mitigate disruption.

Rural areas are unlikely to provide sufficient job opportunities to absorb all of the rural labor released during rural transformation, highlighting the importance of cities and the need to prepare some residents of rural areas for urban lives. Most rural employment in Amazônia is in agriculture (crop and livestock production) (figure 5.1), which accounts for 80 percent of private sector jobs in Rondônia and 42 percent in Roraima (calculated from figure 5.1, excluding public services). Forestry and fishing and aquaculture make smaller, but sizable, contributions to rural employment, especially in the states in Amazônia and the coastal regions. There is some rural manufacturing in Acre, Amazonas, and Pará, mainly near urban areas. Accommodation services, including some tourism, generate minor employment opportunities. Mining (often associated in Amazônia with *garimpeiros*, artisanal or wildcat miners; see chapter 1) also generates some employment, both formal and informal. As the magnitudes in figure 5.1 suggest, these sectors would require substantial employment growth to be able to absorb the large numbers of laborers currently working in agriculture. The employment-generating capacity of rural diversification, including in the rural bioeconomy, is thus relatively limited, highlighting the need for urban areas to absorb most of the excess rural labor and avoid the emergence of favela-like human settlements (see also chapter 2).

This chapter explores rural transformation in Amazônia and derives implications for policy. It reviews the types of land available in the rural transformation

FIGURE 5.1

Most rural employment in Amazonian states is in agriculture

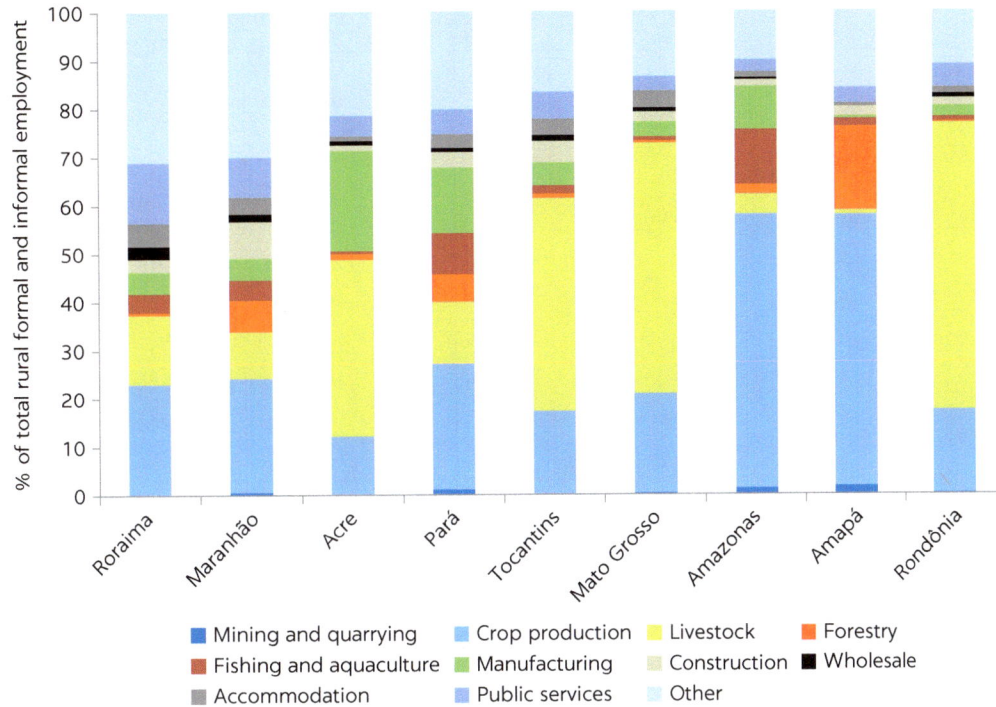

Source: World Bank, using data for the fourth quarter of 2019 from the Brazilian Institute of Geography and Statistics (IBGE) National Continuous Household Sample Survey (PNADC).

process, emphasizing that land designations impose limits on productive use in large parts of Amazônia (see chapter 4); examines transformation in agriculture (including crop and livestock production) and its social and environmental impacts; and suggests implications for policy. One implication concerns the need to prepare rural populations, across generations, for alternative employment opportunities, some in rural areas but most in urban areas. Potential rural job opportunities include diversification in (agro)forestry and nontimber forest products, mining, fishing and aquaculture, and ecological and community-based tourism. Their economic potential is limited, however, and in some cases, such as agroforestry, their viability depends on advancing rural transformation. The key implications from chapters 2–4 also hold for this chapter: by carefully managing both the opportunities and disruptions generated by rural transformation, policy can support rising incomes without undermining the conditions for dignified lives, including in traditional and other rural communities.

RURAL TRANSFORMATION AND LAND USE

More than half of the land in Amazônia is protected and cannot be used for productive purposes or can be used only under severely restricted conditions. Table 5.1 classifies land by public- and private-good dimension, contribution to rural livelihoods, potential for productivity gains, and deforestation risk. Brazil has made considerable advances in protecting public goods in Amazônia by designating various forms of protection of public land. Although some parts of

TABLE 5.1 **Classification of land in Amazônia**

LAND USE CATEGORY	PUBLIC-GOOD DIMENSION	PRIVATE-GOOD DIMENSION	CONTRIBUTION TO RURAL LIVELIHOODS	POTENTIAL FOR PRODUCTIVITY GAINS	DEFORESTATION RISK
Undesignated forest	Very high	Very low	Low	Low if public; high if private	Very high
Indigenous lands	Very high	Very low	Low	Low	Low
Protected areas	Very high	Very low	Low	Very low	Low
Extractive reserves	Medium–high	Low	Low	Low	Low–medium
Public land under forest concessions	Medium–high	Low–medium	Low–medium	Low–medium	Low
Agrarian reform settlements	Medium	Medium	High	High	Very high
Mixed landscapes and agroforestry	Medium–high	Medium	Medium	Medium–high	Medium
Pastures	Very low	High	Medium	High	Very high
Cropland	Very low	Very high	Medium	High	Very high
Degraded lands (unrestored)	Very low	Low	Low	Low	Low

Source: World Bank.

protected public lands can support some production—for example, production through extractive reserves and forest concessions—the regulations that allow for the creation of these sustainable use areas limit the extent of production and choice of technology and thus their level of productivity. The risk of deforestation on public designated land is also lower (see chapter 4). Thus the potential for improved productivity and rural transformation rests mainly with private lands (including agrarian reform settlements or *assentamentos*). Although private land holds the potential for economic growth, certain types of commercial land use are difficult to reconcile with conservation of natural lands, thus tilting the balance toward private rather than public goods. Climate-smart production technologies (including agroforestry systems)[2] and integrated landscape approaches[3] hold some promise for balancing economic development with higher environmental sustainability, but their adoption depends on the level of market development in the region, as discussed in more detail below.

TRANSFORMATION IN AGRICULTURE

This section characterizes agricultural markets and farmers in Amazônia and analyzes the environmental impacts of transformation in agriculture. It shows that, against a background of highly unequal land distribution and dominance of cattle ranching and annual crops in land use, market dynamics are driving a process of rural transformation in Amazônia that increasingly favors large farms with higher total factor productivity (TFP). Growing pressure on competitiveness of small farms in Amazônia and increasing inability of smallholder agriculture to absorb rural labor point toward the need to pay more attention to urban productivity.

Rural transformation and agricultural markets in Amazônia

Much of Amazônia remains an agricultural frontier region, with weakly developed markets (see chapter 1). Markets in frontier areas are remote from centers of economic activity, have inadequate infrastructure, and suffer from market distortions resulting mainly from insecure land tenure (see chapter 4), low access to credit and technical assistance, and low shares of public spending. Production systems in frontier areas tend to be mixed cropping systems, which are labor intensive with low labor productivity, high land productivity, and a high degree of crop diversification. Low levels of technology and economic efficiency result in low TFP, leading to high unit costs of production. The isolation of these areas raises transportation costs, so production mainly serves local markets.

Most farms in Amazônia are family farms, but nonfamily farms account for most of the land area and agricultural output. The Brazilian Family Farm Law (Law 11.326/2006) defines family farmers by farm size, predominant use of family workers, operations managed by the family, and income primarily from farming.[4] Brazilian public policies, such as rural credit programs, further distinguish between poorer family farmers—defined as family farmers who have a gross annual family income (excluding public transfers) of up to R$23,000 (approximately US$4,200) and who use only family labor[5]—and other family farmers.[6] Family farmers, who in Amazônia number about 750,000, account for about 80 percent of farm establishments but for less than 25 percent and 20 percent of agricultural area and gross production value, respectively, while the 170,000 nonfamily farmers hold around 75 percent of all agricultural land (figure 5.2). Land distribution in Amazônia is thus highly unequal: 80 percent of farmers own less than 100 hectares of land and account for 13 percent of total area, while 2.3 percent of farmers own more than 1,000 hectares of land and account for 61 percent of total area.[7]

Among family farmers in Amazônia, livestock raising is the most important agricultural activity, followed by annual crops. About half of family farmers raise

FIGURE 5.2

Shares of nonfamily farms and family farms in gross production value, area, and number of farms, by farm size

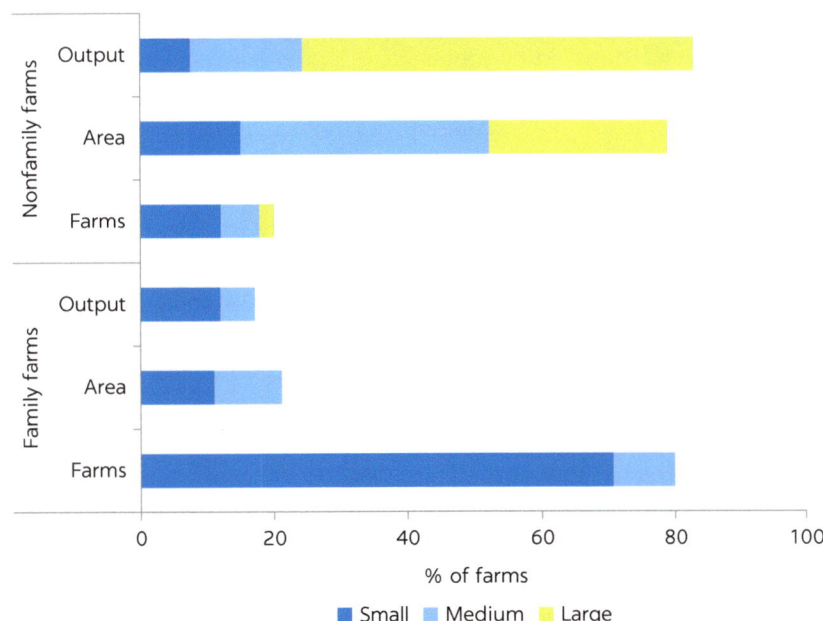

Source: World Bank, based on the 2017 Census of Agriculture by the Brazilian Institute of Geography and Statistics (IBGE).
Note: Small = < 100 hectares. Medium = 100–1,000 hectares. Large = > 1,000 hectares.

FIGURE 5.3

Characteristics of family farms: Distribution of gross production value, area by agricultural activity, and share of farms engaged in each activity

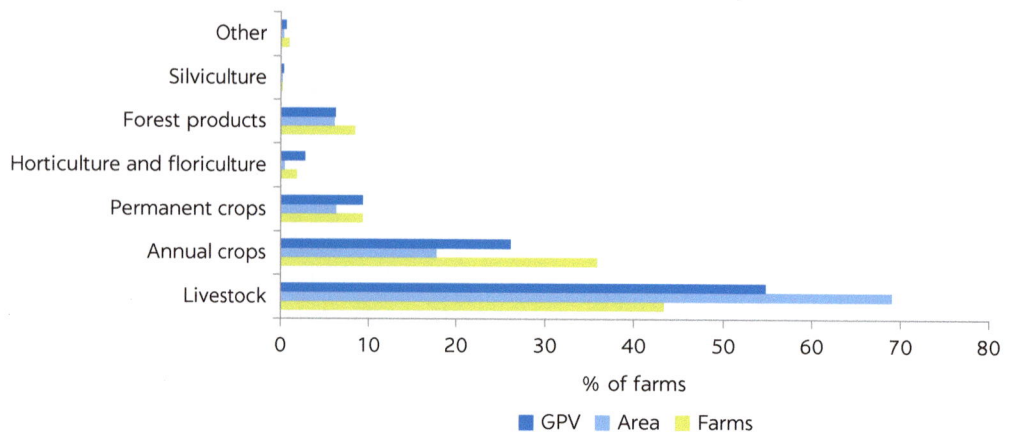

Source: World Bank, based on the 2017 Census of Agriculture by the Brazilian Institute of Geography and Statistics (IBGE).
Note: GPV = gross production value.

livestock, which takes up about 70 percent of the agricultural area and accounts for more than half of agricultural gross production value (figure 5.3). Livestock is followed (in order of importance) by annual crops, permanent crops, and forest products. The shares of other agricultural activities such as agroforestry and horticulture are relatively minor.

Agricultural markets are developing across Brazil, including in Amazônia. Helfand and Taylor (2021) trace farming across three phases, following Brazil's spatial pattern of historical development, with the South and Southeast the most developed regions, the Central-West (which includes Mato Grosso) a developing region, and the North (including the Amazon biome) a frontier region. Producers in frontier areas, where low infrastructure development results in market isolation, face inelastic labor supply and produce mainly for local markets with fairly inelastic demand. Agricultural producers in Amazônia have lower levels of education and less access to credit than their counterparts elsewhere in Brazil, resulting in high labor- and land-intensive farming. But as markets develop, institutions strengthen, distortions diminish, and access to credit and technology improves, production becomes more capital intensive. As natural land is converted into agricultural land (through deforestation), the stock of natural land shrinks and land supply becomes less elastic, eventually resulting in less land expansion for agricultural production. A snapshot of the drivers of market development in Amazônia in figure 5.4 indicates that Mato Grosso (in the New Frontier) is the most advanced state and Amazonas (in the Colonial Frontier) the most lagging,[8] making them good case studies for this chapter.

As markets develop, rural transformation fundamentally alters farming, increasingly advantaging larger farmers. Small and large farmers can coexist when markets are weakly developed, and small farmers may remain competitive as markets develop, provided that they specialize. They may even have similar levels of TFP (see box 5.1) as long as distortions in credit markets limit the ability of larger farmers to replace labor with capital (figure 5.5) and higher costs of labor supervision associated with land size restrict the productivity of larger farmers. However, as markets develop and distortions in land and capital

FIGURE 5.4

Agricultural markets are more developed in the New Frontier than in the Colonial Frontier

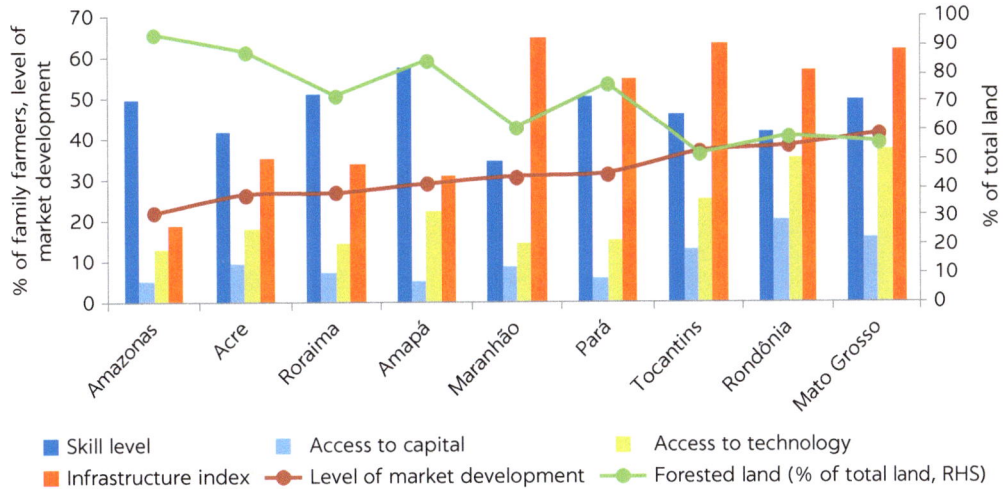

Legend:
- ■ Skill level
- ■ Access to capital
- ■ Access to technology
- ■ Infrastructure index
- ●— Level of market development
- ●— Forested land (% of total land, RHS)

Sources: World Bank, using the 2017 Census of Agriculture by the Brazilian Institute of Geography and Statistics (IBGE) and MapBiomas data.
Note: Skill level = % of family farmers with at least basic education; access to capital = % of family farmers who used credit; access to technology = % of farmers with internet access; infrastructure index = Grupo de Politicas Publicas of the University of São Paulo (https://www.gppesalq.agr.br/) infrastructure index; level of market development = averaged measure for skill level, capital, technology, and infrastructure index.

BOX 5.1

Farm size and farm productivity

Farm productivity can be measured in several ways. This chapter focuses on total factor productivity (TFP), defined as the output generated by all factors of production (land, labor, capital) and other inputs. The higher the output at given levels of production factors and other inputs, the more productive the farm. Like labor productivity, land productivity is a partial measure of productivity: output generated per unit of land, typically referred to as yield. As markets develop further, the resulting improved farm productivity is reflected in increased TFP and land productivity (see figure B5.1.1 for soybean yields).

Across the world, small farms tend to outperform larger farms in land productivity. This performance is often attributed to the relatively higher use of (mostly family) labor and is not necessarily a reflection of high efficiency. For Brazil, Helfand and Taylor (2021) confirm that smaller farmers have higher land productivity, irrespective of their level of market development. However, as markets develop, larger farmers achieve higher TFP. Larger farmers also tend to have higher labor productivity because their capital-labor ratios are higher.

FIGURE B5.1.1

Soybean yields increase with market development

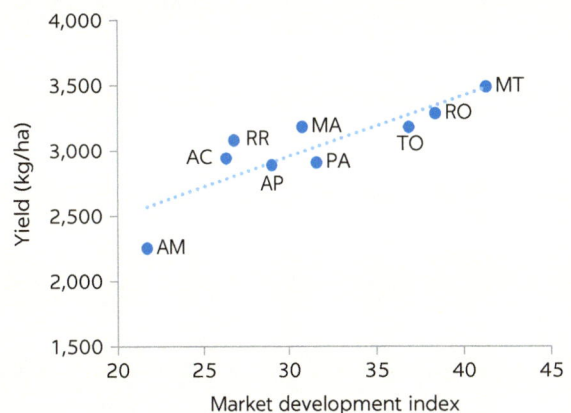

Sources: Market development index from Census of Agriculture by the Brazilian Institute of Geography and Statistics (IBGE) and Grupo de Politicas Publicas of the University of São Paulo (https://www.gppesalq.agr.br/); soybean yield from Conab (Companhia Nacional de Abastecimento).
Note: Market development is an averaged measure of the skill level, capital, technology, and infrastructure indexes. kg/ha = kilogram per hectare. AC = Acre; AM = Amazonas; AP = Amapá; MA = Maranhão; MT = Mato Grosso; PA = Pará; RO = Rondônia; RR = Roraima; TO = Tocantins.

FIGURE 5.5

Three phases of transformation in Amazonian agriculture

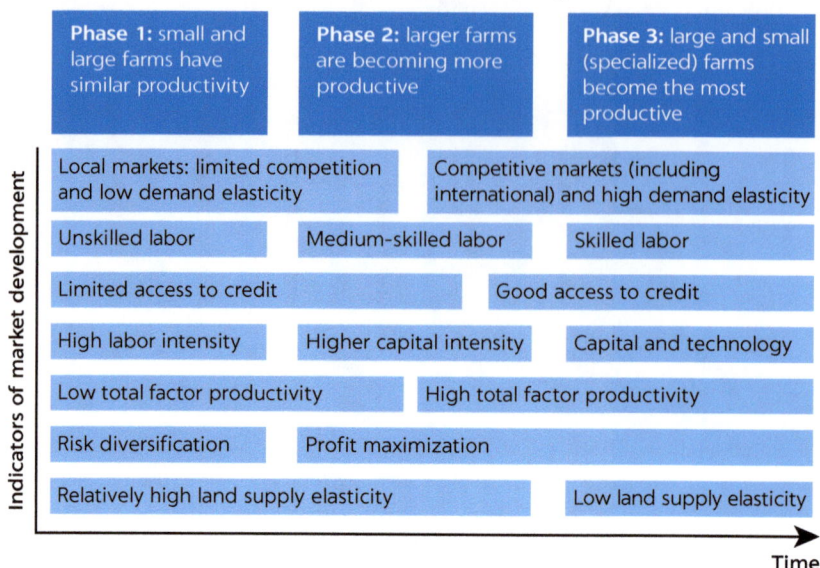

Phase 1: small and large farms have similar productivity	Phase 2: larger farms are becoming more productive	Phase 3: large and small (specialized) farms become the most productive

Indicators of market development

Local markets: limited competition and low demand elasticity	Competitive markets (including international) and high demand elasticity

Unskilled labor	Medium-skilled labor	Skilled labor

Limited access to credit	Good access to credit

High labor intensity	Higher capital intensity	Capital and technology

Low total factor productivity	High total factor productivity

Risk diversification	Profit maximization

Relatively high land supply elasticity	Low land supply elasticity

→ Time

Source: World Bank.

markets diminish (for example, as improved tenure security results in better access to credit),[9] larger farmers substitute capital for labor, thus reducing their supervision costs. Doing so enables them to gain a land productivity advantage in field crops that, coupled with lower unit production costs related to increasing returns to scale, improves their competitiveness relative to smaller farmers. This differentiation between larger and smaller farmers is particularly evident in field crops and may widen as large farmers' access to technology increases (including information and communication technologies and improved inputs) and as more skilled labor (including managerial skills) becomes available.

Smaller farmers can remain competitive in developed markets by focusing on high-value crops with decreasing or constant returns to scale or high-value-added niche markets. Even in developed markets, small farmers can have higher land productivity than larger farmers and continue to produce higher-value commodities for local or regional urban markets (such as horticulture, cacao, black pepper, and coffee).[10] However, as markets develop, larger farmers increasingly outperform smaller farmers in terms of TFP.

As more productive farms crowd out less productive ones, overall productivity increases. A comparison of the impact of market integration in advanced and lagging economies found an increase in TFP in lagging regions as high-productivity producers export to advanced regions, building their market share and putting upward pressure on wages by demanding more labor (Melitz 2003).[11] Low-productivity producers in lagging regions can ill afford the higher labor costs and thus exit. While medium-productivity producers may stay in the market, their productivity levels are too low to allow them to compete in the advanced region (including export markets), and they lose market share to more productive producers. Rural transformation in Amazônia can therefore be expected to result in an overall increase in TFP through a gradual exit of less productive farmers as part of a process of increasing integration with more advanced economies, including regional, national, and global agricultural markets.

Rural transformation and farmers in Amazônia

As is common in agricultural markets with low levels of development, subsistence farming dominates among family farmers in Amazônia. Small farmers consume most of their production of annual crops, mainly grains (figure 5.6), including as animal feed. In contrast, horticultural production is mainly for the market, with production concentrated in peri-urban areas. Permanent crops (cultivated) and forest products (mostly extracted) present a more mixed picture, with own consumption more prevalent among extracted products than cultivated crops.

Compared with nonfamily farmers, family farmers in Amazônia have less access to infrastructure, technical assistance, and capital, and fewer years of education, putting them under increasing competitive pressure. Approximately 30 percent of family farmers in Amazônia do not have access to electricity, less than 8 percent receive some form of technical assistance (mostly from public sources), and less than 4 percent are organized through cooperatives that provide market access and help to bring produce to scale (figure 5.7). Less than 15 percent of family farmers have at least a secondary education. Of these productivity-related variables, membership in a cooperative (Herrera et al. 2018) and education are the most important determinants of smallholder productivity (figure 5.8).

Access to credit facilitates the acquisition of productivity-improving inputs, but the proportion of Amazônian farmers with access to credit is low, and loans to small farmers focus mainly on poverty alleviation. While 29 percent of farmers in Brazil's southern region reported having taken a loan, only about 9 percent of farmers in Amazônia did (the percentage is even lower among women farmers). In addition, most credit consists of short-term working capital

FIGURE 5.6

Consumption of own production was higher on family farms, 2017

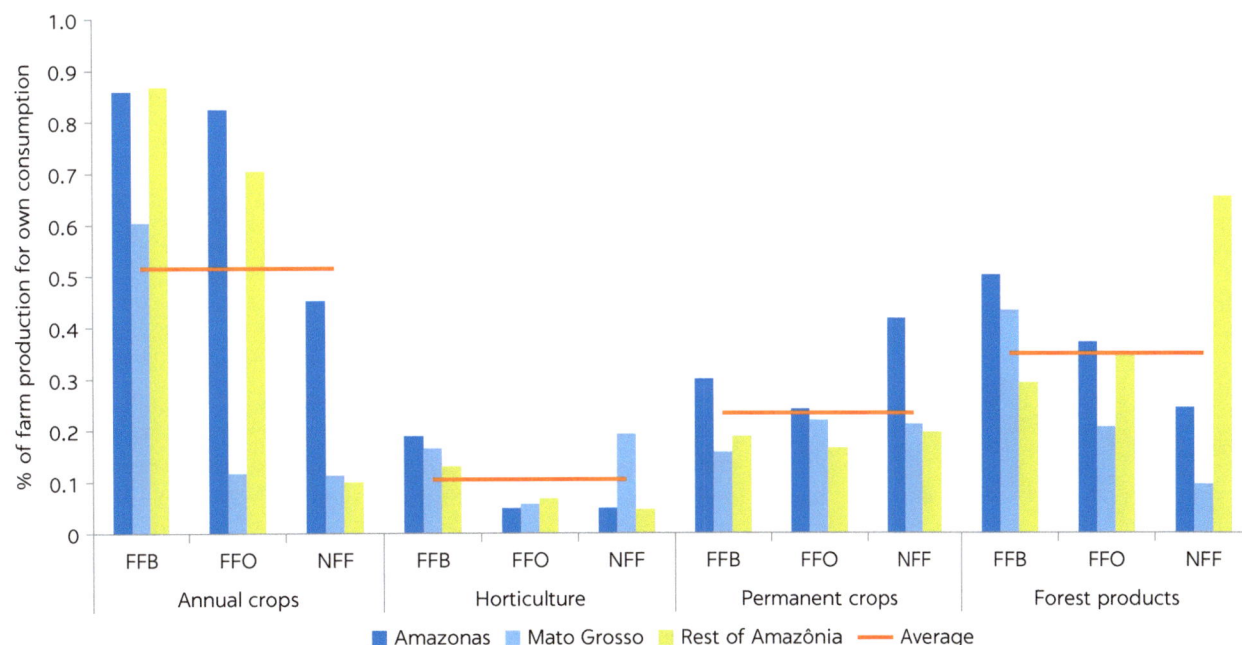

Source: World Bank, using the 2017 Census of Agriculture by the Brazilian Institute of Geography and Statistics (IBGE).
Note: FFB = poor family farmers. FFO = nonpoor family farmers. NFF = nonfamily farmers.

FIGURE 5.7

Changes in the share of farmers benefiting from productivity-increasing measures, by farm size, 2006–17

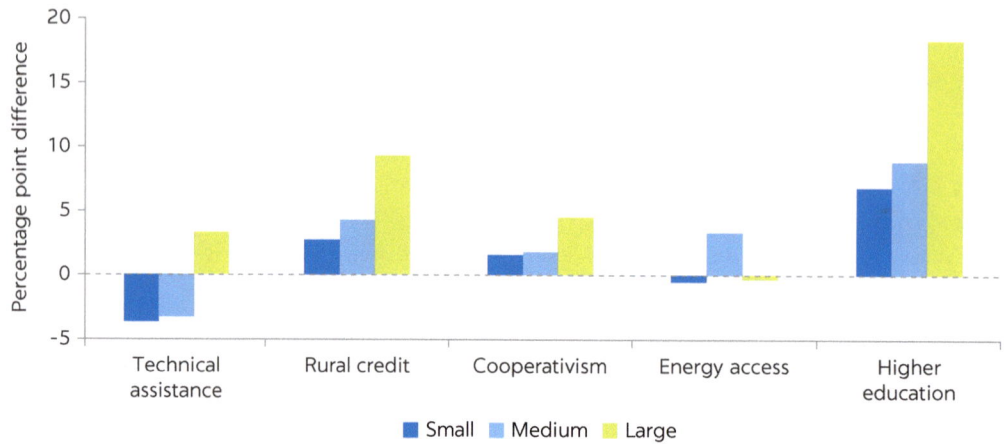

Source: Rocha 2022.
Note: Small = < 100 hectares. Medium = 100–1,000 hectares. Large = > 1,000 hectares.

FIGURE 5.8

The impact of productivity-related variables on changes in total factor productivity, by farm size, 2006–17

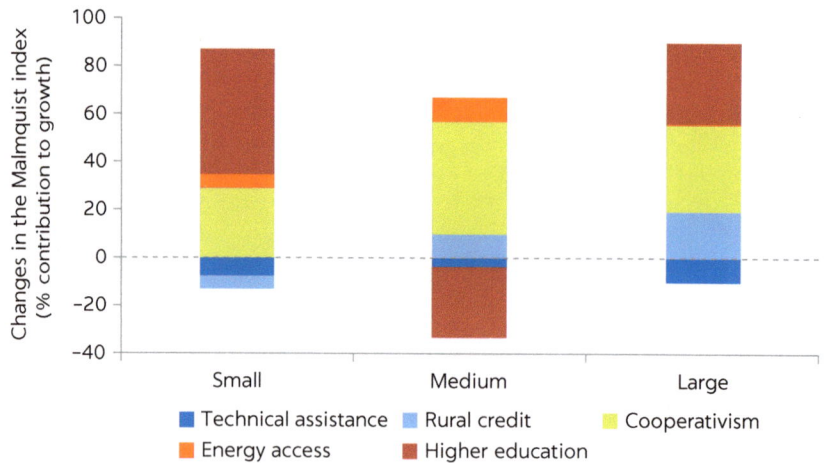

Source: Rocha 2022.
Note: Excludes the contribution from fixed time and residual effects. Small = < 100 hectares. Medium = 100–1,000 hectares. Large = > 1,000 hectares.

rather than longer-term investment loans, which are critical for the adoption of climate-smart agricultural production technologies and thus for simultaneously increasing productivity and sustainability. And small family farmers rely mostly on cooperatives and public banks for credit, whereas larger farmers often borrow from private banks. Private banks are required to earmark a certain percentage of deposits for rural credit, which especially benefits larger farmers, even though they may not be credit constrained. Government-sponsored credit programs such as the National Program to Strengthen Family Farming (PRONAF) and the National Support Program for Medium-Size Rural Producers offer subsidized (low-interest) loans to small and medium family farmers. In 2017 these programs reached about 15,000 family farmers in Amazônia, accounting for about one-third of farmers with a loan (or about 3 percent of all farmers).

However, these government programs have been losing ground over the past few years, as the systematic decline in the proportion of small loans over time has increasingly restricted small farmers' access to credit, and the loans have tended to focus on poverty alleviation rather than on productivity-increasing investments (Brinker 2019; Calice and Kalan 2022; Magalhães and Abramovay 2006; Maia et al. 2012). In addition, the reach of government-supported agriculture insurance programs is very limited in Amazônia.

Several changes to rural credit programs could reduce distortions in rural finance markets and improve access to credit for small family farms. First, instead of interest rate subsidies, which favor larger loans, a fixed subsidy to help banks to cover the administrative costs of loans would work in favor of smaller loans. Second, eliminating interest rate subsidies on loans for large farmers[12] and linking the loans to sustainability objectives would free up resources to strengthen credit programs for small farmers (facilitating the adoption of climate-smart agriculture) and expand agriculture insurance and other risk management programs (World Bank 2020).

The effect of higher education on productivity is strongest for small and large farms (figure 5.8). Small farmers usually work their own land, so any improvement in their technical skills will boost productivity. Many of them engage in off-farm work as well, and education improves their position in the off-farm job market, which may facilitate their purchase of productivity-enhancing inputs. The literature indicates that education has multiple effects on farmers' income, including the probability of obtaining nonfarm employment (Greiner and Sakdapolrak 2013; Yue, Feldman, and Du 2010). Large farmers tend to have agricultural production as their primary source of income, and further improvements in their managerial skills directly benefit farm productivity. A recent study found significant positive effects of education on TFP in Brazilian agriculture for the smallest and largest farmers but not for medium-size farmers (Rada, Helfand, and Magalhães 2019). Earlier studies were often based on the assumption that farmers allocate their labor so as to ensure equal marginal remuneration across different uses (Sumner 1982), leading to ambiguous effects of education on farm and off-farm employment (Tao Yang 1997). The nonsignificant effect of education on time allocation among medium-size farmers may be related to differences in the trade-offs in time allocation between medium-size farmers and small and large farmers. For example, medium-size farmers with a higher education may spend less time on agricultural production activities.

Rapid aging among small farmers undermines the competitiveness of family farmers and is symptomatic of a sector losing attractiveness for youth. Because young people are often more interested in working in urban areas than in rural areas, most farmers are relatively old in Amazônia (as in the rest of Brazil). Aging is particularly pronounced among family farmers (figure 5.9), suggesting that nonfamily farming provides a more attractive value proposition than family farming. Between 2006 and 2017, the proportion of family farmer pensioners in Amazônia almost tripled, while the share of farmers 65 years of age and older also grew significantly. The labor-intensive nature of smallholder farming means that aging puts greater pressure on the labor productivity of family farmers while accelerating the decline in their competitiveness.

Given their struggle to remain competitive, family farmers rely heavily on nonfarm income. While there is variation across states, approximately 50 percent or more of the income of poor family farmers in Amazônia is from nonfarm sources (figure 5.10), mostly from pensions and other retirement payments (figure 5.11). For larger farmers (notably nonpoor, nonfamily farmers), service

FIGURE 5.9

Aging undermines the competitiveness of small family farmers in Amazônia, 2006 and 2017

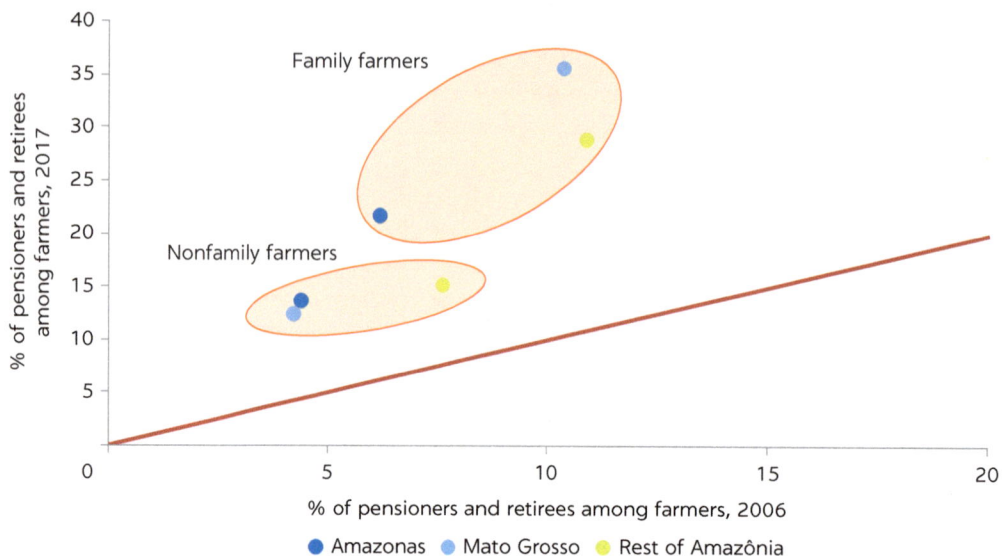

Source: World Bank, using data from the 2006 and 2017 Census of Agriculture by the Brazilian Institute of Geography and Statistics (IBGE).

FIGURE 5.10

Family farmers rely heavily on nonfarm income, 2017

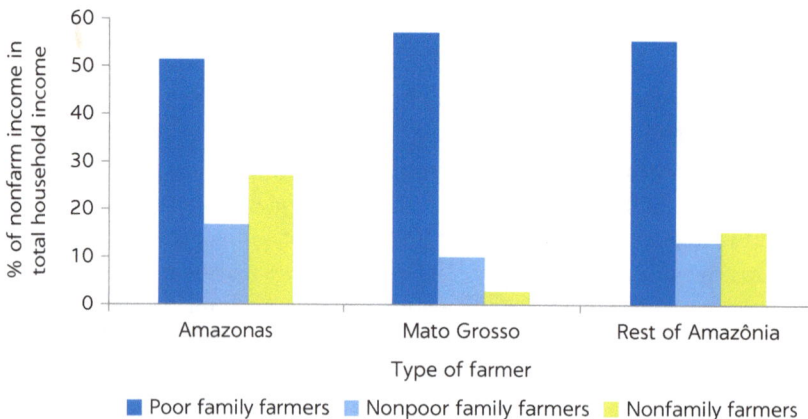

Source: World Bank, using data from the 2017 Census of Agriculture by the Brazilian Institute of Geography and Statistics (IBGE).

and retail activities in urban areas are the main source of other nonfarm income. Because these farms also tend to have higher labor productivity, they can afford to pay higher wages, and some of the nonfarm income of poorer family farmers stems from working on the farms of more productive farmers (Rocha 2022).

Less competitive farmers adapt by changing their production portfolios or seeking other sources of income. Facing competitive pressures, the less competitive, generally smaller and poorer, farmers will sell their labor to other farmers or sell or rent out their land to more productive farmers. Family farmers also adapt to rural transformation by changing their production mix, moving out of products in which they can no longer compete with larger farmers, especially annual crops with increasing returns to scale, such as soybeans. In Amazônia,

FIGURE 5.11

Family farmers rely heavily on pensions and other retirement payments, 2017

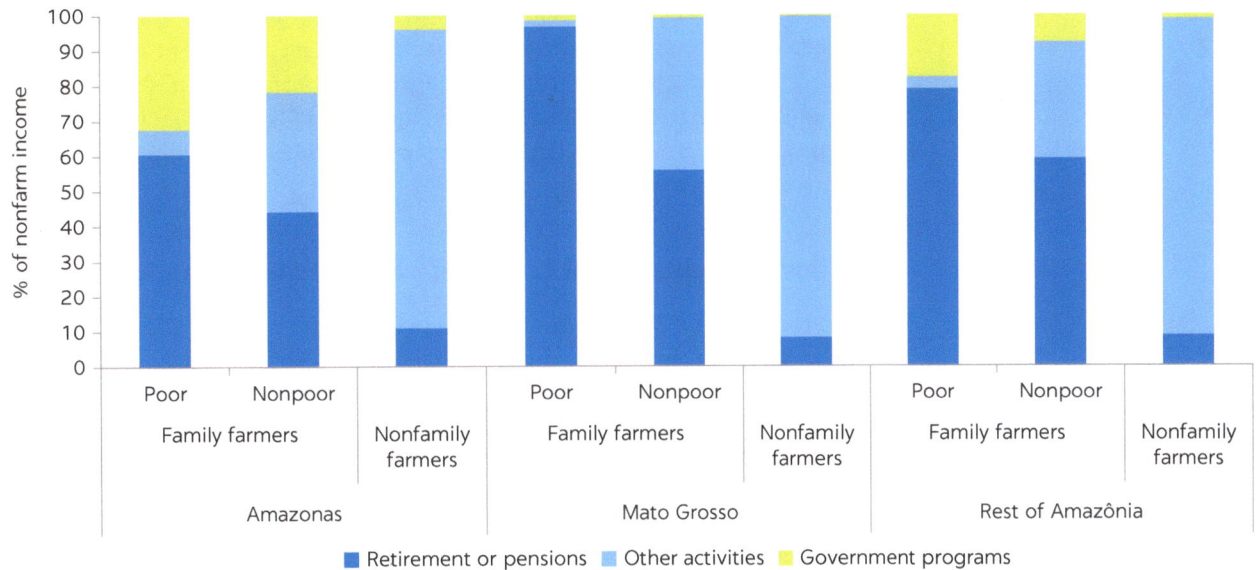

Source: World Bank, using data from the 2017 Census of Agriculture by the Brazilian Institute of Geography and Statistics (IBGE).

FIGURE 5.12

Responding to increasing competitive pressure, family farmers have been changing their production mix, producing fewer annual crops and raising more cattle, 2006–17

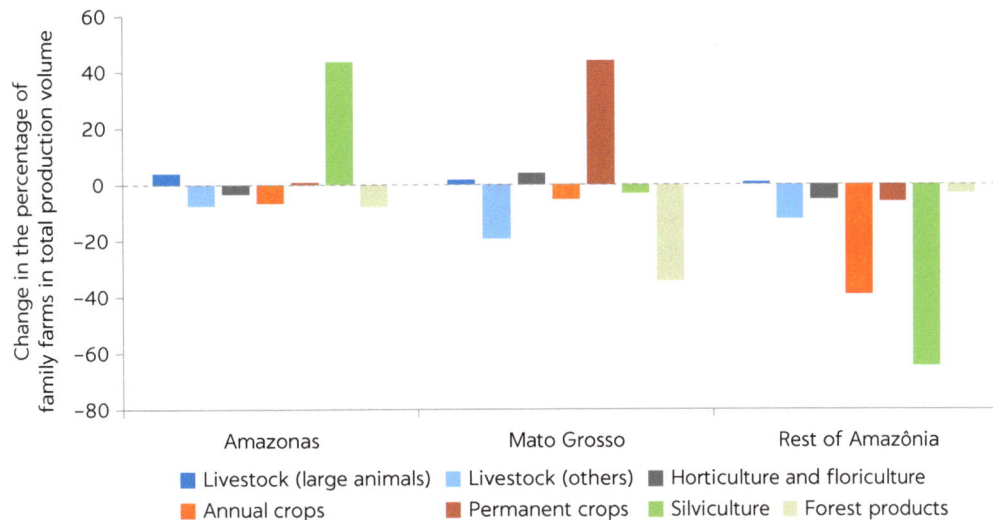

Source: World Bank, using data from the 2006 and 2017 Census of Agriculture by the Brazilian Institute of Geography and Statistics (IBGE).

small farmers also switch from crop production to cattle rearing (figure 5.12), where many manage to remain competitive with larger farmers (Rocha 2022). Family farmers also increase their production of labor-intensive products, such as silviculture in Amazonas and permanent crops in Mato Grosso. Technological innovations—in particular, climate-smart crop and livestock production technologies (climate-smart agriculture) developed by the Brazilian Agricultural Research Corporation (Embrapa)—represent an important, yet not fully tapped, source of support for small farmers in greening their production and making it more sustainable.

Overall, rural transformation will allow agriculture in Amazônia to catch up with agriculture in more advanced regions. Rural transformation is a disruptive process that tends to put smaller and poorer family farmers at a disadvantage.[13] However, it is part of the development process, raising overall productivity in the sector. Rural transformation in Amazônia has allowed more remote areas to catch up, especially in annual crops whose production growth has been higher in Amazônia than in more developed areas.

Environmental impacts of rural transformation in agriculture

Productivity gains as part of rural transformation can lead to deforestation. As shown in chapter 4, gains in agricultural productivity can increase localized deforestation (the Jevons effect), although it should reduce pressure on natural lands globally. Even though TFP gains increase land productivity (through intensification), the relatively high land elasticity in Amazônia still makes it economical to convert forests to productive land to service larger markets when productivity gains improve farmers' competitiveness. As markets develop, demand for commodities becomes more elastic while the supply of land becomes less elastic, putting upward pressure on land prices without increasing output prices. This process will strengthen agricultural intensification as land becomes a more expensive factor of production—resulting in less deforestation. Amazônia has not yet reached this stage; the combination of immature land markets (elastic land supply) and weak forest governance with gradually improving market access will likely cause improvements in agricultural productivity to result in more rather than less deforestation.

Higher agricultural productivity can impact deforestation through direct and indirect channels. More productive farmers may wish to serve larger markets by converting forest to land on their own property. To the extent that they violate the boundaries of the Forest Code, this deforestation would be illegal. Yet the effect may also be indirect, with farmers willing to pay more to buy more productive land legally. Higher demand will raise land prices, which may indirectly fuel deforestation linked to *grilagem* (land grabbing).

Farmers who lose competitiveness during rural transformation sometimes take defensive measures that result in more extensive production and deforestation (Porcher and Hanusch 2022). To date, the only agricultural activity in which family farmers have consistently expanded their market share during rural transformation is cattle raising. Less productive family farmers facing economic pressure can switch into cattle production as a savings instrument, stabilizing or even increasing their purchasing power by expanding (mostly illegally) their access to land through deforestation, with expectations of future increases in land values. Pastures rather than crops are usually the most attractive land use option immediately following deforestation because of biological and soil-related constraints to crop production, low start-up costs of pastures, low input and technology requirements, low price variation for cattle, and greater ease of transporting and marketing livestock than crops. Cultural traditions that assign a higher status to cattle ownership may also play a role.

Expansion of cattle ranching on traditional, low-productivity pastures is typically accompanied by soil nutrient mining, resulting in forest and land degradation. Forest degradation is often a precursor to deforestation, particularly in rural settlements (Gandour et al. 2021). The prevalence of forest degradation around rural settlements is consistent with the transition of less productive producers into extensive cattle farming. Beginning with the felling of trees and the establishment of low-density cattle ranching, the process progresses through a gradual exhaustion of soil nutrients, which forces the farmer to move on to new land and begin the cycle again. This practice may well be economically optimal from an individual farmer's financial perspective.[14] In such cases, forest degradation is followed by land degradation, and economic efficiency is consistent with degraded land and abandoned pastures.

In these situations, reducing deforestation pressure can help to avoid land degradation. When markets develop and demand becomes increasingly elastic, avoiding land degradation requires intensification of beef production (and in some states, including Rondônia and Pará, milk production as well) through sustainable pasture management and higher stocking rates. Sustainable pasture management requires improving soil management and may involve planting legumes, applying fertilizer and limestone, and using more farm machinery. These inputs are expensive, especially for small farmers in Amazônia, in view of high transportation costs, and so the region lags behind the rest of Brazil in the use of these inputs. One way to enable agricultural intensification, as described in chapter 3, is to boost urban productivity in addition to agricultural productivity, altering relative prices, including those of agricultural inputs. In this context, promotion of green technologies, including climate-smart agriculture, is an important policy objective. The national Low-Carbon Agriculture Plan, known as the ABC Plan, supports the restoration of degraded lands and is an important example of such green production technologies (see the discussion below and later in box 5.3).

Improved soil management, including the use of fertilizer and soil conservation technologies, increases land productivity, reduces land degradation and deforestation, and contributes to the competitiveness of agricultural production. Experience in the Brazilian Cerrado illustrates how improved soil management and low land prices can help to maintain agricultural competitiveness (de Rezende 2002). Because soils are of lower quality in Amazônia than in the Cerrado, soil management as a centerpiece of climate-smart agriculture may be especially important for achieving and maintaining land productivity and competitiveness.

Although using more fertilizer can reduce deforestation and land degradation, it can also generate undesirable environmental externalities. Because the level of production that can be sustained using only organic nutrients is generally too low to achieve competitive yields, using more fertilizer often means using more inorganic fertilizers. To the extent that fertilizer use increases productivity and lowers demand for land, it can reduce deforestation. But used improperly, inorganic fertilizers can have harmful environmental impacts, including nitrate leaching, eutrophication (caused by deposits of nitrate and phosphate that lead to excessive growth of algae), greenhouse gas emissions, and heavy metal uptake by plants. Farmers in Amazônia need to have better access to knowledge regarding economically and environmentally sustainable use of fertilizers.

RURAL TRANSFORMATION AND AGROFORESTRY

Agroforestry and small farmers

Agroforestry systems are an important part of the rural bioeconomy and have received increasing attention over the past decade. Insofar as agroforestry systems combine production efficiency with environmental benefits, including climate resilience, nutrient recycling, biodiversity protection, and even climate mitigation,[15] they constitute a key example of climate-smart agriculture and are increasingly attractive in both domestic and export markets.

Agroforestry, though still limited in size, is growing rapidly in Amazônia. Nontimber forest products[16] in Amazônia have an estimated annual production value of about R$2 billion (approximately US$400 million; figure 5.13), three times their value 20 years ago. Production, while dominated by açai and Brazil nuts, also includes cocoa, heart of palm, herbs, oil crops, and fibers. But even though açai is a high-value crop, its production value still accounts for less than 2 percent of agricultural gross domestic product (GDP) in Amazônia.

Agroforestry in Amazônia typically involves extractive methods practiced mainly by small farmers. When demand is inelastic and market access is limited to local markets, production of forest commodities generally consists of simple extraction from forest lands (extractivism). This type of agroforestry is motivated by smallholders' concerns regarding food security and risk minimization rather than profit maximization. Land and labor productivity are low because of intensive use of unskilled labor and low use of capital and technology.[17]

Extractive agroforestry is a common sustainable production system in Indigenous communities. It is also the only production system that is legally permitted in extractive reserves in protected areas and *zoneamento ecológico-econômico* (ecological economic zone) areas. In this sense, agroforestry systems based on extractive methods can help small farmers to cope with loss of competitiveness relative to larger farmers, at least temporarily.

FIGURE 5.13

Agroforestry production in Brazil, 2017

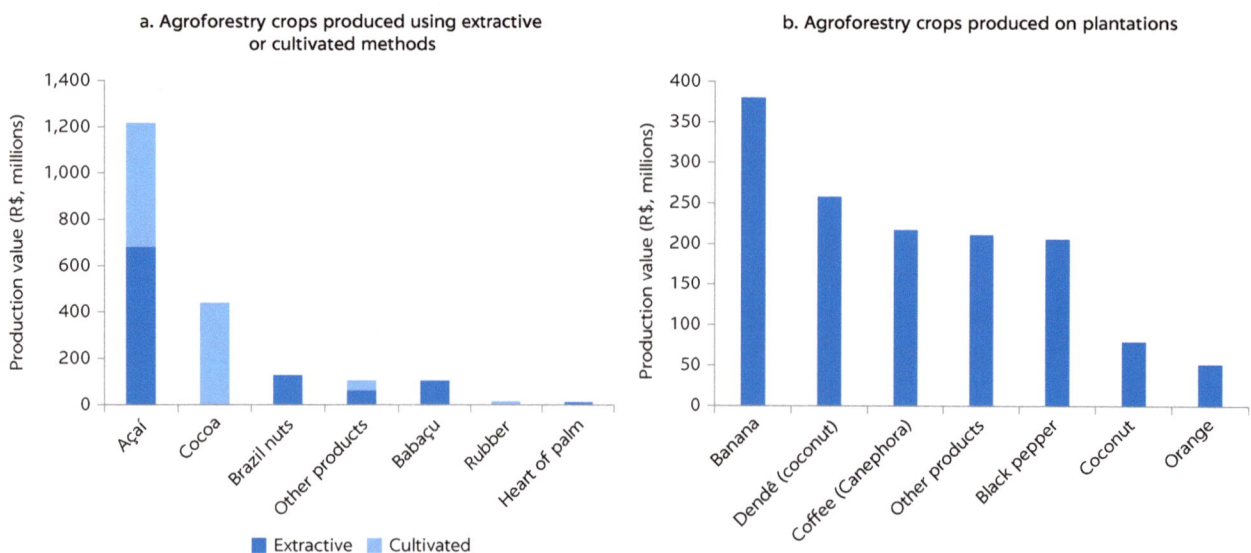

a. Agroforestry crops produced using extractive or cultivated methods

b. Agroforestry crops produced on plantations

Source: World Bank, using 2017 Census of Agriculture by the Brazilian Institute of Geography and Statistics (IBGE).

Extractive agroforestry has only limited potential as an engine of rural growth. This limitation is mainly because market expansion is constrained by two factors: rapidly rising marginal costs of moving deeper into the forest and limited processing capacity. The latter may be addressed to a certain extent by the strengthening of value chains.

Among poorer settlers and farmers, nonextractive agroforestry systems may emerge as part of a pattern of production focused on food security. Households allocate labor, their principal asset, to clearing land and starting productive activities, often exchanging labor with nearby families. The felled trees are burned, and crops are planted among the logs. The process of completely burning the trees typically takes several years, during which crops are interspersed with logs. The first crops following land clearing are often maize, cassava, or rice, all essential food staples. Most poor households are motivated by food security and risk minimization rather than production for the market and profit maximization (de Barros et al. 2009). In addition to extractive methods, other agroforestry systems may also emerge, consisting of a mix of fruit trees, herbs, market garden crops, and staples such as maize and cassava.

The evolving competitiveness of agroforestry and smallholder farming in Amazônia

The suitability and competitiveness of agroforestry systems evolve as markets develop. Figure 5.14 presents a stylized picture of the relationship between market development and competitiveness for agroforestry systems, where market development is defined as in figures 5.4 and 5.5. Because extractive systems have limited capacity to satisfy growing demand at competitive prices (Brazil nuts being a good example), this form of production eventually evolves toward the establishment of plantations. Agroforestry-based bioeconomic production systems gradually lose out to monocultures as markets develop, before regaining some of their competitiveness (even if no longer based on extractivism) as

FIGURE 5.14

The competitiveness of agroforestry-based agricultural production systems change as markets develop

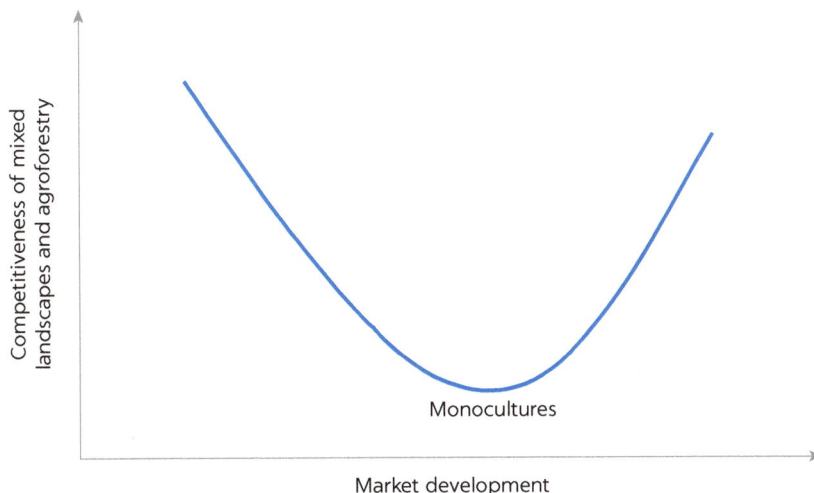

Source: World Bank.

markets develop further and willingness to pay higher prices for products from the bioeconomy increases.

As markets develop, the economic viability of extractivist models is limited to niche markets. Homma (2012) identifies four stages in the transition from an extractivist livelihood based on the bioeconomy to a more managed system of mixed crops or agroforestry: extractivism, stabilization, decline, and planting. Although livelihoods based on extractivism have some early development potential in commodities like timber and açai, Brazil nuts, rubber, and bacuri, the scope for productivity gains is limited. Consequently, as demand expands, the traditional bioeconomy will give way to more modern production methods. For example, guaraná and rubber used to be extractive products, but they are now mostly cultivated (see chapter 1). Extractivism may survive through market segmentation, where its products are differentiated as socially and environmentally sustainable and thus command higher prices in niche markets. By definition, however, niche markets are small, and many tree commodities are increasingly produced on plantations.

As markets develop and favor the production of forest commodities as monocultures over extractive production, small farmers are likely to lose out. Decreasing transportation costs will require farmers to compete with products from more developed and more productive parts of Brazil (or from other countries). Extractive production methods will no longer be competitive, and traditional agroforestry cropping patterns based on risk diversification generally will give way to monoculture production. As access to capital improves, land remains relatively abundant and cheap, and access to skilled labor remains limited, capital- and land-intensive production methods are likely to replace traditional production systems. Subsistence and small family farmers will gradually be crowded out by larger commercial farmers. Unless producers can leapfrog from essentially extractive agroforestry systems to more sophisticated, commercially viable agroforestry, monocultures are the likely transition outcome, with lower carbon benefits and loss of primeval forest.

Increased market competition means that small producers have weaker market power in the value chain, which limits the potential market premiums for bioeconomy products relative to cultivated products (box 5.2). The remoteness of many small producers of bioeconomy products such as forest commodities means that transportation costs are high. Logistics account for up to 67 percent of the production costs of forest commodities, which typically face a steep marginal cost curve (Kohlmann and Licks 2022). Small producers are also disadvantaged by informality, fragmentation, and poor access to sanitary protocols, quality control measures, and processing facilities, all of which reduce their bargaining power relative to large off-takers (Kohlmann and Licks 2022). Amazônia, as well as Brazil more broadly, has been struggling to become competitive in Brazil nuts, despite favorable market prospects and government support—for example, through the minimum price regime administered by the National Supply Company (Conab). Bolivia is now the largest producer of Brazil nuts and the largest exporter. While Brazil has been more successful in developing competitive advantage in açai production and the extractive method is still widely practiced, cultivated açai commands a higher price. This difference may be explained partially by the lower market power of bioeconomy producers within the supply chain and higher transport costs, but it also points to the absence of market premiums for extractive açai and differences in quality.

BOX 5.2

Contrasting extractivist and commercial production in Pará

In Pará, extractive production remains an important element of the bioeconomy, but prices are low. Extractive production of açai and heart of palm exceeds production in managed plantations (figure B5.2.1). Cocoa, another crop with potential for extractive production, is produced mainly as a monoculture in plantations. For all three crops, prices are higher for plantation production than for extractive production (figure B5.2.2), revealing inherent disadvantages of extractive production, including lack of uniform quality, low bargaining power because of producer fragmentation, and high transportation costs because of remoteness. Reflecting strong global demand for açai, price increases between 2006 and 2017 greatly exceeded consumer price inflation (figure B5.2.3), in contrast to the market for extractive heart of palm, which stagnated and faced declining terms of trade. Thus, the bioeconomy based on the sustainable extraction of forest products has limited potential for contributing to economic growth and poverty reduction, especially where markets are not as dynamic as they are for açai.

A successful example of plantation-based commercial agroforestry production in Amazônia is the Mixed Agricultural Cooperative of Tomé-Açu. In Tomé-Açu, a municipality in northeastern Pará

FIGURE B5.2.2

Average prices of produce in Pará, 2017

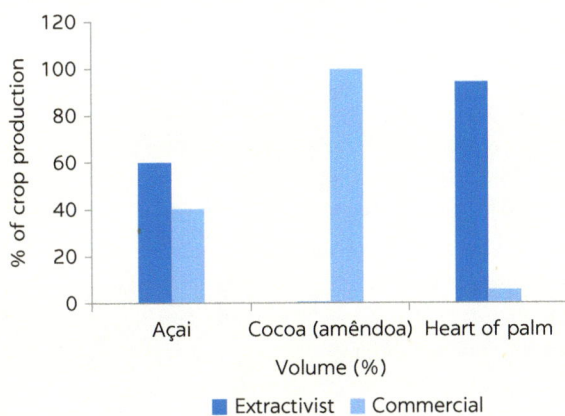

Source: World Bank, using IBGE (Brazilian Institute of Geography and Statistics) data.
Note: The figure displays the price (in Brazilian reais) per kilogram (kg) of each respective crop.

FIGURE B5.2.3

Average price changes in extractive products and consumer price inflation in Belém, 2006–17

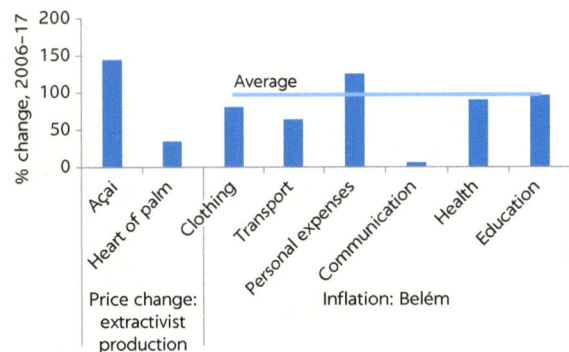

Source: World Bank, using IBGE (Brazilian Institute of Geography and Statistics) data.
Note: The blue horizontal line represents the average consumer price inflation in Belém.

FIGURE B5.2.1

Percentage of produce sold in Pará, 2017

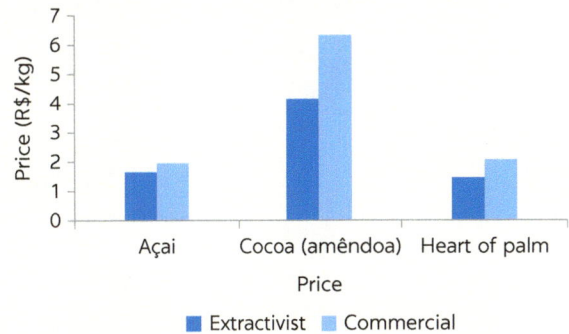

Source: World Bank, using IBGE (Brazilian Institute of Geography and Statistics) data.

settled by Japanese immigrants, some 230 Japanese-Brazilian families farm more than 6,000 hectares of land, growing 70 crop species and 300 intercrop combinations. Their success can be attributed to strong cooperative management, production of highly profitable black pepper, and crop diversification as a deliberate strategy to mitigate the risks of plant diseases and fluctuations in market prices (Yamada and Gholz 2002).

What's next for agroforestry in Amazônia?

As markets develop, improvements in access to skills, technology, infrastructure, and inputs could stimulate a return to agroforestry systems. These systems would necessarily be more intensive and use more technology, capital, and skilled labor than traditional agroforestry systems based on extractivist methods. Modern agroforestry systems (insofar as they are more productive than monocultures) could increase smallholders' land productivity and incomes and restore their competitiveness while preserving native vegetation. The favorable reputation in global markets of agroforestry systems, particularly integrated crop-livestock-forest systems, as "green, climate-smart production systems" could also help. However, the Amazon region in Brazil has probably not yet reached the level of market development required for widespread adoption of such systems, meaning that further public support may be warranted.

Most agroforestry systems, including intensive agroforestry systems, are labor intensive and thus suited to small farmers' factor endowments of abundant family labor, limited access to labor-replacing inputs, and desire to minimize climate and market risks. However, widespread adoption of intensive agroforestry systems as a key part of a strategy that promotes climate-smart agriculture requires dealing with several bottlenecks first:

- Agroforestry systems are relatively management and knowledge intensive, so small farmers in Amazônia would require a technical assistance and knowledge transfer program. Brazil's successful experience in the Cerrado shows that Embrapa is uniquely placed to help to overcome this constraint.
- Despite isolated examples of inelastic land supply and rising land prices, the aggregate supply of land in Brazil remains relatively elastic because the agricultural frontier keeps expanding. This elasticity may discourage the large-scale adoption of production systems with higher land productivity that enable more efficient land use, including agroforestry-based production systems.
- The lag between investment and achievement of the agroforestry system's full production potential means that, at prevailing discount rates in Brazil, the expected returns from agroforestry in terms of discounted cash flow might be insufficient to stimulate large-scale adoption. São Paulo, despite being the most developed Brazilian market, shows only limited adoption of agroforestry and other integrated production systems (Steinfeld 2018).

Still, Brazil has made progress in developing integrated landscape systems that include agroforestry. Led by Embrapa agroforestry research in Brazil focuses on integrated crop-livestock-forest systems. These systems use land more efficiently and also have substantial environmental benefits, including carbon sequestration, soil improvement, erosion control, biodiversity conservation, and improvements in microclimate and animal welfare. In the 2015/16 agricultural year, such systems mostly involved commercial crops (often soybeans), cattle, and eucalyptus and covered 11.5 million hectares (Garrett et al. 2020). Nearly half of them (45 percent) were concentrated in Mato Grosso do Sul, Rio Grande do Sul, and Mato Grosso (the only state in Amazônia). Consistent with the low level of market development in most of Amazônia (figure 5.4), the adoption of integrated crop-livestock-forest production systems outside of Mato Grosso (where market development is more advanced) remains quite limited.

Crop-livestock systems have been adopted more widely in Brazil than crop-livestock-forest systems. Integrated crop-livestock production systems do not include trees, which take a long time to grow and involve sunk costs. Crop-livestock systems still allow the use of crop residues for cattle feed and pasture improvement (especially in no-tillage systems). Integrated crop-live-stock systems are also less complex than crop-livestock-forestry systems and require less management; for these reasons, they are often more attractive to farmers.

The adoption of improved pasture systems in Brazil has been substantial but below potential. The relative success of the ABC Plan in the Cerrado (box 5.3) shows similar promise for Amazônia. The ABC Plan has focused on rehabilitating degraded pastures through the introduction of more productive pasture systems that are able to sustain higher stocking rates by intensifying cattle production. These systems consist of either mixed plantings of improved grasses with nitrogen-fixing legume species or silvopastoral systems that involve cattle grazing combined with forest management. Silvopastoral systems are typically also based on improved pasture species and may include crops. If leguminous trees are planted, they fix nitrogen in the soil and further improve the

---

BOX 5.3

Insights from the ABC Plan

There is evidence that the Low-Carbon Agriculture (ABC) Plan has had a positive impact on the recovery of degraded pastures, income generation, and zootechnical indicators, despite shortcomings related to program implementation, monitoring, and management. Municipalities in Brazil's Northeast region that adopted the ABC Plan during 2013–17 had a 17 percent increase in the area with good pasture and a 19 percent decrease in the area with degraded pasture (Rocha et al. 2019). An evaluation of beef cattle farms in Santa Catarina (in the South region) over 2012–16 found that the ABC Plan increased the number of animals by 21 percent, reduced the slaughter age of animals by 50 percent (from three to two years), and supported the adoption of other zootechnical and management improvements that resulted in a 70 percent increase in capital stock and a 123 percent increase in annual gross revenue (da Costa et al. 2019). However, the allocation of ABC resources has been biased toward the Southeast and Central-West regions of Brazil and the Cerrado biome (Gianetti and Ferreira Filho 2021). Despite these positive results, available resources have not been fully used, and program funding was recently reduced (Observatório ABC 2019).

At least two features of the ABC Plan limit its further expansion. First, farmer credit from the ABC Plan not only carries higher interest rates than credit from other sources but also involves higher transaction costs, as farmers are required to develop a detailed technical plan for sustainable production systems (MAPA 2021). Second, both farmers and technical professionals (such as agronomists, zootechnicians, and veterinarians) often lack sufficiently detailed technical knowledge of climate-smart (low-carbon) agriculture (Assad 2013). Additionally, rather than constrained by limited supply, the ABC Plan seems handicapped by a shortage of demand, mainly because of the economic risks involved in recovering degraded pastures (Barros 2017). The ABC Plan could become more viable and credit uptake could improve if the program would designate priority regions and if its policies would take into account location-specific technical, economic, and environmental aspects beyond differences in stocking rates.

The Brazilian government has launched a new cycle of the ABC Plan for 2020–30—referred to as "ABC+"—as part of its strategy for expanding climate-smart production systems. The new cycle includes the expansion of economic incentives for farmers who adopt such systems, definition of new market instruments for the commercialization of carbon credits, and establishment of an integrated data management system.

production of grass. In addition, silvopastoral systems can sequester higher quantities of carbon and thus mitigate climate change, making them a key example of climate-smart agriculture. Nevertheless, adoption of the technologies promoted by the ABC Plan has been relatively slow, with levels much below potential. Chapter 7 also discusses the potential limitations of implicit subsidies where weak law enforcement may undermine incentives for forest conservation. In such situations, public subsidies for land restoration could act as a disincentive for private individuals to maintain the quality of their land while stimulating illegal deforestation to compensate for land degradation. In this sense, effective environmental protection measures, preferably in tandem with land tenure regularization, are a necessary complementary measure.

An important constraint to the wider adoption of agroforestry systems by small farmers is their low market power as a result of lack of scale and limited market opportunities. Production by small farmers can be brought to scale by aggregating their products, including through cooperatives (but effectiveness is mixed), contract farming (individual farmers contract with a larger buyer), and out-grower schemes (a similar arrangement where the off-taker is also a large producer). These mechanisms can supply small farmers with reliable access to markets, quality inputs, credit, and extension advice. Finally, as experience with açaí has shown, there are opportunities for extractivist producers in growing markets and in cases of decreasing or constant returns to scale (as in cacao). Where markets are not as dynamic, however, low prices can make extractivist production less attractive, especially where cultivated production commands higher prices. To keep extractive methods attractive, product differentiation may be an option for increasing the price premiums for sustainably produced products sold into high-end niche markets, although such markets are, by definition, small.

OCCUPATIONAL TRANSITIONS FOR FARMERS AND SOURCES OF RURAL DIVERSIFICATION

Rural transformation requires less productive farmers to transition to other economic activities, with some opportunities in the rural bioeconomy. Competitive pressures during rural transformation may push less productive farmers toward illegal deforestation unless they have alternative livelihood options (Porcher and Hanusch 2022). Analysis of occupational relatedness (defined as occupations that workers switch to after leaving their original occupation) for three large agricultural activities in Amazônia (cereals, cattle, and soy) shows that workers tend to stay in agriculture, suggesting limited access to nonagricultural occupations (figure 5.15). Farm workers tend to shift from cereal or soybean farming to cattle or other types of crop farming (figure 5.15, panel a and panel c, respectively) as well as to certified, deforestation-free soy production. Cattle workers tend to shift to other livestock-related occupations or take up crop farming (figure 5.15, panel b). Transitions to horticulture are also fairly common, consistent with the analysis in this chapter. Cattle workers seem to be the most versatile: workers transitioning out of cattle production have a significantly larger range of occupational relatedness than workers transitioning out of cereal production (figure 5.15, panel d).

Besides other primary agricultural production, occupational relatedness for agriculture workers is also strong within the agricultural value chain and

FIGURE 5.15

Likelihood of employment transitions from cereal, cattle, and soybean production to other occupations

a. Potential alternative occupations for workers transitioning out of cereal production

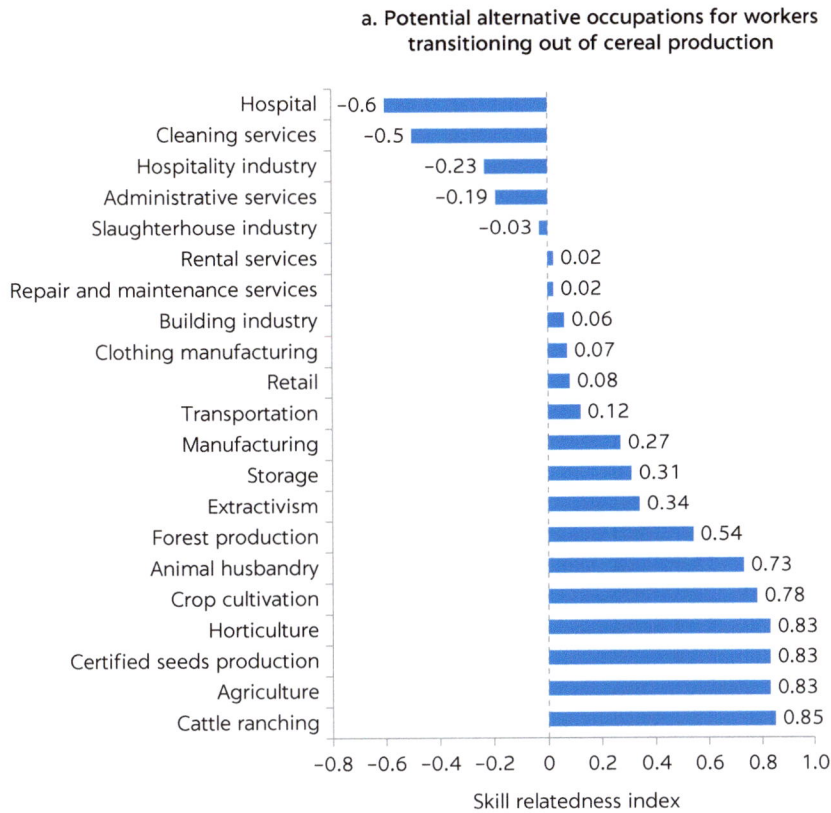

b. Potential alternative occupations for workers transitioning out of cattle ranching

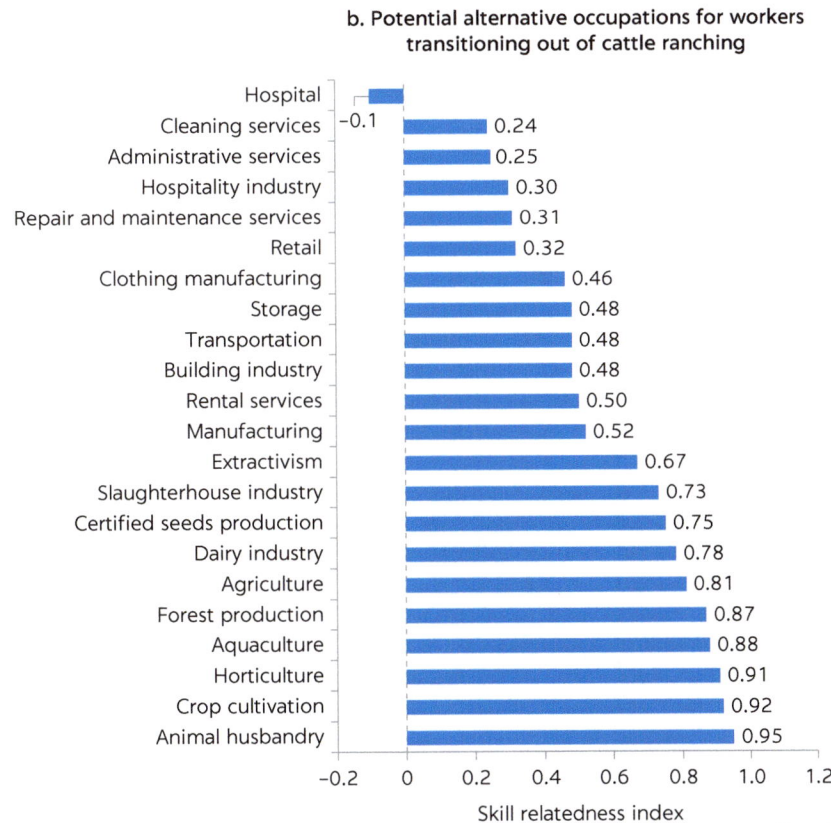

continued

FIGURE 5.15, *continued*

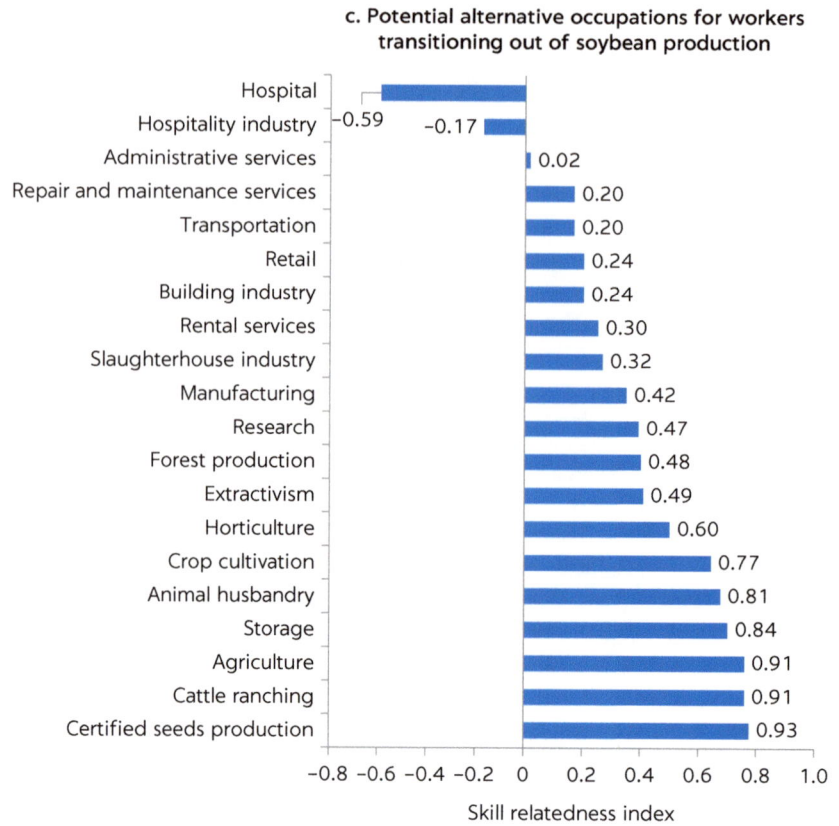

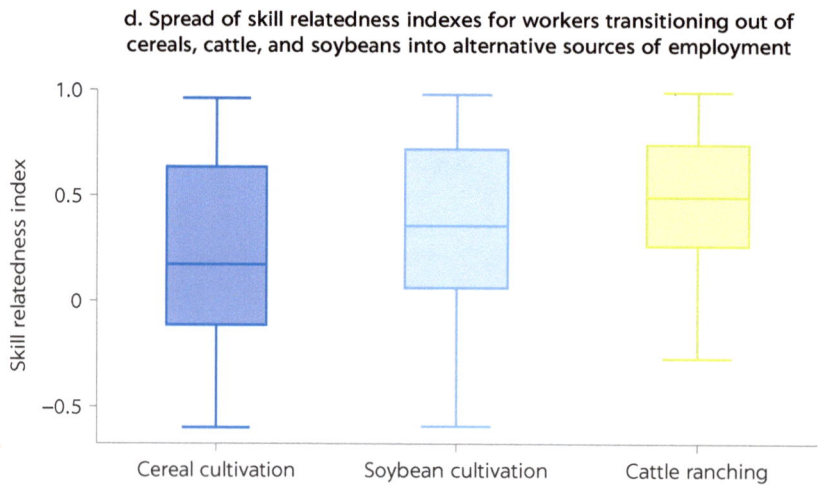

c. Potential alternative occupations for workers transitioning out of soybean production

Occupation	Skill relatedness index
Hospital	−0.59
Hospitality industry	−0.17
Administrative services	0.02
Repair and maintenance services	0.20
Transportation	0.20
Retail	0.24
Building industry	0.24
Rental services	0.30
Slaughterhouse industry	0.32
Manufacturing	0.42
Research	0.47
Forest production	0.48
Extractivism	0.49
Horticulture	0.60
Crop cultivation	0.77
Animal husbandry	0.81
Storage	0.84
Agriculture	0.91
Cattle ranching	0.91
Certified seeds production	0.93

Skill relatedness index

d. Spread of skill relatedness indexes for workers transitioning out of cereals, cattle, and soybeans into alternative sources of employment

Skill relatedness index

Cereal cultivation | Soybean cultivation | Cattle ranching

Source: Cirera and Neto 2022.
Note: Higher values imply greater choice for workers transitioning into alternative employment. Data reflect formal employment only (Annual Social Information Report [RAIS] data from the Population Studies Center, Institute for Social Research). In panel d, outer lines identify the minimum and maximum values, the bottom and top of the box first and third quartile, and the horizontal line in the box is the median.

in the broader rural sector. For cereal, cattle, and soybean workers, occupational transitions to livestock other than cattle (such as pigs or poultry) are relatively common, as are occupational transitions of cattle workers to fisheries and aquaculture. Other than primary agricultural production, occupational transitions are mostly to other parts of the agricultural value chain, such as production of seeds or saplings, milling, production of animal feed, or, for cattle workers, slaughterhouses. Though less common, transitions also occur into mining, including artisanal mining of gold or less precious commodities like sand or limestone (associated with construction).

Occupational switching from agriculture to nonagricultural value chains is rare and mostly limited to low-skill occupations. These sources of employment include freight and taxi transportation services, construction, and sales. Occupational switches to manufacturing are mainly into agricultural value chains (agribusiness). There is almost no occupational switching to the hospitality sector, except in the case of cattle workers.

Providing support in acquiring new skills and generating opportunities outside agriculture are critical, especially for rural youth. During rural transformation, agriculture becomes less labor intensive, so many farmers and farm workers will need to find alternative employment opportunities outside agriculture. As recommended in chapter 2, efforts are needed to improve rural education systems to prepare the rural workforce for new jobs, including in urban areas.

Economically and environmentally sustainable diversification requires a balanced rural transformation in Amazônia. The next sections examine the income potential and rural employment opportunities in forestry; fisheries and aquaculture; tourism (all part of the rural bioeconomy); and mining. Although all four sectors are tradable and could have macroeconomic effects that reduce deforestation, they are also likely to remain small, limiting their ability to affect the macroeconomic forces that drive deforestation. Their income potential for rural populations could still be important, however, depending on balanced development of the region. For example, the forestry sector has long been struggling in Amazônia. Even though oversupply of (often illegal) timber as a by-product of land clearing impedes the development of a sustainable forestry sector, the increasing development of agricultural markets is likely to facilitate the development of sustainable forestry. The development of fisheries and aquaculture depends on "green" farming methods that do not pollute water resources. New urban logistics systems may also facilitate tourism to rural areas in Amazônia. The overall development of Amazônia during the rural transformation process might also reduce some of the opportunistic wildcat mining that has been associated with significant environmental damage.

Forestry

The timber sector in Amazônia has long been volatile. Logging is the only forest activity with significant economies of scale, providing jobs and driving a frontier economy (Merry et al. 2006). Much of this activity has occurred without adequate oversight, enabling loggers to avoid paying taxes or royalties. Combined with windfall profits from access to old-growth timber, the lack of oversight has generated a series of boom-and-bust cycles on the forest frontier. The 10- to 20-year boom phase occurs along the logging frontier because the forest is mature, holding its maximum volume of wood, and the logging industry has unrestricted access to old growth. This phase leaves behind a degraded forest with low or even zero commercial value and a subsequent harvest that is at least 25–30 years away. The abundance of wood in New Frontier areas, coupled with import substitution policies for wood-processing equipment that make the latter expensive, discourages technology adoption and keeps productivity low. Thus, as timber resources become depleted, the benefit–cost ratio of moving to a

New Frontier area to access the stock of old-growth timber is higher than that of staying put and adopting a reduced-impact logging system based on improved processing technologies and rotational timber management (which is the current legal regime on privately owned forest lands in Amazônia). As a consequence, the timber sector thus far has failed to achieve its potential as a constructive partner in the strive for a sustainable future for Amazônia.

Households in *assentamentos* who engage in logging often get involved unwittingly in semilegal sales but achieve only limited welfare gains. Around half of households in agrarian settlements sell timber early in the settlement process (Amacher, Merry, and Bowman 2009). Households usually log the entire legal volume of 60 cubic meters per year permitted on 3 hectares of clearing as well as the approximately 900 cubic meters of commercial timber available on 100-hectare lots.[18] However, households typically do not manage to maximize the value of timber sales because of incomplete market price information, high discount rates (strong preference for immediate cash), and monopsonistic timber markets that leave most sellers as price takers.

Native timber is coming under competitive pressure from substitutes, such as plantation wood, tile, and other construction material. At its peak around 1998, the timber industry in Amazônia consumed an estimated 27 million cubic meters of timber annually.[19] Since then, the volume of timber has declined considerably as enforcement has improved, substitute products have entered the market, and infrastructure challenges along the frontier have raised the price of timber relative to the price of substitute products. Continued expansion of timber plantations into degraded pastures to serve the markets for wood substitutes and paper can be expected.

In 2006 the Brazilian government set out to formalize the timber industry through new forest legislation and timber concessions on public lands. To raise additional funds for managing protected areas and creating a formal structure for timber operations, the government began to offer timber concessions in areas designated for sustainable timber production. The process has been beset by difficulties, including bureaucratic complications (applicants for concessions have to get permission from multiple agencies) and, especially, continued competition from illegal logging.[20] If illegal logging could be controlled, concessions and other forms of legal timber harvest might face more profitable market conditions.[21]

Under current levels of illegal deforestation, timber concessions struggle to deliver on the promise of reduced impact and sustainable timber production (Merry et al. 2006). Although there are success stories, the boom-and-bust cycle continues even as access to profitable commercial timber diminishes. A large volume of timber remains in private forests (and will continue to grow as more undesignated lands are settled and protected areas are degazetted), but extraction of timber on private lands must be regulated better to balance private gains against public goods.

The future of a sustainable timber industry rests not in timber concessions alone, but also in creating a level playing field for timber extraction everywhere. For community forestry and managed forests on private lands to have a role would require stopping the illegal harvesting of timber, which creates an unfair competitive advantage; creating clear incentives for long-term management of community and private forests; reducing the bureaucratic costs of managing timber concessions; and improving access to development finance to allow logging to compete with alternative land uses.

The maturing of the Amazonian economy, coupled with environmental protection measures, would be expected to reduce deforestation and strengthen the prospects for sustainable forestry. In the meantime, logging concessions are likely to continue to be undercut by illegal logging and the high supervision costs needed to fend off illegal loggers. To establish the conditions for a sustainable timber industry, policies need to focus on the macrodrivers of deforestation as well as on the enforcement of environmental protection laws. Innovation and higher use of capital in forestry operations, along with economywide productivity gains, could contribute to higher land productivity while simultaneously improving the environmental sustainability of the industry.

Fisheries and aquaculture

Inland fisheries and aquaculture produce high-value products and can offer attractive income-generating opportunities in Amazônia. These industries represent an underexploited opportunity for green economic development. While the environmental impacts of fish production need to be managed carefully, inland fisheries and aquaculture offer a way to produce protein that is significantly more environmentally sustainable than beef: production of protein through fish cultivation is 30 times less land intensive than protein production through cattle ranching (McGrath et al. 2020). The fisheries sector as a whole is a fast-growing income-earning opportunity: the production value of inland fisheries and aquaculture in Brazil grew at an annual average rate of about 9 percent between 2013 and 2019, totaling around R$5 billion in 2019, R$2 billion more than in 2013.

Despite its potential, performance of the inland fisheries and aquaculture sector in Amazônia has not been uniform. Rondônia leads Amazonian states in inland fisheries and aquaculture, with a total annual production value of approximately R$417 million. The sector is also important in Mato Grosso (R$250 million, though not in the Amazonian part of the state), Pará (R$120 million), Amazonas (R$70 million), and Acre (R$30 million). Pará is the only one of these states experiencing substantial growth in the industry, approximately tripling its production value since 2013. Production value declined considerably in Mato Grosso.

While many households along the Amazon River floodplain engage in small-scale or subsistence fishing, commercial fishing is done by a fleet of larger boats. A study of the commercial fleet operating in the lower Amazon found that smaller boats (less than 4 tons of storage) accounted for almost 90 percent of the catch and more than 70 percent of the product value generated in the region (Almeida, McGrath, and Ruffino 2001). Another study of the fishing fleet in the Amazon-Solimoes River estimated that the fleet of approximately 7,500 fishing boats landed 84,000 tons of fish annually, generating 160,000 jobs and gross product value of approximately R$390 million (Almeida, Lorenzen, and McGrath 2004).

Tilapia and tambaqui account for about half the total aquaculture production value. The production system is thus highly concentrated, focusing on two species that have gained substantial production scale. Other species have not yet achieved scale, possibly because of lower productivity and insufficient market acceptance. For example, the pirarucu, which is being promoted as an important opportunity in inland fisheries, accounts for only 0.5 percent of the value of aquaculture production (SEBRAE 2016).

Other challenges facing inland fisheries and aquaculture include illegal (and therefore unreported and unregulated) fishing and poor enforcement of regulations designed to prevent water pollution. The lack of data needed to establish and enforce quotas and fish population management plans encourages illegal fishing. Regional fish population management plans are needed because some fish species migrate along the entire river. Expansion of aquaculture should proceed cautiously, as fish populations are notoriously difficult to manage; unless proper regulation is in place, aquaculture development could introduce invasive species, with potentially catastrophic consequences for native species and biodiversity. Finally, aquaculture is hampered by more general barriers to development in Amazônia, including underdeveloped markets and logistics.

Tourism

Global tourism markets are growing, presenting opportunities for Amazônia. Amazônia may benefit, in particular, from the growing popularity of ecotourism (including community-based tourism). Some 2.6 million people visited the Amazon region (Bolivia, Brazil, Colombia, Ecuador, and Peru) in 2012, including 2.06 million domestic tourists and 0.56 million international tourists. Although domestic tourists, on average, spend considerably less than international tourists, they spend more overall (US$2.4 billion versus US$1.7 billion a year) because there are so many more of them. More than half of estimated tourist expenditures in the Amazon (US$4.1 billion a year, likely an underestimate) went to Brazil (May 2015).[22]

Surveys among the 640,000 international tourists arriving in Brazil in 2019 by the Ministry of Tourism found that more than half (65 percent) preferred sun destinations in parts of Brazil other than Amazônia and that nearly one in five (18.6 percent) came for ecotourism, nature, or adventure. Only about 65,000 international tourists visited the principal Amazônia destinations of Amazonas and Pará in 2019 (Ministry of Tourism 2020). In 2007 the Institute of Economic Research Foundation (FIPE) found that only about 5 percent (274,000 persons) of international tourists to Brazil visited one or more of the nine Amazônia states (according to the Program for Ecotourism Development in the Legal Amazon). Most international tourism packages to Amazônia enter at Manaus, followed by Belém and São Luis; according to tour operators, the Pico de Neblina in Roraima is a major point of interest.

The Ministry of the Environment has assessed the potential of ecotourism in the nine Amazonian states, with a specific focus on 57 municipalities within 15 ecotourism "poles." Besides the nine state capitals, these poles included Santarém in Pará; Soure on the Island of Marajó; and Parintins (where the *bumba-meu-boi* festivities are held), Barcelos, and Tefé (attracted to the community-based ecotourism site at the Mamirauá biological reserve) in Amazonas; Xapuri (home of Chico Mendes and the rubber tappers' movement in the Vale do Acre) in Acre; and Cáceres (in the Pantanal biome) in Mato Grosso. Other cities cited included Mateiros, Presidente Figueiredo, and São Gabriel das Cachoeiras in Amazonas and Alta Floresta in Mato Grosso. While all regions carry some potential for tourism, tourists identify good infrastructure as an important aspect of their overall experience. In 2017 international tourists in Manaus gave customer service and airport infrastructure a score of 98 out of 100. In the same survey, tourists gave the lowest score to telecommunications services (65 out of 100). Cleanliness of public spaces also received a low score

(Ministry of Tourism 2018). According to the survey, ecotourists expect certain amenities when traveling, suggesting that the region needs to invest more in infrastructure and amenities if it wants to attract more tourists.

Formal employment in the tourism sector has been declining in Amazônia. In 2019 the nine states in Amazônia had a total of 127,516 formal sector jobs in tourism-related occupations, down from 136,050 in 2015 (Information System on the Labor Market in the Tourism Sector [SIMT] of the Institute for Applied Economic Research [Ipea]). Over the same period, the number of formal jobs in the sector in Pará declined from 33,176 to 29,050. Each formal sector job generates an estimated 1.34 informal sector jobs. The types of tourism activities that lead to the largest number of new jobs are dining services (36 percent of jobs), followed by lodging services and transport services (each at about 28 percent). Wages tend to be lower in the tourism sector than in other sectors, possibly due to the high share of female employees (particularly in food preparation and cleaning services) and informal workers (Coelho and Sakowski 2012).

Few national parks in Amazônia receive visitors, since many areas have not yet prepared mandatory environmental management plans. Only a few parks, national forests, and sustainable land use areas currently allow tourist visits, including the Amazônia, Anavilhanas, and Jaú National Parks; the Mamirauá and Juma sustainable land use areas in Amazonas; and the Tapajós National Forest in Pará. Some private natural patrimony reserves and extractive and Indigenous reserves also have established themselves as ecotourism destinations.

As a globally competitive industry, tourism is a challenging sector for the remote Amazonian region of Brazil. Other countries in the Amazon biome offer attractive visits to the Amazon, often in combination with cost-effective visits to other tourist attractions. Brazil has numerous other tourist attractions outside the Amazon that are more established destinations with good infrastructure. As noted, among foreign tourists to Brazil in 2019, 65 percent came to visit beaches and 19 percent came for ecotourism, nature, or adventure (Ministry of Tourism 2020). Consistently over the years, Foz do Iguaçu and Manaus attract the most international tourists looking for ecotourism and nature in Brazil (Ministry of Tourism 2018). The preference for destinations like the Amazon is strongest among domestic tourists: around 26 percent of Brazilians who traveled for leisure opted for ecotourism and nature and adventure trips.

A visit to Amazônia, while not necessarily more expensive than the established sun destinations in Brazil, is relatively time consuming and generally offers fewer amenities. While size and distance are disadvantages for Amazônia as a tourist destination, some places have established infrastructure that offers an excellent experience—fishing for tucunaré near Manaus, for example. However, this is not the case in many other parts of the region, and despite its potential, tourism in Amazônia remains constrained by inadequate logistics and strong competition (including from other regions in Brazil). In 2017 the average international tourist spent US$85.34 daily in Foz do Iguaçu and US$80.34 in Manaus, compared with US$49 in sun destinations such as Fortaleza and Recife and US$72 in Rio de Janeiro. To attract tourists, bureaucratic procedures surrounding visits to public areas need to be streamlined. Equally important, Amazônia needs to offer improved amenities and services, including telecommunication facilities and transport facilities, and will have to do so in a sustainable and ecofriendly way. It is possible to keep tourist visits concentrated in small areas, as demonstrated by Costa Rica, one of the world's most successful tropical ecological tourism destinations, with an area only about one-third the size of the small Amazonian state of Acre. Existing logistics in urban areas (see chapter 6) could serve as hubs and feeders for rural ecotourism in Amazônia, suggesting the potential for synergy effects.

Mining

Most artisanal and small-scale mining in Amazônia is illegal. It is also relatively labor intensive (especially gold and pig iron mining). Modern *garimpeiros,* in contrast, are heavily mechanized and highly capitalized, and they obtain a substantial part of their revenues from gold smuggling and money laundering. They constitute a very important political force at both the state and the federal levels. The Tapajós basin (in southwest Pará), northern Mato Grosso (near Peixoto de Azevedo), and areas close to Porto Velho (Rondônia) and Calçoene (Amapá) are some of the most important gold-mining regions. Brazil produces around 100 tons of gold a year, and about a quarter of that amount is estimated to come from artisanal and small-scale mining, some legal but most illegal. There are more than 450 illegal mining sites in Amazônia, with an estimated 20,000 illegal gold miners in the Yanomami area alone (Brazil's largest protected Indigenous reserve). More than 20 percent of Indigenous lands are affected by mining concessions and illegal mining, covering an area of around 450,000 square kilometers (Vallejos et al. 2020).

The annual rate of deforestation in Amazônia caused by *garimpeiros* increased more than 90 percent between 2017 and 2020, reaching 101.7 square kilometers in 2020 (Siqueira-Gay and Sánchez 2021). While formal mining is required to comply with environmental regulations, most small-scale or artisanal mining (especially illegal mining) areas are abandoned after reserves are exhausted, without proper rehabilitation. Reducing illegality and making mining sustainable will require implementing rules for the traceability of gold production and establishing a system of standards, labels, and certificates that are recognized and valued by global customers and thus enhance the environmental price premiums of artisanal mining products. Such rules would create incentives for artisanal and small-scale mining to adopt green technologies that reduce land degradation and deforestation.

Large-scale mining creates only a relatively small number of jobs in Amazônia. In 2018 there were 15,195 jobs in mineral processing in Pará, mainly in manufacturing ceramic products (34 percent), producing materials for civil construction (27 percent), metallurgy (23 percent), and producing iron, steel, and its alloys (12 percent). When upstream activities are included, mineral extraction employed 32,242 workers in 2018, with a multiplier effect of 0.87 jobs to the mineral transformation industry, according to the National Mining Agency. The Ministry of Mines and Energy has estimated that in 2019 each direct job in mineral extraction generated 13 indirect jobs. Applied to Pará, this would mean 266,000 direct and indirect jobs.

But mining, especially large-scale mining, makes a substantial fiscal contribution to the budgets of affected municipalities through mineral royalties and other nontax payments. In 2020 royalty payments (Financial Compensation for Mineral Exploration, or CFEM) reached R$6.08 billion in Pará, which accounts for 95 percent of the CFEM collections in Amazônia. Parauapebas and Canaã dos Carajás represented 46 percent of the total, followed by Marabá, Paragominas, and Oriximiná. CFEM revenues in other states are much smaller (between

R$5 million and R$60 million per year).[23] Approximately 82 percent of Pará's CFEM revenue is collected from the iron ore industry. Most of the CFEM revenue collected goes to municipalities (65 percent), with smaller shares going to states (23 percent) and the federal government (12 percent). By law, the revenues must be used for projects that directly or indirectly benefit local communities (such as infrastructure, environmental quality, health, and education).

Large-scale mining has also had a positive impact on local economies, although in Amazônia it often comes with environmental harm. Large mining projects often support regional and local infrastructure (such as roads and electricity), either through direct investment or as users of infrastructure services, enhancing the mobility and connectivity of rural populations. The infrastructure built by mining companies, in addition to supporting additional mining projects, can stimulate other economic activities and services. Large mining projects can also foster the growth of urban centers[24] and contribute to the development of local providers of goods and services that, with the right support, can be integrated into domestic and global supply chains and contribute to economic diversification. These impacts are particularly strong during boom periods (Carvalho and Candeira Pimentel 2017). On the negative side, however, the infrastructure and development that mining brings to Amazônia also exacerbate deforestation (see chapters 1 and 4).

As elsewhere, the formal mining industry in Amazônia is increasingly committed to sustainable development. Amazônia is rich in highly sought-after mineral resources such as iron ore and gold, but also in "climate action" minerals that are used to produce the clean energy technologies (wind, solar, batteries) needed for the global transition to a net-zero-carbon future. As long as demand for these minerals is strong and prices remain high, there will be pressure on land for mineral extraction. Reconciling mining and environmental protection is important for sustainable growth. In Amazônia, large-scale mining companies are committed to sustainable land management, effective forest conservation and reforestation, and poverty reduction in their area of operations, including support to municipal governments for the delivery of basic services in remote areas. Large-scale mining can be a positive component of structural transformation in Amazônia through innovative financing (emissions trading, green bonds) of land restoration and management activities. Growing pressure on mining companies to commit to net-zero emissions has stimulated interest in forest carbon offsets, a cost-effective tool for climate mitigation. The development of finance mechanisms that increase private sector investment in the forest sector may protect forests, reduce emissions, and deliver benefits for biodiversity, land conservation, water, and development in local communities and Indigenous areas. Finally, many large-scale mining companies have withdrawn from mineral exploration on Indigenous lands.

CONCLUSIONS AND POLICY IMPLICATIONS

Rural transformation will raise incomes and diversify the rural economy in Amazônia, but it also brings social and environmental disruption that needs to be managed. Most employment in rural Amazônia remains in agriculture, but rural transformation is increasingly releasing rural labor and putting pressure on less competitive farmers. Rural transformation can be facilitated through public policies that focus on developing new sources of economic, social, and environmental resilience. For farming specifically, public policies and programs should focus on the production of high-value crops using climate-smart technologies, support small farmers' incomes and food security, provide assistance to family farmers in transitioning to alternative livelihoods, and limit the impact of structural transformation on deforestation through enforcement of environmental regulations.

Strengthening family farming. A sharper focus on high-value crops as part of a wider green agriculture strategy would entail agricultural extension, farmer training and capacity building, credit programs, and support for organizational structures that help smaller producers to reach scale (such as cooperatives, contract farming, and out-grower schemes). Given the gradual loss of competitiveness of family farmers in the production of annual and permanent crops and the environmental risks linked to cattle ranching, more attention could be given to high-value commodities (such as vegetables and fish farming) that are well suited to family farmers' factor endowments and provide a reliable source of income, especially for farm households near urban centers of demand. The Brazilian government, through Conab, has a minimum price policy for 17 extractive products, 9 of them relevant to Amazônia. However, while the policy supports farmers' incomes in times of low market prices, it is unsustainable in the long run, and the resources could be redirected to raising productivity using green technologies and helping farmers to meet the product standards demanded in private markets. In parallel, training and capacity-building efforts should also focus on greening agriculture and support restoration of degraded lands and forests, agroforestry, and landscape management in general.

Supporting incomes for family farmers. Support for family farmers' incomes and food security is required since subsistence farmers tend to be risk averse and often prioritize production of food staples, even if cash crops would generate higher incomes and offer better food security. Government programs that provide alternative forms of guaranteed income or food security could help farmers to assume more risk and encourage them to make more profitable investments, including in climate-smart agricultural technologies. Existing programs (box 5.4) could be made conditional on participants' not deforesting, in an effort to reduce the high risk that small farmers (agrarian settlers) will deforest in response to competition pressure. Adequate implementation of Brazil's environmental regulation programs is critical to enforce such conditions.

Reforming financial incentives. There is plenty of scope to rationalize the use of public resources in support of commercial farmers. First, instead of interest rate subsidies, agricultural finance for commercial farmers would be improved by focusing on partial credit guarantees and agricultural insurance. Second, allocating public resources to making large-scale production more climate smart would carry both environmental benefits (by reducing greenhouse gas emissions) and economic benefits (by improving resilience and compliance with environmental standards increasingly required in export markets).

Family farmers for whom farming is no longer an economically viable option would benefit from support in transitioning to alternative livelihoods. Chapter 6 demonstrates that raising productivity and generating employment opportunities in urban areas are key elements in a strategy aimed at supporting family farmers' transition. These farmers could receive support for acquiring new, high-demand skills or financial support to start a new business, for example.

BOX 5.4

Evaluation of the impact of public procurement programs on participating farmers

Public procurement provides small farmers with access to markets while supplying food to schools and other public entities. In 2003 the federal government launched the Food Acquisition Program (PAA) to provide food security to vulnerable urban populations. Sustained by the production of family farms, the PAA has become an instrument of inclusive and decentralized development, providing important incentives to family farmers. Another program, the National School Feeding Program (PNAE), financed by the National Education Development Fund (FNDE), requires at least 30 percent of the products it purchases to come from family farms (Law 11,947/2009).

An assessment of the PAA for 2015–17 and the PNAE for 2017 estimated the impact of these programs on the incomes of participating farmers at approximately twice the average value of the purchases, thus confirming the positive impact of the program on market access and family farm households (Rocha, da Silva, and Vian 2019). Despite these positive results, the PAA has been losing influence, as evidenced by a 90 percent reduction in the volume of purchases and an 80 percent reduction in public funding between 2011 and 2017. The PNAE suffered a much smaller reduction in resources of 5.5 percent over the same period.

But while cities are critical for absorbing rural labor in the longer term, there also remains significant scope to support rural livelihoods, especially in sectors that have skills complementary to those of farming, such as forestry, fisheries and aquaculture, selected mining activities, and ecological tourism. Public policy can support a more enabling business environment for these sectors. For some sectors, notably forestry, an enabling environment will depend on lower spillovers from other economic activities, such as deforestation and illegal logging associated with land clearing for agriculture, while fisheries and aquaculture will depend on low pollution spillovers from unsustainable agricultural methods. Rural tourism could benefit from improving logistics associated with urban development in Amazônia.

Some of the policy implications from other chapters are also immediately relevant for rural transformation and economic diversification in Amazônia: strengthening tenure security (chapter 4), education and skills training (chapter 2), and social protection—potentially augmented by payments for ecosystem services (chapters 2, 4, and 7). Focusing on family farmers and traditional producers will be important since many of them are unlikely to survive increased competitive pressure without the support of capacity building and social protection. And last but not least, forest governance remains crucial to limit deforestation pressures from structural change (chapter 4).

NOTES

1. Climate-smart agriculture is defined as land use practices that sustainably increase productivity, enhance climate change adaptation (that is, increase resilience), and contribute to climate change mitigation.
2. The Food and Agriculture Organization of the United Nations uses agroforestry as a collective name for land use systems and technologies that include woody perennials (such as trees, shrubs, palms, and bamboo) on the same land management units as agricultural crops

and livestock in some form of spatial arrangement or temporal sequence. As such, agroforestry incorporates a wide range of systems that vary in complexity.

3. Integrated landscape approaches involve simultaneous consideration of spatial, ecological, and socioeconomic aspects to managing competing demands for land, water, and other natural resources in a given territory, thus creating demand for production systems such as agroforestry that target sustainable intensification. See, for example, World Bank (2014) and Garrett et al. (2020).

4. Area: up to four tax modules, which, depending on the municipality, may comprise 20–440 hectares; labor force: predominantly family members; sources of family income: agriculture accounts for at least half of total income, excluding government benefits and pensions; and farm management responsibility: only family members. Brazil has many public policies aimed at family farms that employ such diverse instruments as rural credit, technical assistance, public procurement, and minimum price.

5. This classification establishes the same criteria as the National Program to Strengthen Family Farming (PRONAF) Microcredit Group B, a government rural credit program. See "Rural Credit," Central Bank of Brazil website (https://www.bcb.gov.br /estabilidadefinanceira/creditorural); and "Pronaf Microcredit (Group 'B')," Brazilian Development Bank (BNDES) website (https://www.bndes.gov.br/wps/portal/site/home /financiamento/produto/pronaf-microcredito-grupo-b).

6. Nonpoor family farms are those with annual income of more than R$23,000 or that use labor other than family members.

7. Figures based on the 2017 Census (Ministry of Regional Development 2020). These aggregate figures for Amazônia do not reflect the large variation in the region. For example, while large farmers account for the bulk of agricultural output in Mato Grosso, small farmers contribute substantially to total production value in Amazonas.

8. This also partially reflects the fact that government support for agriculture has historically focused mainly on field crops rather than forest products.

9. Large farmers may also find it easier to access credit for other reasons, such as the higher collateral value of their land.

10. Urban markets in Amazônia still present substantial opportunities in high-value crops. In Pará, for example, a large share (up to 80 percent) of certain fruits and vegetables are imported from the south and southeast of Brazil.

11. Even though the Melitz (2003) study focuses on industry, its findings are applicable to agriculture.

12. Interest rate subsidies are typically regressive and often do not benefit the target population, leading some researchers to argue that the higher the interest rate subsidy, the larger the probability that the target population will be excluded. See Gonzalez-Vega (1984).

13. As mentioned, the disadvantages of smaller farmers relative to larger farmers stem from multiple factors, including differences in access to credit and technology, lower endowments of land that limit economies of scale, and poorer access to markets.

14. Bulte et al. (2000) discuss how this practice was seen as optimal in the humid tropical lowlands of Costa Rica, an environment similar to the Amazon biome in Brazil.

15. See the literature review in Steinfeld (2018).

16. In this chapter, the term "nontimber forest products" refers to all products produced using extractivist methods according to the 2017 Census of Agriculture (except timber and firewood), plus the cultivation of permanent crops, including açaí, rubber, cacao, heart of palm, camu-camu, and cupuaçu.

17. The discussion in this section focuses on the evolution of the competitiveness of smallholder-based agroforestry systems, not smallholder-intensive mixed cropping systems (often involving intercropping but no trees), where land productivity is relatively high, even though labor productivity may still be low.

18. These permits are readily available and often provide cover for loggers to remove valuable trees from the legal reserve of the lot, degrading the forest quality and "stealing" from the household.

19. See Pereira et al. 2010.

20. Almost all logging outside of concessions is considered illegal in some way.

21. However, profitable market conditions are not guaranteed, since less timber would raise prices and could force consumers to buy substitute products.

22. See the references in May (2015).

23. For data on the biggest CFEM collectors, see the CFEM Extra Collection System tool of the National Mining Agency (ANM) website: https://sistemas.anm.gov.br/arrecadacao/extra/Relatorios/cfem/maiores_arrecadadores.aspx.

24. For example, the 998-kilometer double-track mine-to-port Carajás railroad (Estrada de Ferro Carajás, EFC) serves as an outlet for its mineral production in Pará. Because of its connection to the country's general railroad network, EFC became an important corridor for the export of agricultural bulk and other cargo from Brazil's Central-West region, strengthening agricultural development in the interior of the country. A study by Brauch et al. (2020) shows that shared use of the Carajás railroad infrastructure has brought direct socioeconomic benefits to municipalities along the corridor. Proximity to the export corridor is associated with lower poverty rates and higher socioeconomic indicators. These indicators are higher where mining activities occur and in urban centers like Açailândia, Marabá, and São Luís, where the export terminal of Itaqui is located.

REFERENCES

Almeida, O., K. Lorenzen, and D. McGrath. 2004. "The Commercial Fishing Sector in the Regional Economy of the Brazilian Amazon." In *Proceedings of the Second International Symposium on the Management of Large Rivers for Fisheries, Volume II*, edited by R. Welcomme and T. Petr, 15–24. Bangkok: FAO Regional Office for Asia and the Pacific.

Almeida, O. T., D. G. McGrath, and M. L. Ruffino. 2001. "The Commercial Fisheries of the Lower Amazon: An Economic Analysis." *Fisheries Management and Ecology* 8 (3): 253–69.

Amacher, G. S., F. D. Merry, and M. S. Bowman. 2009. "Smallholder Timber Sales on the Amazon Frontier." *Ecological Economics* 68 (6): 1787–96.

Assad, E. D. 2013. "Agricultura de baixa emissão de carbono: A evolução de um novo paradigma." Report, Observatório ABC, Brasília.

Barros, A. M. 2017. "Avaliação do uso estratégico das áreas prioritárias do Programa ABC." Report, Observatório ABC, Brasília.

Brauch, M. D., N. Maennling, P. Toledano, E. S. Monteiro, and F. B. Tavares. 2020. "Shared-Use Infrastructure along the World's Largest Iron Ore Operation: Lessons Learned from the Carajás Corridor." Columbia Center on Sustainable Investment, New York.

Brinker, I. 2019. "O crédito na agricultura brasileira no período 2013–2018: Um estudo do PRONAF, PRONAMP e demais linhas de crédito rural, com ênfase no investimento." Master's thesis, Universidade do Vale do Rio dos Sinos, São Leopoldo, Brazil.

Bulte, E. H., B. A. M. Bouman, R. A. J. Plant, A. Nieuwenhuyse, and H. G. P. Jansen. 2000. "The Economics of Soil Nutrient Stocks and Cattle Ranching in the Tropics: Optimal Pasture Degradation in Humid Costa Rica." *European Review of Agricultural Economics* 27 (2): 207–26.

Calice, P., and F. D. Kalan. 2022. "Sustainable, Inclusive Growth: Rural Finance in the North Region." Background note for this report, World Bank, Washington, DC.

Carvalho, A. C., and C. A. Candeira Pimentel. 2017. "The Logic of the Valorization of Natural Resources in Brazil: Historical Relationship between the Electricity Sector and the Mining Industry in the Amazon." *Novos Cadernos NAEA* 20 (3): 9–29.

Cirera, X., and A. M. Neto. 2022. "The Role of Skills Relatedness and Spin-offs in Diversification to Green Sectors." Background note for this report, World Bank, Washington, DC.

Coelho, M. H. P., and P. A. M. Sakowski. 2012. "Perfil da mão de obra do turismo no Brasil nas atividades características do turismo e em ocupações. "Discussion paper, Institute of Applied Economic Research (Ipea), Brasília.

da Costa, N. B. Jr., T. C. Baldissera, C. E. Pinto, F. C. Garagorry, A. de Moraes, and P. C. de Faccio Carvalho. 2019. "Public Policies for Low Carbon Emission Agriculture Foster Beef Cattle Production in Southern Brazil." *Land Use Policy* 80 (January): 269–73.

de Barros, A. V. L., A. K. O. Homma, J. A. Takamatsu, T. Takamatsu, and M. Konagano. 2009. "Evolução e percepção dos sistemas agroflorestais desenvolvidos pelos agricultores nipo-brasileiros do município de Tomé-açu, estado do Pará." *Amazônia: Ciência e Desenvolvimento* 5 (9): 121–51.

de Rezende, G. C. 2002. "Ocupação agrícola e estrutura agrária no cerrado: O papel do preço da terra, dos recursos naturais e da tecnologia." Discussion paper, Institute of Applied Economic Research (Ipea), Brasília.

Gandour, C., D. Menezes, J. P. Vieira, and J. J. Assunção. 2021. "Forest Degradation in the Brazilian Amazon: Public Policy Must Target Phenomenon Related to Deforestation." Insight report, Climate Policy Initiative, Pontifical Catholic University of Rio de Janeiro.

Garrett, R. D., J. Ryschawy, L. W. Bell, O. Cortner, J. Ferreira, A. V. N. Garik, J. D. B. Gil, et al. 2020. "Drivers of Decoupling and Recoupling of Crop and Livestock Systems at Farm and Territorial Scales." *Ecology and Society* 25 (1): 24. doi:10.5751/ES-11412-250124.

Gianetti, G. W., and J. B. S. Ferreira Filho. 2021. "The ABC Plan and Program: An Evaluation of Execution and Distribution of Resources." *Revista de Economia e Sociologia Rural* 59 (1): e216524.

Gonzalez-Vega, C. 1984. *Credit-Rationing Behavior of Agricultural Lenders: The Iron Law of Interest-Rate Restrictions.* Boulder, CO: Westview Press.

Greiner, C., and P. Sakdapolrak. 2013. "Rural-Urban Migration, Agrarian Change, and the Environment in Kenya: A Critical Review of the Literature." *Population and Environment* 34 (4): 524–53.

Helfand, S., and M. Taylor. 2021. "The Inverse Relationship between Farm Size and Productivity: Refocusing the Debate." *Food Policy* 99 (February): 101977.

Herrera, G. P., R. Lourival, R. B. da Costa, D. R. F. Mendes, T. B. S. Moreira, U. G. P. de Abreu, and M. Constantino. 2018. "Econometric Analysis of Income, Productivity, and Diversification among Smallholders in Brazil." *Land Use Policy* 76 (July): 455–59.

Homma, A. K. O. 2012. "Plant Extractivism or Plantation: What Is the Best Option for the Amazon?" *Estudos Avançados* 26 (74): 167–86.

Kohlmann, G., and E. Licks. 2022. "Mapping Value Chains for the Amazon Bioeconomy." Background note for this report, World Bank, Washington, DC.

Magalhães, R., and R. Abramovay. 2006. *Acesso, uso e sustentabilidade do Pronaf B.* São Paulo, Brazil: Ministry of Agricultural Development and Economic Research Institute Foundation.

Maia, G. B. da S., V. D. Bastos, B. M. De Conti, and F. B. Roitman. 2012. "O Pronaf B e o financiamento agropecuário nos Territórios da Cidadania do semiárido." *Revista do BNDES* 37 (June): 177–214.

MAPA (Ministry of Agriculture, Livestock and Supply). 2021. *ABC+ plano setorial para adaptação à mudança do clima e baixa emissão de carbono na agropecuária com vistas ao desenvolvimento sustentável (2020-2030): Visão estratégica para um novo ciclo.* Brasília: MAPA Secretariat of Innovation, Rural Development and Irrigation.

May, P. 2015. "Tourism's Contribution to Forest Benefits in the Amazon Basin." Unpublished report, World Bank, Washington, DC.

McGrath, D., L. Castello, M. Brabo, D. Nepstad, S. Gama, B. Forsberg, E. Mendoza, et al. 2020. "Can Fish Drive Development of the Amazon Bioeconomy?" Policy Brief, San Francisco, Earth Innovation Institute.

Melitz, M. J. 2003. "The Impact of Trade on Intra-Industry Reallocations and Aggregate Industry Productivity." *Econometrica* 71 (6): 1695–725.

Merry, F., G. Amacher, D. C. Nepstad, and E. Lima. 2006. "Industrial Development on Logging Frontiers in the Brazilian Amazon." *International Journal of Sustainable Development* 9 (3): 277–96.

Ministry of Regional Development. 2020. "Plano regional de desenvolvimento da Amazônia (PRDA) 2020-2023." Policy document, Ministry of Regional Development, Belém.

Ministry of Tourism. 2018. "Caracterização e dimensionamento do turismo internacional no Brasil, 2013-2017." Descriptive report, Ministry of Tourism and Economic Research Institute Foundation, São Paulo.

Ministry of Tourism. 2020. "Anuario Estatístico de Turismo 2020: Vol. 47, Ano Base 2019." Annual statistical report, Ministry of Tourism, Brasília.

Observatório ABC. 2019. "Análise dos recursos do programa ABC – Safras 2017/18 e 2018/19." Report, Observatório ABC, São Paulo.

Pereira, D., D. Santos, M. Vedoveto, J. Guimarães, and A. Veríssimo. 2010. "Fatos Florestais da Amazônia 2010" [Forest Facts of the Amazon 2010]. Booklet, Amazon Institute of People and the Environment (Imazon), Belém.

Porcher, C., and M. Hanusch. 2022. "A Model of Amazon Deforestation, Trade, and Labor Market Dynamics." Policy Research Working Paper 10163, World Bank, Washington, DC.

Rada, N., S. Helfand, and M. Magalhães. 2019. "Agricultural Productivity Growth in Brazil: Large and Small Farms Excel." *Food Policy* 84 (April): 176–85.

Rocha, A. B. Jr. 2022. "Farm Scale and Productivity in the Legal Amazon." Background note for this report, World Bank, Washington, DC.

Rocha, A. B., G. W. Gianetti, A. N. Almeida, and J. B. S. Ferreira Filho. 2019. "Is the Low Carbon Agriculture Credit Program Impacting Pasture Area and Quality in Brazil's Northeast Region?" Paper presented at Agricultural and Applied Economics Association 2019 Annual Meeting, July 21–23, Atlanta.

Rocha, A. B., R. P. da Silva, and C. E. F. Vian. 2019. "Programa de Aquisição de Alimentos e Programa Nacional de Alimentação Escolar: Dinâmica recente e impacto na receita dos agricultores familiars." Presented at the 57th Annual Meeting of the Brazilian Society of Rural Economy, Administration, and Sociology: Agriculture, Food, and Development, July 21–25, Ilhéus, Brazil.

SEBRAE (Brazilian Support Service for Micro and Small Enterprises). 2016. *Estudo de mercado consumidor do Pirarucu 2016*. Brasília: SEBRAE.

Siqueira-Gay, J., and L. E. Sánchez. 2021. "The Outbreak of Illegal Gold Mining in the Brazilian Amazon Boosts Deforestation." *Regional Environmental Change* 21 (1): 28.

Steinfeld, J. 2018. "Complex Farming Systems: More Ecosystem Services and Higher Labour Requirements: A Case Study from Brazil." Master's thesis, Organic Agriculture, Wageningen University, Wageningen, Netherlands.

Sumner, D. A. 1982. "The Off-Farm Labor Supply of Farmers." *American Journal of Agricultural Economics* 64 (3): 499–509.

Tao Yang, D. 1997. "Education and Off-Farm Work." *Economic Development and Cultural Change* 45 (3): 613–32.

Vallejos, P. Q., P. Veit, P. Tipula, and K. Reytar. 2020. *Undermining Rights: Indigenous Lands and Mining in the Amazon*. Washington, DC: World Resources Institute.

World Bank. 2014. "Moving toward a Sustainable Landscape Approach to Development." Agriculture and Environmental Services Department Note 88433, World Bank, Washington, DC.

World Bank. 2020. "Brazil Rural Finance Policy Note." World Bank, Washington, DC.

Yamada, M., and H. L. Gholz. 2002. "An Evaluation of Agroforestry Systems as a Rural Development Option for the Brazilian Amazon." *Agroforestry Systems* 55 (2): 81–87.

Yue, Z., S. Li, M. W. Feldman, and H. Du. 2010. "Floating Choices: A Generational Perspective on Intentions of Rural-Urban Migrants in China." *Environment and Planning A* 42 (3): 545–62.

6 Toward a New Urban Agenda in Amazônia

PAULA RESTREPO CADAVID AND OLIVIA D'AOUST

KEY MESSAGES

- About three-quarters of the population in Amazônia live in urban areas.
- Amazônia's cities tend to be smaller and farther from national markets.
- Given the vast space, Amazônia's fragmented urban systems center around economic hubs and service hubs.
- Amazônia's cities lag those in the rest of Brazil in access to basic services, digital services, and education and health outcomes, slowing the convergence of incomes per capita.
- Amazônia can move toward the productivity frontier, reduce deforestation pressure, and converge in living standards without expanding the urban footprint.
- There is a long record of developing and implementing regional projects and programs to integrate Amazônia with the rest of Brazil, other Latin American countries, and the world—but a well-defined agenda for Amazonia's cities has been missing.
- *Policy implications:*
  - Developing a tailored and targeted approach to regional development—making cities key economic and service delivery actors in Amazônia.
  - Investing in building local institutions to manage regional and city development better.
  - Investing in urban infrastructure to reduce disparities in living standards in economic and service hubs and increase the competitiveness of cities as regional economic hubs.

- Nurturing existing human capital across the region (for the future) and build local endowments to attract and retain skilled human capital by improving the quality of life, urban amenities, and service levels in economic hubs.
- Carefully choosing interventions to improve connectivity between cities and regional and global markets while protecting the forest.
- Carefully choosing place-based interventions, taking into consideration spatial endowments (population density and proximity to markets).
- Addressing urban issues that persist in Brazilian cities—outside Amazônia—to reduce barriers to mobility and achieve a more efficient urban system. The recently updated National Policy for Regional Development and the National Policy for Urban Development provide a good guiding framework.

POSITIONING CITIES FOR AMAZÔNIA'S DEVELOPMENT

About three-quarters of Amazonians live in urban areas. This chapter focuses on urban areas in Amazônia and their potential contribution to economic development and environmental conservation. It briefly assesses the uniqueness of urban areas and what it would take for Amazônia's cities to improve their economic performance and deliver better futures for their inhabitants. It thus supports implementing the recently updated National Policy for Regional Development (PNDR)—Decree No. 9810/19—which focuses on the foundations and variables needed for Brazil to raise the standard of living, improve the quality of life, and expand the access to opportunities in Amazônia. It calls for a polycentric network of cities, supported by a regional development mandate, to respond to the specific challenges and opportunities of different regions.

Not all cities will contribute to the economy in the same way, for that would be inefficient (and fiscally and environmentally costly). Industries clustering and workers sorting in cities are pulled by market forces, attracted to the advantages of location (natural, physical, or intellectual spillovers) or sometimes by historical accidents (Ellison and Glaeser 1997). Examples include the diamond industry in Antwerp, the wine industry in Mendoza, the automobile industry in Detroit, and technology hubs in Bangalore and Silicon Valley. The forces shaping cities make economic activities lumpy and spatial organization geographically uneven. Economies of scale in production combined with lower transport costs increase the geographic concentration of people and economic activities (Krugman 1991a, 1991b). As economies develop, economic activity generally becomes more concentrated, not less. And the nature of agglomeration seems to be evolving. What mattered in the era of manufacturing (capital and access to shipping) may not weigh as much as it once did. In an era where economies are driven by services, what matters are the interactions between highly skilled workers (Duranton 2020).

Spatial economic concentration need not take place at the cost of inequality in living standards, both within and outside cities. Different policy instruments are available to encourage spatial efficiency while supporting spatial equity (World Bank 2009). Governments can work on achieving the two objectives in tandem, if the instruments to address them are coordinated. The key? To focus on people, acknowledging the challenges of the places where they are, rather than on the places themselves. And achieving spatial equity must not be confused with implementing uniform place-based interventions, which can be costly and do little to improve living standards. The heterogeneous challenges need to be tackled by equally differentiated policies, which requires identifying the payoffs and trade-offs of alternative policy packages. Such policies should be realistic and based on the area's stage of development and its fiscal and institutional capacities (Lall 2009).

Amazonian cities do not provide good alternative jobs for formal rural laborers, nor do they provide quality basic services and a supportive environment to build human endowments for the future. The relatively low transport connectivity and the distance between populated places have led to fragmented urban systems organized around economic nodes, supported by smaller service nodes. Much of Amazônia's urban system functions like isolated island states (Schor and de Oliveira 2011). Cities in the Amazon basin (the Colonial Frontier), in particular, are connected mainly by waterways, and their functional relationships with other populated places are limited by the vast distances between them. These fragmented urban systems are centered around economic nodes, where population and economic activities are lumped and which will be key to fostering urban productivity growth in Amazônia. Given the vast distance between populated settlements, economic nodes are complemented by service nodes, which tend to be smaller but can play a key role in providing services and building endowments (human capital). Economic nodes and service nodes are both essential for developing Amazônia.

Better targeted and tailored policies can enable Amazonian cities to contribute to the region's sustainable and inclusive development without expanding the urban footprint. As chapters 1 to 3 outline, to climb the development ladder, Brazil needs to move toward an urban productivity–led growth model. For Amazônia, cities need to start taking a more central role in development. Federal and state policies need to start putting in place a tailored and complementary set of measures—taking into account the potential of Amazônia's city endowments and economic potential—to foster cities' productivity, improve their livability, and start building the right human capital endowments for the future. It is not necessary to expand the urban footprint; instead, cities need to be enabled to use their spatial, financial, and human endowments more efficiently. In fact, the analysis in chapter 3 suggests that, through general equilibrium effects, higher urban productivity can relieve macroeconomic pressures on natural forests, supporting more sustainable development.

The chapter proceeds as follows. It briefly provides some evidence on how cities in the Amazon have interacted with their surrounding natural areas, with a focus on deforestation, which warrants particular attention as urban productivity has rarely been identified as a deforestation-reducing force (chapter 3).

It next unpacks the theoretical and empirical determinants of urban productivity in Brazil and reviews the potential pathways to higher productivity in Amazônia's cities. It then explores and proposes a dual approach for designing place-based policies in urban Amazônia and in Brazil more broadly.

AMAZONIAN CITIES AND THE FOREST

The growth of cities leads, by definition, to changes in land use. As buildings and infrastructure expand to respond to the growing population, the land surrounding cities is converted. The degree of land conversion usually depends on patterns of occupational and urban growth (compact or sprawled) and is influenced by land use plans that guide the urban growth perimeter and limit expansion in protected or hazard-prone areas. The expansion of cities thus directly converts land use and can drive deforestation or reduce agricultural land. Beyond the direct impacts, it can also lead to deforestation—for instance, when new food-processing industries in a city expand the agricultural activities around it (Porcher and Hanusch 2022).

Amazônia's urban footprint is fairly small, so direct deforestation linked to its urban spaces is limited. The total area of Amazônia's 47 largest cities (accounting for 93 percent of its urban population) is 1,548 square kilometers, or only 0.03 percent of Amazônia's territory.[1] And Amazonian cities tend to be denser than other Brazilian cities, further limiting their direct impact on natural lands.

Deforestation linked to Amazonian cities thus stems from their economic interactions (or value chains) with their environment or through the logistics infrastructure (especially roads) connecting them with the rest of the country. For instance, much more deforestation has occurred around cities on the New Frontier. Map 6.1 illustrates this interaction for two urban clusters: one centered around Manaus, the capital of Amazonas, and one around Porto Velho, the capital of Rondônia. Deforestation is much lower around Manaus and along the

MAP 6.1

Around cities, deforestation is much higher in the New Frontier

a. Manacapuru-Manaus-Itacoatiara

b. Porto Velho-Ariquemes-Ji Parana

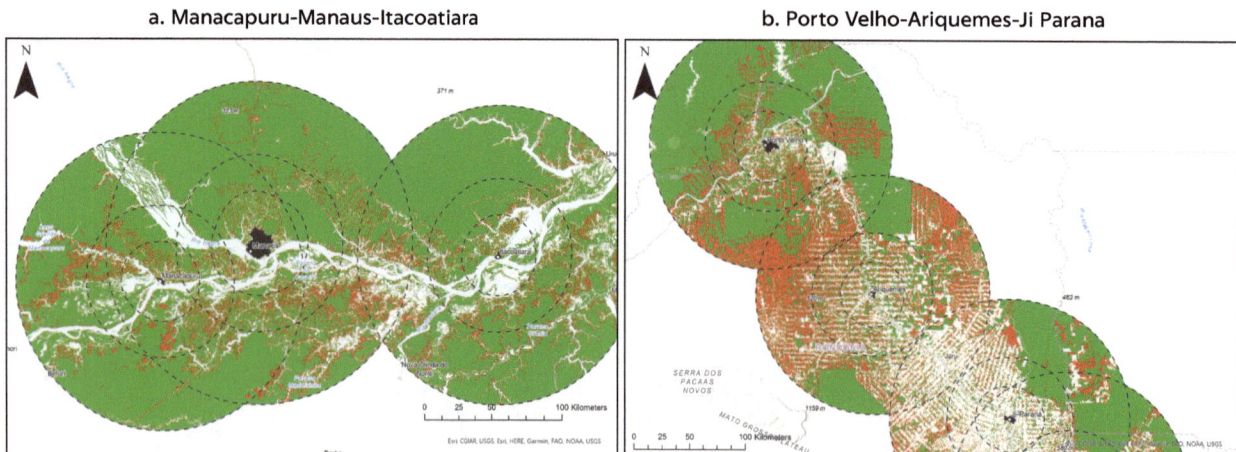

Sources: Hansen et al. 2013 and the Global Human Settlement (GHS) Urban Centre Database 2015 (Florczyk et al. 2019).

Amazon River than around Porto Velho and along BR-364. Rondônia lies on the New Frontier, associated with the Arc of Deforestation. Many cities were established as agriculture expanded into the region.

Deforestation tends to be lower around cities whose value chains are less linked with rural production. Urban areas can be home to industries that process primary commodities (for example, agribusiness or furniture makers), and they often provide services to the hinterland that raise the productivity of land-intensive production (Porcher and Hanusch 2022). So, municipalities where economic activities are related to agricultural production or transformation, including wood processing, tend to be surrounded by areas with higher deforestation (figure 6.1). For example, deforestation around Manaus, an industrial city, is much lower than deforestation around Porto Velho, a strategic port for agriculture (map 6.1, panels a and b, respectively). This initial analysis is consistent with the need for Brazil to move away from its current model of development (based on agriculture and the accumulation of land) and toward one based on the growth of services and manufacturing, which tend to be clustered in and around urban areas.

FIGURE 6.1

The share of economic activity linked to rural production is positively correlated with deforestation

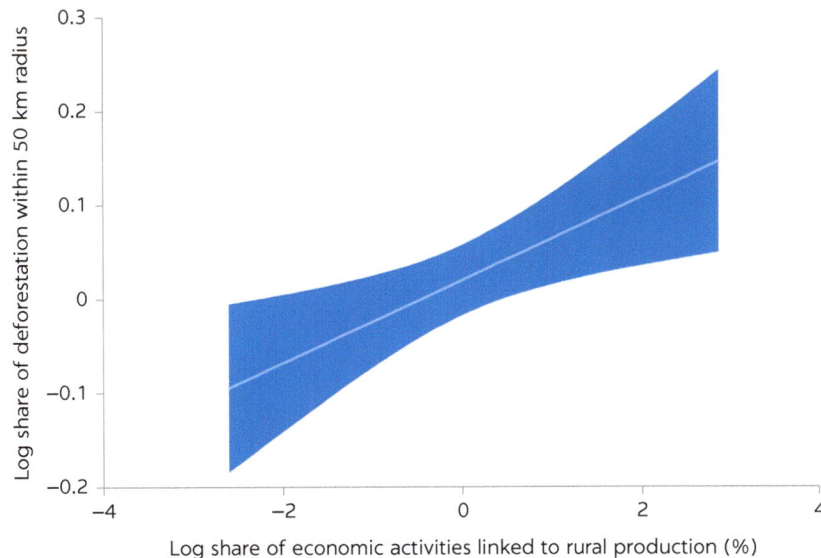

Source: World Bank.
Note: The figure shows a residual-on-residual plot with 90 percent confidence intervals. The y-axis depicts the residuals from an ordinary least squares regression on the log of the annual share of deforestation from existing forest stock (from Hansen et al. 2013) within a 50 kilometer radius from the city defined in the Global Human Settlement (GHS) Urban Centre Database 2015 (Florczyk et al. 2019) controlling for the lag of deforestation rate, travel times via road or waterways to Brasília and state capitals, and year fixed effects (2003–18). The x-axis corresponds to the log of the ratio of location quotient of employment linked to the forest versus not, computed for zip codes falling within 50 kilometers of the city available in the RAIS (Annual Social Information Report) database on the same controls. Each observation is a city. The slope is the resulting coefficient of a linear regression estimating the correlation between deforestation and the share of economic activities linked to rural production with the abovementioned controls, 0.04 ($p < 0.05$).

A TOOLBOX FOR INCREASING URBAN PRODUCTIVITY IN AMAZÔNIA

Theoretical and empirical determinants of urban productivity

A sharper focus on Amazônia's urban productivity is warranted to slow deforestation and boost economic and social development, as outlined in chapters 1 to 3. A new development model involves increasing the productivity of non-land-intensive tradable sectors such as manufacturing and services, which have the power to improve welfare while encouraging forest conservation. As these activities tend to locate in cities, pushing for faster structural transformation and higher urban productivity (inside and outside Amazônia) can have a significant impact on reducing deforestation in Amazônia. How best to achieve this transformation?

Two main reasons explain why one city is more productive than another. First, through skill-selective migration, workers and firms with different characteristics sort into different cities. High-skill workers tend to prefer living in large cities with good amenities, and since those workers tend to be more productive, productivity tends to be higher in the cities where they live. Second, intrinsic city characteristics (population density, urban form) and location characteristics (local endowments, access to markets) that facilitate firm and worker interactions enhance knowledge spillovers and make it easier to match skills to jobs—which makes it less expensive for firms to get supplies and reach markets. In Brazil, college graduates say that they value urban amenities—from trash collection to museums, restaurants, and theaters and to lower crime rates—when choosing where to settle (Fan and Timmins 2017, in Ferreyra and Roberts 2018). These two drivers of productivity reinforce each other: cities (because they have higher economic density) cause workers to be more productive, and cities with higher productivity grow because they attract more productive workers, who are more likely to interact with one another (Duranton and Puga 2020).

How do these positive externalities translate into higher productivity? Urban economics point to three underlying ways that cities can be places where the driving forces of productivity, diversification, and economic growth closely interact (Duranton and Puga 2004).

The first way is agglomeration economies, often captured by population density. Close spatial proximity has many benefits. Some public goods—like infrastructure and basic services—are cheaper to provide when populations are large and densely packed. Firms near each other can share suppliers, which lowers the cost of inputs. Thick labor markets reduce search costs as firms have a larger pool of workers to choose from whenever they need to hire additional labor. And spatial proximity makes it easier for workers to share information and learn from each other (Duranton and Puga 2004). International evidence shows that knowledge spillovers play a key role in determining the productivity of successful cities.

The second way that cities can generate higher productivity is by having more human capital, which gives rise to positive human capital externalities. Workers bring to the workplace a bundle of skills that affect their productivity. As with the theory of agglomeration economies, people learn and interact with each other. Knowledge is embedded in people and passed on by "those who know" (Duranton 2008). Spreading knowledge among large numbers of people increases the generation, accumulation, and diffusion of knowledge.

Larger cities can then be "nurseries" for smaller ones, as knowledge spreads between them (Duranton and Puga 2004).

But learning is more likely for persons with higher skills, predicting that a worker's individual productivity will rise to the average human capital of the city where they live (Moretti 2004; Rauch 1993). In US cities, for example, a 10 percent rise in the percentage of workers with a college degree leads to a 22 percent rise in metropolitan gross domestic product per capita (Glaeser 2011). And larger cities—at least those in the high-income world—reward educated workers more than smaller cities (de la Roca and Puga 2017). This is one reason why larger cities tend to attract more skilled workers. So, it not surprising that cities are often modeled as "interactive systems," in which the urban structure reflects the net benefits of interactions (value of interactions net of transportation costs) (Bacolod, Blum, and Strange 2009). In France, human capital externalities have been shown to affect earnings through greater communication at the workplace. And this effect is greater in bigger and more educated cities (Charlot and Duranton 2004).

The third way for cities to generate higher productivity is that they can benefit from greater and faster access to intermediate inputs and large consumer markets. Higher productivity comes from city size, demand for goods and services, and how well they are connected to other cities and surrounding areas. Greater access to markets and suppliers makes it easier for firms to cover the fixed costs of setting up a new plant, which, in turn, increases profits and productivity (Fujita, Krugman, and Venables 1999; Krugman 1991a, b; Krugman and Venables 1995). This channel reflects the most basic agglomeration economy: reducing transport costs for goods. If a supplier locates near customers, the cost of shipping declines and the array of specialized suppliers of intermediate goods increases. Among the three ways, modifying market access tends to be the most feasible short-term solution to raising urban productivity.

Many of these benefits increase with scale: towns and small cities cannot generate the same productive advantages as larger cities. The elasticity of income to city population is between 3 percent and 8 percent. Each doubling of city size increases productivity by 5 percent (Rosenthal and Strange 2004). But poorly managed urban population growth can increase exposure to pollution and disease, turn density into crowding, increase traffic (and transport costs), and shrink green space. Higher density can also translate into higher land and housing prices, which then add to the social costs (Duranton and Puga 2020). Most cities in Latin America have relatively low productivity, associated with high traffic congestion and dysfunctional land use in areas with illegal settlements. But since urbanization is still fluid, these economies can still be fixed (Duranton 2020; Quintero and Roberts 2018).

Determinants of urban productivity in Brazil

Although much of the productive variation across subnational areas in Latin America is explained by differences in the workforce, an important part relates to the intrinsic characteristics of cities (Quintero and Roberts 2018). In fact, differences in workforce composition cannot explain an important part of the variation in productivity, which is consistent with the existence of the positive externalities and spillovers mentioned earlier. For the Latin America and Caribbean region, having better access to markets and a higher accumulation of human capital (average number of years of schooling) is associated with higher urban productivity (figure 6.2).[2] But no significant relationship is evident between population density and urban productivity, suggesting that cities in this region—contrary to the literature from other countries such as China and India—are not benefiting from higher population density, likely due to congestion forces overwhelming agglomeration economies (Duranton 2020; Ferreyra and Roberts 2018). However, results vary across countries, with Brazil departing from the regional trend, showing the positive correlation between productivity and all driving factors.

For a city in Brazil, closeness to markets, greater concentration of human capital, and higher population density have been linked to higher urban productivity. An increase in urban population density in a given Brazilian city is associated

FIGURE 6.2

Population density, education, and market access are associated with higher urban productivity in Latin America and the Caribbean

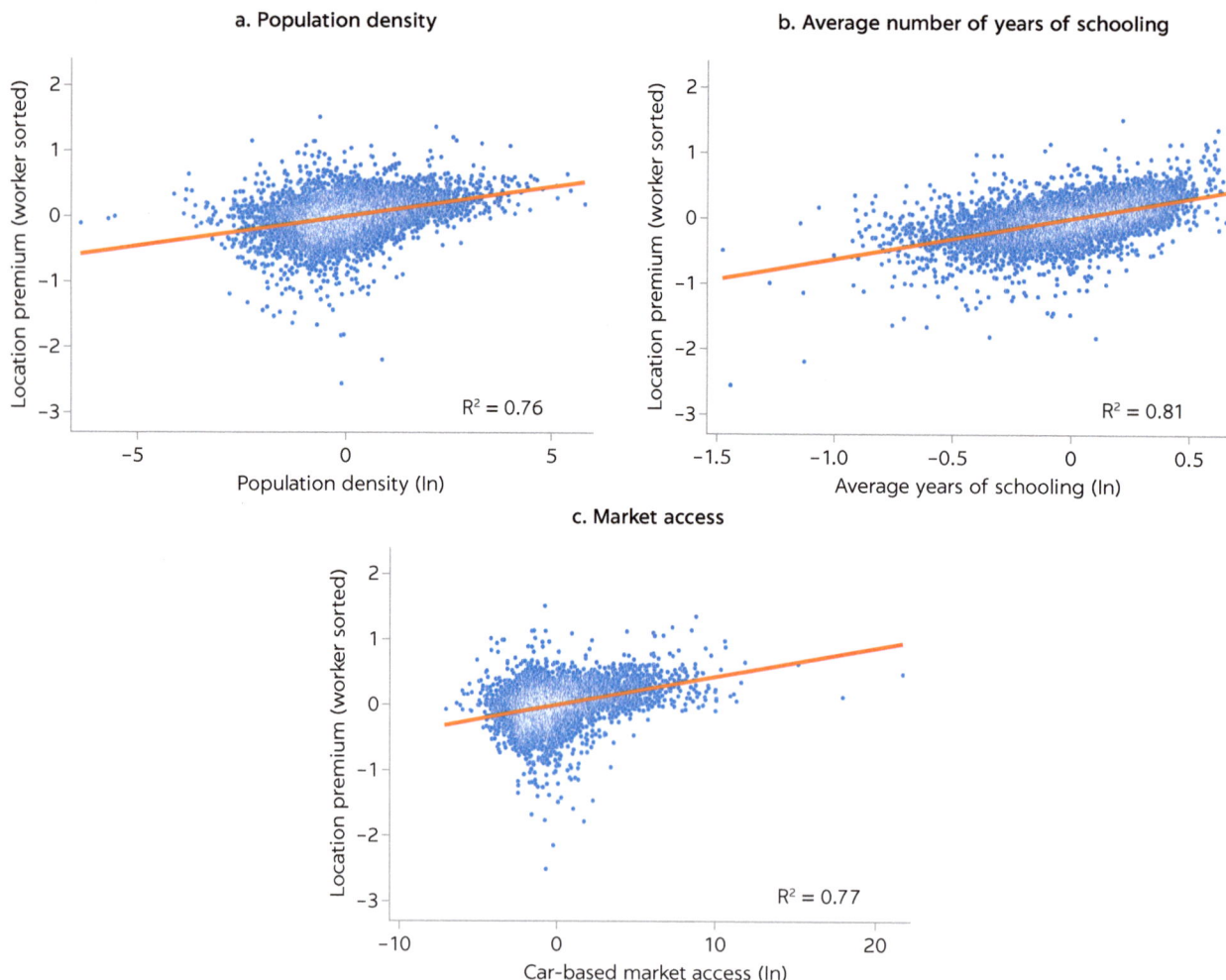

a. Population density

b. Average number of years of schooling

c. Market access

Source: World Bank, based on Quintero and Roberts 2018.
Note: Scatterplots show the correlation between the underlying productivity—estimated location premiums (expressed in natural logs) from Quintero and Roberts (2018)—and the natural logs of population density, average number of years of schooling, and market access controlling for country fixed effects. Subnational administrative areas are the units of observation, and the correlations are estimated on the basis of within-country variation in the data. Market access is measured as $MA_i = \sum_{i \neq j} (P_j / t_{ij}^2)$, where MA_i is the market access of subnational area i, P_j is the population of subnational area j, and t_{ij} is the estimated travel time (by road) between subnational areas i and j.

with a 0.2 percent increase in urban productivity; an equivalent increase in the average years of schooling or market access is associated with a 4.4 percent or 0.2 percent increase in urban productivity, respectively (Quintero and Roberts 2018). While there is evidence of positive agglomeration economies, Brazilian cities could be even more productive if they tackled the negative externalities of density, such as congestion, slums, crime, and inequalities, and invested in institutions and infrastructure to mitigate the costs of congestion (Duranton 2020; Ferreyra and Roberts 2018).

Productivity is highly dispersed across urban areas in Brazil, suggesting inefficient allocations of human capital across the urban system. Subnational differences are lower than in other South American countries, but they exist even after controlling for worker characteristics and thus population sorting. Differentials in nominal wages across metropolitan areas of Brazil declined during the last 15 years, pointing to an improvement in the spatial allocation of workers across metropolitan areas, but Brazilian cities still lag behind their comparators.[3] A shortage of affordable housing in the most productive metropolitan areas is a likely explanation. Inadequate market access is another. In a well-integrated system of cities, the flow of goods, people, and resources across cities closes the productivity gap among cities and maximizes the contribution of the system of cities. And more than in other Latin America and Caribbean countries, high-skill individuals in Brazil sort in large cities, which have high inequalities in skills, leading to large disparities in income.

Pathways to productivity for Amazonian cities

Improving productivity in urban Amazônia requires moving toward the productivity frontier and pushing out its boundaries. As outlined earlier, the productivity frontier of cities is shaped, among others, by their location in relation to national and global markets, their human capital, and their population density. The way to higher productivity thus differs from city to city and needs to take into account a city's relative role in a country's urban hierarchy, its locational assets, and its human capital stock. A small city with a well-grounded and consolidated university campus or near a vibrant large metropolis has much clearer ways to grow its economy than a city in a sparse region with poor locational assets and a small educated workforce.

Cities in Amazônia tend to be smaller than their Brazilian peers. They tend to be toward the lower side of the rank distribution, with only Belém, Manaus, São Luis, and Teresina in the upper ranks (figure 6.3). The average city has 40,738 inhabitants in Amazônia compared with 55,816 in the rest of Brazil. When restricting city size to those with more than 50,000 inhabitants, middle and large cities tend to be smaller in Amazônia than in the rest of Brazil (217,000 in Amazônia and 340,000 in the rest of Brazil). And when restricting it to those with more than 100,000 inhabitants, the average city is 463,000 in Amazônia and 630,000 in the rest of Brazil. So, most of the small cities are likely too small to lift Amazônia's economic performance significantly.

However, Amazonian cities—particularly the larger ones—are denser than their Brazilian peers, suggesting untapped potential. The average Amazonian city has a similar population density of 2,120 inhabitants per square kilometer compared with 2,103 inhabitants per square kilometer in the rest of Brazil. Yet the larger cities in Amazônia (more than 50,000 inhabitants) tend to be much denser than those in the rest of Brazil (figure 6.4). Population densities in Belém

FIGURE 6.3

Most Amazonian cities tend to be small by Brazilian standards

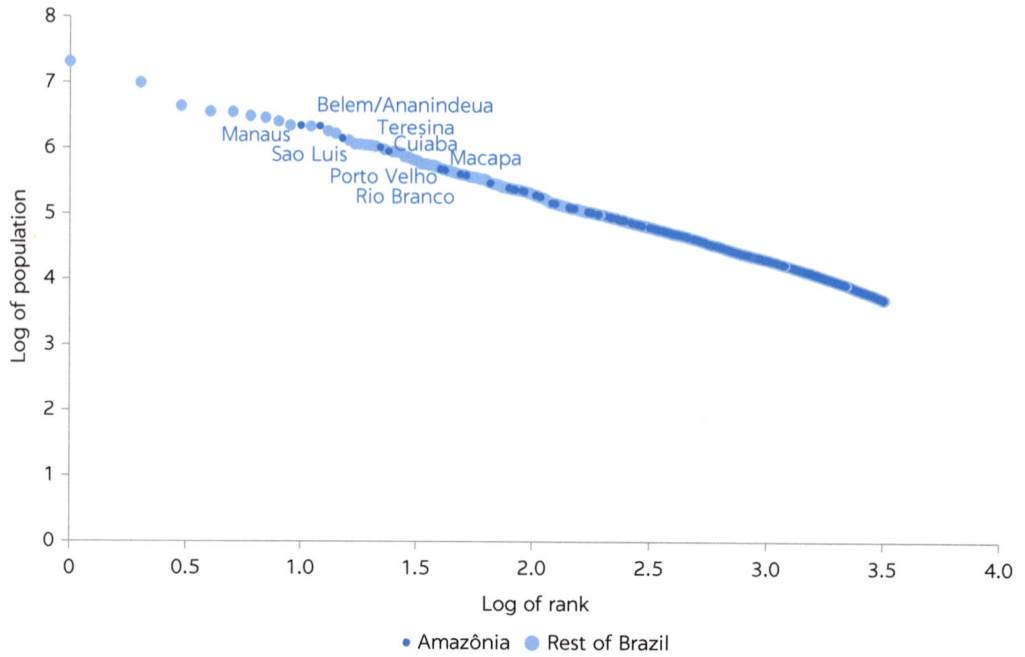

Sources: World Bank, using data from WorldPop 2020 for cities above 5,000 and Dijkstra et al. (2021) for city boundaries.

FIGURE 6.4

Larger cities are denser in Amazônia than in the rest of Brazil

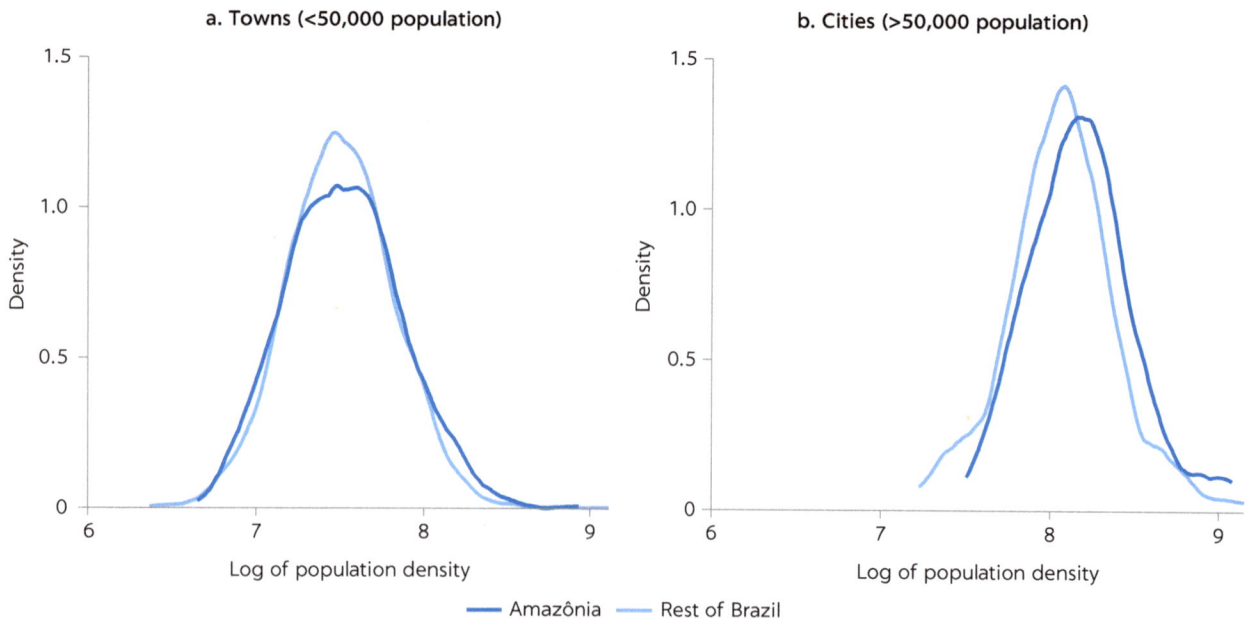

Sources: World Bank, using data from WorldPop 2020 for urban areas above 5,000 and Dijkstra et al. (2021) for city boundaries.

and Manaus are comparable to those in Rio de Janeiro or São Paulo (around 8,000 people per square kilometer) and among the densest cities in the country. Amazonian cities—like most cities in Brazil—also have features of urban form (internal connectivity and smoother and rounder perimeters) linked to higher productivity.[4]

Amazonian cities—particularly those in the Amazon biome—have very limited access to national markets. While most residents of Amazônia have access to a town of 5,000 or more, regional markets are much farther away (map 6.2 and figure 6.5). While 65 percent of localities are within one hour of a town (78 percent are within two hours), they are much farther from regional markets, with only 26 percent within one hour (50 percent within two hours). In the rest of Brazil, 97 percent of localities have access to a town within one hour, and 67 percent are within one hour of a larger market. Distance to national markets is also much farther for cities and localities within the biome, whose main connectivity is through the Amazon River and linked waterways. For example, it takes, on average, 26 hours to reach a city of 50,000 in the state of Amazonas, and only 7 percent of localities are within two hours of a regional market.

The remoteness of Amazonian cities is likely the greatest barrier to delivering higher levels of economic performance in cities. This remoteness is difficult to improve without contributing to deforestation. And while large physical distance has led to disconnected markets, which has implications for trade, improving market access is unlikely to connect very far-off places, as the elasticity of trade with respect to distance is high. To improve connectivity and productivity, interventions could focus on improving and maintaining the transport network, especially water transport, to make it more efficient, along with easing the regulatory environment, to make it more productive (see the companion work to this report for the case of Manaus [World Bank 2023]).

MAP 6.2

Travel times to the most accessible town and most accessible city in Amazônia

a. Most accessible town | b. Most accessible city

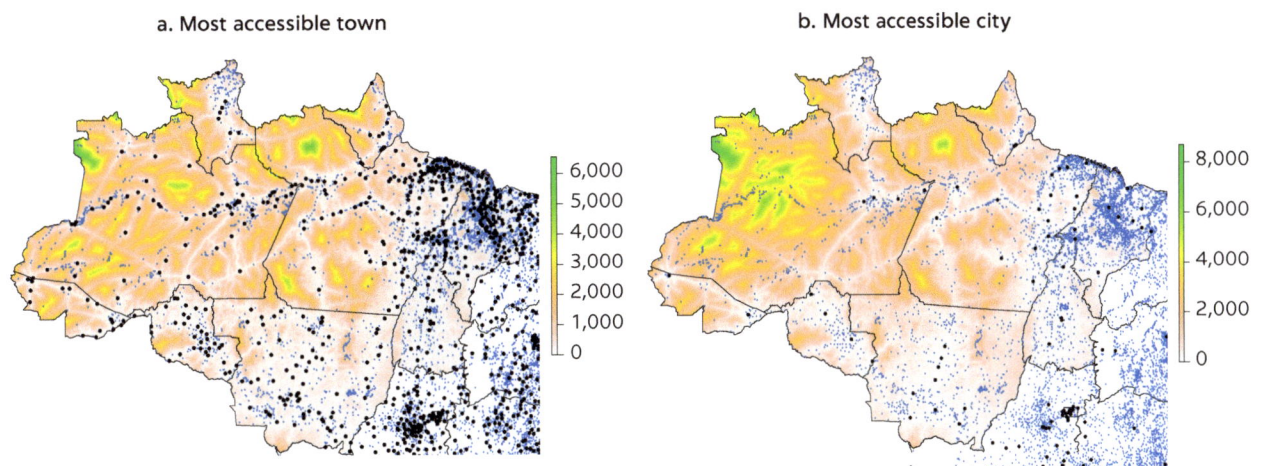

Sources: World Bank, using data from WorldPop 2020 for urban areas above 5,000, Dijkstra et al. (2021) for city boundaries, the Brazilian Institute of Geography and Statistics localities (IBGE 2021), and Weiss et al. (2018) for travel times.
Note: Towns (<50,000 inhabitants) and cities (>50,000 inhabitants) are in black, localities are in blue, overlayed on travel times to towns (panel a) or cities (panel b) in minutes.

FIGURE 6.5

Travel times are much longer in Amazônia

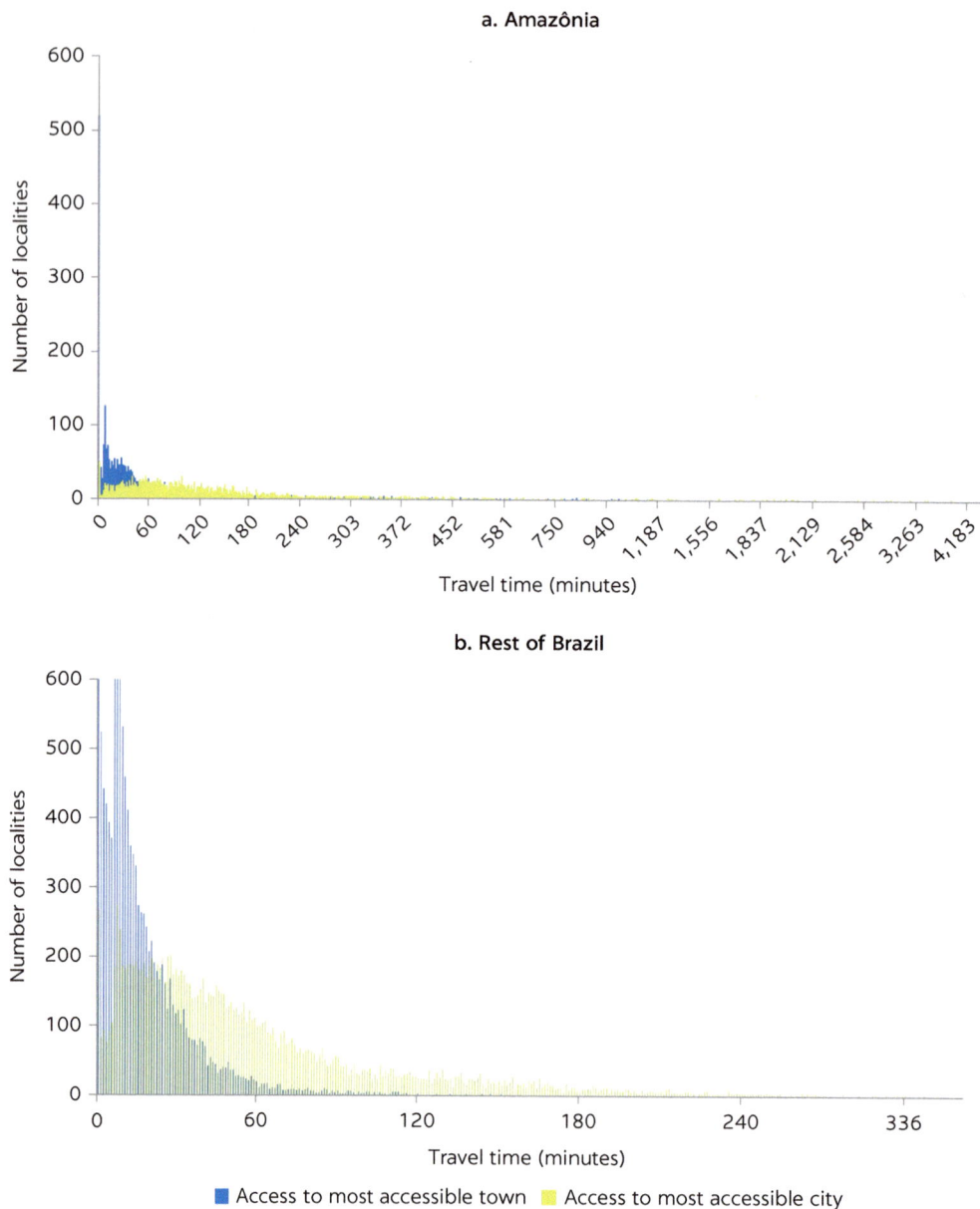

a. Amazônia

b. Rest of Brazil

■ Access to most accessible town   ■ Access to most accessible city

Sources: World Bank, using data from Weiss et al. (2018), Brazilian Institute of Geography and Statistics localities (IBGE 2021), WorldPop (2020), and Dijkstra et al. (2021).
Note: Based on the most accessible town or city from localities. The y-axis was cropped in panel b to highlight differences (there were 2,388 localities with 0-minute travel times to towns).

In addition, workforces in Amazonian cities are not as educated as those in other Brazilian cities. In terms of human capital accumulation, urban areas in Amazônia have the benefit of a younger workforce, which is growing at higher rates than in urban areas in the rest of Brazil but is less educated.[5] The average years of schooling in Amazonian urban areas is 9 years compared with 10 years in urban areas in the rest of Brazil (in 2019), with variations across states (figure 6.6). Enrollments in higher education in Amazonian municipalities are nearly half those in the rest of Brazil (chapter 2). And the probability of

FIGURE 6.6

Average years of schooling are lower in Amazônia, especially in rural areas, 2012–19

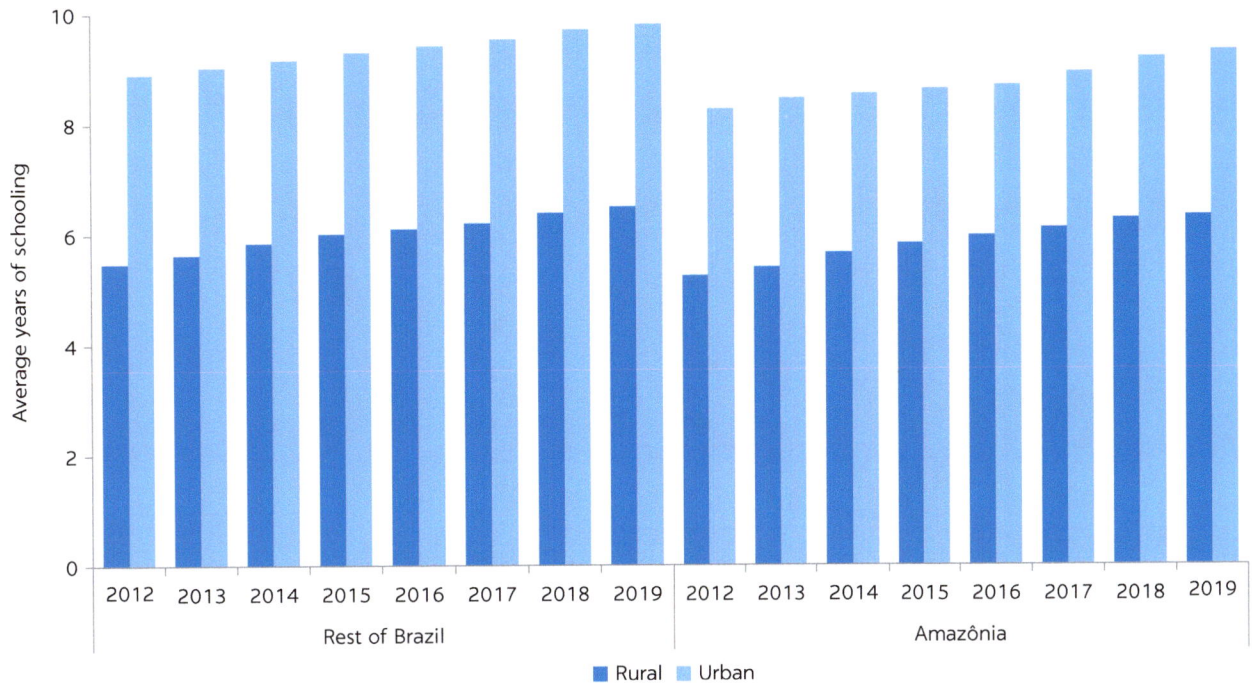

Source: World Bank, using National Household Sample Survey (PNADC) 2012 to 2019 data.

moving out of the region is higher among highly educated people, although the probability of moving out declined in the past decades. Migration out of one's state of birth in Brazil and in Amazônia differs by education, with the most educated having the highest probability of moving out. But trends in out-of-state migration have evolved over time, and, while more educated people used to be more mobile in Amazônia than in the rest of the country, this trend reversed in the 2010s (figure 6.7).

Amazonian cities have much lower access to quality basic services (including digital connectivity). As discussed earlier, the lack of basic services increases the costs of congestion and prevents agglomeration economies from flourishing. Amazonian cities have much lower access to water supply, electricity, wastewater collection and treatment, and solid waste collection and disposal; sewer access is only 33 percent in urban Amazônia, compared with 81 percent elsewhere (figure 6.8) (Arretche 2019). For digital connectivity, a similar proportion of people have cellphones in Amazônia as in the rest of the country, but access to the internet is slightly lower in urban Amazônia. Gaps in the quality of service provision are also persisting and, in some cases, widening, as for electricity, with persistent blackouts and dirty and unreliable energy-generation sources (figure 6.9) (Vagliasindi 2022). The situation is also dire for access to quality broadband services and key assets to assure digital connectivity, such as computers and smartphones (figure 6.10) (Arretche 2019). The low access and poor quality of basic services affect households and firms in different ways—given the need to secure alternative sources and the costly means to assure reliable service provision—making production more expensive and reducing Amazonian cities' attractiveness for private sector development and economic performance.

FIGURE 6.7

People born in the rest of Brazil are more likely to have migrated from their birth state, while educated people in Amazônia were more mobile

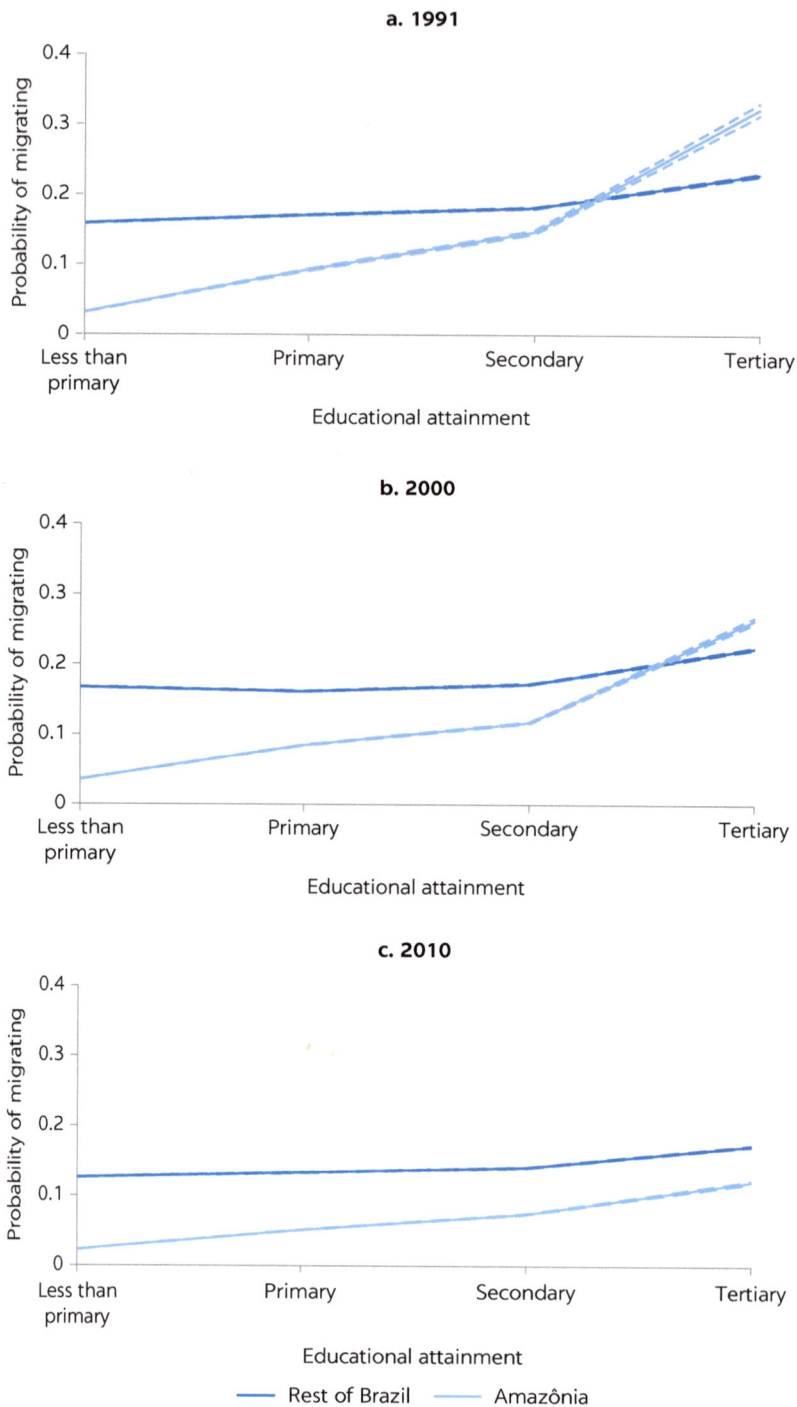

a. 1991

b. 2000

c. 2010

Rest of Brazil ———— Amazônia

Source: World Bank, using Brazil 1990, 2000, and 2010 census data from University of Minnesota's Integrated Public Use Microdata Series (IPUMS) International database.
Note: Estimations are based on a Probit model with the dependent variable being whether one was born in Amazônia and left the region by the year of the census. Controls include gender, age, marital status, educational attainment, area of current residence, employment status at destination (in the absence of information at origin), the average income gap between origin and destination, and the population density at origin (assuming the distribution at the state level has remained the same). Ninety percent confidence intervals are reported.

FIGURE 6.8

Amazonian cities have much lower access to basic services

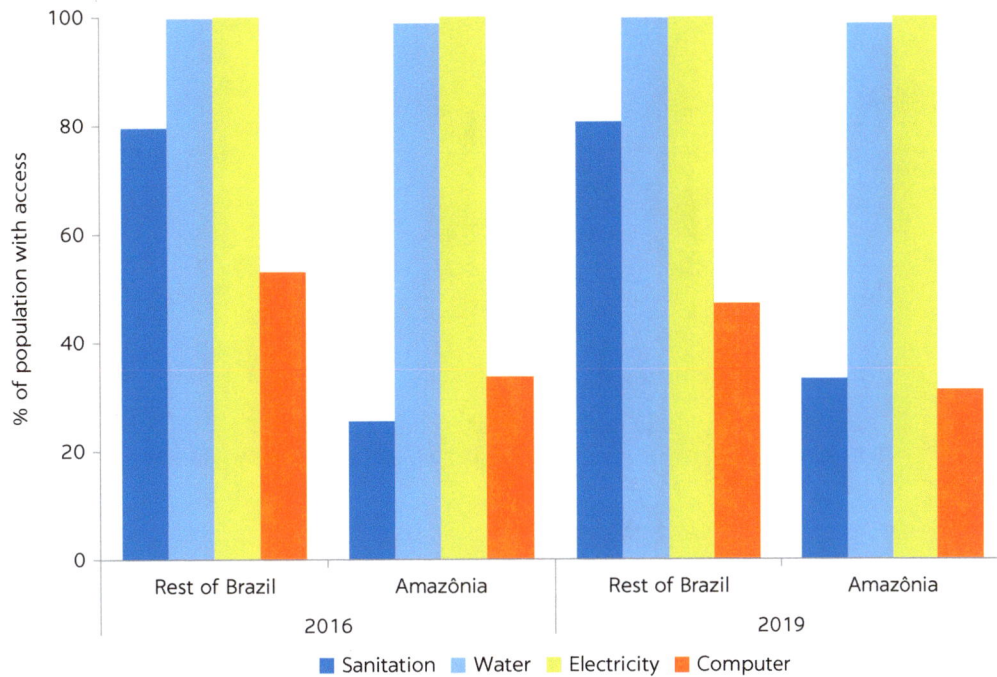

Source: World Bank, using National Household Sample Survey (PNADC) 2016 and 2019 data.

FIGURE 6.9

The reliability of electricity is low in Amazonian states, 2019

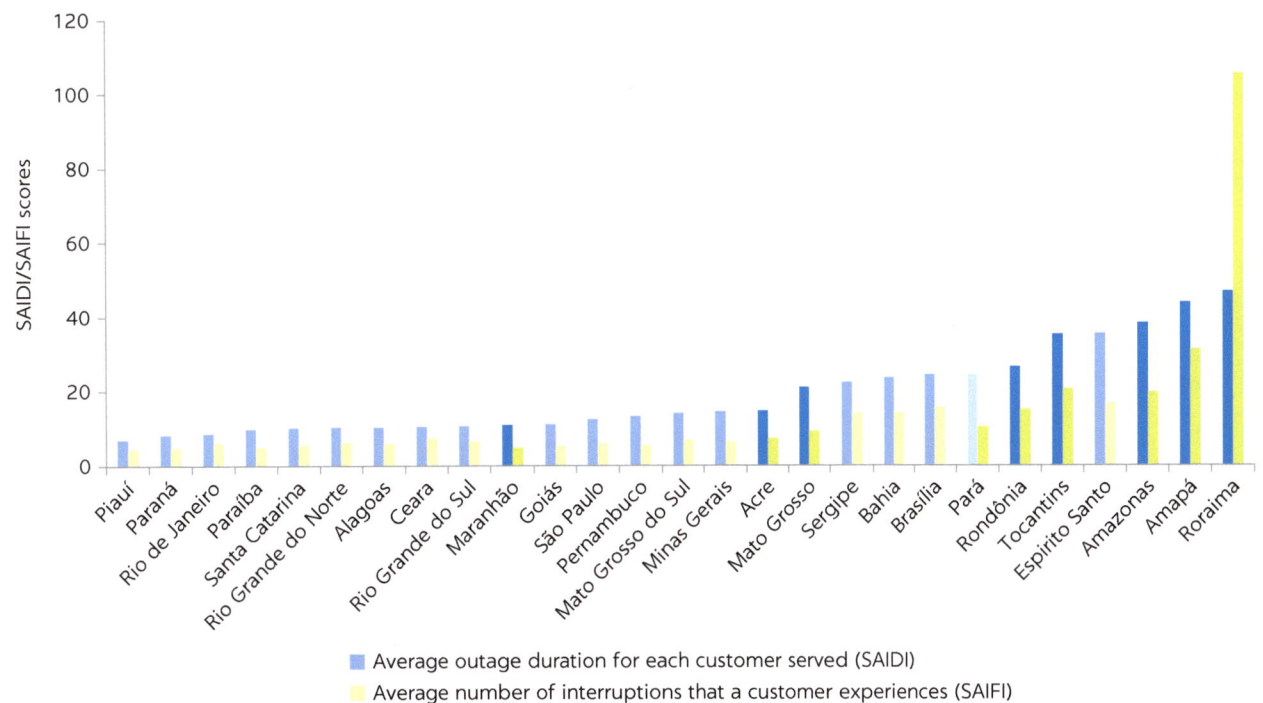

Source: Vagliasindi 2022.
Note: SAIDI = System Average Disruption Index. SAIFI = System Average Interruption Frequency Index. The darker shaded colors indicate Amazonian states.

FIGURE 6.10
Internet speed and reliability also tend to be low in Amazônia, 2019

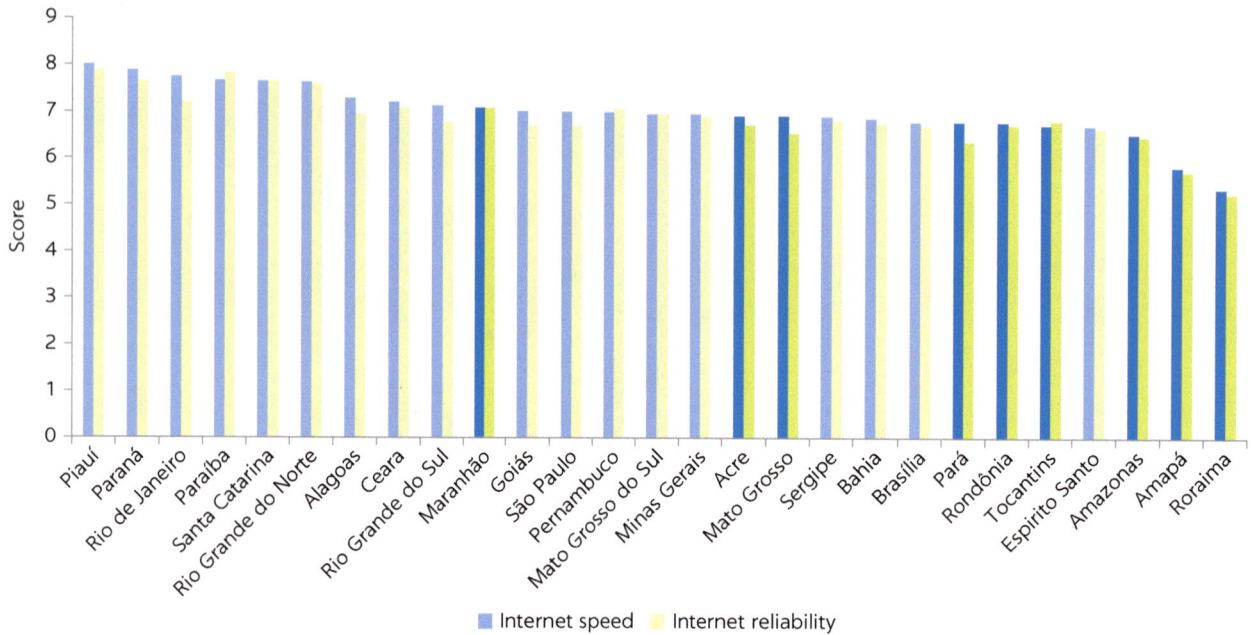

Source: World Bank, based on MelhorPlano and Anatel data.
Note: The darker shaded colors indicate Amazonian states.

A SPATIALLY SENSITIVE APPROACH TO POLICIES FOR AMAZÔNIA'S CITIES

Most—but not all—Amazonian towns and cities lack the spatial endowments and factor inputs required to become economic growth poles. Most cities are likely too small and too far from national and global markets to become economic powerhouses of their regions and Brazil. They also do not have the required factor inputs—human capital and basic services—and business environment to attract private sector development and foster agglomeration economies. In fact, the poor spatial endowments of the region (which are peripheral and sparse, for the most part) are typical of a lagging region. For these reasons, it is essential to have a realistic view of what is feasible and to design place-based policies that reflect territorial challenges and exploit potential productivity and convergence gains (box 6.1). The following discussion looks more deeply into Amazônia's urban system to provide an initial framework for its place-based policies.

The relatively low transport connectivity and long distance between populated places in Amazônia have led to a series of fragmented urban systems organized around economic nodes supported by smaller service nodes. Economic nodes are places where population and economic activities are lumped and will be key to foster urban productivity growth in Amazônia. Given the vast distance between populated settlements, these economic nodes are complemented by service nodes, which tend to be smaller but have a key role to play in service provision and endowment building (human capital) of their population and closely located populated places. Both economic nodes and service nodes are essential for Amazônia's development. This chapter proposes an analytical

BOX 6.1

Avoiding the pitfalls of place-based policies

As outlined in the *World Development Report*: *Reshaping Economic Geography*, lagging regions tend to have poor spatial endowments, to be sparsely populated (with low levels of population density or cities surrounded by sparsely populated territories), and to be far from markets (World Bank 2009). They also tend to have weak local business environments and infrastructure, lower-capacity institutions, and a lower accumulation of human capital. Responding to these challenges, authorities tend to concentrate on implementing spatially targeted policies and investments with the aim of achieving economic convergence. But spatially targeted policies are strategic or sectoral bets and are not guaranteed to be successful. In fact, many interventions—such as the implementation of special economic zones—have proven to be costly failures with a limited number of successes. Experience has shown that more spatially sensitive approaches are warranted and that the design of place-based policies should be informed by their net benefits to national growth, welfare, and social cohesion as well as their practical feasibility given fiscal and political constraints.[a]

Achieving equity across space must not be confused with implementing uniform place-based interventions, which can be costly and lead to little improvement in living standards. The investments and policies to improve living conditions in a sparse, isolated, lagging area are not the same as those needed to address poverty in a slum in a mega-city or in a poor but highly dense region. With the right policy mix for each place, a country can achieve high growth nationally, high living standards in each place, and unity across the territory.

Avoiding the pitfalls of place-based policy requires careful design. There are five main aspects to consider:

- *Address complements together.* Lagging regions often suffer multiple disadvantages; interventions that address only one problem have muted impacts because essential complements are missing. Often, providing all required complements is not feasible. Big pushes are high risk and high cost. Agglomeration economies cannot be implanted. Foundations like a good business environment, fluid factor markets, and human capital are usually needed for place-based policies to succeed.
- *Diagnose and address bottlenecks directly.* Policies often compensate firms for weak outcomes or target high visibility, despite low impacts, instead of addressing underlying bottlenecks.
- *Identify the market failures behind weak outcomes.* Policies need to focus on overcoming market failures and avoid sticking-plaster incentives.
- *Look outward.* Interventions often treat lagging places in isolation, instead of connecting places and their people to external opportunities.
- *Focus on people.* While lagging places stagnate, their people often seek opportunities elsewhere. Ensure decent living standards by providing public services and progressive transfers and develop human capital to broaden access to opportunities and remove mobility frictions.

a. For international experience, see Grover, Lall, and Maloney (2021) and Rodríguez-Pose and Wilkie (2019), among others. For a discussion of Europe, see Farole, Goga, and Ionescu-Heroiu (2018). For special economic zones in particular, see the review of Farole and Akinci (2011). For more details and international experience, see the comprehensive review in Grover, Lall, and Maloney (2021).

framework that could serve as a building block to identify regional economic and service nodes (see annex 6A for details).

Urban productivity gains in Amazônia will likely be limited to a few economic nodes with sufficient endowments for place-based policies to be effective and support competitive industries. As outlined earlier, urban Amazônia has a group of disconnected urban systems, which tend to be located far from markets. The majority of cities and towns are not sufficiently large or strategically located to become prosperous places for private firms to settle or grow. So, urban productivity gains will likely be limited to a few economic nodes.

Economic nodes

Identifying which economic nodes have sufficient locational assets can ensure that place-based policies are well tailored, realistic, and effective. Economic nodes are defined on the basis of their attractiveness—their distance to other populated places and their own population. They need to attract a minimum of five other cities to qualify as economic nodes.[6] That definition does not mean that cities not part of economic nodes are unimportant or inaccessible, but it can start the thinking about how to prioritize place-based policies for boosting productivity around nodes that have sufficient population mass, markets, and economic activities on which to build. Economic nodes have 566,835 inhabitants on average (in 2020). Using this methodology, there is an initial set of 20 potential economic nodes in Amazônia (map 6.3).[7]

The proposed economic nodes appear to have a higher share of university graduates, which is also one of the key factors for urban productivity growth in Amazônia and Brazil more broadly (map 6.4). Criteria other than relative population size and travel time could also be considered (such as existing amenities, service provision, and access to global markets), but that effort would require a deeper engagement. Most of the nodes are state capitals.

MAP 6.3

There are 20 potential economic nodes in Amazônia

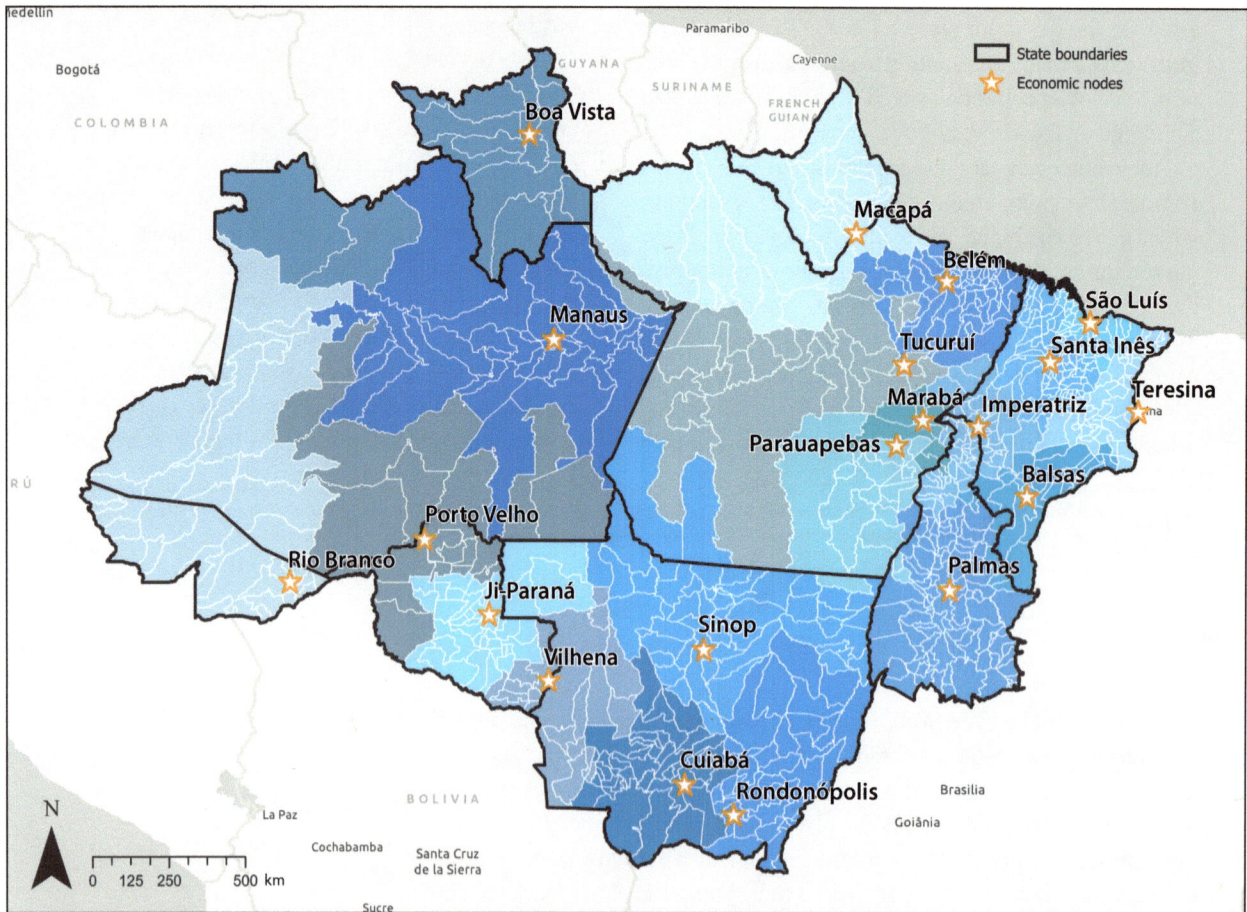

Sources: World Bank, using data from Weiss et al. (2018) for accessibility and WorldPop 2020 for population of cities, based on the global definition described in Dijkstra et al. (2021).
Note: Colors demarcate areas served by the 20 nodes.

MAP 6.4

More university graduates are in economic nodes

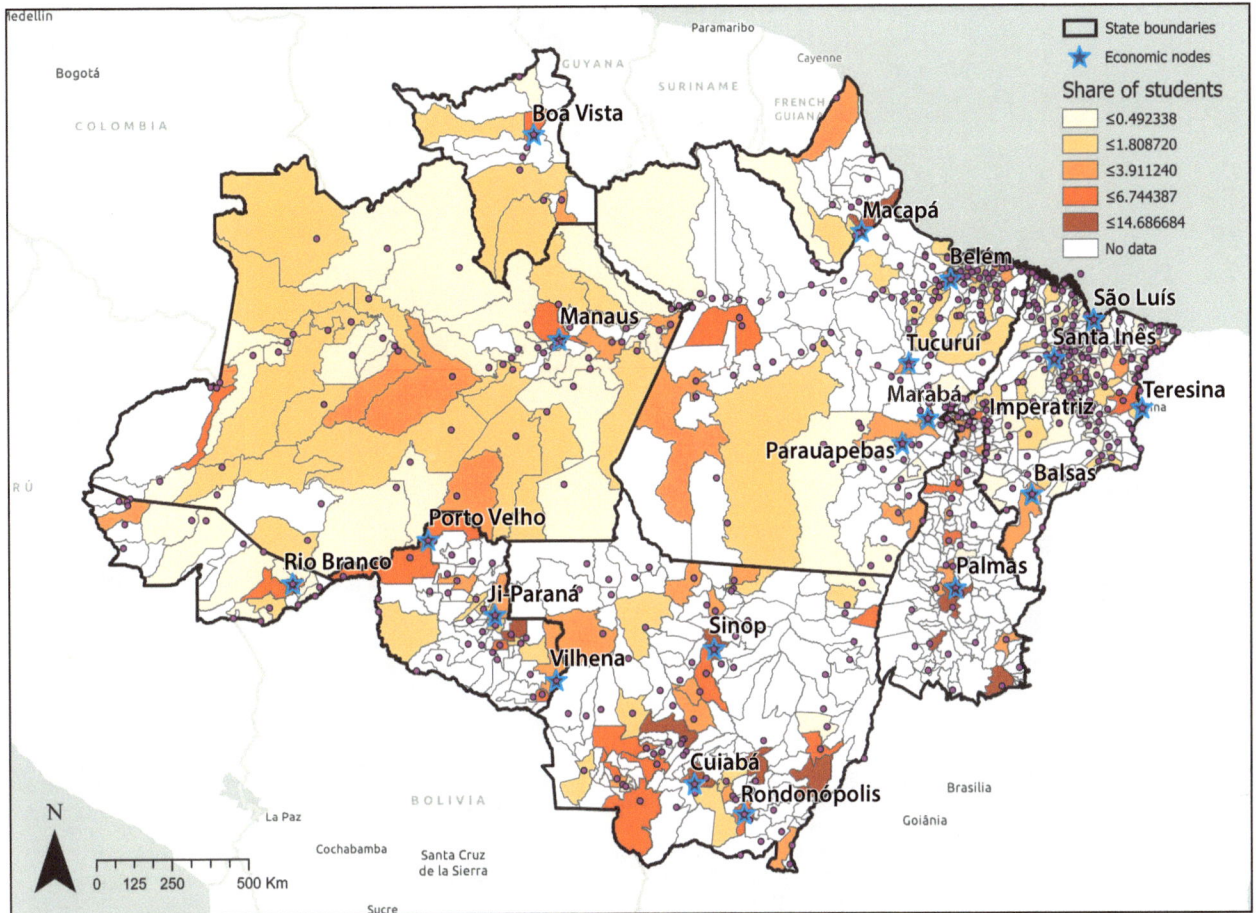

Source: World Bank, based on the National Institute of Educational Studies and Research (INEP) Tertiary Education Census 2014.
Note: Economic nodes are defined on the basis of their attractiveness—their distance to other populated places and their own population. They need to attract a minimum of five other cities to qualify as economic nodes. (Also see annex 6A.)

Some of the identified economic nodes appear better placed to climb the urban productivity ladder. The majority of cities in Amazônia (in green and red in figure 6.11) are in municipalities that have poor spatial endowments: they are far from markets and have relatively low population densities (lower-left quadrant of figure 6.11). Of the 20 economic nodes identified, three are in the lower-left quadrant. Belém, Imperatriz, Palmas, São Luis, and Teresina appear to have the best spatial endowments—they are located in municipalities much closer to markets and have higher population densities. Boa Vista, Manaus, Macapá, and Rio Branco (all on the Colonial Frontier) are relatively dense but located in peripheral municipalities, so the policies implemented there should be different (see box 6.2 and the companion report for Manaus (World Bank 2023).

A coordinated set of actions is needed for several economic nodes to become regional growth poles. This methodology involves devising place-based policies across diverse sectors—as outlined in the companion report on energy, water supply, solid waste, and urban infrastructure in Manaus (World Bank 2023)—and people-focused policies to develop human capital and connect people to opportunities. Ensuring decent living standards and quality of life is also key to retaining and attracting high-skill migration. Beyond those aspects, improving

FIGURE 6.11

Some economic nodes are in municipalities with better spatial endowments—dense and central or dense and peripheral

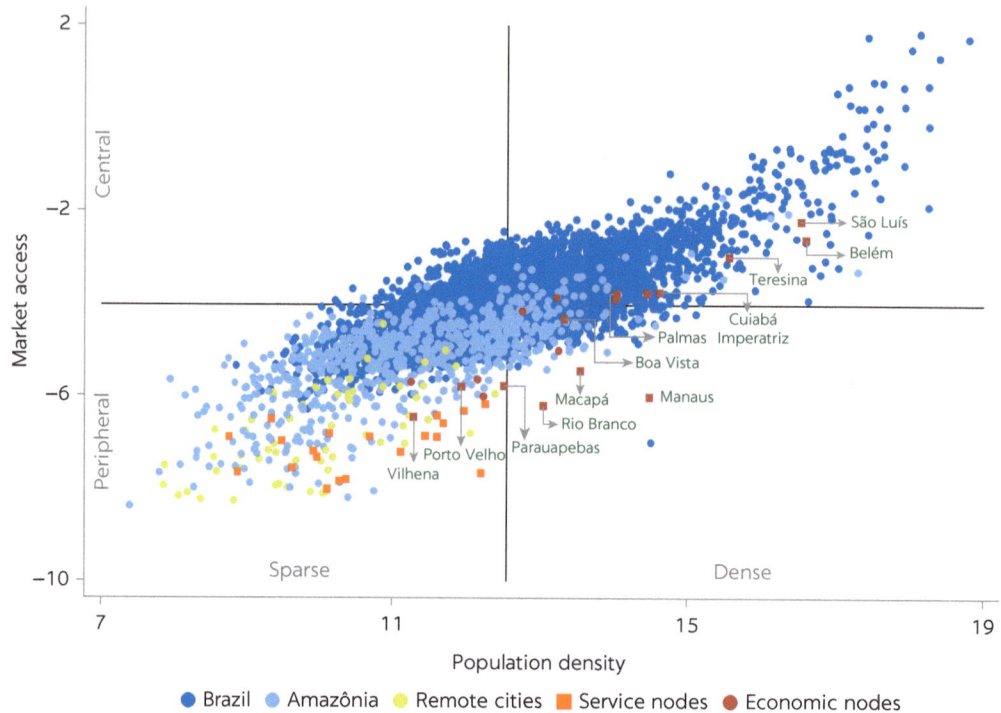

Sources: World Bank, using data from Weiss et al. (2018) and the Brazilian Institute of Geography and Statistics (IBGE) municipal shape files for population and area in 2010 (IBGE 2021).

Note: Each point is a municipality. Remote cities are those more than six hours' driving distance from service nodes. A service node is a populated place sufficiently large to be considered a node and sufficiently close, less than six hours' driving time, to at least three other populated places in Amazônia to serve as a service provision center. Economic nodes are defined on the basis of their attractiveness—their distance to other populated places and their own population. They need to attract a minimum of five other cities to qualify as economic nodes. (Also see annex 6A.)

institutional capacity at the various levels (regional, state, municipal) is essential to ensure that the public sector can lead and coordinate actions at different scales. Finally, improving the business environment and trade and logistics can foster productivity gains in Amazônia's urban private sector (World Bank 2023). However, strategic bets need to be designed properly—with clear objectives, an analysis comparing the benefits of alternative policies, and well-defined exit strategies (box 6.2). There is also a need to conduct a more detailed regional and economic development assessment, strategic exercises, and consultations to establish which economic nodes have the right basic endowments for the highest impact in policies aimed at boosting competitiveness in services and manufacturing and which need complementary interventions.

Service nodes

In potential service nodes and remote cities, additional policies may be warranted to assure the delivery of basic services and build mobile endowments. Interventions should concentrate on improving service delivery in service nodes to reduce spatial disparities. Doing so makes sense both from an equity perspective (so that place does not determine fortune in Brazil) and from a national growth perspective (so that even if people migrate, they have the minimum set

BOX 6.2

Calibrating policies to the difficulties that different areas face

Policies for Amazônia can be calibrated to the difficulties that specific areas face. An important step is to identify key bottlenecks giving rise to weak outcomes. Farole, Goga, and Ionescu-Heroiu (2018) and World Bank (2009) translate these principles into a basic framework for tailoring policy (figure B6.2.1).

Sparsely populated, peripheral places

Institutional reforms and improvements in access to and quality of basic services will have the biggest impact on equity; they can unlock untapped potential, raise living standards, and connect people to opportunities. If these regions have advanced, quality

FIGURE B6.2.1

A framework for approaching policy in lagging regions

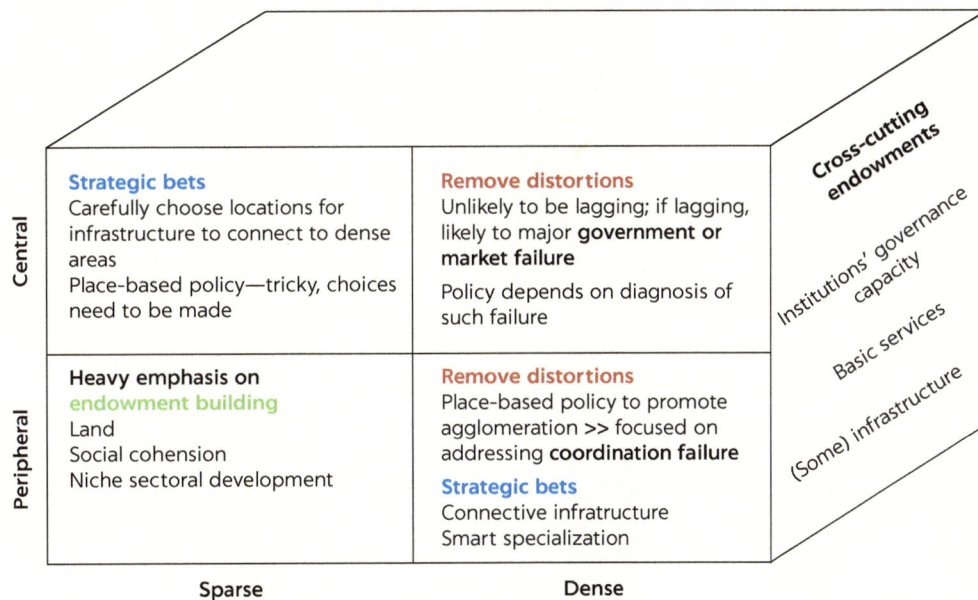

Sources: Farole, Goga, and Ionescu 2018 and World Bank 2009.

Building cross-cutting endowments everywhere

Enhancing institutional capacity to facilitate local governments in delivering their mandates forms the bedrock of public policies to integrate countries spatially, together with facilitating labor mobility across the territory. These policies also include clarifying regulations on property rights and access to land, trade, taxes, and transfer mechanisms—all facilitating product mobility. Assuring minimum levels of basic service provision and some infrastructure also allows leveling the playing field. These policies are essential everywhere, from sparsely populated places like in the far west of the biome to the biggest cities of Amazônia and Brazil.

institutions and human capital has already reached high levels, niche opportunities for regional economic development should emerge through existing institutions.

Densely populated, peripheral places

Connectivity can help poorer places to share in the successes of leading places: it raises the scale of markets that can be accessed from the poorer places and facilitates trade so that places can specialize in what they do best. Better connectivity (transport, energy, logistics) between markets will increase the productivity of activities like agriculture, agroprocessing, or labor-intensive manufacturing to take place and contribute to economic development.[a]

continued

Box 6.2, *continued*

But connective investment needs to be tailored to the place: heavy infrastructure investments need a certain level of economic and population density to have the expected impacts and adequate returns: they should be prioritized around secondary cities and corridors, where opportunities could be broadened and reach more people.

Some lagging regions can be stuck in a situation where they cannot attract investment because there is too little investment; the expected returns to investors depend fundamentally on what investments others will make (coordination failures). Without a dense enough network of firms, underinvestment by all parties results in a low-level trap that is common for lagging regions—more so for regions with lower agglomeration potential. Policy interventions, not market solutions, are needed to address such coordination failures.

Sparsely populated but centrally located regions

These regions are often located near larger agglomerations, so the priority is to improve connectivity to the agglomeration. Targeted sectoral investments may also be relevant in this type of region. Thinking

about developing scale economies around a few nodes and considering the forest, the choice of infrastructure will have to be made carefully (where to place it?) to fill in missing complements around specific nodes rather than spread everything around (and do things piecemeal). The challenge here is that if agglomeration potential is limited, specialization is likely to be particularly important, which raises the typical risk of regional industrial policies that aim to pick winners.

Densely populated, centrally located regions

These regions are the best positioned candidates for place-based policies to address remaining underlying bottlenecks. Costlier, spatially distortive targeted interventions often struggle in less economically dense places due to lack of demand and the necessary complements for their success. However, in places with advanced urbanization (like large cities), more of these complements are present, and markets have revealed the advantages of the location. Here, place-based policies can be powerful to relieve congestion and overcome remaining bottlenecks to fast and inclusive growth.

a. These activities do not exhibit agglomeration economies and therefore are more likely to benefit rather than lose from improved connectivity. Other activities will encourage firms to concentrate in leading areas as improved connectivity allows them to serve markets that are farther away.

of skills to prosper elsewhere). The consolidation and support of service provision in service nodes also makes sense from an efficiency perspective, as some density is necessary for service provision to be delivered at scale, lowering the costs. Different densities will call for different infrastructure and technology of delivery. In sparsely populated areas, considering alternative technologies for service provision (such as solar panels and mobile clinics) that are not dependent on scale economies for achieving efficiency is critical.

But how are service nodes identified? As for economic nodes, service nodes are based on population and distance to other populated places (see annex 6A). A service node is a populated place sufficiently large to be considered a node and sufficiently close, less than six hours, to at least three other populated places in Amazônia to serve as a service provision center (map 6.5). This exercise suggests that around 35 service nodes could potentially serve 465 populated places. The average population of service nodes and remote cities is 326,606 and 14,671 inhabitants, respectively (World Pop 2020).

Some remote cities are too far from the service nodes and thus were not matched with any of them. All of these populated places are much farther than

MAP 6.5

Strengthening service nodes is needed to ensure equity in living standards and opportunities

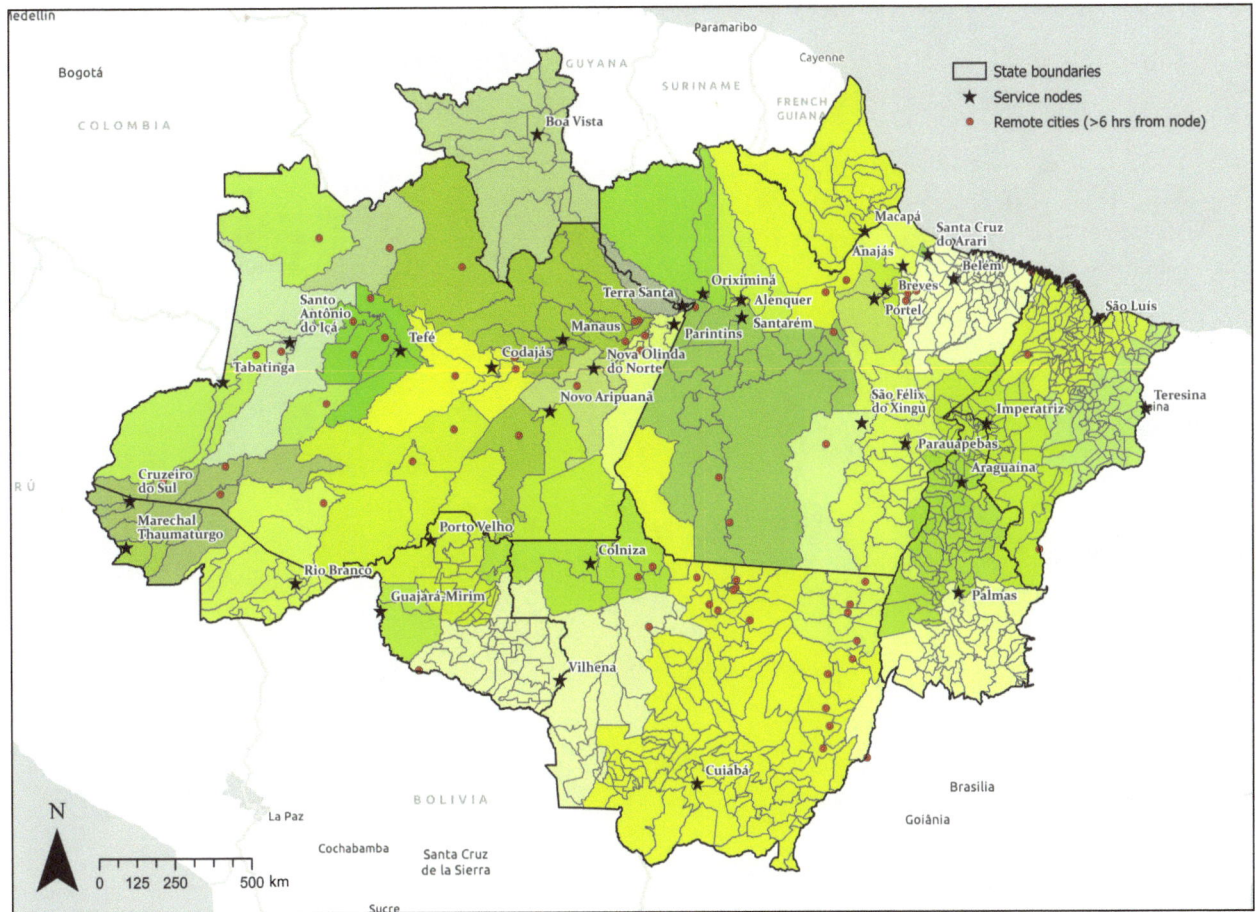

Sources: World Bank, using data from Weiss et al. (2018) for accessibility and WorldPop 2020 for population of cities, based on the global definition in Dijkstra et al. (2021).

Note: A service node is a populated place sufficiently large to be considered a node and sufficiently close, less than six hours' driving time, to at least three other populated places in Amazônia to serve as a service provision center.

the six hours' distance (map 6.6). In addition, given the remoteness of many of these cities and populated settlements and their lack of connectivity with regional markets and the rest of Brazil, the methods and technologies used for service provision will likely need to be tailored to assure both quality and cost-efficient provision. Some examples include simultaneous learning (for children of different ages) and daily-weekly commute for students in remote areas, with student housing close to a few hub schools and e-learning or distance learning programs. Provision of water, sanitation, and electricity should be tailored, depending on local circumstances, to include nonsewerage sanitation and non-conventional sewage options and mini electric grids. The inaccessibility of remote cities is evident on the map. Given the inaccessibility of remote cities, it is highly probable that these places will start (or have started) to lose population as their residents migrate to places with better infrastructure and more opportunities. In those cases, government should continue to emphasize building portable endowments so that people can migrate and use them elsewhere and reduce the barriers to migrate to economic nodes in Amazônia and to cities across Brazil. Policies to manage the shrinking of medium-size cities might be warranted at some point.

MAP 6.6

Economic nodes, service nodes, and remote cities in Amazônia

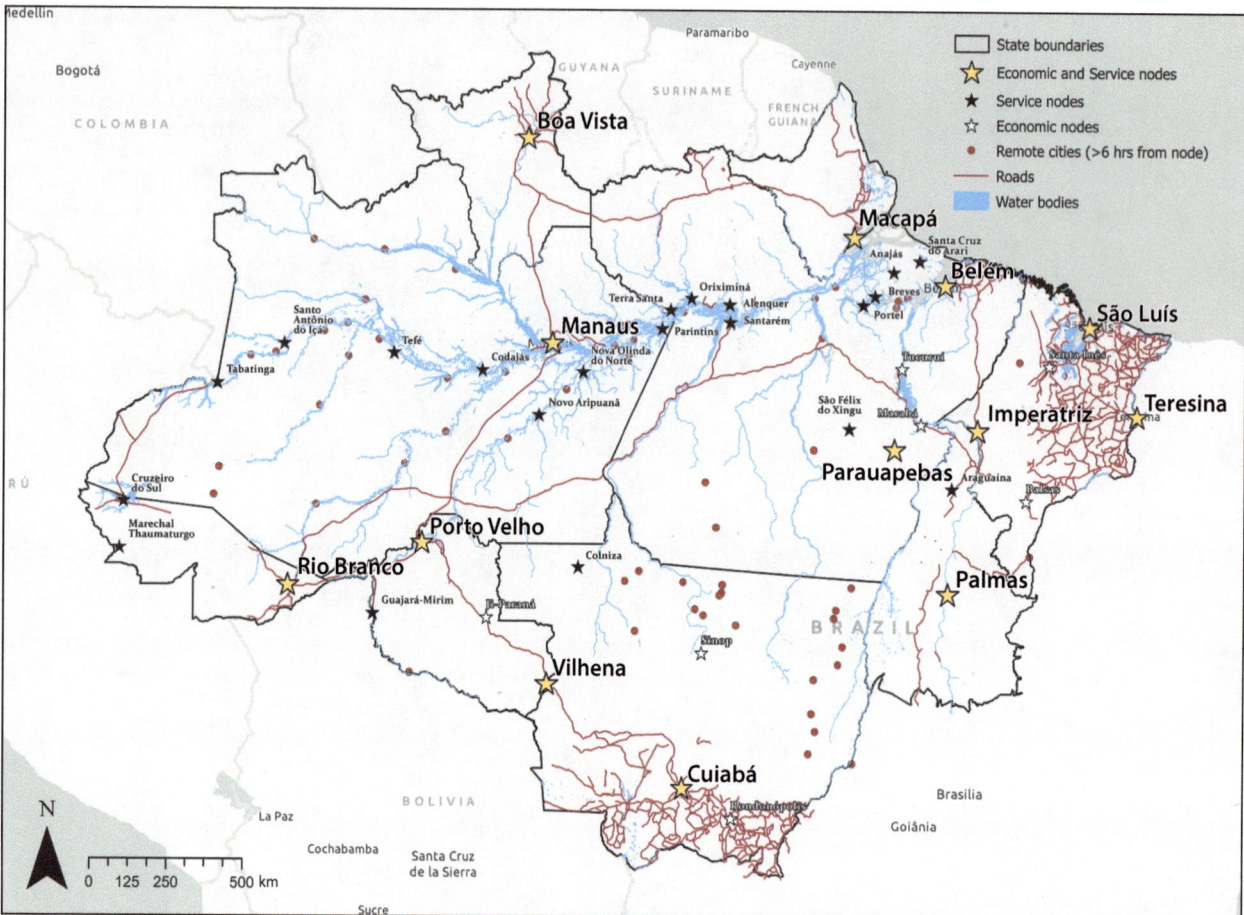

Sources: World Bank, using data from Weiss et al. (2018) for accessibility and WorldPop 2020 for population of cities, based on the global definition in Dijkstra et al. (2021).

Note: A service node is a populated place sufficiently large to be considered a node and sufficiently close, less than six hours' driving time, to at least three other populated places in Amazônia to serve as a service provision center. Economic nodes are defined on the basis of their attractiveness—their distance to other populated places and their own population. They need to attract a minimum of five other cities to qualify as economic nodes. (Also see annex 6A.)

Urban areas outside Amazônia

Urban areas in the rest of Brazil play a key role in achieving greater economic development in Amazônia and having its living conditions converge with the country's leading region—and ensuring a more promising environmental outlook for the forest (chapters 2–4). Brazil's educated workforce is limited, as is its investment in research and development and the efficiency of its transport system, all of which could prove beneficial to raising the country's competitiveness (Artuc, Bastos, and Lee 2021; Grover, Lall, and Maloney 2021). In fact, reducing barriers to migration and solving urban development challenges across Brazilian cities are also the key to boosting urban productivity everywhere and contributing to a more efficient and well-performing system of cities. Ensuring that housing and land markets work well and that people can move where they can get higher returns to their endowments makes sense for Amazônia and beyond. Today, migrants with low levels of skills and human capital could lead to sterile agglomeration, adding to congestion rather than boosting productivity and structural transformation (Grover, Lall, and

Maloney 2021). Investments are needed in people's education, skills, and health in Amazonia and in city housing and amenities to attract high-skill labor. While this subject is beyond the scope of this chapter, it is important to consider such investments as one piece of the puzzle.

The recently updated National Policy for Regional Development is very much aligned with the proposed direction for the regional development of Amazônia and the consolidation of Brazil's urban system (box 6.3). At the federal level, the PNDR is the main policy to promote regional development in Brazil. One of the four objectives of this policy is to "consolidate a polycentric network of cities, in support of de-concentration and the internalization of regional and country development, considering the specificities of each region." To detail this objective further, two plans have been developed: The National Policy for Urban Development (PNDU) and the Regional Development Plan for the Amazon (PDRA). The PNDU's underlying idea is to indicate strategies to strengthen medium-size cities in order to "consolidate a polycentric network of cities." The PDRA aims to reduce regional inequalities, taking into account the Sustainable Development Goals agenda. The PDRA presents a list of types of projects to be promoted and concludes with a list of 251 priority structuring projects listed by each state in Amazônia as follows: Acre (33 projects), Amapá (25), Amazonas (40), Maranhão (27), Mato Grosso (23), Pará (15), Rondônia (25), Roraima (17), and Tocantins (37). More than half the projects are for infrastructure. The rest are divided among social services, education, technology, equipment, tourism, and agriculture, many with a focus on commodity transport and exports.

BOX 6.3

Toward a national policy for regional development

The principles described in this chapter for developing a spatially sensitive approach in Amazônia are well aligned with the recently updated National Policy for Regional Development (PNDR)—Decree No. 9810/19. The PNDR proposes to

- Promote convergence in development levels, quality of life, and access to opportunities in regions with low socioeconomic indicators, such as Amazônia;
- Consolidate a polycentric network of cities, supporting the deconcentration of regional development and considering each region's characteristics;
- Stimulate productivity gains and regional competitiveness (in areas with declining population and high emigration); while this report argues for stimulating productivity gains and regional competitivity, policies in areas with declining populations and high emigration should likely be targeted for promoting convergence in access to services and building human endowments, particularly when dealing with remote places with poor spatial endowments; and
- Foment the creation of added value and economic diversification for regional development, while taking into consideration income generation and sustainability (particularly in regions highly specialized in agricultural and mineral commodities).

CONCLUSIONS AND POLICY IMPLICATIONS

Urban areas of the Amazon have a key role to play in moving toward a convergence of living standards, building human endowments for the future, and moving Brazil toward a pathway of more sustainable growth. Brazil can enhance this role by shifting to an urban-productivity development model and reducing deforestation pressure. But the urban productivity frontier is limited by the poor spatial endowments of Amazônia's cities. A dual approach for place-based policies in urban Amazônia is warranted. The first, concentrating on a selective number of economic nodes to climb the structural transformation ladder, should bring together a set of complementary policies and a sense of realism to succeed. The second, improving service provision and building the capacity of supporting service nodes, should continue building mobile endowments (education, health) even in remote places. Both should consider contextual aspects (Indigenous peoples and minorities) and be tailored to provide cost-effective solutions, adapting service provision technologies where relevant. National urban policies beyond Amazônia also have a role.

More research and analytical work are needed to identify the functional features of Amazônia's urban system and to confirm—including through consultation and qualitative means—the key economic and service nodes and underlying constraints they face in attracting private firms and boosting competitiveness. A more robust and well-defined regional development plan, with deep dives into certain economic and service nodes, could also be useful to update federal priorities in the region and coordinate local and global actors' actions in the short, medium, and long terms.

In considering key investments in Amazônia, carefully identifying the challenges and opportunities is essential. Achieving productivity gains in regions with poor spatial endowments and high emigration is likely to be costly since it requires going against market forces. It is likely that such spatially public investments will not be enough to drive large private investments to this region, so the benefits may remain local and short-lived. In addition, efforts to spread economic activity evenly risk dampening national economic growth. To ensure wider economic benefits, complementary interventions to remove bottlenecks to local economic development—such as strengthening land market regulations and improving access to quality services—can ensure that big public investments bring expected returns to beneficiaries, deliver on social promises, and protect the global public goods of the Amazon forest.

ANNEX 6A: METHODOLOGICAL NOTE: AMAZÔNIA'S FUNCTIONAL REGIONS

Service nodes and regions

Service regions are defined in two steps. Step 1 identifies the regional nodes, and step 2 assigns cities to each region based on their distance to the node.

Step 1 finds, for each city, the largest urban extent in a six-hour radius around its center. The city is classified as a node if one of the following conditions is verified:

- The city has a larger population than the largest city in its proximity (within the six-hour radius around it).

- The city is at least more than half the size of the largest city in its proximity and has a population of at least 50,000 inhabitants.

Step 2, using the node just defined, creates regions by attributing all cities to the closest node. As a result, some cities will be more than six hours away from the regional node (see examples). They are defined as a single node and, while shown as part of the functional region, are considered remote cities.

Example 1

City A has a population of 10,000 and is four hours away from city B (population 15,000), which is four hours away in the same direction from city N (population 250,000). Because city N is a node, city B is not a node, and city A is eight hours away from its node, despite having a city less than six hours away. City A is considered a single node or a remote city.

Example 2

The closest city to city A is 20 hours away, so city A is considered a remote city.

Economic nodes and regions

The economic regions are also defined in two steps.

Step 1 finds, for each city, the most attractive city based on a gravity equation of the form:

$$Gravity_{ij} = \frac{Pop_i \times Pop_j}{d_{ij}^2} \qquad (6A.1)$$

where the numerator is the population of the two cities (in thousands) multiplied and the denominator is the distance (measured as travel time by road or river) between the two cities squared. For each city i, the most attractive city j is the one with the highest gravity score, subject to j's population being at least 30 percent larger than that of i. A city is defined as a node if it is the most attractive city for at least five other cities.[8]

Step 2, using the node just defined, creates regions by attributing all cities to the closest node.

For example, City A has population 15,000 and is one hour away from city B (population 30,000) and three hours away from city C (population 50,000). Cities A, B, and C are isolated and 30 hours away from the next closest city. City A is the most attractive city for city B but cannot be a node because it is smaller. City B is the most attractive city for City C but cannot be a node because it too is smaller. City B is the most attractive city for A and thus is a node, despite being smaller than nearby city C.

NOTES

1. Cities selected in the Global Human Settlement (GHS) Urban Centre Database 2015 with multitemporal and multidimensional attributes (Florczyk et al. 2019) and defined applying the "Degree of Urbanisation," as described in Dijkstra et al. (2021).
2. See also the discussion of education and development in chapter 2.
3. Careful analysis was carried out to select a set of appropriate comparator countries for each Latin America and Caribbean country using a two-stage procedure that classified all countries globally according to their geography in a first stage and then selected the "nearest

neighbors" in terms of population, land area, and overall mean population density within their group. During this process, one country was selected from each of the East Asia and Pacific and Europe and Central Asia regions; the last comparator was chosen unrestricted from the rest of the world. For Brazil, these comparators are (1) China, (2) Türkiye, and (3) United States (as global comparators), and (1) United States, (2) Canada, and (3) Saudi Arabia (as high-income comparators) (Ferreyra and Roberts 2018).

4. In general, urban forms of Brazilian cities tend to support productivity. Beyond density, other spatial dimensions of urban form matter for productivity. Smooth, rounded, compact, and well-connected cities tend to have higher productivity than rugged or elongated cities or cities with poorly connected streets. While the average city in Latin America and the Caribbean is rounded, has smooth borders (perimeters), has a dense street network, and tends to be compactly built, the region is home to cities with a great diversity of urban form (Duque et al. 2021). Cities in Brazil reflect this diversity. They tend to display low smoothness values, indicating unplanned growth patterns, and high roundness indexes, reflected in compact urban areas. Yet cities such as São Paulo have a high-density built urban form, while Brasília has a higher proportion of open spaces within its urban area. These disparities support the finding that high productivity can be achieved by different urban shapes as long as they guarantee inner-city connectivity.

5. City residents are, on average, four years younger in Amazônia than in the rest of Brazil.

6. The nodes have been identified through a methodology inspired by the principle of functional regions first described in Lösch (1938).

7. Although Santarém is a relatively large city with relatively good connectivity, it is not a node because it is near Belém and Manaus and because of its relative size. Belém and Manaus have a much higher weight than other large cities close to Porto Velho, so most nearby small cities are "pulled" in the modeling more by them than by Santarem. As a result, there are fewer than five cities for which Santarem is the city with the highest gravity score; based on our constraints, it is not selected as a node.

8. The same calculations are performed by restricting nodes to be cities that attract at least two or five other cities, respectively.

REFERENCES

Arretche, M. 2019. "A geografia digital no Brasil: Um panorama das desigualdades regionais." In *Desigualdades digitais no espaço urbano: Um estudo sobre o acesso e o uso da internet na cidade de São Paulo*, 55–79. São Paulo: Núcleo de Informação e Coordenação do Ponto BR, NIC.br.

Artuc, E., P. Bastos, and E. Lee. 2021. "Trade, Jobs, and Worker Welfare." Policy Research Working Paper 9628, World Bank, Washington, DC.

Bacolod, M., B. S. Blum, and W. C. Strange. 2009. "Skills in the City." *Journal of Urban Economics* 65 (2): 136–53.

Charlot, S., and G. Duranton. 2004. "Communication Externalities in Cities." *Journal of Urban Economics* 56 (3): 581–613.

de la Roca, J., and D. Puga. 2017. "Learning by Working in Big Cities." *Review of Economic Studies* 84 (1): 106–42.

Dijkstra, L., A. J. Florczyk, S. Freire, T. Kemper, M. Melchiorri, M. Pesaresi, and M. Schiavina. 2021. "Applying the Degree of Urbanisation to the Globe: A New Harmonised Definition Reveals a Different Picture of Global Urbanisation." *Journal of Urban Economics* 125 (September): 103312.

Duque, J. C., N. Lozano-Gracia, J. E. Patino, and P. Restrepo. 2021. "Urban Form and Productivity: What Shapes Are Latin American Cities?" *Environment and Planning B: Urban Analytics and City Science* 49 (1): 131–50.

Duranton, G. 2008. "Viewpoint: From Cities to Productivity and Growth in Developing Countries." *Canadian Journal of Economics/Revue Canadienne d'Economique* 41 (3): 689–736.

Duranton, G. 2020. "Cities in Latin America: Transition Challenges." Unpublished working paper.

Duranton, G., and D. Puga. 2004. "Micro-foundations of Urban Agglomeration Economies." In *Handbook of Regional and Urban Economics*. Volume 4, edited by J. V. Henderson and J.-F. Thisse, 2063–117. Amsterdam: North-Holland.

Duranton, G., and D. Puga. 2020. "The Economics of Urban Density." *Journal of Economic Perspectives* 34 (3): 3–26.

Ellison, G., and E. L. Glaeser. 1997. "Geographic Concentration in U.S. Manufacturing Industries: A Dartboard Approach." *Journal of Political Economy* 105 (5): 889–927.

Fan, L., and C. Timmins. 2017. "A Sorting Model Approach to Valuing Urban Amenities in Brazil." Unpublished paper, World Bank, Washington, DC.

Farole, T., and G. Akinci. 2011. *Special Economic Zones: Progress, Emerging Challenges, and Future Directions*. Directions in Development Series. Washington, DC: World Bank.

Farole, T., S. Goga, and M. Ionescu-Heroiu. 2018. *Rethinking Lagging Regions: Using Cohesion Policy to Deliver on the Potential of Europe's Regions*. Washington, DC: World Bank.

Ferreyra, M. M., and M. Roberts. 2018. *Raising the Bar for Productive Cities in Latin America and the Caribbean*. World Bank Latin American and Caribbean Studies. Washington, DC: World Bank.

Florczyk, A., C. Corbane, M. Schiavina, M. Pesaresi, L. Maffenini, M. Melchiorri, P. Politis, et al. 2019. Global Human Settlement (GHS) Urban Centre Database 2015, Multitemporal and Multidimensional Attributes, R2019A [dataset]. Brussels: European Commission, Joint Research Centre. https://data.jrc.ec.europa.eu/dataset/53473144-b88c-44bc-b4a3 -4583ed1f547e.

Fujita, M., P. Krugman, and A. J. Venables. 1999. *The Spatial Economy: Cities, Regions, and International Trade*. Cambridge MA: MIT Press.

Glaeser, E. 2011. *Triumph of the City: How Our Greatest Invention Makes Us Richer, Smarter, Greener, Healthier, and Happier*. London: Macmillan.

Grover, A., S. Lall, and W. Maloney. 2021. *Place, Productivity, and Prosperity: Revisiting Spatially Targeted Policies for Regional Development*. Washington, DC: World Bank.

Hansen, M. C., P. V. Potapov, R. Moore, M. Hancher, S. A. Turubanova, A. Tyukavina, D. Thau, et al. 2013. "High-Resolution Global Maps of 21st-Century Forest Cover Change." *Science* 342 (6160): 850–53.

IBGE (Brazilian Institute of Geography and Statistics). 2021. "Population." Datasets, IBGE, Rio de Janeiro (accessed January 26, 2022). https://www.ibge.gov.br/en/statistics/social /population.html.

Krugman, P. 1991a. *Geography and Trade*. Cambridge, MA: MIT Press.

Krugman, P. 1991b. "Increasing Returns and Economic Geography." *Journal of Political Economy* 99 (3): 483–99.

Krugman, P., and A. J. Venables. 1995. "Globalization and the Inequality of Nations." *Quarterly Journal of Economics* 110 (4): 857–80.

Lall, S. V. 2009. "Territorial Development Policy: A Practitioner's Guide." Report 70398, World Bank, Washington, DC.

Lösch, A. 1938. "The Nature of Economic Regions." *Southern Economic Journal* 5 (1): 71–78.

Moretti, E. 2004. "Human Capital Externalities in Cities." In *Handbook of Regional and Urban Economics*. Volume 4, edited by J. V. Henderson and J.-F. Thisse, 2243–91. Amsterdam: North-Holland.

Porcher, C., and M. Hanusch. 2022. "A Model of Amazon Deforestation, Trade, and Labor Market Dynamics." Policy Research Working Paper 10163, World Bank, Washington, DC.

Quintero, L. E., and M. Roberts. 2018. "Explaining Spatial Variations in Productivity: Evidence from Latin America and the Caribbean." Policy Research Working Paper 8560, World Bank, Washington, DC.

Rauch, J. E. 1993. "Productivity Gains from Geographic Concentration of Human Capital: Evidence from the Cities." *Journal of Urban Economics* 34 (3): 380–400.

Rodríguez-Pose, A., and C. Wilkie. 2019. "Strategies of Gain and Strategies of Waste: What Determines the Success of Development Intervention?" *Progress in Planning* 133 (October): 100423.

Rosenthal, S., and W. Strange. 2004. "Evidence on the Nature and Sources of Agglomeration Economies." In *Handbook of Regional and Urban Economics*. Volume 4, edited by J. V. Henderson and J.-F. Thisse, 2119–71. Amsterdam: North-Holland.

Schor, T., and J. A. de Oliveira. 2011. "Reflexões metodológicas sobre o estudo da rede urbana no Amazonas e perspectivas para análise das cidades na Amazônia Brasileira" [Methodological Thoughts on the Study of the Urban Network in the State of Amazonas and Perspectives]. *ACTA Geográfica* 5 (11): 15–30.

Vagliasindi, M. 2022. "Key Challenges and Opportunities in the Power Sector of the State of Amazonas." Background note for this report, World Bank, Washington, DC.

Weiss, D. J., A. Nelson, H. S. Gibson, W. Temperley, S. Peedell, A. Lieber, M. Hancher, et al. 2018. "A Global Map of Travel Time to Cities to Assess Inequalities in Accessibility in 2015." *Nature* 553 (7688): 333–36.

World Bank. 2009. *World Development Report 2009: Reshaping Economic Geography*. Washington, DC: World Bank.

World Bank. 2023. "Urban Competitiveness in Brazil's State of Amazonas: A Green Growth Agenda." Companion paper for this report, World Bank, Washington, DC.

WorldPop 2020. Open Spatial Demographic Data and Research. University of Southampton, UK. www.worldpop.org.

A Balancing Act

7 Complementary Policies for Amazônia

MAREK HANUSCH, ANA MARÍA GONZÁLEZ VELOSA,
TANYA LISA YUDELMAN, SANDRA BERMAN, JON STRAND,
AND CLAUDIA TUFANI

KEY MESSAGES

- Sustainable and inclusive development in Amazônia requires rebalancing the development approach through tailored packages of policies that should protect forests and build the longer-term foundations for economic development.
- Given the complexity of the development challenge in Amazônia, policies will be more effective if they complement each other. The synergy of this approach will also limit unintended consequences.
- Complementary policy packages can help the frontier economies of Amazônia to mature economically and institutionally.
- Shared efforts at the global, national, and local levels can support sustainable and inclusive development outcomes in Amazônia, including
    - Sustainable food demand and supply;
    - Sustainable trade systems;
    - Conservation finance;
    - Balanced structural transformation in Amazônia and across Brazil;
    - Improved forest protection in Amazônia; and
    - Tailored social protection, adequate basic services, and a bioeconomy that sustains rural livelihoods in Amazônia.
- Continued investment in the knowledge base on sustainable and inclusive development remains key.
- Policy decisions should be made in an inclusive and consultative way.

WHERE THERE'S SMOKE, THERE'S FIRE

Amazônia's forest fires highlight deep-seated development challenges in Amazônia and in Brazil more broadly. This memorandum has shown that the vast destruction of public value in the Brazilian Amazon is symptomatic of an economy depleting its natural capital rather than generating value by becoming more productive. Poverty—be it rural or urban—and Amazonia's deforestation are on opposite sides of the same coin. Deforestation in Amazônia must not be seen as an isolated concern; it is structural and partly rooted in Brazil's growth model. Likewise, the solutions to Amazônia's deforestation cannot be found in the forest alone.

What is needed is a broader discussion about how Brazil intends to become a richer country, an Organisation for Economic Co-operation and Development (OECD) country, without depleting its natural wealth. For Brazil to become simultaneously a richer and greener country will require complementary policy interventions at the global, national, and local levels, steering the economy toward a more sustainable and inclusive path.

Protecting Amazônia's forests calls for decisive action. Chapter 3 showed that, without external support, such as the past commodity supercycle, the Brazilian economy has been stuttering along, with economic pressures on deforestation rising and past reductions in poverty and inequality reversing. The baseline general equilibrium simulations of chapter 3 suggest that deforestation may in fact further accelerate. Brazil cannot afford to kick the can down the road for at least two reasons: First, the degrees of freedom for stopping climate change are exhausted. Second, Brazilian growth will likely enjoy only limited tailwinds from the global economy. In the end, productivity and governance are within the realm of domestic policy, and Brazil well understands which reforms can boost productivity and protect forests (Dutz 2018). The country urgently needs to make progress on both.

Global climate action may help protect forests but could inflict economic pain on both Amazônia and Brazil unless the growth model becomes more sustainable. Both globally and in Brazil, people have become more attuned to climate change. This holds true especially among younger generations, more-educated individuals, and more-affluent countries (UNDP and University of Oxford 2021)—which also means that global socioeconomic progress will intensify climate awareness.

Adaptations in global consumer behavior and policy efforts to ensure global food security can reduce demand for Brazil's agricultural commodities, which in turn would soften pressure on Brazil's natural forests—most under threat in Amazônia—but at a cost to economic growth. These global preferences could further affect production across Brazil if implemented through trade measures aimed at reducing global greenhouse gas (GHG) emissions.

However, these developments also present an opportunity for change, and Brazil could benefit significantly from global decarbonization (World Bank 2023a). If Brazil, and specifically Amazônia, shift their development approach to emphasize productivity and more balanced structural transformation, paired with stronger environmental protection, they could also unlock larger markets for their sustainably produced agricultural and nonagricultural products while better leveraging the country's green energy matrix in the global decarbonization story.

This concluding chapter reviews how economic, climate, and environmental policies can complement each other so that Amazônia can get ahead of the curve—developing while conserving forests. Higher sustainability in Amazônia will also benefit Brazil more broadly. Financing will be needed to support a strategic shift toward more sustainable and inclusive development.

To promote economic development while protecting natural forests in Amazônia, policies must be carefully balanced. The chapter reviews this balancing act, cutting across the complexity of the development challenges, including *space* (from the global to the local, both rural and urban); *time* (the shorter term and longer term); *society* (public and private, rich and poor, modern and traditional); and *trade-offs* (between consumption and natural assets).

The chapter is also anchored in the four strategic priorities for Amazônia identified in this memorandum, namely (a) fostering productivity through balanced structural transformation, (b) protecting the forest, (c) fostering sustainable rural livelihoods, and (d) marshaling conservation finance. As such, it reviews policies for Amazônia's development through a conservation lens and explores how they can complement each other to help Amazônia's frontier economies mature economically and institutionally, thus fostering sustainable and inclusive development.

DEVELOPMENT IN AMAZÔNIA THROUGH A CONSERVATION LENS

Brazil has invested greatly in developing Amazônia. A return on this investment should not deplete but rather build the country's natural wealth. To do so requires a different approach to development. The decisions made decades ago to populate and develop Amazônia cast a long shadow, currently generating a tension between private land use and the public goods associated with natural forests. It has been a costly undertaking.

Chapter 1 documented Brazil's significant investments in infrastructure, and the companion report to this memorandum—on Amazonas State (World Bank 2023b)—draws attention to the ongoing national fiscal outlays for special economic zones, notably the Zona Franca de Manaus (Free Economic Zone of Manaus). The investments in Amazônia have yielded some returns: notably, significant expansion of agricultural production as well as the emergence of some large Amazonian cities with notable economic capabilities. Taking into account the lost value from destroyed ecosystems in the process, these returns would be much lower overall.

A new development approach would foster economic growth with a much smaller environmental footprint, thus raising income and savings without the large-scale destruction of natural wealth. It would be consistent with Brazil's aspirations to become an OECD country while also helping the country mitigate global climate change and make progress toward achieving its Nationally Determined Contribution under the Paris Climate Accords and its commitment during the 2021 United Nations Climate Change Conference (26th Conference of the Parties, or COP26) to zero illegal deforestation by 2028.

To those ends, action is needed not only in Amazônia but also at the global and national levels (table 7.1) for several reasons:

- Resource-intensive consumer demand (notably, of beef) is a source of deforestation, whether that demand emanates from Amazônia, elsewhere in Brazil, or in the rest of the world.

- The growth model fueling deforestation is an Amazonian problem as much as it is a broader Brazilian problem.
- Although some actions are within the responsibility of Amazonian authorities, others require the commitment of entities across federal levels in areas such as law enforcement, land regularization, reform of the rural credit system, or structural economic reforms.
- There is an important regional dimension given the economic and environmental spillovers across the eight countries in the broader Amazon region (box 7.1).

BOX 7.1

Protecting the Amazon biome through regional collaboration

The diverse habitats and species in all countries sharing the Amazon are intricately linked and provide ecosystem services essential to humans across national borders and globally. Those countries depend on the integrity of the whole biome for ecological sustainability, maintenance of the hydrological cycle, biodiversity conservation, and climate change resilience. The notion of a connected Amazon beyond political boundaries also mobilizes traditional ethnic groups and their knowledge of the region. Recognizing and protecting the biological and cultural connectivity of the Amazon ecosystems not only ensures the provision of their services but also promotes community, scientific, and institutional relations and partnerships toward common interests.

Threats across countries

Ecosystem connectivity can also influence the range and impact of threats across Amazon countries. For example, poor decisions that result in unsustainable infrastructure development upstream in shared water systems may alter freshwater dynamics and divert water resources away from tributaries or rivers, leaving downstream users (like Brazil) to manage the adverse impacts of reduced water availability and frequently erratic flows.

Overfishing in one country may also affect fish populations in other countries—especially migratory fish species, which are most of the species fished. For instance, Bolivian fish stocks are affected by overfishing in the Madre de Dios region in Peru and in the

low and medium basin of Brazil's Madeira River (Van Damme et al. 2011). Even criminal activities, such as illegal wildlife and timber trade, cut across borders, and perpetrators take advantage of the different laws and policies in each Amazon country and exploit the gaps that arise from insufficient cooperation between international agencies and destination countries.

Examples of regional collaboration

Brazil has been an active participant and leader in designing multiple efforts to promote regional cooperation in addressing challenges affecting the biome and in promoting integrated solutions aligning with national and subnational development plans. One such important effort is the 1978 Amazon Cooperation Treaty, which led to the establishment of the intergovernmental Amazon Cooperation Treaty Organization (ACTO), a platform for political and regional dialogue to encourage sustainable development and social inclusion.[a] The latest national-level coordination initiative is the 2019 Leticia Pact, signed by seven Amazon countries to address the drivers of deforestation and environmental crimes in the region.[b]

Collaboration has also been promoted subnationally or thematically, as in the following examples:

- The Governors' Climate and Forests Task Force advances jurisdiction-wide approaches to protecting forests, reducing emissions, and enhancing livelihoods.[c]
- The integrated watershed management of the Putumayo-Içá basin project has been jointly

continued

Box 7.1, *continued*

prepared by Brazil, Colombia, Ecuador, and Peru.[d]

- The Regional Initiative for the Conservation and Sustainable Use of Amazon Wetlands includes Bolivia, Brazil, Colombia, Ecuador, and the República Bolivariana de Venezuela.
- The Amazon Network of Geo-Referenced Socio-Environmental Information, established in 2007, is a consortium of civil society organizations from Amazon countries to produce and disseminate knowledge, statistical data, and geospatial socio-environmental information.[e]

Finding common ground

There are competing sectoral agendas and unharmonized systems. There is limited capacity to supervise compliance of agreements that are not legally binding. And there is a lack of continuity because of changes to governments. But several benefits of collaboration still outweigh the costs:

- Improving governance and law enforcement to tackle cross-border illegal activities, including wildlife trafficking and illegal logging[f]
- Strengthening socioeconomic development along borders
- Enhancing nature-based tourism networks
- Sharing lessons and best practices on protected area management, sustainable forestry, and productive value chains
- Harmonizing knowledge protocols and basin-wide monitoring systems
- Facilitating dialogue on trade, infrastructure, migration, and managing transmittable (zoonotic) diseases

The Amazon Sustainable Landscapes Program, financed by the Global Environment Facility and managed by the World Bank, gives Brazil a platform to participate in such collaboration in areas and topics of interest.

a. The permanent secretariat of ACTO is hosted by Brazil, in Brasília.
b. The Leticia Pact was signed in September 2019 by Bolivia, Brazil, Colombia, Ecuador, Guyana, Peru, and Suriname (https://www
.cancilleria.gov.co/en/newsroom/news/siete-paises-suscriben-pacto-leticia-amazonia), and its corresponding Action Plan was issued in
December 2019 (https://www.cancilleria.gov.co/sites/default/files/planofactionfinaltext-5dicen12.pdf).
c. The task force is a subnational collaboration between 39 states and provinces from Brazil, Colombia, Côte d'Ivoire, Ecuador, Indonesia,
Mexico, Nigeria, Peru, Spain, and the United States. One of its results was the San Francisco Declaration (September 2018) by Amazon
governors within five countries (Bolivia, Brazil, Colombia, Ecuador, and Peru) to implement actions against climate change and
deforestation (https://www.gcftf.org/wp-content/uploads/2020/12/San_Francisco_Declaration_ENG.pdf). The following Brazilian states
(which also comprise Amazônia) are task force members: Acre, Amapá, Amazonas, Maranhão, Mato Grosso, Pará, Rondônia, Roraima, and
Tocantins.
d. This project, to be financed by the Global Environment Facility, is being led by the State Secretariat for the Environment (Sema) of
Amazonas State and the Ministries of Environment from the other three neighboring countries (Colombia, Ecuador, and Peru).
e. The network includes eight institutions from six Amazon countries: Bolivia's Friends of Nature Foundation (FAN); Brazil's Socio-
Environmental Institute (ISA) and Amazon Institute of People and Environment (Imazon); Colombia's Gaia Amazonas Foundation; the
Ecuadorian Foundation for Ecological Studies (EcoCiencia); Peru's Institute for the Common Good (IBC); and República Bolivariana de
Venezuela's Provita and the Social-Environmental Work Group for the Amazon (Wataniba).
f. Although the relative importance of illegal wildlife trade as a driver of environmental degradation is smaller than others, its
reduction through detection and stronger enforcement efforts has the potential to leverage long-term cooperation across regional
and national governments with positive collateral effects to improve the general perception about environmental governance.
For example, an interesting case from which Brazil and other Amazon countries can learn is Peru's efforts to strengthen the
capacities of its national and subnational institutions and to promote citizen participation and monitoring to prevent and reduce
environmental crimes.

Any policy focus on Amazônia must be attuned to the need to protect the region's forests. Table 7.1 summarizes the high-level policies discussed in this memorandum—at the global, national, and Amazonian levels—from global agricultural markets to Brazilian and Amazonian structural transformation, sustainable livelihoods in Amazônia, and conservation finance.

Figure 7.1 then applies a conservation lens to the policies discussed in this memorandum, revisiting the framework introduced in chapter 1 (figure 1.5).

TABLE 7.1 Shared efforts to support sustainable and inclusive development in Amazônia at the global, national, and local levels

OBJECTIVE	GLOBAL LEVEL	NATIONAL LEVEL	AMAZÔNIA
Global sustainable demand and supply			
Consuming more sustainably (C1a)	✓	✓	✓
Closing crop yield gaps (C1a)	✓	✓	Yes, guarding against the Jevons effect[a]
Promoting sustainable trade integration (C1b)	✓	✓	
Balanced structural transformation across Brazil (C2a and C2b)			
Removing distortions in product and factor markets		✓	✓
Fostering sustainable infrastructure and logistics and strengthening urban networks and municipal services in rural and urban areas		✓	✓
Reforming implicit incentives to extensive agriculture (including rural credit and land taxes) and foster climate-smart agriculture (C3)		✓	✓
Strengthening human capital		✓	✓
Improved forest protection in Amazônia			
Accelerating land regularization (C4a)		Yes, for federal lands in Amazônia	✓
Strengthening law enforcement, including forest governance (C4b)		Yes, for relevant federal agencies and regional collaboration	✓
Avoiding deforestation, promoting reforestation (C5a), and restoring degraded lands (C5b)		Yes, for example, through the CRAs	Yes, guarding against deforestation leakage
Sustainable rural livelihoods in Amazônia (C6)			
Strengthening the bioeconomy			✓
Tailoring social protection			✓
Conservation finance			
Providing financing	✓	✓	✓
Receiving financing		Yes, for federal efforts in Amazônia	✓

Source: World Bank.
Note: Conservation-informed policies are denoted by a "C," as further elaborated in this chapter's "complementary policies" section and figure 7.1.
a. The "Jevons effect" refers to "intensification inducing extensification," whereby agricultural productivity gains locally increase deforestation.
CRAs = Environmental Reserve Quotas (Cotas de Reserva Ambiental).

The figure enables an examination of how policies can break the pernicious logic of deforestation and their economic impacts in both the shorter and longer term.[1] Some policy scenarios entail trade-offs between natural capital and consumption, but the risk of tipping points in Amazônia tilts the balance further toward forest conservation. If tipping points are triggered, welfare impacts will be unambiguously negative (chapter 1). However, this chapter shows that synergies can prevail under well-balanced packages of complementary policies, especially if they are carefully timed.

FIGURE 7.1

Policy levers to change the pernicious logic of deforestation

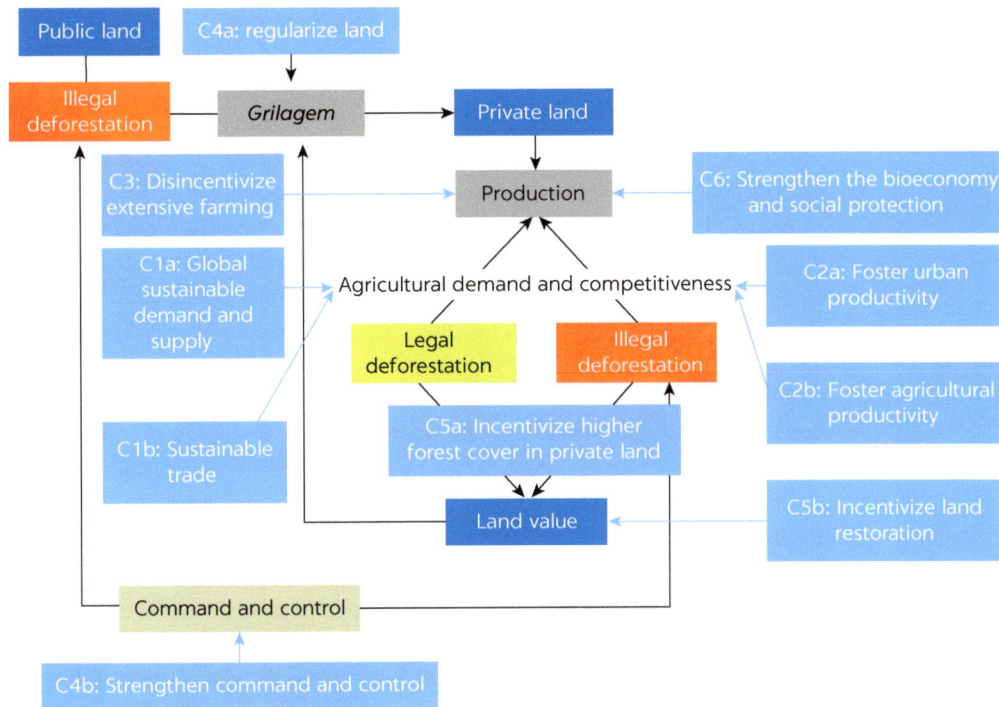

Source: World Bank, drawing on figure 1.5 in chapter 1.
Note: The boxes and lines shaded in light green show the relationship of proposed conservation-informed policies (denoted by "C" and a number) that address various causes of changing forest cover in Amazônia. "Illegal deforestation" includes unauthorized logging in public lands (such as protected areas or Indigenous territories) and forest clearing as part of the *grilagem* (land grabbing) process. Illegal deforestation also occurs in private lands violating the Forest Code. "Legal deforestation" occurs in private lands within the limits of the Forest Code. Agricultural demand and competitiveness affect land use choices, land values, and consequently incentives for *grilagem*. Command and control interventions aim to curb illegal deforestation. The figure does not account for legal logging, deforestation for infrastructure development, or legal forms of small-scale sustainable production in public lands.

COMPLEMENTARY POLICIES

Effective, well-balanced policy packages can help Amazônia protect its forests and at the same time develop faster and more inclusively. A growth model focused on higher productivity (policy scenarios C2a and C2b in figure 7.1)—including in the currently lagging urban sectors—is consistent with measures to reduce inefficient support to extensive agriculture (C3) and to intensify agriculture through a more inelastic land supply by regularizing and protecting natural lands (C4a and C4b), all propelling structural change while conserving forests in Amazônia. At the same time, structural change can bring both social and environmental disruption, making it critical to provide alternative sustainable livelihoods to small farmers and forest communities (C6) while guarding against the deforestation caused by social or environmental shocks. Building resilience will be particularly important as climate change intensifies. Policy should thus focus on enabling structural transformation while carefully mitigating its adverse impacts.

One critical issue is that deforestation can leak across territories. This makes complementary policies even more important to reduce incentives to deforest more in one location, legally or illegally, when deforestation is reduced in another.

Conservation finance, in addition to better-structured public budgets, can support complementary policy packages policies. It will require effective forest protection and can fund efforts to directly strengthen land and forest governance (policy scenarios C4a and C4b) and promote higher forest cover (C5a and C5b) but also more broadly to foster sustainable development in Amazônia (C2a, C2b, and C6). Conservation finance can emanate from within Brazil but also from other parts of the world—for example, through donations or global carbon and financial markets.

Although some policies could have rapid impacts once implemented, they might not be implemented rapidly for political economy reasons. Effective policy packages could help overcome this. Chapter 3 drew attention to potential trade-offs between forest protection and consumption under the current growth model, while chapter 4 developed this thought further to stress the political economy implications and how they can be overcome. Environmental protection is more difficult when there are immediate welfare losses. Combining the various policies shown in figure 7.1 would tend to increase overall welfare, which could also help to generate political will to implement them. Conservation finance can further help to generate the required political will and is thus an important component of an effective policy mix.

The following subsections survey the economic and environmental (with a focus on forest cover) impacts from policies discussed across this memorandum as well as their likely shorter- and longer-term effectiveness. As much as possible, the discussion captures both direct and indirect effects. In the case of welfare, this often requires an understanding of how interventions are financed (generally requiring some redistribution and in some cases introducing distortions), which goes beyond the scope of this discussion.

Global sustainable demand and supply

Policy scenario C1a: More sustainable consumer preferences and closing global crop yield gaps

- *Economic impact:* Lower agricultural prices, at least for resource-intensive goods → lower real income for Amazonian producers cushioned by higher prices for sustainable producers; for consumers, higher purchasing power due to expanded agricultural supply and ambiguous impacts due to shifts to sustainable production
- *Environmental impact:* Lower demand for agricultural land → higher natural forest cover
- *Impact over time:* Longer term

Consuming more sustainably. What happens in Amazônia is partly determined elsewhere. Even though Amazônia is remote and isolated in some ways, it is deeply integrated into the world in other ways. Therefore, the global demand and supply for commodities—and the consumer demand underlying them—matter for what happens in Amazônia.

The unsustainable agricultural expansion into Amazônia, and into other natural lands globally, is driven partly by rising international demand. An extractive growth model is partly enabled by a global opportunity: buoyant food markets. The global population continues to grow, though the pace is slowing.

Without a change in global consumption patterns, this growth will continue to raise the demand for food and agricultural commodities—as well as other commodities associated with deforestation, like minerals and timber.

For food demand, consumers across the world (including Brazil) have several ways to adapt their behavior to help reduce pressures on natural lands (Searchinger et al. 2019). Animal products (meats, dairy, fish, and eggs) are associated with highly resource-intensive production. Modeling suggests that reducing the intake of animal-based foods by 30 percent could eliminate all cropland expansion globally by 2050 (considering demand-side factors only). A similar effect could be achieved if consumers in richer countries adjusted their meat intake downward to the global average. A 30 percent reduction of ruminant meat demand (beef, sheep, goat) in Europe, Latin America, the Russian Federation and other countries of Eastern Europe and Central Asia, as well as in Canada and the United States would have a similar effect on croplands. In all cases, this shift in consumer preferences would require an expansion of vegetarian diets, which are associated with much higher resource efficiency.

The various policy entry points range from advocacy to changing social norms and awareness around healthy and sustainable diets, reducing food waste, and fiscal interventions to discourage unsustainable foods and encourage sustainable ones (Searchinger et al. 2019).

Consumers increasingly care about sustainable production methods. This can translate into a willingness to pay a premium for higher production costs. Figure 7.2 looks at two types of agricultural producers—those who deforest (extensive agriculture) and those who intensify production instead. Because of the cost involved in intensifying production (through greater use of machinery, inputs, and so on), intensive farmers have a steeper supply curve: they need to be paid a marginally higher price for each additional unit produced than extensive farmers.[2]

Figure 7.2 simulates a shift of demand away from extensively farmed products toward more sustainable production, thus lowering deforestation. It shows that the price for extensively farmed products falls, thus reducing deforestation. Consumers continuing to purchase those products will pay lower prices. The steeper supply curve for *intensive* farmers requires the market price to increase more sharply than the corresponding fall in prices for *extensive* farmers. In other words, consumers must be willing to pay a higher price for the intensively produced goods to conserve the forest. And this behavior will provide incentives for producers to increasingly switch to sustainable methods that will increase their overall welfare.

Closing crop yield gaps. Interventions are also needed in agriculture policy to help the world meet its food needs more efficiently. Countries across the world vary greatly in agricultural productivity, with African countries especially lagging the rest. Closing crop yield gaps would increase the food supply by using land more efficiently, thus reducing the encroachment on natural lands. But there are risks: as agricultural productivity gains reduce pressures on natural lands globally, they can increase them locally owing to the Jevons effect.[3]

Overall, closing crop yield gaps globally could eliminate pressures on natural lands globally. The alternative could be an expansion of cropland into global natural forests by 26 percent (or 3.4 million square kilometers) between 2010 and 2050—with significant increases in GHG emissions and biodiversity loss (Williams et al. 2020). In those simulations, 87.7 percent of species would lose parts of their habitats, and 1,280 species would lose more than 25 percent of their habitats across the world. Intensifying agricultural production in Brazil could

FIGURE 7.2

The impact of sustainable demand on market prices and forests

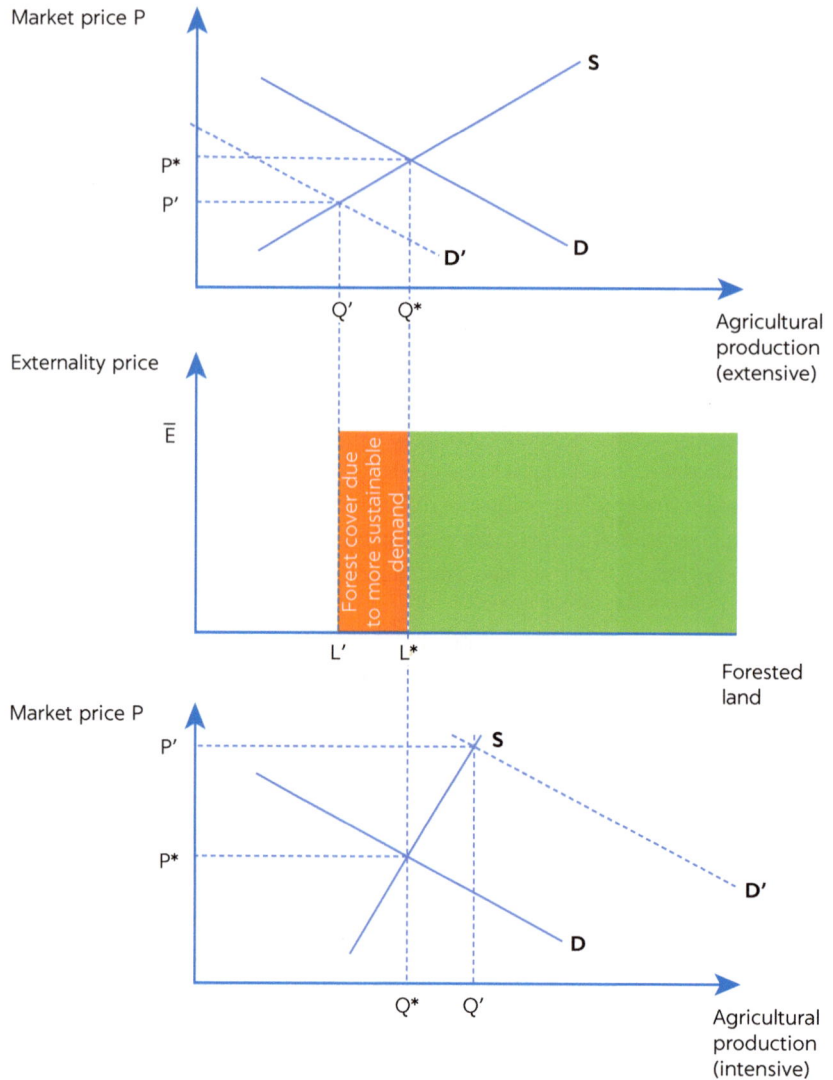

Source: World Bank.
Note: The figure illustrates how a shift in consumer demand toward sustainable products changes prices for sustainable and unsustainable producers and conserves natural land otherwise at risk of deforestation.

take pressure off ecosystems in other parts of the world, but it necessitates preventing the Jevons effect in Amazônia (see policy scenario C2b).

Lower agricultural prices associated with a global increase in supply would benefit consumers' purchasing power, while it would put pressure on producers to raise their own productivity.

Getting ahead of the curve. Both less bouyant food demand and higher global agricultural productivity pose a threat to an extractive growth model, whereas a more sustainable growth model harbors many global opportunities. As climate change accelerates, people globally are focusing increasingly on sustainability. Changing consumer preferences and making greater efforts to meet food needs more efficiently will only intensify. Brazil and Amazônia must prepare for this because it will reduce global market opportunities. An export basket based on primary products is not fit for the future, and Brazil must diversify. For Amazônia specifically, betting on development through extensive agriculture for export is risky (both economically and environmentally) and unlikely to be future-proof.

Brazil and Amazônia alike should prepare for a more sustainably minded future. A focus on more balanced structural transformation (policy scenarios C2a, C2b, and C3) and more effective land and forest governance (scenarios C4a and C4b) could build a foundation to compete successfully in global markets and benefit from the global decarbonization drive in sectors as diverse as sustainable agriculture and green manufacturing (World Bank 2023a).

Policy scenario C1b: Trade liberalization

- *Economic impact:* Greater market access and productivity gains from trade liberalization → higher overall income
- *Environmental impact:* Higher demand for agricultural goods (putting pressure on forests) and higher overall productivity, including in urban sectors (reducing pressure on forests) → ambiguous impact on natural forest cover
- *Impact over time:* Longer term

Trade liberalization could help Brazil overcome its legacy of import substitution industrialization (chapters 1 and 3). Liberalization tends to raise overall income, but it can bring significant social and environmental disruption. Raising productivity (policy scenarios C2a and C2b), to make the economy more competitive externally, and social protection interventions (scenario C6), to cushion adverse impacts on the poor, are thus important complementary policies.

International trade agreements harbor significant environmental risks (World Bank 2023a). Brazil is a counterparty to the recent EU-Southern Common Market (MERCOSUL) agreement, which intensifies trade between the two trading blocs. Brazil is expected to gain better access to European markets, especially for primary commodities, including ethanol. Given the association with deforestation, European beef liberalization was more modest. Brazil has committed to opening up certain manufacturing sectors over a 15-year period.

The gains from trade are estimated to benefit the Brazilian economy overall, but the impacts on natural forests, especially in Amazônia, are more complex (World Bank 2023a). Exposing Brazilian manufacturing to more competition can be expected to help raise the productivity of that sector, and this memorandum has suggested that such a productivity boost will reduce deforestation. But opening trade will also increase demand for Brazilian agricultural products. Even though products directly associated with deforestation have been somewhat exempted from trade liberalization,[4] land competition is still likely to intensify, and production decisions responding to an overall increase in demand are not confined to specific geographic areas within Brazil. The displacement of production across the Brazilian economy can fuel deforestation.

Thus the relative timing of opening manufacturing markets across Brazil (which could help reduce Amazonian deforestation) matters. Future trade agreements should focus on this balance to support Brazil's and Amazônia's sustainable development.

International trade policy will put increasing pressure on Brazil to guarantee deforestation-free value chains. Various safeguards are in place to avoid the export of commodities produced in illegally deforested land, but the effectiveness of such safeguards is currently mixed (Abman, Lundberg, and Ruta 2021; Rajão et al. 2020).

Several countries are considering making access to their markets conditional on meeting more ambitious environmental standards. Although the European Union (EU) Carbon Border Adjustment Mechanism currently focuses on fuel-related carbon content, it will conceivably be extended to agricultural products, such as a requirement to prove they were produced in deforestation-free areas. Some countries (like Belgium) are already considering such measures.

As long as other major markets do not impose similar standards, trade diversion is likely, with sustainability-certified Brazilian products reaching markets with the highest standards and uncertified products reaching markets (global or domestic) with lower standards. However, as higher standards are increasingly adopted across countries, pressure will increase on Brazil to strengthen sustainable certification systems. "Feebate" systems (discussed in chapter 4) could help Brazil to achieve this goal and get ahead of the curve by providing fiscal incentives for producers to join credible certification schemes.

Balanced structural transformation

Policy scenario C2a: Foster urban productivity

- *Economic impact:* Higher employment and higher real wages → higher income
- *Environmental impact:* Higher relative competitiveness of non-land-intensive sectors → higher natural forest cover (especially if urban production sources are sustainable)
- *Impact over time:* Longer term

Brazil needs to update its growth model to tip the balance more strongly toward urban productivity, driving diversification beyond commodities. This memorandum has built upon a foundation of research pointing to Brazil's productivity challenges, showing that they affect Amazônia in at least two important ways: A stagnant Brazilian economy provides little uplift to the lagging Amazonian economies. And Brazilian growth challenges like "Custo Brasil"—the high cost of doing business in Brazil—are shared challenges.

A sharper focus on urban productivity and competitiveness across the country would benefit Brazil overall and support Amazônia in catching up with the rest of the country. As this memorandum has discussed (chapters 1 and 3), an excessive focus on rural production, and especially on extensive agriculture, can be distortionary and undermine development because it directs factors of production in the opposite direction of structural transformation. Greater urban productivity across the country would rebalance urban and rural competitiveness, helping to alter the pressures that contribute to large-scale deforestation in Amazonian natural forests. Notably, urban productivity will have a larger impact on slowing deforestation when it does not generate additional agricultural demand as through deep rural value chains in areas and value chains where forest governance is weak.

A focus across Brazil would also help to avoid a divergence in growth models that could undermine the economic cohesion of the Brazilian federation (chapter 3). At the federal level, fostering urban productivity includes accelerating the structural reform agenda, which can range from resuming reforms to the country's byzantine tax system and raising efficiency in logistics to strategically leveraging new trade agreements to open urban sectors to greater competition (discussed earlier under scenario C1b). In addition, states should eventually reflect a sharper urban focus in their four-year Multiannual Plans (Planos Plurianual, or PPAs) and develop an agenda for productive, green towns and cities. Urban priorities would eventually need to find better expression in federal and subnational budgets as well.

Transport infrastructure. An emphasis on urban productivity can also reduce the need for rural roads, a key driver of deforestation. The current risk in Amazônia is that the Arc of Deforestation keeps shifting north, supported by (often informal) rural roads. Strengthening urban productivity would reduce the need for those roads; cities are already connected to markets by road or rail (especially on the New Frontier) and by waterway (on the Colonial Frontier) as well as airports.

In principle, expanded transport infrastructure in Amazônia should have low priority when development is urban-focused. River transportation, where feasible, can be a relatively sustainable logistics solution for shipping goods (acknowledging that environmental challenges also exist for rivers). Rather, prioritizing road investments in other parts of Brazil—strengthening connectivity, especially between the coastal urban hubs—would bring large welfare gains to the whole country, including Amazônia (which would benefit from the growing markets) (Gorton and Ianchovichina 2021).

Market distortions. Removing market distortions will be important for productivity. Brazilian industrial policy has a history of "picking winners." In Amazônia, this is still reflected by the tax incentives given directly to companies in the Zona Franca de Manaus (World Bank 2023b). An approach to industrial policy focused on strengthening the broader business environment would reduce economic distortions, including implicit competition issues, hence raising the overall competitiveness of urban centers. Some investments in this regard will not require significant fiscal outlays; for example, many interventions to reduce the Custo Brasil in Amazônia and beyond require regulatory changes. One critical area for structural reforms lies in the national transport sector (water transport in particular), whose inefficiencies disproportionately hurt remote Amazônia.

Eventually, as Amazônia develops the urban foundations it needs for economic convergence with the rest of the country, financial support to the region can be reduced. In the meantime, public funding is justified by the positive environmental externalities of sustainable development in Amazônia. Funding could be raised through conservation finance or by repurposing distortionary incentives in other sectors (such as those disincentivizing extensive agriculture, as discussed under policy scenario C3).

Urban networks. A network of green towns and cities should support structural transformation and poverty reduction in Amazônia. Policy would focus on productivity in and across Amazonian cities that have already developed economic capabilities, infrastructure, density, skills, and logistics (economic nodes). In the Amazon biome, these towns and cities tend to be lined along major rivers. In developing cities, particular attention should be paid to greening energy, logistics, transport, and waste.

Vertical cities. More-vertical cities are also consistent with more productive cities, meaning that urban development does not require a larger physical footprint—particularly important for reducing the direct impact of urban Amazônia on its forests.

Human capital. Balanced structural transformation also requires a strong human capital foundation (chapter 2). Growth and structural transformation require skilled workers, but Amazônia has significant human capital constraints. Investing in human capital is important to create the skills for economic diversification. It is also important for people to adapt to structural change by upgrading skills, switching professions, or migrating to faster-growing areas across the country.

This memorandum has highlighted the critical need to invest in teachers as well as the important role of Amazônia's urban nodes in providing basic public services such as health and education. Improving human capital outcomes tends to be a slow process, however, and is partly endogenous to the structural transformation process itself, in a virtuous circle of economic development and human capital development. To enhance the skills of the Amazonian labor force faster and drive productivity, attracting skilled migrants to urban Amazônia can help, highlighting once more that Amazônia is nested within Brazil and that policies to advance development in other parts of the country will also benefit Amazônia.

In the shorter term, a complementary policy focus on the poorest is essential to cushion the shocks from economic disruption (scenario C6).

Basic infrastructure services. Beyond productivity, raising living standards requires that infrastructure gaps be met, including housing and water and sanitation. (For example, the new Marco do Saneamento Básico [Basic Sanitation Framework] law is an opportunity to attract private capital to water and sanitation in the region.) Notably, basic infrastructure services are not an urban priority alone but also one for rural areas, both to provide adequate basic living standards and to avoid excessive push factors for rural-urban migration beyond the usual urbanization process associated with structural transformation.

While urban productivity reduces deforestation in Brazil (chapter 3), it may displace some deforestation to other parts of the world. To counter this, agricultural productivity gains across Brazil and the world are complementary (policy scenarios C2b and C1a).

Policy scenario C2b: Foster agricultural productivity

- *Economic impact:* Higher real wages and rural-urban migration → higher income (especially when coupled with urban productivity and jobs)
- *Environmental impact:* Agricultural intensification (lower deforestation) but potentially more demand for land to expand market share (higher deforestation, as per the Jevons effect) → positive effects on global natural forests but ambiguous impact in Amazônia
- *Impact over time:* Longer term

Amazônia's agricultural productivity is already catching up with that of other parts of Brazil, but this convergence has been accompanied by high deforestation. The sector's growth has been supported by buoyant international markets but also by improved infrastructure and market access. Yields tend to be higher in states with more developed agricultural markets, and many of the interventions listed under policy scenario C2a (such as transport infrastructure and human capital) also matter for agricultural productivity and broader structural transformation. Growth in the agriculture sector has allowed many Amazonian states, especially in the New Frontier, to contribute to the local and global food supply while reaching higher levels of development. Yet the agricultural frontier is also synonymous with the Arc of Deforestation, making this a model that is not fit for purpose in the sensitive ecosystems of Amazônia.

Mitigating the Jevons effect. To reduce the risk of deforestation, fostering agricultural productivity should be sensitive to the maturity of agricultural markets and leverage complementary interventions to contain the Jevons effect. Although the jury is out on whether the Jevons effect holds in Amazônia, modeling for this memorandum suggests that it does. At a minimum, this flags the Jevons effect as an important risk that policy makers should mitigate, which could be done in several ways:

- *Fostering agricultural productivity in other parts of Brazil* where production volumes are much larger, land markets are more mature, and deforestation is less of a concern could raise the food supply without putting pressure on Amazônia's agricultural frontier. This logic could also apply to the more mature markets in Amazônia (for example, the southeastern parts of Mato Grosso State).
- *Complementing Amazônia's agricultural productivity gains with stronger land and forest governance* such as land regularization (policy scenario C4a), command and control (C4b), land restoration (C5b), disincentivizing extensive farming (C3), and improving tracing systems and incentive systems (like feebates) could deter illegal forest clearing.
- *Fostering urban productivity* (C2a) is another important complementary policy focus, supporting agricultural intensification through the impact on capital and input prices (relative to land prices).

Addressing social implications. When fostering agricultural productivity, policy must also account for the social implications, not least because agricultural productivity gains tend to reduce agricultural employment. Chapter 5 showed that intensifying competition between more productive and less productive farmers is one source of overall productivity growth. Among the social implications, however, are that the less productive farmers, who tend to be poorer and have smaller farms, are crowded out. To support their livelihoods while preventing a rotation to less sustainable production modes, policy should stimulate alternative sustainable opportunities in rural areas, notably the bioeconomy (C6).

At the same time, adequate social protection systems must be in place to cushion the adverse impacts of structural transformation on rural populations, including traditional communities. Eventually, urban areas will play a critical role in absorbing rural migrants, again highlighting the role of urban productivity (C2a) as an important complementary policy focus.

Policy scenario C3: Disincentivize extensive farming

- *Economic impact:* Lower distortions in agriculture and stronger structural transformation → higher income
- *Environmental impact:* Agricultural intensification → higher natural forest cover (and further enhanced ecosystem services if reforms strengthen climate-smart agriculture)
- *Impact over time:* Shorter to longer term

Reducing implicit policy support for extensive agriculture is expected to have positive impacts on forests and on income (by reducing distortions and fostering structural transformation).

One focus is rural credit reform. Much regulatory progress has already been made in reducing the adverse environmental impacts from rural credit (as with Resolution 3,545 of the Brazilian Central Bank) while also promoting low-carbon agriculture (Resolution 3,896) and introducing broad regulations to promote socioenvironmental sustainability and for financial institutions to address climate risks (Resolutions 4,327 and 4,557). Yet traditional sources of rural credit continue to be distortionary while undermining the effectiveness of more sustainable credit programs such as Brazil's Low-Carbon Agriculture (ABC) Plan to promote low-carbon agriculture.

To reduce pressure on natural lands, credit for rural production should not be increased overall; existing budgets should instead be repurposed to focus on more specific objectives (as in the ABC Plan) focused on public goods and sustainable, climate-smart agriculture, including integrated landscape approaches and climate insurance. Notably, encouraging higher yields through measures like crop-livestock or crop-livestock-forestry integration are more likely to succeed when the land supply is more inelastic (chapter 5), making them complementary to policies focused on land and forest governance (scenarios C4a and C4b) and a reformed rural land tax (Imposto sobre a Propriedade Territorial Rural, or ITR).

The ITR should be reformed to make the land supply less elastic while aligning it with environmental laws and systems (notably the Rural Environmental Cadastre).[5] Reforms to disincentivize extensive farming are consistent with efforts to promote productivity (Souza-Rodrigues 2019) and structural change away from extensive agriculture; their political feasibility can accordingly be enhanced through progress in shifting the overall growth model (scenarios C2a and C2b), as well as revenue recycling and conservation finance.

Improved forest protection

Policy scenario C4a: Regularize land through land designation

- *Economic impact:* Improved tenure rights and higher expected production costs by constraining the future supply of land → higher income for beneficiaries but lower overall expected income from restricting the supply of land (not accounting for indirect positive economic effects from curbing ecosystem loss)

- *Environmental impact:* Promote agricultural intensification and less *grilagem* (land grabbing) → higher natural forest cover (especially if undesignated areas are designated as protected areas or Indigenous territories)
- *Impact over time:* Shorter to longer term (depending on political will and implementation capacity)

Land regularization is a multidimensional issue in Amazônia, affecting various stakeholders, with nuanced economic and environmental implications. Land regularization matters for poor settlers in Amazônia. Weak land tenure is a constraint for National Institute for Colonization and Agrarian Reform (INCRA) settlers in agricultural reform settlements (*assentamentos*), preventing more productive farming. Due to the effects on farmer productivity, guarding against the Jevons effect remains relevant here.

At the same time, traditional livelihoods are threatened by tenure insecurity, because there are still significant areas of unregistered Indigenous land. Land rights for many communities of *quilombolas* still must be strengthened and recognized in Amazônia.[6] There are important synergies between this agenda and forest protection. Vast areas of still undesignated land have stimulated *grilagem* (land grabbing), land speculation and rural violence—so land designation is critical to eliminate that source of deforestation and conflict and there are good arguments for designations as protected areas or Indigenous territories.

If undesignated land is turned into *private land*, the Forest Code allows for 20 percent *legal* deforestation in the Amazon (and even higher percentages in other biomes). At the same time, it would increase the supply of agricultural land and could thus reduce deforestation elsewhere; even though overall deforestation impacts are relatively ambiguous then, risks for Amazonian forests remain high.

Notably, this form of frontier expansion— handing public land to private individuals—reaches back at least to colonial times and forms part of many states' growth model, anchored in the availability of artificially cheap land. This makes it politically more difficult to remedy the underpricing of land in the regularization process or to designate it as protected land altogether.

Designating undesignated areas as protected areas or Indigenous territories would likely reduce deforestation. *Grilagem* would not be economically viable, because this land could not be sold and curtailing land expansion would incentivize agricultural intensification. However, risks remain even here. For as long as illegal deforestation is not controlled and areas that can be legally deforested remain, the demand for land not met by expanding production into undesignated lands could be met by converting forests into agricultural land in other areas.

Complementary measures (for example, C2a, to take pressure off the agricultural frontier, or conservation finance) could strengthen the political will to rebalance the current policy emphasis toward the protection of forests. Conservation finance can also help resource the complex legal and administrative process associated with land regularization. Other complementary measures to make land regularization more impactful and reduce deforestation leakage include more effective command and control (C4b) and balanced structural transformation (C2a, C2b, and C3).

Policy scenario C4b: Command and control

- *Economic impact:* Higher production costs by constraining the supply of land, reducing employment, and raising food prices → lower income (not accounting for indirect positive effects from curbing ecosystem loss)
- *Environmental impact:* Prevention of illegal logging and forest clearing, promotion of agricultural intensification → higher natural forest cover due to lower illegal deforestation (potential leakage into legal deforestation)
- *Impact over time:* Shorter term (depending on political will and enforcement capacity)

Natural forests must be protected by enforcing existing environmental protection laws, including the Forest Code. Effectively applying these laws in Amazônia could in principle eliminate illegal deforestation. When laws are fully and consistently enforced, illegal deforestation is eliminated or kept to an absolute minimum. When they are not, substantial deforestation is likely to occur over the foreseeable future. This means that enforcement of these laws is of overriding importance for the survival of an intact Amazon rainforest close to its current level, as well as Amazônia's other forests.

The institutional basis for full enforcement of the Forest Code and other environmental laws already exists, but the will to enforce them may not. Sophisticated surveillance systems (remote sensing, including the Real-Time Deforestation Detection [DETER] system) can detect illegal deforestation and guide enforcement officers. And "blacklisting" municipalities (by concentrating protection efforts) in deforestation hot spots can yield strong results although risks for deforestation leakage remain. What is lacking are incentives to actually enforce the Brazilian forest laws, including the Forest Code, and to do so at all levels of government—local, state, and federal.

Effective law enforcement is critical and requires stable and adequate resourcing as well as capacity strengthening of key enforcement agencies, such as the Brazilian Institute of the Environment and Renewable Natural Resources (IBAMA) and the Chico Mendes Institute for Biodiversity Conservation (ICMBio) at the federal level. But it also requires a change in attitudes toward Forest Code enforcement at all levels, including the local level. At subnational levels, states and municipalities must provide their respective monitoring and enforcement bodies with adequate resources and capacity. Perhaps more difficult, an enabling environment must also be provided to give local enforcement agents the correct incentives to enforce existing laws.

At all levels of government, political will is critical to providing an authorizing environment for effective law enforcement. A shift in the broader growth model away from extensive agriculture (C2a, C2b, and C3) should also help to align political incentives with better environmental protection, further supported by conservation finance.

The overall welfare impacts of forest governance interventions depend on potential indirect effects, especially if tipping points are triggered in the Amazon. A growth model based on extensive agriculture implies that restricting the land supply—be it by curbing *grilagem* or by strengthening command and control—reduces real incomes, lowering agricultural employment and raising food prices. This is a central factor in the political economy of the protection of Amazonian forests, undermining political will. Yet these estimates do not take into account broader impacts such as the disastrous consequences of triggering a tipping point in the Amazon. Acknowledging these risks is yet another reason to shift the economy toward a more sustainable growth model. A productivity-focused growth model (policy scenarios C2a and C2b) raises income and is fully consistent with forest protection.

Avoiding legal deforestation, promoting reforestation, and restoring degraded lands

Policy scenario C5a: Incentivize higher forest cover on private land

- *Economic impact:* Alternative revenue source for landowners → higher welfare for landowners
- *Environmental impact:* Higher forest cover in specific properties potentially partly offset by (legal or illegal) deforestation in other areas → higher natural forest cover (but some deforestation leakage)
- *Impact over time:* Increasingly effective as illegal deforestation is controlled and balanced structural transformation advances

It is critical to make farmers in Amazônia compliant with the forested areas minimums under the Forest Code. The environmental reserve quota (CRA) scheme is one way of doing this for land deforested before 2008, whereby farmers comply by buying forest credits from overcompliant farmers as a compensation mechanism. In principle, this could strengthen the credibility of the Forest Code and ensure that legal deforestation is controlled within its boundaries and forest stocks are preserved. Operationalizing the CRA scheme is thus an important component of managing legal land use changes.

To increase forest stocks, various other options can be deployed. Yet possible deforestation leakage can undermine the effectiveness of programs aimed at raising the forest stock in private lands. Farmers could be encouraged to be overcompliant with the Forest Code (for example, by selling forest credits, as under the REDD+ framework)[7] or by obtaining support in reforesting their lands (as through Brazil's Programa Reflorestar [Reforest Program]).

Possible innovations in financial regulations are also being discussed that could allow for forested land to be included in collateral value, thus raising its value. These interventions will directly or indirectly generate income for participating landowners. Yet as long as forest governance is weak in Amazônia, these efforts can result in deforestation leakage (Dasgupta 2021). They would reduce the agricultural land supply, raise land values, and make it economical to grab land or deforest elsewhere on private lands. Such interventions are thus more effective when complemented by measures that reduce overall deforestation pressures (see, for example, policy scenarios C1a, C2a, C3, C4a, and C4b).

Policy scenario C5b: Incentivize land restoration

- *Economic impact:* Raise returns on land → higher income for landowners
- *Environmental impact:* More available productive land, reducing the need to clear forests (but subsidies for restoration can inadvertently generate incentives to let land degrade) → ambiguous impact on forest cover (unambiguously positive impact if converting degraded land to forest)
- *Impact over time:* Increasingly effective as illegal deforestation is controlled and balanced structural transformation advances

Financing to restore degraded lands for productive use can lower deforestation—or displace it. Restoring degraded land—for example, through the ABC Plan—would in principle increase the supply of productive land, enabling more agricultural production without clearing additional forest while also lowering incentives for *grilagem*. In addition, land under agricultural use also provides higher ecosystem services than degraded land.

Public subsidies can generate incentives for land restoration, raising the return on land. Yet subsidies could also cause deforestation if they create an expectation that public financing will be available to restore degraded private lands in the future—inadvertently creating incentives to let land degrade[8] and reversing the intended impact of lowering deforestation. Such adverse incentives could be avoided if restoration activities only prepare *public* degraded lands for agricultural use and then sell them to farmers. Adverse incentives might also be reduced if only *currently existing* degraded lands are eligible for public financial support, thus limiting expectations for any future financial support—but governments have low credibility in Amazônia on enforcing cutoff dates (as with land regularization). Such programs are likely to become more effective with institutional maturity and higher government credibility.

Reforesting or afforesting *public* degraded lands (for example, through public-private partnerships) would raise the forest stock without unintended consequences on deforestation. Such interventions do not affect the land supply and therefore do not generate market incentives that can result in deforestation. There would be no market return, requiring that such interventions be supported with various forms of conservation finance. Trading of carbon offsets under Article 6 of the Paris Agreement could play a significant role for this activity (chapter 4).

Sustainable livelihoods

Policy scenario C6: Strengthen the bioeconomy and social protection

- *Economic impact:* Higher and more resilient incomes for poor farmers and communities → lower rural poverty
- *Environmental impact:* Fewer transitions into unsustainable activities, and higher sustainable natural capital use → higher forest cover and enhanced ecosystem services
- *Impact over time:* Shorter to longer term

Given high rural poverty rates, it is important to promote rural livelihoods. The disruption associated with economic development lends additional urgency to this. Less productive farmers will increasingly come under pressure from more productive farmers as rural transformation advances. Policy should not artificially support inefficient production in the longer term, but support is needed until alternative livelihoods can be developed. This support can include social programs for farmers, such as the Programa de Aquisição de Alimentos (Food Acquisition Program), which should be made conditional on not deforesting. Public resources should also finance technical assistance and reskilling for other activities within agriculture (with a focus on more sustainable techniques) or beyond agriculture. There are potential links with the urban agenda (policy scenario C2a) if farmers are supported in seizing opportunities from high-value-added agriculture (notably horticulture) in peri-urban areas.

Strengthen the bioeconomy. The bioeconomy can play an important role. For one, it can provide alternative livelihoods for rural populations, unlocking the natural capital of standing forests and reducing incentives to switch into unsustainable activities, especially as agricultural competition intensifies. There are also opportunities for small bioeconomy activities as auxiliary activities associated with legal reserves. Finally, several activities linked to the bioeconomy have high cultural value in Amazônia. These activities include the production of nontimber forest products (like açai or cocoa), production of nonforest products through fisheries and aquaculture, and ecological tourism.

Policy makers must, however, remain vigilant about risks associated with the bioeconomy, such as the following:

- Markets are relatively small, and overly promoting production could quickly result in falling prices for producers, both in Amazônia and in other parts of the world (which are often among the poorest).
- There are also risks of slipping into monoculture production, which would belie the original idea of the bioeconomy and be harmful to forests.
- Stimulating the bioeconomy (including associated processing industries) could raise demand for land, which, in an environment of weak land and forest governance, could indirectly harm forests.

To mitigate these risks, policy could focus on sustainable small-scale production for niche markets that is supported by sustainability labels and strong sustainability standards across the bioeconomy value chain. Complementary forest protection policies (see, for example, scenarios C4a and C4b) will help to reduce unintended consequences.

Tailor social protection. Brazil already has a strong social protection system in place, also benefiting Amazonians. Brazil's advanced social safety nets (including Auxílio Brasil, rural pensions, unemployment insurance, and others) will provide a crucial role in maintaining minimum living standards where shocks are unsuccessfully mitigated.

In Amazônia, there are opportunities for complementary social protection interventions, building on programs like Bolsa Floresta or the discontinued Bolsa Verde. They would support traditional ways of life and reward rural populations for their sustainable livelihoods in Amazônia's sensitive ecosystems. Such programs may reduce deforestation arising from economic destitution. But they also have limitations (Dasgupta 2021):

- Such programs tend to focus on communities that *already* practice sustainable livelihoods.
- Conditioning support on measurable reductions in deforestation may put beneficiaries, who tend to be among the most vulnerable, in conflict with illegal loggers and other criminals—in an environment where the rule of law is weak.
- Even if deforestation can be reduced, it may "leak" to other parts of the forest, undermining the efficiency of the fiscal outlay (Porcher and Hanusch 2022).

A deliberate narrower focus on protecting the poor, coupled with support for sustainable livelihoods, will reduce the risk of disappointment (and program discontinuation) if such programs do not necessarily effectively reduce deforestation.

POLICY PACKAGES FOR DIFFERENT LEVELS OF ECONOMIC AND INSTITUTIONAL MATURITY

Different policy packages may be most appropriate depending on the level of economic and institutional maturity across Amazônia. This memorandum has shown (in line with figure 1.9 in chapter 1) how the frontier economies of Amazônia can become more prosperous through more balanced structural transformation (economic maturity), with economic growth turning increasingly productivity- and urban-led and by strengthening public and private sector governance (institutional maturity). Various policy interventions complement each other as economies mature (figure 7.3), with human capital investments remaining critical throughout—such investment perhaps being the most important driver of long-term inclusive growth.

Weak institutional and economic maturity

Where overall levels of maturity are still low—as in the most remote states of Amazônia (like Acre, Amapá, and Roraima) or in selected municipalities of other states (like Amazonas, Maranhão, or Pará)—the first challenge is to bolster institutional maturity. This should acknowledge the strength of existing, traditional institutions, including Amazônia's Indigenous peoples. Beyond this, institutional maturity requires strengthening governance (a) in the public sector (for example, capacity for public administration, law enforcement, judicial functions, and so on); and (b) in the private sector (for example, stronger environmental, social, and governance [ESG] standards and practices). Institutional maturity also includes governance for land markets and forest protection. Policy should ensure that basic infrastructure is available to all Amazonians, including in remote areas.

Economies are not diversified at this point, dominated mostly by the public sector (and often, informal) services in the urban areas and by relatively unproductive agriculture in the rural areas. Under traditional development approaches, these states would aim to strengthen agricultural productivity, but this is risky if forest governance is weak, because it could lead to deforestation (due to the Jevons effect). Policy should support sustainable rural production (including the bioeconomy) and strengthen land and forest governance as a foundation for investments in agricultural productivity. Systems for

FIGURE 7.3

Policy interventions, by level of economic and institutional maturity

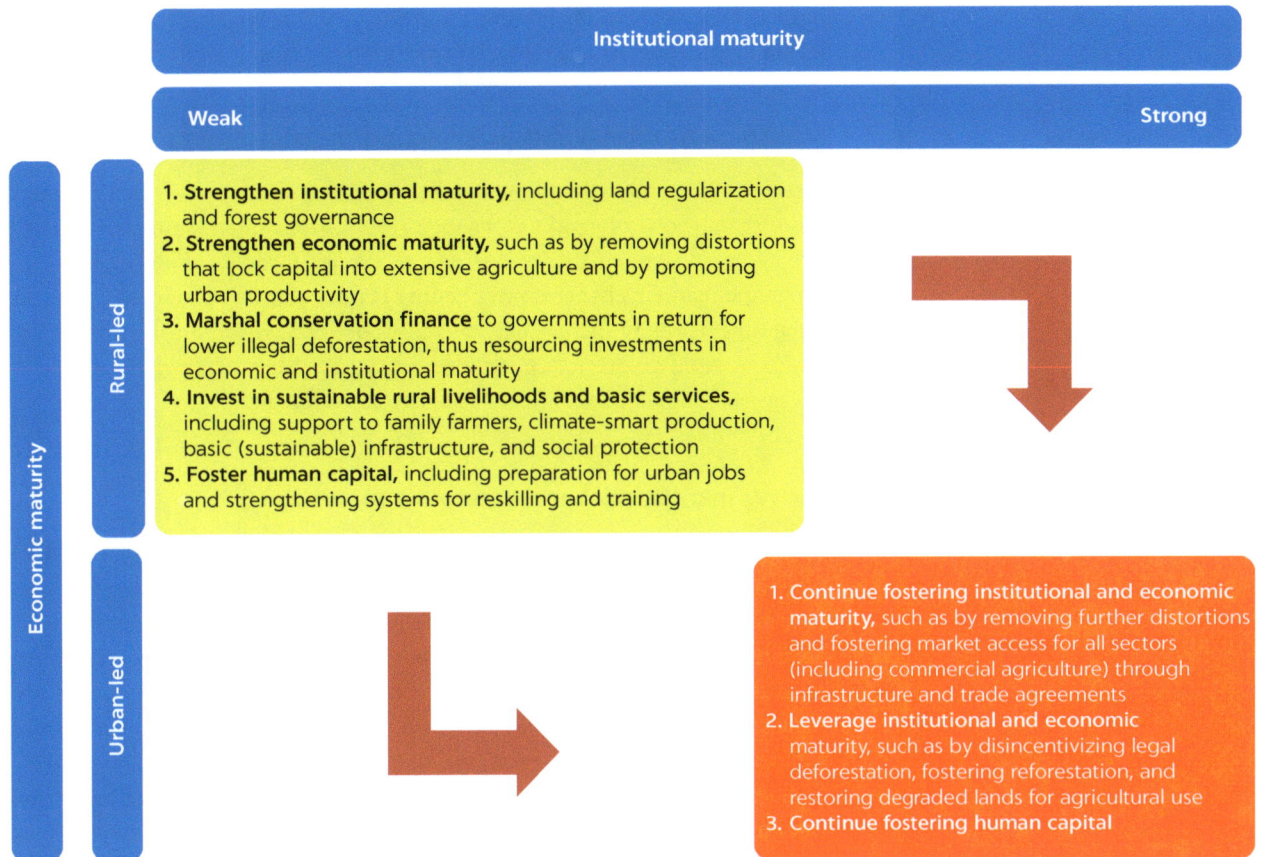

Institutional maturity

Weak — **Strong**

Economic maturity

Rural-led

1. **Strengthen institutional maturity,** including land regularization and forest governance
2. **Strengthen economic maturity,** such as by removing distortions that lock capital into extensive agriculture and by promoting urban productivity
3. **Marshal conservation finance** to governments in return for lower illegal deforestation, thus resourcing investments in economic and institutional maturity
4. **Invest in sustainable rural livelihoods and basic services,** including support to family farmers, climate-smart production, basic (sustainable) infrastructure, and social protection
5. **Foster human capital,** including preparation for urban jobs and strengthening systems for reskilling and training

Urban-led

1. **Continue fostering institutional and economic maturity,** such as by removing further distortions and fostering market access for all sectors (including commercial agriculture) through infrastructure and trade agreements
2. **Leverage institutional and economic maturity,** such as by disincentivizing legal deforestation, fostering reforestation, and restoring degraded lands for agricultural use
3. **Continue fostering human capital**

Source: World Bank.

conservation finance should be developed at this stage and be available at all levels of maturity, certainly for as long as the forest is under threat. At this stage, human capital needs include the building of foundational skills while preparing Amazonians for the structural transformation of the economy.

Weak institutional and high economic maturity

This is a relatively hypothetical scenario, since institutions are critical for economic development. To an extent, Amazonas State reached this maturity level at the cost of a high fiscal outlay, though it has struggled to make its relatively urban economy productivity-led—and it thus risks slipping back into low institutional and economic maturity.

In relatively mature economies, economic pressure on natural forests is lower, which could provide a political opportunity to reform the systems that implicitly support extensive agriculture (for example, the current structure of the rural land tax or reforming the rural credit system, mindful of respective responsibility at the federal and state levels). However, governments should not wait to institute these reforms, because removing the underpricing of natural capital could release productive capital for structural transformation. Where urban productivity is strong, policy should ensure that rural populations can meet urban job demand, including through training and reskilling. Systems also need to be in place as economies transition to this stage to protect traditional livelihoods through adequate social protection systems.

Strong institutional and weak economic maturity

Institutional maturity is still relatively low on the Amazonian frontier, though there are pockets of good governance across Amazonian states (chapter 4). Where institutional maturity is strong, the policy focus would be on fostering economic maturity, hence strengthening rural and urban productivity. At the same time, it would increasingly become more efficient to incentivize private agents to avoid deforestation, reforest, and restore degraded agricultural land, because potential leakage effects would be more contained.

Strong institutional and economic maturity

The objective, of course, is strong institutional and economic maturity. Both types of maturity should help Amazônia converge with Brazil and the world, so reforms must be sustained to foster the catching-up process. Deforestation risks are already likely to be lower along the southeastern border of Amazônia where most deforestation has already occurred and structural transformation and regional convergence are more advanced, but gaps in the enforcement of environmental laws continue to exist even there.

Because strong land and forest governance, jointly with balanced structural transformation, will contain extensive agriculture and the Jevons effect, this is the stage where fostering commercial agriculture will be the least risky for Amazônia's forests. Strong institutions will also limit the potential environmental costs associated with trade and infrastructure. Institutional and economic maturity can be expected to curb both legal and illegal deforestation.

CONCLUDING THOUGHTS AND THE FUTURE RESEARCH AGENDA

This memorandum has provided some food for thought on sustainable development in Amazônia. It should be complemented with further research. It has built upon a significant Brazilian and international knowledge foundation and drawn attention to some gaps in this foundation, notably on the macroeconomic drivers of deforestation and on broader questions about Brazil's and Amazônia's growth model. It has also identified links between macroeconomic forces, the strength of institutions in a frontier economy, and their joint impact on the ability of public institutions to protect the forest. In a nutshell, it calls for greater emphasis on balanced structural transformation coupled with stronger institutions for forest protection. This memorandum should be seen as one contribution to the discussion about sustainable development in Amazônia, and its core insights should be thoroughly interrogated and developed further in the future.

For Amazônia, most policies discussed in the memorandum tend to be aligned with local development plans, especially the four-year plans (PPAs) and the 2021 Green Recovery Plan (chapter 1). However, this memorandum also calls for some potential strategic shifts, notably a sharper urban focus. Incorporating thinking on urban productivity for Amazônia in policy planning would require more preparation, consensus building, and implementation time—and it requires adequate funding and platforms for collaborating and exchanging ideas.

Knowledge gaps remain. This memorandum has generated new insights into urban productivity, but this remains a relatively nascent area of research that requires strengthening. In addition, Amazonian cities need to be not only more productive but also greener: the sustainability of cities takes on particular importance considering the highly sensitive ecosystems in which they are located. This memorandum has also provided some new ideas for conservation finance, but further research is needed into both the mechanics and potential implementation arrangements. Whether conservation finance can provide incentives sufficient to generate political will and resources to protect Amazônia's forests remains an area for further study.

In addition, informing development policy for Amazônia requires better data. This memorandum has been constrained by the data available. In some cases, its preparation helped to pilot new approaches for using data, including tax receipts (*notas fiscais*), which, in the companion report to this memorandum, enable analysis of subnational trade flows (World Bank 2023b). There is scope to further develop this administrative data source for policy research, especially if more recent data can be leveraged for research (taking into account the relevant confidentiality requirements associated with tax data).

Another shortcoming was the unavailability of a recent census, since Brazil's 2020 population census had to be postponed because of the COVID-19 pandemic. The expected completion of the census later in 2022 will provide much needed information, if mainly for the longer term.

Because poverty is high in Amazônia, policy makers also need a good database for formulating their policy interventions. In the shorter term, household surveys (like the Continuous National Household Sample Survey, or PNADC) could be revamped to provide samples large enough to better understand the livelihoods in communities that are more difficult to reach in Amazônia.

Finally, consultations and advocacy are both key. Development is always a shared agenda, and it is critical for stakeholders to be consulted in all policy discussions. For this memorandum, the COVID-19 pandemic imposed some limits on consultations, especially on face-to-face interactions with communities, though online consultations were held with a broad set of stakeholders. As the research agenda continues beyond the pandemic, opportunities will be sought for more interactions and inputs.

Of course, consultations will also be indispensable in developing policies and projects in Amazônia, from preparation through implementation and closing. And where consensus emerges, advocacy can support decision-making in the public and private sectors. What is clear is that Amazônia's forests must be protected, and this memorandum has provided some suggestions on how to promote socioeconomic development in Amazônia while conserving its exceptional natural and cultural wealth.

NOTES

1. Most of the displayed mechanisms are also modeled in Porcher and Hanusch (2022).
2. For a comparison of different intensification strategies and costs from the Brazilian Amazon, see Pedrosa et al. (2019).
3. The "Jevons effect" refers to "intensification inducing extensification" whereby agricultural productivity gains locally increase deforestation. For further discussion, see chapters 3 and 5.
4. There is some evidence that such provisions in regional trade agreements can reduce deforestation (Abman, Lundberg, and Ruta 2021).
5. In 2012, Brazil updated its 1965 Forest Code and introduced the Rural Environmental Cadastre (CAR), an innovative database and environmental management tool.
6. The communities of *quilombolas*, descendants of African fugitive slaves, are further discussed in chapter 1.
7. REDD+ is a framework created by the United Nations Framework Convention on Climate Change (UNFCCC) Conference of the Parties (COP), standing for "reducing emissions from deforestation and forest degradation in developing countries."
8. This risk was also identified in Dasgupta (2021, 205).

REFERENCES

Abman, R., C. Lundberg, and M. Ruta. 2021. "The Effectiveness of Environmental Provisions in Regional Trade Agreements." Policy Research Working Paper 9601, World Bank, Washington, DC.

Dasgupta, P. 2021. *The Economics of Biodiversity: The Dasgupta Review*. London: HM Treasury.

Dutz, M. A. 2018. *Jobs and Growth: Brazil's Productivity Agenda*. International Development in Focus Series. Washington, DC: World Bank.

Gorton, N., and E. Ianchovichina. 2021. "Trade Networks in Latin America: Spatial Inefficiencies and Optimal Expansions." Policy Research Working Paper 9843, World Bank, Washington, DC.

Pedrosa, L. M., A. K. Hoshide, D. C. de Abreu, L. Molossi, and E. Guimarães Couto. 2019. "Financial Transition and Costs of Sustainable Agricultural Intensification Practices on a Beef Cattle and Crop Farm in Brazil's Amazon." *Renewable Agriculture and Food Systems* 36 (1): 26–37.

Porcher, C., and M. Hanusch. 2022. "A Model of Amazon Deforestation, Trade, and Labor Market Dynamics." Policy Research Working Paper 10163, World Bank, Washington, DC.

Rajão, R., B. Soares-Filho, F. Nunes, J. Börner, L. Machado, D. Assis, A. Oliveira, et al. 2020. "The Rotten Apples of Brazil's Agribusiness: Brazil's Inability to Tackle Illegal Deforestation Puts the Future of Its Agribusiness at Risk." *Science* 369 (6501): 246–48.

Searchinger, T., R. Waite, C. Hanson, J. Ranganathan, and E. Matthews. 2019. *Creating a Sustainable Food Future: A Menu of Solutions to Feed Nearly 10 Billion People by 2050*. Washington, DC: World Resources Institute.

UNDP (United Nations Development Programme) and University of Oxford. 2021. "People's Climate Vote: Results." Survey report, UNDP and University of Oxford.

Van Damme, P. A., F. M. Carvajal-Vallejos, M. Pouilly, T. Perez, and J. Molina Carpio. 2011. "Threats to Fish and Fisheries in the Bolivian Amazon." In *Los peces y delfines de la Amazonía boliviana: Hábitats, potencialidades y amenazas* [The Fish and Dolphins of the Bolivian Amazon: Habitats, Potentialities and Threats], edited by P. A. Van Damme, F. M. Carvajal-Vallejos, and J. Molina Carpio. Cochabamba, Bolivia: Editorial INIA.

Williams, D. R., M. Clark, G. M. Buchanan, G. F. Ficetola, C. Rondinini, and D. Tilman. 2020. "Proactive Conservation to Prevent Habitat Losses to Agricultural Expansion." *Nature Sustainability* 4: 314–22.

World Bank. 2023a. *Brazil Country Climate and Development Report*. Washington, DC: World Bank.

World Bank. 2023b. "Urban Competitiveness in Brazil's State of Amazonas: A Green Growth Agenda." Companion paper for this report, World Bank, Washington, DC.

www.ingramcontent.com/pod-product-compliance
Lightning Source LLC
Chambersburg PA
CBHW061134030426

42334CB00003B/30